PRIVATE SECURITY LAW
Case Studies

PRIVATE SECURITY LAW
Case Studies

David A. Maxwell, J.D., CPP

BUTTERWORTH–HEINEMANN

Boston   London   Oxford   Singapore   Sydney   Toronto   Wellington

Recognizing the importance of preserving what has been written, it is the policy of Butterworth-
Heinemann to have the books it publishes printed on acid-free paper, and we exert our best
efforts to that end.

Library of Congress Cataloging-in-Publication Data

Maxwell, David A. (David Alexander), 1930–
    Private security law case studies / David A. Maxwell.
      p. cm.
    Includes bibliographical references.
    ISBN 0-7506-9034-8 (case bound)
    1. Private security services—United States—Cases. 2. Police,
Private—United States—Cases.   I. Title.
KF5399.5.P7M39   1992
344.73' 05289—dc20
[347.3045289]
                                   91-41572
                                       CIP

British Library Cataloguing in Publication Data

Maxwell, David A.
    Private security law case studies
I. Title
347.306

ISBN 0-7506-9034-8

Butterworth–Heinemann
313 Washington Street
Newton, MA 02158–1626

10 9 8 7 6 5 4 3

Printed in the United States of America

To Jane V. Brown,
without whose uncompromising and committed
support in time, talent, energy, superb
skills, and administrative assistance, this
effort would not have been possible,

and to Tom and Mike

Contents

Chapter 2   Intentional Torts   55

Chapter 3   Agency   91

Preface

This case book is uniquely designed for the special needs of private security practitioners, students, and instructors. Cases provide a basic orientation to problems causing loss from litigation. They cover some fundamental principles of law. And they serve as a point of departure for the further study of these problems and issues and their resolutions. Appendix A contains some traditional legal resource material that may be helpful for future study.

Information, presented through the case law study system, comes from cases chosen for their factual, realistic, and practical connection to the private security industry. This focused approach addresses specific problem areas of the industry. It is not by any means an attempt to teach law school courses. By using factual situations directly linked to the responsibilities and everyday duties of those associated with the industry, this system will enable a private security practitioner to develop a deeper interest and understanding of legal problems encountered in some security actions. The rationale of the court should be closely examined. It may provide information a security manager could apply to forestall potential future loss.

Given the space constraints and voluminous amounts of material available, the material in this book only begins to touch on the issues. This is an effort to promote serious, critical, and thoughtful study of issues faced in the private security industry. It is hoped that the reader will pursue more education, gain more understanding, and then use this knowledge to reduce the loss from litigation.

In a note to Felix Frankfurter on December 12, 1915, Oliver Wendell Holmes, Jr., wrote, "Of course . . . the eternal effort of art, even the art of writing legal decisions, is to omit all but the essentials . . . 'the point of contact' is the formula . . . the place where the boy got his fingers pinched . . . the rest of the machinery doesn't matter."[1]

Thus, material irrelevant to the specific issue or topical matter of this book and the private security industry has been excised from the decisions. Those desiring a more complete treatment of a case or more extensive case citations should consult the case and other traditional legal resource material. Excisions are not represented by ellipses (. . .). Titles and citations to the cases are simplified. Most footnotes have been omitted.

Since many cases are concluded by settlement, a small sampling of settlements germane to the subject matter of this book are contained in Appendix B. Appendix C contains several different codes of ethics, since the activity in some of the cases appears to be unprofessional and unethical. And since some private security employees are, or may be found to be, governmental actors, Appendix E contains selected portions of constitutional amendments, and Appendix F contains selected federal deprivation of rights statutes. Appendixes G and H deal with private citizen arrest authority, while Appendix I is one state's use of a physical force statute. A glossary of some of the basic legal terms follows the Appendixes.

The intent of this book is to be gender neutral, and reference to either gender shall be construed as including both male and female.

A few passages from *Corporate Security Administration and Management* by J. Kirk Barefoot and David A. Maxwell (Boston: Butterworth–Heinemann, 1987) have been excerpted for use in this book.

The author and publisher are not engaged in the giving of legal advice or rendering legal service, and merely intend to make the reader aware of certain problem areas and resolutions peculiar to the industry. This book should not be consulted as giving legal advice. Appropriate legal counsel should always be consulted.

REFERENCES

1. Novick, Sheldon M. *Honorable Justice: The Life of Oliver Wendell Holmes.* Boston: Little, Brown and Company, 1989, p. 320.

Acknowledgments

Thanks go to Philippa K. LeVine, M.S., and Robert A. Moffatt, J.D., for their research, administrative help, and encouragement in the early stages of this project, and to Daniel K. Maxwell, M.S., Nancy S. Jasiurkowski, and Jane V. Maxwell for their time, administrative help, and encouragement.

Special thanks and appreciation to Patricia A. Morrissey, J.D., for her considerable time, research efforts, administrative help, assistance, and guidance in the latter stages of writing this book.

And thanks to Greg Franklin, Senior Editor, Butterworth-Heinemann, for his patient support, suggestions, advice, and recommendations.

Introduction

Private security personnel, both proprietary (in-house) and contract, long have had the responsibility of protecting life (employee, customer, invitee, and guest), property (real and personal), and information and ideas. They are dedicated to preventing loss from, for example, crime, fire, accidents, and hazards (either natural or man-made). Disasters, such as explosions, fires, tornados, and sabotage, can adversely affect the profitability or even the very existence of a company.

Because of the litigious nature of our society, another hazard—the legal pitfall—can be added to this group. A lawsuit has the potential to cause a devastating loss. It can result directly from errant actions in the security operation or from the fault, intentional or otherwise, of security personnel.

The Hallcrest Report II findings show that the private security industry continues to grow, with employment in 1990 estimated to be approximately 1.5 million. Four of the major reasons which account for this increasing growth and the limited growth of public law enforcement are

- increasing fear of crime;
- increasing crime in the workplace;
- decreasing rates of spending for public protection; and
- increasing awareness and use of private security products and services as cost-effective protection measures.[1]

Concomitantly, this report predicts that legal actions regarding the duty to protect, foreseeability of crime risk, negligent hiring and retention, and other civil wrongs (torts) will likely continue to evolve throughout the 1990s. That the litigation explosion in security-related matters may be the catalyst for setting security standards or codes, which should help reduce claims and ultimately improve security services and products, also is discussed.

In supporting this contention, the *Hallcrest Report II* noted that there are now four newsletters devoted to security law and liability issues. Virtually all corporate and contract security managers in reconnaissance interviews in 12 metropolitan areas expressed growing concern over lawsuits. This concern was manifested in a variety of security management issues such as hiring, training, equipment, personnel deployment, crime incident response, supervision, security systems, and other matters covering nearly the whole spectrum of public and private security.

The report also noted that a litigation explosion began in 1979. By 1982, research indicated that the average major award of reported cases had risen to more than one million dollars. For 1990 and beyond, it predicted that more security-related lawsuits will be filed and that more large punitive damage awards will be awarded, perhaps increasing at a rate of 25% per year. Claims are expected to include inadequate security, crimes, wrongful deaths, and a variety of torts. Hallcrest interviewees and security practitioners predicted that liability cases involving crime and security incidents will most frequently involve

- shopping malls, convenience and retail stores;
- apartments and condominiums;
- hotels, motels, casinos, bars, and restaurants;
- health care and educational institutions;
- security service and equipment companies;
- common carriers, airports, rail and bus stations;
- governmental and private buildings and parking lots; and
- sports and special events centers.

The report noted that interviews indicated a growing concern over lawsuits. It predicted that during the 1990s, as a secondary outcome of litigation, evaluative measures of crime prevention effectiveness would emerge regarding the use of security guards, alarms, locks, cameras, lighting, and security training. Additional concerns for the security manager involve the lack of legal knowledge by security employees[2] and a growing body of case law on tort actions on the status of police officer arrests when working off-duty (moonlighting) as private security officers.[3]

THE LAW AND PRIVATE SECURITY

A word about the purpose of our law in the United States and a way to look at and interpret it so that the security manager, supervisor, personnel, or student can reasonably interpret decisions in order to combat potential future losses. Although decisional or statutory law may vary in some degree from jurisdiction to jurisdiction, the legal system attempts to strike a balance between the rights of persons and private organizations to protect lives and property from outside interferences and the rights of private citizens to be free from the power or intrusions of others. This attempt to balance the competing and conflicting interests is nowhere more apparent than in the field of security.

The private sector uses proprietary (in-house) or contractual security employees to protect their own lives and property and that of their customers, invitees, and guests. In the balancing interest standard, all citizens are entitled to be free from incidents such as assault and battery, false arrest and imprisonment, defamation of character, invasion of privacy, intentional infliction of emotional distress, malicious prosecution, unreasonable use of force, outrageous conduct, and other invasions of private citizen interests.[4] In addition, liability potentially exists for the failure to protect certain interests of employees and visitors.

The thrust of this book is to review case decisions that deal with private security activities which resulted in loss. By reviewing these decisions, various principles of law can be extracted which the security manager can use to thwart or reduce potential future loss. Case decisions form a body of jurisprudence in any given area. Lending stability, order, and certainty to these legal principles is the doctrine of *stare decisis*. *Stare decisis* is where the courts follow or stand by precedents of decided cases in which the factual situations are substantially the same. These precedents, established by the courts, can guide the security manager to take proper action in the never-ending quest of preventing loss. Although there may be departures from precedent from time to time, general legal precedents are usually adhered to, thus offering guidance to the security manager. Note, however, that exact and precise legal guidelines and parameters, which would cover all situations, cannot be drawn in all instances from the cases in this book.

But an understanding of the factual settings and rationale for decisions will help orient and direct the security manager to past and present major problem areas by focusing on what went wrong. Systems and controls can then be put in place that will eliminate or reduce as much as possible similar scenarios and damage awards. If, for example, the security manager detects or forecasts a use-of-deadly-force problem involving armed guards, he may reduce this risk by more training, closer supervision, or eliminating some or all of the arms.

Even if a case is won in court, however, there is a loss: loss in the expense of preparing a defense, loss in the expense of employee time away from the job, and loss from the expense of legal fees. The best legal loss prevention tactic is not having to go to court at all.

THE RIGHTS AND LIMITATIONS OF SECURITY

The conduct and activities of private security personnel and the private security industry have limitations, restrictions, and obligations placed on them by law or administrative regulation. Businesses and people have the right to protect their property or persons, and the authority of private security is derived from the extension of those rights. Basic authority is limited to private citizens who act on behalf of private citizen employers, unless they are sworn, deputized, or commissioned by some law or regulation. If sworn, they may have full or limited police powers and be confined or restricted to a particular area and time. Some of the major categories or branches of law which may have a controlling or obligating effect on private security are as follows:

1. **The United States Constitution.** While generally not applicable to private citizens, provisions in the Constitution may control the activities of a private citizen if that private citizen acts as an agent for, at the behest of, or in concert with public law enforcement, or those deputized or commissioned with police powers by a licensing or regulatory agency. If the governmental nexus is met, a citizen may be subject to sanctions, such as the Fourth and Fifth Amendments of the Bill of Rights. The Fourth Amendment deals with

arrests, stop and frisk, and search and seizure. The Fifth Amendment deals with interrogations and confessions. Some state constitutions may have a tighter interpretation than the United States Constitution relative to the rights of its citizens.

2. **Federal Statutes, such as Title 42, United States Code, Section 1983** (civil remedy for rights deprivation) and **Title 18, United States Code, Section 242** (criminal charges against those who deprive others of rights) if there is linkage to governmental police agents may have a controlling or obligating effect on private security.

3. **Tort law** deals with private or civil wrongs, other than contract, and affects or controls relationships between people in any given situation.

4. **Contract law** involves obligations created through voluntary promises. If the promises are not carried out, a breach of contract may exist, and penalties may be assessed.

5. **Agency law** deals with the relationships when one acts for another, by the latter's authority, and the attendant responsibilities of the latter.

6. **Criminal law** covers sanctions imposed on violators of the various local, state, and federal ordinances and statutes.

7. **Administrative, regulatory, state, and federal laws** govern security activities, operations, and personnel such as:

- licensing;
- registration;
- qualifications;
- education;
- minimum age;
- experience;
- training;
- insurance;
- bonding;
- weapon permits;
- patch, badge, and uniform requirements;
- shoplifting detention parameters;
- closed circuit television use in certain areas;
- polygraph use;
- employee identification cards;
- use of force; and
- citizen arrest powers.

Tort Law

Negligence and intentional torts are areas of tort law of great concern to the private security industry. Tort law, which governs civil relationships between people, is designed to remedy wrongs. In effect, it limits or restrains conduct by threat of financial loss through actions at law. Duties exist in this relationship; and a breach of the duty, either negligently or intentionally, can create a legal cause of action. One of the problem areas dealt with in this book includes negligent hiring, training, entrustment, supervision, retention, investigation, detention, and use of weapons. Another problem area examined is intentional torts (Chapter 2). This is a tort done by a person who intended to do it. Examples are assault and battery, false arrest and false imprisonment, defamation of character, malicious prosecution, invasion of privacy, and outrageous conduct. While a tort is usually a positive act (commission), it may also be an omission or failure to do something. Even though a tort is a civil wrong, in some instances it may also be a crime. One can be sued civilly for assault and battery and also be prosecuted criminally for the same thing.

Law of Agency

In Chapter 3, attention is paid to some aspects of the law of agency. Again we are dealing in relationships, namely that of the employer and employee or independent contractor. Of great concern is who controls the employee or independent contractor and whether or not liability may be imputed to the employer. The amount of control exercised by the employer over the employee may have a direct and telling bearing on whether or not liability is imputed. Scrutiny is also given to another aspect of the agency relationship, namely scope of employment. Should the employer be held liable for a wrong committed by the employee outside the scope of his employment and which does not further the employer's interests?

Contract Law

A third type of relationship deals with contract law (Chapter 4). A contract—an agreement between two or more persons—is usually formal and can be express or implied. The terms of the contract, which should be in clear, precise, definite, and express language, define the obligations of the parties and set forth respective responsibilities and duties. It is possible that a person not a party to the contract may benefit from the contract. Some contracts limit or disclaim liability. Of course, failing to act as promised may result in a breach of contract lawsuit.

Liability and Damages

An additional avenue of inquiry deals with the eventuality that something went wrong in one of the above relationships and that an action for damages may be brought against the perceived offender by the party claiming injury (Chapters 5 and 6). Some damages can be compensatory or actual in nature. The purpose of this type of damage award is to place the injured party in the same position he was in before the injury occurred. Another type of damage award is punitive or exemplary. It may be assessed if the harm done was aggravated by malice, oppression, fraud, or wicked or wanton conduct. The purpose here is to punish and make an example of the perpetrator. Liability for the faulty actions of an employee may extend to the employer or corporate parent. If the injured party contributes to the harm done, a portion of the damages may possibly be assessed to him. Sometimes the injured party fails to reasonably avoid the harm or seek proper medical attention. This could be a factor in mitigating the damages. And, sometimes people who sue for damages will not receive any because of the lack of jurisdiction.

Probable Cause and Arrest

The authority of the private citizen is considered in Chapter 7. The security manager should know whether his or her employees are legally classified as sworn police (governmental agents) or whether they are acting purely as private citizens. If the employees are acting as governmental or state agents, they must abide by constitutional sanctions and rules that govern the activities of sworn law enforcement officers. For example, the Fourth (arrest and search and seizure) and Fifth (*Miranda*) Amendments indicate that constitutional sanctions might apply to private citizen security personnel if they act in concert with the police; if they act at the behest, or as agents, of the police; if they are granted police power through commissioning, deputizing, or licensing regulation; if they are performing a public function; or if a nexus with the state is met. If the employees are not governmental actors, then the authority they possess is the same as that for other private citizens in their jurisdiction. They possess only the same power and authority as does their employer.

Probable cause, which is explored in Chapter 8, deals with the type and amount of knowledge needed to make a valid arrest. For those with police powers, the standard is uniform throughout the country because of federal interpretations. Different standards for a citizen arrest exist in different states, and this type of knowledge requirements are noted in Appendix G. What is the difference between reasonable grounds, reasonable cause, probable cause, information, and immediate knowledge? Probable cause is an affirmative defense in false arrest/imprisonment actions.

From earliest times private citizens have had the authority to make arrests. Today private citizens may make arrests under certain conditions for certain crimes the requirements of which vary from state to state. Chapter 9 examines cases dealing with arrests by private persons. Appendixes G and H will help to sort out the crimes and conditions. Presence may be a requirement to make a valid arrest. Must there be actual presence or can presence be construed by the senses and the circumstances? Arrest authority is derived by statute in some states and by common law in others. In some states, a stringent arrest requirement is that a felony has been committed in fact. Examples of unreasonableness and outrageous conduct are also examined in Chapter 9.

Search

There are times when private citizen security employees conduct searches in order to protect property and life. Cases involved in this area are presented in Chapter 10. The basic permissibility to conduct a search flows from consent (actual or implied) and in some instances (and then limited) as incidental to a valid arrest or detention. Some of the areas examined in this chapter include: joint private security/police operation, stop-&-frisk, emergency doctrine, found property, items in plain view, locker searches, and noncoercive search tactics and alternative procedures. Take good note of the last case in the chapter (*People v. Stormer*). Will this ruling stay confined to one county or might it possibly expand to other jurisdictions?

Interrogation

Private security employees interview people in order to obtain information. The Fifth Amendment may apply to private citizens if they are operating under the mantle of state authority, work jointly with the police, or meet the public interest/public function/public accommodation tests. Cases in Chapter 11 look at various treatments the courts have given in these areas. Also examined is union representation at an investigatory interview should the results of the interview lead to disciplinary action.

Use of Force

Chapter 12 looks at some of the principles involved in the use of physical force by private citizens. The force used may be deadly or nondeadly. Use of force requires justification of the necessity for its use and of the amount that is used. Examples of nonjustifiable and inexcusable use of force are looked at as are the confrontation-aggression concept, self-defense, defense and recovery of property, ejection from premises, pushing, and the notion of retreat.

Deprivation of Rights

If a security employee is acting under color of law, he or she may be subject to federal civil and criminal deprivation of rights statutes. Cases in Chapter 13 deal with the conversion of the private citizen to a government actor, which may take place because of statutory provison, through joint operation with the police, or because the significant involvement/public function/nexus tests are met. Note the court's comments that vicarious liability may also attach to the employer.

Chapter 14 deals with the nonapplicability of the entrapment doctrine to purely private citizen interests.

For many years, the private security industry has been engaged in a variety of activities to help professionalize the industry. These activities include annual professional organization chapter and national seminars, workshops, research, scholarships, and periodicals and journals. A factor that has driven the private security industry to greater professionalism is litigation. Successful actions by plaintiffs against security wrongs are forcing improvements in security standards.[5]

Every corporation is potentially vulnerable to devastating financial loss from mishaps, faults, errors, or negligence, intentional or otherwise, by members of its proprietary or contract staff.[6] Thus, familiarity with civil and criminal liabilities attached to security activities is important for security professionals. Awareness of the ways in which security operations can legally jeopardize an organization is a prerequisite for most security professionals.[7] Liability is both personal and expensive.

About 11 percent of security decision makers, according to a 1990 *Security* survey, were involved in a liability action in 1989. A security director turned lawyer, who is currently updating a mid-1970s study, says today's average settlement is $550,000, with average jury awards of 1.2 to 1.4 million dollars.[8]

Private enterprise, of which private security, either proprietary or contractual, is a part, is profit oriented. It is not funded with tax dollars nor is it clothed with the concept of governmental immunity. Legal damage awards against a company because of fault or omission by security personnel could adversely affect the profit margin of the company. Since security implies order, stability, and predictability, it is much better for the security manager to avoid or control litigation loss than have the control come from the courtroom via a plaintiff's successful legal remedy. Just as there is no such thing as 100 percent security, there is no such thing as being 100 percent free from potential litigation. Since the task of the security manager is to try to reduce security breaches as much as possible, the parallel and perhaps greater task is to reduce opportunities for costly adverse legal action.

The alert and knowledgeable security manager can have a significant affect in reducing or forestalling loss from litigation. Keeping abreast of the law related to security practices will help the manager make more intelligent and correct decisions in guarding against the legal hazard.

REFERENCES

1. Cunningham, William C., John J. Strauchs, and Clifford W. VanMeter. *Hallcrest Report II: Private Security Trends 1970-2000.* Boston: Butterworth–Heinemann, 1990, p. 237.
2. Cunningham, William C., and Todd H. Taylor, *The Hallcrest Report: Private Security and Police in America.* Portland, Ore.: Chancellor Press, 1985, p. 103.
3. Reiss, Jr., Albert J., *Private Employment of Public Police,* National Institute of Justice, United States Department of Justice, Washington, D.C., 1988, p. 52.
4. *Scope of Legal Authority of Private Security Personnel,* Private Security Advisory Council, Law Enforcement Assistance Administration, Washington, D.C., 1978, p. 3.
5. McCrie, Robert D. "The Development of the U.S. Private Security Industry," *The Annals of the American Academy of Political and Social Science,* vol. 498, July, 1988, p. 32.
6. Barefoot, J. Kirk, and David A. Maxwell, *Corporate Security Administration and Management.* Boston: Butterworth–Heinemann, 1987, p. 17.
7. Gallery, Shari Mendelson, ed. *Security Management: Readings from 'Security Management' Magazine,* Boston: Butterworth–Heinemann, 1984, p. 251.
8. Zalud, Bill, ed. "Where Are The Bad Guys?" *Security*, vol. 27, Feb., 1990, p. 9.

PRIVATE SECURITY LAW
Case Studies

PART I

Negligence, Intentional Torts, Agency, Contracts, Alarms, Damages

1
Negligence

Tort law governs civil relationships between people; and in our society, people have many varied and different interests and needs. Some fundamental needs and interests associated with the person are having sufficient food, water, rest, warmth, and being safe and secure. The societal importance given or attached to these varying interests and needs differs, and, coincidentally, the type and amount of legal protection afforded to these needs and interests differ also. Some interests are given greater legal protection than others. Societal recognition has been given to the notion that all people in this country have a duty not to intentionally or negligently invade or interfere with the safety and security of another.

The law is in a continuous state of evolvement and changes as time goes on. Thus, legal protections given to particular interests change with the times. The litigious nature of our society today is evidence that the scope and nature of legal protections in certain areas is on the increase. Tort law controls relationships through threat of lawsuit by the injured party and sets guidelines for reasonable conduct between people.

A tort is a civil wrong or injury other than a breach of contract. It is a violation of some duty owed to the individual who claims to have been injured or damaged. Elements in a tort action include

1. the existence of a legal duty from the defendant to the plaintiff,
2. a breach of that duty, and
3. damage or harm or injury as the proximate result of the breach.

This wrong may be committed upon the person or property of another and may be the direct invasion of a legal right of that person. The wrongdoer is called a tort-feasor. If more than one is involved, they may be called joint tort-feasors. A tortious or wrongful act has also been defined as the commission or omission of an act, without right, wherein another receives an injury to his or her person, property, or reputation.

The cases involving tortious activity are basically either by negligence (discussed in this chapter) or by intentional tort (discussed in Chapter 2).

Negligence can be defined as the failure or omission to do something which a reasonable and prudent person would do, and the doing of something a reasonable and prudent person would not do. It is the failure to use such care as a reasonable and prudent person would use under similar circumstances. It can be characterized by thoughtlessness, inadvertence and inattention, and other similar words. It is conduct which departs from that which a reasonably prudent person under like circumstances would do. Negligence can reach the criminal level, the crimes for which are spelled out in penal codes, when it attains a level of wickedness, wantonness, gross recklessness, or is evil in nature. That aspect will not be dealt with in this book.

Negligence can be imputed to another because of certain relationships, e.g., employer/employee, which will be discussed in Chapter 3. The doctrine of comparative negligence, addressed in Chapter 4, basically deals with proportional liability for the harm done.

DUTY

In negligence cases, duty may be defined as conduct based on a legal obligation to which the law will give recognition and effect to conform to a particular standard of conduct toward another. The word *duty* denotes the fact that the actor is required to conduct himself in a particular manner at the risk that if he does not do so he becomes subject to liability to another to whom the duty is owed for any injury or damage sustained by the other, of which the actor's conduct is the legal cause.

The word *care* in connection with this means diligence, careful heed, close or watchful attention, concern, and discretion. It is prudence, regard, and vigilance. The opposite is carelessness, unconcern, indifference, or negligence. In the law of negligence, the amount of care granted by the standard of reasonable conduct must be in proportion to the apparent risk. As the danger becomes greater, the actor is required to exercise caution commensurate with it. Ordinary care is that degree of care which persons of ordinary care and prudence are accustomed to use and employ under the same or similar circumstances. It is that degree of care which may reasonably be expected from a person in the party's situation. Reasonable care is such a degree of care, precaution, or diligence as may fairly and properly be expected or required having regard to the nature of the action and the circumstances surrounding the action. It is such care as an ordinarily prudent person would exercise under the conditions existing at the time he is called upon to act.

Duty Owed

BROWN v. JEWEL COMPANIES, INC.
530 N.E.2d 57 (1988)

Presiding Justice Green delivered the opinion of the court:

On October 26, 1987, plaintiff filed suit in the circuit court of Macon County against defendants Jewel Companies, Inc., and Osco Drug, Inc. After that complaint was dismissed on defendants' motion, an amended complaint was filed against the same defendants, who again moved to dismiss for failure to state a cause of action. On March 2, 1988, the court allowed that motion, granting plaintiff a further opportunity to amend. Plaintiff elected to stand on the amended complaint and, on March 23, 1988, the court entered judgment in bar of action in favor of both defendants. Plaintiff has appealed. We determine that each count contains allegations of a cause of action but also purports to impose liability based on allegations which do not set forth a tort. Accordingly, we reverse the order of dismissal and remand for further proceedings with directions that much of the complaint be ordered stricken.

Plaintiff's amended complaint is apparently directed against each defendant in separate counts, but each count makes the same allegations because plaintiff contends defendants together were the operators of a combined grocery and drug store in a mall in Decatur on April 7, 1987, the date of the alleged incident in question. She alleged defendants employed security guards to protect against shoplifting. She also alleged the "guards customarily pursued and apprehended suspected shoplifters on the store premises," and "some of * * * those apprehended had fled or attempted to flee through the exit" of the store in the past. The amended complaint further set forth that defendants (1) knew their self-service method of operation made shoplifting on the premises more likely; and (2) should have anticipated shoplifters would be pursued by the guards and injure customers in the course of their flight.

The amended complaint then alleged: (1) on April 7, 1987, plaintiff was a customer in defendants' store, and was in the process of leaving, when a suspected shoplifter, being chased by guards, knocked plaintiff through a door and onto a sidewalk, whereupon a chasing security guard kicked or stepped on plaintiff's foot, injuring her further. That complaint maintained the security guard had stopped the accused shoplifter near the exit to the store, but the guard's effort to seize the shoplifter was unsuccessful.

The complaint further alleged defendants were negligent and violated their duty under section 2 of the Premises Liability Act (Ill. Rev. Stat. 1985, ch. 80, par. 302), in that their security guard:

(a) * * * failed to restrain the suspect;
(b) * * * failed to block the suspect's path to the exit;
(c) * * * pursued the suspect when he knew or should have known that customers would thereby be endangered;
(d) * * * failed to keep a proper lookout while pursuing the suspect;
(e) * * * failed to avoid plaintiff's foot;
(f) * * * failed to apprehend the suspect at a place where her flight would not jeopardize other persons on the store premises; and
(g) * * * defendants failed to properly train its security guard in the restraint and pursuit of suspected shoplifters.

Finally, the complaint contained allegations of proximate cause and plaintiff's injury.

Any contention that the complaint here is multifarious because any cause of action for the pursuing security guard's negligence in stepping on or colliding with plaintiff was separate from a cause of action for the defendants' negligence arising from the suspected shoplifter's flight from the security guard and collision with plaintiff is not of significance.

Section 2 of the Premises Liability Act abolishes the common law distinction between invitees and licensees in regard to duty owed by owners and occupiers of premises to such persons and describes the duty owed to both invitees and licensees as "that of reasonable care under the circumstances regarding the state of the premises or *acts done or omitted on them.*"

The allegation contained in the two counts which charges the pursuing guard with failing to keep a proper lookout during the chase and failing to avoid plaintiff's foot sets forth a cause of action in favor of plaintiff for an act of negligence by that guard which was a proximate cause of injury to plaintiff. Clearly, under the allegations, the guard owed a duty to plaintiff to use care not to injure her while chasing the shoplifter.

We hold that no other grounds for relief were stated in plaintiff's complaint because the defendants owed no duty to plaintiff in regard to the other allegations of commission or omission. In *Kirk v. Michael Reese Hospital & Medical Center*, 513 N.E. 2nd 387, *cert. denied* (1988), 108 S.Ct. 1077, the supreme court again set forth the elements for determining whether one has a duty to exercise care in regard to another. The most important element was stated to be foreseeability, provided the foreseeability was reasonable. The court then recited with continuing approval the other factors set forth in the leading case of *Lance v. Senior*, 224 N.E. 2nd 231. These include the likelihood of injury, the weight of the burden in guarding against the injury, and the consequences of putting the burden on the defendant.

The substance of the charges, besides those which we deem sufficient to state a cause of action, are that (1) defendants should have anticipated shoplifters would be in their store; (2) upon stopping a suspected shoplifter, defendants' guard should have restrained the shoplifter; (3) once the shoplifter ran, the guard should not have chased the shoplifter; and (4) defendants should have trained their guards how to properly restrain and pursue shoplifters. Because we conclude the allegations fail to set forth ultimate facts giving rise to the other elements imposing a duty on defendants, we need not decide whether defendants should reasonably have foreseen shoplifters would (1) frequent their store; (2) run, if apprehended and not restrained; and (3) run into and injure customers while they ran.

To make sure persons suspected of shoplifting are not able to run from security guards who stop them would place an enormous burden upon the operators of retail establishments. It would require a large force of guards and would also require the guards to use substantial force against each suspect. In the process, guards would be likely to use an amount of force very inappropriate for the arrest of persons charged with the nonviolent and usually misdemeanor classification of the crime involved. Moreover, the guards required to perform those functions would usually not be peace officers and would have authority to arrest only when possessed of "reasonable grounds to believe that an offense * * * *is being committed.*" (Ill. Rev. Stat. 1987, ch. 38, par. 107-3.) Imposing such a duty on retailers and their security guards would place too difficult a burden upon them, considering that the likelihood of very serious injury, resulting from a fleeing shoplifter running into a customer, is not very great. Moreover, as we have indicated, a likely consequence of placing this burden on retailers would be use of excessive force by security guards.

Whether a security guard owes a duty to customers not to chase fleeing suspected shoplifters because of the danger the shoplifter will run into a customer presents a closer question. Decisions from other States in this regard are not uniform. In *Williams v. McCrory's Department Store*, 354 So. 2d 725, such a duty was held to exist under the foregoing circumstances, while in *Graham v. Great Atlantic & Pacific Tea Co.*, 240 So. 2d 157; *Knight v. Powers Dry Goods Co.*, 30 N.W.2d 536; and *Radloff v. National Food Stores, Inc.*, 121 N.W.2d 865, the courts found no such duty.

We hold that security guards have no duty to refrain from pursuing suspected shoplifters under the facts alleged. As we have pointed out, the likelihood of very serious injury resulting to customers from a collision with a customer is not great. The likelihood of such an injury occurring is not increased very much because of the guard's pursuit, since most shoplifters will flee as quickly as possible when they have been stopped, regardless of whether pursuit takes place. The consequence of a rule against pursuit would be a substantial encouragement to shoplifting and would place an unreasonable burden upon the retailer. The duty of the guard is not to refrain from pursuit, but, as we have held in upholding part of the allegations of the complaint, the duty of the guard is to use ordinary care that he not collide with and injure a customer in that pursuit.

Plaintiff relies upon various Illinois decisions concerning customers' causes of action against business proprietors for injuries by criminals occurring on the premises. These cases differ materially from the case on review. In *Cross v. Wells Fargo Alarm Services,* 412 N.E.2d 472, *Neering v. Illinois Central R.R. Co.*, 50 N.E.2d 497, and *Duncavage v. Allen*, 497 N.E. 2nd 433, recovery was sought from owners or occupiers of premises known to be in dangerous areas based upon failure to provide security guards. The danger of injury in those cases was much greater than that from an occasional fleeing shoplifter in the instant case. In *Welsh v. White Castle Systems, Inc.*, 479 N.E.2d 944, and *Jacobsma v. Goldberg's Fashion Forum*, 303 N.E.2d 226, store customers were injured by fleeing thieves when they attempted to stop the thieves at the request of store employees. In *Jacobsma*, the store employees had knowledge that the shoplifter had three days earlier attempted to steal from the store. In none of the cases did the court impose upon the merchant or employees of the merchant the duty to use care to restrain the shoplifter or to refrain from chasing the shoplifter.

Because the allegations concerning negligence on the part of the defendant and their servants in regard to negligence on their part in (1) permitting the suspected shoplifter to run from the guards, and (2) chasing the shoplifter do not concern any duty owed by defendants to plaintiff, we treat those allegations as surplusage. However, as we have indicated, when chasing the suspected shoplifter the security guard would have a duty to use care to avoid colliding with or otherwise injuring a customer. Accordingly, we reverse the judgment dismissing the amended complaint but direct that on remand the circuit court order such surplusage be stricken from the complaint.

Reversed and remanded with directions.

CASE COMMENT

The duty owed is that of reasonable care under the circumstances. An important element is foreseeability. Some factors to consider in connection with this are the likelihood of injury, the weight of the burden in guarding against the injury, and the consequences of putting the burden on the defendant. Here, the guard, while chasing a suspected shoplifter, would have a duty to use care to avoid colliding with or otherwise injuring a customer.

Duty To Perform Satisfactorily

ERICKSON v. CURTIS INVESTMENT COMPANY
432 N.W. 2d 199 (1989)

Syllabus by the court
1. Respondents CIC, AAP, AMP, and Leadens owed a duty to Erikson to provide reasonably safe parking conditions.
2. Respondents breached that duty.
3. There was a causal relationship between the breach and the assault.

FORSBERG, Judge.

This is an appeal from the trial court's grant of summary judgment in favor of respondents State of Minnesota, Curtis Investment Company (CIC), Allright Parking Minnesota, Inc. (APM), Allright Auto Parks, Inc. (AAP), and Leadens Investigation and Security, Inc. (Leadens). It is also a cross-appeal by CIC, APM, and AAP from the trial court's grant of summary judgment dismissing third-party claims against Nu-Way House, Inc. (Nu-Way). We affirm in part and reverse in part.

FACTS

Appellant Garnet Erickson was assaulted and raped at about 5:00 p.m. on December 7, 1983, at the Curtis Parking Ramp in downtown Minneapolis. Erickson worked downtown and was a monthly contract parker at the Curtis Ramp. The ramp was attached to the Curtis Hotel by a skyway. CIC owned and operated the Curtis Hotel and owned the Curtis Ramp. CIC had leased the Curtis Ramp to APM, a subsidiary of AAP. Leadens was hired by CIC to provide security guards for the hotel.

The alleged rapist, Thomas Sabo, was out on parole when he allegedly raped Erickson. Sabo was referred to Nu-Way for alcohol treatment by the Minnesota Department of Corrections.

ISSUES

1. Was there a duty on the part of CIC, APM, AAP, and Leadens to provide adequate security measures in the parking ramp?
2. If a duty so exists, is there material issue of fact as to its breach?
3. Was there a material issue of fact as to a causal relationship between the alleged breach of duty and the assault?

Courts vary in their approach to the duty of possessors of property to protect others from crime. Some courts refuse to recognize any duty at all to protect patrons from the criminal acts of third persons merely because they occur on a business' property. *Shaner v. Tucson Airport Authority, Inc.*, 573 P.2d 518; *Davis v. Allied Supermarkets, Inc.*, 547 P.2d 963. Other courts recognize that a landowner may be under a duty to protect others from crime under certain carefully limited "special" circumstances. Some courts hold, for example, that no duty arises unless the landowner knows or has reason to know that "acts are occurring or about to occur on the premises that pose imminent probability of harm to an invitee." *Cornpropst v. Sloan*, 528 S.W.2d 188; *Henley v. Pizitz Realty Co.*, 456 So.2d 272. In *Schmanski v. The Church of St. Casimir of Wells*, 67 N.W.2d 644 the Minnesota court held:

> The occupant of premises, although not an insurer of their safe condition, *is bound to exercise ordinary or reasonable care to keep them in a safe condition for those who come upon them by his express or implied invitation.* Such duty of reasonable care includes the duty of making the premises safe as to dangerous conditions or activities upon the premises of which the occupant knows or of which he ought to have knowledge in the exercise of reasonable care.

See also Ponticas v. K.M.S. Investments, 331 N.W.2d 907 (a landlord was liable under a negligent hiring theory when the resident manager, who had a history of criminal convictions, used a pass key to enter a female tenant's apartment and raped her).

Yet, other courts hold that a criminal attack may be sufficiently foreseeable to ground a duty to prevent it *if and only if* substantially similar crimes have occurred on the premises in the past. *See e.g., Butler v. Acme Markets, Inc.*, 445 A.2d 1141 (seven muggings in previous year made eighth sufficiently foreseeable). Similarly, in *Roettger v. United Hospitals of St. Paul*, 380 N.W.2d 856, a local hospital in the Twin Cities was found negligent for its inadequate security procedures when a trespasser assaulted a patient. The jury concluded that the hospital's failure to provide adequate security on the patient's floor was a substantial factor in bringing about the patient's injuries. This court affirmed the verdict, recognizing that the hospital owed a duty of care to take reasonable steps to ensure the safety of Roettger while on the hospital premises.

We believe that such a duty exists in this case. First of all, there is evidence that this is a high crime area and that crimes had been committed both in the Curtis Hotel and ramp. Secondly, concern was expressed by Curtis about the number of "street" people and crime in the area. While there were no reported rapes in the ramp, there were many crimes against property. The security expert's testimony and common sense clearly indicate that property crimes can easily escalate to violent crimes. An interrupted thief is unpredictable and can easily turn on the one who interrupts. The rape was a foreseeable event.

Respondents rely strongly on *Pietila v. Congdon*, 362 N.W.2d 328, contending that foreseeability is lacking. But *Pietila* involved a private residence unlike this case of *Roettger*. As stated in *Roettger*,

> *Pietila* is easily distinguished from the present case; it involved a private residence where the defendants neither acknowledged nor undertook any special duty to deter crime on the premises. Here, United is a large urban hospital that had hired a security staff to protect its patients and employees.

CIC, APM, and AAP had a duty to provide a reasonably safe parking ramp. As the security firm hired by CIC, Leadens had a duty to perform their security function in a satisfactory manner.

II.

There are sufficient facts asserted by appellants to raise a material issue of fact as to causation. First of all, a consultant testified that Curtis failed in providing adequate patrol and adequate lighting. Curtis failed to control the ramp's perimeters and elevator areas. Experts also testified to the lack of training of Leadens security people. Erickson further argues that Leadens failed to maintain a regular foot patrol schedule, or even utilize existing hardware such as punch clock devices to ensure patrolling. As to APM, there were also no signs alerting possible criminals of the existence of security or emergency communicators (telephones or emergency buttons) to alert security personnel nor were there closed circuit televisions. Many other security breaches were listed or noted by the consultants.

Moreover, the security guard on duty may have been negligent in not detecting the rape. The alleged rapist, Thomas Sabo, stated that he never saw a security person and if he had, he would have left. He also said the ramp was so dark, you could barely see but a few cars away. Therefore, there is certainly a fact issue as to a causal relationship between the breach of duty and the sexual assault.

Leadens also argues that it was an agent of CIC and therefore it was not liable for injury to anyone other than customers of CIC. Erickson was not a customer of CIC, but only a contract parker of AAP and APM. This argument would lead one to the conclusion that absolutely no security was provided by AAP and APM which is simply not true. Leadens' guard assumed the duty of provided security for the entire ramp. It certainly did not separate CIC customers for special protection.

III.

There is also an issue raised by AAP claiming that they are not liable for the negligent acts of their subsidiary APM. There would seem, however, to be such a close relationship between the parent company AAP and its subsidiary APM to raise at least a fact issue of control.

All advertising came from AAP; the Employees' Handbook was issued by AAP. To facilitate and ensure the leasing agreement, AAP provided CIC with AAP literature. APM agreed to provide as consideration to CIC, AAP's design division. There are several instances of control exhibited by AAP, such as financial data, compilation, profit sharing, training and others.

Although we are inclined to believe that punitive damages should not be awarded in this case, we feel that such a decision should be made after appellants' case-in-chief is presented, and not by summary judgment.

AFFIRMED IN PART, REVERSED IN PART.

CASE COMMENT

Here the court noted that the security firm had a duty to perform their security function in a satisfactory manner, and specifically there was a failure to maintain regular foot patrol, a failure to utilize hardware to ensure patrolling, and a lack of training. Other failures connected to another corporation were inadequate lighting, failure to control the perimeter and elevator areas, a lack of security signs, emergency communicators, and closed circuit television. The court also suggested there may have been negligence in detecting the crime involved.

NEGLIGENT HIRING

A security company has the duty to exercise ordinary care in hiring persons who, because of the nature of employment, could present a threat of harm or injury to a third party. In this situation, the third party is the company they are hired to protect. The preselection investigation is related to the degree of risk a potential employee poses and should be commensurate with the risk involved. In selecting employees, a security company may be duty bound to exercise a greater amount of care to ascertain if the employees are honest and not likely to commit theft. When an employer does not use reasonable care in selecting employees fit for the work assigned, the employer may be liable even though the harm was brought about by the willful act of the employee beyond the scope of his employment. (Scope of employment is addressed in Chapter 3.) The failure of the employer to exercise reasonable care in selecting employees who the employer knew or should have known were unfit for employment exposes third parties to an unreasonable risk of harm.

In the following case, the security company was obliged to conduct a reasonable investigation into the employee's work experience, background, character, and qualifications. The standard of care does not vary. The greater the risk of harm, the greater the degree of care necessary to constitute ordinary care.

WELSH MANUFACTURING, DIVISION OF TEXTRON, INC.
v. PINKERTON'S, INC.
474 A.2d 436 (1984)

KELLEHER, Justice

This is an action for negligence wherein the plaintiff, Welsh Manufacturing (Welsh), brought suit against a security guard company, Pinkerton's, Inc. (Pinkerton's), for losses sustained as a result of three major thefts. Welsh claimed that Pinkerton's was negligent in the hiring, training, supervision, or assignment of a guard who was later found to have been a co-conspirator in connection with the Welsh thefts and that such negligence was the proximate cause of its losses. A Superior court jury returned a verdict in favor of Welsh, judgment was rendered in accordance therewith, and Pinkerton's now appeals.

On appeal, Pinkerton's contends that there was insufficient evidence relative to each theory of liability to warrant their individual submission to the jury. Additionally, it challenges the propriety of the trial court's refusal to grant its motion for a new trial. We affirm the judgment of the Superior Court.

Pinkerton's is a long-established security service- corporation serving Rhode Island and neighboring areas of Massachusetts. It was engaged by Welsh for approximately thirty years to provide for the security of Welsh's manufacturing facility, which in 1973 was located in the Olneyville section of Providence. Welsh, a division of Textron, manufactured gold sunglass frames for the United States government. The Welsh complex consisted of two buildings, one across the street from the other. There were always sizable quantities of gold on the Welsh premises, and Pinkerton's agents were aware of this fact.

Under the contract between the parties, Pinkerton's assessed the security requirements of Welsh's premises and daily provided one uniformed and unarmed security officer therein for twenty-four hours. During the night shift, that is, approximately midnight to early morning, the guard was required to make periodic checks of all floors in the complex, registering his presence at designated locations. Between August 24, 1973, and October 7, 1973—a span of about forty-five days—three thefts at Welsh's facility resulted in losses of gold in excess of $200,000. All three thefts were carried out by the same persons. The first two incidents occurred while Pinkerton's employee, Donald Lawson (Lawson), was guarding Welsh's facility during the night shift. On both of these occasions, Lawson admitted the perpetration of the thefts. At the time of the third theft, Lawson had quit working for Pinkerton's, but he testified later that he had provided vital information to parties who subsequently, on the Saturday evening of the 1973 Columbus Day weekend, broke into Welsh's plant, put a gun to the head of the Pinkerton guard on duty, handcuffed him to a nearby machine, and "cleaned out" Welsh's gold inventory, which had a value of close to $180,000.

Lawson was a twenty-one-year-old part-time employee who worked for Pinkerton's on weekends. During the time of the Welsh thefts he had been employed by Pinkerton's for less than six months. He was at this same time a member of the United States Navy. In July 1972 he had been transferred to Quonset Point Naval Air Station in North Kingstown, Rhode Island, and thereafter took up residence in a West Warwick apartment building. The jury heard Lawson's deposition, which revealed that after having made the acquaintance of the occupant of the adjoining apartment, one Anthony Fiore, a person with known criminal proclivity, Lawson had agreed to procure a security-guard position at Pinkerton's for the purpose of assisting the neighbor in stealing the valuable commodities stored on premises to which he might be assigned. In return, Lawson too would share in the fruits of such thefts. Accordingly, Lawson had applied to Pinkerton's in March 1973, and in alleged violation of what Welsh claimed at trial to be a duty to make a reasonable investigation, Pinkerton's hired him.

We consider briefly the principles of law involved in the action before us. In deciding this case, we align ourselves with the majority of jurisdictions that recognize the direct liability of an employer to third parties who are injured by acts of unfit, incompetent, or unsuitable employees. Illustrative of these are *Ponticas v. K.M.S. Investments*, 331 N.W.2d 907, and *C.K. Security Systems, Inc. v. Hartford Accident & Indemnity Co.*, 223 S.E.2d 453. In *Ponticas*, a tenant who was sexually assaulted by the manager of her apartment complex brought suit against the owner of the complex. The tenant alleged that the owner was negligent in hiring the manager, who had a criminal record. On his application for the position, the manager had provided the names of two references, one without an address, the other without a phone number. When asked if he had ever been convicted of any crimes, he entered "traffic tickets." The owner of the complex did not investigate further. It was adduced at trial that, in fact, the two references were his mother and his sister and at the time of his application he was on parole following a conviction in California for burglary and receiving stolen goods. The court stated that an employer has the duty to exercise ordinary care in hiring persons who, because of the nature of the employment, could present a threat of injury to members of the public. The court further stated that the scope of an employer's pre-selection investigation is related to the degree of risk a potential employee poses to the third party but imposed no duty upon the employer to inquire into an applicant's criminal record. The *Ponticas* court found, however, that because the employment involved the manager's access to the apartment by use of a passkey, the scope of the owner's preselection investigation was not commensurate with the risks involved.

In *C.K. Security Systems, Inc. v. Hartford Accident & Indemnity Co.*, 223 S.E.2d 453, a guard who had been furnished by a security company to a landlord pursuant to a contract entered the office of one of the landlord's tenants and stole a blank check. He made the check payable to himself for an amount representing a six to seven thousand dollar overdraft, forged the tenant's signature, and deposited the check in the guard's own account in another bank. The tenant's bank authorized payment, having failed to check the signature. The bank and its insurer brought an action against the security company and its employee, claiming that the company had negligently hired its guard. In support of its motion for summary judgment, the guard's employer offered an affidavit showing the following: the guard has passed a personnel test with a high grade; he had been granted a permit to serve as a guard by the local police department; the security company had contacted the guard's prior employers; the guard had passed a criminology course. There was evidence that the police department in granting its permits only inquired into felony convictions. The court, in affirming the trial justice's denial of the motion, held that the evidence did not demand a finding that the company had exercised ordinary care in its selection of the guard. The court stated:

> The defendant was offering a security service and the use of its employees to patrol the premises for the purpose of protecting persons and property. In the selection of its employees it may have been duty bound to exercise a greater amount of care to ascertain its employees were honest and were not likely to commit thefts, where one employing others to perform a different type of service may meet the standard of care required with a lesser amount or quantum of care.

The action before us is distinguishable from that which arises under the doctrine of "respondeat superior" where the wrongful conduct of the employee is attributable to the master vicariously. Indeed, an action for negligent hiring provides a remedy to injured third parties who would otherwise be foreclosed from recovery under the master-servant doctrine since the wrongful acts of employees in these cases are likely to be outside the scope of employment or not in furtherance of the master's business. *See Di Cosala v. Kay*, 450 A.2d 508.

In *Di Cosala* the Supreme Court of New Jersey expressed this distinction aptly:

> The tort of negligent hiring or failure to fire addresses a different wrong from that sought to be redressed by the *respondeat superior* doctrine. One court has stated that:
>
>> One dealing with the public is bound to use reasonable care to select employees competent and fit for the work assigned to them and to refrain from retaining the services of an unfit employee. When an employer neglects this duty and as a result injury is occasioned to a third person, the employer may be liable even though the injury was brought about by the wilful act of the employee beyond the scope of his employment. *Fleming v. Bronfin*, 80 A.2d 915.
>
> Thus, the tort of negligent hiring addresses the risk created by exposing members of the public to a potentially dangerous or dishonest individual, while the doctrine of *respondeat superior* is based on the theory that the employee is the agent or is acting for the employer. Therefore the scope of employment limitation on liability which is a part of the *respondeat superior* doctrine is not implicit in the wrong of negligent hiring.

Our recognition of direct employer liability for its negligence is consistent with section 213 of the Restatement (Second) *Agency* (1958):

> A person conducting an activity through servants or other agents is subject to liability for harm resulting from his conduct if he is negligent or reckless:
> * * * (b) in the employment of improper persons or instrumentalities in work involving risk of harm to others.

Furthermore, our reasoning that the employer may be directly liable for wrongful acts of its negligently hired employee comports with the general tort principles of negligence long espoused by this court. Although the facts of this case present a question of first impression in this jurisdiction, we do not view this case as presenting a novel concept in our negligence law; rather, we see it as an application of the standard of due and reasonable care under the same or similar circumstances. See *Leonard v. Bartle*, 135 A. 853. Liability of the employer is premised on its failure to exercise reasonable care in selecting a person who the employer knew or should have known was unfit or incompetent for the employment, thereby exposing third parties to an unreasonable risk of harm.

The initial considerations in every negligence action are the determination whether there is a duty running from a defendant to a plaintiff and the definition of the scope of that duty. A duty of care may arise by virtue of a relationship created or existing between a plaintiff and a defendant. In this case, the relationship was a contractual one, wherein Pinkerton's agreed to provide security-guard services to Welsh for a consideration. Accordingly, we find that arising out of that relationship was Pinkerton's duty to Welsh to exercise reasonable care in selecting an employee who, as far as could be reasonably known, was competent and fit for the task of guarding the Welsh facility. This duty included Pinkerton's obligation to conduct a reasonable investigation into Lawson's work experience, background, character, and qualifications.

We have held that the standard of ordinary care does not vary; "it is a question of degree only." *Leonard v. Bartle*, 135 A. at 854. The greater the risk of harm, the higher the degree of care necessary to constitute ordinary care. In the instant case, the risk of harm to clients like Welsh was a significant loss of property, and Pinkerton's was hired to protect against that risk. Pinkerton's was offering a service the very essence of which required honest, trustworthy, and reliable personnel. The sensitive nature of the employment, coupled with the opportunity and temptations incident to it, would lead to the conclusion that a prudent employer in these circumstances should rely on more than the absence of specific evidence or statements that a potential employee is dishonest or criminally inclined. We believe that a reasonable investigation would call for affirmative statements attesting to an applicant's honesty, trustworthiness, and reliability and perhaps also require the disclosure of the basis upon which the recommending person has relied. Realizing that job applicants generally provide references who are certain to produce favorable reports, we think that background checks in these circumstances should seek relevant information that might not otherwise be uncovered. When an employee is being hired for a sensitive occupation, mere lack of negative evidence may not be sufficient to discharge the obligation of reasonable care. Section 302B, part D, of the Restatement (Second) of *Torts* (1965) states that an actor must take precautions:

> Where the actor has brought into contact or association with the other a person whom the actor knows or should know to be peculiarly likely to commit intentional misconduct, under circumstances which afford a peculiar opportunity or temptation for such misconduct.

Whether an employer exercises the quantum of care required is ordinarily a jury question.

An employer's duty does not terminate once an applicant is selected for hire. Other courts have stated that an employer has a duty to retain in its service only those employees who are fit and competent. We agree. At trial, Welsh proceeded on three additional theories of Pinkerton's liability: negligent supervision, negligent training, and negligent assignment. Pursuant to its broad duty to retain suitable and competent employees, we conclude that Pinkerton's owed Welsh a duty to exercise due and reasonable care in the preparation and assignment of its security officers for the sensitive task of guarding large quantities of gold.

At the close of all the evidence, Pinkerton's moved for a directed verdict, which the trial justice denied. The court charged the jurors that Welsh was seeking to prove Pinkerton's negligence in the hiring, the training, the supervision, or the assignment of its guard, Lawson. He instructed them that if they found that Pinkerton's failed to exercise reasonable care in any one of these areas, they could find for Welsh, provided the negligence was the proximate cause of Welsh's losses. The jury returned a general verdict in favor of Welsh with no special findings to indicate the theory or theories upon which it relied. Consequently, we must test each theory separately to determine whether sufficient evidence was adduced at trial to warrant its submission to the jury. *Davis v. Caldwell*, 429 N.E.2d 741. The *Davis* court held:

> When multiple theories of liability have been submitted to a jury which is instructed to return a general verdict only, a judgment entered on such a verdict in favor of the plaintiff must be reversed when the proof was insufficient for submission as to one or more of those theories.

NEGLIGENT HIRING

We conclude that a rational trier of fact could infer that Pinkerton's had failed to exercise due and reasonable care in hiring Lawson for the purpose of assigning him to guard such a valuable commodity as the gold possessed by Welsh. Pinkerton's preselection process in hiring Lawson was as follows. Lawson filled out a general application form calling for, among other things, the names of his former employers and three persons who had known him for more than five years. Pinkerton's did not contact the three character references. Instead, it forwarded reference forms to Lawson's high school principal and to the Rhode Island Hospital, where Lawson had worked as an emergency room technician for approximately one month. The reference forms consisted of one question that asked whether the person queried could recommend the applicant without reservation and a request for any adverse comments on aspects of Lawson's character.[3]

The high school principal commented that Lawson possessed many of the qualifications for Pinkerton's work, stating that his average academic ability would be an asset in following directions and taking orders from his superiors. The comments did not address matters pertaining to Lawson's honesty and trustworthiness. Rhode Island Hospital attached an employment-termination form wherein his supervisor rated Lawson as follows: "Average" for (a) ability to work under supervision, (b) manners with public, and (c) attitude toward work; "Good" for (a) quality of work, (b) ability to work with co-workers, (c) honesty, and (d) appearance; and "Poor" in attendance. In the space provided for comments, the supervisor remarked that on two occasions Lawson had failed to report to work; and in response to the single question about recommending Lawson without reservation, the supervisor entered "see attached", referring to its aforementioned form. Pinkerton's also

[3]Pinkerton's reference form read in part: "Please use the reverse side of this letter to inform us of any known inaccuracies in the above statement, and tell us of any adverse comment in connection with his honesty, character, domestic life, integrity, financial status, ambition, health, mentality, sobriety, agreeableness, or any other adverse characteristic of which you may be aware. If you prefer to indicate adverse comments by phone, please feel free to contact me."

phoned a person who Lawson indicated was his superior officer in the Navy. He responded that he would recommend Lawson for the Pinkerton's job. Testimony showed that this man had been Lawson's superior officer for about two months. Pinkerton's requested Lawson's authorization for release of any police records. It requested those records from the State of Rhode Island, which reported that Lawson had no criminal record. Pinkerton's did not conduct any further background check. We think that Pinkerton's cursory investigation prior to Lawson's employment provided it with little current intelligence on him and could well support an inference of negligence in hiring for such a sensitive assignment as the guarding of gold. Therefore, Welsh's claim of negligent hiring was properly one for the jury's consideration.

TRAINING AND SUPERVISION

We find that proof was sufficient to submit these theories to the jury. There was evidence in the case that Pinkerton's did not have a training program of a formal and inculcative nature to which Lawson was subjected prior to his first assignment. There was evidence, however, that Lawson was assigned to various duties of low-level responsibility at other establishments before his assignment to Welsh. There was testimony also that Pinkerton's had a policy whereby supervising officers made unannounced checks of its guards once a week for each shift. From this evidence, reasonable minds could infer that preparation for a task involving grave temptations toward dishonesty, such as the Welsh assignment, was a function of on-the-job training combined with Pinkerton's supervision of its employee in ascending levels of responsibility over a period of time. Thus, training and supervision in these circumstances could well be viewed simply as two aspects of a single concept under the facts of this case. The record shows that Lawson had no prior work experience of the type involved in Pinkerton's business. Lawson's assignments prior to guarding the Welsh complex do not evidence ascending levels of sensitivity. Moreover, notwithstanding Pinkerton's policy of surprise checks, there was testimony that the checks were rarely conducted on weekends when Lawson usually worked, and Lawson could not recall ever having been supervised. In addition, there was evidence that at least one supervisor in the course of these earlier duties had reason to suspect Lawson of "having sticky fingers" in relation to a theft of proceeds of a vending machine. Although this suspicion fell short of probable cause, it was a factor that should have been considered under reasonable standards of supervision prior to assigning Lawson to the guarding of such a commodity as gold. Evidence in the case indicates that this suspicion was not so considered by Pinkerton's in accordance with those reasonable standards prior to Lawson's assignment to Welsh. In the face of such proof, the trial justice did not err in declining to direct a verdict in regard to training and supervision.

ASSIGNMENT

In respect to this theory, the evidence is more than ample to survive a motion for directed verdict. Lawson had been hired after a cursory investigation. He had been employed by Pinkerton's for approximately six months. During that time he had been assigned to no duties that would affirmatively demonstrate his reliability and honesty, save possibly a short assignment at United Wire, a metals plant, during which his supervisor became suspicious of him as the result of the vending-machine incident. Despite the lack of a positive record of honesty and despite the suspicion, although founded on less than probable cause, Pinkerton's assigned this relatively new and untried employee to safeguard a valuable quantity of gold. A rational trier of fact might certainly infer that the Welsh assignment was premature for this employee and, further, that it did not comport with the reasonable standard of care required to protect a client's interest under such circumstances. The trial justice was certainly correct in declining to direct a verdict on this theory of liability.

We hold therefore, that all theories of liability were appropriately submitted to the jurors for their consideration and determination.

Pinkerton's challenges the propriety of the trial justice's submission of the issue of proximate cause to the jury. This challenge would relate to all alternative theories of negligence and is based upon Pinkerton's assertion that Lawson's criminal intervening act broke the chain of causation. We reject this challenge. We have enunciated the test for proximate cause in terms of foreseeability.

> The test in these cases must be whether the intervening act could reasonably have been foreseen as a natural and probable result of the original act of negligence of the defendant.

We are of the opinion that Lawson's succumbing to temptation and his participation in the criminal thefts might be found by a rational trier of fact to be a reasonably foreseeable result of Pinkerton's negligence in taking reasonable steps to assure its employee's honesty, trustworthiness, and reliability. When considering foreseeability in respect to the issue of proximate cause, this court observed in a somewhat analogous case that "[i]t was for the jury to determine what dangers a racetrack operator should have perceived and what precautions and safeguards it should have taken for the benefit of its paying patrons***" In the case at bar it was similarly for the jury to determine what dangers, including criminal conduct, Pinkerton's should have perceived and what precautions and safeguards it should have taken for the benefit of its client, from whom it received a fee for the purchase of security. This foreseeability would be as applicable to the $180,000 robbery, by which time Lawson had ceased to work for Pinkerton's, as to the earlier thefts since Lawson later admitted to furnishing the robber with information helpful to implementing the third crime.

We turn now to the issue of the trial justice's denial of Pinkerton's motion for new trial. In passing upon this motion, it would also be necessary that the trial justice exercise his independent judgment in evaluating the general verdict with respect to each theory of liability. In this instance the trial justice gave a comprehensive and detailed analysis of all the evidence. He did not expressly outline the evidence relative to each theory of liability, but he did reach an overall determination that there was sufficient evidence to support the verdict of the jury in respect to hiring, training and supervision, and assignment. Although he did not discuss training in this instance as a separate theory, we reiterate that under the evidence in this case, training and supervision are related aspects of the same theory, particularly in the absence of a formal training program. In his instructions to the jury and in his analysis of the evidence, the trial justice did not suggest that the absence of a formal training program was negligence per se. He correctly regarded training and supervision as constituting ascending levels of responsibility in the course of on-the-job observation and evaluation.

For reasons stated, Pinkerton's appeal is denied and dismissed. The judgment of the Superior Court is affirmed, and the case is remanded to the Superior Court.

CASE COMMENT

The majority of jurisdictions recognize the direct liability of an employer to third parties who are injured by acts of unfit, incompetent, or unsuitable employees. This case is distinguished from *respondeat superior* or vicarious liability as the employee's wrongful act would likely be outside the scope of his employment. The tort of negligent hiring addresses the risks created by exposing members of the public to a potentially dangerous or dishonest individual. The liability of the employer is premised on its failure to exercise reasonable care in selecting a person who the employer knew or should have known was unfit or incompetent, thereby exposing third parties to an unreasonable risk of harm. Here the duty included an obligation to conduct a reasonable investigation into the employee's work experience, background, character, and qualifications. The standard of ordinary care does not vary: it is only a question of degree. The greater the risk of harm, the higher the degree of care necessary to constitute ordinary care.

NEGLIGENT TRAINING

Employees should be subjected to training prior to assignment. The standards for training are reasonable and should be commensurate to accomplish the task at hand. When the task at hand involves a potential for harm or injury, the standard for training rises according to the risks. Employing guards in a situation such as in the following case (providing security at a wrestling match) is likely to lead to contact with patrons and has the potential for altercations. In fact, the security company knew that violence was pervasive at similar events at the auditorium. The guards were issued guns, nightsticks, and handcuffs. The failure of a security company to adequately train employees in the use of dangerous instrumentalities issued to them exposes the company to liability.

GONZALES v. SOUTHWEST SECURITY AND PROTECTION AGENCY, INC.
100 N.M. 54, 665 P.2d 810 (1983)

LOPEZ, Judge.

Plaintiff sued for damages resulting from false imprisonment, battery and negligent hiring, training, supervision and retention of certain personnel. A bench trial was had and plaintiff was awarded $15,000.00. Defendant appeals. We affirm.

FACTS

Plaintiff, Raymond Gonzales (Gonzales), sued the City of Albuquerque (City), Fundamentals, Inc. (Fundamentals), Southwest Security and Protection Agency (Southwest) and five security guard employees of Southwest. The suit arose out of an episode where Gonzales received injuries while attending a wrestling match sponsored by Fundamentals. The match was held in the civic auditorium owned by the city, which it rented to Fundamentals. Southwest was hired by Fundamentals to provide security services for the event.

Gonzales sustained a broken jaw and lost four teeth in an incident involving five of Southwest's security men. He claims he was handcuffed by the security men, taken to a small room in the auditorium and beaten. The incident occurred as Gonzales and a friend were leaving the auditorium and a woman accosted him for having thrown beer during the matches. Security guards intervened and told Gonzales and his friend to leave. Once outside the auditorium the woman again accosted Gonzales' friend, setting off a substantial disturbance. When the security guards arrived Gonzales was a bystander. Nevertheless, the guards threw Gonzales to the ground, handcuffed him and took him to a small room where he was beaten. Throughout the incident Gonzales apparently was calm and did not provoke the guards.

Default judgment was entered against Southwest employees Mike and Alex Sedillo and David Chavez. At trial the City, Fundamentals and Southwest employee Ysidro Victor Vigil were found to be free of fault. Judgment in favor of Gonzales was entered against Southwest and its employee Denny Sanchez. Southwest appeals.

On appeal Southwest contends (1) that it should not be held responsible for the intentional torts of its employees; and (2) that substantial evidence does not support the trial court finding it negligent.

POINT 1: AN EMPLOYER'S LIABILITY FOR THE INTENTIONAL TORTS OF ITS EMPLOYEES.

An employer is liable for the intentional torts of its employees if the torts are committed in the course and scope of employment. Whether an employee's conduct is within the course and scope of employment is a question of fact. In the case at bar, the question is whether the security guards' imprisonment and battering of Gonzales was within the course and scope of their employment. In resolution of this question we note that local decisions exist regarding an employee's intentional torts; however, none address the activity of private security personnel.

The definition of "the course and scope of employment" is variable. In *Miera v. George*, 237 P.2d 102, the court adopted the following test of whether conduct was within the course of employment:

> But in general terms it may be said that an act is within the "course of employment" if (1) it be something fairly and naturally incident to the business, and if (2) it be done while the servant was engaged upon the master's business and be done, although mistakenly or illadvisedly, with a view to further the master's interests, or from some impulse of emotion which naturally grew out of or was incident to the attempt to perform the master's business, and did not arise wholly from some external, independent, and personal motive on the part of the servant to do the act upon his own account.

In addition to the test delineated above, the instant case requires additional considerations because of the nature of Southwest's and the security guards' work. The Restatement of Agency addresses the use of force as follows:

> A master is subject to liability for the intended tortious harm by a servant to the person or things of another by an act done in connection with the servant's employment, although the act was unauthorized, if the act was not unexpectable in the view of the duties of the servant.

Restatement (Second) of Agency § 245 (1958). Comment c to § 245 adds the following:

> c. **Nature of employment.** Whether or not an employment involves or is likely to lead to the use of force against the person of another is a question to be decided upon the facts of the individual case. To create liability for a battery by a servant upon a third person, the employment must be one which is likely to bring the servant into conflict with others. The making of contracts, or the compromise, settlement, or collection of accounts, does not ordinarily have this tendency. On the other hand, *the employment of servants to guard or to recapture property*, to take possession of land, or to deal with chattels which are in the possession of another, *is likely to lead to altercations, and the master may become liable, in spite of instructions that no force shall be exerted against the person of the possessor.*

In this case Southwest provided the security personnel with uniforms, handcuffs, guns, nightsticks and the authority to keep peace. Evidence at trial showed that Gonzales' injuries were inflicted, at least in part, by a guards' use of a nightstick. Moreover, Gonzales was handcuffed during the beating. We therefore have a situation where not only did Southwest's employees beat a person, but the beating was facilitated by instrumentalities provided by Southwest.

According to the foregoing facts and authority, we conclude that the trial court properly determined that the guards' conduct was naturally incident to Southwest's business. The trial court also properly determined that the guards' conduct substantially arose out of an attempt to perform Southwest's business. Finally, from our review of the record, we hold that substantial evidence supports the trial court's finding that Southwest was liable for its employees' intentional torts.

POINT 2. WHETHER SUBSTANTIAL EVIDENCE SUPPORTS FINDING SOUTH-WEST NEGLIGENT.

Southwest contends the trial court's finding of negligence is not supported by substantial evidence. This argument is based on the New Mexico Supreme Court decision in *F & T Co. v. Woods*, 594 P.2d 745. In *Woods* the court held that defendant could not be liable for negligently hiring or retaining an employee because there was no showing that defendant's omissions proximately caused plaintiff's injuries. The principle reason proximate causation was lacking was because defendant's employee was acting outside the scope of employment, without defendant's authority and without instrumentalities provided by defendant, when plaintiff was harmed. In the case at bar, however, we have held that the guards were acting within the scope of their employment, and were using instrumentalities provided by Southwest, when Gonzales' injuries occurred. We therefore begin with a vast factual disparity between *F & T Co. v. Woods* and the case at bar.

The specific error alleged by Southwest is that the guards' intentional torts were neither foreseeable nor the cause of Gonzales' harm. While the terms "foreseeability" and "proximate causation" evade precise definition, the meaning of these terms is well known in the law. The existence of causation is ordinarily a question of fact. In the case at bar the court concluded that Southwest negligently equipped, trained, supervised and retained the guards, and that Southwest's negligence was the cause of Gonzales' harm. These conclusions were based on the following findings:

12. Southwest Security did not adequately investigate the background and the character of the individual Defendants herein prior to hiring them as security guards.
13. Southwest Security did not adequately supervise their security guards in general and in particular on the evening of August 19, 1979.
14. Southwest Security failed to adequately train the security guards in the use of weapons such as clubs and handcuffs which were provided to Mike Z. Sedillo, Alex Sedillo, Denny Sanchez and David Chavez.
15. Southwest Security failed to adequately instruct its employees in the proper method of restraining and arresting individuals.
16. There was at least one other prior beating of an individual by employees of Southwest Security and in particular Mike Z. Sedillo which occurred at a wrestling match and Southwest Security was or should have been aware of such incident(s) and failed to take appropriate action to avoid further incident(s) of this nature.
17. The negligence of Southwest Security as specified above proximately caused the damages which resulted to Raymond J. Gonzales.

The findings quoted above are supported by evidence in the record. Testimony at trial revealed that Southwest's guards previously had mistreated people, that supervisors or owners of Southwest knew or should have known of such treatment, and that Southwest knew violence was pervasive at similar events held in the auditorium. From these facts we conclude that substantial evidence supports the trial court's findings that Southwest was negligent and that its negligence caused Gonzales' injuries.

The judgment of the trial court is affirmed. Appellate costs are to be paid by Southwest.

IT IS SO ORDERED.

CASE COMMENT

The security agency provided its employees with handcuffs, guns, and nightsticks. The beating in this case was facilitated by the instrumentalities provided. The court found, among other things, that the security agency failed to adequately train their employees in the use of the weapons. If provided tools, employees should be trained when and how to use them and when and how not to use them.

NEGLIGENT ENTRUSTMENT

To entrust is to give something over to another for its care, its protection, or for its use in the performance of some activity. In the private security industry, one very serious concern is the issuing of firearms to members of the security staff.

A firearm securely locked away in a metal cabinet without ammunition is not a dangerous instrumentality as long as this condition exists. Neither is a car, without keys in it, parked in a securely locked garage. But, taken from these sites and respectively furnished with ammunition and keys, they can become a dangerous instrumentality if not handled properly or operated by a competent, trained, or satisfactorily licensed individual. A dangerous object is one that poses a high risk of injury. The care to be exercised in entrusting an object to someone is proportionate to the potential danger involved. In other words, the degree or measure of care to be used depends on the dangerousness of the object. Examples of inherently dangerous instrumentalities are explosives, fireworks, gun powder, electricity, and combustibles.

Liability may extend to the person or company that entrusts a dangerous object to a person who lacks competency and skill in handling the object. Therefore, the security manager should see that those entrusted with firearms are competent, fit, skilled, experienced, mature, trained, and licensed, if required. Conditions that may signal fitness or competency problems relative to the entrustment of firearms include aggressiveness, violent disposition, recklessness, quickness of temper, physical or mental handicap, or substance abuse.

The Hallcrest Report II indicates that there has been a dramatic decrease in the number of armed security personnel in recent years. One reason for the decrease was the higher liability and greater risk for employers. In the following two cases (Horn and Langill), notice the lack of supervision and adequate storage of the weapon and the lack of training and experience of the new employee.

HORN v. I.B.I. SECURITY SERVICE OF FLORIDA, INC.
317 So. 2d 444 (1975)

WALDEN, Judge.

Wrongful death action brought by Administratrix. Jury trial resulted in judgment for the defendant. Administratrix appeals. We reverse and remand for a new trial.

Erroneous jury instructions form the basis for our decision. They were:

> The issues for your determination on the claim of Cecil Westfall against IBI are: Whether IBI was negligent in the entrustment of the weapon to George David Lowe. And if you further find George David Lowe was negligent, whether such negligence of *IBI and* George David Lowe was a legal cause of the death of the decedent, Mr. Westfall.

Negligence is a legal cause of loss, injury or damage if it directly and in natural and continuous sequence produces or contributes substantially to producing such loss, injury or damage, so that it can reasonably be said that, but for the negligence, the loss, injury or damage would not have occurred.

The facts. Defendant employed Westfall and Lowe as security guards. Defendant entrusted Lowe with a revolver for use in the job.

While off the job and playing "quick draw," Lowe shot and killed Westfall with the revolver, or with another which was missing from the job.

Please look back to the instructions. They clearly require as a basis for recovery four things:

1. A finding that defendant negligently entrusted the weapon to Lowe.
2. A finding that defendant's negligent entrustment in 1 above was the legal cause (as defined) of Westfall's death.
3. A finding that Lowe was negligent in the use of the weapon.
4. A finding that Lowe's negligence in 3 above was the legal cause (as defined) of Westfall's death.

It is the inclusion and imposition of number two requirement above that makes the jury instruction erroneous and causes us to reverse. For the owner of a firearm to be liable for injury negligently caused by the person to whom he has entrusted a gun, he need only be negligent in the entrustment of that firearm.

In *Langill v. Columbia,* the court held there should not have been a summary final judgment for defendant, Wackenhut Security Corporation, when one of its off-duty security guards had shot and killed a man with a firearm provided the guard by Wackenhut. The court found there existed genuine issues of fact as to whether Wackenhut negligently entrusted the weapon to its employee. The court held:

> The owner of a firearm, a dangerous instrumentality, may be found liable for injury if there *was negligence in the entrustment* of the firearm. (Emphasis added.)

In this case, the additional requirement that the negligent entrustment, itself, directly and in natural and continuous sequence produced the death of Westfall constituted an almost impossible burden, particularly under the facts of this case. The jury instruction imposed a burden of proof on plaintiff that is erroneous under the law. As such, it is reversible error.

We reverse and remand for a new trial.

Reversed and remanded.

LANGILL v. COLUMB IA
289 So . 2d 460 (1974)

PER CURIAM.

Plaintiff-appellant seeks review of an adverse final summary judgment entered in favor of the defendant Wackenhut Corporation.

Defendant James Columbia was employed by the defendant Wackenhut Corporation as a bank security guard. On May 4, 1971 Wackenhut issued to Columbia a pistol and five rounds of live ammunition to be used by him the following day on his job. The next morning, defendant Columbia while dressing for work partially loaded the weapon. Plaintiff and another man drove up to defendant's trailer, his place of residence, to discuss some work to be done thereon. Columbia came outside and joined them and during the course of the discussion without provocation or reason, he pointed the pistol at plaintiff and the other man and pulled the trigger discharging a bullet which passed through and killed the other man and lodged in plaintiff's side. Plaintiff filed suit against Columbia and Wackenhut Corporation to recover damages for the injuries sustained as a result of the shooting. Wackenhut filed a motion for summary judgment which was granted by the trial court, which continued the cause against Columbia at the request of plaintiff pending the outcome of this appeal.

We find merit in plaintiff-appellant's contention on appeal that the trial court erred in entering summary final judgment in favor of Wackenhut Corporation where there existed genuine issues of fact as to whether or not Wackenhut negligently entrusted one of its weapons to its employee Columbia.

This court has held that the owner of a firearm, a dangerous instrumentality, may be found liable for injury if there was negligence in the entrustment of the firearm.

After reviewing the record in a light most favorable to plaintiff-appellant, the party against whom the summary judgment was entered, we found the following facts to which defendant Columbia testified in his deposition. Defendant Columbia was approximately seventy (70) years of age when hired by defendant Wackenhut Corporation; he was given no special or personal physical instruction in the use and loading of firearms; he had little or no experience in firing a weapon; and the defendant Wackenhut Corporation along with the pistol and live ammunition merely issued to Columbia a guard manual which contained some information as to the proper handling of a weapon.

A jury, having had the opportunity to consider the above facts, may have determined that the defendant Wackenhut Corporation was negligent in entrusting the pistol with five rounds of live ammunition to the defendant Columbia. Thus, we find it was error for the trial court to have entered summary final judgment in favor of Wackenhut .

Accordingly, the judgment of the trial court is reversed and the cause is remanded with directions to hold a jury trial on the issue of negligent entrustment.

Reversed and remanded with directions.

CASE COMMENT

Negligence is the absence of due diligence. A firearm is a dangerous, deadly weapon. The owner of a weapon may be liable if he negligently entrusts the weapon to another. The higher the risk, the higher the degree of care.

NEGLIGENT SUPERVISION

A security company's duty to third parties does not terminate once an applicant is selected and trained. The company has a duty to exercise due and reasonable care in supervising its employees. The standard of reasonable supervision corresponds in extent and degree to the ascending or descending levels of responsibility and activity of the employee. The greater the degree for potential harm by the employee requires corresponding supervision of a like or equal degree. In the following cases, one employee normally drank at work while being entrusted with the job of ejecting patrons. In the other, employees burglarized customers while privileged to enter their property.

An employer has a duty to exercise reasonable care to avoid harm to patrons by exercising supervisory care when the employer knows, or by reasonable diligence ought to know, that his employee is about to eject a patron. The employer also has a duty to exercise supervisory care when employees are privileged to enter another's property. The duty to supervise extends to intentional torts by the employee in furtherance of the employer's objectives and to activities like theft, which is outside the scope of employ-ment, when the employee is privileged to enter another's property because of their employment.

AMERICAN AUTOMOBILE AUCTION v. TITSWORTH
730 S.W. 2d 499 (1987)

DUDLEY, Justice.

The appellees, Ralph Titsworth and Joe McPeek, filed a tort suit under a negligent supervision theory, seeking to hold the employer, appellant American Automobile Auction, Inc., liable for the intentional acts of its employees. The jury returned verdicts of $50,000.00 for appellee Titsworth and $1,000.00 for McPeek. We affirm the judgment on the verdicts.

The appellant's first point of appeal is that there is no proof of negligence because, it argues, the employees committed intentional torts against the appellees. The proof was undisputed that the employees committed intentional torts, but such proof does not exclude the theory of negligent supervision of the employees who committed the intentional torts. The appellees' theory of the case was not based upon imputed liability, and they did not seek an instruction on vicarious liability for the intentional torts, but rather, they sought recovery on the theory of direct liability for the negligent failure to supervise employees.

In determining the sufficiency of the evidence an appellate court reviews the evidence, and all reasonable inferences from it, in the light most favorable to appellee. In so reviewing the evidence we find that the appellant corporation conducted automobile auctions. It hired David Doster and Don Ball, both ex-convicts. Doster was hired as a sales director and repossessor of vehicles while Ball was hired as an auction ring man and bouncer. At the time of the intentional torts, an auction was being conducted, and employee Ball, who normally drank while at work, had a bottle of beer in his hand.

The president of the appellant corporation, Don Moak, had barred appellee McPeek from attending a different automobile auction which he owned because Moak had previously had trouble collecting a debt from McPeek and his partner. In fact, Moak and employee Doster had repossessed a truck from McPeek's partner. Even so, appellant corporation mailed a written invitation to McPeek to attend the auction.

On the night of the auction, McPeek went to Moak's office and asked if he was invited to or barred from the auction. Moak asked him to leave and come back some other time and discuss it. Moak then watched appellee McPeek go into the auction. McPeek caused a disturbance. The appellant's employees, Doster and Ball, commenced to forcibly eject appellee McPeek. Appellee Titsworth, a large man, attempted, without fighting, to protect McPeek and, at the same time, get him out of the auction area. Employee Doster told appellee Titsworth: "Turn him loose, we're going to teach him a lesson. This is the reason I pay this boy [Ball] $100.00 a week is to take care of punks like him." Employees Doster and Ball then viciously attacked appellee McPeek in the auction area. McPeek drew a knife and started to fight back. Appellee Titsworth pleaded with them to stop before someone was killed. Appellee Titsworth then got appellee McPeek away from the auction and led him across the street to Titsworth's truck. The employees, Doster and Ball, got a shovel and a bumper jack, went across the street to appellee Titsworth's truck, and severely beat both appellees.

The beatings were so tumultuously administered that a crowd of 50 people gathered before it ended. Even so, the president of the appellant corporation remained in his office.

These facts and the reasonable inferences therefrom establish that appellant corporation hired Ball, an ex-convict, for the purpose of forcefully ejecting people from the auction and teaching "punks" "a lesson." Ball was paid $100.00 per week but only worked one day a week. Ball normally drank at work and had a bottle of beer in his hand when the intentional torts occurred. Doster, another ex-convict, knew that appellee McPeek and his partner owed the appellant's president, Moak, a debt and he had repossessed a truck from the partner. On the night at issue, Don Moak told appellee to leave the premises, but saw him walk into the auction area. At this point, the president of appellant corporation knew, or by the exercise of reasonable diligence should have known, that appellee McPeek might be forcibly ejected by the corporation's employees, Doster and Ball. Still he did not exercise any supervisory care on behalf of the appellant corporation.

Clearly, an employer who hires two ex-convicts, one of whom is normally drinking, and entrusts to them the job of forcibly ejecting patrons, has a duty to exercise reasonable care to avoid harm to those patrons by exercising supervisory care when the employer knows, or by the exercising of reasonable diligence ought to know, that such employees are about to forcibly eject a patron.

Appellant next argues that the evidence is insufficient to support the amount of the awards. The argument is without merit. McPeek, who received the $1,000.00 verdict, suffered a permanent scar, plus pain, suffering, and anguish. Titsworth, who received the $50,000.00 verdict, had medical expenses in excess of $3,700.00, is still under medical care, has suffered loss of income, has suffered pain, and according to his medical witness, will continue to do so.

Affirmed.

CASE COMMENT

An employer who hires people to teach "punks" a lesson and forcefully eject patrons, coupled with the employees background and drinking habits, has a duty to exercise reasonable care to avoid harm to the patrons by exercising supervisory care over those employees.

INTERNATIONAL DISTRIBUTING CORPORATION v. AMERICAN DISTRICT TELEGRAPH COMPANY
569 F. 2d 136 (1977)

ROBB, Circuit Judge:

This case arises from the theft of thousands of dollars worth of merchandise from a liquor store operated by International Distributing Corporation (IDC). IDC sued American District Telegraph Corporation (ADT), the company which provided a burglar alarm service to IDC. The theory of the suit was that two of ADT's employees committed the thefts.

The District Court granted summary judgment to the plaintiff (IDC) on the count of the complaint which alleged a breach of contract but granted summary judgment to the defendant (ADT) on the remaining counts. Both parties appealed.

We affirm the summary judgment on the contract count and reverse with respect to the counts sounding in tort.

The dispute in this case arises from a contract in which ADT agreed to provide burglar alarm service to IDC. The contract provided that when ADT received an alarm signal at its central monitoring station it would dispatch its employees to IDC's store. The employees would gain entry by using keys which IDC provided to ADT for this purpose. Unfortunately, this practice proved tantamount to letting the wolf into the sheepfold. Two of ADT's employees, Smith and Hines, repeatedly stole large quantities of liquor after using their keys to enter and check on real or bogus alarms.

IDC sued ADT in both contract and tort, basing the tort counts upon the theory of *respondeat superior*. Defendant ADT moved for summary judgment on the tort counts, and the District Court granted the motion. The court also granted summary judgment to the plaintiff *sua sponte* on the counts sounding in contract. However the court awarded damages of only $446.00 in accordance with a limitation of damages clause in the contract. We shall consider each of these actions briefly.

I. CONTRACT COUNT

The summary judgment was based upon two documents. The first was an affidavit by the police officer who obtained confessions from Smith and Hines describing the perpetration of the thefts. The second was a transcript of Smith's and Hines' testimony at the criminal trial of one of their alleged co-conspirators. These two documents establish that Smith and Hines regularly stole from IDC by disabling the burglar alarms and misusing the keys IDC provided to ADT.

Notwithstanding ADT's assertion to the contrary, the affidavit and trial transcript proffered admissible evidence sufficient to support summary judgment on the contract claim. Smith's and Hines' incriminating statements would be admissible at trial, either through their own testimony, or if the culprits proved to be unavailable as witnesses, as statements against interest. Furthermore, either an affidavit or a certified transcript of prior testimony may provide the basis for summary judgment.

The affidavit and transcript establish *prima facie* a breach of ADT's contractual duty to provide continuous alarm service, and are opposed only by ADT's bare allegation that Smith and Hines did not commit the thefts. But a party may not avoid summary judgment by mere allegations unsupported by affidavit. Hence, summary judgment for IDC on the contract count was proper.

IDC, of course, agrees that this summary judgment in its favor is proper, but maintains that the District Court improperly limited damages to $446.00. The District Court fully analyzed this contention before rejecting it, and we need not repeat that analysis, which we think is correct.

II. TORT COUNTS

We turn next to the counts of the complaint sounding in tort. The District Court concluded that the defendant ADT was not liable on the theory of *respondeat superior* and granted summary judgment accordingly. We agree that ADT would not be vicariously liable. However we reverse because ADT may be *directly* liable under another theory: negligent supervision of its employees.

We first consider IDC's argument that ADT is liable on the theory of *respondeat superior*. IDC argues that ADT should be liable if the torts committed by ADT's employer were foreseeable, regardless of whether the thefts were committed in furtherance of the employer's interest. In support of this proposition the IDC cites our decision in *Lyon v. Carey*, 533 F.2d 649. But *Lyon v. Carey* did not purport to establish such a rule. In the District of Columbia, "'unless an assault, or other tort, is actuated in part at least by a purpose to serve a principal, the principal is not liable.'" *Meyers v. National Detective Agency, Inc.*, 281 A.2d 435. Nothing in *Lyon v. Carey* changes this rule. In the *Lyon* case we held that a department store may be liable for an assault committed by one of its deliverymen. The assault grew out of a dispute over payment for the delivered goods, and the lynchpin of our decision was that the dispute was originally undertaken *on the employer's behalf*. We noted that the employer would be liable if the assault "was the outgrowth of a job-related controversy", but not if the assault was "simply a personal adventure of the deliveryman . . . ." We remarked that the assault by the deliveryman "was perhaps at the outer bounds of *respondeat superior* . . . ."

It is clear that the thefts in this case were "simply a personal adventure" which did not spring from any purpose to serve the employer. Hence the District Court correctly refused to impose vicarious liability upon ADT.

Nevertheless the District Court should not have granted defendant ADT summary judgment on the tort claims, for a jury could have held ADT directly liable for negligent supervision.

It is true that plaintiff IDC did not plead the theory of negligent supervision. However federal courts grant the parties the relief to which the facts entitle them, even if the proper theory has not been pled.

The facts on the record to date would plainly support an inference that ADT was negligent in its supervision of Smith and Hines. It is clear that an employer may be liable for negligent breach of its duty to supervise its employees. Restatement (Second) of Agency § 213(c); *see* W. Seavy, Law of Agency 138 (1964). And an employer has a duty to supervise those of its employees who are privileged because of their employment to enter another's property. This duty extends even to activities which, like theft, are outside the scope of employment. Restatement (Second) of Torts § 317 and accompanying comments.

On the record established to date in this case, a jury could reasonably conclude that ADT did not exercise reasonable care to supervise its employees. The thieves were able to bypass the alarm system and enter the protected premises at will, conducting a burglary of one of ADT's customers nearly every other day and looting IDC's store ten to fifteen times. A jury might conclude from these facts that the occasional spot checks conducted by ADT were inadequate in view of the ease with which employees could conduct major thefts. Consequently, the summary judgment on the tort counts must be reversed and the case remanded for trial.

The judgment is *Reversed in part, Affirmed in part.*

CASE COMMENT

When employees are privileged by their employment to enter another's property, the employer has a duty to supervise those employees. In this case of repeated burglaries over an extended period of time occasional spot checks were inadequate, especially in view of the ease with which the thefts were carried out.

NEGLIGENT RETENTION

Security managers may, from time to time, receive information in the form of complaints, or otherwise, about the conduct of a security employee. Depending on the depth, breadth, and type of abnormal, irregular, or faulty activity complained about, the manager's failure to take some type of corrective action may result in litigation for negligently retaining the unfit employee. Examples of complaints include incompetency, propensity towards violence, use of abusive or defamatory language, over-reaction to situations likely to be encountered, use of excessive force, and substance abuse.

To resolve or correct the activity complained about may require one or more of the following positive actions: discharge of the employee, discipline, reassignment of the employee to other duties so as to obviate the activity complained of, retraining in the particular area, rehabilitation, or closer supervision and control. For example, an employee with a bad driving record is required to attend and pass a safe driver education course before being allowed to drive the company's vehicles again. Successfully completing and passing the safe driver course basically recertifies the driver, and the slate is wiped clean. Likewise, if an employee with a substance abuse problem successfullly attends an appropriate rehabilitation program, the employee can be reintroduced into the work force. Positive actions of this nature will diminish the threat of successful negligent retention litigation.

In the following case the guard's superiors had received reports of his threats of physical violence; however, no disciplinary action was taken in response to the reports.

LINDSEY v. WINN DIXIE STORES, INC.
368 S.E. 2d 813 (1988)

BANKE, Presiding Judge.

The appellant, Bret Allen Lindsey, brought this action to recover for injuries allegedly inflicted upon him by a co-worker, Charlie Whitehead, while the two of them were in the employ of the appellee, Winn Dixie Stores, Inc. Both Winn Dixie and Whitehead were named as defendants in the action. This appeal is from the grant of Winn Dixie's motion for summary judgment. The action presumably remains pending below against Whitehead.

The following facts may be assumed for purposes of this appeal. The appellant was employed as the store's produce manager, while Whitehead was a city policeman hired to work at the store as a part-time security guard. The two had no relationship outside of work. Prior to the incident giving rise to this action, they had maintained a pleasant and friendly relationship at work, marred only by one incident several months previously in which Whitehead had accused the appellant, in the presence of other store employees, of stealing merchandise. The appellant had immediately reported the incident to the store manager, and Whitehead had later apologized to him for making the accusation.

On the day prior to the alleged assault, Whitehead confronted the appellant on the job with a report that someone had told him that the appellant had called him stupid. The appellant denied having made such a statement and considered the matter closed. The following day, however, Whitehead approached the appellant while the latter was in the back of the store unpacking produce and told him, "I'm off the clock . . . . If you want to call me stupid, you can call me stupid." The appellant replied, "Charlie, I told you yesterday that I didn't call you stupid but if you insist I will call you stupid." The appellant thereupon proceeded to do so, whereupon Whitehead grabbed him from behind in a choke hold, continued choking him until he passed out, and dropped him to the floor. As a result of the fall, the appellant suffered a fractured jaw, a lacerated chin, and the loss of three teeth.

The appellant's superiors had previously received reports from other store employees to the effect that Whitehead had threatened them with physical violence; however, no disciplinary action had been taken against Whitehead in response to those reports. On the evening before he committed the alleged assault on the appellant, Whitehead announced to the store's acting manager that "he was going to take the appellant's face and mop the back room with it."

The evidence of record in this case does not establish as a matter of law the existence of any causal relationship between the appellant's performance of his duties at the supermarket and the incident which gave rise to this action. Instead, it may be inferred from the evidence that Whitehead attacked the appellant for reasons which were purely personal, within the contemplation of OCGA § 34-9-1(4). It follows that Winn Dixie was not entitled to summary judgment on the basis of OCGA § 34-9-11.

Winn Dixie contends that even if it is not insulated from liability for Whitehead's alleged misconduct pursuant to the Workers' Compensation Act, it is insulated pursuant to the "fellow-servant doctrine." We disagree.

The fellow-servant doctrine is set forth at OCGA § 34-7-21 as follows: "The employee shall not be liable to one employee for injuries arising from the negligence or misconduct of other employees about the same business." While this doctrine would appear to insulate the appellee from any *vicarious* liability for Whitehead's alleged conduct which might otherwise be imposed pursuant to the doctrine of respondeat superior, it has been held that the fellow-servant doctrine does not protect an employer from being charged with direct liability for *its own* negligence in hiring or retaining an employee with knowledge that the employee's presence or the manner in which the employee performs his duties poses a danger to co-employees.

There is, as has previously been indicated, evidence of record in this case indicating that the appellant's superiors had been placed on notice prior to the alleged assault on the appellant that Whitehead had threatened other co-workers with physical violence. More-over, there is evidence that, less than a day prior to the alleged assault, Whitehead had announced to the assistant store manger (who was serving at that time as the acting manager) an intention to "take the appellant's face and mop the back room with it." As this evidence is supportive of the appellant's claim that his injuries were proximately caused by the appellee's negligence in allowing Whitehead to continue to work at the store with knowledge of his alleged violent propensities, we hold that the trial court erred in granting the appellee's motion for summary judgment.

Judgment reversed.

CASE COMMENT

Management had knowledge of prior reports of threats of physical violence by the security guard. The guard announced the night before to the acting manager that the next day he was going to mop the back room with plaintiff's face. No disciplinary action was taken by management. An employer is not protected from being charged with liability for its own negligence in retaining an employee when they have knowledge that the employee poses a danger to co-employees.

NEGLIGENT INVESTIGATION

An investigation is one of the tools of the trade a security manager uses in his efforts to prevent loss. It can help determine what actually was lost and the value of the loss. And it may provide information that could help counter future losses. Through an investigation, the culprit hopefully can be identified. When an individual is identified as the perpetrator, any one of a number of actions can take place: request for restitution, discharge of the employee, arbitration hearing, or criminal charges. In any event, the alleged culprit has rights to be won or lost. It is important, therefore, that the investigation be conducted fully, fairly, and properly. Failure to do so, coupled with an accusation against an individual, might possibly lead to litigation, such as malicious prosecution, wrongful discharge, defamation of character, and infliction of emotional distress. The investigation should be complete, fair, proper, and leave no stone unturned.

Some examples of an incomplete, and thus negligent, investigation can be found in *Wainauskis v. Howard Johnson Company*, 488 A.2d 1117 (1985), a malicious prosecution case successfully won by an employee charged with the theft of four deposits. The court noted the following delinquencies:

- failure to interview any of the other seven employees who knew the combination to the safe;

- failure to interview the employee's superior to whom she reported finding hidden cash and asked to have the combination to the safe changed;
- failure to determine the employee's procedure for making deposits;
- failure to verify that the employee did not work on one of the days during which the daily deposits were missing;
- failure to investigate the employee's prior employment history and personal background;
- failure to make a full and fair disclosure to prosecuting authorities; and
- failure to take the time, when no immediate action was called for, to devote time to an adequate investigation as the protection of the individual demanded such because of the hardship, humiliation, suspense, and expense to which an innocent person may be subjected.

SHAFFER v. SEARS, ROEBUCK AND CO.
734 S.W. 2d 537 (1987)

CRANDALL, Judge.

Defendants Sears, Roebuck and Company (Sears) and Patricia Zoeller (Zoeller) appeal from a judgment entered pursuant to a jury verdict in a malicious prosecution action in favor of plaintiff, Carleton B. Shaffer, in the amount of $20,000 compensatory damages against both defendants and $50,000 punitive damages against Sears only. Zoeller is a security guard employed by Sears. We affirm in part and reverse in part.

Defendants instigated an unsuccessful criminal prosecution of plaintiff for shoplifting which gave rise to this malicious prosecution action. This is the second appeal of this case. At the first trial plaintiff obtained judgment for $15,000 actual damages against Sears, Zoeller and two other defendants and $275,000 for punitive damages against Sears only. On appeal, we reversed and remanded in light of *Sanders v. Daniel International Corporation*, 682 S.W. 2d 803, which substantially changed the law of malicious prosecution as it existed in Missouri. *Shaffer v. Sears, Roebuck and Co.*, 689 S.W.2d 683 (Shaffer I). On remand plaintiff filed an amended petition naming Sears and Zoeller as the only defendants. The case is an appeal from the second trial.

Defendants first contend that plaintiff failed to make a submissible case for compensatory damages in malicious prosecution. The evidence at the second trial was essentially the same as the first trial. Since the facts are set forth in detail in Shaffer I, we need not reiterate them in this opinion. In that case we noted at page 687:

> We turn to defendants' contention that the plaintiff failed to present evidence sufficient to make a submissible case under the newly articulated standards and that outright reversal is required. As to compensatory damages we believe the evidence to be sufficient. A jury could have found (but was not compelled to find) that one or more of the individual defendants proceeded consciously to persecute plaintiff with such wanton disregard for the rights of plaintiff as to infer an improper motive. That finding is one of legal malice sufficient under *Sanders* to support the cause of action. Here defendants were advised before prosecution was instigated of plaintiff's explanation of the occurrence. They made no effort to check out his story which could have been done by simply contacting another of Sears employees. That employee in fact verified plaintiff's story. That, coupled with the physical viewing point of the store security officer who purported to see the theft, plaintiff's payment of items worth six times the value of what he purportedly stole, the condition of the items when taken from plaintiff indicating the possibility of prior purchase, and the inflexible policy of prosecution of Sears testified to, support a finding of wanton disregard for plaintiff's rights. In addition no

investigation was conducted even after plaintiff's attorney advised the company of the results of his investigation, and prosecution was continued without further review.

Defendants' challenge to the compensatory damage award is basically a re-argument of the same point they raised in *Shaffer I*. We concur with our prior opinion. Defendants' first point is denied.

Defendants next contend that plaintiff failed to make a submissible case on the issue of punitive damages. Since this malicious prosecution action arose from proceedings which were criminal in nature, proof of actual malice is required to support a punitive damage award.

In *Shaffer I*, we held:

> As to the punitive damages, proof of actual malice is required. As defined in *Sanders* that proof is lacking. Wanton disregard sufficient for legal malice is not sufficient for actual malice under the *Sanders* case. We cannot say, however, that plaintiff would be unable to provide evidence of actual malice now that he is aware of the requirements of *Sanders*.

Plaintiff has not adduced any additional evidence on the issue of actual malice. Further, we decline to follow plaintiff's suggestion that we carve out a new exception to the actual malice requirement where a private police or security force is involved. We therefore find defendants' second point meritorious.

The judgment for $20,000 compensatory damages is affirmed as to both defendants. The judgment for $50,000 punitive damages against Sears only is reversed.

CASE COMMENT

The defendant was advised of the plaintiff's explanation prior to instigating prosecution, yet made no effort to check it out by contacting an employee of the store. No investigation was conducted even after the plaintiff's attorney advised the store of the results of his investigation. These, among other things, led the court to support a finding of wanton disregard of the plaintiff's rights.

NEGLIGENT DETENTION

In this country, a duty is imposed on society not to intentionally or negligently invade or interfere with the safety or security of another. Freedom from illegal confinement (the restriction of one's locomotion) and intrusion into their privacy interests (such as a search) are legally protected interests. Although, in the following case, the security guard was authorized by state law to use reasonable force to question and detain, he also was required to have reasonable cause to believe a theft had been committed. Lacking reasonable cause to believe a theft had occurred, his detention of the customer and subsequent method and extent of inquiry were found to be excessive. Note in this state law that a detention shall not constitute an arrest.

The merchant's privilege statute in this case (LSA - C.C. Art. 2315) does not obviate or shield the merchant from civil liability when the reasonable cause standard is not met.[1]

---

[1] For an excellent treatise on this subject see *Prosecuting the Shoplifter: A Loss Prevention Strategy*, James Cleary, Jr., Butterworth Publishers, Stoneham, Mass , 1986.

THOMAS v. WINN DIXIE LOUISIANA, INC.
477 So.2d 925 (1985)

ARMSTRONG, Judge.

Defendant, Winn Dixie Louisiana, Inc. (Winn Dixie), appeals from a trial court judgment finding it negligent in the manner in which it treated a suspected shoplifter.

Plaintiff, Mary Louise Thomas, is the sole chef and half owner of Mais Oui Restaurant on Magazine Street in New Orleans. Ms. Thomas frequently shopped for provisions for her restaurant at the Winn Dixie store on Prytania Street.

On July 15, 1980 she went to Winn Dixie to shop. As Ms. Thomas often did, she obtained a brown bag from the front of the store. Ms. Thomas decided to purchase 24 boxes of cornbread mix which she placed in the brown paper bag inside of the shopping cart. Another customer, Richard Baum, saw Ms. Thomas place the cornbread mix in the paper bag. Mr. Baum thought that Ms. Thomas might be shoplifting so he reported her actions to the manager and the security guard, an off-duty New Orleans Police Officer.

Eventually Ms. Thomas reached the check out counter, where she paid for all of her purchases including the 24 boxes of cornbread mix. Mr. Bowman, the security guard, then inquired of Ms. Thomas and the cashier whether Ms. Thomas had paid for all of the groceries. The cashier responded that Ms. Thomas had paid for her purchases. Ms. Thomas responded to the question by saying, "Are you kidding?" At the request of the security guard Ms. Thomas was then ushered to the rear of the store. There is controverted testimony at this point. Ms. Thomas testified that the security guard examined her purse and told her that she could go. The security guard testified that Ms. Thomas shoved her purse at him in a belligerent manner and said, "Check my purse if you think I'm shoplifting". At any rate the security guard searched Ms. Thomas' purse and found nothing. Ms. Thomas then left the store.

After a trial on the merits the trial court held that Winn Dixie was negligent in its treatment of the plaintiff and awarded her $22,500 in damages.

In its reasons for judgment the trial court states:

> This Court is of the opinion he (the security guard) was negligent in not doing two things. One: Following her right in the aisles to ascertain himself as to what was going on rather than taking the word of a lay person ... Secondly: He was negligent in not coming to the conclusion that if a person goes through the shopping line and puts all of their groceries on a conveyor, then that person would not be in the process of shoplifting. Also, I find that Officer Bowman was guilty of negligence in saying to the cashier in an audible voice, did Ms. Thomas, did Ms. Thomas pay. In essence, did Ms. Thomas pay for all of the groceries, more particularly everything in the bag.

For the afore-quoted reasons the trial court determined that Winn Dixie was negligent under LSA-C.C. Art. 2315.

On appeal defendant asserts that the trial court erred in finding defendant negligent under LSA-C.C. Art. 2315 rather than applying the standards set forth under LSA-C.Cr.P. Art. 215.[1] Furthermore, defendant asserts that Ms. Thomas was never actually detained. Additionally, defendant claims that the damages awarded by the trial court are excessive.

[1] Art 215. Detention and arrest of shoplifters. A. (1) A peace officer, merchant, or a specifically authorized employee or agent of a merchant, may use reasonable force to detain a person for questioning on the merchants' premises, for a length of time not to exceed sixty minutes, when he has reasonable cause to believe that the person has committed a theft of goods held for sale by the merchant, regardless of the actual value of the goods. The merchant or his employee or agent may also detain such a person for arrest by a peace officer. The detention shall not constitute an arrest.

We do not agree with the appellant. There is civil liability under LSAC.C. Art. 2315. Not only must the storekeeper have reasonable cause to initiate an investigation of a customer in regard to shoplifting, but the method and extent of the inquiry must also be reasonable to afford the store immunity from civil liability under LSA-C.C. Art 2315.

In this instance the extent of the inquiry was excessive. Once the security guard determined that Ms. Thomas had paid for all of her groceries his inquiry should have ended. Instead, Ms. Thomas was taken to the rear of the store and her purse searched.

Ms. Thomas testified that as a result of her experience in defendant's store she suffered a great deal of emotional trauma. Ms. Thomas' emotional distress was corroborated by her daughter and Fred Davis, Ph.D., who testified that Ms. Thomas suffered from post traumatic stress reaction as a result of this incident. Patricia Sutker, Ph.D., also testified that Ms. Thomas suffered a psychological reaction to the incident at Winn Dixie; however, Dr. Sutker characterized Ms. Thomas' reaction as milder than Dr. Davis characterized it. Dr. Davis examined Ms. Thomas 18 months after the incident, and Dr. Sutker examined her over 2 years after the incident. Both doctors agreed that when they talked to Ms. Thomas she was still suffering from the psychological effects that the incident had upon her. In making its award the trial court stressed how impressed it was with Ms. Thomas' sincerity and with the conclusions of the psychologists.

When damages are not susceptible of precise measurement, much discretion shall be left to the court for the reasonable assessment of these damages.

The law is plain and means what it says, and it is the duty of all appellate courts to follow it. Under this rule the amount of damages assessed by the judge or jury should not be disturbed unless the appellate court's examination of the *facts* reveals a clear abuse of the discretion vested in the trial court.

Under these circumstances we cannot say that the trial judge abused his discretion in awarding Ms. Thomas $22,500.

In sum we hold that under the circumstances of this case defendant should be held liable for the emotional trauma suffered by Ms. Thomas. We also hold that the amount of the trial court's damage award was not excessive.

For the foregoing reasons the judgment of the trial court is affirmed.

AFFIRMED.

CASE COMMENT

A regular and frequent customer paid for her purchases. This was verified by the cashier. The case should have ended here. In order to detain under this shoplifting statute, the merchant must have reasonable cause to initiate a shoplifting investigation. There was none. Note that there can be civil liability even with the merchant's statute.

NEGLIGENT USE OF WEAPONS

A gun is a dangerous, lethal instrumentality. The rules for the use of a gun are stringent not only for the purpose for which it is being used, but also in terms of the duty owed to the public at large. A gun user must act in a reasonable manner so as not to invade the personality interests of members of the public. One must take into consideration the probability that any person, other than the felon as in the following case, might be hit. Lacking skill in the use of a weapon and shooting into a crowded thoroughfare makes for a reasonable chance to cause grave harm to bystanders.

The facts and circumstances of the situation are taken into consideration in determining the reasonableness of the action taken. In civil liability, if the evidence shows that the armed security guard acted without due regard to the danger caused to third parties, both the guard and the employer may be held liable.

GIANT FOOD, INC. v. SCHERRY
444 A.2d 483 (1982)

WILNER, Judge.

Appellant employed William Joyner as an armed security guard to protect its store located in the Blair Plaza Shopping Center in Silver Spring. On the evening of November 11, 1978, while on duty, Joyner observed a man brandish a pistol and rob one of appellant's cashiers. He allowed the robber to leave the store, and began to pursue him across the parking lot.

As the robber reached a car parked at the far end of the lot, Joyner pulled his pistol and twice shouted to the man to stop, identifying himself as a police officer. The robber ignored the warnings, got into the car, and began to drive quickly away. Joyner, standing between fifteen and forty feet from the fleeing vehicle, fired two shots at the car.[1] One, aimed at the driver's side window, hit the rear quarter panel. The other, aimed at the rear window, sparked this litigation. Instead of hitting the car, the bullet went through Geraldine Scherry's fifth floor apartment window across the street.

Ms. Scherry was just walking into her living room when the bullet shattered her window, strewing glass all over the apartment. Thinking that someone was trying to kill her, she became hysterical. The episode was so unnerving as to cause nausea, insomnia, headaches, and general mental and emotional distress, leading to the need for some psychotherapy, one hospitalization, and lost time from work.

Ms. Scherry and her husband sued appellant in the Circuit Court for Montgomery County on a variety of theories. Ultimately, the case was submitted to the jury on the theory of Joyner's negligence in firing the second shot, for which appellant would be vicariously liable, and appellant's direct negligence in hiring Joyner and entrusting him with a firearm without proper training. The jury returned a general verdict of $15,000 compensatory damages, $12,000 attributable to Ms. Scherry's injuries and $3,000 for loss of consortium.

In this appeal, appellant raises three issues: (1) is appellant immune from liability to appellees because Joyner had a right to use deadly force in attempting to capture the fleeing felon, (2) was the damage award based upon inadmissible expert testimony given in response to an impermissible hypothetical question, and (3) did the court err in its instructions to the jury with respect to damages?

(1) *Liability*

Appellant's theory of immunity, or non-liability, proceeds thusly: (1) as a result of his direct observations, Joyner had probable cause to arrest the fleeing felon; (2) he had the right to use reasonable force to effect that arrest, and, in the circumstances presented here, that included the use of deadly force; (3) his actions were therefore "privileged"; and (4) by reason of that "privilege," no liability would accrue to an unintended third party victim.

Appellant argues this theory in two contexts: the denial of its motion for directed verdict, and the court's refusal "to instruct the jury on Restatement of Torts section 143(2) relating to the use of force and pursuit of a fleeing felon."

[1] Joyner testified that he fired the second shot from a distance of about fifteen feet. Detective William Crieder, who investigated the incident, stated that, according to what Joyner told him at the time, Joyner "was 40 feet from the car" when he fired the second shot.

We have no difficulty with appellant's first premise. Under Maryland law, "a private person may make an arrest if he ha[s] reasonable grounds (probable cause) to believe that a felony was committed and that the person whom he arrests committed it." Certainly, in light of his own observations, Joyner had probable cause to believe that the person he was pursuing had just committed an armed robbery, and he therefore had the right and authority to arrest him.

We agree also that a person authorized to make an arrest may use reasonable or "necessary" force to accomplish that result. Prosser, *Law of Torts*, 134 (4th Ed. 1971). We do not necessarily concur, however, with appellant's argument that the use of deadly force—the firing of shots—was justified, at least not as a matter of law. Given the fact that the robber was in the process of fleeing and, at the time, presented no immediate danger to Joyner or anyone else, and given the alternative option of noting the license tag number of the getaway car (which Joyner neglected to do) and summoning help from the police, a permissible inference could be drawn that Joyner's actions exceeded the use of reasonable or necessary force under the circumstances and therefore were not privileged. See Restatement of Torts (2d) § 79 (1965).

We need not rest our decision on that doubt alone, for there is a more significant weakness in appellant's argument. Joyner's conduct has to be viewed not only in the context of the duty he owed to the robber not to use excessive (i.e., unreasonable, unnecessary) force in effecting an arrest, but also in terms of a duty he owed to other persons to act in a reasonable manner. A finding of "privilege" with respect to the robber does not, in other words, end the inquiry *vis a vis* any responsibility to third parties such as Ms. Scherry; it would, at best, merely serve to insulate Joyner and appellant against liability *to the robber*, had *he* been shot.

Restatement of Torts (2d) § 137 (1965), states that "[l]iability for the invasion of any of another's interests of personality, by the exercise of the privilege of effecting the arrest or recapture, or of maintaining custody of a third person, is determined by the rules stated in §§ 74 and 75 (of the Restatement)." Section 75, which deals with the situation of one acting in self-defense, provides:

> An act which is privileged for the purpose of protecting the actor from a harmful or offensive contact or other invasion of his interests of personality subjects the actor to liability to a third person for any harm unintentionally done to him *only if the actor realizes or should realize that his act creates an unreasonable risk of causing such harm.*

See also §§ 83 and 111, expressing the same principle in the context of acting in defense of property and in the recaption of chattels.

These sections of the Restatement make clear that, in attempting to make a warrantless arrest, a person has, in effect, a double responsibility—one to the prospective arrestee not to use unnecessary force against him, and one to the public at large to use even reasonable force in a reasonable manner. This is illustrated in Comment c to § 137, which states, in relevant part:

> Thus, if an actor is privileged to shoot at an escaping felon, he is not liable to a third person harmed by a stray bullet, *if when he shot there was little or no probability that any person other than the felon would be hit.* But when he shoots into a crowded thoroughfare, and unintentionally hits a passerby, his act is unprivileged if, in view of the surrounding conditions, including the nature of the crime for which he seeks to arrest, recapture, or maintain custody, the harm which may ensue if he does not act, and his skill or lack of skill in the use of the weapon, it is unreasonable for him to take the chance of causing grave harm to bystanders. (Emphasis supplied.)

In light of the case law that has developed, we think that the reference in the second sentence of Comment c to shooting into a crowded thoroughfare is merely one of example, not one of limitation. The reasonableness standard set forth in §§ 75, 83, and 111, incorporated by reference into § 137, and otherwise explicated in Comment c, would apply whether the shot is fired into a "crowded thoroughfare" or any other place or circumstances in which there is some prospect that an innocent person may be hurt.

These kinds of situations, in which an innocent bystander is injured or killed in the course of an attempt to apprehend a criminal or defend an attack on one's person or property, arise in a variety of contexts—some more life-threatening to the actor than others, some involving felons and felonies, others involving misdemeanants and misdemeanors. The context is important in determining the reasonableness of the action taken, but the basic standard seems to be the same. Where the evidence shows that the actor, whether a police officer or a private citizen, acted without due regard to the danger caused to innocent third parties, he (and his employer) have been held liable.

Conversely, where the evidence establishes that the defendant acted reasonably, liability has been denied.

The question, then, is whether, under all of the circumstances in which Mr. Joyner found himself at the moment he took the second shot, it was reasonable for him to have fired that shot. Was there a prospect of injuring someone else?

In *Fowler v. Smith*, 213 A.2d 549, in an oft-quoted passage, stated:

> Negligence is a relative term and must be decided upon the facts of each particular case. Ordinarily it is a question of fact to be determined by the jury, and before it can be determined as a matter of law that one has not been guilty of negligence, the truth of all the credible evidence tending to sustain the claim of negligence must be assumed and all favorable inferences of fact fairly deducible therefrom tending to establish negligence drawn . . . . *And Maryland has gone almost as far as any jurisdiction that we know of in holding that meager evidence of negligence is sufficient to carry the case to the jury. The rule has been stated as requiring submission if there be any evidence, however slight, legally sufficient as tending to prove negligence, and the weight and value of such evidence will be left to the jury.*

Against this standard, we find no error in the court's refusal to grant either the motion for directed verdict or the instruction "on Restatement of Torts section 143(2). . . ."

Mr. Joyner described the episode thusly:

> As soon as he (the robber) set foot on the parking lot he got into a slight trot across the parking lot. At this time I had already unbuckled my holster, and I jumped up and followed suit. I unholstered my revolver.
>
> I was running to the parking lot, and I called for the subject to halt, 'police officer'. He looked around and kept trotting.
>
> I am still in pursuit as he reached the car. I noticed that he did not have an accomplice, and he reached in the car, he reached down into his inside coat and pulled his revolver back and brandished it up in the air like this. (Witness indicating.) He did it as if he was going to turn and fire. He did not fire.
>
> He put his weapon back in his pants, stuck it back down in his pants and got in the car. This is when I hollered for him to halt again. At this time the subject got in the car and proceeded to pull off, and I fired my first shot which hit the rear panel of the car.
>
> He was pulling off in kind of a hurry. He burned a lot of rubber on the parking lot getting off the parking lot. I fired another shot at the back window of the car.

Earlier, he had stated:

> Q The robber never pointed his gun at you at any time during this chase, is that correct?
> A No, he didn't point at me—at me directly.
> Q He didn't point it directly at anybody else in the area, is that correct?
> A   No."

In a subsequent testimony, Joyner confirmed that the robber "put his weapon back in his belt *before he got in the car.*"

Montgomery County police personnel arrived at the scene "a couple seconds" after the shooting incident, according to Joyner. From the description given by him, the suspect was arrested the next day.

From that evidence, permissible inferences arise that (1) the fleeing robber posed no imminent danger to Joyner or anyone else; (2) Joyner could have assisted in recovering his employer's property and effecting the robber's arrest simply by noting his description and the license tag number of the "getaway" car and summoning the more mobile county police; and (3) Joyner was literally shooting into the dark at a rapidly moving target. [4] From the fact that his first shot, aimed at the driver's window, hit the rear quarter panel, a fair inference arises that Joyner's aim was not the best, and that he should have realized that to be the case. Finally, from other evidence in the record, a further inference arises that Joyner should have been aware that he was shooting in the general direction of the apartment complex in which Ms. Scherry resided and that, if he missed his intended target (or the bullet ricocheted off of it), the bullet might strike someone therein.

These inferences are clearly ones of negligence. From them, a trier of fact could rationally conclude that Joyner did not act reasonably, that he should have realized he was creating an unreasonable risk of harm to innocent bystanders by taking that second shot. The issue, then, was one for the jury.

With respect to the instruction, the record reveals that it was merely a recitation of the Restatement of Torts (2d) § 143(2), which has no relevance whatever to this case.

Section 143 deals with the force which a person is authorized to use to *prevent* the commission or consummation of a felony. Subsection (2), and the requested instruction, provides:

> The use of force or the imposition of a confinement intended or likely to cause death or serious bodily harm is privileged if the actor reasonably believes that the commission or consummation of the felony cannot otherwise be prevented and the felony for the prevention of which the actor is intervening is of a type threatening death or serious bodily harm or involving the breaking entry of a dwelling place.

There was no evidence to support such an instruction. Joyner did not fire his gun to prevent a felony, but to apprehend the felon. There was, at the time, no threat of death or serious bodily harm (except from Joyner), and the felony in question did not involve the breaking and entry of a dwelling place. Most important, even if the privilege mentioned in the instruction were applicable, for the reasons stated above it would not preclude liability to appellees.[5]

---

[4] The episode occurred at about 7:30 p.m. on November 11. Joyner stated that "it was dark that time of the year, but the parking lot was light."

[5] We need not consider whether appellant would have been entitled to an instruction along the line of § 137, as such an instruction was not requested. The court gave general instructions on the law of negligence, and specifically told the jury that it was to consider "whether his actions in shooting at the subject under the existing circumstances was reasonable; whether his conduct was such as to produce an unreasonable risk of harm to members of the public in the vicinity,

Because we believe that the case was properly submitted to the jury on the issue of Joyner's negligence, for which appellant would be vicariously responsible, and in light of the general verdict returned by the jury (there being no request by appellant for submission of the case on issues), it is not necessary for us to consider whether the evidence sufficed to sustain the verdict on the alternative basis of negligent employment and entrustment.

JUDGMENT AFFIRMED; APPELLANT TO PAY THE COSTS.

CASE COMMENT

One may have the authority to arrest and to use reasonable or necessary force to make the arrest. When the danger subsides and alternative ways to make the arrest are apparent, the alternative ways may be best depending on the conditions. Two duties are owed here: one to the robber and one to the public at large. Some factors to take into consideration are the nature of the crime, the harm which may ensue if one does not act, one's skill or lack of skill in use of the weapon, and the chance of grave harm to bystanders. Liability can attach when one acts without due regard to the danger caused to innocent third parties.

In the following case, two shots were fired by the guard. The first was a warning shot in the air; the second was fired at the ground in the general direction of the decedent's feet. The guard apparently was not aiming at him and had no intention of wounding him. The voluntary act of shooting a pistol is an intentional act and negligence may be found in an intentional act if the act is done carelessly. Even if the use of force was justified, it will not insulate the guard from liability if the conduct was performed negligently.

JONES v. WITTENBERG UNIVERSITY
634 F.2d 1203 (1976)

CELEBREZZE, Circuit Judge.

This is an appeal from a jury verdict for Appellee in an action under Ohio's Wrongful Death Act and survival statute brought within the District Court's diversity jurisdiction. The jury found Appellants Wittenberg University and Chester Phillips liable for decedent's death and injuries and awarded $27,000 damages in the wrongful death action and $100,000 damages for pain and suffering in the survival action. Decedent's estate was also awarded $1,331.72 for funeral expenses.

This case arose out of the shooting death of John Lobach, hereinafter referred to as decedent, a student at Wittenberg University, on May 10, 1969 by Chester Phillips, a security guard employed by the university. The incident began at 2:40 a.m. when Phillips and Frank Lytle, university security guards, discovered decedent on a second story ledge of a women's dormitory on campus. He descended when ordered to do so by the guards and was placed in custody. Under interrogation at the scene the decedent explained that he was there to meet a girl he had met earlier in the evening and who had invited him up. He gave a false name and informed them that he was a local high school student. The security guards were hesitant to place the decedent under arrest. Although they had radio contact with the local police, they did not report the incident. No attempt was made to ascertain what, if anything, had occurred in the dormitory. Instead, they placed decedent in the backseat of the patrol car and drove around the campus looking for a supervisor to make the decision whether or not to place decedent under arrest. Decedent was not searched though a search

and whether Mr. Joyner realized, or should have realized in the exercise of reasonable care that his action might be dangerous to persons on adjoining property."

That is the essence of § 137.

would have disclosed that he was carrying correct identification. He was not handcuffed, according to guard Frank Lytle, because to handcuff him would mean that he was under arrest. After driving around for a half hour they returned to the dormitory and Lytle went inside to talk with the housemother. While he was inside he heard two shots being fired.

The only direct testimony on the shooting came from Chester Phillips, the security guard who fired the fatal shot. He testified that decedent bolted from the car ignoring several orders to "halt" and only sped up after he fired the first warning shot in the air. He testified that he then fired a second shot at the ground in the general direction of decedent's feet. Phillips claimed that he was not aiming at decedent and had no intention of wounding him. He assumed that he had missed and decedent had escaped when he heard the sound of something hitting a parked car. Phillips raced to the spot and found decedent's body sprawled on the ground. The second shot had pierced his chest. A thirty to forty yard trail of blood indicated that decedent had run that distance after being struck by the bullet.

The section creating an action for wrongful death provides:

> When the death of a person is caused by wrongful act, neglect, or default which would have entitled the party injured to maintain an action and recover damages if death had not ensued, the corporation which or the person who would have been liable if death had not ensued, or the administrator or executor of the estate of such person, as such administrator or executor, shall be liable to an action for damages, notwithstanding the death of the person injured and although the death was caused under circumstances which make it murder in the first or second degree, or manslaughter.

Although wrongful death actions must be brought in the name of the personal representative of the deceased, the action is "for the exclusive benefit of the surviving spouse, the children and other next of kin of the decedent." Wrongful death actions are designed to recompense a decedent's beneficiaries for any "pecuniary injury" they may have suffered by virtue of his untimely death. Survival actions, by contrast, are not concerned with the wrong to the beneficiaries but with the wrong to the injured person. The survival statute provides that any cause of action which a person would have for personal injury during his lifetime survives his death and may be brought on behalf of his estate. The same act may provide a basis for an action in tort saved by the survival statute and an action for wrongful death if the injuries sustained thereby result in a person's premature death.

The trial below was bifurcated. Along with instructions on the question of liability, the District Judge submitted a list of special interrogatories to the jury. These interrogatories reflected the various theories of counsel and were designed to disclose the bases for the jury's verdict. After finding Appellants liable for the wrongful death of the decedent and for the conscious pain he suffered prior to his death, the jury answered the following written interrogatories:

1. Do you find that the death of John Lobach was caused by the wrongful act of defendant Chester Phillips?
   Yes   No X
2. Do you unanimously find that the death of John Lobach was caused by the negligence of defendant Chester Phillips?
   Yes X   No
3. Do you unanimously find that the death of John Lobach was caused by the default of defendant Chester Phillips?
   Yes X   No
4. Do you unanimously find that John Lobach assumed known risk as defined to you in charge 5084.2?
   Yes   No X

5. Do you unanimously find that John Lobach suffered conscious pain prior to his death?
   Yes X   No

6. Do you unanimously find that the conscious pain suffered by John Lobach prior to his death resulted from an assault and battery upon him as defined in charge 5924 by defendant Chester Phillips?
   Yes   No X

7. Do you unanimously find that the conscious pain suffered by John Lobach prior to his death was a proximate result of the negligence of Chester Phillips?
   Yes X   No

8. Do you unanimously find that John Lobach assumed a known risk as defined for you in charge 5084.2?
   Yes   No X

The answers to the interrogatories disclose that the jury found that the decedent's injuries were caused by the negligence of Chester Phillips, the security guard who fired the fatal shot. Wittenberg University, having stipulated that Mr. Phillips was acting within the scope of his employment at the time of the shooting, was held liable for his negligence under the theory of *respondeat superior.*

Appellant contends that the jury's finding of negligence is contrary to the weight of the evidence because Phillips' uncontroverted testimony was that he intended to shoot in the direction of the fleeing student, although he did not intend to wound him. Appellant argues that a finding of negligence may not be grounded on a wilful and intentional act. However, this argument overlooks the principle of tort law that an intentional act may be so negligently performed that it results in civil liability for the actor. To a degree all negligent conduct is intentional in that it is *voluntary.* Even though injury may be unintended, the act which leads to the injury to be actionable negligence must be the product of the actor's will.

> To constitute negligence the conduct involved, be it act or omission, must be voluntary conduct. This does not mean that the actor intended the injurious result of his conduct or intended that it should produce some intermediate result which ultimately brought about the injury. The requirement is not that any particular state of mind must accompany the act, but simply that the act or omission itself be a conscious manifestation of the actor's will. Thus . . . the bodily movement or rest of a man asleep or in a trance will not itself constitute negligence.

The voluntary act of firing a pistol is an intentional act, even though harm was not intended, but it may constitute negligence if it was done so carelessly as to result in foreseeable injury. In this case Phillips testified that the second shot which struck decedent was meant to be a warning shot which was fired at the ground in decedent's direction rather than in the air as the first shot had been. Based on this testimony the jury could reasonably find that decedent's death was caused by Phillips' negligent firing of the second warning shot.

Appellants further argue that the jury's answers to the interrogatories are inconsistent with a finding of liability. Appellants conclude that the jury impliedly found that the force used by Chester Phillips was not unreasonable under the circumstances. This conclusion is tenuous at best, based on unfounded assumptions and faulty premises, and contradicts the jury's express finding that the decedent's death was caused by Phillip's negligence. In Ohio any person who has reasonable grounds to believe a felony has been committed may detain a suspect until a warrant may be obtained. A police officer may accomplish this detention by the use of "reasonable force".[1] However, it is well established under Ohio law

---

[1] There was a controversy at trial whether Chester Phillips, as a private security guard, was a police officer entitled to use reasonable force in detaining a suspect. Although this issue was

that a police officer may be held personally liable where use of excessive *force or negligence* results in personal injury or death.

An allegation that an officer had reasonable grounds to believe a felony had been committed and that reasonable force was used in detaining a suspect is an affirmative defense to a charge of assault and battery by way of justification for the force employed. However, even a justifiable use of force will not insulate an officer from liability if this otherwise justifiable conduct is negligently performed. Phillips may have been justified in firing a warning shot to frighten the fleeing decedent but if that shot was fired so carelessly as to negligently injure the suspect he may be held liable for damages. The jury's verdict in this case reflected the state of the evidence and applicable state law. The responses to the interrogatories were entirely consistent with the finding that Phillips' negligence caused the decedent's injuries and death.

The District Judge did not charge the jury on the issue of contributory negligence although he did instruct them as to assumption of risk. This was not error. In Ohio, contributory negligence is ordinarily a question for the jury. However, a court in a wrongful death action may refuse to charge on the issue of contributory negligence if there is no evidence tending to establish it.

Phillips' uncontroverted testimony was that decedent bolted from the patrol car and fled custody despite Phillips' order to "halt" and the firing of a warning shot. While decedent's flight may have been an exercise in faulty judgment, it does not constitute negligent conduct. The trial judge was correct in concluding that the circumstances were more appropriate for instruction on assumption of risk rather than on contributory negligence. Although contributory negligence and assumption of risk may overlap in appropriate cases, they are separate and distinct defenses. It is often said that assumption of risk is based on "venturousness" and contributory negligence on "carelessness". Decedent's flight was a deliberate attempt to escape custody and was not the sort of careless conduct which one generally associates with negligence. Since there was no evidence tending to establish negligence on the part of decedent it was not error to refuse a charge on contributory negligence.

The jury found that decedent had not assumed the risk that he would be injured by Phillips' negligently fired warning shot. Appellants contend that they were entitled to a judgment that the decedent assumed the risk of being shot as a matter of law. The question of assumption of risk is ordinarily for the jury to determine in light of all the facts and circumstances of the case. It is only when reasonable minds can come to but one conclusion that the assumption of risk issue becomes one for the court. Such was not the case here, particularly in view of the fact that decedent was not placed under arrest. The only direct testimony on the shooting came from the defendant, Chester Phillips. His credibility and the accuracy of his reporting of the events which led to decedent's death were issues for the jury to decide. More importantly, however, assumption of risk arises only if the danger is so obvious that one is presumed to have assumed a known risk. Normally one is not bound to anticipate another's negligence. It is for that reason that Ohio courts have held that the doctrine of assumption of risk cannot be applied if the negligence of an individual, which the injured party could not have foreseen or expected, was the proximate cause of *his* injury. One cannot be held to assume the risk of subsequent negligence. Decedent should not be deemed to have assumed the risk of injury from the negligently fired warning shot as a matter of law when even Phillips who fired the shot could not have anticipated its striking decedent.

not presented to the jury or resolved by the court, we assume for purposes of decision that Phillips was a police officer with authority to arrest and detain a felony suspect.

Appellants also argue that Appellee has not borne the burden in the survival action of proving by expert medical testimony that decedent sustained conscious pain and suffering during the period between the shooting and his death. Under Ohio law, lay persons may reach conclusions on matters within their common experience absent expert testimony. The evidence unquestionably demonstrates that decedent ran approximately forty yards after being shot. From this the jury could reasonably conclude from their common experience that decedent was conscious during that period and experiencing pain and suffering from the gunshot wound.

At trial the District Court admitted evidence of Chester Phillips' background including testimony by two doctors who had treated him for physical and emotional distress over a period of years. Both doctors agreed that Phillips was suffering from an "anxiety reaction" which was manifested in a chronic state of nervousness, general irritability toward people, and an inability to cope with stress. At the time this evidence was presented it was relevant to at least two issues at trial: the negligence of the university in hiring someone with Phillips' background as an armed security guard and the availability of punitive damages. Subsequently both of these issues were removed from the case,[6] and defense counsel motioned that all evidence of Phillips' employment background and physical and mental disability be stricken from the record as irrelevant to any remaining issues. The motion was denied. Admittedly much of this evidence had become irrelevant at this stage of the case, but the evidence of Phillips' psychological disability continued to be relevant to two issues remaining in the case: (1) Phillips' mental state at the time of the shooting, and (2) his credibility as the sole eyewitness.

Normally evidence of an actor's subjective state of mind is irrelevant to the issue of negligence because his conduct is evaluated according to the objective standard of a "reasonably prudent person under the circumstances." In this case, however, the jury had to determine whether Phillips consciously intended to shoot decedent. If the shooting was intentional or reckless his conduct would constitute an assault and battery and not simple negligence. Evidence of Phillips' state of mind at the time of the shooting was relevant to the scienter element of assault and battery under Ohio law. If the jury had determined that Phillips intended to shoot decedent, recovery would have been barred by the running of the statute of limitations for assault and battery actions. Evidence of Phillips' state of mind might also be relevant to his credibility, i.e., his ability to make critical judgments concerning the actual events and circumstances surrounding this case. Since evidence of Phillips' mental state had continued relevancy to issues remaining in the trial, its admission was not reversible error.

The parties have made various other arguments which we have considered and find to be without merit. Accordingly the judgment of the District Court and its award of damages is affirmed.

CASE COMMENT

When decedent was originally placed in custody, no attempt was made to ascertain if an incident had occurred. He was not searched nor was he handcuffed. He was driven around

---

[6] The negligent hiring issue was removed from the case by Wittenberg University's admission that Chester Phillips was acting within the scope of his employment at the time of the shooting. This meant that the University assumed automatic liability should Phillips be found negligent. This obviated the necessity of Plaintiff proving that the university was separately liable for negligently hiring Phillips. The punitive damage issue was removed from the case when the Judge determined that the statute of limitations had run on assault and battery and that punitive damages were not recoverable in Ohio for negligence.

in the patrol car for half an hour looking for a supervisor to make a decision on whether or not to place him under arrest. The guard who claimed he was not aiming at him and did not intend to wound him fired two warning shots: the first in the air and the second into the ground. The second shot pierced decedent's chest. Firing a pistol is a voluntary and intentional act, and even though harm was not intended, it may constitute negligence if done so carelessly as to the result in foreseeable injury.

FAILURE OR OMISSION

Negligent actions can be either positive or negative. A positive act would be doing something a reasonable and prudent person would not do under like or similar circumstances. A negative act would be the failure (omission) to do something a reasonable and prudent person would do under like or similar circumstances. Thus, the security manager must think in terms of civil liability not only about positive actions taken by employees, but also about the failure of employees to do something they should have done.

When one undertakes to perform a service, the act itself may give rise to a duty to another person who might foreseeably be harmed by the first person's failure to perform the undertaking with reasonable care. When one promises to perform a task (such as calling the police), the failure to do so may breach the applicable standard of care. Note the use of expert witnesses in the following case.

To Call Police

TUCKER v. SANDLIN
337 N.W.2d 637 (1983)

PER CURIAM.
Defendants appeal as of right from the judgment entered on the jury's verdict of $80,000 in favor of plaintiff. On appeal, defendants raise numerous issues, none of which require reversal.

Defendants first urge that the trial court erred as a matter of law in denying their motion for judgment n.o.v. According to defendants, plaintiff failed to present sufficient evidence to raise a jury question as to the issues of negligence, duty and proximate cause. We disagree.

In *Samson v. Saginaw Professional Building, Inc.*, 224 N.W.2d 843, the Supreme Court held that a cause of action had been stated against the lessor of a building where a tenant was stabbed in an elevator by the patient of a co-tenant. This Court quoted 2 Restatement Torts, 2d, § 302B, p. 88 as follows:

> An act or omission may be negligent if the actor realizes or should realize that it involves an unreasonable risk of harm to another through the conduct of * * * a third person which is intended to cause harm, even though such conduct is criminal.

See also 2 Restatement Torts, 2d, § 324 A, p. 142, which provides:

> One who undertakes, gratuitously or for consideration, to render services to another which he should recognize as necessary for the protection of a third person or his things, is subject

to liability to the third person for physical harm resulting from his failure to exercise reasonable care to perform, his undertaking, if

(a) his failure to exercise reasonable care increases the risk of such harm, or
(b) he has undertaken to perform a duty owed by the other to the third person, or
(c) the harm is suffered because of reliance of the other or the third person upon the undertaking.

See also *Smith v. Allendale Mutual Ins. Co.*, 303 N.W.2d 702, where the Court recognized that an undertaking to perform a service may give rise to a duty to one who might foreseeably be injured by that person's failure to perform the undertaking with reasonable care. Other courts have applied this reasoning to uphold a cause of action where security guards for a school or college have failed to exercise due care in following up on reports that a person on the premises threatens to cause foreseeable harm to a student. In the present case, plaintiff presented evidence which could support findings that (1) the security guard, Rothgeb, had actual notice of a life-threatening assault on the fifth floor of the student parking ramp, (2) that Rothgeb promised the victim of this first assault that he would "take care" of the task of informing police of the assailant's presence, thereby undertaking a duty to all users of the ramp that he would do so, and (3) that Rothgeb failed to immediately notify police, an omission which certain expert testimony indicated was a breach of the standard of care applicable to a security guard in Rothgeb's position. Plaintiff's proofs not only precluded judgment n.o.v. as to the issues of duty and negligence but also as to the issue of proximate cause. A jury could reasonably find that Rothgeb's omission directly caused plaintiff's injuries, by enabling the assailant to remain on the premises and carry on his criminal conduct without interruption. We conclude that the trial court acted properly in denying defendants' motion for judgment n.o.v.

Defendants next urge that the trial court erred in admitting Sergeant Beauchamp's hearsay testimony that he received a call reporting the assault at 8:16 p.m. on the night in question.

Defendants' third argument on appeal is that the trial court erred in allowing plaintiff's attorney to pose certain hypothetical questions which, according to defendants, were not supported by evidence of record. We find no basis for reversal. Plaintiff's appeal brief clearly demonstrates that each element of the first challenged hypothetical was supported by trial testimony. This initial question was properly asked for the purpose of establishing Rothgeb's standard of care. To the extent that certain follow-up questions assumed facts not in evidence (*e.g.*, the fact that police were called promptly at 8 p.m.), the trial court still properly admitted them for the limited purpose of showing what might have happened had Rothgeb immediately reported the first assault to the police. The trial court recognized that such questions, although somewhat "speculative" in nature, were necessary to allow plaintiff to establish her theory that she would not have been assaulted had Rothgeb in fact complied with plaintiff's conception of the applicable standard of care. The jury was informed that this was the sole purpose of the follow-up questions and plaintiff did not claim or assume that the facts underlying these questions had been proven. Accordingly, the jury could not have been misled into believing that plaintiff had proven the facts underlying the follow-up hypotheticals. There is no basis for defendants' claim of prejudice as to this issue.

Defendants' fourth argument has even less merit. According to defendants, the trial court erred in admitting Deputy Chief Crawford's deposition testimony describing how a police officer would have responded to the situation confronting the security guard, Rothgeb. Defendants insist that it was an abuse of discretion to admit this evidence because Rothgeb did not have police training and should not be held to the police officer's standard of care. We assume *arguendo* that the standards of care applicable to police officers may differ from those applicable to security guards such as Rothgeb. However, we note that plaintiff never attempted to create the impression that Rothgeb would be held to the police officer's standard of care. On the contrary, Crawford stated clearly that a security guard such as Rothgeb would not be expected to apprehend a suspect as would a police officer but that he would instead only be expected to call for assistance. Crawford's testimony was certainly relevant to the issue of whether Rothgeb complied with the lesser standard of care applicable to security guards. The determination of relevancy was properly left to the trial court.

Defendants next challenge the admission of evidence of the police department's average response time. According to defendants, the evidence was neither relevant nor supported by an adequate foundation. We disagree. The foundation for the response time figure was probed and tested during the course of extensive cross-examination. Questions regarding the accuracy of the figure go to its weight rather than to its admissibility. Furthermore, the figure was certainly relevant in determining whether police could have arrived in time to prevent the assault had Rothgeb promptly reported the assailant's presence. Defendants insist that the response time figure is irrelevant because it only applies to "serious" calls, whereas Rothgeb's belated call was treated as "non-serious" in nature since the complainant had left the scene. This argument begs the question because certain trial testimony indicates that if the first assault had been promptly reported the police would still have treated the matter as a "serious" one warranting immediate response. Under the circumstances, we cannot agree with defendants that the response time figure was either irrelevant or so lacking in foundation as to be inadmissible.

Defendants next urge that two of plaintiff's experts, Dr. Weaver and Deputy Chief Crawford, lacked sufficient practical experience to qualify as experts on the subject of a security guard's standard of care. We believe that this issue was properly left to the trial court's discretion. The court's decision to qualify these witnesses as experts was not an abuse of discretion where trial testimony indicated (1) that Dr. Weaver had over 20 years' experience as a teacher and consultant in the field of security administration and (2) that Crawford had worked with the city police department for over 25 years and had worked on various occasions with security guards. Even if it were error to qualify Crawford as an expert, the error was harmless as his "expert" testimony regarding the standard of care was substantially similar to, and therefore cumulative with, that of Dr. Weaver.

Defendant's seventh argument is that the trial court erred in denying their motion for a mistrial based upon the nonproduction of police documents. According to defendants, police witnesses relied upon certain undisclosed documents to demonstrate that police cars were available at the time of the assaults. We find no basis for reversal. It was the negligence of defendants' attorneys, rather than any surprise tactics of plaintiff, which resulted in defendants' failure to obtain copies of the subject documents. At the time of Deputy Chief Crawford's November, 1979, deposition, defendants' attorneys not only had learned of the subject records (officers' daily reports and "call sheets" as well as police emergency response time reports) but actually had an opportunity to question Crawford about them. At one point, Crawford went beyond merely explaining the records and offered to show defense counsel a copy of "the actual report". Crawford made clear that copies of the records were available. Still, defendants did not request copies prior to trial. Defense counsel not only had prior notice of the availability of these records but also had an opportunity to review them during trial and to extensively cross-examine Sergeant Beauchamp regarding their contents. We conclude that there can be no basis for any claim that defendants were prejudiced by the nonproduction of police records.

Finally, we find no merit in defendants' claim that the award of damages was so clearly and grossly excessive as to shock the judicial conscience. There was no showing that the award was secured by improper methods, prejudice or sympathy. Reasonable minds could decide that the award of $80,000 was just compensation for the substantial physical injuries and for the severe and lasting mental anguish which plaintiff described in her testimony.

In concluding review of this appeal, we state our finding that the trial court's opinion was sufficiently clear and detailed in its review of the issues presented in defendants' motions for a new trial to comply with the requirements of GCR 1963, 527.7.

Affirmed.

CASE COMMENT

An undertaking to perform a service may give rise to a duty to one who might foreseeably be injured by that person's failure to perform the undertaking with reasonable care. Here there was evidence that the guard was on notice of a life-threatening assault, that the guard promised he would inform the police of the assailant's presence (thereby undertaking a duty to all users of the ramp), and that the guard failed to immediately notify the police. Expert witnesses testified that the guard was not expected to act as a police officer in apprehending the assailant, but he was expected to call for assistance. Also he breached the standard of care applicable to a guard in his position.

In the following case, evidence was presented by a rape victim that neither her rape nor any other rape would have been attempted if the guard had been performing the duty they were hired to do: patrol the premises. Instead of patrolling, the guards slept, watched television, stayed in their apartments, socialized with their girlfriends, and left the premises. Additionally they also failed to prepare written reports or notify the police of a series of rapes.

To Patrol

WILLIAMS v. OFFICE OF SECURITY & INTELLIGENCE, INC.
509 So.2d 1282 (1987)

PER CURIAM.
This is an appeal from the trial court's entry of a directed verdict in favor of the defendants and an order conditionally granting defendants a new trial should the directed verdict be reversed on appeal. We reverse the judgment and order appealed from and reinstate the jury verdict based upon the following analysis.

Briefly stated, the relevant facts are as follows. On August 18, 1981 plaintiff Mabel Hamilton Williams was attacked and raped by an intruder who broke into her apartment at Westview Terrace Apartments.[1] At the time of the rape, this apartment complex was allegedly being protected and guarded by defendant Office of Security and Intelligence, Inc. (OSI).[2]

A jury found that the negligence of OSI, of defendant Barnard Ferron, its president, and of defendant Ray Overcash, the OSI supervisor at Westview, was a proximate cause of Ms. Williams' injuries and awarded her $800,000 in compensatory damages.

However, while the jury was deliberating, the trial court granted OSI's motion for a directed verdict. The trial court's ruling was based upon the reasoning that "no matter how grossly negligent the evidence showed the defendants to have been, only by sheer coincidence could the defendant's guards have been in the right place to prevent this rape and, therefore, their negligence was not a proximate cause of the plaintiff's injuries."

[1] Evidence presented at trial indicated that another tenant committed the rape.

[2] A review of the record shows that OSI guards negligently carrried out their duty to patrol the apartment complex twenty-four hours a day.

A motion for a directed verdict should be treated with care, and this is especially true in negligence cases where the role of a jury to weigh and evaluate the evidence is particularly important since reasonable individuals can draw various conclusions from the same evidence.

We have carefully reviewed the record, briefs and argument of counsel in accordance with the foregoing principles and conclude that the evidence presented at trial established not only that OSI was negligent, but also that OSI's negligence was a proximate cause of the rape of Ms. Williams.

The guards were hired to patrol the apartment complex premises. Instead, they slept, watched television, stayed in their apartments, socialized with their girlfriends, and left the premises. Moreover, they also failed to prepare written incident reports or notify the police of the series of rapes occurring at Westview.

In the instant case, Ms. Williams presented testimony that neither her rape nor any other rape would have been attempted if the guards had been performing their duties. *See Holley v. Mt. Zion Terrace Apartments, Inc.,* 382 So.2d 98, "It is peculiarly a jury function to determine what precautions are reasonably required in the exercise of a particular duty of due care."

Ms. Williams also showed that because the guards were negligent in their performance, they encouraged criminals to commit crimes, including rapes, at the apartment complex, rather than deterring such behavior. For their part, the defendants did not show that the intruder would not have been seen and stopped from entering the apartment if reasonable security had been present or "that the crime would not even have been attempted in the face of the deterrent effect of such protection." *Holley,* 382 So.2d at 101.

Based on the reasons and authorities set forth above, the judgment and order appealed from are reversed with instructions to the trial court to reinstate the jury verdict.

Reversed and remanded with instructions.

CASE COMMENT

Sleeping, watching television, staying in their apartments, socializing with girlfriends, leaving the premises, failing to prepare written incident reports, and failing to notify police of a series of rapes can hardly be said to be patrolling, which the guards were hired to do. Because of this negligence, criminals were encouraged to commit crimes at the complex, rather than being deterred from such behavior by guard patrols.

In the next case, the company had a policy for immediate compliance and cooperation in the event of a robbery. Supervisors were required to have a thorough working knowledge of all company policies. A policy to comply imposes a duty on the employees. Failure to use due care in connection with the duty to act reasonably under the circumstances leads to liability. Here the supervisor failed to follow company policy by not doing what the robbers told him to do—initially not letting them have the money. This apparently provoked the criminals and helped to create a hostile situation. Experts testified that the response to the robbery was substandard.

To Comply With Policy

MASSIE v. GODFATHER'S PIZZA, INC.
844 F.2d 1414 (1988)

WESLEY E. BROWN, Senior District Judge.
Mary Massie brought this negligence action against her former employer, Godfather's

Pizza, claiming damages for a rape and assault she sustained during a robbery of a Godfather's Pizza restaurant in Salt Lake City, Utah, on October 5th-6th, 1983. She claimed that she was injured because of the negligence of Godfather's and its employee, James Head, who failed to comply with the demands of the robbers, contrary to company policy.

The jury returned a special verdict in favor of plaintiff for $200,000 in general damages, and an additional $36,000 in special damages. After trial the court sustained defendant's motion for remittitur, and reduced the special damage award to $10,000.

Both parties appeal from the judgment—the defendant upon various grounds, including the absence of negligence, and upon the argument that worker's compensation is plaintiff's exclusive remedy—while plaintiff appeals the trial court's action in reducing the jury award of special damages from $36,000 to $10,000.

The issues on appeal are whether or not the trial court properly denied Godfather's Motion for Judgment Notwithstanding the Verdict, whether the trial court erred in denying Godfather's Motion for New Trial, and whether the jury's damage awards were appropriate and supported by substantial evidence. In the appeal, Godfather's claims that state worker's compensation is plaintiff's exclusive remedy; that neither Godfather's Pizza nor its employees owed a duty to comply with the demands of the robbers; that the policy of Godfather's Pizza to comply with the demands of robbers did not impose a duty on its employees; that any alleged negligence on the part of Godfather's was not the proximate cause of plaintiff's injuries; that plaintiff's counsel's plea for punitive damages in his closing argument was prejudicial, and that his incorrect statement of law concerning the "coming and going rule" was prejudicial, so that a new trial is required; and finally, that the general and special damages awarded to plaintiff were excessive.

Our review of the record discloses that the evidence, viewed in the light most favorable to the plaintiff, entitled the jury to make the following findings of fact:

Plaintiff was employed by defendant Godfather's at its restaurant located at 2100 South 900 East, Salt Lake City, Utah through October 5, 1983. She worked as minimum wage "counter help", taking orders, cleaning tables and running the cash register. She had no supervisory responsibility at work and she had nothing to do with the safe that was in a back room at the restaurant. Her uniform consisted of navy blue pants, a blue and tan striped pullover shirt, and while working, an apron, hat and name tag. Neither the shirt nor the pants had the Godfather's name or logo on them.

James Head, originally hired as a cook and a dishwasher, was made a shift supervisor for Godfather's in May, 1983, at which time his wage was raised from the minimum wage of $3.35 per hour to $3.50 per hour. As a shift supervisor, Head was considered a part of the management team, who was to have a thorough working knowledge of company policies and procedures. He had all of the keys to the restaurant and he possessed the combination and key to the safe located on the premises. Management personnel, including the shift supervisor, wore a vest and tie, which signified their special position of authority.[1]

Prior to October 5, 1981, Head had been a shift supervisor for approximately six months but had not yet learned how to close out the books at the end of the evening shift.

According to Head's job description in the company manual, he was required to "maintain positive community relations at all times, *both on and off* the job", and he was expected "even when he was off the clock" to be representing Godfather's Pizza.

Carl Satchell was the manager of the Godfather's restaurant in October, 1983. He had not previously checked into Head's prior employment or Army background, and he testified that prior to October 5th, Head had "acted macho and cocky" during working hours.

---

[1] As shift supervisor, Head was required to "Maintain a thorough working knowledge of and follow all company policies and procedures", according to the company manual, and Carl Satchell, the manager of the restaurant.

Satchell also knew that on one occasion, Head had brought a gun that was wrapped up and concealed on the Godfather premises.

Prior to October 5, 1983, plaintiff knew that there was a safe in the employee break room, and she had requested Head to get change for her on several occasions. She assumed that Head had access to the safe, although she had never actually seen him open it.

Godfather's usually closed at 11:00 p.m., but on October 5, 1983, the restaurant became busy late in the evening, causing the shift to run later than usual. Plaintiff, who was scheduled to work until closing, did not have a car at work that day. Although her husband usually picked her up after work, plaintiff made arrangements to walk home with Head after work that day, so her husband would not have to get their small son out of bed at that time of the night to come and pick her up. Plaintiff had walked home from work on many prior occasions, but not after dark.

After the last customers were served, plaintiff, Head, and Carl Satchell began cleaning up and preparing to leave. Satchell left about midnight, leaving plaintiff and Head still at work. Prior to leaving, Satchell asked plaintiff to estimate when she would finish her work so he could fill out her time card. She estimated another half hour, so Satchell "clocked her out" at 12:30 a.m. In fact, plaintiff did not complete her work in that time, and worked another 45 minutes or so beyond the time noted on her card. Plaintiff was not paid for the extra time.

While cleaning up, plaintiff observed someone pull on the locked door of the restaurant, but she did not see the individual well enough to identify him. The restaurant did not have "open" or "closed" signs on the door, and it was not unusual for people to walk by to see if the place was still open.

After their work was done, Head and plaintiff played a video game and then left the restaurant, Head locking the door behind them. They did not observe anyone around the restaurant when they left. At the time they left the store, plaintiff was wearing her dark slacks and striped shirt, covered by a long navy seater coat. Her apron was rolled up and put in her pocket, and her hat and name tag had been left at the restaurant. Head had removed his tie and wore a black jacket or vest over his clothes.

About two blocks from the restaurant they were accosted by two men, who ordered them to go back to the restaurant to get money. Head noticed that one of them had a knife in one of his pockets. Head agreed to cooperate and they walked back to the store, but Head told one of the men that he could not open the safe, although he had the knowledge and ability to do so. Head knew that there was only $500 in the safe.

On the way back, the men checked Head's wallet and asked plaintiff for her money. She had only a nickel which the men did not take. At the store, the men took Head's keys and made plaintiff unlock the restaurant. All four went in, and the men locked the door after them and kept Head's keys.

Head led plaintiff and the men around to check the tills, which were empty, and into the break room. Head and one of the men went on to the manager's office for a search for money, and then Head's hands were tied and he was returned to the break room. There, one of the men began manipulating the safe, trying to open it; Head again was asked to open the safe, but he again denied that he could do so. The men became frustrated and disgusted at their inability to get any money. One man made a statement to the effect that "if we can't get any money, we're going to get some pussy." The jury was entitled to find that this statement was made in the break room in Head's presence.

One of the men then took plaintiff to a different part of the restaurant, forced her to undress and raped and sodomized her. Then, the second man did likewise. During this, Head heard Mary crying and screaming. After the second assault on plaintiff began, Head finally agreed to open the safe, but not until the first man went to Head, zipped up his pants in front of him, and threatened him with a roll of cellophane wrap. After getting the money, the two men left on foot, taking plaintiff with them, and leaving Head tied up in the restaurant. Plaintiff was forced to run down an alley and over an eight foot fence, injuring her foot and both hands. She was able to escape when a policeman came into view. The men separated and ran; they were never caught.

Head told the robbers that he could not open the safe because he felt that, as a representative of Godfather's, he was left in charge of it and it was his responsibility. He told an investigator that he didn't want to lose his job, and didn't want Godfather's to lose any money.

Prior to the incident involving plaintiff, Godfather's had formulated a written policy which called for immediate compliance and cooperation in the event of a robbery. The company Manual set out procedures to be followed:

> No amount of money is worth the safety and well being of Godfather's Pizza employees. The criminal is usually interested only in money and, if not provoked to any other violence, will 'take the money and run.' The real key to safety of the victim is to allow the criminal to get in and get out as quickly as possible. "Godfather's Pizza, in cooperation with law enforcement agencies, has established the following standard procedures in the event of a holdup or robbery.
> * Above all, remain calm.
> * Do not create a hostile situation.
> * Do exactly what the criminal tells you.
> * Do not provoke the criminal.
> * Offer no resistance.
>
>   *   *   *   *   *   *   *
>
> Above all, cooperate. Do not try to overcome the criminal. Do not resist. Do exactly what the criminal says.

When making bank deposits, Satchell had discussed with Head that he should comply with robber's demands, but he did not review the written policy with Head. Godfather's had no organized training program with regard to employee conduct during a robbery, and the robbery policy was not posted in the restaurant. The Company Manual was kept in the locked manager's office and was not generally available to employees. Head testified that he had received no training whatsoever regarding robbery, and he was not aware of Godfather's written policies.

The two men made all of their demands and efforts to Head to get money, not to the plaintiff. Prior to the one man's statement that if they could not get money they would attack plaintiff, there had been no indication that the men intended a sexual assault of any sort.

Two experts testified to the effect that Head's response to the robbery, and Godfather's methods of hiring and training its personnel, were substandard. Both of these experts also established proximate cause, testifying that if Head had reacted properly and turned over the money, the robbers probably would have taken the money and left, without harming plaintiff.

Prior to the assault, plaintiff enjoyed life, enjoyed dealing with the public, was outgoing and had a good marriage with a satisfying sex life. Since this incident, her marriage has suffered, her sex life has been significantly impaired, and she feels frightened, threatened, and insecure. She obtained psychiatric and emotional counseling from several professionals. At the time of trial, she was being seen by Dr. Victor Cline, whom she had seen about six times. Dr. Cline diagnosed plaintiff as suffering from post-traumatic rape syndrome, from which she will never recover. This doctor testified that the memories of the assault were permanently etched into her recollection by a chemical produced in high stress situations, locking vivid memories in place to recur from time to time. Dr. Cline and plaintiff planned future appointments, which would become less frequent when progress was made, or more frequent, in time of stress. The doctor's usual charge for counseling was $75 per hour at time of trial.

Plaintiff has tried to return to restaurant work, but gave up one job when they wanted her to work nights. She is afraid to walk past "scruffy looking" men, and will cross the street to avoid them. At the time of trial she was employed cleaning houses for two or three hours a day.

In her complaint, plaintiff alleged that the response of the shift supervisor, James Head, was negligent, for which Godfather's was responsible under the principle of *respondeat superior*, and that Godfather's was directly negligent in the manner of hiring, screening, and failing to train its supervisory-management personnel. Godfather's denied the allegations, and raised the affirmative defense that worker's compensation was plaintiff's exclusive remedy, and that Godfather's had no separate duty to plaintiff, and that its negligence, if any, was not the proximate cause of injury and damage to plaintiff.

The case was submitted to the jury upon a general theory of negligence, and upon instructions which covered Godfather's affirmative defense based upon workmen's compensation. The jury was instructed that in order for the plaintiff to prevail, she was required to prove three propositions.

1. That the defendant Godfather's Pizza, Inc. was negligent in that either, (a), Godfather's failed or omitted to give adequate training, supervision and education to James Head as to appropriate measures he should have taken in the event of a robbery; and/or (b), that James Head failed to act as a reasonably prudent person should have acted during the course of the robbery and at a time when he was acting in the scope of his employment for Godfather's.

2. That the negligence of the defendant in either or both of the particulars that I've just referred to was a proximate cause of the incident to the plaintiff.

3. That as a result of said incident, she suffered injuries and damages.

The trial court provided the jury with a lengthy and detailed definition of "negligence" as it pertained to the case before them:

Negligence is the failure to exercise due care under the circumstances. The degree of care required increases in proportion to the risk of harm which is known or under the circumstances ought to be known to exist.

Negligence may be the doing of some act which a reasonable and prudent person would not do under the same or similar circumstances, or it may be the failure to do something that such a person would have done under the same or similar circumstances. The mere fact that an incident happened, considered alone, does not support an inference that any party to this action was negligent.

You'll note that the person whose conduct we set up as the standard is not the extraordinarily cautious individual nor the exceptionally skillful one, but a person of reasonable and ordinary prudence. While exceptional caution and skill are to be admired and encouraged, the law doesn't demand them as a general standard of conduct.

In determining whether plaintiff Mary Massie or James Head was negligent, you should consider the following: A person who, without negligence on their part, is suddenly and unexpectedly confronted with peril arising from either the actual presence or the appearance of imminent danger to themselves or to others is not expected nor required to use the same judgment and prudence that may be required of them in calmer and more deliberate moments. In such a situation their duty is to exercise only the degree of care which an ordinary prudent person would exercise under the same or similar circumstances. If, at that moment, they exercise such care, they do all the law requires of them, even though, in light of after events, it might appear that a different choice and manner of action may have been better or safer.

The scope of Godfather's liability under the principle of *respondeat superior*, was set out for the jury in this manner:

> The defendant … is liable for the negligent acts of its employee, James Head, provided such acts were done within the course and scope of his employment. In determining whether or not James Head's conduct at the time of the incident was within the course and scope of his employment for this purpose, you should consider whether or not the conduct was of the kind he was employed to perform, whether or not the conduct occurred substantially within time and space limits, and what extent, if any, the conduct was motivated by a purpose to serve the employer.

As to the issues of proximate cause and intervening cause, the jury was instructed that an intervening cause "is one which actively operates to produce harm and occurs after the purported negligent act … and which was not foreseeable to the defendant." It was explained that even though the injury was the result of criminal conduct by third parties, such conduct could be a proximate cause, if the criminal conduct was itself "foreseeable to the defendant". The court instructed that:

> Foreseeable means to know or reasonably anticipate beforehand. Thus, you should determine, in the case of the defendant … whether it was negligent, and if so, whether at that time, as a reasonably prudent corporation, it should have reasonably anticipated or foreseen that a criminal assault generally of the same kind as occurred here could have occurred as a result of its negligence. And the same thing as to James Head. If you find that he was negligent and acting in the scope of his employment at the time, you should then determine whether, at that time, as a reasonably prudent person, James Head should have reasonably anticipated or foreseen that a criminal assault, generally of the same kind that occurred here, could have occurred as a result of his negligence.

1. Godfather's Pizza and/or James Head while acting within the scope of his employment, was negligent;
2. That such negligence was a proximate cause of plaintiff's injury;
3. That plaintiff was not negligent;
4. That the negligence of Godfather's–James Head was 100%;
5. That at the time of the incident in question, plaintiff was *not* acting within the course and scope of her employment with defendant;
6. That plaintiff's special damages were in the sum of $36,000 and that her general damages were in the sum of $200,000 for total damages of $236,000; and
7. That plaintiff did not fail to mitigate her damages.

Defendant next contends that if plaintiff was not within an employment situation, then in effect, it had no duty at all toward plaintiff since no duty is imposed in law upon a proprietor of a business establishment to comply with a demand of a robber. This precise argument was presented to—and rejected by—the trial court at the close of plaintiff's evidence, and the case was submitted to the jury upon general principles of common law negligence, which required an element of "foreseeable harm."

Under Utah law, Godfather's had a duty to act reasonably under the circumstances. In Utah, the possessor of land may be liable when harm is caused by the negligent or intentional acts of third parties, if the landowner failed to exercise reasonable care to discover that such acts were being, or were likely to be done. *Pagan v. Thrift City, Incorporated*, 460 P.2d 832. The rule applies, even though criminal conduct by third persons is involved, if such conduct is foreseeable.

In *Pagan*, the Utah rule was stated in this manner, 460 P.2d at 834:

> A possessor of land who holds it open to the public for business purposes is subject to

liability for injuries to members of the public where harm is caused by negligent or intentional acts of third persons provided the possessor of the land failed to exercise reasonable care to discover that such acts are being done or likely to be done, or to give a warning adequate to enable visitors to avoid harm.

The trial court ruled, and the evidence established, that Godfather's had recognized foreseeable harm, and created its own duty to the public when it established its written "robbery policy," quoted above. There was no error in the submission of the question to the jury, under the instructions of the court which are quoted above.

Defendant contends that any alleged negligence on its part was not a proximate cause of plaintiff's injuries, because there was no evidence that Head would have acted any differently had he received formal "robbery training"—and because there was "no evidence" that this particular rape would not have occurred even if Head had immediately opened the safe. Defendant has ignored the testimony of plaintiff's expert witnesses who described the formal training required to insure that an employee's reaction to a robbery situation would be automatic—and the testimony of both expert witnesses to the effect that in their opinion the sexual assault on plaintiff would not have occurred if Head had opened the safe promptly. A jury question existed, and the issue was properly submitted for determination.

For all of the foregoing reasons, the Judgment is AFFIRMED.

CASE COMMENT

The shift supervisor, who claimed he was not aware of company policies, was required to maintain a thorough working knowledge of and to follow all company policies and procedures. The policy called for immediate compliance and cooperation in the event of a robbery. Also the company had a policy that no amount of money was worth the safety and well-being of the employees. Experts testified that the supervisor's response was substandard, that formal training would have ensured automatic employee reaction to a robbery, and that the assault would not have occurred if the safe was opened promptly. The store had recognized foreseeable harm and created its own duty to the public when it established its written robbery policy.

In the next case, the company failed to provide the police with exculpatory information after it had asked them to conduct a theft investigation. In one statement, the company investigator agreed with the head cashier that the prime suspect had probably not been responsible. They suspected someone else. This statement was never turned over to the police. Only two out of five statements were given to the police. When an investigation is undertaken, there is an obligation to furnish police with not only inculpatory information, but exculpatory information as well. Liability may not be avoided in a malicious prosecution case unless a full disclosure of all material facts relative to the charge has been made. Malicious prosecution is examined in Chapter 2.

To Provide Exculpatory Statements

BROWN v. DART DRUG CORPORATION
551 A.2d 132 (1989)

GARRITY, Judge.

Kellie Renee Brown appeals from the grant of a summary judgment motion by the Circuit Court for Prince George's County, that effectively terminated her claims against Dart Drug Corporation of Maryland (Dart Drug). Appellant's claims, for malicious prosecution and negligence, were based on Dart Drug's failure to provide exculpatory information concerning Ms. Brown to the Prince George's County Police Department after it had asked the police to conduct an investigation of a theft and had furnished the police with information tending to indicate that Ms. Brown was the thief.

Facts

Ms. Brown had been employed by Dart Drug for approximately two months as a part-time cashier at the time of the alleged theft.

On the evening of October 23, 1983, after finishing her evening shift, Ms. Brown followed the routine procedure for balancing her register before leaving. On this particular night, Ms. Brown discovered a shortage of $6.20. After recounting the money several times with the manager, Joel Croteau, the shortage remained. The remaining money was then sealed in an envelope and deposited in the store safe by Croteau.

The following morning, the safe was opened by two Dart Drug employees, Norma Peloquin and Mary Overton. Upon opening the envelope, a cash shortage of $900, specifically 45 twenty-dollar bills, was discovered. The matter was turned over to two investigators, Ali M. Muhammed and Donald Cooper, of Dart Drug's internal investigations unit. On the same day, the two investigators interviewed and obtained statements from Ms. Brown, Mr. Croteau, Ms. Peloquin and Ms. Overton, and then contacted the Prince George's County Police Department to report the theft. The case was assigned to Detective Joseph W. Frohlich, and Dart Drug's investigators turned over to him the statements they had previously taken from Ms. Brown and Mr. Croteau. Subsequently, Mr. Cooper obtained a statement from the head cashier, Clevetta Forrester, in which Ms. Forrester voiced her suspicions that Ms. Peloquin had both a motive and an opportunity to commit the theft. She further averred that Ms. Peloquin had severe financial problems at the time, that she was behind in her rent, and that bill collectors were calling the store for her. Moreover, according to Ms. Forrester, Ms. Peloquin had previously acted in a suspicious manner while in her presence when removing cash tills from the safe, and that several days earlier a $47 shortage had been discovered in one of the cash tills which Ms. Peloquin had removed from the safe. Allegedly, after Mr. Cooper took this statement, he agreed with Ms. Forrester that Ms. Brown, who had been targeted by Dart Drug as the prime suspect, had probably not been responsible for the theft.

Although the Forrester statement taken by Mr. Cooper was never turned over to Detective Frohlich, Mr. Muhammed attested that he contacted the detective to relate that as a result of an investigation involving other incidents in the store, Ms. Peloquin should also be considered a suspect.

Detective Frohlich conducted an independent investigation and interviewed a number of Dart Drug employees. He did not interview Ms. Forrester, however, because she was not made known to him. After concluding his investigation, Detective Frohlich brought charges against Ms. Brown for theft over $500 in value. The matter went to trial in the District Court for Prince George's County. Ms. Brown was acquitted of the charge.

Ms. Brown subsequently brought this action for malicious prosecution and negligence. In opposition to a motion for summary judgment, Ms. Brown included affidavits from

Detective Frohlich and the prosecuting attorney in which each stated that if he had known of Ms. Forrester's statement Ms. Brown would not have been prosecuted.

Discussion of Law

On appeal, the appellant posits that there was sufficient evidence to submit the counts of malicious prosecution and negligence to the jury. Specifically, the appellant alleges that, once Dart Drug investigators undertook to make an investigation of the incident and supply the police with information, they had an obligation to furnish the police with not only inculpatory information, but any exculpatory information as well.

Before an action for malicious prosecution may be brought, the complaining party must show:

(a) a criminal proceeding instituted or continued by the defendant against the plaintiff, (b) termination of the proceeding in favor of the accused, (c) absence of probable cause for the proceeding, and (d) "malice," or a primary purpose in instituting the proceeding other than that of bringing an offender to justice.

Dart Drug denies responsibility and avers that Detective Frohlich commenced the criminal action against Ms. Brown based on his independent investigation.

In *Wood v. Palmer Ford*, 471 A.2d 297, Judge Orth cited Prosser, *Law of Torts* (4th ed. 1971) p. 836–7, for the proposition that:

The defendant may be liable either for initiating or for continuing a criminal prosecution without probable cause. But he cannot be held responsible unless he takes some active part in instigating or encouraging the prosecution. He is not liable merely because of his approval or silent acquiescence in the acts of another, nor for appearing as a witness against the accused, even though his testimony is perjured, since the necessities of a free trial demand that witnesses are not to be deterred by fear of tort suits, and shall be immune from liability. On the other hand, if he advises or assists another person to begin the proceedings, ratified it when it is begun in his behalf, or takes any active part in directing or aiding the conduct of the case, he will be responsible. The question of information laid before prosecuting authorities has arisen in many cases. If the defendant merely states what he believes, leaving the decision to prosecute entirely to the uncontrolled discretion of the officer, or if the officer makes an independent investigation, or prosecutes for an offense other than the one charged by the defendant, the latter is not regarded as having instigated the proceeding; but if it is found that his persuasion was the determining factor in inducing the officer's decision, or that he gave information which he knew to be false and so unduly influenced the authorities, he may be held liable.

In the case at bar, Dart Drug directly aided the conduct of the police investigation by examining witnesses and taking statements. The manager, Stanley Klutz, filed a Crimes Against Property report the same day that the money was discovered missing and listed Kellie Brown as the number one suspect. Of the five statements that were taken by Dart Drug investigators, only two were furnished to Detective Frohlich. Most importantly, neither the exculpatory statement executed by Ms. Forrester nor Ms. Forrester's identity was ever made known to the police.

It is settled law that a civil defendant may not avoid liability for malicious prosecution by relying on the independent judgment of a prosecutor or attorney unless that defendant has made a full disclosure of all material facts relative to the charges being made.

We believe it clear that once Dart Drug had failed, for whatever reason, to provide the police with the exculpatory evidence regarding Ms. Brown, the issue of whether Dart Drug was liable on the theory of either malicious prosecution or negligence became a question for the fact finder. Accordingly, we hold that the trial court erred in granting the motion for summary judgment on behalf of Dart Drug.

JUDGMENT REVERSED; CASE REMANDED TO THE CIRCUIT COURT FOR PRINCE GEORGE'S COUNTY FOR FURTHER PROCEEDINGS IN ACCORDANCE WITH THIS OPINION; COSTS TO BE PAID BY APPELLEE.

CASE COMMENT

The store failed to provide exculpatory statements to police after it had asked the police to investigate a theft and had furnished police with information that the plaintiff was suspected. The store investigator agreed with the head cashier that the plaintiff probably had not been responsible for the theft. This statement was never turned over to the police, thus the investigating detective never interviewed her. Out of the five statements taken by the store only two were given to the police. One may not be in a position to avoid liability in a situation like this if full disclosure of all material facts is not made.

2

Intentional Torts

People in the United States have certain legally protected interests and certain legally protected freedoms. This chapter deals with the intrusion or invasion of some of these freedoms and interests. These are translated into intentional torts as follows:

- Freedom from the fear or apprehension of harmful or offensive contact—Assault;
- Freedom from harmful or offensive bodily contact—Battery;
- Freedom from illegal confinement—False Arrest and False Imprisonment;
- Freedom from wrongful criminal prosecution or unjustifiable litigation—Malicious Prosecution;
- Freedom from the invasion in the interest in one's reputation—Defamation;
- Freedom from the invasion of, or intrusion into, one's privacy interests—Intrusion Upon Seclusion or Invasion of Privacy; and
- Freedom from being emotionally distressed—Infliction of Emotional Distress and Outrageous Conduct.

An intentional tort is a tort or wrong done by a person who intended to do that which the law has declared to be wrong. This is opposite of negligence where the tortfeasor failed to exercise a particular degree or standard of care. It may also be a willful tort, which involves intent, and because of the indifference to the safety of others may have the elements of malice or ill will. Some intentional torts, such as assault and battery, can be prosecuted as crimes, as defined in various penal codes.

ASSAULT AND BATTERY

An assault is an unlawful or illegal threat or attempt to do physical harm or inflict injury on another person, together with an apparent present ability or capacity to do so. It can be committed without physical contact such as touching or hitting. It is an intentional show or display of force that gives the victim reason to fear or expect immediate bodily harm. An element of the apprehension of the victim is required for it to be a tort.

Battery is the unlawful or illegal application of force to another. It requires physical contact, which may be an offensive touching or a beating with bodily injury, either directly or with an object.

Assault is the offer of the use of force; and battery is the use of that force.

CAPPO v. VINSON GUARD SERVICE, INC.
400 So.2d 1148 (1981)

CHIASSON, Judge.

Frank J. Cappo, plaintiff-appellant, filed this appeal alleging that the trial court erred in applying the doctrine of mitigation and in fixing the amount of damages awarded to him against the defendants, Vinson Guard Service, Inc., Sam Cooke, and Ground Pat'i, Inc. All of the defendants have answered the appeal.

On June 9, 1978, Cappo along with three companions entered the parking lot of the Ground Pat'i Restaurant on Jamestown Avenue, in the city of Baton Rouge. Sam Cooke, an elderly security guard employed by Vinson Guard Service to patrol the parking lot of the Ground Pat'i confronted Cappo, and informed him that if he was not patronizing the restaurant that he would have to park his car elsewhere. Cappo, who had been drinking, testified that his intention was to proceed to a nearby nightclub along with his friends. He told Cooke that he knew the owner of the Ground Pat'i, who had given him permission to park in the lot.

Abusive language and threats ensued until the manager of the Ground Pat'i, Lawrence Prather, was notified and came out to settle the dispute. Standing in between Cooke and the plaintiff, Prather tried to learn what the difficulties were, so he could resolve them. Cappo explaining the situation called Cooke, an "old bastard." Whereupon, Cooke from behind Prather, struck plaintiff causing him to fall, injuring a bone in his left wrist. Prather dismissed Cooke, and allowed Cappo and his party to remain.

Plaintiff filed suit against Sam Cooke, individually; Vinson Guard Service, Cooke's employer; Ground Pat'i, Cooke's employer; and the Travelers Insurance Company, the liability insurance carrier of Vinson. On plaintiff's motion to dismiss, Travelers was dismissed from the case. Ground Pat'i filed a third party demand against Cooke and Vinson seeking indemnity of any award it would be called upon to pay.

At the trial on the merits, the trial court found no question of liability holding that the abusive language used was no excuse for the tortious conduct. It held that Cooke, with Vinson Guard as Cooke's employer under La.C.C. art. 2320, and Ground Pat'i as Cooke's special employer under *LeJeune v. Allstate Ins. Co.*, 365 So.2d 471, were liable *in solido* for the damages sustained by the plaintiff.

On the question of damages, the trial court found an award of $13,490.00 to be reasonable, but reduced it to $7,500.00 on mitigating factors. The two reasons cited for mitigation were: 1. Plaintiff played a major part in provoking the incident; 2. Plaintiff's failure to minimize his damages through surgery. The court granted Ground Pat'i's third party demand against Cooke, only, but concluded that Vinson Guard was liable for contribution as a solidary obligor. From this judgment plaintiff appealed complaining of the assessment of damages and the application of the doctrine of mitigation. Vinson Guard and Cooke answered the appeal seeking a reversal or, in the alternative, that the damages be reduced. Ground Pat'i answered the appeal seeking to reverse the trial court's holding that Cooke was its employee and that it was a solidary obligor along with Vinson Guard and Cooke. In the alternative Ground Pat'i submits that the court erred in failing to grant its third party demand against Vinson Guard for indemnity.

The issue of liability of the three defendants will be discussed first. There is no merit to Sam Cooke's contention that the trial court erred in finding him liable. The intentional battery committed upon the plaintiff is a sufficient basis for finding Cooke liable as a tortfeasor under La.C.C. art. 2315. As found by the trial court, the verbal provocation cannot excuse the commission of a battery upon a person.

There is also no merit to Vinson Guard's argument for not being held liable. Vinson Guard was the general employer of Cooke; the one who paid him and the one who had the ultimate power to terminate him. Under La.C.C. art. 2320 and the decision in *Foster V. Hampton*, 381 So.2d 789, Vinson Guard is solidarily liable to the plaintiff with Cooke.

Ground Pat'i contends that it should not be held liable as Cooke's special employer since the relationship between Ground Pat'i and Vinson Guard was that of independent contractor and not that of master and servant. In addition Ground Pat'i argues that if Cooke is considered its employee, he was not acting within the course and scope of his employment when he struck the plaintiff. We find that the trial court correctly treated both of these points in its written reasons for judgment and we approvingly quote therefrom the following:

> At trial the manager of the Ground Pat'i, Lawrence Prather, testified that he periodically checked on the parking lot as a part of his duties. He further testified that he could tell Cooke who to admit and who to exclude from the lot. Additionally, Prather said that he had authority to have Cooke replaced by another Vinson guard. Prather stated that he exercised his authority over Cooke on the night of the incident by sending Cooke home. Also, there is no question that Cooke's activities during the performance of his duties benefitted the Ground Pat'i as well as Vinson Guard Service. Thus, the Ground Pat'i had supervision and direction of Cooke's activities during the performance of his duties and for that reason must be considered Cooke's special employer for the purpose of this suit.
>
> The Ground Pat'i argued in the alternative that even if it were found to be Cooke's employer, it should not be held liable because Cooke's action in striking the plaintiff was outside the course and scope of his employment. Again, the court cannot agree. Cooke did not turn aside from his employment to pursue a personal motive such as revenge. The argument with the plaintiff occurred as a part of Cooke's duties, and the battery was committed during the argument. Cooke was attempting to enforce the parking regulations that he had been charged to enforce. The blow, though probably sparked by a personal insult, never became separate from Cooke's employment.

Our attention next turns to the issue of the assessment of damages and whether the trial court erred in finding the plaintiff failed to mitigate his damages. Appellate review of an award for damages was discussed by the Supreme Court in *Reck v. Stevens*, 373 So.2d 498. In that decision the court outlined the test for appellate courts to use in reviewing awards as follows:

> It is only after articulated analysis of the facts discloses an abuse of discretion, that the award may on appellate review, for articulated reason, be considered either excessive or insufficient.

Based on the injury and treatment hereinafter discussed we do not find any abuse of discretion in the trial court's award of $13,490.00.

The trial court after making its award, reduced it to $7,500.00 because plaintiff failed to mitigate his damages. The necessity for a plaintiff to mitigate his damages is well founded in Louisiana Law. The first factor in reducing the award was the provocatory words used by the plaintiff before he was struck by Cooke. As stated by the court in *Watts v. Aetna Casualty & Surety Company*, 309 So.2d 402,

Provocation by words, however, can be considered in mitigation of damages although rejected as justification for an unlawful act.

The plaintiff called Cooke an "old bastard" right before he was struck. The trial court found that these words spoken about Cooke to a third party, Lawrence Prather, was a fact that was proper to use in mitigating damages. We agree with this finding of fact and conclusion of law.

In regards to the second basis for mitigation, the trial court was correct in finding that the plaintiff failed to submit to reasonable medical treatment for his injury. Plaintiff was being treated by Dr. Alan Farries, who had put a cast on the wrist following the incident. No improvement was shown and finally in November, of 1978, Dr. Farries recommended surgery. However, plaintiff failed to undergo the surgery because of other commitments.

The surgery recommended had a sixty to sixty-five percent success rating and would have left the plaintiff with a ten percent disability to the left wrist. Without the surgery his disability is estimated to be thirty to thirty-five percent. We agree that this surgery would have been beneficial to the plaintiff and was reasonable medical treatment. Therefore, the trial court was correct in reducing the award because plaintiff failed to mitigate his damages.

For the reasons assigned, the judgment of the trial court is affirmed at appellant's cost.

CASE COMMENT

Verbal provocation cannot excuse the commission of the intentional tort of battery upon a person in a situation like this. However, the words can be considered in mitigation of damages. This is not a "fighting words" First Amendment–type event. Plaintiff failed to submit to reasonable medical treatment, which enhanced the mitigation claim.

FALSE ARREST AND FALSE IMPRISONMENT

A false arrest is the forceful and unlawful restraint of the liberty of another without proper legal authority. Inasmuch as the arrest itself restrains liberty, it also becomes false imprisonment. The thrust of this tort lies in the protection of the personal interest in the freedom from restraint of movement or locomotion. Malice and ill will are not elements of this tort; however, if shown, they can be a cause for punitive or exemplary damages. False arrest and false imprisonment can be viewed as being synonymous.

The following case takes the major definition "confinement without legal justification" a step further. It considers the purpose of an arrest—which is to bring the person arrested before a court. One may be liable for false arrest if he encourages, promotes, or instigates the arrest. There is a difference between the mere supplying and furnishing of information to the police and the urging, procuring, or instigating of an arrest. No liability attaches to the former, and the latter usually consists of false, misleading, incomplete, or unsubstantiated information.

False Arrest

DAY V. WELLS FARGO GUARD SERVICE CO.
711 S. W.2d 503 (1986)

BILLINGS, Judge.

Plaintiff Paul M. Day filed an action against his former employer, defendant Wells Fargo Guard Service, (hereinafter Wells Fargo) for instigating and encouraging the St. Louis Police Department to falsely arrest plaintiff. The jury returned a verdict awarding plaintiff $15,000 in actual damages and $30,000 in punitive damages. We affirm.

The primary issue in this appeal is whether plaintiff produced sufficient evidence of defendant's instigation of plaintiff's false arrest to warrant submission of the case to the jury. Defendant contends plaintiff's proof on this issue was fatally deficient, and it was not shown that defendant caused plaintiff to be restrained against his will.

Before examining the quality of plaintiff's evidence, a few basic principles underlying an action for false arrest should be noted. A false arrest occurs when there "is confinement without legal justification by the wrongdoer of the person wronged." Section 112 of the Restatement of Torts (Second) defines an arrest in the following manner:

> An arrest is the taking of another into custody of the actor for the actual or purported purpose of bringing the other before a court, or of otherwise securing the administration of the law.

In Comment C to § 112, the Drafters of the Restatement state that "an arrest is usually made for the purpose of bringing an actual or supposed criminal into court for the purpose of *investigation* or trial." And the arrest of a person can occur without actual physical restraint—that is without the application of force or the handcuffing of the suspect. See *State v. Maxwell*, 395 N.E. 2d 531, (officer's order to defendant to appear the following morning at police station was sufficient restraint on defendant's liberties to constitute arrest, notwithstanding the fact usual trappings of arrest did not occur). Furthermore, an arrest can be accomplished without a formal declaration of such. Section 544.180, RSMo 1978, describes the necessary elements of an arrest and nowhere mentioned is a requirement that the arresting officer make a formal declaration to the arrestee that he is under arrest.

We also concluded that "a person may... be liable for false arrest if he... merely instigates the arrest, as in the case of providing information on the basis of which a subsequent unlawful arrest is made." Plaintiff need not prove that the defendant actually ordered or directed the plaintiff's arrest, but only that defendant encouraged, promoted or instigated the arrest. And, plaintiff is entitled to prove these facts by either direct or circumstantial evidence.

The crux of plaintiff's theory of the case is that for a period of approximately six weeks in 1982, Wells Fargo wrongly accused him of stealing a missing pistol that had been issued to him on March 17, 1982. And that after defendant recovered the weapon and learned it was not stolen, but had been in the possession of another employee who was out sick until May 27, 1982, defendant, nevertheless, intentionally instigated the false arrest of plaintiff by St. Louis police officers on June 8, 1982.

Plaintiff's evidence consisted of seven live witnesses, deposition testimony, and a number of documentary exhibits. In this connection, we note that some of plaintiff's proof included the prior inconsistent statements of a number of Wells Fargo's employees. Such statements are admissible as substantive evidence.

On March 17, 1982, plaintiff, a security guard in the employ of defendant, was issued a revolver for use in connection with the performance of his job. At the time that plaintiff was given this weapon, he routinely signed a firearm agreement which, among other things, identified by serial number the revolver being issued.

Plaintiff presented testimony that in the early morning hours of April 3, 1982, Carlos Sampson, a field inspector for defendant, visited plaintiff where he was stationed that day and told plaintiff that he needed plaintiff's weapon for use on the firing range where other employees were being qualified in the use of firearms. Plaintiff at that time gave Sampson the pistol that he was issued on March 17, 1982.

Plaintiff testified later the same morning he asked Mike Fingerhut, one of his superiors at the agency, to make a record of the fact that his weapon was no longer in plaintiff's possession—so as not to conflict with the firearm agreement. Plaintiff testified further that Fingerhut refused on the ground that the pistol would be returned immediately to plaintiff. Plaintiff, however, produced further evidence showing that after April 3, 1982, the weapon he was issued on March 17, 1982, was never again in his possession. On April 19, 1982, plaintiff resigned his position with Wells Fargo.

On direct examination, Mr. Fingerhut denied that he knew before June 8, 1982 that the revolver had been recovered and since its disappearance had been in the possession of another Wells Fargo employee, Eugene Bennett, who was on sick leave until May 27, 1982. However, in deposition testimony taken prior to trial and which plaintiff read into the record, Mr. Fingerhut testified that he learned that Mr. Bennett was in possession of the missing pistol sometime after the first part of May, 1982.

Daniel Bradshaw, the branch manager for Wells Fargo, testified that it was a matter of policy to notify the police when a missing gun is recovered, and he testified further that he was uncertain whether he instructed Mr. Fingerhut to notify the police that the gun had been found.

It was virtually undisputed that defendant first reported the gun missing to the St. Louis Police on May 20, 1982. Prior to this report Mr. Fingerhut had contacted plaintiff in April at plaintiff's new place of employment, National Industrial Security, and threatened plaintiff with arrest unless the weapon was returned. Additionally, Mr. Fingerhut made similar threats over the telephone to plaintiff's pregnant wife, and he also informed plaintiff's new employer of the controversy.

During the course of his testimony, Mr. Fingerhut admitted that he was interested in having the police investigate the matter. Both Mr. Fingerhut and Mr. Bradshaw testified that plaintiff was not notified prior to June 8, 1982, that Wells Fargo had found the missing weapon.

The false arrest of plaintiff occurred on June 8, 1982 when two police officers, White and Loftin, confronted plaintiff while he was on duty at his new job. The officers did not declare to either the plaintiff or his supervisor that he was about to be placed under arrest. Instead, plaintiff's evidence showed that the officers told the supervisor that "we have to take him with us." Plaintiff testified that the two officers told him that he had to go with them, and that he was afraid not to go with the officers and that he believed he had no choice in the matter.

Upon "taking" plaintiff, Officers White and Loftin directed and controlled his movements for nearly three hours. First, plaintiff was taken to defendant's offices where he was confronted by Mr. Fingerhut. Next, the police took plaintiff to his apartment to look for a receipt for the weapon he was presently using in connection with his new job. Then plaintiff was taken to a district police station where he was further questioned. From the police station, plaintiff was then taken by Officer Loftin to a Union Carbide facility to obtain additional information from another Wells Fargo employee.

We have reviewed the entire transcript and conclude that plaintiff presented sufficient evidence on the element of instigation by defendant to warrant submitting the case to the jury. And notwithstanding the fact that the entire trial was filled with sharply conflicting testimony and facts with respect to whether plaintiff was actually arrested, the jury was presented with sufficient evidence to warrant a conclusion that despite the absence of the customary trappings of an official arrest, Officers White and Loftin, nevertheless, intended to restrain plaintiff against his will, that they suspected him of committing the crime, that plaintiff did not voluntarily accompany the police for three hours and that at no time during the three hours was plaintiff free to remove himself from their control.

We hold that the jury could reasonably find that plaintiff was falsely arrested and that Wells Fargo instigated the false arrest. For these reasons, we find defendant's principal point to be without merit. Plaintiff made a submissible case and the trial court was correct in allowing the case to go to the jury.

We think the evidence presented would allow a jury composed of reasonable men and women to conclude that Wells Fargo's employees knew before June 8, 1982 that the weapon had been found and that plaintiff had never stolen it or was even in possession of it after April 3, 1982. Reasoning upon these facts, the jury could conclude that defendant instigated plaintiff's false arrest without just cause or excuse. Assuming that the jury accepted plaintiff's evidence that when he was taken by the police to defendant's offices on June 8, 1982, and again accused by Mr. Fingerhut of a crime that never occurred and which Mr. Fingerhut knew never happened, it would not be unreasonable for the jury to conclude that such conduct was committed with malice, and was willful and wanton. We disagree with defendant's contention that this evidence was legally insufficient on the issue of punitive damages.

The judgment is affirmed.

CASE COMMENT

A false arrest occurs when there is confinement without legal justification by the wrongdoer of the person wronged. A person may be liable for false arrest if he merely instigates the arrest, i.e., such as providing information on the basis of which a subsequent unlawful arrest is made. The wrongdoer need not actually order or direct the arrest, but merely encourage, promote, or instigate it. An arrest is the taking of a person into custody for the actual or purported purpose of bringing that person before a court. It can occur without actual physical restraint. It can be accomplished without a formal declaration and without the application of force or handcuffs.

False Imprisonment

The next set of cases show that restraint of movement or locomotion may not necessarily need to consist of actual physical holding, confinement, or detention in order to constitute false imprisonment. The length of time of restraint need only be for a brief period. False imprisonment may arise out of acts, gestures, or words or similar means which induce a reasonable apprehension that force will be used. Tapping on a shoulder or using a harsh, rough, determined tone of voice to an elderly person may be sufficient to bring a cause of action. Reasonable actions on the part of a security employee, coupled with probable cause, will do much to obviate this intentional tort.

MENDOZA v. K-MART, INC.
587 F.2d 1052 (1978)

HOLLOWAY, Circuit Judge.
As to the false imprisonment claim, the district court's rationale for granting judgment n.

o. v. is that "Mendoza, herself, testified that the March 1975 occurrence had involved no detention." One basic element of such a claim is that the plaintiff be confined or restrained in some unlawful way by the defendant. Restatement, Second, Torts—§ 37 (False Imprisonment). The restraint constituting false imprisonment may arise out of words, acts, gestures or similar means which induce reasonable apprehension that force will be used if the plaintiff does not submit and it is sufficient if they operate upon the will of the person threatened and result in a reasonable fear of personal difficulty or personal injuries.

Confinement in jail or holding in custody is not necessary, and the restraint need only be for a brief time.

FISCHER v. FAMOUS-BARR COMPANY
646 S.W. 2d 819 (1983)

DOWD, Presiding Judge.

A false imprisonment case.

Defendant appeals from the trial court's order sustaining plaintiff's motion for new trial on the ground that the verdict finding defendant, Famous-Barr Company, not liable for false imprisonment was against the weight of the evidence.

This case was tried before and resulted in a $20,000 verdict for plaintiff for false imprisonment. The trial judge granted defendant's motion for a new trial because of the failure of plaintiff to present expert medical testimony concerning the cause of plaintiff's injuries. We affirmed. *Fischer v. Famous-Barr Co.,* 618 S.W.2d 446.

On May 28, 1977, plaintiff, a 74 year old woman, purchased two pantsuits from the fourth floor of defendant's downtown St. Louis store; the salesperson who attended plaintiff, however, failed to remove the security wafers attached to the clothing. As a result, when plaintiff walked under the sensormatic device in the ceiling on her way to the escalator with the security wafers in her bag, she activated the security alarm. Defendant's employee, Mrs. Lela Creason, alerted by the alarm, saw that plaintiff was the only person within range of the sensormatic device and followed plaintiff down the escalator. Mrs. Creason tapped plaintiff on the shoulder as she descended the escalator and said, "You have something in that bag that don't belong to you." She also stated, "Give me that, I will have to have your bag." Mrs. Creason took the bag from the plaintiff, saw the security wafers still attached to the clothing, found the receipt for the purchase and told plaintiff she would "have to come back up on the fourth floor" with her. Plaintiff did not go willingly or voluntarily with Mrs. Creason. Plaintiff testified, "I had to go." Mrs. Creason retained the bag of clothing and they returned to the fourth floor where the security wafers were mechanically removed. Defendant's employee then said, "you may go." Mrs. Creason's tone of voice was harsh, rough, and determined. Plaintiff was then permitted to leave the store.

Plaintiff filed this action for damages sustained as a result of her false imprisonment by defendant's employee. Following the jury verdict for defendant, plaintiff moved for and was granted a new trial "on the ground that the verdict was against the weight of the evidence . . ."

The record here shows that plaintiff pleaded and proved the elements of a false imprisonment case.

False imprisonment consists of the direct restraint of personal liberty. The required restraint may be from fear of force as well as from force itself. Words alone may suffice to bring about the actual restraint of liberty. False imprisonment may be committed by words alone or by acts alone or by both and by merely operating on the will of the individual.

In the instant case, the evidence on record shows that the plaintiff was on her way down the escalator when she was stopped by defendant's employee and ordered to return to the fourth floor sales desk. Plaintiff did not go voluntarily or willingly with defendant's employee. Although no actual force was used other than a tap on the shoulder, it may be inferred that the harsh words of defendant's employee, her possession of the bag containing plaintiff's purchases, and plaintiff's belief that she must return to the fourth floor were sufficient to operate on plaintiff's will and to restrain her personal liberty. Accordingly, plaintiff made a submissible case of false imprisonment and defendant's second point is denied.

For the foregoing reasons the trial court's order sustaining defendant's motion for new trial is affirmed.

Judgment affirmed.

DENT v. MAY DEPARTMENT STORES COMPANY
459 A.2d 1042 (1982)

PER CURIAM:

Appellant appeals from an order of the trial court which granted appellee's motion for summary judgment in her action for false arrest and imprisonment. We affirm.

Uncontradicted evidence before the trial court established that on the afternoon of March 8, 1980 appellant, a customer in appellee's department store, The Hecht Company, purchased a skirt. The cashier apparently failed to remove a magnetized sensormatic device designed to apprehend shoplifters and, consequently, appellant activated a buzzer near a store exit as she attempted to leave.

A security guard assigned to monitor the sensormatic detector then approached appellant and asked whether she had made a purchase in the store. She responded that she had bought a skirt and the guard asked to see it. Appellant showed him her shopping bag, which contained bags with purchases from various other stores, whereupon the guard removed a Hecht Company bag and discovered that, while a sensormatic device was still attached to the skirt, appellant had a receipt for her purchase.

At this point the guard asked appellant to follow him and touched her elbow with his hand. When appellant responded that she could walk by herself without his assistance, he dropped his hand and again asked that she follow him. As they proceeded toward a small room near the exit, the guard explained that there was no problem, that incidents of this nature occurred frequently. Appellant overheard other shoppers who observed the incident comment that a shoplifter had been apprehended.

Inside the small room the guard used a machine to remove the magnetic tag from the skirt and wrote a report about the incident in appellant's presence, explaining that he was required to record such incidents. He then returned the skirt to appellant and she departed.

Appellant filed a complaint against appellee in the trial court alleging false arrest and false imprisonment. Following the deposition of appellant, appellee moved for summary judgment. The trial court granted this motion on the ground that the undisputed facts revealed as a matter of law that no false arrest or imprisonment had occured.[1]

"The gist of any complaint for false arrest or false imprisonment[2] is an unlawful detention . . . ." "The unlawful detention of a person without a warrant or for any length

[1]Although appellant captioned her complaint "False Arrest and False Imprisonment" the trial court also analyzed the undisputed facts to determine whether appellant could recover based on a theory of negligent infliction of emotional distress. The court properly concluded that, since no physical injury was established, appellant could not recover for any humiliation, shock, embarrassment, and mental anguish she may have suffered as a result of the cashier's negligent failure to remove the sensormatic device from the skirt.

[2]As a practical matter—at least for our purposes here—there appears to be no real difference between false arrest and false imprisonment. Accordingly, we review appellant's claims without distinguishing these theories of recovery.

of time whereby he is deprived of his personal liberty or freedom of locomotion . . . by actual force, or by fear of force, or even by words" constitutes false imprisonment. In determining whether particular conduct constitutes false arrest or imprisonment it is not the subjective state of mind of the plaintiff but, rather, the "actions or words of the defendant which must at least furnish a basis for a reasonable apprehension of present confinement."

Once a prima facie case of false arrest or false imprisonment has been established, however, "a showing of probable cause constitutes a valid defense to such an action . . . and probable cause exists if the facts and circumstances known to the arresting officer warrant a prudent man in believing that an offense has been committed."

While probable cause is a mixed question of law and fact in false imprisonment cases in this jurisdiction, *Lansburgh's, Inc. v. Ruffin*, 372 A.2d 561, "where the facts are not in dispute the question of probable cause is one of law to be decided by the court." In determining whether a detention is based upon probable cause we view the evidence of probable cause from the perspective of the arresting officer.

In the instant case the trial court correctly ruled that the appellee was entitled to judgment as a matter of law based on the undisputed facts as established by the pleadings and supporting materials. Assuming for purposes of this appeal that the words spoken and actions taken by the guard when the sensormatic alarm sounded created a reasonable apprehension of present confinement the guard nevertheless had probable cause to detain and question appellant. The undisputed facts reveal that the alarm sounded as appellant attempted to exit the store, an event sufficient to support an inference that she was attempting to remove merchandise from the store illegally— particularly in light of the sophistication and selectivity of the sensormatic equipment. See *Lucas v. United States*, 411 A.2d 360.

Our conclusion that the security guard had probable cause to detain appellant does not end our inquiry, however, since a detention which is unreasonable in length or manner could constitute a false imprisonment despite the legality of the initial confine-ment. However, we hold that the trial court correctly concluded that no false imprison-ment occurred in the instant case as a matter of law. Following his inspection of appellant's parcels, the guard neither detained her for an unreasonable length of time nor acted unreasonably. To the contrary, he merely asked appellant to accompany him so that he could remove the magnetic tag from her purchase, completed a written report of the incident, and returned the skirt to her. *See id.* (detention of suspected shoplifter for questioning for approximately one hour does not rise to gravity of false imprison-ment where initial detention was based on probable cause).

Affirmed.

CASE COMMENT

Restraint may arise out of words, acts, gestures, or similar means which induce reasonable apprehension that force will be used if the plaintiff does not submit. The required restraint may be from fear of force as well as from force itself. Words alone may suffice to bring about the actual restraint of liberty. The unlawful detention can be for any length of time. As a practical matter, there appears to be no real difference between false arrest and false imprisonment. Probable cause constitutes a valid defense to a false arrest or false imprisonment action.

DEFAMATION: PRIVILEGE

Defamation is the holding of one up to ridicule, scorn, or contempt. It includes both slander and libel. Defamation tends to injure a person's reputation, lessen the esteem or respect in which that person is held or excite unpleasant or derogatory opinions or feelings against that person. The defamatory statement exposes the individual to contempt, hatred, or ridicule. Defamation is the unprivileged publication of false statements. Private security personnel may, under certain conditions, publish statements that are derogatory in nature if it is done in the course of their work. Libel is defamation expressed in writing or printed material. It is generally not a problem in the private security industry. Slander is the oral or spoken publication of a defamatory message, which can include false and malicious words concerning another's reputation. The basic elements of slander are a defamatory statement concerning another, unprivileged communication of this statement, and fault on the part of the publisher. The publication required here is to third parties. If there are merely words between two persons not heard by a third party, there is no tort.

JACKSON v. J.C. PENNEY COMPANY, INC.
616 F. Supp. 233 (1985)

O'NEILL, District Judge.

Plaintiff, an at-will employee of defendant, J.C. Penney Company, Inc., was suspected of stealing merchandise from defendant's store and was discharged. She then filed this action charging wrongful discharge, slander, false imprisonment, and intentional infliction of emotional distress. Defendant has moved for summary judgment.

The facts that give rise to the present action occurred on January 29, 1984. Plaintiff was entitled to purchase merchandise at a 15% employee discount. On her lunch break, plaintiff made purchases in the girl's department. When she returned to her work station, pursuant to store policy, her shopping bag was inspected by a co-worker and it was discovered that the bag contained 17 items; the attached sales receipt showed payment for only 16. Plaintiff was asked to go to the office of the personnel manager, Charles McGowan, where in the presence of two store security guards she was told that she was suspected of theft and was terminated. She was then led out of the store by one of the guards.

In Count 2 plaintiff claims to have been slandered by her termination. A communication is defamatory when it tends to harm the reputation of another so as to lower him in the estimation of the community. However, one is not liable for a publication of defamatory matter made on a conditionally privileged occasion, absent proof of abuse of that privilege.

A communication is privileged when it is made on a proper occasion, from a proper motive, in a proper manner and based upon a reasonable cause. Furthermore, the privilege exists only when the circumstances lead any one of several persons having a common interest in a particular matter to believe that another sharing such common interest is entitled to know a given fact.

The defamatory communication in this case is the accusation by Mr. McGowan that plaintiff had "conspired to steal" a nightgown. When this statement was made only plaintiff, McGowan and two security guards were present. Plaintiff claims that there was no reason for the security personnel to participate in the proceeding. However, one security guard was the person responsible for the initial investigation that discovered the unpaid for item, while the other escorted plaintiff out of the store. This was a privileged occasion since all present shared a common interest.

Abuse of the privilege may be found when the publication is actuated by malice or negligence, or is made for a purpose other than that for which the privilege is given, or to a person not needed to accomplish the purpose of the privilege, or contains matter not necessary to accomplish the purpose. There are no such facts alleged.

Plaintiff also asserts that it was known throughout the store that she was being discharged for theft. However, she points to no communication published by the defendant that resulted in this common knowledge. In order for liability to exist, there must be a publication of defamatory matter.

Count 3 asserts a claim for false imprisonment, but plaintiff admits that the facts of this case do not support this claim.

Count 4 asserts a claim for intentional infliction of emotional distress. Pennsylvania recognizes this cause of action where one intentionally causes severe emotional distress by conduct that goes beyond all reasonable bounds of decency. The conduct complained of must be so extreme and outrageous so as to be regarded as atrocious, and utterly intolerable in a civilized community. There are four elements necessary to this action: 1) the conduct must be extreme and outrageous; 2) the conduct must be intentional or reckless; 3) it must cause emotional distress; and 4) the distress must be severe.

Plaintiff claims she was falsely charged with theft, and was humiliated, embarrassed and mocked in front of her fellow employees at the time of her discharge. It is reasonable to expect that plaintiff would feel embarrassed under the circumstances. However, no reasonable person would consider defendant's conduct outrageous. The termination was based on the discovery that plaintiff had an item in her shopping bag that had not been paid for. One permissible inference is that plaintiff was responsible for the item being in her bag. The conduct attributed to defendant in this complaint was not so extreme and outrageous to support an action for intentional infliction of emotional distress. Furthermore, there is no showing that defendant intended to cause emotional distress to plaintiff. The evidence shows that defendant had a legitimate basis for the termination, and plaintiff has asserted no facts showing another motive to cause her harm. As alleged, defendant's conduct did not cross the threshold of decency and was not utterly intolerable in a civilized society.

For the foregoing reasons, defendant's motion for summary judgment will be granted.

CASE COMMENT

If there is no publication of defamatory matter, there is no liability. One is not liable for publication of defamatory matter when made with a privilege, that is, when it is made on a proper occasion, from a proper motive, in a proper manner, and based on reasonable cause. Truth is a defense in a defamation case.

MALICIOUS PROSECUTION

Malicious prosecution, an intentional tort, deals with the liability of persons who initiate prosecution for purposes other than enforcing the criminal law or bringing an offender to justice. Unjustifiable and oppressive litigation of criminal charges can cause the person charged pecuniary loss, distress, and loss of reputation. Proceedings in these cases are normally initiated for some improper purpose and without probable cause.

The accuser does not believe in the guilt of the accused, and the proceedings are initiated primarily because of hostility, spite, hatred, or ill will toward the accused, or to obtain a private advantage from the accused such as forcing the payment of money or the turning over of property.

Malice can be distinguished from mere negligence in that the malice arises for some purpose, whereas negligence arises from the absence of purpose (inattention or thoughtlessness). Malice is an intentional action without justification. Malice equates with ill will, the desire to do harm, and the willful, wanton, reckless disregard of rights. Malice exists where a charge is made with the knowledge of the accuser that the charge is false or the charge is made with a reckless disregard for whether it is false. Malice can be inferred from a lack or want of probable cause, circumstances surrounding the prosecution, or the motives of the accuser or instigator. There may be no malice connected with the inaccurate reporting of criminal conduct when there is no intent to mislead.

The elements of malicious prosecution are

1.   the commencement of a prosecution against the now or present plaintiff;
2.   its legal causation by the now or present defendant against the plaintiff who was the defendant in the original proceeding;
3.   the termination of the case in favor of the now or present plaintiff;
4.   the absence of probable cause for such proceeding;
5.   the presence of malice; and
6.   damages suffered by the original defendant.

EASTMAN v. TIME SAVER STORES, INC.
428 So.2d 1163 (1983)

GAUDIN, Judge.

Appellant is Mrs. Alice P. Eastman, who was unsuccessful in a malicious prosecution action in the 24th Judicial District Court. On appeal she contends that the trial judge erred in finding that Time Saver Stores, Inc., and its employees had probable cause for having her arrested and that appellees acted without malice.

Considering the record, we cannot say that there was no factual basis for the district court's decree or that the judgment was manifestly erroneous. There *was* cause for suspicion and very little if any maliciousness, and we affirm the decree in appellees' favor.

Eleven people testified during this two-day trial, including Carlos Sosa, the supervisor of the Time Saver Store where Mrs. Eastman was employed on the 3 p.m. to 11 p.m. shift. There were, he said, repeated cash shortages in that store.

On November 24, 1979, Sosa and William Tolar of the Time Saver security department decided to conduct a surveillance. They helped another Time Saver employee, Arturo Sosa, climb into an air conditioning vent above the cash registers. From this viewpoint, Arturo Sosa said he saw Mrs. Eastman take "two handfuls of quarters and put one on her pocket and the other one in the register." He also saw, he said, Mrs. Eastman receive a $20 bill from a customer and ". . . put it in her pocket."

Arturo Sosa then described how Mrs. Eastman removed another $20 bill from a special envelope and ". . . put it in her pocket and put the plastic envelope back to where it was originally." Store procedure required that monies received from sale of gasoline be placed in these envelopes and deposited in a safe. The envelope in question, Arturo Sosa said, had become ". . . caught in the slot . . .", allowing Mrs. Eastman to extricate it and remove its monetary contents.

Store employees then closed the store and called the police.

Mrs. Eastman's explanation was that she was only temporarily holding the money in her pocket and that she fully intended to place the funds in their proper places.

The trial judge said in his "Reasons for Judgment":

"Plaintiff's testimony explaining why she had store money on her person at the time of her arrest seems implausible. The fact that she even carried property on her person was suspicious in and of itself. The explanation by plaintiff does not overcome the other circumstances which led Time Saver to have her arrested. The store employees observing her testified she acted suspiciously when pocketing the money. There had been systematic cash shortages in the store which always coincided with her shift, regardless of whom she worked with." The Supreme Court of Louisiana defined the elements necessary to support a malicious prosecution claim:

(1)   The commencement or continuation of an original criminal or civil proceeding;
(2)   Its legal causation by the present defendant against plaintiff who was defendant in the original proceeding;
(3)   Its bona fide termination in favor of the present plaintiff;
(4)   The absence of probable cause for such proceeding;
(5)   The presence of malice therein; and
(6)   Damages suffered by the original defendant.

Considering the facts and circumstances of the instant case, the trial judge could not say, nor can we, that there was an absence of probable cause or that there was any actionable malice.

Reasonable efforts toward crime suppression should not be punished and therefore curtailed by civil liability for simple mistake. However, the efforts must be reasonable; the individual remains obliged to act as a reasonable person would, taking into consideration all of the circumstances. Not every mistake in defending one's self or community against crime is an actionable fault, but only such mistake as is not reasonably justified by the surrounding circumstances.

Clearly, the systematic shortages during Mrs. Eastman's shifts and her questionable behavior on the date in question gave Time Saver employees reason to believe that appellant was responsible for at least some of the shortages.

For these reasons, we affirm the judgment in favor of Time Saver and its employees against Mrs. Eastman.

AFFIRMED.

CASE COMMENT

The presence of probable cause and the absence of malice eliminate two of the six elements that are necessary to support a malicious prosecution claim. Whenever one or more elements of a legal action are eliminated, that action will fail.

JONES v. GWYNNE
306 S.E.2d 574 (1983)

HEDRICK, Judge.

This is a civil action for malicious prosecution. Evidence presented at trial tended to show the following. On 9 May 1979 Ramona Galarza, a cashier at McDonald's restaurant, told the second assistant manager, Sheila Stewart, that she had seen Ray Jones, the plaintiff, take money from customers and deposit it in the cash register without reporting the sale on the cash register. Galarza said the plaintiff did this by ringing "no sale" instead of the purchase amount on the register. Sheila Stewart reported this to the first assistant manager, Steve Winstead, and to the Fayetteville Area Supervisor, Paul Craddock who in turn called his supervisor, J.D. Bell, and McDonald's Regional Security Manager, Matt Gwynne.

On 16 May 1979 Gwynne and Craddock conferred with Detectives Post and Kraus of the Fayetteville Police Department and requested assistance in the investigation. Craddock and Gwynne then took written statements from three McDonald's cashiers, Ramona Galarza, Christal Newton and Stephanie Williams, who said they had seen Jones take money from customers and ring up "no sales." Gwynne and Craddock did not take statements from two other McDonald's employees, Pam Lawson and Hazel Bido, who testified they had never seen Jones take money without recording the sale in the cash register. During their investigation Craddock and Gwynne reviewed the store records and register tapes and found a number of "no sales" on the register tapes from the days Jones was managing the restaurant. On 18 May 1979 Detectives Post and Kraus went to McDonald's and observed Jones at work for about an hour. They saw nothing unusual, and they reported this to Gwynne and Craddock. Gwynne, Craddock, Kraus and Post returned to McDonald's on 18 May 1979 where they arrested Jones and took him to the Fayetteville Law Enforcement Center for questioning. He cooperated fully with the police and denied embezzling any money from McDonald's.

After questioning Jones, Detective Post again conferred with Gwynne and Craddock. According to his testimony at trial, he told them that Jones denied any wrongdoing and that ". . . if we were going to act, we would have to act on whatever we have, and that we had enough probable cause to go to court already." Detective Post then spoke with Assistant District Attorney Michael Winesette. Winesette testified at trial regarding their conversation:

> I did not tell him (Post) he had real problems with the case. Based on what he told me, I told him it sounded like he had a good case, but that he needed evidence of the conversion of the money. That is one of the elements of the case. I told them they needed more evidence. I don't know if those were the exact words, but basically I told him that he should try to get as much evidence as he could on the fourth element.

Detective Post informed Gwyne of his conversation with Winesette. After discussing the matter with his superiors, Gwynne told Post that McDonald's wanted to prosecute Jones. Warrants were then taken out against Jones charging him with embezzlement of $1.50 on or about 15 May 1979 and "an indeterminant amount" on or about 14 April 1979.

On 26 June 1979 the assistant district attorney took voluntary dismissals on both charges. Plaintiff filed the present action three days later. After this action was filed but prior to trial, the grand jury indicted the plaintiff on three counts of embezzlement from McDonald's Restaurant. Plaintiff was tried on these charges in February, 1980. After hearing the State's evidence on one of the charges, the trial judge dismissed the case and the assistant district attorney took voluntary dismissals as to the remaining charges.

The present action came to trial in January, 1982. At the close of plaintiff's evidence motions of defendants Christal Newton and Ramona Galarza for a directed verdict were allowed. The motions of defendants Matt Gwynne and McDonald's Corporation for a directed verdict were denied. The following issues were submitted to and answered by the jury as indicated:

1. Did the Defendant, Matt Gwynne, maliciously prosecute criminal charges of embezzlement, issued on May 18, 1979, against the Plaintiff, Ray Jones?
   Answer:Yes.
2. Did the defendant, McDonald's Corporation, maliciously prosecute criminal charges of embezzlement, issued on May 18, 1979, against the Plaintiff, Ray Jones?
   Answer: Yes.
3. If so, what amount, if any, is the Plaintiff, Ray Jones, entitled to recover for actual damages?
   Answer: $200,000.
4. What amount of punitive damages, if any, should be awarded to the Plaintiff, Ray Jones?
   Answer: $100,000.

From a judgment entered on the verdict, defendants appealed.

In order to succeed in an action for malicious prosecution, the plaintiff must show "that defendant initiated the earlier proceeding, that he did so maliciously and without probable cause, and that the earlier proceeding terminated in plaintiff's favor." The defendants argue that the trial court erred by excluding evidence of probable cause. They contend the court erred by (1) instructing the jury that it could not consider the grand jury indictments of Jones as evidence of probable cause, (2) excluding Matt Gwynne's testimony that he had been told the assistant district attorney believed probable cause existed to prosecute Jones, and (3) refusing to admit into evidence the warrants issued for Ray Jones' arrest.

Defendant first assigns error to the court's charge to the jury that "you may not consider the evidence of the return by the Grand Jury of the bills of indictment as true bills on this question of probable cause because it occurred after the filing of this action." Defendants assert that "the three grand jury indictments of Ray Jones on August 13, 1979 are prima facie evidence that probable cause existed for Jones' arrest and prosecution."

Defendants are correct in their contention that a bill of indictment has been characterized by our Supreme Court as "prima facie evidence" of probable cause in cases involving malicious prosecution. In discussing this rule, Prosser notes:

> Where the accused is committed or held to bail by a magistrate, or indicted by the grand jury, it is evidence that there was probable cause for the prosecution. It is very often said that this establishes a "prima facie" case; but since the plaintiff has the burden of proving lack of probable cause in any case, and is free to do so, this apparently means nothing more than that the commitment is important evidence on the issue.

W. Prosser, Handbook of the Law of Torts Sec. 119, at 846 (4th ed. 1971). While competent, evidence of indictment by a grand jury is not conclusive on the issue of probable cause; it is to be considered by the jury along with all the other evidence in the case.

While the general rules governing the admissibility of grand jury indictments in malicious prosecution cases are clear, it is true, as defendants concede in their memorandum of additional authority, that "the factual situation in this case has never been ruled upon by a North Carolina appellate court." In this case, the indictments defendants sought to introduce were issued after the present action for malicious prosecution was commenced. Plaintiff in the present case based his complaint not on the indictments, but rather on the arrest warrants issued months before. When the district attorney took a voluntary dismissal on the warrants, the criminal proceedings against Jones terminated for the purpose of this action, and the tort was complete. While we could avoid deciding the question by agreeing with plaintiff that the challenged instruction, if error, was not prejudicial, we choose to be more definitive and declare that the better rule in such a case bars consideration of later indictments on the issue of probable cause. We note that the inquiry into probable cause seeks to establish whether there existed "such facts and circumstances known to the defendant at the time, as would induce a reasonable man to commence a prosecution." We do not believe that a grand jury determination of the existence of probable cause, issued after the alleged tort is complete and the complaint filed, is relevant to this inquiry. We thus hold that the trial judge did not err in giving the challenged instructions.

Defendants also contend that Gwynne should have been allowed to testify that "he knew, before warrants were sworn out against Jones, that Assistant District Attorney Winesette believed probable cause existed to prosecute Jones." We do not believe defendants were prejudiced by the exclusion of this testimony. Mr. Winesette testified that he told Detective Post that Post had "a pretty good case" but needed evidence of the conversion of money to make a case of embezzlement. Also, the following testimony by Gwynne, allowed into evidence, indicated Gwynne's awareness of Post's conversation with Winesette:

MR. JOHNSON (defendant's attorney): What, if any, conversation did you have with Detective Post about contacting the District Attorney's Office?
A. I asked him, let's contact the District Attorney's Office and discuss the case with them. And at that point Detective Post called the District Attorney's Office and talked with a District Attorney about the case. He was on the telephone for ten or fifteen minutes, I suppose. And following the telephone conversation, he came back in the room . . . and told me that he had talked with the District Attorney's Office . . . .
MR. JOHNSON: After Detective Post contacted the District Attorney's Office, did he advise you of the District Attorney's response—yes or no?
GWYNNE: Yes. He did.

Detective Post also testified:

I talked to the District Attorney staff and explained to them exactly what I had, what the evidence tended to show and what testimony would appear to be from the employer's standpoint . . . . We felt that we had plenty to go on as far as the charges, or I wouldn't have signed a warrant.

The substance of the conversation between Post and Winesette and Gwynne's knowledge of that conversation were allowed into evidence. Therefore, the exclusion of Gwynne's statement that Detective Post told him the assistant district attorney thought there was probable cause in no way prejudiced the defendants.

We also find no error in the court's exclusion of the two warrants issued for Jones' arrest on 18 May 1979. Both arrest warrants were identified at trial and read into evidence by Lloyd Clifford Brisson, an assistant district attorney. Furthermore, Brisson explained the notations "V-O-L" "D-I-S" " to go to GJ," which he had made on the shucks containing the warrants. He testified the notations meant he had taken a voluntary dismissal and the cases would go to the grand jury. The judge also instructed the jury it could consider the warrants relevant to the issue of probable cause. This assignment of error is overruled.

Plaintiff also argues that evidence of Mr. Gwynne's conduct of the investigation supports a finding of actual malice on the part of Mr. Gwynne. This evidence is relevant to the issues of probable cause and legal malice, as well as to the question whether punitive damages may be supported on the basis of "reckless and wanton disregard of the plaintiff's right." This evidence bears no relation, however, to actual malice "in the sense of personal ill will" on the part of Mr. Gwynne.

The defendants also contend that there was insufficient evidence that the prosecution was instituted " in a manner which showed the reckless and wanton disregard of the plaintiff's right," the second asserted ground for imposition of punitive damages. That the defendants instituted the prosecution without probable cause was established by the evidence to the satisfaction of the jury and has not been successfully contested on appeal. But plaintiff must show more than a lack of probable cause to be entitled to jury consideration of punitive damages. The evidence must show "reckless and wanton disregard" of the rights of the plaintiff. We hold that there was insufficient evidence of such aggravated conduct to permit the jury to consider the issue of punitive damages. We note the undisputed evidence that Gwynne examined records that indicated large numbers of "no-sales", that he interviewed witnesses who claimed to have seen plaintiff take money from the register, and that he consulted with the police and with his superiors before instituting proceedings. Although sufficient to permit a finding that defendants acted without probable cause, the evidence was insufficient as a matter of law to establish reckless and wanton conduct on the part of the defendants.

The result is: in the trial for malicious prosecution and compensatory damages, we find no error; that portion of the judgment awarding plaintiff punitive damages must be vacated.

No error in part, vacated in part.

CASE COMMENT

While competent, evidence of an indictment, which has been characterized as *prima facie* evidence of probable cause, is not conclusive on the issue of probable cause. It is to be considered by the jury with all the other evidence in the case. When the prosecutor in this case took voluntary dismissal on the warrants, criminal proceedings were terminated and the tort was complete. As to probable cause, there either existed or did not exist such facts and circumstances, known to the defendant in this case at the time, that would induce a reasonable man to commence prosecution.

TRESPASS

Trespass is entering or going on another's land or property without permission, consent, lawful authority, or right. It is an illegal or unlawful act or interference against another's person, property, or rights and may injure or damage their health, reputation, or property.

KING v. LOESSIN
572 S. W. 2d 87 (1978)

COLEMAN, Chief Justice.

This is an appeal from an order overruling a plea of privilege. The question is whether the action of a purported agent is chargeable to the defendant where the purported agent is the employee of a corporation who was employed to do investigative work for the defendant. The plaintiff asserts that a trespass was committed in the county of suit which authorized venue in that county under Subdivision 9 of Article 1995, VATS. The judgment will be affirmed.

Delcer King, appellant, contracted with Smith Protective Services, Inc. to investigate a number of his competitors in the equipment business. Smith's employee, Thompson, along with another employee burglarized the offices of appellee in order to obtain certain sales invoices. Appellee sued Smith Protective Services, Inc., Cal Meyers, the investigations manager for Smith, and appellant, King, for damages incurred as a result of the alleged break-in. King filed his plea of privilege to be sued in his county of residence. Appellee, Loessin, filed a Controverting Plea and incorporated his original petition into the pleading by reference. This pleading sufficiently alleged that an agent or representative of the defendant, King, committed a trespass at Loessin's business office in the county of suit.

It is undisputed that Thompson entered the premises of Loessin with out permission of Loessin and removed certain items. The appellant contends that the plaintiff failed to prove that Thompson was an agent of King at the time of the trespass and that he was acting within the course and scope of his employment.

A contract between King and Smith Protective Services, Inc., is in evidence. It reflects that King contracted with Smith to conduct certain investigative services and agreed that the services would be performed by licensed investigators if required by law.

There was testimony that Mr. King told Mr. Meyers, who was acting for Smith Protective Services, Inc. that he desired an investigation of tool thefts and sabotage at his John Deere Tractor Agency and certain other matters. In particular, he wanted to determine who was selling parts to a competitor "at a lowest cost than what was the normal rule within his area." Mr. Meyers testified that King explained to him what was required in order to satisfy the John Deere people that someone was infringing upon his region. Meyers stated that King told him that the only thing that would satisfy the John Deere people would be an invoice showing a 20% discount and that he wanted to secure one of those invoices. " He didn't particularly care how he went about getting it and said money was no object."

Mr. Meyers testified that while Mr. King did not specifically discuss a violation of the law in connection with the investigation, he did stipulate that he didn't particularly care about how he went about getting the information he needed. Mr. Meyers hoped that his employees would not exceed the law because they had been warned not to, but he stated that he had given Mr. Jerry Dolly permission to discuss the matter with Mr. King. Mr. Meyers stated that he told Mr. King that if anything criminal came up he was going to have to bear the burden if he was going to coach the Smith investigators.

Mr. Thompson was a Smith employee before the contract with King was executed. Thompson took his instructions from Meyers. Mr. Thompson testified that he went with Jerry Dolly to see Delcer King and that Dolly did all the talking. He didn't hear Mr. King say anything about committing a burglary. Mr. Dolly gave him his instructions. Thompson admitted that he burglarized the Loessin Implement Company located in Weimar, Colorado County, Texas. He reported to Mr. Meyers after he "pulled the burglary". Meyers paid him for "conducting such burglary" with a Smith Protective Services, Inc. payroll check.

The corporation was employed to secure, among other things, an invoice. Thompson and Dolly were assigned to this case. They talked with Mr. King and there is testimony that he furnished them a broken part to take to Loessin's place of business for repair in order to give them an excuse for an entry.

There is nothing in the testimony of Mr. King which would support the conclusion that he had any right to control Smith as to the method or means by which the work contracted for was to be accomplished. There is no testimony that King in fact instructed either Meyers, Thompson, or Dolly concerning the methods to be used in conducting the investigations.

A crucial question for determination is whether Smith Protective Services, Inc. was an independent contractor or whether the corporation and its employees had the status of agents or employees of King. The written agreement merely provides that Smith Protective

Services, Inc. will be compensated at the rate of $20 per hour plus expenses for its investigative services. It does not specify the services to be rendered.

Although there is no single rule that is absolute and definite, the outstanding and ultimately decisive consideration in determining the independence of the contract is the employers right to control the details of the work. The basic test of a contractor is that he render service in the course of an independent occupation, representing the will of his employer only as to the result of his work, and not as to the means by which it is accomplished. Thus, if the employer is interested only in the results, and there is left to the party performing such services complete control of the details as to the method and manner of such performance, then the relationship of independent contractor exist.

An employer is not responsible for the acts or omissions of an independent contractor and his subcontractors or servants, committed in the prosecution of work that is not in itself unlawful or attended with danger to others. The doctrine of respondeat superior has no application.

A person who contracts with another to perform a service unlawful in itself, even as an independent contractor, is responsible in damages for injury which might result from the performance of that service.

There is evidence which will support an implied fact finding of contemplated illegal activity on the part of Smith Protective Services, Inc. in conducting the investigation and of authorizing such activity if necessary to the successful completion of the investigation. This fact will be presumed found in support of the trial court's judgment. Under such circumstances the employer would not be insulated from liability by reason of the fact that the person perpetrating the offense might otherwise enjoy the status of an independent contractor.

Where an agent's act is done within the scope of his authority, while acting in the furtherance of the principal's business, the principal is liable for his actions regardless of whether he had authority to do the particular act complained of, and regardless of whether he may have performed the act in the ordinary manner.

A "trespass" within the meaning of Subdivision 9 of Article 1995, supra, includes injuries to property resulting from wrongful acts, either willfully inflicted or the result of affirmative active negligence on the part of the wrongdoer, as distinguished from injuries that are the result of a mere omission of duty.

One who enters on land of another without having the consent of the owner commits a trespass on land. A common law action of trespass is included within the meaning of the word "trespass" as used in Subdivision 9 of Article 1995, supra.

To sustain venue under Subdivision 9, Article 1995, supra, the plaintiff must establish by a preponderance of the evidence (a) that a trespass has been committed; (b) that it was committed in the county of suit; and (c) that the defendant asserting his privilege committed the acts, or that they were committed by another under circumstances that make the defendant legally responsible.

The venue facts required to be established in order to maintain venue under Subdivision 9, Article 1995, supra, have been established by a preponderance of the evidence.

Affirmed.

CASE COMMENT

One who enters the land of another without consent of the owner commits a trespass on the land. Burglary—breaking and entering into various kinds of structures—is a crime. Here the court felt there was evidence supporting the implied fact of the employer authorizing such activity.

INVASION OF PRIVACY

Invasion of privacy deals with the right of individuals to withhold themselves or their property from public scrutiny, if they so choose. It is the right to be let alone. There are four general classes of tort actions for invasion of privacy:

1. appropriation of the plaintiff's name or likeness to the benefit or advantage of the defendant;
2. intrusion upon the seclusion or solitude of the plaintiff by invading his home or eavesdropping;
3. the public disclosure of private facts; and
4. publicity which places the plaintiff in a false light in the public eye.

A security manager should be most concerned with number 2: intrusion upon seclusion or solitude. The concern comes about because of the great amount of investigative activity conducted by the private security industry. The right to privacy is a personal right, and the invasion of that right is a willful tort which constitutes a legal injury. Physical intrusion, analogous to trespass, is the unwarranted invasion to the right of privacy when highly offensive and objectionable to the reasonable person. Surveillance may be so overzealous as to render it actionable in a court of law. It is the right of every citizen to be let alone. Intrusion is wrongful when the manner in which it is done is outrageous and causes mental suffering, shame, and humiliation to a person of ordinary sensibilities.

While the right of privacy may be waived by one who files an action for damages resulting from a tort, it is only waived to the extent of the defendant's intervening right to investigate and ascertain for himself the true state of the injury. The waiver is only for a reasonably unobtrusive type of investigation which would be in the defendant's interest in preparing its case.

In the following case, overt, extended, and prolonged activities, such as trailing in a conspicuous manner sufficient to excite speculation in the neighbors, constant following in public places, pursuit tactics openly conducted late at night so as to alarm the average person, coupled with other acts amounting to trespass and eavesdropping, which resulted in fright, shock, and physical and mental impairment, were not reasonable conduct within the bounds of the implied waiver.

PINKERTON NATIONAL DETECTIVE AGENCY, INC. v. STEVENS
132 S. E. 2d 119 (1963)

Syllabus by the Court.

2. (a, b) Where the violation of the right of privacy is alleged by way of overt and extended activities of the defendant in causing the plaintiff to be followed, harassed and terrified over an extended period of time as a result of unreasonable surveillance, allegations showing that these activities resulted in fright, shock, and physical and mental impairment of a more or less permanent nature are sufficient to sustain the action regardless of whether or not the course of conduct was wilfully and wantonly pursued in an effort to intimidate the plaintiff and cause her to abandon a pending damage suit against a third party, or merely undertaken in a negligent manner.

(c) The right of privacy may be implicitly waived and it is waived by one who files an action for damages resulting from a tort to the extent of the defendant's intervening right to investigate and ascertain for himself the true state of injury. However, this includes only a waiver of that reasonably unobtrusive type of investigation which would be to the best interests of the defendant in preparing its case. Activities consisting of overt and prolonged "trailing" of the defendant in a conspicuous manner sufficient to excite the speculation of neighbors, constant following in public places, pursuit tactics openly conducted late at night such as would ordinarily alarm an average person together with other acts amounting to trespass and eavesdropping, cannot as a matter of law be said to be reasonable conduct in defense of the damage suit within the implied waiver of investigation resulting from filing such an action.

3. Count 1 of the petitions in this case is construed as being founded upon the invasion of the right of privacy in a negligent manner by the commission of intentional acts; that is, with the intent to commit acts alleged to be wilful and wanton but without specific intent to injure the plaintiff. Count 2 of each petition is founded upon a wilful and intentional tort. The separate counts of each petition are not duplicitous.

Ruth Stevens filed an action for damages in the Superior Court of Fulton County against Pinkerton National Detective Agency, Inc. and its employer, United Services Automobile Association, alleging that the insurance company, which was obligated to defend the action under its contract of motor vehicle insurance with a defendant in a pending damages suit in which she was the plaintiff, invaded her right of privacy by the manner in which an investigation of her activities by private detectives was conducted, as a result of which she suffered severe mental, physical and emotional injury. Her husband, James A. Stevens, filed a companion action against the same parties seeking recovery for medical expenses and loss of consortium.

RUSSELL, Judge.

2. (a) The amended petition set out substantially the following facts: Ruth Stevens was injured in a collision with an automobile driven by one Bell who was insured under a motor vehicle liability insurance policy by the defendant United Services Automobile Association, in which collision she suffered physical injury and severe shock to her "nervous and emotional system." She thereafter filed an action for damages against Bell alleging these facts. The insurance company, through its attorney, employed the defendant Pinkerton National Detective Agency, Inc. to follow the plaintiff and furnish reports of her activities in an effort to determine the extent of injury. Employees of this defendant commenced shadowing plaintiff, stealthily at first and then with progressively increasingly objectionable behavior. She was constantly under surveillance. The detectives would peep through the hedge adjoining plaintiff's house, slink around her house, snoop and eavesdrop upon her activities therein, park near the house where they could watch her through a hole in the hedge, and later park across the street from early morning until late at night, follow her, especially at night, in automobiles staying only a few car lengths behind. In particular, they drove past the house several times on several days before April 13, 1957, and almost every day toward the end of April; parked different colored automobiles beyond the hedge and peeped through the hedge several times on several days after April 13, and almost every day towards the end of April, during May and June, July 2, six occasions between July 25 and August 13, August 20, and two occasions between August 20 and the first part of September; came on her premises at night near her windows and ran on being observed several nights shortly after May 9 and shortly after June 6, and between July 2 and 10; peeped in the windows of her house several nights shortly after May 9, shortly after June 6, and on July 2, 11, and 12; eavesdropped and listened in on conversations inside the house on July 2 and 11, several nights shortly after June 6, and June 11; went into the woods behind her house on July 2, snooped behind the hedge, eavesdropped, and peeped in, moved about at night

in the woods and on the premises around the house several nights between July 2 and 10 and on July 10 in the daytime; on July 2 cut a hole in the hedge alongside the street in order to peep into the windows; came to the door on June 27 pretending to be television salesmen and on July 12 pretending to have business with her; followed her closely in an automobile on given dates, into stores and public places; on July 10 followed her into a named restaurant and were waiting outside a restroom door when she came out, and so on. On one occasion the plaintiff returned home at night and was so closely followed that she ran into the house in panic, hit a piece of furniture, and knocked herself unconscious. On another occasion at a given date her automobile was followed from Atlanta to Forrest Park where police intercepted it and the identity of the persons shadowing her was discovered. During the early part of the surveillance plaintiff, who was already emotionally upset as a result of the collision, had a continuous feeling of being followed and spied upon, which her doctor and members of her family thought to be hallucinatory, and she suffered extreme mental torment in the belief that she was losing her mind. Later the disturbance manifested itself in nervous spasms, sleeplessness, nightmares, and the appearance of rash and lesions at dermal nerve endings over her entire body, accompanied by unbearable itching. She was forced to employ both medical and psychiatric aid. After finally discovering the identity of the defendants on August 13, her attorney contacted the attorneys for defendants and informed them of her condition and that their conduct had almost made her lose her mind, and defendant's attorney stated he would request his client to discontinue these activities; nevertheless, the surveillance was continued in as aggravated a form as before, and plaintiff was forced to undergo electroconvulsive shock treatment from August through November. The conduct of the defendants in shadowing, snooping, spying and eavesdropping upon plaintiff was done in a vicious and malicious manner not reasonably limited and designed to obtain information needed for the defense of plaintiff's lawsuit against Bell but deliberately in a way calculated to frighten and torment her. Plaintiff's neighbors also noticed the espionage and thereby gained the impression that she was engaged in some wrongful activity and began to discontinue any association with her. The shock and injury to her nervous system is permanent.

The petition is brought in two counts, count 2 alleging that the acts complained of were wilful, vicious and malicious, done with the intention of terrifying her to the extent that she would drop the lawsuit against Bell, and count 1 averring that the acts were wilfully done as matter in aggravation of damages but not alleging any malicious intention to injure the plaintiff.

(b) Pavesich v. New England Life Ins. Co., 122 Ga. 190, 50 S.E. 68, still remains a leading case on the action for violation of the right of privacy, but it is no longer a lonely pioneer in the field. The many jurisdictions following its lead are impressively listed in *Eick v. Perk Dog Food Co.*, 106 N.E. 2d 742, with the comment that "against this massive weight of authority there is pitted a small, largely inconclusive group of opinions written for the most part before the bulk of the cases upholding the right of privacy were decided." If it is necessary to relate the action to trespass, eavesdropping, injury to reputation, physical injury resulting from the fright these elements appear in the petition. Prosser, Law of Torts, 2d Ed., p. 639 states that the tort actions grouped in this field are only a phase of the larger problem of the protection of peace of mind against unreasonable disturbance. "When the 'new tort' of the intentional infliction of mental suffering becomes fully developed and receives general recognition, the great majority of the privacy cases may very possibly be absorbed into it * * * There remains, however, a large and growing field in which privacy becomes important because no other remedy is available." Whether or not there is express malice, that is, a motive to harm the plaintiff by the activity engaged in, is immaterial, because the absence of the motive will neither insulate the defendant if the tort is in fact committed nor will its presence create a cause of action if none otherwise exists. "Each person has a liberty of privacy, and every other person has, as against him, liberty in reference to other matters, and the line where these liberties impinge upon each other may in a given case be hard to define; but that such a case may arise can afford no more reason for denying to one his liberty of privacy than it would to deny to another his liberty, whatever it may be. In every action for a tort it is necessary for the court to determine whether the right claimed has a legal existence, and for the jury to determine whether such right has been invaded, and to assess the damages if their finding is in favor of the plaintiff. This burden which rests upon the court in every case of the character referred to is all that will be imposed upon it in actions brought for a violation of the right of privacy." Pavesich, supra. Acts merely resulting in fright or shock are not actionable in the absence of wilful and intentional misconduct on the theory that there has been no injury to purse or person. But where physical *or mental* impairment flows naturally as a direct consequence of the tort, there has been *injuria* in its legal sense, and recovery may be had both for it and the accompanying fright and mental suffering. Allegations of permanent mental impairment having physical manifestations and necessitating medical care, treatment by electric shock therapy and psychiatric aid are allegations of fact which show injury resulting in mental impairment as opposed to mere fright, shock and hurt feelings. The tort and resulting damage are thus sufficiently alleged in both counts of each of the petitions.

(c) It is contended by the plaintiff in error that under one of the well recognized exceptions to the right of privacy, the defendants were justified in their actions, especially those alleged in count 1, for the reason that the plaintiff filed a damage suit against Bell alleging certain physical injuries and the defendant in that suit and his insurance company and Pinkerton, who was employed by the latter, had a right to make such investigation as it deemed necessary in order to ascertain whether the claim for damages was well founded. The recently decided case of Forster v. Manchester, 189 A.2d 147, upholds this view. In that case the detectives employed by the insurance company assigned a team of two men to take moving pictures of the plaintiff for possible use in a pending damage suit and at least twice followed her very closely in traffic, causing her to become extremely nervous and upset so that she required medical treatment. There as here the defendants were notified of the effect of their conduct on the plaintiff but ignored the letter, and the plaintiff was aware of being followed on four subsequent occasions. The court stated, with two justices dissenting:

> By making a claim for personal injury appellant must expect reasonable inquiry and investigation to be made of her claim and to this extent her interest in privacy is circumscribed. It should also be noted that all of the surveillances took place in the open on public thorough-fares, where appellant's activities could be observed by passersby. To this extent appellant has exposed herself to public observation and therefore is not entitled to the same degree of privacy that she would enjoy within the confines of her own home * * * There was nothing unreasonable in the manner in which appellant was followed nor in the taking of motion pictures. In regard to the surveillance, it was conducted by experienced investigators who did not use improper techniques * * * there was no trespassing on appellant's property nor spying through her windows.

The test of reasonableness is that stated in Restatement of the Law, Torts, 398, § 867. It is implicit in Souder v. Pendleton Detectives, 88 So.2d 716, where the cause of action in a similar case was upheld because of allegations suggesting a violation of the Louisiana "Peeping Tom" criminal statutes. In Schultz v. Frankfort Marine Accident & Plate Glass Ins. Co., 139 N.W. 386, which alleged "rough shadowing" on the part of the detectives for the purpose among others of intimidating the plaintiff from leaving town the court held that, omitting the alleged acts of trespass and eavesdropping, threats, slander and alleged restraint of the plaintiff's liberty, the open and repeated acts of surveillance were sufficient of themselves to publicly proclaim the plaintiff suspect and subject him to public disrepute so as to constitute "the analogue of libel." This petition does not limit the defendants' acts to that reasonable and unobtrusive observation which would ordinarily be used to catch one in normal activities unaware, but sets out a course of conduct beyond what would be sufficient for the purpose intended, and certainly one which would disturb an ordinary person without hypersensitive reactions. Both counts of both petitions set out a cause of action.

Judgment affirmed in part; reversed in part.

CASE COMMENT

Claimants in a lawsuit must expect reasonable inquiry and investigation. To this extent, their privacy is circumscribed. People do not enjoy the same degree of privacy when exposing themselves to public observation as they enjoy in the privacy of their own home. Trespass and eavesdropping are not reasonable methods of investigation and may well be criminal, unprofessional, and unethical.

Theft, background, worker's compensation claims, insurance claims, and competitive intelligence are some of the types of investigations conducted by private security. Surveillance is one of several investigative tools. Investigative surveillance, if not done properly, may compete with the legally protected interests of a person. In other words, liability may ensue if there is an intrusion of a person's seclusion or privacy. This type of intrusion must be highly offensive to the reasonable person and would consist of overzealous and extensive shadowing and monitoring. Conversely, there is no intrusion if a person is observed or photographed while in a public place, since the person's appearance is public and open to the public eye. Reasonable persons cannot find highly offensive matters known to the public. If there is no intrusion into a person's privacy, there should be no successful cause of action because the activity is reasonable.

REASONABLE ACTIVITY

Contrary to the previous case, the next case demonstrates that while an investigation may be one of the regrettable aggravations of living in today's society, it can be done in a reasonable manner and not intrude in one's privacy. Note that there was a limited amount of activity; the conduct of the investigators did not go beyond all possible bounds of decency; and their conduct was not outrageous, atrocious, extreme, or utterly intolerable. The investigator's activity did not involve unreasonable intrusions.

FIGURED v. PARALEGAL TECHNICAL SERVICES, INC.
555 A.2d 663 (1989)

STERN, J.A.D.

Plaintiff commenced this action against two investigators and the corporation which employed them. The complaint alleged, among other things, that defendants' surveillance of her activities invaded her privacy and caused her severe emotional distress. Plaintiff sought damages for invasion of privacy and both negligent and intentional infliction of emotional distress. A judge of the Law Division concluded that, based on the undisputed facts and all reasonable inferences derived therefrom, no cause of action had been established and granted defendants' motion for summary judgment. We now affirm the judgment of the Law Division.

I.

Plaintiff was in an automobile accident on January 23, 1983 as a result of which she claimed to have suffered physical, emotional and psychological injuries. The liability carrier for the other vehicle involved in the accident retained defendant Paralegal Technical Services, Inc. to investigate plaintiff's injury claims and Paralegal assigned the investigation to the individual defendants, their employees.

Plaintiff complains in particular about two separate incidents which occurred during defendants' surveillance. The first occurred on the morning of June 6, 1984. Plaintiff received a telephone call from a neighbor who said that she had noticed two suspicious-looking vehicles going up and down the road in front of plaintiff's home. Later, when plaintiff left her home with her mother to keep a doctor's appointment, she noticed two cars parked in a wooded area near the road and saw two men standing alongside the road, watching her as she left. As plaintiff drove to her appointment, she noticed that both cars were following her. Eventually, plaintiff pulled into the parking lot of a store about five miles from her home and noticed that the two cars had followed her into the parking lot. The driver of one car parked in the back of the store and then walked around the front of plaintiff's car, looking "straight into her face" while "within arms reach" of her. He "kept peering" at plaintiff and walked very slowly, "staring" as he passed, but said nothing to her.

The second incident occurred on September 11, 1985. Plaintiff left a family birthday party in Scranton, Pennsylvania, and drove onto Route 380, when she noticed that one of the same vehicles involved in the June 6, 1984 incident was again following her. The vehicle proceeded to follow plaintiff closely for over forty miles until she pulled into a rest area. After plaintiff stopped, she noticed that the other vehicle had "pulled around" and parked facing her.

The motion judge granted summary judgment in favor of defendants on the issue of negligent infliction of emotional distress because he found that there was no breach of duty, apparently on the ground that any harm to plaintiff was unforeseeable. He also granted summary judgment in favor of defendants on the issue of intentional infliction of emotional distress, finding that defendants' conduct did not rise to the required level of outrageous-ness. Finally, the judge granted summary judgment in favor of defendants on the issue of invasion of privacy, because he found that, viewing the facts in the light most favorable to plaintiff, the cause of action was not established.

II.

Our Supreme Court recently considered the proofs necessary to sustain a claim for negligent or intentional infliction of emotional distress in the absence of physical injury. In *Buckley v. Trenton Savings Fund Society*, 544 A.2d 857 the Court first considered "negligent infliction of emotional distress" and the development of case law thereunder, indicating that recovery seemed to be permitted, even in the absence of physical injury to the plaintiff, under circumstances where there was a "sufficient guarantee" of the "genuineness" of the claim and the emotional distress was sufficiently "severe," such as involving actual observation of severe injury or death to a loved one. The *Buckley* Court then discussed "intentional infliction of emotional distress" and the developing case law thereunder, stating that "generally speaking, to establish a claim for intentional infliction of emotional distress, the plaintiff must establish intentional and outrageous conduct by the defendant, proximate cause and distress that is severe." See *Restatement, Second, Torts* (1965), § 46. The Court determined that initially, the plaintiff must prove that the defendant acted intentionally or recklessly. For an intentional act to result in liability, the defendant must intend both to do the act and to produce emotional distress. Liability will also attach when the defendant acts recklessly in deliberate disregard of a high degree of probability that emotional distress will follow. . . .

Second, the defendant's conduct must be extreme and outrageous. . . . The conduct must be "so outrageous in character, and so extreme in degree, as to go beyond all possible bounds of decency, and to be regarded as atrocious and utterly intolerable in a civilized community. . . . Third, the defendant's action must have been the proximate cause of the plaintiff's emotional distress . . . Fourth, the emotional distress suffered by the plaintiff must be "so severe that no reasonable man could be expected to endure it.

With respect to both negligent and intentional infliction of emotional distress, therefore the *Buckley* Court concluded that

the severity of the emotional distress raises questions of both law and fact. Thus, the court decides whether as a matter of law such emotional distress can be found, and the jury decides whether it has in fact been proven. . . . When conduct is directed at a third party, proof of bodily harm is required, . . . but when the intentional conduct is directed at the plaintiff, he or she need not prove any physical injury. . . . It suffices that the conduct produce emotional distress that is severe.

We conclude that the Law Division judge did not err in determining that there was insufficient evidence as a matter of law to present the emotional distress claims to a jury.

There was insufficient proof of severity of emotional distress, whether negligently or intentionally inflicted, to support a valid cause of action. Whether an insurance investigation following a claim may be deemed "one of the regrettable aggravations of living in today's society", *Buckley, supra,* here the evidence was "insufficient as a matter of law to support a finding that the mental distress was so severe that no reasonable man could be expected to endure it."

III.

We are also satisfied that the facts, viewed in a manner most favorable to plaintiff, do not give rise to a cause of action for invasion of privacy.

. . .The law of privacy comprises four distinct kinds of invasion of four different interests of the plaintiff, which are tied by the common name, but otherwise have almost nothing in common . . . : (i) commercial appropriation of one's name or likeness, (ii) intrusion, (iii) public disclosure of private facts and (iv) publicity which places the plaintiff in a false light in the public eye. *Galella v. Onassis, 353 F. Supp.* 196, 487 F.2d 986 *See also Restatement, Second, Torts* (1977), § 652A.

This case concerns a claim for "unreasonable intrusion upon seclusion of another." According to the *Restatement,*

one who intentionally intrudes, physically or otherwise, upon the solitude or seclusion of another or his private affairs or concerns, is subject to liability to the other for invasion of his privacy, if the intrusion would be highly offensive to a reasonable person. *Restatement,* § 652B.

According to the comments to this section, a defendant is subject to liability

. . . only when he has intruded into a private place, or has otherwise invaded a private seclusion that the plaintiff has thrown about his person or affairs. . . . There is no liability for observing the plaintiff or even taking his photograph while he is walking on the public highway, since he is not then in seclusion, and his appearance is public and open to the public eye. . . .

There is likewise no liability unless the interference with the plaintiff's seclusion is a substantial one, of a kind that would be highly offensive to the ordinary reasonable man, as the result of conduct which the reasonable man would strongly object.

It may well be that "freedom from extensive shadowing and observation has come to be protected in most . . . jurisdictions", and that "overzealous" shadowing and monitoring may, therefore, be actionable. However, the facts of this case—even accepting plaintiff's version as true in every respect—do not warrant relief. *Bisbee*, 452 A.2d 689. The allegations do not reveal an intrusion which would be "highly offensive" to a reasonable person:

> The thrust of this aspect of the tort is, in other words, that a person's private, personal affairs should not be pried into. . . . The converse of this principle is, however, of course, that there is no wrong where defendant did not actually delve into plaintiff's concerns, or where plaintiff's activities are already public or known.

Bisbee affirmed a grant of summary judgment in favor of defendant, denying plaintiff's claim that his seclusion was unreasonably intruded upon, because reasonable men could not find any highly offensive intrusion and because all the matters at issue were otherwise known and public. The photograph which was published in that case had been taken from the public thoroughfare and thus represented a view available to any bystander. *See also N.O.C., Inc. v. Schaefer*, 484 A.2d 729. Similarly, in *Forster v. Manchester*, 189 A.2d 147, the Pennsylvania Supreme Court held that detectives employed by an insurance company to make an investigation did not invade the privacy of a claimant since their surveillance "took place in the open or public thoroughfares where the claimant's activities could be observed by passers-by." The *Forster* court concluded that the conduct of the investigation was not "unreasonable," and therefore not actionable, adding that "by making a claim for personal injuries appellant must expect reasonable inquiry and investigation to be made of her claim and to this extent her interest in privacy is circumscribed."

Similarly, here plaintiff, in her deposition and answers to interrogatories, asserts that defendants drove past her home, and were seen to do so, on several occasions on one day; that they parked their cars about half a mile from her home and stared at her as she drove past them; that they followed her on a public street to a store; and that after she parked in the store's parking lot, one defendant walked slowly around her car and stared her straight in the face. She also asserts that she was followed on Route 380 in Pennsylvania, and that when she stopped at a rest area the investigators did so as well. These allegations do not include acts which involve an unreasonable intrusion upon plaintiff's seclusion. Rather, the defendants' activities all took place in the open, either on public thoroughfares or in areas where members of the public had the right to be. As noted by Judge Haines in *Schafer, supra*, "*Bisbee* supports the proposition that whatever the public may see from a public place cannot be private."

An individual who seeks to recover damages for alleged injuries must expect that her claim will be investigated. Although the investigation must be reasonably conducted, and may not involve an intrusion into the privacy of the claimant which could be deemed highly offensive to a reasonable person, we conclude that here, even giving plaintiff the benefit of all legitimate inferences, the facts submitted in opposition to defendants' motion for summary judgment reveal no objectively unreasonable or highly offensive conduct on the part of the defendants. Accordingly, the judgment is affirmed.

CASE COMMENT

One is not in seclusion in public areas where his appearance is public and open to the public eye. Freedom from extensive shadowing has come to be protected in most jurisdictions, and overzealous shadowing and monitoring may be actionable.

INTRUSIVE INVESTIGATION

In the next case, an investigator gained admittance to a hospital room where the plaintiff was confined and where she had an exclusive right of occupancy. The investigator used deception to secure an address for the defendant. An unreasonably intrusive investigation, which would be objectionable or offensive to the reasonable person is actionable. An investigation must be done within legal bounds and in a proper manner.

NOBLE v. SEARS, ROEBUCK AND CO.
109 Cal. Rptr. 269 (1973)

KINGSLEY, Associate Justice.

Plantiff Noble sued Sears, Roebuck and Co., Sears' attorneys, Sam Pruitt Investigations, and certain persons working for Sam Pruitt Investigations, charging 10 counts. The 10 counts alleged: trespass; battery; fraud; negligently caused physical, mental and emotional injuries; invasion of attorney-client relationship; invasion of privacy; negligent entrustment of agents (two counts); conspiracy; violation of statutory duties; and violation of attorneys' ethics. We are here concerned only with the counts which charged respondents Sears and its attorneys, namely the fifth, sixth and seventh causes of action. Respondents' demurrers to those causes of action were sustained and plaintiff has appealed from the resulting order of dismissal.

We set out certain facts alleged which form the background for the three causes of action in the complaint which are before us on this appeal.

Mrs. Noble was the plaintiff in an action against Sears for personal injuries allegedly caused while she was shopping in a Sears store. The attorney defendants were employed by Sears to defend that action. Defendant Pruitt, an investigator, was hired to assist in preparing the defense. The attorneys desired to take the deposition of a man named Bohm, who had accompanied plaintiff on her shopping trip. That effort was frustrated because plaintiff either could not procure or did not have an address for Bohm. In an effort to secure the address from plaintiff, an employee of Pruitt, named Lemon, gained admittance to a hospital room where plaintiff was confined and, by deception, secured the address. It is that alleged invasion, and Lemon's conduct while in the room, which form the basis for plaintiff's claim of injury.

Plaintiff argues that an "unreasonably intrusive" investigation, which plaintiff has alleged in her sixth cause of action, is a tort for which damages are recoverable. We agree. Various courts have recognized that an intrusive investigation may give rise to a cause of action for damages. The Florida Supreme Court recognized that an investigation done by trailing and shadowing a claimant could amount to an actionable invasion of privacy, if it is unreasonably intrusive.

A Georgia court also has held that an investigation done in a frightening manner may provide a cause of action against a detective agency. The Louisiana court has held that an investigation by detectives hired by an insurance company must be conducted within legal bounds and failure to investigate in a proper manner may amount to a cause of action for breach of privacy.

In California, the Supreme Court has recognized, in dicta, that a private investigation may give rise to a cause of action for damages for invasion of the right to privacy. The court said "In such cases, the private investigators may well make an intrusion into the individual's right of privacy which would be objectionable or offensive to the reasonable man. Courts have permitted such an individual to maintain an action for damages against the intruders."

Therefore, we hold that an unreasonably intrusive investigation may violate a plaintiff's right to privacy. The theory of plaintiff's complaint, as set forth in the first cause of action (incorporated by reference into the sixth) is that she had, at least as against Sears, Pruitt, Lemon and respondent attorneys, an exclusive right of occupancy of her hospital room. Assuming that that theory is sustained by proof, the other conduct alleged against Lemon would seem to fall within the concept of unreasonably intrusive investigation.

Insofar as the sixth cause of action is concerned, plaintiff's case involves a second step, namely that, assuming that Pruitt and Lemon are liable for the allegedly unlawful invasion of plaintiff's room and for Lemon's conduct thereafter, the attorneys and Sears, who hired Pruitt and Pruitt's staff, are liable for the torts of those investigators.

Plaintiff relies on *Martin v. Leatham*, 71 P.2d 336, in which the proprietor of a skating rink was held liable for the torts of an employee of a detective service which had been retained to protect the property. In *Martin* the evidence showed that the alleged actor had acted under orders directly given to him by the rink owner's wife. In the case at bench, the complaint alleges, in paragraph IV of the sixth cause of action, "that each and every of the wrongful and intrusive acts complained of herein were committed under the instructions and prior approval, express or implied, of" Sears and its attorneys, which allegation would seem to bring the sixth count within the *Martin* ruling. But we must discuss the problem further.

Plantiff also argues that Sears and its attorneys are liable because, where a corporation undertakes an activity involving possible danger to the public under a license or franchise granted by public authorities, these liabilities may not be evaded by delegating performance to an independent contractor. Plaintiff points out that a common carrier's duties are non-delegable, and that the statutory duty of motorists to maintain their brakes is non-delegable. None of these cases, or the theory behind them, has any application to the practice of law or the business of private investigations. These latter two activities, when performed properly, cannot be considered inherently hazardous to the public by their very nature, nor do we regard them as so "dangerous" as to be non-delegable. It is clear that both common carriers and drivers of automobiles may present serious dangers to the public safety and that special rules may be developed in order to protect the public from physical danger. If we are to find liability on the part of hirers of private investigators, it must be on a theory other than the non-delegability of dangerous activities.

Different jurisdictions have examined problems similar to the one before this court, and they have reached a variety of conclusions. A brief examination of the case law elsewhere reveals that a hirer is not liable for the torts of security personnel supplied by an independent agency where the hirer did not exercise control, although where the hirer of the detective agency does exercise control, the hirer may be liable. However, even though hirers of an independent security or protective agency have generally been held not liable for *negligent* torts of agency personnel, where the hirer did not exercise control over them, hirers have been held liable for the *intentional* torts of the agency's personnel committed, in the scope of the agency's employment, against the hirer's invitees.

Other courts have found that the hirer of a detective bureau agency is not liable for the intentional tort of the detective agency, on the theory that the relationship was that of independent contractor and employer and there was an absence of right to control.

Some courts distinguish the use of detective personnel on a temporary contract investigating a single event, from security personnel hired for the general protection of property, finding that the hirer is not liable for intentional torts, such as false arrest, committed by the personnel of the investigatory agency focusing on the fact that such an intentional tort is outside the scope of the limited employment.

In California there is little law directly on the subject before us. Respondent Sears' cases, are of little assistance since in those cases the special officers were in performance of their duties as quasi-public officials, appointed by city authority.

Our research has disclosed some rather weak authority on the question before us. In another case the court held an oil company liable for an intentional tort namely, unlawful imprisonment, participated in by employees of a private detective agency that was hired by the company. Without any discussion as to whether the private detective was an independent contractor or agent, and without any discussion as to possible differences in liability where the agency is hired to protect rather than investigate, the court held that there was sufficient evidence to support the jury's finding that the company was liable.

The appellate court has upheld an award of compensatory damages against a turf club and a private security agency, hired by the club to police its ground, for intentional torts, i.e.: battery and "wrongful arrest," committed by an employee of the security agency. Again, the court did not discuss an agency theory.

The case of *Draper v. Hellman Com. T. & S. Bank*, 263 P. 240, is perhaps closest in point. Allegedly libelous statements were made in a telegram sent by a private detective agency, hired by a bank to locate a former employee for questioning about misappropriated funds. Although the hiring bank did request the agency to send the telegram, it in no way authorized the use of libelous language. Without making any distinction between an agency hired to investigate and an agency hired to protect, the court held that the bank could not avoid liability by claiming that the detective agency acted as an independent contractor. The court held the principal liable for the torts of its agent committed in the scope of employment.

Thus it appears that in California the hirer of a detective agency for either a single investigation or for the protection of property, may be liable for the intentional torts of employees of the private detective agency committed in the course of employment.[8]

Thus, plaintiff has stated a cause of action against the hirer for the intentional tort of the private detective agency. Whether or not the tort was committed in the scope of employment is a question of fact not to be decided on demurrer. What we have said above is consistent with the related rule that the attorney at law who, as principal, employs other attorneys to collect a judgment and who authorized them to levy on property owned by the debtor may be held responsible for the acts of the agent attorneys within the scope of their authority. The analogy between one who collects on a judgment and one who is a private investigator is clear. The demurrer to the sixth cause of action should not have been sustained.

The seventh cause of action appears to allege liability on two theories: (1) negligent supervision, and (2) negligent entrustment.

Plaintiff appears to be attempting to allege a duty on the part of Sears and its attorneys to supervise their agents, and that failure to exercise supervision constitutes negligence. Although a principal may be liable for the torts of an agent committed in the scope of authority, that theory of vicarious liability is not based on the fact that the principal is negligent if he fails to supervise the agent. The principal is held liable as a matter of public policy, in order to promote safety for third persons. The theory of liability is that the principal

---

[8] We do not consider herein the liability or nonliability of the hirer for negligent torts of the employees of a detective agency.

is holding out the agent as competent and fit to be trusted, and thereby, in effect, warranting good conduct and fidelity of the agent.

The Restatement of Agency (2d ed. 1958) § 213, states: "A person conducting an activity through servants or other agents is subject to liability for harm resulting from his conduct if he is negligent or reckless . . . (c) in the supervision of the activity . . ." As will be noted, the liability thus stated attaches only where the supervision (or lack thereof) is negligent or reckless. We are cited to no authority, nor have we found any authority basing liability on lack of, or on inadequate, supervision, in the absence of knowledge by the principal that the agent or servant was a person who could not be trusted to act properly without being supervised. As so limited, the concept adds little, if anything, to the concept of liability for wrongful or negligent entrustment, which we now discuss.

Plaintiff alleges negligence in choosing the Pruitt detective agency to do its investigation. Under this allegation, whether defendants were negligent in choosing Pruitt is a matter of fact to be determined, based on the evidence. The fact that Pruitt was a licensed detective agency is one fact to be considered in determining whether the lawyers and Sears were negligent in their choice, but we cannot say on the record before us that, as a matter of law, this was sufficient to show that Sears and its attorneys exercised reasonable care in their choice.

The demurrer to the seventh cause of action should not have been sustained.

The judgment (order of dismissal) is affirmed as to the fifth cause of action; it is reversed as to the sixth and seventh causes of action. Appellant shall recover her costs in this court.

CASE COMMENT

An unreasonably intrusive investigation, an investigation done in a frightening manner, and failure to investigate in a proper manner may provide a cause of action against the investigator and/or the employer.

OUTRAGEOUS CONDUCT

Outrageous conduct is the intentional and wrongful invasion of one's right to privacy which results in harm. It is an invasion of one's solitude or seclusion in his private affairs. As a trespass on a person's right to privacy, it is a serious interference with the privacy right.

The intrusion is one that is highly offensive or objectionable to the reasonable person. The intrusion is one that is unreasonable and unwarranted and the interference must be substantial. The outrage can cause mental suffering, shame, or humiliation to a person of ordinary sensibilities. The conduct goes beyond the limits of social toleration.

Look at the particular relationship of the parties involved and at the actual or apparent authority of one party over the other. The victim of this intentional tort may be young, inexperienced, vulnerable, or perhaps have a perception of being economically dependent. The level of conduct in this tort is extreme, atrocious, and goes beyond all possible bounds of decency. It is utterly intolerable conduct in a civilized community. Outrageous conduct does not extend to mere insults, indignation, annoyances, or petty oppression. Outrageous conduct is wrongful behavior which causes grave injury or serious wrong to a person. It is basically a mode of action rather than an omission.

An example would be the late night calling by a collection agency which used abusive and threatening language to bully payment. Or, it might be the strip search of a young, inexperienced, vulnerable female employee, as is reported in the following case.

BODEWIG v. K-MART, INC.
635P.2d 657 (1981)

BUTTLER, Presiding Judge.

In this tort action for outrageous conduct, plaintiff seeks damages against her former employer, K-Mart, and a K-Mart customer, Mrs. Golden. Both defendants moved for summary judgment, which the trial court granted. Plaintiff appeals from the resulting final judgments entered. We reverse and remand.

Our review of the pleadings, depositions and affidavits is in the light most favorable to the party against whom the motion is filed. On the evening of March 29, 1979, plaintiff was working as a part-time checker at K-Mart. Defendant Golden entered plaintiff's check out lane and plaintiff began to ring up Golden's purchases on the cash register. When plaintiff called out the price on a package of curtains, Golden told plaintiff the price was incorrect because the curtains were on sale. Plaintiff called a domestics department clerk for a price check. That clerk told plaintiff the curtains in question were not on sale. Upon hearing this, Golden left her merchandise on plaintiff's counter and returned with the clerk to the domestics department to find the "sale" curtains.

After Golden left, plaintiff moved Golden's merchandise to the service counter, voided the register slip containing the partial listing of Golden's items and began to check out other customers. Three to ten minutes later, Golden returned to plaintiff's checkstand, where another customer was being served. Golden "looked around" that customer and asked what plaintiff had done with her money. When plaintiff replied, "What money?", Golden said that she had left four five-dollar bills on top of the merchandise she was purchasing before she left with the domestics clerk. Plaintiff told Golden she had not seen any money. Golden continued in a loud, abrupt voice to demand her money from plaintiff and caused a general commotion. Customers and store personnel in the area began to look on curiously.

The K-Mart manager, who had been observing the incident from a nearby service desk, walked over to plaintiff's counter. After a short discussion with Golden, he walked up to plaintiff, pulled out her jacket pockets, looked inside and found nothing. Then he, plaintiff and two or three other store employees conducted a general search of the area for the money. When this effort proved fruitless, the manager explained there was nothing more he could do except check out plaintiff's register. Golden said, "Well, do it." The manager and an assistant manager locked plaintiff's register and took the till and the register receipt to the cash cage. While the register was being checked, Golden continued to glare at plaintiff while plaintiff checked out customers at another register. The register balanced perfectly. When the manager so advised Golden, Golden replied that she still believed plaintiff took her money and continued to "cause commotion" and glare at plaintiff. A further general search of the surrounding area was conducted without success. Golden still would not leave; another employee was trying to calm her down.

The manager then told[1] plaintiff to accompany a female assistant manager into the

---

[1] In her deposition, plaintiff stated that the manager "asked" her to disrobe. Plaintiff stated in a later affidavit that the manager "told" her to disrobe. Given the plaintiff's youthful age and subservient position as an employee, her consistent statements in both her deposition and her affidavit that she believed she had no choice but to disrobe outweighs the semantic inconsistency of the two words. Whether she truthfully believed that, and if so, whether it was a reasonable belief, is for the jury.

women's public restroom for the purpose of disrobing in order to prove to Golden that she did not have the money. As plaintiff and the assistant manager walked to the restroom, the manager asked Golden if she wanted to watch the search; Golden replied: "You had better believe I do, it is my money." In the restroom, plaintiff took off all her clothes except her underwear while Golden and the assistant manager watched closely. When plaintiff asked Golden if she needed to take off more, Golden replied that it was not necessary because she could see through plaintiff's underwear anyway.

Plantiff put on her clothes and started to leave the restroom when the assistant manager asked Golden how much money she had in her purse. Golden replied that she did not know the exact amount, but thought she had between five and six hundred dollars. She did not attempt to count it at that time.

Plaintiff then returned to her checkstand. Golden followed plaintiff to the counter and continued to glare at her as she worked. Finally, the manager told Golden nothing more could be done for her, and after more loud protestations, Golden left the store.

Upon arriving home, Golden counted the money in her purse. She had $560. She called plaintiff's mother, whom she knew casually, and related the entire incident to her, stating that she had told K-Mart that plaintiff had taken her money. She described the strip search to plaintiff's mother and stated that when she was asked if she wanted to watch the strip, she responded, "Damn right." The mother expressed concern that plaintiff would lose her job; Golden said she would call the store and ask them not to let her go. Golden did make that call. After the conversation with Golden, plaintiff's mother, father and sister went to K-Mart to see if plaintiff was all right and to take her home.

Plaintiff returned to work the next day and was told that the keys to the cash register were lost and she was to work on a register with another employee. That procedure is known as "piggy-backing," and plaintiff had been told three months earlier that the store would no longer "piggy-back" checkers. Plaintiff believed the store was monitoring her by the "piggy-back" procedure; she quit at the end of her scheduled shift that day.

Because the questions relating to each defendant differ, we consider the trial court's ruling as to each of them separately.

K-MART

K-Mart contends that the trial court properly granted its motion, because the facts presented do not constitute outrageous conduct as a matter of law. Its principal argument is that plaintiff consented to the strip search, either expressly as its manager stated, or tacitly by not expressly objecting. Plaintiff stated, variously, that she was told or asked by the manager to disrobe, but, whether asked or told, she did not consider that she had a choice. She thought she would lose her job if she refused, and she needed the job. The issue of lack of consent to that search is an issue of fact, but whether it is an issue of material fact depends upon whether, assuming plaintiff's version to be true, the facts are sufficient to submit the case to the jury on the outrageous conduct theory.

The relatively short history and development of the tort of outrageous conduct, at least in Oregon, is summarized by the court in *Brewer v. Erwin*. As the court pointed out, the exact elements of the tort are still in process of clarification. There are at least two versions of the tort. One is represented by *Turman v. Central Billing Bureau*, and involves intentional conduct, the very purpose of which is to inflict psychological and emotional distress on the plaintiff. The other is represented by *Rockhill v. Pollard*, where the wrongful purpose was lacking, but "the tortious element can be found in the breach of some obligation, statutory or otherwise, that attaches to defendant's relationship to plaintiff * * *." The court concluded its discussion as follows:

* * *This court has not had occasion to consider whether in the absence of such a relationship a recovery for solely emotional distress can be based on a defendant's conduct, not otherwise tortious, that a jury may find to be beyond the limits of social toleration, though the conduct is not deliberately aimed at causing such distress but only reckless of the predictable effect.

In *Brewer*, the court did not consider the question posed in the foregoing quote, because it found the defendant's conduct was intentional. Here, we are faced with the issue, unless there was the type of special relationship between plaintiff and K-Mart justifying recovery for emotional distress based on that defendant's conduct, which was not deliberately aimed at such distress but was reckless of the predictable effect of that conduct.

Neither the Supreme Court nor this court has been presented with the question of whether the employer-employee relationship falls into that special category. This court, however, has treated the landlord-tenant relationship as a "prime consideration" in evaluating the defendant's conduct. We reached that conclusion because landlords were in a position of authority with respect to tenants and could affect the tenants' interest in the quiet enjoyment of their leasehold. An employer has even more authority over an employee, who, by the nature of the relationship, is subject to the direction and control of the employer and may be discharged for any or no reason, absent an agreement restricting that authority. Clearly, that relationship is not an arm's length one between strangers. Accordingly, we conclude that the relationship between plaintiff and K-Mart was a special relationship, based on which liability may be imposed if K-Mart's conduct, though not deliberately aimed at causing emotional distress, was such that a jury might find it to be beyond the limits of social toleration and reckless of the conduct's predictable effects on plaintiff.

We conclude that a jury could find that the K-Mart manager, a 32-year-old male in charge of the entire store, after concluding that plaintiff did not take the customer's money, put her through the degrading and humiliating experience of submitting to a strip search in order to satisfy the customer, who was not only acting unreasonably, but was creating a commotion in the store; that the manager's conduct exceeded the bounds of social toleration and was in reckless disregard of its predictable effects on plaintiff.

GOLDEN

Because there was no special relationship between plaintiff and Golden, the evidence must be such that a jury could find Golden's conduct not only socially intolerable, but that it was deliberately aimed at causing plaintiff emotional distress. Golden contends the evidence does not permit those findings, because she was merely trying to get her money back from plaintiff. To sustain that position, it would be necessary to resolve the disputed facts relating to Golden's conduct in her favor. As in the case against K-Mart, those factual issues are material only if, after resolving them in plaintiff's favor, the evidence would permit a jury to find for plaintiff.

We conclude that the facts, viewed most favorably to plaintiff, would permit a jury to find that Golden's entire course of conduct was intended to embarrass and humiliate plaintiff in order to coerce her into giving Golden $20, whether rightfully hers or not; that Golden did not know how much money she had in her purse, variously stated to be between $300 and $600, made no effort to determine if she was, in fact, missing four five dollar bills until she returned home, at which time she found she was mistaken; that Golden's insistence on a check of plaintiff's cash register, her insistence that plaintiff still had her money after the register checked out perfectly, her eager participation in the strip search of plaintiff and her continuing to stare angrily at plaintiff over an extended period, even after all efforts to find her money failed, would permit a jury to find Golden's conduct deliberately calculated to cause plaintiff emotional distress and exceeded the bounds of social toleration.

A jury could also find in Golden's favor, but the mere fact that her stated ultimate objective was to get her money back is not sufficient to defeat plaintiff's claim. In *Turman v. Central Billing Bureau*, the defendant's objective was to collect a bill, but its methods of achieving that objective were held actionable as outrageous conduct. There are lawful (socially tolerable) ways to collect money from another, and there are unlawful (socially intolerable) ways to do so.

EMOTIONAL DISTRESS

Common to her claims against both defendants is the requirement that plaintiff prove that she suffered severe emotional distress. If the facts presented are believed, plaintiff suffered shock, humiliation and embarrassment, suffering that was not merely transient. Plaintiff characterized herself as a shy, modest person, and said that she had two or three sleepless nights, cried a lot and still gets nervous and upset when she thinks about the incident. Concededly, this element of the tort has been, and still is, troublesome to courts. K-Mart contends there is no objective evidence of the distress, such as medical, economic or social problems. In *Rockhill v. Pollard, supra*, plaintiff became nervous and suffered from sleeplessness and a loss of appetite over a period of about two years. The court said:

> * * * Defendant belittles these symptoms, but it is the distress which must be severe, not the physical manifestations. * * *

Defendant Golden contends that the purpose of requiring proof of severe emotional distress is to guard against fraudulent or frivolous claims and that some degree of transient and trivial distress is a part of the price of living among people. Here, however, it is not unreasonable to expect that a shy, modest, young woman put in plaintiff's position would suffer the effects she claims to have suffered from the incident, and that her distress was more than that which a person might be reasonably expected to pay as the price of living among people.

We cannot say as a matter of law that plaintiff's evidence of severe emotional distress is insufficient to go to a jury.

* * *

Because neither defendant was entitled to judgment as a matter of law, neither motion for summary judgment should have been granted.

The judgment for each of the defendants is reversed. The case is remanded for trial.

CASE COMMENT

This tort, which is still in the process of clarification, contains two variations. One involves intentional conduct to inflict psychological and emotional distress. The other is where the wrongful purpose is lacking, but the tortious element can be found in the breach of some obligation that attaches to the relationship. Here a jury could find the alleged victim's conduct was intended to embarrass and humiliate the plaintiff and was coercive in nature. Also a jury could find that because of the degrading and humiliating experience of a strip search, the conduct of the store went beyond the limits of social toleration. There also may have been a lack of true voluntariness to the claimed consent: submit to the search or lose the job, which can be characterized as a form of economic coercion.

3
Agency

In the United States today, there are two general types of private security: proprietary (in-house) and contract security services. Some businesses choose not to hire their own security staff and hire a contract security service to perform a variety of functions, such as guards, investigations, armored delivery, etc. Usually a written contract, detailing the various conditions and requirements of employment, is entered into. Thus, a relationship is created by voluntary, consensual agreement between the parties which authorizes one party to act for the other.

Agency is a relationship wherein one party is empowered to represent or act for the other under the authority of the latter. It is the delegation of some lawful business activity of the employer, with more or less discretionary power, to another. The latter (the contract security agency) undertakes to manage or perform the activity (providing security) and renders an accounting to the employer. Agency means more than tacit permission; it involves a request, instruction, or command. In other words, one party is authorized to do certain acts for the other which the other could do but has for some reason elected not to do. It is the delegating of some activity of the business to another.

There are three types of agency relationships: principal and agent, master and servant (employer and employee), and proprietor and independent contractor.

A *principal* directs or permits another (agent) to act for his benefit. The other is subject to his direction and control. An *agent* is authorized by another (principal) to act for or represent him in some type of business affair. In this relationship, the use of some discretion by the agent to accomplish the means is worthy of notice.

A *master* is a principal who employs another (servant), and who has the right to control the other's physical conduct. The master controls the results of the work and may also direct the manner in which it is done. A *servant* is employed by another (master). His physical conduct in the performance of the job is controlled or is subject to control by the master. Note the lack of discretion here.

A *proprietor* owns or operates a business or has exclusive title or legal right to anything. An *independent contractor* contracts with another to do a job, but is not controlled by the other nor subject to the other's right to control, with respect to the physical conduct in the performance of the undertaking.

The amount and extent of control by either party is a very important determinant when liability is involved and is addressed in a latter part of this chapter.

RELATIONSHIP

In the first case in this chapter, the plaintiff alleged an implied master-servant relationship. The court concluded the guard was acting on his own volition, there being no master-servant relationship by which the defendant store had the right to control the conduct of the work of the employee of another store, thus there could be no vicarious liability.

MAPP v. GIMBELS DEPARTMENT STORE
540 A.2d 941 (1988)

WEIAND, Judge:

The issue in this appeal is whether a department store is liable for injuries sustained by a shoplifter while being pursued and apprehended by a person who was not employed by the store. The trial court held that in the absence of a master-servant relationship by which the store acquired a right to control the pursuer, there could be no vicarious liability for the conduct of the pursuer in restraining the thief. We affirm.

On March 29, 1983, Barry Mapp was observed in the J.C. Penney department store in Upper Darby by security personnel who suspected that he might be a shoplifter. Michael DiDomenico, a security guard employed by J.C. Penney, followed Mapp when he left the store and proceeded to Gimbels department store. There, DiDomenico notified Rosemary Federchok, a Gimbels security guard, regarding his suspicions. Without any request for assistance, DiDomenico determined that he would remain to assist in case Federchok, a short woman of slight build, required help in dealing with Mapp in the event he committed an offense in Gimbels. It came as no surprise when Mapp was observed taking items from the men's department of the store. When Mapp attempted to escape, he was pursued. Although Federchok was unable to keep up, DiDomenico continued to pursue Mapp and ultimately apprehended him in the lower level of the Gimbels parking lot. When Federchok arrived with Upper Darby police, merchandise which had been taken from Gimbels was recovered. Mapp, who had been injured when he jumped from one level of the parking lot to another, was taken to the Delaware County Memorial Hospital where he was treated for a broken ankle.

On March 27, 1985, Mapp commenced an action against Gimbels for injuries sustained while being chased and apprehended by DiDomenico. Mapp alleged in his complaint that DiDomenico, while acting as an agent of Gimbels, had chased him, had struck him with a nightstick, and had beat him with his fists. After the pleadings were closed and pretrial discovery completed, Gimbels moved for summary judgment. The trial court determined that there was no issue of fact regarding Gimbels' possible liability and entered the requested summary judgment. DiDomenico, the trial court concluded, "was acting of his own volition as an employee for J.C. Penney in instigating surveillance of Mapp and following him into the parking lot." On appeal, Mapp argues that there was an implied master-servant relationship between Gimbels and DiDomenico which was sufficient to make Gimbels vicariously liable for DiDomenico's conduct. We disagree and affirm the judgment entered by the trial court.

It is beyond dispute in the instant case that DiDomenico was not at any relevant time employed by or subject to a right of control by Gimbels. An agency results only if there is an agreement for the creation of a fiduciary relationship with control by the principal. *Smalich v. Westfall,* 269 A.2d 476. "The basic elements of agency are 'the manifestation by the principal that the agent shall act for him, the agent's acceptance of the undertaking and the understanding of the parties that the principal is to be in control of the undertaking.'" Restatement (Second) of Agency § 1, Comment b (1958).

"'A master is a principal who employs an agent to perform service in his affairs and who controls or has the right to control the *physical conduct* of the other in the performance of the service.'" *Smalich v. Westfall, supra,* quoting Restatement (Second), Agency § 2(1) and (2) (emphasis in original). "The relation of employer and employee exists when a party has the right to select the employee, the power to discharge him, and the right to direct both the work to be done and the manner in which such work shall be done."

There was no agreement between Gimbels and DiDomenico that DiDomenico would act on behalf of Gimbels or that he would become subject to the right of Gimbels to oversee and direct the manner in which his surveillance was to be conducted. While working for J.C. Penney, DiDomenico had followed Mapp into Gimbels. He remained there without invitation and at his own instance. His assistance was neither requested nor sought by Gimbels or by anyone on its behalf. Therefore, DiDomenico was acting on his own and not as an agent or employee of Gimbels when he chased Mapp through the parking area and apprehended him in the lower parking area. Contrary to appellant's contention, there is no evidentiary basis for asserting the existence of an agreement of assistance between Gimbels and J.C. Penney whereby the security personnel of one store was authorized to provide assistance to the other in apprehending shoplifters.

In the absence of a right to control the conduct of DiDomenico's work, Gimbels cannot be liable for injuries which he inflicted during his chase and apprehension of appellant, a shoplifter. The trial court properly entered summary judgment in Gimbels favor.

Affirmed.

CONTROL

Vicarious (imputed) liability may attach to the employer of an independent contractor for the actions of the independent contractor's employee. Whether or not liability attaches depends on the amount of control exercised by the employer over the independent contractor's employee. The basic question is whether the principal or master can be liable for the intentional tort of the servant of the independent contractor. Keep in mind that an independent contractor contracts with another to do something for him but is not controlled by the other nor subject to the other's right to control with respect to his physical conduct in the performance of the undertaking.

In the following case, the court pointed out some specific instances of control over the duties of a store guard in its finding of liability of the store. The store manager had operational control over the guard: the guard was under general direction of the store manager, the guard would follow specific requests of the store manager, and the store manager instructed guards to keep juveniles out, lock certain doors, and watch for shoplifters. In other words, the greater degree of control exercised over an independent contractor's employee, the greater the chance for vicarious liability.

SAFEWAY STORES, INC. v. KELLY
448 A.2d 856 (1982)

PRYOR, Associate Judge:

This is an appeal from a jury finding of liability against Safeway Stores, Inc., for assault and battery, and false arrest arising from the actions of a security guard working at a Safeway grocery store. Appellant contends that it is not liable in respondeat superior for these actions and that in any event probable cause existed for the arrest of appellee. Preliminarily, we hold that Safeway is vicariously liable for the actions of the guard acting within the scope of his employment. Finding probable cause for the arrest of appellee but sufficient evidence to support the jury finding of excessive force in making the arrest, we reverse the jury verdict of false arrest but affirm the verdict of assault and battery.

One evening in February 1976, as George I. Kelly entered a Safeway store in Southeast Washington, D.C. to shop for groceries, he noticed that an automatic exit door was not working properly and that it was necessary to exert pressure on the door to push it open. According to appellee's testimony, he completed his shopping and later advised a cashier that he wanted to make a complaint about the broken door. The cashier suggested that Kelly talk to the assistant manager, Mr. Wheeler. When Kelly did so, the assistant manager responded that the door would be fixed in two or three months, and that Kelly was always making trouble for him. Kelly testified that he had never made a complaint to Mr. Wheeler before that night and also stated that the assistant manager said to him, "Boy, if you don't get out of this store, I'm going to have you arrested." Kelly responded, "Well, call the police, I want to file a complaint." He explained that it was unclear to him that the assistant manager was directing him to leave the store. Holding his bag of groceries, Kelly stood in the front of the store to await the police. The assistant manager beckoned to a security guard, Larry Moore, who was assigned to the store by Seaboard Security Systems, Ltd., and at the same time asked someone in the back of the store to call the police. Within a few minutes Officer Knowles of the Metropolitan Police Department came into the store. According to appellee, Knowles first spoke with the assistant manager, who had called him over, and then approached appellee and said, "The manager wants you to leave the store." Kelly testified that he was about to respond to the officer when the security guard approached from the rear and grabbed him around his throat; simultaneously, the police officer stuck his knee into Kelly's chest. The two pushed him to the ground, and handcuffed him. Without resistance from Kelly, the officer and the security guard took Kelly to the back of the store where he stood in handcuffs in view of store customers. After 10 or 15 minutes a police car arrived and transported him to the precinct where the police charged him with unlawful entry,[2] and subsequently released him.

The chief security investigator for Safeway Stores, Inc., Mr. Kubicek, stated that Safeway did not hire, pay or train the Seaboard guards or tell them specifically how to do their work. He said that there was an oral understanding between Safeway and Seaboard that Seaboard would supply security guards for 16 Safeway stores. Safeway paid for their services in one lump sum to Seaboard. Kubicek explained that a guard was under the general direction of the store manager, who had operational control over the guard. Specifically, he said that the store manager would normally set the hours the guards worked, and could ask Seaboard to replace a guard with whom he had become dissatisfied. Kubicek also testified that if a store manager encountered problems with a customer and needed a guard's assistance, the guard would act under the general direction of the manager.

Testifying for appellant, Seaboard security guard Moore contradicted appellee's version in some respects. Moore stated that he noticed Kelly and the assistant manager in the front

────────────────────

[2]The criminal charge was subsequently dropped.

of the store talking loudly. Contrary to appellee's assertion that the assistant manager motioned to the guard, Moore said he approached the assistant manager on his own initiative in an attempt to resolve an emerging problem. At the same time, Moore stated, Officer Knowles of the Metropolitan Police Department entered the store and came directly over to the assistant manager and Kelly. When Kelly became louder, the police officer decided to place him under arrest. The security guard grabbed Kelly, who then swung at the officer. A scuffle broke out between the guard, the officer and Kelly, resulting in Officer Knowles handcuffing Kelly and placing him under arrest with the assistance of the guard.

Although Moore differed with Kubicek as to the question of who determined a guard's working hours, he generally supported the latter's testimony in other respects. Moore also explained that Seaboard trained the guards placing primary emphasis on apprehension and arrest of shoplifters. He added that he would follow specific requests of the manager, such as locking the doors in the evenings, and would act under the general direction of the manager if he were having a problem with a customer.

Also testifying for appellant, the assistant store manager Wheeler recollected that the police officer first came over to talk to him, and then approached Kelly and told him the assistant manager wanted him to leave the store. Wheeler also said that Kelly threw a punch at the officer before the security guard touched Kelly to assist in the arrest. The store manager denied that he had called Kelly a troublemaker. He explained that, in response to Kelly's boisterous complaints about the broken door, he told Kelly that if he could not "keep it down", Wheeler would call the police to remove him. Wheeler also stated that the only instructions Safeway gave to the guards were to keep juveniles out of the doorway and to watch for shoplifters.

Officer Knowles stated that a short interval after entering the store on routine patrol, he heard loud shouting on the premises. Seeing the assistant manager and Kelly in the front of the store, he approached the assistant manager, who told him that he had asked Kelly to leave but Kelly refused. The officer approached Kelly and informed him that he would have to leave if he would not quiet down. When Kelly continued to shout, Officer Knowles told him he was under arrest. The officer could not tell if Kelly swung at him, but did know Kelly raised his fist or fists. The officer grabbed Kelly around the neck, and pulled him to the ground. Moore then grabbed Kelly and helped the officer handcuff him.

In his suit against Safeway, Kelly alleged assault and battery, and false arrest. The jury entered judgment against Safeway for compensatory damages in the amount of $25,000 for assault and battery, and $40,000 for false arrest. Safeway moved for judgment notwithstanding the verdict or alternatively for a remittitur and/or a new trial. On May 7, 1980, the trial judge granted a remittitur, thereby reducing appellee's verdict for assault and battery to $2,000, and for false arrest to $13,000. He conditioned denial of Safeway's motion for a new trial on Kelly's acceptance of the remittitur. Kelly filed a timely acceptance of the remittitur and Safeway appealed the court's ruling.

II

The threshold determination is whether Safeway is liable for the alleged assault and battery and false arrest of appellee by a security guard who was working at a Safeway store and was employed by an independent security service. Safeway argues that it avoids liability since the guard service company was an independent contractor[8] and not a servant of Safeway.

---

[8]An independent contractor is defined as "a person who contracts with another to do something for him but who is not controlled by the other nor subject to the other's right to control with respect to his physical conduct in the performance of the undertaking." Restatement (Second) of Agency § 2 (3) (1958).

Determining whether a master and servant[9] relationship exists depends upon the particular facts of each case. See Restatment (Second) of Agency § 220, Comment (c) (1958). The leading case in our jurisdiction lists the following factors to be considered:

> (1) the selection and engagement of the servant, (2) the payment of wages, (3) the power to discharge, (4) the power to control the servant's conduct, (5) and whether the work is part of the regular business of the employer. Standing alone, none of these *indicia*, excepting (4), seem controlling in the determination as to whether such relationship exists. The decisive test * * * is whether the employer has the *right to control and direct the servant in the performance of his work and manner in which the work is to be done. LeGrand v. Insurance Company of North America*, 241 A.2d 734, quoting *Dovell v. Arundel Supply Corp.*, 124 U.S. App.D.C. 89, 361 F.2d 543, *cert. denied*, 385 U.S. 841, 87 S.Ct. 93, 17 L.Ed.2d 74 (1966).[10]

In characterizing the right to control as the determinative factor, we mean the right to control an employee in the performance of a task and in its result, and not the actual exercise of control or supervision.

In a similar case, we held that a guard employed by an independent security service at a Safeway store was a servant acting within the scope of employment when he assaulted a customer. *Safeway Stores, Inc. v. Gibson*, 118 A.2d 386, *aff'd*, 99 U.S.App.D.C. 111, 237 F.2d 592. However, in that case, this Court did not discuss the distinction between an independent contractor and a servant since Safeway only challenged whether the guard was acting within the scope of his employment, and whether Safeway was liable for punitive damages.

A discussion of the factors relevant to determining whether a store's security service is in a master/servant relationship or is an independent contractor appears in *Adams v. F.W. Woolworth Co.*, 257 N.Y.S. 776. The court held that a detective agency, which was employed to protect the store's property, was a servant and not an independent contractor of the store

---

[9]The terms "master" and "servant" are defined as follows:

(1) A master is a principal who employs an agent to perform service in his affairs and who controls or has the right to control the physical conduct of the other in the performance of the service.

(2) A servant is an agent employed by a master to perform service in his affairs whose physical conduct in the performance of the service is controlled or is subject to the right to control by the master. Restatment (Second) of Agency § 2(1) & (2) (1958).

[10]Similarly, the American Law Institute distinguishes a servant from an independent contractor as follows:

(a) the extent of control which, by the agreement, the master may exercise over the details of the work;

(b) whether or not the one employed is engaged in a distinct occupation or business;

(c) the kind of occupation, with reference to whether, in the locality, the work is usually done under the direction of the employer or by a specialist without supervision;

(d) the skill required in the particular occupation;

(e) whether the employer or the workman supplies the instrumentalities, tools, and the place of work for the person doing the work;

(f) the length of time for which the person is employed;

(g) the method of payment, whether by the time or by the job;

(h) whether or not the work is a part of the regular business of the employer;

(i) whether or not the parties believe they are creating the relation of master and servant; and

(j) whether the principal is or is not in business. Restatment (Second) of Agency § 220(2) (1958).

owner. The court found the following factors relevant: the contract was performed at the store; the store could determine which people the guards should investigate; the agency had no specific job or piece of work to perform; the agency rendered continuous service for which the store paid it weekly; and the store could terminate the particular service whenever it chose. The court emphasized that no single fact is more conclusive of a master and servant relationship than the unrestricted right of the employer to terminate the employment whenever he chose.

Appellant argues that the trial court should have granted its motion for judgment notwithstanding the verdict since Safeway did not have the right to control the manner in which the guard performed his work, thereby making the guard an independent contractor. Analyzing the facts in this case against the *LeGrand* factors, we reach the opposite conclusion. Although Seaboard hired the guards, Safeway had the right to discharge an individual guard, subject to Seaboard's approval. Safeway hired the guards to work on a continuous basis at several of its stores and paid for their services on a monthly basis in a lump sum payment to the agency. Most importantly, Safeway enjoyed the right to control the guards' conduct. As Kubicek testified, the store manager had operational control over the guards, who worked under his general direction. The guard's testimony provided some specific instances of control: on occasion he would lock the doors at the manager's request or would act under the manager's general direction if he were having a problem with a customer. The store manager's testimony added further examples: the manager instructed the guards to keep juveniles out of the doorway and to watch for shoplifters. Finally, Kelly's description of the events at issue in this case revealed that the manager motioned for the guard to come to his assistance after Kelly complained about the doors to the manager. Thus, the record reflects that the Safeway manager identified specific problems requiring the guard's assistance and directed the guard to those problems. These specific instances of actual control are evidence of the general right of Safeway to control the guard in the performance of his duties. Thus, we find there was evidence upon which a reasonable jury could properly have found that the guard was a servant and not an independent contractor of Safeway[12] and that accordingly, Safeway is liable for the guard's allegedly tortious conduct which gave rise to this action.[13]

III

Next we turn to appellant's allegation that the trial court should have granted judgment n.o.v. on the false arrest claim since probable cause existed to arrest appellee for unlawful entry. "In this jurisdiction the gist of a complaint for false arrest or false imprisonment is an unlawful detention." Once shown, the defendant has the burden of establishing probable cause for the arrest. To prevail, the arresting officer need not prove probable cause in the constitutional sense, but rather must prove that he had a reasonable good faith belief that

---

[12]Even where the guard agency is an independent contractor, the hirer of the agency may still incur liability in certain circumstances. For instance, due to the actions of the Safeway assistant manager in requesting Kelly's arrest, Safeway might have incurred liability if the elements of false arrest had been shown. However, our holding in Part III *infra* that probable cause existed for Kelly's arrest precludes us from reaching this issue.

In addition, courts have held a grocery store liable for the intentional torts committed by their independent contractors based on the store's personal nondelegable duty to protect its property and customers.

[13]The mere existence of a master and servant relationship does not impose liability on the master unless the servant is acting within the scope of employment. However, in this case, it is undisputed that the guard was acting within the scope of employment when he assisted the police officer in arresting appellee.

the suspect committed the offense. We must view the evidence of probable cause from the perspective of the arresting officer and not the plaintiff.

The issue of probable cause for false arrest is a mixed question of law and fact. Where the facts are in dispute, the issue of probable cause is for the jury, but where the facts are undisputed or clearly established, a question of law arises for the court. Where the undisputed facts considered in the light most favorable to the appellee establish probable cause, then a directed verdict or judgment n.o.v. is appropriate.

In this case security guard Moore assisted Officer Knowles in arresting Kelly for unlawful entry. Absent a constitutional or statutory right to remain, a person lawfully on the premises of a commercial establishment is guilty of unlawful entry if he refuses to leave the premises after a demand by the person lawfully in charge. *Grogan v. United States*, 435 A.2d 1069, (individuals protesting abortions declined to leave clinic after ordered to do so); *Kelly v. United States*, 348 A.2d 884, (unregistered guest failed to leave after returning to hotel despite warning not to); *Feldt v. Marriott Corp.*, 322 A.2d 913, (barefoot woman refused manager's request to leave restaurant); *Drew v. United States*, 292 A.2d 164, 166, *cert. denied*, 409 U.S. 1062, 93 S.Ct. 569, 34 L.Ed.2d 514 (man failed to leave restaurant after owner asked him to leave despite previous warning not to return); *United States v. Bean*, D.C.Sup.Ct., (Cr. No. 50426-70, May 12, 1971) (man with prior arrest for shoplifting failed to leave store after ordered to do so).

Appellee does not allege any constitutional or statutory basis to remain on the premises against the wishes of the Safeway manager. Rather, he argues that he had a good faith belief in his right to remain since he had not yet completed the business transaction for which Safeway had invited him onto the premises and that the manager did not specifically ask him to leave. The facts, considered in the light most favorable to appellee, do not support this contention. According to the testimony of Officer Knowles and the assistant manager, the latter told Knowles that he (the manager) wanted Kelly to leave the store and that when Knowles conveyed this information to Kelly, Kelly refused to leave. As appellee himself testified, the manager told him that if he did not leave, the manager would call the police and have him arrested. This testimony renders incredible Kelly's subsequent statement that he did not know the manager wanted him to leave. Thus, the record reflects that it was undisputed that probable cause existed to arrest Kelly for unlawful entry. Accordingly, we reverse the judgment against Safeway for false arrest.

IV

Safeway also argues that the trial court should have granted judgment n.o.v. on the assault and battery claim. If the person making a lawful arrest used excessive force, the person arrested may have a claim for assault and battery. In this case the action of the Seaboard guard may impose liability on Safeway. As we have said:

> A master may be liable in compensatory damages where he has confided to his servant duties which in the natural and ordinary course may involve the use of force upon third persons, and he has expressly or impliedly committed to the servant the determination of the particular occasion upon which such force is to be used and the particular degree of force which is to be applied.

Appellee alleges that although he offered no resistance, the Seaboard guard grabbed him from behind around the throat and pushed him to the ground before handcuffing him. Although witnesses for appellant each told different versions of the events, we find that there was sufficient evidence upon which a jury could properly have found Safeway liable for assault and battery. Accordingly, we affirm the jury finding of liability on that count.

Affirmed in part and reversed in part.

CASE COMMENT

One of the determinative factors in this case was the right of the store to control the employee of the security service in the performance of a task and in its result. The court found that the store enjoyed the right to control the guard's conduct; therefore, the guard was a servant of the store and not an independent contractor.

In the following case, a cafe paid a city police department for the services of an off-duty police officer. Because his task was similar to that of a bouncer and because of the cafe's control over him, he was found to be an employee of the cafe.

DAVIS v. DELROSSO
359 N.E.2D 313 (1977)

KAPLAN, Justice.

The plaintiff Gary H. Davis sued the defendants Steven DelRosso, Millbury Cafe, Inc. (Millbury), and the city of Worcester for damages for an assault on him by DelRosso, a Worcester police officer who was serving in off-duty hours on paid detail at Millbury's premises. At trial to a jury, the city of Worcester's motion for a directed verdict was granted, and the plaintiff took no appeal from the ensuing judgment. Verdicts of $45,000 each having been returned against Millbury and DelRosso, Millbury moved for judgment notwithstanding the verdict or a new trial; DelRosso moved for a new trial. The trial judge denied the motion for judgment n.o.v. but granted each defendant a new trial unless the plaintiff agreed to remit $20,000 from the verdicts. When the plaintiff agreed to the remittiturs, the judge denied the new trial motions and entered judgments for $25,000. Appealing from the respective judgments, Millbury claims error in the denial of judgment n.o.v. or a new trial; DelRosso claims error in the denial of a new trial.

Under the verdicts, the jury can be taken to have accepted the following version of the facts. The plaintiff, thirty-one years old, an executive of a computer service company, on finishing end-of-month work on Friday, December 29, 1972, about 11:15 P.M., drove a few blocks to Millbury's cafe, called "Steeple Bumpstead," located on Millbury Street, Worcester. In the evenings the cafe provided music, dancing, and other entertainment, besides food and drink. The place was crowded as the plaintiff entered. He stood at the bar and ordered a beer, his only alcoholic drink of the day. He recognized a young woman with whom he was casually acquainted—a registered nurse, as it happened—and began to chat with her at the bar.

A man approached and asked the young woman for a dance. She declined. He returned in a few minutes, and, on being again refused, took the young woman by the arm. The plaintiff said, "Leave her alone." At this point the man grabbed the plaintiff by the shirt. The plaintiff pushed him away. Neither landed any blows or, it seems, attempted any.

Almost instantly—perhaps in response to a call by a bartender for "Stevie"—DelRosso, evidently in uniform, appeared and stepped between the two. Without inquiring into the merits, he pushed the plaintiff against a wall, and as the plaintiff rebounded, or was pulled from the wall by DelRosso, DelRosso struck him a blow on the mouth with his right fist. This did considerable damage to the plaintiff's upper teeth and bridgework and he began to bleed profusely. DelRosso seized the plaintiff by the hair, pulled or dragged him outside, and shoved him to the ground. The young woman followed outside and asked DelRosso whether she might help the plaintiff; DelRosso rebuffed her and ordered her back into the cafe. After perhaps ten minutes, a police wagon arrived and the plaintiff was driven to a hospital where, after waiting a half hour, he was given medication, and a cut in his upper lip was stitched. He was then driven to the Waldo Street jail; there he spent the night in a cell.

(The record does not indicate on what charges he was held. DelRosso said he had "arrested" the plaintiff in the cafe for disturbing the peace, and outside the cafe for drunkenness.)

Reconstruction of the plaintiff's teeth required visits to a dentist over a period of several months. The medical bills came to about $3,000.

On this evidence, DelRosso's own liability for the use of excessive force, and for his subsequent behavior, is clear enough. The jury could find the involvement of Millbury was as follows. Millbury had an informal arrangement with the Worcester police department by which the department cooperated in supplying the cafe with an off-duty policeman for the hours from about 9 P.M. to closing each night, Tuesdays through Saturdays. Millbury paid for these services at an hourly rate by checks to the order of the police department; after tax withholding, the policemen received their shares. (It may be surmised that the routing through the police department was intended, at least in part, to assure fairness in the allocation of the work to the volunteers.) DelRosso had worked at the cafe on a previous occasion and knew the manager. It was understood, without need for express instructions, that the policeman was there to inhibit disturbances and, if any arose, to quell them.

Whether one who uses the services of policemen on paid detail may be held responsible as a principal for their particular conduct has been made to depend on whether the policemen were properly classified, in respect to conduct of that sort, as "independent contractors" or as "servants" or "employees." This in turn has depended on a multifactored estimate which expresses itself mainly in a conclusion regarding the principal's "right to control" the policemen's activities. See *Luz v. Stop & Shop, Inc., of Peabody*, 202 N.E.2d 771; *Cowan v. Eastern Racing Ass'n, Inc.*, 111 N.E.2d 752; *Posner v. Paul's Trucking Serv., Inc.*, 380 F.2d 757, (1st Cir. 1967).[3]

In the present case we are to assume that the judge instructed the jury correctly, since the defendants do not complain of the instructions and indeed the record appendixes do not reproduce them. Except for very plain cases, the discrimination and determination are for the jury as a question of fact. So they were here. In reaching verdicts for the plaintiff, the jury were entitled to attach significance to the circumstances, among others, that DelRosso's task (as the jury might believe) was similar to that which has been customarily confided to the bartender or "bouncer"; that his work was to be performed on the principal's premises though it might spill over to the sidewalk and that he was engaged alone and not, as in some decided cases, in company with other policemen under the command of a superior officer. The jury could find that DelRosso was "acting not as a public officer in a public place but as an employee of the defendant for its private purposes on its private premises." That DelRosso, implicitly authorized by the principal to use force in appropriate situations, in fact used force inappropriately or excessively, would not relieve the principal here by putting those tortious acts beyond the scope of the employment. We perceive no error in the denial of judgment n.o.v.

CASE COMMENT

Here there was an informal arrangement where the cafe paid the police department and the police department supplied off-duty officers. There was also an understanding that the off-duty policeman, evidently in uniform, was there to inhibit and quell disturbances and was implicitly authorized to use force. His task was similar to that of a bouncer. Because of the cafe's right to control, he was found to be an employee of the cafe.

[3]Our cases have not always been entirely in accord with the nomenclature of Restatement (Second) of Agency § § 2, 220 (1958) but they have tended to like results. The problem can sometimes be put as one of "borrowed servants"; see *id.* at § 227, comment *c* (regarding special police).

JOINT CONTROL

Sometimes joint liability will attach to both the employer of the independent contractor and the independent contractor. In the following case, the guard, furnished by contract from a third agency, was held to be a borrowed employee of the gas station, as well as being on loan from the security agency. The court found that both the gas station and the security agency exercised joint control over the guard. Factors showing joint control came from conflicting testimony, which included the following:

- The security agency hired the guards, assigned the guards their duties, and directly supervised the guards.
- The gas station had the power to hire and fire the guards, set standards for the guards, evaluate the guards' work, require the guards to be armed, schedule the guards' times and place of work, give direction to them at each station, and directly supervise and control them.

GULF OIL CORPORATION v. WILLIAMS
642 S.W.2d 270 (1982)

CORNELIUS, Chief Justice.

Gulf Oil Corporation and Empire Security Agency, appeal from a jury verdict awarding Thomas Williams $94,719.77 actual damages and $50,000.00 punitive damages for personal injuries.

Thomas Williams purchased gasoline at a Gulf Station in Houston. Robert Gory, a security guard employed by Empire Security Agency and furnished to Gulf through a contract between Gulf and Manpower, Inc., believed that Williams had robbed or was attempting to rob the cashier. He followed Williams to his car and shot him in the head and hand. The jury found that Gory was the borrowed employee of Gulf, on loan from the Empire Security Agency, Inc. They also found that Empire ratified Gory's conduct. Judgment was rendered against Empire, Gulf and Gory for the actual damages, and against Empire and Gory for the punitive damages. We will modify the judgment to eliminate the award of punitive damages and will affirm the judgment as modified.

Empire's third point contends the trial court erred in awarding damages against it because the security guard had been found to be the borrowed employee of Gulf. It is argued that if Gory was the employee of Gulf he could not have been acting also as the employee of Empire. We disagree. There was evidence that Empire and Gulf had joint control over Gory, and that Empire ratified his conduct on the occasion in question. This evidence is sufficient to sustain the joint liability of Empire and Gulf for actual damages. Restatement (Second) of Agency § 226 (1958). The complaints in Points 3 and 9 concerning punitive damages are rendered moot because of our disallowance of those damages pursuant to Point of Error 2.

Empire's fifteenth and sixteenth points urge there was no evidence that Gory was incompetent or that Empire was negligent in hiring an incompetent and entrusting him with a weapon. Testimony was given by two eyewitnesses that Gory walked up to William's car, stuck a gun through the car window, and shot him. We find this sufficient for the jury to infer that Gory was incompetent and unfit as a security guard. However, on the question of Empire's negligence in hiring Gory, evidence was presented that a notation appeared on Gory's application to the effect that "Capt. Benham called New York, okay." Testimony also showed that Empire checked with Gory's Houston employer. There is no evidence that Empire knew or should have known that Gory was incompetent. Thus, there can be no liability on the issue of negligent hiring. This does not require reversal, however, because other evidence and findings justify the award of actual damages.

Gulf also complains of the judgment, contending that the evidence is legally and factually insufficient to support the finding that Gory was Gulf's borrowed servant. There was testimony at trial that: Empire hired the security guards for work at Gulf Stations and assigned them their duties; Gory was never employed by Gulf while working for Empire; Empire was responsible for the direct supervision of the guards; Empire had a contract with Manpower, Inc. to supply security guards at Gulf Stations; the guards took no direction from Gulf; Empire directed the guards in the amount of force to be used; and all complaints about the guards were sent to Manpower, Inc. However, there was other evidence tending to show that Gory was the borrowed employee of Gulf on the occasion in question. There was testimony that Gulf had the power to hire and fire the guards; it set the standards for the guards; it evaluated their work; it required that the guards be armed; it scheduled which guards would work at what stations and at what times; the guards took direction from Gulf marketers at each station; and Gulf directly supervised and controlled the guards. Thus, the evidence was conflicting and it was not conclusively established that Gory was not Gulf's borrowed employee. There was evidence supporting both sides of the issue and we find it sufficient to support the jury's finding of fact.

The judgment of the trial court is modified to exclude the award of punitive damages against Empire. In all other respects, it is affirmed.

BLEIL, Justice, dissenting.

While I agree that the judgment against Empire Security Agency, Inc. should be affirmed to the extent that it awards actual damages, I would reverse the judgment against Gulf Oil Corporation and render judgment that Thomas Williams take nothing against Gulf.

Gulf's evidentiary points are well taken. The court errs in affirming judgment against Gulf because the evidence is legally and factually insufficient to support a finding that Gory was the borrowed employee of Gulf at the time of the shooting.

Gulf had a written contract with Manpower, Inc. by which Manpower furnished guards for security at Gulf stations. Pursuant to this agreement, Gulf paid Manpower. Under a separate contract, Empire Security Agency agreed with Manpower to furnish security guards. Empire hired and fired these guards and furnished them to Gulf stations pursuant to its contract with Manpower.

In determining the threshold question of whether sufficient evidence supported the jury's finding that Gory was the borrowed employee of Gulf, Section 220(2), Restatement (Second) of Agency (1958), gives solid assistance. It provides,

> (2) In determining whether one acting for another is a servant or an independent contractor, the following matters of fact, among others, are considered:
> (a) the extent of control which, by the agreement, the master may exercise over the details of the work;
> (b) whether or not the one employed is engaged in a distinct occupation or business;
> (c) the kind of occupation, with reference to whether, in the locality, the work is usually done under the direction of the employer or by a specialist without supervision;
> (d) the skill required in the particular occupation;
> (e) whether the employer or the workman supplies the instrumentalities, tools, and the place of work for the person doing the work;
> (f) the length of time for which the person is employed;
> (g) the method of payment, whether by the time or by the job;
> (h) whether or not the work is a part of the regular business of the employer;
> (i) whether or not the parties believe they are creating the relation of master and servant; and
> (j) whether the principal is or is not in business.

Regardless of any disputed testimony certain matters are conclusively established: (a) that Gulf had no agreement with Gory or Empire; (b) that Gory was engaged in the distinct occupation of being a security guard; (c) that Empire, not Gulf, furnished Gory his uniform and firearm; (d) that Empire, not Gulf, paid Gory for the work done; (e) that Empire, not Gulf, provided training and instruction for the security guards; and (f) that Empire, not Gulf, regularly engages in the business of security services. Application of Section 220(2) compels a conclusion that the evidence does not support a finding that Gory was the borrowed employee of Gulf.

The case of *Producers Chemical Company v. McKay*, 366 S.W.2d 220, sets out the general rule for determining when the employee of one employer becomes the borrowed employee of another. Under its guidelines, if Gory had been placed under the control of Gulf in the manner of the performance of his duties, he might become the special or borrowed employee of Gulf. The evidence showing this control is not found in the record. Gulf did not hire Empire or Gory. Gulf did not contract with Empire or Gory. Empire's president stated that no person with Gulf instructed Empire concerning the security duties at the Gulf station.

When a contract exists between a general employer and a special employer, that contract controls the question of employment at the time in issue. No contract existed between Empire and Gulf. Therefore, the question is whether Gulf had the right to control the manner and details of Gory's work. This control must be authoritative rather than suggestive, and any sporadic acts of control by Gulf should not be considered. Under the facts of this case I conclude that the evidence is both legally and factually insufficient to support the finding that Gory was a borrowed employee of Gulf Oil Corporation.

I dissent from the Court's decision to the extent that it holds that the judgment against Gulf Oil Corporation is affirmed.

CASE COMMENT

Although the dissent felt that evidence showing control was not found in the record, the majority found evidence that the security company and the oil company had joint control over the guard and therefore there was joint liability. The majority found that the oil company, although working through a third company to get its guards, had the power to hire and fire, set standards, evaluate their work, require that they be armed, set their schedules, give them direction, and directly supervise and control them.

RESPONDEAT SUPERIOR/VICARIOUS LIABILITY

Respondeat superior means "let the master answer for the acts of his servant." This means that the master is liable in certain cases for the wrongful acts of his servant. The master is responsible for the want of care on the part of his servant toward those to whom the master owes a duty to use care, provided the failure of the servant to use such care occurred in the course of his employment. This doctrine applies only when the relation of master and servant existed between the defendant and the wrongdoer at the time of the injury sued for, and in respect to the transaction from which it arose. It is not applicable where the injury occurred while the servant was acting outside the legitimate scope of his authority. However, if the deviation of the servant is only slight or incidental, the employer may still be liable. Along with this doctrine is "vicarious liability," which means an indirect legal responsibility. That is, an employer can be liable for the acts of an employee.

SCOPE OF EMPLOYMENT

Under the doctrine of *respondeat superior*, a principal is liable for the torts of his agent committed within the scope of his employment. An employee acts within the scope of his employment when he is doing something in furtherance of the duties he owes to his employer and where the employer is, or could be, exercising some control, directly or indirectly, over the employee's activities. An employee is in the scope of employment whenever he is engaged in activities that fairly and reasonably may be said to be incident of the employment or logically and naturally connected with it.

Some factors to be considered in determining if the activity was done within the scope or course of employment include: time, place, and purpose of the act; authorization of the act by the employer; common performance of the act by employees on behalf of their employer; extent to which the employee's interest was advanced by the act; extent to which the private interests of the employee were involved; the length of departure of the employee from company business to take care of personal affairs; the furnishing of the means and instrumentalities by the employer which inflicted the injury; and knowledge on the part of the employer that the employee would do the act or had done the act before.

In *Gonzales v. Southwest Security and Protection Agency, Inc.*, which is reported under "Negligent Training," (Chapter 1, page 15), the security guards responsible for the false imprisonment and battery were held to be acting within the scope of their employment. An employer is liable for the intentional torts of its employees if the torts are committed in the course and scope of employment. The security company provided the guards with uniforms, handcuffs, guns, nightsticks and the authority to keep peace. The beating was facilitated by instrumentalities provided by the security agency. The guard's conduct arose out of an attempt to perform the agency's business. For a more in-depth explanation, please refer to the case.

BEYOND THE SCOPE OF EMPLOYMENT

The following five cases demonstrate that some activities by security company employees are outside the scope of their employment. Activities such as murder, rape, arson, burglary, and wrongful death are not in furtherance of the employer's business. These activities cannot be fairly and reasonably said to be incident to the employment or logically and naturally connected with it. Note, however, that although a company may escape liability because its employee went beyond the scope of employment, the company may be liable for negligent hiring or negligent supervision.

Rape/Murder

MARTIN v. UNITED SECURITY SERVICES, INC.
373 So.2d 720 (1979)

PER CURIAM.

The question on this appeal is whether the court erred in granting summary judgment in favor of appellee as to Count Two of the complaint. Count One alleged negligence on the part of appellee in the employment of a security guard. Count Two sought to impose liability upon the grounds that the security guard was acting within the scope of his employment at the time he raped and killed appellant's decedent. The trial court granted summary judgment as to Count Two, finding there was no genuine issue of material fact and that the appellee's security guard at the time was not acting within the scope of his employment. We agree with the trial court and affirm.

The record reveals that appellee's employee, a security guard, originally went to the home of appellant's decedent, Joyce Atchley, to call his employer and ask why the relief guard had not yet arrived at the apartment complex to which he was assigned. He then left Atchley's home, but returned a few moments later to call his wife and tell her he was delayed. It was at this point that the rape and murder took place. The employee, Turner, was subsequently convicted of second degree murder and sentenced for the offenses.

On this record, we have no difficulty in finding that the employee had "stepped away" from appellee's business at the time of the criminal attack upon Atchley. It seems clear that the attack upon Atchley was unrelated to the employee's duties as a guard and that the motive for the attack was the furtherance of the employee's interests, not appellee's. In these circumstances, the master cannot be held liable for the servant's acts.

ERVIN, Judge, specially concurring.

I concur in the opinion of the majority solely on the basis of the pleadings as drafted under Count II, which alleged that the employee "was acting within the scope of his employment with the defendant." Aside from the pleaded issue of respondeat superior, an issue which was not pleaded is whether an implied contractual relationship exists between the employer and the person assaulted, which may result in tort liability to the employer. Such a theory has been permitted in other jurisdictions under particular circumstances. That question is of course not decided by our opinion and in my view remains an open one.

Assault/Rape

HEINDEL v. BOWERY SAVINGS BANK
525 N.Y.S.2d 428 (1988)

HARVEY, Justice.

Appeal from an order of the Supreme Court, entered June 4, 1987 in Sullivan County, which partially granted a motion by defendant Interstate Security Service North for summary judgment dismissing the complaint against it.

Defendant Robert Turner was employed as a security guard by defendant Interstate Security Service North (hereinafter Interstate). On December 31, 1983 he was assigned to work at the Mid-Valley Mall in the Town of Newburgh, Orange County. At approximately 8:30 P.M., Turner forced a 15-year-old girl who was in the mall to accompany him to the mall's security office where he assaulted, raped and sodomized her. Turner was subsequently convicted upon his plea of guilty to the crime of rape in the first degree and sentenced to a term of imprisonment.

The victim's father (hereinafter plaintiff) commenced this action alleging, *inter alia*, that Interstate was vicariously liable for Turner's acts. Interstate moved for summary judgment. Supreme Court granted partial summary judgment dismissing the first and second causes of action which were premised upon the theory of respondeat superior. This appeal by plaintiff followed.

We affirm. While an employer can be held vicariously liable for the torts of his employee committed in the course of the employer's work, even if the acts are done irregularly or with disregard of instruction, there is no respondeat superior liability for torts committed by the employee for personal motives unrelated to the furtherance of the employer's business. Here, Turner's outrageous conduct was in no way incidental to the furtherance of Interstate's interest. The acts were committed for personal motives and were a complete departure from the normal duties of a security guard. Accordingly, we conclude that Supreme Court correctly dismissed the causes of action which were based upon the theory of respondeat superior.

The other arguments advanced by plaintiff on appeal have been considered and found meritless.

Order affirmed, with costs.

Arson

WATSON v. AQUINAS COLLEGE
268 N.W.2d 342 (1978)

R.B. BURNS, Presiding Judge.

The issue presented in this case is whether the Private Security Guard Act of 1968, M.C.L. §338.501 *et seq.*; M.S.A. § 18.185(1) *et seq.*, imposes vicarious liability upon a security guard agency or its insurer for damages caused by the wrongful act of an agency security guard where the act was not within the scope of the agency's business. We hold that it does not.

Security guards Reitz and Smith deliberately set fire to the Aquinas College Faculty Arts Building in order to provide an excuse for not making rounds. Reitz was employed by Aquinas College and Smith was employed by Engineered Protection Systems, Inc. and assigned to duties at Aquinas College. Ronald Watson, an art department professor who lost personal property in the fire, brought this action against Reitz, Smith, Aquinas College, Engineered Protection, and Engineered Protection's insurer, California Union Insurance Company. Aquinas College cross-claimed against the other defendants. Both Watson and Aquinas College (hereinafter plaintiffs) alleged that the Private Security Guard Act of 1968 made Engineered Protection and California Union (hereinafter defendants) vicariously liable for the action of Smith. Defendants asserted as an affirmative defense that Smith's action was outside the scope of employment. Plaintiffs moved for summary judgment under GCR 1963, 117.2(3), and defendants moved to strike the allegation of liability under the Private Security Guard Act, GCR 1963, 115.2. The trial court denied plaintiffs' motion and granted defendants' motion. Properly labeled, however, it appears that the trial court granted summary judgment, GCR 1963, 117.2(3), in favor of defendants. GCR 1963, 117.3. We affirm.

Unless the Private Security Guard Act modified the common law, defendants are not liable, for "under the doctrine of *respondeat superior* there is no liability on the part of an employer for torts intentionally or recklessly committed by an employee beyond the scope of his master's business".

Plaintiffs rely upon two sections of the act. Section 9(1), which requires as a condition of licensing the filing of a bond or policy of insurance, provides in part:

The bonds shall be taken in the name of the people of the state, and a person injured by the *wilful, malicious, and wrongful act* of the licensee or any of his agents or employees may bring an action on the bond or insurance policy in his own name to recover damages suffered by reason of the act. M.C.L. § 338.1059(1); M.S.A. § 18.185(9)(1).

Section 17(1) provides:

A licensee may employ as many persons as he deems necessary to assist him in his work of alarm system contractor or private guard or agency and in the conduct of his business, and *at all times during the employment may be accountable for the good conduct in the business of each person so employed.* M.C.L. § 338.1067(1); M.S.A. § 18.185(17)(1).

It is plaintiff's theory that these two sections create a cause of action independent of the common law. They reason as follows:

It is a familiar rule of construction that it will not be presumed that the legislature intended to do a useless thing and that if possible every part of a statute must be given effect.

Unless the emphasized "may" in Section 17(1) is read as "shall" the Section merely restates the obvious, since an employer is accountable at common law under the doctrine of *respondeat superior.* This would be a useless act. If read as "shall", the Section creates a cause of action. The conduct the employer will be accountable for is that set forth in § 9(1): "wilful, malicious, and wrongful act(s)". Neither Section limits liability to acts within the scope of employment. Since Smith's act was wilful, malicious, and wrongful, the employer and his insurer are liable.

Plaintiffs' analysis is defective. "Statutes will not be extended by implication to abrogate the established rules of common law." From the Legislature's use of the words "may" and "shall" in the act it is readily apparent that it understood the permissive-mandatory distinction between the two words. See particularly the remainder of § 9(1). The Legislature's use of the word "may" in § 17(1) indicates that it intended liability to be dependent upon the existence of liability at common law. Since codification of the common law is not a useless act, we see no reason to adopt plaintiff's strained interpretation of the act.

Affirmed. Costs to defendants.

Burglary

SEXTON BROTHERS TIRE COMPANY v. SOUTHERN BURGLAR ALARM COMPANY OF GEORGIA, INC.
265 S.E.2d 335 (1980)

SOGNIER, Judge.

Southern Burglar Alarm Co. of Georgia, Inc. (Southern) installed a burglar alarm system for Sexton Brothers Tire Co. (Sexton) in 1971. The system was tied into Southern's office and the police department, and if the alarm went off one of Southern's employees would go to Sexton's building, meet an employee of Sexton's who would unlock the building and inspect the alarm system to see if a burglary had occurred or if the system malfunctioned. In December 1974 or January 1975 Brooks, an employee of Southern, and Brocato, an employee of Sexton, entered into a plan to steal tires from Sexton. Brooks would trip the alarm at Sexton, Brocato would be called to let Brooks into Sexton's building, and the two of them would then steal one or two truckloads of tires and sell them. Brooks' girlfriend was also an employee of Southern who monitored alarms from Sexton and always called Brocato; she then destroyed records of the incoming alarm from Sexton. This scheme was followed for approximately six months; in October 1975 Brocato confessed to stealing tires and indicated that he and Brooks had stolen about 300 to 350 tires.

Sexton filed this action against Southern to recover the cost of the tires stolen, alleging they suffered a loss as a result of a conspiracy between some of their employees and Southern. The jury rendered a verdict for Sexton, but the trial court granted a motion by Southern for a judgment notwithstanding the verdict. Sexton appealed, and its sole enumeration of error is that the trial court erred in granting the motion for a judgment n.o.v. as Southern was not entitled to judgment as a matter of law.

While the gist of Sexton's argument is that the exculpatory clause in its contract with Southern is not enforceable, the only issue in this case is whether Brooks was acting as Southern's agent at the time he and Brocato stole tires from Sexton. It is apparent that Brooks was not at that time acting as Southern's agent. Southern's obligation under its contract was to install an electric burglar alarm and to maintain it in good working order. Whenever the alarm sounded in Southern's office, one of its agents would go to Sexton's to determine the cause of the alarm. To accomplish this, one of Sexton's designated employees would meet Southern's agent and let him enter the premises to inspect the alarm system and make repairs if necessary. Nothing in the contract authorized the agent to enter Sexton's building for any other purpose.

Code Ann. § 105-108 provides, in pertinent part:

> Every person shall be liable for torts committed by his . . . servant, by his command or in the prosecution and within the scope of his business, whether the same shall be by negligence or voluntary. This court has held that "(i)n determining the liability of the master for the negligent or wilful acts of a servant, the test of liability is, not whether the act was done during the existence of the employment but whether it was done within the scope of the actual transaction of the master's business for accomplishing the ends of his employment."

The evidence presented by Sexton did not show that stealing tires was within the scope of Brooks' employment; on the contrary, the testimony by deposition of Brocato, Sexton's former employee, stated that he wouldn't consider Brooks to be acting on behalf of Southern when he was stealing tires and "I am sure he wasn't getting paid by the company to do that." It is well-settled that the mere fact that a tortious act of an employee amounts to a crime does not, per se, relieve his employer from liability. The test of liability is the same as in cases where a non-criminal act is involved; the act must have been one authorized by the employer prior to its commission, ratified after its commission, or committed within the scope of the employment. The evidence shows that Brooks was not acting within the scope of or in the prosecution of the business of Southern when he was stealing tires, and Southern did not ratify Brooks' actions. Sexton produced no evidence which connected the theft of tires with Southern's business or which showed that Brooks acted on behalf of Southern when he stole the tires. The several thefts involved Brooks only and did not involve the employer. "There is no liability on the part of the master arising from the mere relationship of master and servant. There is a long line of decisions to the effect that if the servant steps aside from his employment and acts without the scope of his master's business, and commits a tort, the master is not liable."

As the only business of Southern was to install and maintain electric burglar alarm systems, any action by Brooks in stealing tires would be personal and outside the scope of his employment. This court has held that an agent was acting on his individual responsibility, not on his master's business, when he committed an offense (assault and battery) arising out of a personal matter. Accordingly, the trial court did not err in granting the motion for a judgment n.o.v. In view of our decision on this issue, we need not address the questions relating to validity of the contract provisions.

Judgment affirmed.

Wrongful Death

VALLEJO v. OSCO DRUG, INC.
743 S.W.2d 423 (1988)

TURNAGE, Presiding Judge.

The widow, child and parents of Paul Vallejo brought a common law action against Osco Drug, Advance Security and Marvin Duncan for the wrongful death of Paul Vallejo. The court entered summary judgment in favor of Osco and denominated the judgment as final for purposes of appeal. The action still pends against Advance and Duncan.

The contention on appeal is that Duncan was the alter ego of Osco and when he intentionally killed Vallejo such act was the act of Osco. Affirmed.

The petition alleged that Vallejo was working as the manager of an Osco Drug store in June of 1986. Osco had contracted with Advance Security to supply armed guards. One of the guards stationed by Advance was Marvin Duncan.

In June of 1986, Duncan conspired with an accomplice to stage a robbery of the store. During the robbery, Vallejo was shot and killed with Duncan's gun. It was alleged that Duncan had pleaded guilty to a criminal charge of intentionally killing Vallejo.

It was further alleged that Osco had a duty to provide a safe place to work for Vallejo and to do this had hired Advance to police the store. The petition alleged that the duty of Osco to provide a safe workplace was nondelegable and that Duncan became the alter ego of Osco in the performance of his duty to keep the store safe. It was further alleged that when an employer acts through an alter ego to perform a nondelegable duty, the act of the alter ego is the act of the employer and not the act of the alter ego himself. It was pleaded that when Duncan intentionally killed Vallejo such intentional act was the act of Osco. It was further pleaded that because the act of killing Vallejo was intentional and was attributed to Osco, a common law suit would lie against Osco since an intentional injury inflicted on an employee by an employer is not covered by workers' compensation laws.

The premise of the petition that an employer owes a duty to its employees to furnish a reasonably safe place in which to work is correct. However, an employer is not an insurer of the safety of the employee and the failure to exercise ordinary care to provide a safe workplace constitutes negligence.

The further contention that the duty to furnish a reasonably safe workplace is one which cannot be delegated so as to relieve the employer from liability for the negligent performance of that duty is also correct. The significance of the nondelegable nature of the duty to provide a safe workplace has largely disappeared with the advent of the Worker's Compensation Law. Prior to the adoption of that law, it was important to determine whether negligence in furnishing a safe workplace was the act of a fellow employee, which barred a suit for damages, or was the act of the employer which would allow such a suit. Since the Workers' Compensation Law abolishes the defense of negligence by fellow servant, cases are few which discuss the nondelegable duty to furnish a safe workplace.

While it is true that Osco owed Vallejo a nondelegable duty to make the workplace safe, and that the act of an alter ego in making the workplace safe is the act of the employer, it does not follow that the intentional act of Duncan in killing Vallejo constituted an intentional act on the part of Osco. In *Gens v. Wagner Electric Mfg. Co.*, 31 S.W.2d 785, the court considered a case in which an employee was knocked from her chair when another employee pushed or tilted her chair. There was an allegation that the floor was covered with dirt and grease but the court pointed out that the condition of the floor had nothing to do with the injury. The court held that the sole and proximate cause of the fall and injury was the act of the employee in tilting the chair and was entirely outside of the scope of the duties of that employee. The court held that there was no showing that the condition of the workplace contributed in any way to the injury.

In *Sherrill v. American Well & Prospecting Co.*, 176 S.W. 658, a group of employees with the consent of their foreman decided to make a homemade cannon to celebrate New Year's Eve. The employees were gathered in the workroom pounding gun powder into a piece of iron when the powder exploded and injured an employee. The court held that while the law imposes a duty on the employer to furnish a safe place to work for its employees it does not make the employer responsible for the acts of employees when such acts are not within the scope of employment and in the performance of the employer's business. The court further held that even if the foreman had been the vice principal of the employer and had known that the employees were loading the cannon, the evidence fails to show that the accident should have been contemplated because the plan was to explode the cannon outside. The court held that because the injury arose from acts performed by parties who turned aside from the employer's business and were engaged in an act on their own, the employer would not be liable for the injury.

In this case the allegation is that Duncan intentionally engaged in a robbery of the very store that he was hired to protect. There can be no question that he turned away from the duty he was hired to perform and engaged in conduct contrary to the purpose of his employment. The act of Duncan was clearly outside the scope of his employment and outside the performance of Osco's business. Further, the proximate cause of death was not the condition of the premises but the unlawful act of Duncan. For these reasons the act of Duncan could not be considered the act of Osco to constitute the infliction of an intentional injury on Vallejo by Osco.

The summary judgment in favor of Osco is affirmed.

CASE COMMENT

Although the acts done in these cases—murder, rape, assault, arson, burglary, and wrongful death—were carried out during the existence of employment, they did not accomplish the ends of their master's business. The acts were beyond the scope of employment. The employees stepped away from their employer's business, their activities were unrelated to their duties, their motives were not in furtherance of their employer's interests, and they engaged in conduct contrary to the purpose of their employment, which was a complete departure from their normal duties. The possibility of actions for negligent hiring and/or negligent supervision may exist.

INDEPENDENT CONTRACTOR

An independent contractor contracts to do work or render service according to his own methods. He is subject to the control of the employer only for the result or end product of the work. The control is to the extent that the desire of the employer is followed only as to the results and not as to the means as to how it is accomplished. The greater the degree of control by the employer, the lesser the degree of independence by the contractor. The converse, of course, is also true, in that the lesser degree of control by the employer results in a greater degree of independence of the contractor. Some factors in determining whether or not the independent contractor relationship exists include: the extent of control by the employer over the details, whether or not the occupation of the independent contractor is distinct from that of the employer, and whether the work is done under the employer's direction or without supervision. Generally, the employer who bargains with the independent contractor only for results and retains no control over the method used is not expected to be held responsible.

GLENMAR CINESTATE, INC. v. FARRELL
292 S.E. 2d 366 (1982)

RUSSELL, Justice.

The question presented in this case is whether an off-duty police officer, directing traffic out of a drive-in theater onto a state highway, is acting as an independent contractor or an employee of the theater management.

Shortly after midnight on June 25, 1978, Sergeant James D. Lilly of the Goochland County Sheriff's Department was directing traffic out of the Patterson Drive-In Theatre onto Route 6 in Goochland County. Route 6 (Patterson Avenue, extended) is an east-west highway divided by a median strip, with two lanes of traffic in each direction.

Sergeant Lilly stood near the center line between the two westbound lanes. He wore a brown Sheriff's Department uniform and directed traffic with a three cell flashlight. In response to Lilly's signal, Mr. Herbert K. Rae drove his car out of the theater entrance and headed across the westbound lanes of Route 6 toward a break in the median strip. As his vehicle crossed the first lane, it was struck broadside by a car driven by plaintiff's decedent, John G. Farrell, travelling west on Route 6. John Farrell died as a result of the injuries received in the collision.

Robert T. Farrell, John Farrell's father and administrator, brought this action for wrongful death against Glenmar Cinestate, Inc. the owner of the drive-in theater, and Ray Bentley and Neighborhood Theatre, Inc., partners trading as Ray Bentley Productions, who leased the theater for the exhibition of the late movie. Plaintiff's motion for judgment alleged that Sergeant Lilly was negligent in his direction of traffic, that his negligence was the proximate cause of the injuries which resulted in John Farrell's death, that Lilly was an employee of the defendant operators of the theater, and that his negligence should be imputed to them under the doctrine of *respondeat superior*. Neither Sergeant Lilly nor Mr. Rae was joined as a defendant.

At the close of the plaintiff's case, the defendant moved to strike the plaintiff's evidence on the ground that no evidence had been presented in support of plaintiff's theory that Lilly was an employee, agent, or servant of the defendants. The motion was denied. It was renewed at the end of the case and again denied.

Over the defendant's objection, the court instructed the jury that the question whether the defendants were responsible for any negligence on Lilly's part depended upon whether the jury found Lilly to be an independent contractor or an employee. The jury was further instructed that the overriding factor to be considered in deciding this question was whether the defendants had the right to control Lilly's activities in directing traffic.[1]

The jury returned a verdict against all defendants in the amount of $52,911.30. Defen-

---

[1]Instruction #14, given at the request of the plaintiff, told the jury: One of the determinations that you must make in this case is whether, when he was directing traffic, Lilly was an employee

dants' motions to set aside the verdict were denied. The defendants' appeal is based upon the following contentions: (1) that the legal relationship between Sergeant Lilly and the defendants was that of an independent contractor as a matter of law, and therefore the matter should not have been submitted to the jury, (2) that John Farrell was contributorily negligent as a matter of law, and (3) that the court improperly refused certain instructions. Since we view the first contention as dispositive of the case, it is unnecessary to discuss the others.

The evidence concerning the question of agency is undisputed. The Goochland County Sheriff's Department performs local police functions. The Sheriff's deputies are sworn law-enforcement officers who are technically "on duty 24 hours a day" in the sense that they are authorized to make arrests, enforce the laws, and respond to emergencies at any time. The Department has a policy prohibiting the deputies from holding regular part-time jobs. They are, however, permitted to provide traffic control and other help "on various functions" outside their usual working hours, for which they may receive private compensation. The officers who perform such services are required to work in pairs and appear in uniform.

Over a period of several years, the drive-in theater and the Sheriff's Department had developed a routine procedure. During the week preceding a late show, Margaret Weston, the theater manager, would call the Goochland County Sheriff's Office and request the services of two deputies for a late night movie. Each officer who performed these services at the drive-in was paid $25.00 by the theater management. Mrs. Weston was not informed of the arrival of the police officers. The officers knew from frequent repetition and experience what was expected of them, and received no instruction from the theater as to their duties. The officers were generally on hand to quell disturbances, to watch for gate-crashers, and primarily to direct traffic.[2]

Chief Deputy Sheriff M.H. Clements, Jr., testified that he had formerly worked at the drive-in theater, directing traffic. He was asked how he would have reacted if one of the theater employees had come out and said, "I don't like the way you are doing it, I want you to do it another way, would you have paid attention to him?" Clements replied: "No sir, I would not have listened to him, as I felt I was doing my job in a safe manner." He further testified that he directed traffic according to the training that he had received as a police officer, and not with regard to the instructions of anyone at the theater.

Prior to the night of the collision, Sergeant Lilly had performed these duties at the theater

or agent of the defendants, or one of them, or whether he was acting as an independent contractor in his business relationship with them.

There is no question but that the services of Lilly were engaged by one or both defendants and that he was paid by funds belonging to the defendant Bentley.

In determining the employment status you may consider the method of payment, who made the payment, who set the hours and place of employment, who provided instructions as to Lilly's work, and who had contact with Lilly.

But the overriding factor to be considered is whether either or both defendants had the right to control the traffic directing of Lilly. If Lilly was under the control and direction of either or both defendants as to this work, or if either or both defendants had the right to control and direct such work, then he was an employee. If Lilly had a contract to perform this service for the defendant but he controlled and determined how this service was to be accomplished without direction or control from the defendants, then he was an independent contractor.

[2]The plaintiff offered the following instruction, which was given without objection: "In all instructions of the court, the point in time is that moment when Lilly is directing traffic onto Patterson Avenue." Since all the instructions offered by both parties restricted the jury's attention to Lilly's activities in directing traffic, we shall confine our consideration to those functions. Accordingly, we do not reach the effect, if any, which his other duties might have had upon his relationship with the defendants.

"half a dozen or more" times. On the night of the collision he was given no particular instruction. He did not check in at the box office, but arrived at the theater shortly after midnight and immediately began directing the departing traffic onto Route 6, as had become customary. Deputy Sheriff J.T. Payne was to have assisted Sergeant Lilly. However, en route to the Patterson Drive-In, he had stopped to issue a summons to a motorist speeding on Route 6. This delayed his arrival at the scene until after the collision. Both deputies testified that the direction of traffic is police work and that they considered themselves to be on duty as police officers when at the theater.

The plaintiff concedes that no actual direction was given to Sergeant Lilly as to the manner in which he was to carry out his duties. However, plaintiff contends that the defendants reserved the right to do so, based on the following testimony:

> THE COURT: Who, if anyone, did you have any dealings with or whoever would tell you what to do when you got there, if anyone, or did you just do what you needed to do?
> THE WITNESS (Sgt. Lilly): Well, I really didn't know. I figured if there is anything specific they wanted done, somebody at the theater, management-wise or whoever, would tell us what to do, otherwise we would just go down and walk in the concession stand, say hello, let them know you were there, and go out on the lot, walk around.

The plaintiff also read in evidence the following testimony of the defendant Bentley, from a discovery deposition, describing the usual activities of the deputies on duty:

> They generally sat in the patrol cars in the back of the theater, in the concession building and watched the movie, and if we had someone run the gate, that is someone coming in without paying and just driving past the gate, or if we had a rowdy crowd and bothering someone, had a complaint, then they would assist. If the manager wanted them for any purpose, they reported directly to the manager, to this woman, and they were to do so. Other than to just greet them and observe that they were paid on a couple of evenings, I never talked to them myself.

In *Craig v. Doyle*, 19 S.E.2d 675, we defined independent contractor as "one who undertakes to produce a given result without being in any way controlled as to the method by which he attains the result." There, we quoted with approval from *Kelley's Dependents v. Hoosac L. Co.*, 113 A. 818.

> If under the contract the party for whom the work is being done may prescribe not only what the result shall be, but also direct the means and methods by which the other shall do the work, the former is an employer, and the latter an employee. But if the former may specify the result only, and the latter may adopt such means and methods as he chooses to accomplish that result, then the latter is not an employee, but an independent contractor. So the master test is the right to control the work. And it is this right which properly differentiates service from independent employment.

In *Ross v. Schneider*, 27 S.E.2d 154, we stated that:

> The test of the relationship is the right to control. It is not the fact of actual interference with the control, but the right to interfere, that makes the difference between an independent contractor and a servant or agent.
> One of the means of ascertaining whether or not the right to control exists is the determination of whether or not if instructions were given they would have to be obeyed.
> The measure of compensation is also important for where it is based upon time or piece the workman is usually a servant, and where it is based upon a lump sum for the task he is usually a contractor.

The testimony upon which the plaintiff relies to show that the defendants reserved the right to control the officers applies, not to their direction of traffic, but to other duties which they might be called upon to assume at the theater. Even then, it is evidence of a right to specify results rather than means or methods.

Sergeant Lilly chose his own method of directing traffic. There was no evidence which indicated that the defendants reserved the power to direct his means of doing so, or that he would have obeyed them if they had attempted to so instruct him. We find no evidence in the record that warrants submitting to the jury the issue of the defendants' liability for Lilly's negligence. The defendants' motion to strike the evidence or set aside the verdict should have been granted because of the plaintiff's failure to produce any credible evidence to support the application of the doctrine of *respondeat superior*.

Moreover, we held in *N. & W. Ry. Co. v. Haun*, 187 S.E. 481, that a special police officer appointed by public authority, but employed and paid by a private party, does not subject his employer to liability for his torts when the acts complained of are performed in carrying out his duty as a public officer. The test is: in what capacity was the officer acting at the time he committed the acts for which the complaint is made? If he is engaged in the performance of a public duty such as the enforcement of the general laws, his employer incurs no vicarious liability for his acts, even though the employer directed him to perform the duty. On the other hand, if he was engaged in the protection of the employer's property, ejecting trespassers or enforcing rules and regulations promulgated by the employer, it becomes a jury question as to whether he was acting as a public officer or as an agent, servant, or employee.

The alleged negligence on Lilly's part of which the plaintiff complains, consisted in his directing the Rae car to proceed out of the theater entrance, into the westbound lanes of Route 6, without due regard to Farrell's approach. Lilly was then standing in the public highway, engaged in the performance of a public duty. Thus the defendants incurred no vicarious liability for his conduct. For these reasons, the judgments will be reversed and final judgment entered for each defendant.

Reversed and final judgment.

CASE COMMENT

An overriding factor in determining whether or not one is an independent contractor is the right to control and direct the work. If the worker controls and determines how the service is to be accomplished, then he is an independent contractor. Here the activity was traffic control on a public street. During this time, the deputy considered himself to be on duty as a police officer. No direction was given by theater management about the manner in which the deputy was to carry out his traffic control. The deputy chose his own method of directing traffic; thus the theater incurred no vicarious liability for his conduct.

DELEGABLE OR NON-DELEGABLE DUTY

A business may decide to hire an independent contractor for many reasons. The business may not have expertise in a particular area, orders may have increased and additional temporary help is needed to transport the finished goods, or it may cost less to have someone else perform certain tasks. Another reason may be to shift the risk.

When hiring an independent contractor, business should exercise due care in the selection of the contractor. Under the doctrine of negligent selection, the employer may be found liable if the employer knew or should have known that the contractor was not competent and the incompetency caused harm to others.

The normal principle of delegability is that the employer of the independent contractor is relieved of liability for the negligence of the independent contractor where the contractor is in exclusive control of the work. There are, however, two exceptions to this general rule. Duties of the principal, or employer of the independent contractor, are non-delegable or non-assignable where the work to be performed is inherently dangerous or if the duty is of a personal character.

In reviewing the following case, remember that negligence, or the absence of due diligence, is distinguished from the intentional tort category. Also a corporation may not always be able to immunize itself from responsibility by hiring an independent contractor.

DUPREE v. PIGGLY WIGGLY SHOP RITE FOODS, INC.
542 S.W. 2d 882 (1976)

NYE, Chief Justice.

Plaintiffs, Margaret Dupree and husband, Charles Dupree, Jr., brought suit against Denco Security Systems, Piggly Wiggly Shop Rite Foods, Inc., R.B. Denson and I.B.I. Security Service, Inc., for false imprisonment and malicious prosecution. The case was tried before a jury which answered special issues favorable to Mrs. Dupree concerning false imprisonment, but found that Denco Security Systems on the occasion in question was acting as an independent contractor for Piggly Wiggly. Based on such findings, the trial court denied plaintiffs any recovery against Piggly Wiggly. Mrs. Dupree has timely perfected her appeal to this Court.

The plaintiff, Margaret Dupree, was a married woman, 56 years of age and mother of four children. At the time of the incident in question, Mrs. Dupree was very active in both school and church activities and had never, before the occasion in question, been charged with a criminal act.

Defendant, Denco Security Systems, is a private investigation company who, at the time in question, worked exclusively for Piggly Wiggly Shop Rite Foods, Inc. The two security guards who participated in the false imprisonment of Mrs. Dupree were Eddie Bo Wilson and J.O. Harris, both being employees of Denco. The defendant, Piggly Wiggly, is a corporation doing business in the State of Texas, in the retail grocery business. Piggly Wiggly had a contract with Denco whereby Denco was to provide external and internal security services for its stores. The store manager of the Piggly Wiggly store at the time the incident made the basis of the lawsuit occurred, was Mr. Jerry Michalik.

Mrs. Dupree testified during the trial that on the afternoon of October 23, 1969, at about 2:30 p.m., she entered the Piggly Wiggly store, located on Cavalcade Street in Houston, Texas, for the purpose of buying some groceries and other non-food items. The evidence reflects that she had been a frequent customer in this store for the past year. Mrs. Dupree testified that while in the store, she purchased some cupcakes, a package of salami, a small toy rocket, two pairs of beads, a candy bar and a pair of panties. Mrs. Dupree was checked out by Thelma Feak, one of the store's checkers. She received a sales receipt for the above items and then left the store.

Upon arriving home, Mrs. Dupree noticed that she was out of milk. Her daughter complained that the type of salami her mother had purchased was a type which she did not like. Mrs. Dupree then decided it would be necessary for her to return to the store for the milk and try to exchange the salami for another kind. Upon entering the store, the second time that day, Mrs. Dupree carried with her a large shopping bag which she stated contained those items she had purchased earlier in the day.

Mrs. Dupree testified that she went back to the meat counter to exchange the package of salami, but could find no other type of salami. She then went by the toy section to look at the toy rocket and beads to see if she could find some that were better packaged than the ones she had previously purchased, but found them to be the same. She then picked up some other items (bread, root beer, chicken, milk and ice cream) and proceeded through the check out stand at which time she paid for them.

After Mrs. Dupree left the store, two men approached her, told her that they were the police and that she was under arrest. Those two individuals were later identified as J.O. Norris and Bo Wilson, security agents for Denco Security Systems. Although the evidence is conflicting, it appears that Mrs. Dupree was told by the two security guards that they were arresting her for shoplifting. Mrs. Dupree was then taken back into the store by the two guards and back to a storeroom in the rear of the store. Everything was then taken out of her purse and billfold. Mrs. Dupree testified that she gave one of the guards the sales receipt she received earlier in the day showing that those items she was accused of shoplifting had been paid for. One of the guards admitted that Mrs. Dupree gave him the sales receipt covering the questioned items, but he testified that it did not correspond with the prices of those items she was accused of shoplifting. He said that he gave the sales receipt back to Mrs. Dupree.

Mrs. Dupree testified that she stayed in the storeroom for approximately an hour and forty-five minutes and was not allowed to leave nor was she allowed to use the telephone. She repeatedly denied that she had taken any merchandise without first paying for it. Mrs. Dupree reiterated to the guards that she had purchased the items earlier that same day and requested the security guards to talk with the checker (Thelma Feak) so that her story could be verified. The two guards refused to do so. Although the value of the merchandise allegedly stolen was only of the approximate value of $2.12, the security guards decided to file criminal charges for shoplifting against her. The evidence showed that the store manager, Mr. Michalik, was in the back storeroom with the two security guards and Mrs. Dupree approximately half the time that she was back there.

One of the guards called the police department and requested that police officers be sent to pick her up. Two Houston uniformed police officers subsequently arrived and led her out of the store and took her to the Houston Police Station. Mrs. Dupree was fingerprinted, photographed, booked and then placed in jail. She stayed in jail until later that evening when she was finally released on bond. The criminal complaint against her by the security guards was subsequently dismissed on February 17, 1970.

On June 6, 1970, Mrs. Dupree initiated this lawsuit. The defendant, Piggly Wiggly Shop Rite Foods, Inc., answered the lawsuit contending that the incident complained of was proximately caused by the acts of a third party (Denco) over whom it had no control and that Denco was not an agent, servant or employee of Piggly Wiggly.

The trial of the cause commenced on January 13, 1975, and was tried before a jury. In answer to certain special issues submitted, the jury found that: Mrs. Dupree did not commit the offense of shoplifting; that Mrs. Dupree was falsely imprisoned; that Norris and Wilson (guards) participated in the false imprisonment of Mrs. Dupree; that Michalik (store manager) did not participate in the false imprisonment of Mrs. Dupree; that guards Norris and Wilson participated in the filing of the criminal complaint against Mrs. Dupree; that Mr. Michalik (store manager) did not participate in the filing of such complaint; that Norris and Wilson (guards) did not have probable cause to believe Mrs. Dupree had committed a criminal offense; that Norris and Wilson (guards) were not acting as employees of Piggly Wiggly on the occasion in question; that Denco was acting as an independent contractor on the occasion in question; that the reasonable and necessary medical and legal expense incurred by Mrs. Dupree was $650.00; that the sum of $25,000.00 would reasonably compensate Mrs. Dupree for the damages she sustained; and found no exemplary damages should be assessed against Piggly Wiggly.

The plaintiff then moved for judgment regarding defendant, Piggly Wiggly Shop Rite Foods, Inc., contending that by reason of the jury's answers and as a matter of law, judgment should be entered against Piggly Wiggly for the amount of actual damages of $25,650.00. The trial court entered a Default Judgment against Denco Security Systems for the sum of $50,650.00 (the actual damages plus $25,000.00 exemplary damages), but adjudged that plaintiff should not recover anything from defendant Piggly Wiggly Shop Rite Foods, Inc.

Mrs. Dupree brings forward five points of error on appeal. No complaint has been raised by the appellees concerning the jury's findings that: Mrs. Dupree did not commit the offense of shoplifting; that she was falsely imprisoned; or to the amount of damages. The primary question on appeal is whether under these facts and circumstances, Piggly Wiggly is responsible for the acts of Denco and its employees.

The appellant contends that the trial court erred in failing to enter judgment for her on the verdict because the defendant Piggly Wiggly had a "non-delegable duty" to afford Mrs. Dupree a safe place in which to shop, and liability attached to Piggly Wiggly as a matter of law when the duty was breached by the two security guards who were acting in behalf of Piggly Wiggly.

Appellee, Piggly Wiggly, contends that where an employer (Piggly Wiggly) contracts with an agency (Denco) for private police or security service, in order to be liable for the acts of personnel supplied, it is dependent upon a factual determination of the nature of the employment relationship between the employer (Piggly Wiggly) and the agency (Denco) supplying the personnel and the nature of the tort committed. Appellee says in effect that since the jury found that Denco was an independent contractor, Piggly Wiggly is not liable regardless of what the security guards did. The question is whether or not Piggly Wiggly is liable as a matter of law for the tortious conduct of Denco's employees or agents under the facts.

There are two types of relationships easily recognized in Texas that could exist between Piggly Wiggly and Denco which would cause liability to attach to Piggly Wiggly for the tortious acts of Denco's agent or employee. One is that of master-servant and the other is Principal-Agent. A master or principal is liable to one falsely imprisoned by the acts of an employee or agent acting within the scope of his employment. If the act of the employee or agent is done within the scope of his authority as an employee or agent and while acting in furtherance of the employer's or principal's business, then the employer or principal is liable in damages for the false imprisonment.

Under the rule of the aforesaid cases, in order to cause liability to attach to Piggly Wiggly for the tortious acts of the two guards, it would be incumbent upon a plaintiff to establish that: 1) the relationship between Piggly Wiggly and the two security guards was that of either master-servant or principal-agent; 2) that the servant or agent actually caused or participated in the illegal restraint; and 3) that he acted within the scope of employment or authority either implied or express; or 4) that the act was ratified by the master or principal. In the case at bar, the jury found that the two security guards were not acting as employees of Piggly Wiggly but were employees of Denco and that Denco was acting as an independent contractor.

This brings us to appellant's main contention which presents a more difficult problem. That is, even though the jury found that Denco was an independent contractor, such relationship will not relieve Piggly Wiggly from liability because Piggly Wiggly had a "non-delegable" duty to afford Mrs. Dupree a safe place in which to shop. As a consequence, liability attached as a matter of law when such duty was breached by the acts of the security guards who were acting on behalf of Piggly Wiggly from the outset.

We have found no Texas case which has had before it the exact question of whether or not the *"duty"* owed by a business establishment seeking to protect its property from shoplifters is "non-delegable" or "non-assignable" under circumstances where a store owner attempts to insulate itself from such responsibility to an innocent victim of a false arrest or false imprisonment by a security guard of an independent contractor employed for such purpose.

In view of the absence of Texas case law on this subject, we look to the numerous out-of-state cases relating to the liability of an employer for acts of security guards who are employees of an independent contractor. Many of such cases can be found in 38 A.L.R.3rd 1332. Under Section 5 of this article entitled "non-delegable duty of hirer", there are two exceptions prevalent to the general overall principal, that an employer of an independent contractor is not liable for the *negligent acts* committed by such contractor or his employees.

Under one exception, it is generally recognized, (Texas included), that where the work to be performed is "inherently dangerous", duties commensurate therewith cannot be delegated to an independent contractor so as to relieve the delegator of liability.

The first aspect of the question presented is, whether the task of guarding one's property from possible shoplifter by security guards is of such an inherently dangerous character, that such work constitutes a dangerous non-delegable duty of the owner. The theory upon which this liability is based is that a person who engages a contractor to do work of an inherently dangerous character, remains subject to a duty (an absolute, non-delegable duty) to see that it is performed with that degree of care which is appropriate to the circumstances. Liability of the employer depends upon his antecedent knowledge of the danger inherent in the work or in a finding that a reasonable prudent man (or corporation) should in the exercise of due diligence, have known of such dangerous work.

The question of what type work is considered inherently dangerous so as to impose liability upon an employer, is not always readily soluble. It usually is dependent on the facts of each particular case.[1] For instance, it has been held that the protection of one's property with firearms does not, in and of itself, constitute an inherently dangerous activity. This type of duty can, in some instances, be delegated to an independent contractor, thereby relieving the hirer of a security agency from liability for acts of ordinary negligence committed by the agency's personnel. The record before us does not readily point out the inherent dangers of the security work. Therefore, under the state of the facts in this case we cannot hold as a matter of law that the work of the security guards in protecting Piggly Wiggly's property from shoplifters was inherently or intrinsically dangerous. If plaintiff was to prevail upon this theory, (inherently dangerous work), it would have been incumbent upon her to request special issues thereon. This she did not do.

The other exception is that because of the "personal character" of duties owed to the public by one adopting measures to protect his property, owners and operators of enterprises cannot, by securing special personnel through an independent contractor for the purposes of protecting property, obtain immunity from liability for at least the intentional torts of the protecting agency or its employees. False imprisonment is an intentional tort.

In *Adams v. F.W. Woolworth Co.*, the leading case, the plaintiff, a customer in the defendant's store, recovered damages for false arrest. The defendant contended the plaintiff's arrest was caused by employees of one Lowenthol, (an independent contractor),

---

[1]For a list of work held inherently dangerous and not inherently dangerous, see 57 C.J.S. Master-Servant § 590, pp. 362-363.

who had contracted to provide the defendant with detective service. In rejecting this contention, the court said:

> A store owner who places a detective agency on his premises for the purpose of protecting his property by various means, including arrest, should not be immune from responsibility to an innocent victim of a false arrest made by the detective agency, even as an independent contractor . . . customers of Woolworth Company are invited into the store to buy its merchandise, for the profit of Woolworth Company. Can it be said that Woolworth Company can disclaim all duty of protecting them from the tortious acts of detectives brought by it into its own premises for the very purpose, among others, of making arrest of its customers? This is not the case of a contractor doing his work negligently. Where negligence is the sole basis of the liability, the doctrine of respondeat superior has been held inapplicable to independent contracts. Negligence does not enter into the tort of false arrest. The act itself, if not justified under statute . . ., is tortious, irrespective of negligence. Lowenthol was brought onto the premises to watch and also to arrest. Immunity from vicarious liability would permit any store keeper to subject his customers to the hazards of an irresponsible detective agency without peril to himself. He would obtain all the benefit of the surveillance and punishment of shoplifters; he would be subject to none of the penalties for unjustified or unlawful arrest of law-abiding citizens. The opportunities for gross injustice afforded by such a doctrine are too manifest to permit its incorporation into the jurisprudence of our state, without compelling reason.

The weight of the above authorities seems to be that one may not employ or contract with a special agency or detective firm to ferret out the irregularities of its customers or employees and then escape liability for the malicious prosecution or false arrest on the ground that the agency and/or its employees are independent contractors. Consideration of public policy requires the necessity for holding a responsible person liable for the acts done by others to its patrons in the prosecution of its business. Such cases adopting this policy have been founded on the principle that he who expects to derive advantage from an act which is done by another for him, must answer for any intentional injury which a third party may sustain from it. We believe that a holding to the contrary immunizes the corporation from the responsibilities imposed by law, thereby permitting it to subject its patrons to the hazards of an irresponsible detective agency while escaping all danger of the legal ramifications adverse to itself.

The undisputed facts before us show that Denco Security Systems was employed by and worked exclusively for Piggly Wiggly Shop Rite Foods, Inc. providing both external and internal security for the various Piggly Wiggly stores in Houston, Texas. When a security problem arose in one of the stores, Piggly Wiggly would contact Denco, inform them of the specific problem, and request that Denco send security guards out to the particular store. When the guards arrived at the particular store to which they were assigned, they would report in to the store manager (which in this case was Michalik) making him aware that they were on the premises. At this time, the store manager would either brief the guards on the problem as he believed existed or point out to the guards a customer who he suspected of shoplifting. The guards would then proceed to walk around the store keeping the suspected shoplifter under surveillance until they saw the allegedly illegal conduct occur, at which time an arrest would ensue.

It is clear that Piggly Wiggly provided the place in which these security guards were to work thereby intentionally exposing its customers to the possible tortious conduct of the guards. The jury made several findings, none of which were complained of or attacked by Piggly Wiggly. Those findings are that Mrs. Dupree did not commit the offense of shoplifting; that she was falsely imprisoned; and that Norris or Wilson participated in the false imprisonment. At the time Mrs. Dupree was arrested and taken back into the Piggly

Wiggly store, the manager (Michalik) was fully aware of the situation and, in fact, remained in the back storeroom at least half the time Mrs. Dupree was retained there. It is undisputed that Piggly Wiggly did not make any effort to investigate the propriety of the arrest or detention through its management or through other employees.

There are certain duties that an owner of a store cannot absolve itself from liability by delegating the performance thereof to an independent contractor. Such non-delegable duty cases hold the store operator liable for the negligence of the contractor although he himself has done everything that could reasonably be required of him.

We hold that Piggly Wiggly by securing through the guise of an independent contractor, security guards to protect its property by various means, cannot obtain immunity from liability for false imprisonment which such store owner would not be equally entitled to if such owner itself directly selected and paid the agents expressly retaining the power of control and removal. When a store owner undertakes these functions its duties are *personal* and non-assignable and where the company arranges for and accepts the service, it will not be permitted to say that the relationship of master and servant as far as responsibility is concerned, does not exist. Negligence does not enter into the tort of false imprisonment. The act itself is tortious irrespective of negligence. The appellant's second point of error is sustained.

Because of the disposition hereinafter made, it is not necessary for us to consider appellant's other points of error. The jury found that Plaintiff had been damaged in the amount of $25,650.00. Those damages are here rendered against Piggly Wiggly Shop Rite Foods, Inc. The judgment of the trial court is accordingly reversed as to appellee Piggly Wiggly Shop Rite Foods, Inc. and judgment is here rendered for the Plaintiffs Margaret Dupree and husband Charles Dupree, Jr. in the amount of $25,650.00 with interest from date of judgment and for costs. The judgment as to appellee R.B. Denson is affirmed.

REVERSED AND RENDERED IN PART AND AFFIRMED IN PART.

CASE COMMENT

Although the jury found that the security company was an independent contractor, the question was whether the store was responsible for the acts of the security company and its employees. The plaintiff argued that the store had a non-delegable duty to provide a safe place to shop, and therefore the store is not relieved from liability. In its rationale, the court discussed the principle that he who expects to derive an advantage from an act which is done by another for him, must answer for any intentional injury which a third party may sustain from it. The court believed that a holding contrary to this principle immunizes the corporation from responsibilities imposed by law, thereby permitting it to subject its patrons to the hazards of an irresponsible security agency while escaping the danger of legal ramifications adverse to itself.

DEL SIGNORE v. PYRAMID SECURITY SERVICES, INC.
537 N.Y.S.2d 640 (1989)

WEISS, Justice.

Appeal from an order of the Supreme Court (Connor, J.), entered October 26, 1987 in Columbia County, which denied a motion by defendant Saratoga Performing Arts Center, Inc. for summary judgment dismissing the complaint against it.

Plaintiffs, who are brother and sister, commenced this action to recover damages for injuries sustained at a concert on August 14, 1984 on premises owned by defendant Saratoga Performing Arts Center, Inc. (hereinafter SPAC). The pleadings indicate that plaintiff Claire

Del Signore left the concert area at the main gate, with permission from several security guards, to look for a companion. Plaintiff Christopher Del Signore waited for her inside the gate and Claire returned minutes later. As the two proceeded back to the concert, they were physically assaulted by defendant John Verro, an employee of defendant Pyramid Security Services, Inc. (hereinafter Pyramid). The complaint, as expanded by the bill of particulars, predicates SPAC's negligence on a failure to supervise and avoid such an unprovoked and wanton assault despite notice of prior disturbances by Pyramid personnel. Following depositions, SPAC moved for summary judgment on the premise that Pyramid, as an independent contractor, was solely responsible for the acts of its employees. Supreme Court denied the motion, finding that a triable issue of fact existed as to whether SPAC was negligent in hiring Pyramid to provide the required security. SPAC has appealed.

We reverse. Initially, we observe that the record substantiates Supreme Court's characterization of Pyramid as an independent contractor. The depositions of both Frank Carlucci, SPAC's operations manager, and Eugene Cole, president of Pyramid, establish that Pyramid provided security pursuant to a written contract, with Pyramid retaining control over the manner of performance.

Generally, an employer is not liable for the torts of an independent contractor or an employee thereof. An exception exists where the employer engages an unqualified or careless contractor or, when on notice of deficient performance, fails to prevent the continuance of such negligence. SPAC maintains that there is no evidence to establish any negligence on its part in hiring Pyramid and, in any event, that plaintiffs failed to raise this theory in their pleadings. We agree that there is no indication that SPAC was negligent in contractually engaging Pyramid's services in the first instance. The further question, which is viably presented in the pleadings, is whether SPAC was placed on notice of improper performance by Pyramid personnel and yet failed to take corrective measures.

Supreme Court based its decision on the combined testimony of Carlucci, that it was likely that Pyramid guards utilized force on concert patrons, and Cole, that prior lawsuits had been commenced against Pyramid based on assaults by their employees. Reviewing these depositions in context, however, we find no basis to substantiate that SPAC was on notice of improper conduct by Pyramid personnel by virtue of prior disturbances at the concert facility. Carlucci indicated that it was "possible" SPAC was a party to an assault-based lawsuit, but with no correlation to Pyramid. Similarly, Cole acknowledged that Pyramid had been named in assault suits prior to August 14, 1984, but with no connection to SPAC. When asked whether any previous incidents occurred on SPAC's property where "individuals were struck or in any way detained physically by" Pyramid guards, Carlucci initially responded "I would assume so", but then stated, "No, I don't know." This statement does not factually substantiate negligence on SPAC's part in failing to supervise Pyramid's security procedures or otherwise implement enforcement guidelines.

Even according plaintiffs the benefit of every favorable inference, we find no evidence that SPAC was on notice of Verro's assaultive nature or that Pyramid personnel were utilizing undue force prior to the subject assault. The fact that SPAC participated in determining how many security guards would be needed at a particular concert and pursued a no-reentry policy at this concert may indicate control over the results to be achieved, but does not establish active participation in the manner of performance. Nor do we agree with plaintiffs' assertion that the services provided were so specialized or hazardous as to impose a nondelegable duty on SPAC to ensure proper performance by Pyramid. Accordingly, we conclude that SPAC was entitled to summary judgment dismissing the complaint against it.

Order reversed, on the law, without costs, motion granted and complaint dismissed against defendant Saratoga Performing Arts Center, Inc.

CASE COMMENT

Control over the results and not over the manner of methods in which the work is performed does not establish active participation in the manner of performance. This court felt that the security services were not so specialized or hazardous so as to impose a nondelegable duty on the arts center to ensure proper performance by the security agency.

4

Contracts

A contract is a consensual agreement between two or more persons or parties which creates an obligation to do or not to do a particular thing. A contract contains terms and conditions. In an express contract, the terms are openly declared on the making and are stated in distinct and explicit language.

A corporation may enter into contracts to hire guards, investigators, executive protection personnel, or consultants. It may also enter into contracts to purchase fencing, locks, fire extinguishers, or closed-circuit television. A contract security company may enter into contracts to purchase uniforms, equipment, or provide security personnel. In any event, the needs and requirements should be clearly spelled out so that there is no ambiguity about what is to take place.

The cases in this chapter describe situations which deal with the intent of the parties to a contract, duties and responsibilities of the parties, the type of language to be used, and the validity or non-validity of an oral contract. Also discussed are the failure to perform a duty or breach of contract, whether an implied contract exists, whether one may benefit from a contract even though not a party to it, and limitations and disclaimers to a contract.

INTENT OF THE PARTIES

The signatory to a contract should know precisely what duties and responsibilities are expected and required. The existence of the duties will turn on the terms of the contract. Because the intent and meaning of the parties is expressed in the language used, the language in a contract should accurately convey the meaning intended. A contract is construed or interpreted according to the intention of the parties, and that intention is manifested by the terms. The security manager should know what is meant by the language of the contract at the time of the signing of the contract. The following case raises the question about whether or not the security company contracted to provide protection that the store may have owed its patrons.

BROWN v. NATIONAL SUPERMARKETS, INC.
679 S.W.2d 307 (1984)

KAROHL, Presiding Judge.

Plaintiff-appellants Pauline and George Brown appeal from a summary judgment in favor of the three defendants, National Super Markets (National), Sentry Security Agency (Sentry) and T.G. Watkins, a security guard, employed by Sentry. The issue is whether defendants as a matter of law had a duty to protect the plaintiff from an assault by an unknown third party on defendant National's parking lot.

Pauline and George Brown brought a negligence action against the defendants after Pauline was shot and seriously injured by an unknown assailant in National's parking lot. The Browns allege that the defendants have a duty to protect National's patrons both in the store and in the parking lot and that they breached that duty. Defendants denied that they have such a duty and filed a motion for summary judgment. The trial court granted the motion.

Appellants maintain that summary judgment should not have been granted because as a matter of law their petition properly stated a claim of actionable negligence. The petition asserts that while Pauline Brown was on the National premises she was assaulted, battered and shot by an unknown assailant as a direct and proximate result of the negligence of the defendants. The petition also claims that in the two years prior to Mrs. Brown's assault there were sixteen incidents of reported robbery involving a firearm and seven incidents of reported strong arm robberies as well as 136 other reported crimes on the National's premises. Appellants maintain that this known criminal activity and conduct create special facts and circumstances giving rise to a duty on behalf of the defendants to protect store patrons against assaults. Respondents deny that the reported robberies or other crimes create special circumstances giving rise to a duty on the part of defendants to protect Mrs. Brown from injuries caused by the criminal activities of an unknown third party.

As to National the question here is whether as a matter of law a store owner, the security company it has hired under a contract to provide security services and an on-duty security guard have a duty to protect store patrons from criminal assaults by third parties when the store owner knows that repeated violent crimes have occurred recently on the premises.

Our court addressed this issue in *Meadows v. Friedman Railroad Salvage Warehouse*, 655 S.W.2d 718. In *Meadows* a woman was assaulted and shot on the warehouse premises. We there noted that while there is no general duty for the owner of a business to protect a plaintiff against the intentional criminal conduct of unknown persons, the duty can arise where special relationships or special circumstances exist. Included among the special circumstances and facts there discussed was the frequent and recent occurrence of violent crimes on the business premises. The court in *Meadows* affirmed the dismissal for failure to state a claim because the person there did not "allege that *specific prior crimes occurred on the premises*, or that specific individuals committed violent acts on the premises . . . ." In *Nappier v. Kincade*, 666 S.W.2d 858, we noted that if a business owner has notice, actual or constructive, of prior acts committed by third parties on the premises which might cause injuries to the patron, he or she may be liable if reasonable care to provide appropriate precautions are not taken. The court stated that in order to prevail under this rule a plaintiff must allege that specific crimes occurred on the premises. In the case at bar the plaintiffs have attached and incorporated a detailed list of prior violent crimes that have occurred on National's premises.

Based on the legal theory approved in *Meadows* and *Nappier*, that a business owner may have a duty to patrons summary judgment as to National was error.

The question as to Sentry and its employee is whether they assumed a duty to plaintiff if, as alleged, they contracted with National to provide protection National may owe to its patrons. The cases do not clearly establish whether a security company or security guard working for a business owner under contract have a duty to protect patrons from crime. It is the general rule that a private person has no duty to protect another from a deliberate criminal attack by a third person. We find that Sentry may or may not have assumed such a duty when it entered into the security contract. The existence of a duty will turn on the terms of the contract and the circumstances.

Plaintiffs allege in their amended petition that Sentry contracted with National to provide security against criminal activities for National *and its patrons* (our emphasis). In effect plaintiffs claim that the contract between National and Sentry is an attempt to perform National's previously established duty. The provisions of the contract are not in evidence. However, the National store manager testified by deposition that although he had never seen the contract he understood it to cover the area both inside and outside the store. T.G. Watkins, the security guard, stated in his deposition that he was never told to patrol the parking lot. As it is unclear whether the security company assumed any duty through the contract an issue of facts remain and summary judgment was error.

Plaintiffs may be third party beneficiaries to this contract. As such they may sue in tort or contract for any contract breach by Sentry or its employees.

> Third party beneficiary is the nomenclature given to one who is not privy to a contract nor its consideration but to whom the law gives the right to maintain a cause of action for breach of contract. . . . Only those third parties for whose primary benefit the contracting parties intended to make the contract may maintain an action. . . . The intention of the parties is to be gleaned from the four corners of the contract, and if uncertain or ambiguous from the circumstances surrounding its execution.

Privity of contract is no longer always necessary to maintain a suit for breach of contract.

> There are situations in which the making of the contract creates a relation between the defendant and the promise, which is sufficient to impose a tort duty of reasonable care . . . .
> . . . Where an agent or servant has accepted the control of property under a contract with his principal, and under circumstances where there is an obvious risk of harm to outsiders if he does not use reasonable care, the obligation of affirmative conduct has been imposed upon him.

As a matter of law both National and Sentry *may* have a duty to protect National patrons from criminal assaults. Summary judgment was inappropriate because questions of fact remain.

We reverse the trial court decision for summary judgment and remand the cause for an action consistent with this opinion.

CASE COMMENT

The security company was hired to provide security services to the store. One question raised is whether or not the security company contracted to provide protection that the store may have owed its patrons. The court found that it may or may not have assumed such duty when it entered into the security contract, and that the existence of the duty would turn on the terms of the contract and the circumstances surrounding it. The intention of the parties to the contract may be gleaned under the "four corners" rule (taking the instrument as a whole). If uncertainty and ambiguity exist, intention also may be taken from the circumstances surrounding its execution. Details of contractual conditions, duties, and obligations should be spelled out clearly and in terms of certainty. This will decrease future ambiguity and uncertainty and be more in line with some of the definitional terms for the word *security*: freedom from doubt and a sense of certainty.

CLEAR AND EXPRESS LANGUAGE

When an agreement (contract) is reduced to writing, the terms should be plain, unequivocal, and not susceptible to interpretation, to avoid any misunderstanding. The terms should be complete and sufficient, and the commitments spelled out with definite meaning so there is reasonable certainty about the obligations. To accomplish this, use clear, distinct, plain, definite, explicit, and unambiguous language. Avoid vague, incomplete, indefinite, and ambiguous language, since the meaning and intention of the parties to the contract may be construed from the language expressed in the document. In the following case, notice how the clear and express language spelled out the obligations of the security company. The language clearly showed the security company had no duty as alleged in the breach of contract action.

BLUE JEANS CORPORATION v. PINKERTON, INC.
275 S.E.2d 209 (1981)

WELLS, Judge.

Plaintiff, a North Carolina corporation engaged in the manufacture of garments, brought this action seeking to recover from defendant, a corporation engaged in the security field, damages sustained by plaintiff, based on breach of contract and negligence.

Plaintiff alleged in its complaint the existence of a contract between the parties wherein defendant promised to provide to plaintiff an asset protection service. This service included furnishing security guards who would routinely inspect the manufacturing and storage buildings at plaintiff's plant in Whiteville. Such inspections were to be performed at least once every hour and defendant's guards were to notify plaintiff of any hazard whatsoever threatening plaintiff's assets.

Plaintiff further alleged that at some time during the weekend of 12 November to 15 November 1976 while defendant's security guards were on duty, one of the plaintiff's warehouses sprang tremendous leaks in its roof due to unusual weather, and that fabrics stored in the warehouse suffered water damage in the amount of $7,300 as a result. By failing to observe and/or to report to plaintiff the hazardous condition of the warehouse roof, the security guards were negligent and such negligence caused the damage to plaintiff's property. Plaintiff also alleged that the guard's failure to inspect the warehouse and/or to report the leaks constituted contract breaches that caused the property damage.

In its answer, defendant relied *inter alia* on the contract between the parties. The service authorized by the contract was as follows: "Guard will be alert and respond to and report on conditions of fire, theft, trespass and vandalism." Defendant alleged that under the contract there was no duty to seek out leaks in the plaintiff's building.

Defendant moved for summary judgment. In ruling on defendant's motion, the trial judge considered the following: the affidavits of the two security guards assigned to plaintiff's plant on 12–15 November, stating that they were instructed to be on the lookout for fire, theft, trespass and vandalism, and not weather conditions or leaks; the affidavit of defendant's district manager, including a copy of the agreement between the parties; the affidavit of plaintiff's vice president, stating that the pre-contractual negotiations between the parties included representations by defendant that it would provide security with regard to fire as well as other acts of God including weather; a letter from defendant to plaintiff detailing the security services defendant offered; and the security service reports prepared by defendant's two guards with regard to their shift at plaintiff's plant on 12–15 November.

The trial court granted defendant's motion for summary judgment and plaintiff has appealed.

Defendant's evidence properly before the court established the existence of the written contract between the parties in the form of a letter confirming plaintiff's order for services, signed by both parties, and specifying the service authorized, the hours of service, and the charges and rates. In clear and unambiguous language, the contract stated the conditions to which defendant's guards would be alert and respond: fire, theft, trespass and vandalism. Clear and express language of a contract controls its meaning, and neither party may contend for an interpretation at variance with its language on the ground that the writing did not fully express his intent. Considered alone, the contract shows that an essential element of plaintiff's claim is nonexistent, *i.e.*, defendant had no contractual duty to be alert to and report on weather conditions or roof leaks. Having carried its burden, defendant forced plaintiff to produce a forecast of its evidence.

In its affidavit in response to defendant's motion for summary judgment, plaintiff's vice president stated that in pre-contractual oral negotiations, defendant's agents represented that defendant's service would provide a complete asset protection respecting all emergencies and acts of God including weather. Plaintiff also submitted a copy of a letter from defendant to plaintiff detailing the services defendant offered. Plaintiff's forecast of evidence fails to establish the existence of a genuine issue of material fact. Plaintiff has not controverted the validity of the written contract. Even if the parties did in fact discuss duties in addition to those named in the contract, such prior or contemporaneous negotiations are presumed to be merged in the written contract, and are therefore without effect.

Defendant's evidence also established the lack of any genuine issue of material fact with regard to plaintiff's negligence claim. To recover damages for injury resulting from actionable negligence of defendant, plaintiff must show the existence of some legal duty owed to plaintiff by defendant, as well as defendant's breach of that duty, and that the breach was the proximate cause of plaintiff's injury. Because defendant's uncontroverted evidence proved that the contract created no duty of defendant to be alert and respond to weather conditions and roof leaks, plaintiff has failed to show an essential element of its negligence claim, *i.e.*, the existence of the duty.

Considering all the evidence before the trial court on defendant's motion for summary judgment, we conclude that defendant established his right to judgment as a matter of law and that summary judgment for defendant was properly granted.

Affirmed.

CASE COMMENT

The security company prevailed because the contractual conditions were expressed in clear, express, and unambiguous language. The court found that the clear and express language of a contract controls its meaning. Neither party may contend for an interpretation at variance with its language on the grounds that the writing did not fully express intent.

ORAL CONTRACT

A contract can be oral or verbal and is thus expressed by speech only, as opposed to writing. The reduction of terms and conditions of a business agreement to writing eliminates problems. Writing is the best evidence of the intention of the parties to a contract. Generally speaking, most business contracts are in writing. In the following case, the manager of a park and the security contractor spent much time discussing such things as the number of men needed; the hours involved; the material needed; the structure of the security plan; the location, keys and paper dials of the time clocks; and insurance coverage. After the discussion, they apparently shook hands and said, "It's a deal." The park manager later hired another firm to provide security for the park. Under the law of this state the security licensee is required to give in writing what he has agreed to do and what the cost would be. If the licensee proceeds without complying with this requirement, he does so with the risk of later being without recourse if the client rejects his services. An old saying from law school days is that an oral contract isn't worth the paper it's written on.

CAPOZZELLA v. WATERFUN ACQUISITION, INC.
532 N.Y.S.2d 653 (1988)

JAMES C. HARBERSON, Jr., Judge.

The plaintiff seeks $2,000 in damages for breach of contract. The respondent claims there was no contract as a matter of fact and law.

The plaintiff runs a security business. He was contacted by Ed Bouchard in March of 1988. He was acting as an independent contractor for the defendant's Waterfun Theme Park. He wanted to determine if the plaintiff was interested in providing security for the Park when it opened in May of 1988.

The plaintiff testified that Bouchard arranged a meeting with a Steven Africk, the manager, on May 4, 1988. When Bouchard and the plaintiff arrived at the office they were advised that Mr. Africk had become ill and another appointment was arranged on 5/5/88 at 11:00 a.m. The plaintiff went to this meeting alone.

Mr. Africk and the plaintiff met for less than an hour. The plaintiff advised Africk of his extensive background in police and security work comprising of, among other things, over twelve years with the F.B.I. in various roles including security, as well as his extensive work in security for private business.

They discussed the number of men needed, the hours involved, the material needed and the structure of the security plan for the geography of the Park. The price per hour suggested by the plaintiff was $7.50. Africk explained that he was also considering another firm who had a cheaper hourly rate.

The plaintiff countered with a $7.00 per hour rate and, according to the plaintiff, Africk stood up, reached across the desk, shook the plaintiff's hand saying, "It's a deal."

After this meeting concluded, Africk introduced the plaintiff to his Park foreman Dale Mallette. There had been a question about the time clocks used in the past and, according to the plaintiff, he was going to determine if they could be used on the job. The plaintiff and Mallette spent some time together discussing the keys for the time clocks, the number of locations where they would be placed for the watchman and where the keys were at that time. The plaintiff then left the Park with the time clocks so he could determine if they were working properly. Mr. Mallette gave him these clocks.

The plaintiff called Lathem Time Recorder Company on 5/11/88 to order paper dials for the time clocks and had them shipped to the Park. The plaintiff also inquired about insurance coverage if he acted as courier to take the daily receipts to the bank. The job was to begin on 5/18/88.

On 5/13/88 Bouchard advised the plaintiff that he heard Africk had entered into a security agreement with another firm. The plaintiff called Africk on 5/13/88 and he was advised he had been quoted a better price from another person and he had decided not to hire the plaintiff.

Mr. Africk testified that he had an extensive management background but that he had no experience with security services. He confirmed a meeting took place but that the discussions were not as detailed as the plaintiff related. He said the meeting took place on 5/12/88 and that at the termination of the meeting no firm agreement had been reached. He also affirmed that he gave no permission to have the time clocks removed from the Park and that the plaintiff had taken them without his consent.

Mr. Africk testified that he hired another firm on 5/13/88 (the day after he consulted with the plaintiff, according to Africk's testimony). This same day the plaintiff called Africk upon hearing from Bouchard that another person had been hired to provide security. Africk agreed that he informed the plaintiff on 5/13/88 he did not need his services.

Mr. Africk submits as Exhibit A of his lawyer's brief (and raised the issue during cross examination of the plaintiff) a newspaper story where the plaintiff said there had been an agreement firmed up by a handshake that was terminated before it began. The story reported:

> He charges that about a week before the security job was to begin, he and Mr. Africk shook hands after agreeing to terms, with Mr. Africk saying, "Then it's a deal". "I learned three days later, by telephone, that he decided to go with someone else," Mr. Capozzella said. *Watertown Daily Times*, 6/9/88.

A review of the testimony and exhibits is necessary to ascertain the date these events took place and from it discern, to the extent possible, the true story.

The plaintiff says the arranged meeting occurred on May 5, 1988, while Africk says it occurred on 5/12/88. While the actual date is in dispute, there is no question a meeting of short duration did take place between the plaintiff and Africk. The telephone bill shows the plaintiff called the Lathem Time Recorder Company on 5/11/88 at 12:36 p.m. The invoice from the same company shows a shipment of paper dials to Waterfun Theme Park on 5/16/88.

If the testimony of Africk is correct then why would the plaintiff call the company supplying time clock dials on 5/11/88? This is the day *before* Africk even met the plaintiff and, certainly, before the plaintiff could have even seen the time clocks to determine the make of the clocks and whether the dials were needed. In other words, the plaintiff could not have called (nor would he have had any reason to call) before he secured the clocks subsequent to meeting with Africk. The Court concludes that the meeting took place on 5/5/88 and not on 5/12/88.

The plaintiff testified in detail about the proposed security arrangements he and Africk agreed about at their meeting. Africk denies the discussion was anything more than a general review of needs and prices to meet those needs. It is the impression of the Court that the plaintiff's detailed understanding of the operation of the Park could have only come from a complete discussion of the whole operation in order to assess the security needs and, for that matter, the attendant cost to provide it. That is why he had knowledge of the animals, key locations, rain gear, *et cetera*, when he testified; that is why he examined the time clocks (and ordered the paper dials); and that is why he made additional inquiry into courier insurance if he was going to carry money to the bank under a separate agreement.

It is fair to assume if Africk had no experience with security contracts then he was either using the plaintiff to obtain information concerning what the Park needed under the guise of negotiating an agreement or, once he had the plaintiff's price, he went to the other security firm to force their price lower having the plaintiff to return to if the other firm would not reduce the cost for services. As it turned out, whatever the scenario, the plaintiff was not hired.

Exhibit A is a security service bid made by the firm the defendant hired. It is dated 5/11/88. There is a document dated May 18, 1988, submitted as part of Exhibit A which includes a security service agreement. This second document sets out information required by the General Business Law Section 84 and 19 N.Y.C.R.R. 173.1. It is interesting to note that this document is devoid of any details concerning the manner in which the services were to be carried out for the defendant by the security force. It was this detail that the plaintiff and Africk discussed at their meeting in addition to dates, hours and price. It was during this same time period that the successful firm was negotiating with Africk (5/11/88 to 5/18/88).

The question remains whether a contract exists under the events heretofore described.

LAW

The agreement between the plaintiff and defendant was to be completed within one year and would not be barred by General Obligations Law, Section 5-701 (a.) (1.) because it was not in writing. The obligation to provide a written statement of services and charges is imposed to an extent required by the General Business Law, Article 7 and 19 N.Y.C.R.R. 173.1.

Section 173.1(a) states:

> No licensed private investigator, watch, guard or patrol agency shall undertake to perform any services on behalf of a client unless such licensee shall have delivered to the client a written statement, signed by the licensee, which shall set forth the specific service or services to be performed and the charge or fee therefor . . . 19 N.Y.C.R.R. 173.1(a).

The intent of the legislature in establishing Article 7 of the General Business Law as implemented by such rules and regulations deemed appropriate by the Secretary of State, was to act under the police power of the state to protect the public in this area of business endeavor.

There is no question then, of the obligation of the plaintiff to have complied with Section 173.1(a) of N.Y.C.R.R. before he undertook an action to perform services for the respondent. The defendant's counsel urges the Court to adopt the conclusion of the Court of Appeals in *Weir-Metro Ambu-Service v. Turner*, 57 N.Y.2d 911, 442 N.E.2d 1268, 456 N.Y.S.2d 757 wherein the Court disallows a cause of action based on an oral agreement because it ". . . contravened the requirement that a contract to perform services for a medical facility . . ." be in writing (10 N.Y.C.R.R. 400.4 (a) (1) . . .).

The plaintiff's counsel rejects this point comparing 10 N.Y.C.R.R. 400.4(a) (1) requirement, with those of 19 N.Y.C.R.R. 173.1. His position is that the writing required for the former must be a written contract while in the case of the latter the written statement is only a licensing requirement. The conclusion suggested is the same language that would have been used in the 19 N.Y.C.R.R. 173.1 Section if a written contract was needed to have an enforceable agreement. This position is not tenable.

Article 7 of the General Business Law empowers the Secretary of State with the authority to regulate the activity of security agencies. To be licensed, the plaintiff was required to comply with such rules and regulations. Section 173.1(c) of 19 N.Y.C.R.R. requires the licensed agency, like the plaintiff, to refrain from doing any service for a client until the same was outlined in writing, delivered to the client, and:

> The licensee shall obtain an acknowledgment in writing from the client of receipt of any statement of services or charges or executed agreement delivered. 19 N.Y.C.R.R. 173.1(c).

The exception to this obligation of 19 N.Y.C.R.R. 173.1(a) is found at paragraph (b) of the same section:

> ... if the client and the licensee have entered into an agreement in writing, setting forth the services to be rendered and the fee or charge therefor ...

The statement required in paragraph (a) would only be required in addition to a written agreement, if the written agreement was silent as to the limits of the service to be rendered. 19 N.Y.C.R.R. 173.1(b).

It is clear that the Secretary of State's rules made a written contract a part of any agreement between a licensee like the plaintiff and a client like the defendant and, if the writing lacked certain specifics, 19 N.Y.C.R.R. 173.1(b) provided them. Thus, while the language of 10 N.Y.C.R.R. 400.4(a)(1) varied with that of 19 N.Y.C.R.R. 173.1(a)(b)(c), the intent was the same—certain business relationships regulated by the State of New York must be in writing to be enforceable as a matter of public policy. Because the plaintiff failed to comply with this requirement of 19 N.Y.C.R.R. 173(a)(b)(c) the contract he alleges between himself and the defendant is void and unenforceable by the *Weir* rationale.

The plaintiff argues that even if the writing required by the Statute was not presented to the defendant before he learned that another company had been hired, he had the right to the claim under the contract as long as he prepared the writing before he commenced to do the job. The Court disagrees.

The State of New York's legislation in this area was to inoculate the client of the licensee against an obligation that was not first presented to him in a form outlined at 19 N.Y.C.R.R. 173.1. It was a condition precedent to an enforceable agreement and not, as the plaintiff would urge, a condition subsequent to be complied with after an oral agreement to terms had been negotiated—even with some part performance prior to the required document being given to the client by the licensee.

The purpose of the law and regulation is to allow the client to have in writing what he has agreed the licensee do and what the cost will be. If the client determines upon receipt of the "advance statement of services and charges" to reject it, there is no obligation to accept the agreement; and, if the client accepts it, the licensee:

> ... shall obtain an acknowledgment in writing from the client of receipt of any statement of services or charges or executed agreement delivered. 19 N.Y.C.R.R. 173.1(c).

If a licensee proceeds without complying with this requirement, he does so with the risk of later being without recourse if the client rejects his services. The burden by regulation rests upon the licensee and he avoids it at his peril.

It is the decision of the Court that the plaintiff's request for judgment is denied without costs.

IMPLIED OR NOT IMPLIED CONTRACT

An implied contract is one that is not evidenced by the explicit agreement of the parties. It can be inferred from the acts, conduct, or circumstances surrounding a particular situation. The obligation is not stated in direct words but is obtained by deduction or implication of the circumstances and conduct of the parties involved in the particular activity.

The problem here for the security manager is that the company may have voluntarily assumed a duty to protect without having formally said so. The duty may be fashioned from various representations made as to safety and security at the site, because it totally and exclusively controls the property, or because a special relationship between it and the plaintiff has arisen. Implications of the duty may be gleaned from company documents, brochures, leaflets, pamphlets, and other material which may contain representations about safety and security. The next two cases explain how a plaintiff goes about trying to show that an implied contract to provide safety and security existed.

NIESWAND v. CORNELL UNIVERSITY
692 F. Supp. 1464 (1988)

CHOLAKIS, District Judge.

In September 1983, Erin Nieswand enrolled as a freshman at Cornell University where she shared a room in a dormitory known as North Campus 7 with two other students, Jane Niehaus and Young Hee Suh. During the course of the fall term, Young Hee received love letters and presents from Su Yong Kim who was not a Cornell student. At some point during the semester, Kim came to Cornell and took Young Hee out to dinner. In late October, around Halloween, Kim went to Young Hee's room asking to see her. It appears that Young Hee was no longer interested in Kim and went to the room of Ken Sepe, her resident advisor, and asked him to tell Kim that she was not around. Sepe testified that his offer to have Kim removed was rejected by Young Hee who subsequently left the room to talk with Kim.

In the early evening of Saturday, December 17, 1983, Kim somehow gained access to North 7. The dormitory's doors were supposed to be locked for the weekend. A "Memorandum on Residential Hall Security Policy and Procedures", which was drafted after the incident by Lieutenant Boice of Cornell's Department of Public Safety, did not definitively conclude how Kim gained entry to the dormitory. Among the possibilities is that either the front door or fire escape doors to the suites were not adequately secured or were propped open, that someone let Kim in, or that he simply walked in while a resident either left or entered the dormitory. The deposition testimony of various witnesses conflicts on the exact manner by which Kim entered the dormitory.

Erin saw Kim and left a note on her dormitory room door that Kim was on campus. Young Hee returned to her room at some point after 11:00 p.m. Sitting in the corridor of the suite were other residents of the suite including Diane Nielsen and Melissa Paulson. Kim was apparently down the corridor around the corner. After being informed of Kim's appearance in the suite, Young Hee went into Nielsen's room where she was followed by Nielsen and Paulson and the door was closed.

Young Hee called her roommate, Erin, who was elsewhere on the Cornell campus. Sometime thereafter, Erin, accompanied by Peter Browning, another Cornell student, arrived at and entered Nielsen's room. At some point, Young Hee also phoned David Kang, a Cornell student, and asked him to come to her room and talk with Kim in Korean. Through an open door, Young Hee conversed with Kim who remained in the corridor. Young Hee returned to her own room to talk with Kim who attempted to close the door behind him. Nieswand, Browning and Paulson entered the room. Nielsen also returned to the suite. Shortly thereafter, Kang arrived.

From an undisclosed location, either on his person or in the suite, Kim suddenly pulled out a rifle and ordered Nielsen and Paulson, who were standing in the doorway, into the room. Kim announced his intention to kill all six persons in the room, Suh, Nieswand, Nielsen, Paulson, Browning and Kang. Sometime thereafter, Jane Niehaus, the third roommate, attempted to enter her room, but was told to stay out by Young Hee.

Kim subsequently allowed Nielsen, Paulson, Browning and Kang to leave the room. Kim refused to permit Erin to leave, apparently because she allegedly had teased him on the phone in the past. Shortly after the four students were released, two series of shots were heard.

Upon entering the room, it was apparent that Young Hee, who was shot three times, was dead. Erin, who was shot twice, was alive and removed to Tompkins Community Hospital. She was subsequently transported to the Upstate Medical Center in Syracuse where she died.

Plaintiffs have brought fifteen separate counts against Cornell arising out of the tragic incident. These counts can be summarized as follows:

> Counts I and II   Cornell failed to provide adequate security for its students and, in particular, was aware of Kim's antisocial behavior
> Counts III and IV   Cornell voluntarily assumed the duty to protect students from harm and breached this duty
> Count V   Cornell's representations of safety and its total and exclusive control of campus security rendered Cornell strictly liable for Erin's death
> Count VI   Pain and suffering caused by Erin as a result of the breach of duty set forth in the previous counts
> Counts VII and VIII   Cornell security personnel were unprepared, untrained and unequipped to handle reasonably foreseeable criminal activity and failed to render aid
> Counts IX and X   Cornell breached a contract existing between it and Erin
> Count XI   Cornell breached its obligations towards Erin's parents who were third party beneficiaries of Cornell's contract with Erin
> Count XII   Cornell inflicted emotional distress on Erin's parents by not promptly notifying them of a shooting; by failing to make travel arrangements to Cornell after the incident; and by mailing Erin's grades which included an incomplete grade for two classes
> Counts XII, XIV, and XV   Punitive Damages

Cornell has brought a third-party action against the convicted murderer, Su Yong Kim.

By its motion, Cornell seeks summary judgment, on all of plaintiff's counts. In their opposition papers and at oral argument, plaintiffs withdrew the strict liability claim (Count V) and the third-party beneficiary claim (Count XI). At oral argument on this motion, this Court dismissed the infliction of emotional distress claim (Count XII).

Negligence Claims

Cornell seeks to dismiss Counts I through IV, and VI through VIII on the ground that, as a matter of law, it cannot be held liable for its alleged failure to provide Erin Nieswand with adequate security. Plaintiffs' allegation of negligence is based on two theories of liability: (1) Cornell, as a landowner, failed to provide adequate security and (2) Cornell, by virtue of its relationship with its students, was obligated to provide adequate security.

To prove a case of negligence under New York law, a plaintiff must establish: (1) the existence of a duty on the part of a defendant to plaintiff; (2) defendant's breach of that duty; and (3) an injury proximately caused by the breach. The question presented by this motion is whether Cornell owed to Erin Nieswand the duty to undertake security or protective measures for the dormitories it operated.

New York law imposes a duty on a landowner to exercise reasonable care under the circumstances to maintain his property in a safe condition. However, a landowner is not an insurer of safety. Instead, a landowner "cannot be held to a duty to take protective measures unless he knows or has reason to know that there is a likelihood of conduct on the part of third persons which would endanger the safety of the visitor." Besides foreseeing harm from a particular assailant, however, a landowner can be put on notice if past history of criminal activity indicates that a criminal incident is a significant, foreseeable possibility. As a result, a college will have breached its duty if it fails to take minimal precautions to protect its students from the reasonably foreseeable acts of third persons.

Cornell maintains that there is no evidence that it knew or should have known that Kim would endanger the life of any Cornell student. It refers to the depositions of student witnesses who described Kim as a well-dressed man who never caused a disturbance. In furtherance of its argument, Cornell contends that, in the past and on the night of the tragedy, Young Hee rejected suggestions by certain students to contact the Department of Public Safety and/or the Resident Advisor. Finally, the University's Department of Public Safety has no records of any reported problems with Kim prior to the incident.

Cornell also contends that there is no evidence of an extensive history of criminal conduct on the campus sufficient to impose a duty to provide security for the dorms. It points out that prior to this tragedy there had been no murder or attempted murder in the history of the university. As a result, it maintains that it had no duty, as a matter of law, to provide adequate security. See, e.g., *Iannelli*, 498 N.Y.S.2d 377 (minor incidents of crime did not put landowner on notice); *Whitney v. State*, Claim No. 65293, slip op. at 5 (Court of Claims, July 19, 1982) (one prior violent incident in the preceding 10 months); *D'Aquanni v. State*, Claim No. 62627, slip op. at 4 (Court of Claim, September 8, 1980) (three other violent attacks in two years prior to incident).

Plaintiffs have countered by submitting evidence that Cornell was specifically aware of the threat posed by Kim. At his deposition on April 17, 1985, Dr. George Nieswand, Erin's father, testified that either Mr. Paleen or Mr. Daly, Director and Assistant Director of the Department of Residential Halls, respectively, advised him that Kim "had been there on a previous visit and had to be escorted off of the campus by university security." On another occasion, plaintiffs assert that one of the victims, Young Hee Suh, hid in the room of her Resident Advisor, Ken Sepe, in an attempt to avoid Kim.

Plaintiffs have also submitted statistical evidence of the amount of crime which occurred on the Cornell campus during the three school years prior to Erin's death. From 1980–1983, the following crimes were reported: 4 rapes, 8 robberies, 9 assaults, 42 "other assaults", 19 sex offenses, 793 burglaries and 2582 larcenies.

In its Reply Papers, Cornell has attempted to refute plaintiffs' contentions. It has submitted the deposition of Ken Sepe, a Resident Advisor, who testified that although Young Hee did, on one occasion, hide in his room, she left the room to talk to Kim. He further described Kim as patient and nonviolent. Cornell has also submitted the testimony of Jane Niehaus, Erin and Young Hee's roommate, who confirmed this view of Kim. Niehaus also testified that while she saw Kim in the dorm on consecutive days on a prior weekend, she wasn't sure where he stayed, but guessed he stayed in the lounge.

In *Miller*, the Court of Appeals held that the State of New York had a duty to take the minimal security precaution of locking a dormitory's doors when it had notice of the likelihood of criminal intrusion. 467 N.E.2d at 497. Notice in that case consisted of nonresidents twice loitering in the dormitory's lounges and hallway and numerous crimes in the dormitories such as armed robbery, burglaries, criminal trespass, and a rape by a nonstudent.

In *Nallan*, the plaintiff was shot by an unknown assailant while he was registering as a guest in defendant's Manhattan office building. The plaintiff introduced evidence that there were 107 reported crimes in the office building during the 21 months before the shooting, at least 10 of which were crimes against the person. Although there was no proof that any of these crimes occurred within the lobby of the building where the shooting occurred, the Court of Appeals wrote:

> A rational jury could have found from the history of criminal activity in the other parts of the building that a criminal incident in the lobby was a significant, foreseeable possibility. If the jury found that defendants knew or had reason to know of the prior crimes in the building and further found that defendants should have anticipated a risk of harm from criminal activity

in the lobby, it properly could have gone on to conclude that defendants failed in their obligation to take reasonable precautionary measures to minimize the risk and make the premises safe for the visiting public. 407 N.E.2d at 458.

From the evidence submitted, it is apparent that a question of material fact exists as to whether Cornell University could have foreseen the criminal activity in this case so as to give rise to a duty on its part to provide adequate security measures.

Cornell raises for the first time in its Reply Papers that it did not breach its duty, even if such a duty existed. However, as noted by the New York Court of Appeals:

> What safety precautions may reasonably be required of a landowner is almost always a question of fact for the jury. Conceivably, in assessing the reasonableness of the landowner's conduct, the jury might take into account such variables as the seriousness of the risk and the cost of the various available safety measures.

As a separate basis for dismissing these counts, Cornell maintains that no special relationship existed between it and Erin which would give rise to a duty on Cornell's part to provide police protection. New York courts have long recognized the principle that, in the absence of a special relationship, a government entity owes no duty to provide police protection to the public. This governmental immunity has been extended to cover nongovernmental entities, such as the New York City Transit Authority, which perform a governmental function. *Wiener v. Metropolitan Transp. Auth.*, 433 N.E.2d 124.

In *Wiener*, the New York Court of Appeals noted that the Legislature had declared in Public Authorities Law § 1202(2) that the New York City Transit Authority "shall be regarded as performing a governmental function in carrying out its corporate purpose and in exercising the powers granted by this title." Furthermore, the court noted that the Legislature authorized the Authority to maintain a transit police force whose members are designated as police officers for purposes of the Criminal Procedure law, and whose powers, while geographically limited, are just as broad as a municipal police officer.

Cornell maintains that its status is analogous to the transit authority in *Wiener*. It notes that in Education Law § 5709, the Legislature authorized Cornell to maintain a police force whose duties were geographically limited. They were also given the power of peace officers as set forth in the Criminal Procedure Law. Based upon this Legislative enactment, Cornell maintains that it cannot be held liable for failure to provide police protection to Erin.

This Court need not rule on Cornell's argument. The special relationship rule is inapplicable when a purported governmental entity is acting in a proprietary capacity. Plaintiffs' assertion of liability against Cornell is not based upon its alleged failure to provide police protection. Instead, plaintiffs claims are premised on Cornell's status as a landowner in its operation, maintenance, and supervision of its dormitories. In such cases, the purported governmental entity is "held to the same duty of care as private individuals and institutions engaging in the same activity". As previously discussed, liability will only arise if there has been a failure to exercise reasonable care to prevent or minimize reasonably foreseeable danger. Cornell's motion for summary judgment on plaintiffs' claims of alleged inadequate security is, in all respects, denied.

Contract Claims

In Counts IX and X, plaintiffs allege that an implied contract was created between Cornell and Erin. This contract allegedly arose out of a series of documents, brochures, leaflets and pamphlets Cornell sent to prospective students and to students accepted for enrollment. In their motion papers, plaintiffs have cited two provisions containing representations which they contend constitute part of this contract. A brochure entitled "Living on Campus,

Cornell University 1983–1984" contains, on page 19 under the heading "Policy", the following representation:

Security. Concern for personal safety and security of property is shared by all segments of the University community. The Department of Residence Life provides facilities and programs that reflect this concern. Each building is locked during the evening and night, and periodic personal security programs are offered within the residence areas.

The ultimate responsibility for personal security, however, rests with each resident. Complying with security measures and reporting incidents immediately will greatly assist in making the residence halls secure. The Department of Residence Life, on behalf of all residents of the halls, asks you to cooperate in this effort.

Furthermore, the "Residence Hall Policy and Safety Procedures, 1983–84" provides:

Security. Personal safety and security at Cornell are both community and individual responsibilities. The Department of Residence Life maintains facilities and programs that reflect this concern and that assist residents of the living units in providing for their own security. Each building is locked at night and kept locked until early morning, and personal security programs are periodically offered in the residence areas.

The ultimate responsibility for personal security is that of each resident. If you follow the procedures listed below and immediately report any incidents, you will help make the residence halls secure:

1. Lock your room whenever you leave it, even for a few minutes
. . . .
5. Do not prop open outside exit doors when they should be locked.
. . . .
9. Report suspicious behavior or individuals to the Department of Public Safety immediately (dial 6-1111 or use a Blue Light telephone).

Cornell first asserts that no contract exists between it and Erin. It cites a number of cases in which the courts have refused to recognize a contractual obligation based upon provisions in college booklets, etc.

Numerous courts in New York have recognized that once a student is admitted to a university, an implied contract can arise between the student and the university.

None of the cases addressing the issue of an implied contract between student and university involve facts remotely similar to the present case. For the most part, these cases involve students seeking monetary refunds of tuition, or enforcement of post graduation guarantees of employment. Cornell expresses a concern that if the language set forth in its bulletins is given a construction as desired by plaintiffs, it would, in effect, be a "guaranty of security". Contrary to this suggestion, it is apparent that, by these provisions, Cornell only assured that each building would be locked at night and that periodic security programs would be offered. It also made clear, however, that its students had certain obligations to maintain adequate security.

Finally, Cornell raises for the first time in its Reply Papers, that if it had a contractual duty to provide security then Erin had a similar duty, under the same provisions, to report suspicious behavior to the Department of Public Safety and to refrain from propping open the outside doors with soda cans. Because Erin allegedly breached this obligation, Cornell maintains that she cannot now recover against Cornell for breach of contract.

From the deposition testimony submitted by the parties, it is apparent that a question of fact exists as to whether either party failed to meet his or her obligations under the contract. Plaintiffs have submitted the testimony of numerous students and staff members who testified that the problem of propped open doors was well known. Despite this alleged knowledge, plaintiffs contend that the University failed to take steps to resolve the problem. Cornell has countered that Erin herself propped open the doors. Based upon these conflicting contentions, a question of fact exists. Cornell's motion for summary judgment on plaintiff's claims for breach of contract is, in all respects, denied.

In sum, after a review of the entire file in this matter, Cornell University's motion for summary judgment is denied in so far as it seeks dismissal of Counts I through IV, VI through X, and XII through XV. The emotional distress claim (Count XII) is dismissed for the reasons stated at the oral argument of this motion on January 15, 1988. Finally, Counts V and XI are dismissed on the consent of the parties.

IT IS SO ORDERED.

CASE COMMENT

In this case, the plaintiffs alleged that an implied contract existed between the deceased and the university. They claimed that representations of safety and control of security by the school arose out of a series of documents, leaflets, and pamphlets. The school asserted that no contract existed between it and the deceased. The court felt that because of conflicting contentions a question of fact existed and denied the school's motion for summary judgment.

In the next case (*K.M.H. v. Lutheran General Hospital*), the plaintiff alleged that there was a professional contract whereby the hospital agreed to provide her with a safe, secure environment for her care and to protect her privacy, safety, and security. Here the court noted that the facts and circumstances creating the implied promise, together with the duties and obligations to be performed, are material fact questions and set aside the summary judgment. This court also noted an earlier case in which a patient is generally admitted to a hospital under an implied obligation to receive such reasonable care and attention for safety as the patient's mental and physical condition may require. In *G.L. v. Kaiser Foundation Hospitals, Inc.,* 757 P.2d 1347 (1988), the court found, after lengthy discussion of implied contracts, that an act of admission does not make the hospital absolutely responsible for the safety of a patient.

K.M.H. v. LUTHERAN GENERAL HOSPITAL
431 N.W. 2d 606 (1988)

COLWELL, District Judge, Retired.

Plaintiff appeals from a summary judgment entered in favor of defendants Lutheran General Hospital and Lutheran Medical Center in a contract case wherein plaintiff, a hospital patient, claims the terms of an implied contract requiring defendants to provide privacy, safety, and security were breached when she was sexually assaulted by a male nurse employee of the hospital. Plaintiff claims error in that there are genuine material fact issues remaining. We reverse and remand for further proceedings.

Concurrently with this case, plaintiff filed in the same court a companion case in tort against the same defendants, alleging the same basic facts. That action was also dismissed on summary judgment.

The petition alleges that plaintiff entered the hospital as a surgery patient on November 26, 1983, where she remained as a patient until discharged on January 6, 1984. Upon her admission to the hospital, there was a professional contract with the defendants whereby they agreed to provide plaintiff "a private, safe, secure, environment for her care and to protect her privacy, safety and security." There are no allegations of consideration, and it is assumed that the alleged terms are somehow implied. While still a hospital patient occupying private room 532, on January 5, 1984, plaintiff received pain and sleeping medication in the late hours. About 3 a.m. on January 6, 1984, she was awakened by an employee of the hospital dressed in hospital uniform, later identified as Thomas Eckles, who touched her and announced the purpose was a "bed check", then sexually assaulted plaintiff. Plaintiff alleges defendant breached the professional contract in six particulars that we summarize as (1) neither providing for nor protecting plaintiff's privacy, safety, and security by staff, facilities, or otherwise; and (2) failing to provide the required degree of care to protect plaintiff from sexual indecencies by male personnel, considering her weakened and stressful condition. The prayer was for special and general damages. The petition contains some allegations appropriate in tort; however, such do not change the theory of the contract action. Defendants answered by a general denial followed by their motion for summary judgment, which, after hearing, was granted. For the purpose of the motion, defendants admitted that an intentional tort had been committed by Eckles.

The evidence adduced at the summary judgment hearing is summarized. By affidavit and supporting documents, defendants show that proper and acceptable procedures were followed by the hospital in hiring Eckles and, if plaintiff was assaulted by Eckles, that such act by Eckles was not in the performance of his assigned duties at the time; therefore, defendants were not liable on the theory of respondeat superior.

Plaintiff's affidavits and supporting documents attempted to discredit defendants' defense theories by showing that staff nurses in hospitals are expected and required to assist all patients in a hospital by tasks such as bed checks, answering call lights, and helping patients in and out of chairs and beds, whether or not nurses are assigned to the area where the patient is found. It also included a copy of a letter dated January 16, 1984, signed by Thomas Eckles, stating that he did not assault plaintiff and that he was not in her room at the alleged time and place, but that he passed room 532 on four occasions on the night of the alleged assault.

Throughout their brief, defendants argue that the issues presented at the hearing were whether defendants were responsible for an intentional tort of an employee and whether the hospital was negligent in the hiring and supervision of that employee; further, they argue that the summary judgment should be sustained as demonstrated by their evidence that Eckles committed an intentional tort that was clearly shown not to be within the scope of his employment.

It is true that the evidence did generally relate to alleged tortious acts of Eckles; however, it is not necessary to determine whether this evidence supports the summary judgment. Rather, our attention is first directed to the petition, which on its face shows that there are genuine questions of material fact remaining. "In order to recover on an action for a breach of contract, the plaintiff must plead and prove the existence of a promise, its breach, and damage . . ." The petition appears to allege in general terms an implied contract, imposing upon the hospital the duty and obligation to provide plaintiff a private, secure environment for her care and to protect her privacy, safety, and security. The facts and circumstances creating the implied promise, together with the duties and obligations to be performed, are material fact questions whether the same are oral, express, assumed, or imposed by law; or, as stated in a 1914 case, "A patient is generally admitted to a hospital . . . under an implied obligation that he shall receive such reasonable care and attention for his safety as his mental and physical condition . . . may require."

Summary judgment should not be used to deprive a litigant of a formal trial if there is a genuine issue of fact . . .

> . . . Without that prima facie showing, a plaintiff faced with a motion for summary judgment is not required to reveal the evidence he expects to produce to prove the allegations of the petition.

Plaintiff was not obligated to supply any other information at the hearing. There being genuine issues of material fact remaining, the judgment was in error. The summary judgment is set aside, and the cause is remanded for further proceedings.

REVERSED AND REMANDED FOR FURTHER PROCEEDINGS.

DUTY

A legal duty is an obligation one is required to obey. It is an obligation of performance to do what the law requires to be done. One may be bound by a legal obligation and be required to obey it. Performing the duty may be mandatory, and a cause of action may result if the duty is not performed or if it is performed unsatisfactorily. Failure to perform a contractual duty may result in a breach of contract claim. If there is a duty, a concomitant issue arises about whether or not the duty was performed satisfactorily. Failure to satisfactorily perform a duty may result in a negligence claim. One of the allegations in the following case is that the security company assumed a duty to protect after the guard informed an employee that the building was safe and that the security company was negligent in performing its duty to provide security.

GARDNER v. VINSON GUARD SERVICE, INC.
538 So. 2d 13 (1988)

PER CURIAM.

Appellants, Hazel S. Gardner and her husband Henry Lee Gardner, sued Vinson Guard Service ("Vinson Guard"), alleging negligence or wantonness, breach of contract, and legal fraud in that the defendant allegedly failed to prevent injury to Hazel. The injury occurred as a result of a break-in at a business at which the defendant company was employed as a security service. Summary judgment was granted in favor of Vinson Guard.

Hazel was employed by Van's Photo, Inc.; her shift began at 5:00 a.m. Vinson Guard was employed, via an oral contract, to provide security guards at Van's Photo.

Although operating under an oral contract, special instructions were given the security officers working at Van's Photo. These instructions stated:

> Security Officer will report at 8:15 PM and will remain on duty until 6:00 AM, Sunday through Thursday.
>
> Report for duty in full uniform at 8:15 PM. There will be a group of female employees coming to work from about 8:30 PM until 11:30 PM. The Security Officer will remain in front of the building during these hours. After 11:30 PM, each hour he will make a security check of sides and rear of Van's building. (Note: Be sure and vary times these checks are made, so as not to set a pattern.)
>
> At 5:00 AM each morning, there will be three (3) more female employees reporting for work. The security officer will be in front of the building so that he can make sure these ladies get into the building safely.
>
> Parking is to be directly in front of the building under the Van's sign, and across Emogene Street in front of Van's small building. If this is not sufficient, parking will be allowed along the wall of the building (behind the guard house) starting at far end and coming toward the guard house.
>
> Guards will use the bathroom facilities in Van's building, but will not visit or linger in building for any extended period of time.
>
> The guard house has been provided for Security Officers by Van's Photo and will be kept locked at all times. It will be kept neat and clean at all times by the Security Officers.
>
> Any Security Officer found in violation of any of the above will be TERMINATED.

The uncontroverted affidavit testimony was that Vinson Guard was to provide protection for vehicles in the parking lot of Van's Photo and to protect employees travelling to and from their vehicles. A secondary responsibility of the security guards was to patrol the perimeter around the facility and to make their presence evident.

On the morning of November 18, 1983, Hazel arrived at work, to learn that a burglary had occurred. The security guard informed the employees, including Hazel, that he had interrupted someone trying to break into the cigarette machine and that there was no need to call the police because the man had left and he (the security guard) had recovered all of the merchandise. The security guard then proceeded to show the employees where the rear door had been forced open. Hazel testified during her deposition that the security guard represented to her that it was safe to enter the building; she and her fellow employees then went inside to begin work. Approximately 15 minutes later, Hazel went upstairs to the restroom, where she was struck in the abdomen by a second burglar, who then fled, unseen, from the building.

The Garners alleged that Vinson Guard committed legal fraud through its agent by falsely representing to Hazel that it was safe to enter the building; was negligent or wanton in performing its duties of providing security for the building; and breached its contract to provide security services for the building. Hazel claimed damages for personal injuries and Henry claimed damages for loss of consortium.

On appeal, the Gardners argue that the trial court erred in granting summary judgment in favor of Vinson Guard and they raise the following issues:

1. Whether Vinson Guard had a duty to protect Hazel against the criminal attack of a third party, who injured her, and, if so, whether the record created an issue of fact as to whether Vinson Guard was negligent or wanton in performing this duty.
2. Whether Hazel was a third-party beneficiary of the contract for security services between Vinson Guard and Van's Photo and, if so, whether a material issue of fact was presented as to whether Vinson Guard breached that contract, causing injury.
3. Whether the Gardners have a claim for fraud against Vinson Guard where Hazel, relying on a statement made by an employee of Vinson Guard that it was safe to enter the Van's Photo place of business, suffered an injury when attacked by the second burglar, when Vinson Guard knew the building had been burglarized and had failed to find that burglar or to notify police.

In light of the evidence that the security guard informed Hazel that the premises were safe, a jury question was created as to whether Vinson Guard had assumed a duty to protect the Van's Photo employees while they were inside the building. We, therefore, hold that the trial court erred in granting summary judgment on the negligence count.

However, the Gardners' contentions regarding the next two issues must fail. In their brief, the Gardners argue that a cause for action may exist for a third-party beneficiary for a breach of contract. We do not dispute that a cause of action may exist, but we can find no contractual duty imposed upon Vinson Guard. Likewise, having thoroughly examined the record in a light most favorable to the Gardners, we can find no genuine issue as to any material fact regarding the Gardners' fraud claim. The trial court, therefore, did not err in granting summary judgment as to either the Gardners' contract count or their fraud count. Nor do we find any evidence to support the Gardners' claim for wantonness.

Due to the foregoing, we hold that there was evidence presented supporting the Gardners' claims under the negligence count, but that no evidence was presented to support the wantonness, contract, or fraud theories.

AFFIRMED IN PART; REVERSED IN PART; AND REMANDED.

CASE COMMENT

This guard service operated under an oral contract modified by special instructions. The court found no evidence to support a verdict favorable to the plaintiff under the contract theory that the guard service had a duty imposed on it.

SIMMONS v. BALTIMORE ORIOLES, INC.
712 F. Supp. 79 (1989)

GLEN M. WILLIAMS, Senior District Judge.

The plaintiff brought suit against the defendants for $1,000,000 in compensatory damages and $1,000,000 in punitive damages for injuries to his face and jaw arising out of a fight with defendants Champ and Hicks, minor league baseball players employed by the Baltimore Orioles. Specifically, Simmons alleges that he was the victim of an assault by Champ and Hicks which ended with Hicks breaking Simmons' jaw with a baseball bat. Defendant Baltimore Orioles, Inc., has moved to dismiss the charges, and defendant Bluestone Security Agency has filed a motion for summary judgment. No motions are pending on behalf of Champ and Hicks individually.

Certain facts are not in dispute. Simmons, along with a friend, attended the Fourth of July, 1988 game between the Martinsville Phillies and the Bluefield Orioles, a Baltimore farm team, at Bluefield, Virginia. Bluefield was not having a good year, and whether for this or some other reason Simmons moved down to the third baseline along about the eighth inning, and started to heckle the Oriole players sitting in the bullpen. Champ stated in his deposition that Simmons was accusing the ballplayers of stealing the local women, and that he (Simmons) would show the Orioles what West Virginia manhood was like by blowing the players' heads off. Whatever was precisely said, the pitching coach then asked Simmons to leave.

After the game (Bluefield lost, 9-8, stranding three runners in the bottom of the ninth), Champ encountered Simmons in the parking lot. Simmons, in his complaint, offers no details of what ensued other than that he was punched and kicked by Champ and then hit in the jaw by a baseball bat wielded by Hicks, causing his jaw to be broken in two places. Champ's version was that Simmons saw him carrying a bat, made a gesture as if he were shooting Champ with his finger, and said "Oh, so you need a bat, huh?" Champ said "No, I don't," and threw his bat down. Simmons gestured toward his car and said, "Let's go over to my car, and I'll blow your head off." Another player tried to intervene, and Champ said "Just get out of here." Simmons then advanced threateningly upon him, and Champ hit Simmons in the face. Simmons was unfazed, and Champ kicked him in the chest, causing Simmons to stagger back. According to Champ he then smiled and said "I'm drunk. I didn't feel that." Champ turned to walk away, and at that point defendant Hicks hit Simmons. Simmons said Hicks hit him with a bat, but Hicks says that he used only his fist. Hicks had not been near any of the heckling and says he intervened because he was afraid Simmons was about to pull a gun on Champ.

Defendant Bluestone Security Agency has moved for summary judgment. The plaintiff alleges that Bluestone had a contract with the Orioles to supply a security guard at the ballpark, and that its negligence in performing these duties was a proximate cause of Simmons' injuries.

A party moving for summary judgment is entitled to it as a matter of law where the party opposing the motion has failed to make a sufficient showing of an essential element of his case on which he has the burden of proof.

The claim against Bluestone rests on the assertion that it had a duty to be present at the time the fight took place. The exact time is not precisely established in the record, but was clearly after 10:00 p.m.: Officer Brewster, the Bluefield, Virginia town policeman who arrived on the scene immediately after the fight listed the time in his report as 10:20 p.m., and Hicks and Champ recall it as occurring even later.

Jack Asbury, the Chief of Police of Bluefield, Virginia and the co-owner of Bluestone, deposed that Bluestone had a contract with the City of Bluefield, West Virginia, to provide security services for its city park. The park is located in both Virginia and West Virginia, but Bluestone's contract was with Bluefield, West Virginia only. As Mr. Asbury recalled it, Bluestone had had an agreement to provide a guard for the entire length of the ballgame some years previously, but this became too expensive and the special guard was dropped. He was not sure what specific hours the guards were supposed to work.

Herbert Sims, the Director of Parks and Recreation for the City of Bluefield, West Virginia, deposed that "maybe a couple weeks" before the fight he had cut Bluestone's patrol hours back from 5:00 p.m.–11:00 p.m. to 7:00 p.m.–10:00 p.m. in order to save money. He said that the agreement was for Bluestone to patrol the City Park, and that there was no agreement with them to provide security to Bowen Field, the ballpark.

William Asbury, Chief Asbury's son, was the supervisor, or general manager, at Bluestone. He was patrolling the park on the night of the incident. He stated that their agreement was to patrol the park from 7:00 p.m. to 10:00 p.m., Monday through Thursday, and 6:00 p.m. to 11:00 p.m. Friday, and 4:00 p.m. to 9:00 p.m. weekends. July 4th, 1988 was a Monday. Mr. Asbury recalled that on holidays such as Independence Day, he started work earlier, but still quit at 10:00 p.m. Officer Brewster also stated that Bluestone's quitting time was 10:00 p.m.

Against this, there is only the testimony of George Fanning, the Orioles general manager, who recalled that "in recent years" Bluestone was patrolling within the ballpark and the parking lot outside. The only thing he knew about the city's agreement with Bluestone, however, was what he had been told by Mr. Sims and the City Manager of Bluefield, West Virginia. He said that he had seen them parked outside his office at the park, but "I don't know whether they're there all the time."

Based on these depositions, the court concludes that the plaintiff has failed to meet his burden under *Celotex*. There can be little doubt that Bluestone had no duty to patrol the park after 10:00 p.m. The only evidence to the contrary came from Mr. Fanning, who recalled seeing Bluestone officers present in the past, but was not directly involved with the provision of security services and would not, in the ordinary course of his duties, have known whether Bluestone's hours had been cut back by the City of Bluefield a week or so before the incident. In the face of the unequivocal evidence of the individuals directly involved, plus the corroboration of a disinterested police officer, there can be no genuine dispute that Bluestone had any duty to be present after 10:00 p.m.

Therefore, it is proper to grant summary judgment in favor of Bluestone.

Therefore, the Baltimore Orioles' motion to dismiss the plaintiff's claims will be granted, as will Bluestone's motion for summary judgment.

An appropriate Order will enter this day.

CASE COMMENT

Based on testimony in depositions, the court had little doubt that the security firm had no duty to patrol the park after 10:00 PM. This reaffirms the proposition that having clear terms of contractual obligations can be very helpful.

PROFESSIONAL SPORTS, INC. v. GILLETTE SECURITY, INC.
766 P.2d 91 (1989)

GREER, Judge.

This appeal raises questions concerning a security company's liability as a joint tort-feasor. Since this is an appeal from a summary judgment, we review the facts most favorably to the appellant.

The appellant, Professional Sports, Inc., also known as the Phoenix Giants (Professional), leased and operated the Phoenix Municipal Stadium, including the internal concessions stands. The appellee, Gillette Security, Inc. (Gillette), had a contract with Professional to provide security at the stadium during baseball games. Pursuant to the contract, guards employed by Gillette were required to "patrol and secure" the stadium and adjacent parking lot. Gillette told its guards to do whatever the Phoenix Giants requested them to do, and the Phoenix Giants instructed the guards to monitor alcoholic beverage service and consumption inside its grounds. This included the detection of underaged persons attempting to purchase and consume alcohol. Guards were assigned to posts near the concession stands where Professional's employees sold beer. They were also assigned to patrol the stands and had the authority to "take necessary action," which included ejecting people from the stadium.

This case arises out of an accident which occurred near the stadium in July, 1983. David Ford, then 16 years old, attended a Phoenix Giants baseball game at the stadium with two friends, both 17 years old. The legal drinking age at that time was 19 years. The game that evening was promoted and advertised on the radio as "KDKB 50¢ Beer Night." A major attraction was the reduced price for beer. Although David does not recall purchasing any beer, his friends purchased between six and eight rounds at the stadium's concession stands. During the course of the game, David drank and became increasingly intoxicated and unruly.

Late in the game, David and his friends left the stadium. David was obviously intoxicated —he was stumbling and slurring his speech. The three boys wandered about the parking lot and eventually made their way to Van Buren Street. As David attempted to cross the street, an automobile struck and severely injured him.

David filed an action against Professional and various other defendants not pertinent to this appeal. The complaint alleged, in part, that Professional was negligent in furnishing alcohol to David, then a minor, and allowing him to become intoxicated. Professional filed a third-party complaint against Gillette for contribution pursuant to A.R.S. § 12-2501 *et seq.* (Supp. 1987).[1] Professional later settled with David. Gillette then moved for summary judgment, claiming it owed David no duty and therefore could not be a joint tortfeasor with Professional for the purpose of contribution. The trial court granted Gillette's motion, and Professional brought this appeal.

The issues raised on appeal include:

(1) Did the contract between Professional Sports and Gillette Security create a duty?
(2) Did Gillette voluntarily undertake conduct so as to acquire a duty to David?
(3) Did Gillette have a statutory duty pursuant to A.R.S. § § 4-241(A) and 4-244(9)?[2]
(4) Did Gillette have a duty to protect David from further harm after he became intoxicated?

---

[1] *But see* Laws 1987, ch. 1, § 1, effective January 1, 1988, abolishing joint and several liability of tortfeasors.

[2] At the time of David Ford's accident, A.R.S. § 4-241(A) provided:

A licensee, employee or other person who questions or has reason to question whether or not a person ordering, purchasing, attempting to purchase or otherwise procuring or attempting to procure the serving or delivery of spirituous liquor, is nineteen years old, shall require the person

Since we conclude that the contract between Professional and Gillette created a duty in negligence to protect minors such as David Ford from illegally consuming alcohol, we need not consider the remaining issues.

NEGLIGENCE IN GENERAL

To maintain an action in negligence, four elements must be shown: (1) duty, (2) breach of duty, (3) causation, and (4) damages. The question on appeal is whether Gillette had a duty to persons such as David Ford. A duty must be recognized by law and must obligate the defendant "to conform to a particular standard of conduct in order to protect others against unreasonable risks of harm." Whether a duty exists is usually a question of law for the court to decide.

In Arizona, a supplier of liquor has a common law duty to use reasonable care in supplying liquor to underage individuals who, "by reason of immaturity or previous overindulgence, may lack full capacity of self-control and may therefore injure themselves, as well as others." There is no doubt that , as a matter of law, Professional, the supplier of liquor at Phoenix Municipal Stadium, had a duty to protect minors such as David Ford. Further, there is no doubt that Professional breached its duty. The question here, however, is whether Gillette *also* had a duty to protect Ford and others like him, even though it was not the supplier of liquor and therefore did not have a duty at common law.

On appeal, Professional argues (1) that Gillette acquired a contractual duty when it agreed, as an independent contractor, to help control the purchase and consumption of alcohol at the stadium, and (2) that the general responsibilities of a security company would include such a duty. Gillette, on the other hand, argues that, because it never undertook such a duty and had no duty as a matter of law, summary judgment in its favor was proper.

GILLETTE'S DUTY

In *Papastathis v. Beall*, 723 P.2d 97, this court held that a franchiser who undertook the responsibility of recommending and inspecting certain soft drink racks to be used by its franchisees could be liable to third parties for the negligent performance of those duties. A customer of one of the franchisees was injured when a soft drink can fell off a rack which had been inspected and endorsed by the franchisor. The court relied upon § 324(A) of the *Restatement (Second) of Torts* (1984), which states:

> One who *undertakes*, gratuitously or *for consideration*, to render services to another which he should recognize as necessary for the protection of a third person or his things, is subject to liability to the third person for physical harm resulting from his failure to exercise reasonable care to protect his undertaking, if
>
> (a) his failure to exercise reasonable care increases the risk of such harm, or
> (b) he has undertaken to perform a duty owed by the other to the third person, or
> (c) the harm is suffered because of reliance of the other or the third person upon the undertaking.

to exhibit an identification card and on a card to be retained by the licensee to sign his name, the date, and number of such identification card. . .

See Laws 1983, ch. 91, § 2. The provision was amended by Laws 1984, ch. 67, § 4, making the legal drinking age twenty-one years.

Pursuant to A.R.S. § 4-244(9) as it read then, it was unlawful

> for a licensee or other person to sell, furnish, dispose of, give or cause to be sold, furnished, disposed of or given to a person under the age of nineteen years, or for a person under the age of nineteen years to buy, receive, have in possession or consume, spirituous liquor. . . .

See Laws 1983, ch. 91, § 4. This provision was similarly amended by Laws 1984, ch. 67, § 5, to read "twenty-one years" instead of "nineteen years."

The court concluded that the franchisor's failure to exercise reasonable care increased the risk of harm to the third party, the injured plaintiff. *Papastathis*, 723 P.2d at 100.

Section 324(A) of the *Restatement* has been applied in many types of situations, including those involving security guards. For example, in *Gold Mills, Inc. v. Orbit Processing Corp.*, 297 A.2d 203, a New Jersey court held that a security company which negligently performed its contract to guard certain premises was liable for the theft of a third party's goods stored on the premises. The court concluded:

> The context of the facts in our case also falls within the provision of § 324A(b) *[Restatement (Second) of Torts]*. Defendant, by undertaking the contract to provide guards at the plant of Orbit, assumed in part at least a duty which Orbit owed to plaintiff, and it did so with the reasonable foreseeable consequence that if it failed to exercise due care, the owners of the goods at Orbit processing plant might be damaged. The Restatement rule would impose liability under such set of facts.
>
> The court noted, however, that liability will attach only if the contractor has commenced performance of the contract. *Gold Mills*, 297 A.2d at 206. Thus, the contractor is not liable if he fails entirely to perform the contract. *Id.; see also, Abel Holding Co. v. American Dist. Tel. Co.*, 350 A.2d 292, *aff'd*, 371 A.2d 111; *Tucker v. Sandlin*, 337 N.W. 2d 637.

The uncontroverted evidence in this case shows that Gillette had a contract with Professional requiring it to patrol and secure the stadium premises. Gillette told its guards to do whatever the Phoenix Giants management asked them to do towards that end; and Ethan Blackaby, the general manager of the Giants, who was also an officer with Gillette, instructed Gillette's security guards to police the concessions where beer was sold, check for underaged persons attempting to purchase beer, check the stands for underage drinkers, control the crowd (including patrons who became drunk and unruly), and to take whatever action was necessary to maintain the peace on the premises. Thus, these instructions were given by both Professional and Gillette.

Professional argues that Gillette undertook certain responsibilities when it accepted these instructions pursuant to the contract and agreed to supervise the purchase and consumption of alcohol on the premises. Gillette, however, maintains that it did not undertake any affirmative action by which it acquired a duty to third persons such as Ford. This, it claims, distinguishes this case from the cases discussed above. *E.g., Gold Mills; Abel; Tucker, supra*. It points out that in *Randolph v. Arizona Board of Regents*, 505 P.2d 559, Division 2 concluded there were no allegations in the complaint from which it could be inferred that the University of Arizona had assumed a duty to protect the plaintiff from disease or sickness, and it argues that the same reasoning should apply here.

Gillette acknowledges that instructions were given, but argues that giving "mere instructions," without some affirmative action, *see, e.g., Gold Mills*, does not mean that it acquired a duty. It points out that there is no evidence in the record that, on the night of the accident, the security guards 1) sought to check the age of David Ford or his friends, 2) attempted to detect underaged alcohol purchasers, 3) attempted to prevent the sale of alcohol to minors, or 4) attempted to prevent David Ford from consuming alcohol. Therefore, Gillette reasons, it never commenced performance of its obligation to control underaged drinking.

Gillette's reliance on the absence of this evidence is misplaced. This evidence goes to the question of the specific details of Gillette's conduct, rather than whether it acquired a duty by agreeing to perform these functions. We therefore disagree with Gillette's characterization of these facts as indicating it did not undertake conduct to acquire a duty. It is undisputed that Gillette's guards were on duty the night of the accident. Thus, at the very least, Gillette commenced performance of its obligation to provide security services pursuant to its contract, which included the control of underaged drinking.

Viewing the facts most favorably to Professional Sports, the only reasonable inference is that Gillette commenced performance of its contract with Professional, which included preventing underaged persons such as David Ford from purchasing and consuming alcohol. In so doing, Gillette undertook, for consideration, to render services to Professional which it should have recognized were necessary to protect third-party patrons of the ball park, including underaged drinking patrons. More specifically, it undertook to perform Professional's duty under *Brannigan*, 667 P.2d at 216, to use reasonable care in supplying liquor to underaged individuals. See also, A.R.S. § § 4-241(A), -244(9), and -311 (Supp.1986). Thus, it is potentially liable to David Ford for physical harm he suffered if it failed to exercise reasonable care in performing the duties it undertook pursuant to contract. *Restatement (Second) of Torts* § 324(A), subsections (a), (b) and (c); *Papasthathis*, 723 P.2d 97.

Professional also relies on *Forbes v. Romo*, 601 P.2d 311, for the premise that a duty to a third party to exercise due care may arise from a contractual relationship. It again points out that, pursuant to the contract, Gillette instructed its employees to follow the instructions given by Professional Sports and that Professional instructed the guards to prevent the purchase and consumption of alcohol by minors. Gillette argues, on the other hand, that *Forbes* does not apply because it concerns only the duty arising out of a contractual relationship between a landlord and his tenants.

Under *Forbes*, a contractual relationship can give rise to an obligation in tort. In *Forbes*, Division 2 held that, because of the contractual relationship between a tenant and a landlord, the duty to exercise due care arose toward a third party who, in that case, was another tenant. The court noted that, although generally a relationship (i.e., privity) between the negligent and injured party is necessary for there to be a duty, in some situations, it is not required. The court further concluded that, although a duty might have been owed in that case, reasonable minds could not differ that the tenant was not negligent. It therefore affirmed the summary judgment in the tenant's favor.

In this case, it is undisputed that Gillette had a contract with Professional requiring it to patrol and secure the stadium premises. This included patrolling for the detection and prevention of underaged drinking. Therefore, reasonable minds could not differ that Gillette had a duty to exercise due care for the benefit of third parties like David Ford. As in *Forbes*, privity of contract between Gillette and Ford, the injured third party, was not necessary.

Gillette's reliance on *Contempo Constr. Co. v. Mountain States Tel. and Tel. Co.*, 736 P.2d 13, is misplaced. In that case, Division 2 held that Mountain States Telephone had no duty to the City of Phoenix' contractor to move Mountain States utility poles. The court held that there was neither a contractual relationship between the parties nor a duty in negligence. It based the latter holding on the fact that there was no relationship between the utilities and the contractor to give rise to a legal duty. The court did not address the issue presented here, whether a duty to *third parties* could arise from a contractual relationship. Thus, its holding that a relationship between the injured party and alleged tortfeasor was necessary to show a duty existed has no bearing on this case, where a relationship between the injured third party and alleged tortfeasor is not required.

In its discussion of duty, *Contempo* quoted Prosser on Torts: "No better general statement can be made than that the court will find a duty where, in general, reasonable persons would recognize it and agree that it exists." Reasonable persons would agree that security guards who undertake for hire to patrol a stadium have a duty to exercise due care for the protection not only of the stadium, but of the stadium's patrons.

GILLETTE'S BREACH

Gillette next argues that, even if it owed a duty, it did not commit a breach. It points out in its discussion of its second issue on appeal (whether it acquired a duty) that it provided crowd control on the night Ford's friends illegally purchased alcohol and that it exercised reasonable care in performing these duties. The question of breach is generally one of fact. Gillette argues, however, that there is no evidence that it fell below the applicable standard of care and that summary judgment was therefore proper. We disagree. There is evidence in the record which may indicate that, although Gillette's guards were on duty, they failed to detect or prevent underaged persons from purchasing and consuming alcohol or to take any action in response to David Ford's obviously loud and unruly behavior.

Unlike *Forbes* then, the question of whether Gillette breached its duty is one on which reasonable minds could differ; therefore, it must be resolved by the finder of fact. On remand, the factfinder must determine whether Gillette failed to exercise reasonable care, thereby increasing the risk of harm to third parties such as David Ford. At this point, the evidence Gillette claims is lacking becomes relevant in determining whether Gillette exercised reasonable care or acted as a reasonable security service. Thus, Gillette's guards' admitted failure to check the ages of David Ford and his friends, and their failure to attempt to detect or prevent underaged persons from purchasing or consuming alcohol in general can be considered in determining whether Gillette breached its duty.

CONCLUSION

We therefore conclude that the contract between Professional and Gillette was an undertaking for consideration within the meaning of § 324(A), *Restatement (Second) of Torts*, which created a duty on Gillette's part to exercise reasonable care to protect minor patrons of the stadium such as David Ford from illegally consuming alcohol. Whether it breached its duty and its degree of fault as a joint tortfeasor with Professional Sports are questions to be determined by the finder of fact.

In accordance with this decision, the summary judgment in favor of Gillette is reversed and this matter remanded to the trial court for a trial on the merits.

CASE COMMENT

The security staff was told to monitor alcoholic beverage consumption, including detecting underage purchase and consumption. They also had the authority to take necessary action, including ejecting people from the stadium. The court found that the security company had a contract requiring it to patrol and secure the stadium, and this included detecting and preventing underage drinking. This created a duty for the security firm to exercise reasonable care to protect minor patrons of the stadium. Also note that a contractual relationship can give rise to an obligation in tort.

THIRD PARTY BENEFICIARY

A third party beneficiary is one who may benefit by a contract, but who is not a party to the contract, and one who may have legally enforceable rights in the contract.

In *Brown v. National Supermarkets* (see page 124), a security company contracted with a store to provide security. When entering into this contract with the store, did the security company assume a duty the store may have owed its patrons? The plaintiffs claimed the contract between the store and the security company was an attempt to perform the store's previously established duty. The plaintiffs were not a party to the contract. The notion here is that the third party beneficiary is one who is not privy to a contract nor the contract's considerations, but to whom the law gives the right to maintain a cause of action for breach of contract. Here the security company, by contracting with the store, may have a duty to protect the store's patrons from criminal assaults. The patrons to be protected, who were not signatories to the contract, are the third party beneficiaries. The security company manager should inquire about the duties of the client prior to entering into a contract.

BREACH OF CONTRACT

A breach of contract is the violation of a legal promise or obligation. It is the failure, without legal excuse, to perform any promise which is a part of the contract. A party to a contract assumes an obligation, and it is the duty of that party to comply. Nonperformance or failure to comply with the obligation constitutes a breach. Parties to a contract have the duty of good faith compliance and fair dealing in the performance of the contract. When bound by promise, people should do what they said they would do. The law will require that they do what they promised or it will exact a penalty for not doing so. A party to a contract may not flout its obligations so as to be injurious to the other party who has the right to receive the benefits of the contract. One of the remedies for a breach of contract is damages for failure to perform or for not performing in a manner according to the terms of the contract. The following two cases illustrate breach and nonperformance principles. Both security companies suffered judgments against them for, respectively, failure to reimburse the client for the loss of money and failure to meet its duties or contractual obligations of guarding the plant.

BROOKLYN UNION GAS COMPANY v. JOHN SHIELDS
DETECTIVE BUREAU, INC.
503 N.Y.S. 2D 852 (1986)

Before BROWN, J.P., and RUBIN, EIBER and SPATT, JJ.
MEMORANDUM BY THE COURT.

In an action, *inter alia*, to recover damages for breach of contract, (1) the plaintiff Brooklyn Union Gas Company appeals from so much of an order of the Supreme Court, Kings County, dated July 5, 1985, as denied its motion for summary judgment, and (2) the third-party defendant Hartford Accident and Indemnity Company separately appeals from so much of the same order as denied its motion for summary judgment dismissing the third-party complaint.

Order modified, on the law, by deleting the provision thereof which denied the plaintiff's motion for summary judgment and substituting therefor a provision granting that motion to the extent that the plaintiff is awarded judgment on its cause of action to recover damages for breach of contract, in the principal sum of $82,911.14, and, upon searching the record, the complaint is otherwise dismissed. As so modified, order affirmed, with costs to the plaintiff on its appeal, payable by the defendant third-party plaintiff-respondent, and with costs to the defendant third-party plaintiff-respondent payable by the third-party defendant on its appeal, and matter remitted to the Supreme Court, Kings County, for entry of an appropriate judgment.

On August 21, 1981, the plaintiff Brooklyn Union Gas Company (hereinafter Brooklyn Union) and the defendant John Shields Detective Bureau, Inc. (hereinafter Shields) entered into an agreement in which it was provided that, for a fee, Shields would furnish armed guards to transfer funds from Brooklyn Union's offices to certain banks. The agreement provided that in the event of loss, Shields was to reimburse Brooklyn Union for the amount thereof within 15 days. It also contained a provision requiring Shields to pay any costs, expenses and attorney's fees incurred by Brooklyn Union in connection with any claims or actions brought against it arising out of the performance of Shields' duties.

On April 12, 1983, two Shields employees, William F. Buckley and Frank Slater, were engaged in making collections on behalf of Brooklyn Union pursuant to the contract. Buckley, who was armed, made the pickups and deliveries, while Slater, who was not armed, drove the vehicle in which they were making their collections. During the course of the day, Buckley left the car to make a pickup from Brooklyn Union's Bedford-Stuyvesant office while Slater remained behind. Buckley was given two bags which he was told contained a total of $129,261.61 in cash and checks, and he was instructed to take the bags across the shopping plaza in which the office was located to a branch of the Chemical Bank. According to Slater, he remained in the car in order to serve as a lookout for Buckley. Immediately upon leaving the Brooklyn Union office, Buckley was struck from behind by an unknown assailant and the bags were taken from him. The attack took place in a blind spot in the plaza so that Slater was unable to see what had occurred. Neither the bags nor the money were recovered.

Because the stolen checks were either replaced or, since payment was stopped, Brooklyn Union sustained a cash loss of only $77,933.70. In addition, however, it claimed that it had incurred expenses of $4,977.44 in obtaining replacement checks and that its total loss therefore amounted to $82,911.14. It made demand for repayment of said amount under the terms of the agreement in letters to Shields dated April 14, 1983, and June 10, 1983, respectively. Shields, however, refused to reimburse Brooklyn Union for its loss.

At the time of the incident, there was in effect a Comprehensive Dishonesty, Disappearance and Destruction policy issued to Shields by Hartford Accident and Indemnity Company (hereinafter Hartford), which covered Shields' work under its contract with Brooklyn Union and contained provisions with respect to indemnifying Shields for "Loss Outside the Premises". As part of the loss outside the premises coverage, the policy provided "that each messenger while conveying monies, securities and other property . . . in excess of $10,000.00 shall be accompanied by at least 1 guard". The term "Guard" was defined as "any male person not less than seventeen, nor more than sixty-five years of age, who accompanies a Messenger by direction of the Insured, but who is not a driver of a public conveyance".

In a complaint dated January 26, 1984, Brooklyn Union commenced this action asserting claims against Shields for breach of contract and negligence and sought damages therefor in the amount of $97,108. Apparently the moneys in excess of the actual loss of $82,911.14 represented legal fees and other costs expended in prosecuting the action. Thereafter, Shields served a third-party summons and complaint on Hartford setting forth causes of action sounding in indemnification and breach of contract and requesting money damages in the amount of $20,666.67. In its answer, Hartford pleaded as an affirmative defense that the "Loss Outside the Premises" endorsement placed the robbery outside the coverage of the policy, because Buckley had not been "accompanied" by Slater at the time of the robbery.

Thereafter, both Brooklyn Union and Hartford moved for summary judgment. By order dated July 5, 1985, Special Term denied both motions finding that "sufficient triable issues of fact requiring a plenary trial exist, including, but not limited to, whether defendant Shields exercised due care in its bailment of the funds in issue, the parties' intent and understanding of pertinent provisions in both Brooklyn Union Gas' contract with Shields and Shields' insurance contract with Hartford, the accuracy of sketches and investigation of the crime scene submitted by Hartford and whether Shields assumed all risk of loss".

We have examined the disputed provisions in the contract between Brooklyn Union and Shields and find them to be unambiguous. Therefore, the intent of the parties can be gleaned from the contract itself and evidence extrinsic to it may not be considered. The agreement between Brooklyn Union and Shields plainly requires that Shields reimburse Brooklyn Union for the losses it actually incurred as a result of the robbery and summary judgment thereon should have been granted in favor of Brooklyn Union. However, the provision concerning Shields' obligation to reimburse Brooklyn Union for its costs, expenses and attorneys' fees is clearly intended to apply to claims brought against Brooklyn Union by third parties and is not applicable to this action. Accordingly, the plaintiff's right of recovery is limited to the actual loss occasioned by the robbery, i.e., $82,911.14, and should not include its costs, expenses and attorneys' fees. We find Shields' other contentions with regard to the main action to be without merit.

With respect to the third-party action, on the other hand, we find that the question of whether Shields' employee, Buckley, was "accompanied" by Slater while he was sitting in the car acting as a lookout, as required under the Dishonesty, Disappearance and Destruction policy issued by Hartford presents a question of fact and we accordingly affirm so much of the order appealed from as so held.

SANDVIK, INC. v. STATEWIDE SECURITY SYSTEMS, DIV. OF STATEWIDE GUARD SERVICES, INC.
469 A.2D 955 (1983)

ANTELL, P.J.A.D.

Defendant, a licensed private detective agency, contracted June 28, 1974 with plaintiff, a manufacturer of tungsten carbide inserts, to provide security guard service. On January 22, 1977 the employee assigned by defendant to guard the plant on the 12:30 a.m. to 8:00 a.m. shift, William Milnes, was bribed to leave his post at 4:00 a.m. for 30 minutes. During his absence 4205 kilograms of tungsten carbide powder worth $118,000 was stolen.

The complaint herein filed alleged liability for breach of contract, two theories of negligence, and liability based on the claim that as a licensee under The Private Detective Act of 1939, *N.J.S.A.* 45:19-8 *et seq.*, defendant is "accountable" for the good conduct of its employees. See *N.J.S.A.* 45:19-15. The trial judge, who heard the case without a jury, found a breach of contract by defendant and awarded damages of $1,994.33, being one-twelfth of the annual contract price of $23,932. On this appeal plaintiff contends that the judge applied the incorrect measure of damages, arguing that he should have allowed full recovery of all consequential losses, that is, $118,000, the value of the stolen inventory. Plaintiff also appeals from an order for summary judgment dated December 21, 1981 dismissing its demands asserted in the second and third counts of the complaint for recovery grounded in negligence. On its cross-appeal defendant maintains that the trial judge erred in his finding of contractual liability.

We deal first with plaintiff's appeal from the order for summary judgment dismissing the second and third counts of the complaint. The second count alleged that plaintiff's loss resulted from the negligence of defendant through its agents, servants and employees. The third count asserted negligence in defendant's hiring and training of employees. Defendant's motion, accompanied only by a brief and without supporting certifications or affidavits, relied entirely upon the deposition testimony of its executive vice president to the effect that the employment application of William Milnes, the errant guard, was "as clean as any application I've ever seen" and that there was "no way in the world that we could have found anything wrong with this guy." As against this, plaintiff described its claim of hiring negligence in the following answer to one of defendant's interrogatories:

> Defendant hired employees without investigating same for predisposition hence [sic] to criminal activities. No psychological evaluation to determine same and no program to encourage honesty or to alert employees to potential embezzlers.

Apart from the fact that a material issue was raised by the foregoing answer, counsel for plaintiff explained on the motion that she was still engaged in a search for Milnes' personnel file which, as the judge found, had been misplaced through defendant's negligence. Although plaintiff's 150 day discovery period had expired, the circumstance of the missing file should have been weighed heavily in favor of denying the motion, particularly since the facts upon which liability was predicated lay peculiarly within defendant's knowledge.

Under all the circumstances the motion for summary judgment should not have been granted. For reasons which will become evident from our disposition of the contract aspect of the case, the summary judgment as to tort the claims is no longer of any practical significance, but the granting thereof must nevertheless be reversed.

We agree with the trial court's finding that defendant had breached its contract with plaintiff. Defendant's argument before us is that this result conflicts with the rule that an employer is not answerable for the acts of an employee outside the scope of his employment. It maintains that Milnes' behavior, for which he was indicted and convicted on charges of embezzlement, was not in furtherance of defendant's business and therefore could not support a finding of civil liability against defendant. The argument, however, confuses an agency principle applicable to tort cases with the elements of contractual liability.

The judgment under review does not impose vicarious liability arising from Milnes' wrongful conduct. It results only from defendant's failure to meet its obligation of guarding the plant. Obviously, there was no other way that defendant could perform this contract except through its employees. Whether defendant performed or failed to perform can therefore only be determined by the conduct of the employee it chose for this purpose, and Milnes' deliberate 30 minute absence from the premises supports the trial judge's finding that defendant's contractual obligation had been breached.

We find, however, that the trial judge erred in limiting recovery to the amount of defendant's fees for the month in which the theft occurred. He reasoned that because defendant had not been fully informed as to the value of the tungsten carbide powder being guarded the parties could not reasonably have intended that defendant's liability for loss resulting from breach of contract should extend to the value of stolen inventory.

The applicable rule is that generally "the *prima facie* measure of damages for the breach of contract is the *quantum* of loss consequent thereon. The injured party is entitled to the value of the contract to him," subject to the following limitations:

> First, the damages shall be those arising naturally, i.e., according to the usual course of things, from the breach of the contract, or such as may fairly and reasonably be supposed to have been in the contemplation of the parties to the contract at the time it was made, as the probable result of the breach; and, second, they must be the reasonably certain and definite consequences of the breach, as distinguished from mere quantitative uncertainty.

As Williston explains, this allows recovery "for only such consequences as would follow such a breach in the usual course of events." That is, a defendant "is liable only for consequences which were reasonably foreseeable at the time when the contract was entered into, as probable if the contract were broken." 11 *Williston, Contracts* (3d ed. Jager 1968), § 1344 at 226-27.

The consequences may have been foreseeable because they would occur in the natural course of events, or because, although unusual, the defendant knew special facts making them probable. For all such consequences, the defendant is liable whether they were actually foreseen or not, or whether even the criminal act of a third person intervenes.

The only purpose of the contract was to avoid the precise loss suffered. Although defendant might not have been specifically told the value of tungsten carbide powder, it knew that plaintiff's plant was likely to contain movable property in the form of inventory and capital assets of substantial value. Furthermore, as defendant acknowledged in a preliminary letter, it knew that plaintiff had an internal theft problem, that the purpose of the hiring was to "help abolish inventory loss," and that for this service plaintiff obliged itself to pay a yearly charge of nearly $24,000. Under the circumstances, we find unavoidable the conclusion that the inventory loss of $118,000 was a reasonably foreseeable, natural and proximate consequence of defendant's breach.

Defendant's contention that the result here reached constitutes defendant a guarantor against loss is rejected. Nowhere do we suggest that defendant's obligation to keep a guard on plaintiff's premises carries with it a guarantee against loss. Not before us for consideration is a case of the kind hypothesized by defendant wherein the security service's basic obligation to provide a guard on the premises is fulfilled, but the guard is stricken by illness or overpowered by robbers or immobilized by other factors beyond his control. We leave the question of whether breach of contract could be found in such cases to be decided on the facts of each particular case. Here we deal only with a case in which defendant failed in its duty to provide a guard, thus committing a breach proximately related to the loss.

Our research discloses that courts which have elsewhere considered this question have reached substantially similar results. In *Cooper v. IBI Security Service of Florida*, 281 So.2d 524, a life insurance premium collector was shot while making his collections when an armed guard failed to accompany him into a dangerous area as contracted for by the guard's employer. The complaint by the collector sought recovery of damages for injuries on the ground that the security service failed to provide the contracted for protection. On appeal from a trial court's dismissal of the complaint the Court of Appeals reversed. In so doing it stated:

> It was the purpose and object of the contract to obviate or protect the plaintiff from exactly that which occurred when he went unprotected, with foreseeability and likelihood thereof, and the basis therefor, sufficiently alleged to be known to exist. On the allegations of the amended complaint it could not be held that the facts disclosed showed absence of proximate cause as a matter of law.

In *Homan v. County of Dade*, 248 So.2d 235, the Court said:

> Foreseeable acts of third persons are not superseding causes which insulate a prior tort feasor from liability as a matter of law, where such acts combine with the tort feasor's negligence to bring about harm to an innocent party; they are merely concurrent causes." The same principle as to proximate causation is applicable under the count on breach of contract, asserted by the plaintiff in the capacity of a third party beneficiary.

In *Better Food Markets v. American Dist. Tel. Co.*, 253 P.2d 10, plaintiff sued in tort and contract for damages resulting from defendant's failure to respond promptly to burglar alarm signals as it had contracted to do. The form of analysis employed by the Supreme Court of California in reversing the judgment for defendant entered by the trial court is seen in the following language of its opinion:

There is evidence upon which it could have been found that the loss was the proximate result of the defendant's delay in responding to the alarms. There was but one individual committing the burglary. He acted deliberately and there is reason to believe that the agreement between the parties was entered into with the intention of providing for the apprehension of such a person before he left the premises. The time and distance factors indicate that this particular burglar may have been caught had the police and guards been called to the premises a few minutes earlier, and that the delay of nine minutes after the safe had been opened permitted the escape. Such probabilities are to be weighed in the light of common experience in such matters and present a triable issue of fact. There was substantial evidence from which a jury could have found that the plaintiff's loss was the proximate result of the defendant's breach of its contract. Therefore it was error for the trial court to order judgment for the defendant on its motion for a directed verdict.

The underlying operative principle in both these cases is that the security service will be held answerable for all reasonably foreseeable losses ensuing from the nonperformance by its employees of the security service's contractual undertakings.

The order for summary judgment dated December 21, 1981 is vacated without remanding for further proceedings. The judgment in favor of plaintiff is modified so as to award damages in the amount of $118,000 and as modified the judgment is affirmed.

LIMITATION

A limitation is a restriction which defines the time or extent of any particular activity. A limitation, which fixes the extent of the activity, may be made by express words of the contracting parties. It circumscribes the continuance of the activity to be performed in positive and certain terms or by reference to some other event.

In the following case, the security company and the apartment complex had an agreement, evidenced by written instructions, which expressly limited the security objective to the reduction of vandalism, i.e., crimes against property. The plaintiff's position was to try to extend or enlarge the protection duties of the security company to protect persons as well as property. The court found that the plaintiff failed to demonstrate the existence of a duty on the part of the security company which would encompass protection of persons. The security company could have contracted to provide security for persons if it so desired. This express limitation prevented financial loss by the security company. The court also pointed out that if one undertakes an act one has no legal duty to perform, one must, in the performance of that act, exercise ordinary care and may be liable if the failure to exercise ordinary care increased or caused the risk of harm.

DEEDS v. AMERICAN SECURITY

528 N.E. 2d 1308 (1987)

PER CURIAM.

This cause came on to be heard upon the appeal from the Court of Common Pleas of Hamilton County.

Plaintiff-appellant/cross-appellee Suzanne Deeds ("Deeds") has taken the instant appeal from the judgment entered below in favor of defendants-appellees/cross-appellants American Security and Robert Justice on Deeds' complaint seeking damages for Justice's negligent execution of his duties as a security guard.

On appeal, Deeds advances two assignments of error in which she challenges the trial court's refusal to permit expert testimony and to instruct the jury on the duty of a security guard. American Security and Justice have filed a cross-appeal in this matter in which they contend, in a single assignment of error, that the trial court erroneously denied their motion for a directed verdict.

In 1980, American Security was retained by Olde Montgomery Apartments ("Olde Montgomery") to provide security services for its apartment complex. Pursuant to its oral agreement with Olde Montgomery, American Security developed a set of written "on the job instructions" for its employees which set forth patrolling and reporting procedures and which expressly limited its security purpose to the reduction of vandalism.

In the early morning hours of July 29, 1984, Deeds arrived at the complex to visit her fiance and was accosted in the parking lot by a man armed with a knife. Justice, a security guard employed by American Security, was patrolling the parking lot in his car. He stopped his vehicle within five feet of the prone figures of Deeds and her assailant, observed what he perceived to be a consensual sexual act, and advised Deeds and her assailant that behavior of that nature would not be tolerated there. He then departed with the promise that he would return. When Justice returned, Deeds freed herself from her assailant, ran to Justice, and informed him that she had been raped. Upon the assailant's assurances that he and Deeds were acquainted and that the sexual conduct that Justice had witnessed was consensual, Justice permitted the assailant to leave the premises. He then contacted the county authorities with a description of the assailant and the license number of his vehicle. The assailant was subsequently apprehended and convicted.

In May 1985, Deeds instituted the action underlying the instant appeal in which she sought compensatory damages from American Security and its employee, Justice, for physical injuries and psychological trauma suffered as a result of Justice's negligent execution of his duties as a security guard. The matter was tried to a jury, which returned a verdict in favor of American Security and Justice, and the trial court entered judgment accordingly.

On appeal from the judgment entered below, Deeds essentially challenges the trial court's refusal to recognize a specialized duty on the part of a private security guard which would extend to the general public and which would encompass protection of persons as well as property. Thus, in her first assignment of error, Deeds contends that the trial court erred in refusing to permit a security expert to testify to the generally accepted standard of conduct for a private security guard or to express his opinion as to whether Justice, in his conduct with respect to Deeds, adhered to that standard. We find no merit to this contention.

Liability for negligence is predicated upon injury caused by the failure to discharge a duty owed to the injured party. Thus, to sustain an action founded upon negligence, a plaintiff must demonstrate:

(1) that the defendant had a duty, recognized by law, requiring him to conform his conduct to a certain standard for the protection of the plaintiff;
(2) that the defendant failed to conform his conduct to that standard; and
(3) that the defendant's conduct proximately caused the plaintiff to sustain actual loss or damage.

Evid.R. 702 and 704 govern the admissibility of expert testimony and provide as follows:

RULE 702. Testimony By Experts
If scientific, technical, or other specialized knowledge will assist the trier of fact to understand the evidence or to determine a fact in issue, a witness qualified as an expert by

knowledge, skill, experience, training, or education, may testify thereto in the form of an opinion or otherwise.

RULE 704. Opinion of Ultimate Issue

Testimony in the form of an opinion or inference otherwise admissible is not objectionable solely because it embraces an ultimate issue to be decided by the trier of fact.

Thus, Evid.R. 702, in conjunction with Evid.R. 704, permits expert testimony and expert opinion on "an ultimate issue to be decided by the trier of fact" if the witness is qualified as an expert with "specialized knowledge" and if his testimony or opinion will assist or help the trier of fact to understand the evidence or to decide an issue of fact.

In Ohio, neither statutory nor common law imposes a specialized standard of care upon a private security guard in the execution of his duties. Although a duty to protect residents of an apartment complex and their guests from crimes against persons may arise under contract, the agreement between Olde Montgomery and American Security, as reflected in the "on the job instructions" issued by American Security, expressly limited Justice's security objective to the reduction of vandalism, *i.e.*, crimes against property. We, therefore, find that Deeds failed to demonstrate the existence of a duty on the part of Justice in the execution of his employment duties as a security guard which would extend to her or would encompass the protection of her person on the premises. Resultantly, the expert testimony and opinion sought to be elicited by Deeds in the proceedings below as to the generally accepted standard of conduct for a security guard and Justice's adherence to that standard would not have been helpful to the jury, within the meaning of Evid.R. 702, either in its understanding of the evidence presented or in its determination of the factual issues material to Deeds' claim. Thus, we conclude that the trial court properly excluded the proffered expert testimony and, accordingly, overrule Deeds' first assignment of error.

In her second assignment of error, Deeds contends that the trial court erred in its refusal to instruct the jury on the standard of care of a "reasonably prudent security guard." Again, and for the reasons set forth in our disposition of the first assignment of error, we are unpersuaded.

At trial, Deeds requested the court to charge the jury as follows:

A private security guard has a legal duty to protect members of the general public from assaults by third persons. If the security guard fails to act as what a reasonably prudent security guard under similar circumstances, and that failure is the proximate cause of the Plaintiff's injuries then your finding must be for the Plaintiff.

The court refused the requested charge but instructed the jury on the general legal duty to exercise ordinary care to avoid injuring another. The court further charged that one who undertakes an act which he has no legal duty to perform must, in the performance of that act, exercise ordinary care and may be subject to liability to an injured plaintiff for resultant physical harm if his failure to exercise ordinary care increased or caused the risk of harm.

As we determined, *supra*, neither the state legislature nor the state courts have recognized a higher duty on the part of a privately retained security guard to protect members of the general public from offenses against their persons. We, therefore, conclude that the requested instruction, having no basis in law, was unwarranted. Accordingly, we overrule Deeds' second assignment of error.

Although, as we determined *supra*, a privately retained security guard, by virtue of his status, owes no specialized duty to the general public to protect against crimes against their persons, the trial court properly found and so instructed the jury that one who intervenes to aid another has a duty, in the course of his intervention, to exercise ordinary care. Thus, construing the evidence most strongly in favor of Deeds, we determine that reasonable minds could come to differing conclusions on the evidence submitted. We, therefore, conclude that the court below properly overruled defendant's motion for a directed verdict and, accordingly, overrule the sole assignment of error advanced on cross-appeal.

Having thus found the two assignments of error asserted by Deeds and the sole assignment of error advanced by American Security and Justice to be untenable, we affirm the judgment of the court below.

JUDGMENT AFFIRMED.

CASE COMMENT

Here there were written on-the-job instructions which set forth patrolling and reporting procedures and which expressly limited the security purpose to the reduction of vandalism, i.e., crimes against property. The court, therefore, found that the plaintiff failed to demonstrate the existence of a duty on the part of the guard which would encompass the protection of her person.

BANNER CHEVROLET v. WELLS FARGO GUARD SERVICES
508 So. 2d 966 (1987)

WARD, Judge.

Banner Chevrolet contracted with Wells Fargo Guard Services for security services at Banner's car dealership on Chef Menteur Highway in New Orleans. While this contract was in effect, during business hours on June 6, 1983, a car was stolen from Banner's service department. The vehicle was recovered the following day but had sustained damage which Banner repaired at a cost of $411.89. Additionally, Banner paid $245.56 to the car's owner to rent another automobile while his was being repaired. Banner's insurer, Bellefonte Underwriters Insurance Company, partially paid for Banner's losses, and exercising its subrogation rights, joined Banner in suing Wells Fargo for the cost of repairing the car and rental expense. Wells Fargo appeals from a judgment in favor of Banner Chevrolet and Bellefonte Underwriters Insurance Company for $657.45.

Wells Fargo contends that the Trial Court erred in failing to apply the following limitation of liability clause contained in the contract between the parties to relieve Wells Fargo of liability.

> 8. LIABILITY: It is understood that Wells Fargo is not an insurer; that insurance shall be obtained by Client, if any is desired; that the sums payable hereunder to Wells Fargo by Client are based upon the value of services offered and scope of liability undertaken, and such sums are not related to the value of Client's interest protected or of property belonging to Client or to others located on Client's premises. While Wells Fargo will do its best to protect the assets and employees of Client, Wells Fargo makes no warranty, express or implied, that the services it furnishes will avert or prevent occurrences, or the consequences therefrom, which may result in loss or damage to the Client. Client agrees that Wells Fargo shall not be liable for any of Client's losses or damages, irrespective or origin, to person or to property, whether directly or indirectly caused by performance or nonperformance of obligations imposed by this Agreement or by negligent acts or omissions of Wells Fargo, its agents or employees.

A party may legally contract with another party to exclude liability for his negligence if the exculpatory agreement clearly expresses that intent. As long as one's negligence does not cause physical injury to another, contractual provisions are valid to eliminate completely or to partially limit liability for losses due to negligence, but not for losses caused by intentional acts or gross fault. La.C.C. art. 2004; *Carriage Meat Co. v. Honeywell, Inc.*, 442 So.2d 796. The question to be resolved in this appeal is, therefore, whether the actions of Wells Fargo were mere negligence for which Wells Fargo is not liable or whether the actions amounted to intentional misconduct or gross fault which would be outside the scope of the exculpatory clause.

Wells Fargo argues that the conduct of its employee was at worst simple negligence and that the proximate cause of the theft was the negligence of Banner employees. Relying on *Carriage Meat, supra, Haspel v. Rollins Protective Services, Inc.*, 490 So.2d 530, and *Lazybug Shops, Inc. v. American District Telegraph Co.*, 374 So.2d 183, *writ refused*, 376 So.2d 1271, Wells Fargo contends the exclusionary clause is applicable to this case.

Banner responds that the Trial Court correctly held Wells Fargo liable because its fault was gross negligence, greatly below the applicable standard of care, and the exculpatory clause therefore has no effect. Banner further contends that *Haspel* and *Lazybug Shops*, cited by Wells Fargo, are distinguishable from the present case. Banner argues that those cases involved exculpatory clauses which were clear and unambiguous, whereas the clause in the instant case is unclear because of the language that Wells Fargo ". . . will *do its best* to protect the assets and employees of the client." Ambiguous provisions should be construed against the party that prepared the agreement. Wells Fargo drafted the contract at issue here. Therefore, Banner asserts that Wells Fargo had to do its best to protect the client's property before the exculpatory clause applies. Banner argues the "do its best" clause was a condition precedent to the application of the exculpatory provisions; otherwise Wells Fargo could escape liability even if its employees did nothing to protect Banner.

The record before us shows that at the time of the theft from Banner's premises, access to the parking lot adjoining the service department was regulated by a wooden railroad crossing type arm which was raised to permit cars to enter and exit. Beyond this arm was a gate in the chain link fence surrounding the lot which could be folded open like an accordion. Normally, only one of the two sections of the gate was kept open so that the crossing arm blocked the opening in the fence. The gate when half open was kept in place by a 4-by-4 timber so that it would not swing into a fully open position which would leave a gap between the end of the crossing arm and the gate through which a car could be driven. During business hours, gate control was the responsibility of a Wells Fargo employee posted in a gatehouse who kept a log of vehicles leaving the premises and who raised the crossing arm to permit entry and exit. About three hours before the theft, Banner employees had removed the timber which held the gate closed and the timber had not been replaced. The thief was thus able to drive through the open gate and around the end of the crossing arm.

On the day of the theft, Melanie Smith was the Wells Fargo employee in charge of gate control. Her report of the incident states that the unknown thief walked up to her and asked for "Dennis." Smith replied, "Dennis who?" but the thief did not respond and walked on. Approximately thirty minutes later, having found an unattended car in the service department with the keys inside, the thief sped off the lot. Smith reported the theft to her Wells Fargo supervisor who instructed her to call the police.

In determining whether Wells Fargo should be liable for Banner's loss, we emphasize that this case is a claim for damages due to a breach of the contract for security services, and that the defense is denial of breach because a provision of the contract expressly denies that Wells Fargo will be liable for negligent acts of employees. This is not a negligence claim for damages; Wells Fargo's obligations are determined by the terms of the contract, not by the law of negligence. Accordingly, the question is whether the conduct of Wells Fargo's employee constitutes a breach of Wells Fargo's obligation to provide security services or whether the exculpatory clause allows Wells Fargo to avoid financial responsibility for the loss even though caused by negligent acts or omissions of its employee.

The evidence produced at trial established that Melanie Smith failed to properly carry out her gate control duties. Although it was Banner employees who moved and carelessly failed to replace the timber which held the gate closed, Smith was at her post, only a few feet from the gate and the misplaced timber, for three hours while the gate stood open, and she did not close the gate and replace the timber. Additionally, Smith was aware of the presence of an unauthorized individual on Banner's premises for approximately thirty minutes before the theft and did nothing to alert other security personnel or Banner employees. On this record, the Trial Judge correctly found that the conduct of the Wells Fargo employee fell below the standard of conduct for security guards. Clearly, the Wells Fargo employee was negligent.

We do not, however, agree with the Trial Judge's conclusion that the negligence constitutes a breach of the contract for security services, and we hold that the exculpatory clause is effective to relieve Wells Fargo of liability for damages. The clause to which Banner agreed plainly provides that Wells Fargo is not to be liable for losses "irrespective of origin. . . whether directly or indirectly caused by performance or nonperformance of obligations. . . or by negligent acts or omissions. . . ." The facts surrounding Banner's loss indicate that it is within the terms of this clause and therefore Wells Fargo is not liable. We decline to hold as Banner urges that the "do its best" phrase in the exculpatory clause is a condition precedent to the application of the clause. All contracts must be performed in good faith, and in our opinion good faith performance implies that an obligor will do his best. Accordingly, express inclusion of the promise to do one's best in the performance of a contract adds nothing to the contractual undertaking, and we will not interpret the phrase to mean that the exculpatory clause has no effect if Wells Fargo fails to do its best.

Accordingly, the judgment of the Trial Court is reversed. All costs to be paid by the parties jointly.

REVERSED.

CASE COMMENT

A limitation of liability clause in the contract relieved the security company of liability. Note the phrase that the security company "is not an insurer," and that the client agreed that the security company would not be liable for any of the client's losses or damages irrespective of origin. The court held that one party may legally contract with another party to exclude liability for negligence if the exculpatory agreement clearly expressed that intent.

DISCLAIMER

A disclaimer is a repudiation or denial of a claim or a refusal to accept responsibility beyond what is specifically contracted for or stated. This is important because it is a limitation on the liability of the disclaimant. The following two cases point out that one party to a contract can be relieved of liability by disclaimer language conspicuously printed on the agreement between the parties. Also pointed out is that if the complaining party had read the contract or if they could have read it, they would have known of the limitation; the fact they didn't was immaterial. This reinforces the notion that parties can make a valid contract which exempts one of the parties from liability.

NEW ENGLAND WATCH CORP. v. HONEYWELL, INC.
416 N.E.2d 1010 (1981)

Before GRANT, KASS and NOLAN, JJ.

RESCRIPT.

A motion for summary judgment for the defendant was allowed. There was no error because there was no genuine issue of material fact, and the defendant was entitled to judgment as matter of law.

In count one of its complaint, the plaintiff alleged the defendant's breach of contract and warranties under an agreement for burglar alarm protection and in count two, the defendant's negligence. 1. In boldface type in the contract, the defendant disclaims liability for breach of the warranties of merchantability and fitness. Even if, arguendo, this contract is within the article of the Uniform Commercial Code (Code) governing sales, G.L. c. 106, § 2-101, et. seq. (and we do not so decide), the defendant is relieved of liability by its disclaimer language, which is conspicuously printed on the agreement entered into by the parties. General Laws c. 106, § 2-316. Whatever other terminology may be used to describe the burglar alarm system which is the subject of the contract, no one can seriously contend that this subject matter constitutes "consumer goods" as that term is used in G.L. c. 106, § 2-316A, inserted by St. 1970, c. 880, which operates to limit the right to disclaim liability on warranties. See G.L. c. 106, § 9-109(1), as appearing in St.1979, c. 512, § 7, which defines "consumer goods" as goods which "are used or bought for use primarily for personal, family or household purposes." 2. The contract also disclaims responsibility "for any losses ... even if due to contractor's negligent performance or failure to perform any obligation under the agreement." This disclaimer is clearly sufficient to protect the defendant from claims of negligence. A party may "make a valid contract exempting the defendant from liability to it for injuries resulting from its negligence or that of its employees." 3. The language of the disclaimer of liability is sufficiently broad to cover the failure of the alarm system which occurred. 4. As the plaintiff's argument as to c. 93A, § 11, is made for the first time on appeal, we do not consider it.

Judgment affirmed.

FLORENCE v. MERCHANTS CENTRAL ALARM CO., INC.
412 N.E. 2d 1317 (1980)

OPINION OF THE COURT MEMORANDUM.

The order of the Appellate Division should be affirmed, 73 A.D.2d 869, 423 N.Y.S.2d 663, with costs.

The contract provided that "The sole duty of the Contractor is to notify the Police Department and the Subscriber by calling on the telephone if a signal is received in the Central Station which might indicate illegal entry" (par. 4) and that "the Contractor assumes no responsibility whatsoever for the condition of said Police Alarm transmitter or for any loss sustained by the Subscriber through burglary or through any other cause, during the period within which the contract is in force. It is agreed that the Contractor is not an insurer and that the payments hereinbefore named are based solely on the value of the service described and, in case of failure to perform such service and a resulting loss, the Contractor's liability hereunder shall be limited to and fixed at the sum of Fifty Dollars ($50.00) as liquidated damages and not as a penalty, and this liability shall be exclusive" (par. 7).

Despite its erroneous reference to "liquidated damages", defendant's contract, unlike the sprinkler contract involved in *Melodee Lane Lingerie Co. v. American Dist. Tel. Co.*, 218 N.E.2d 661, is not one "affecting real property" or for "services rendered in connection with the construction, maintenance and repair of real property" within the meaning of § 5-323 of the General Obligations Law. Defendant was, therefore, free to limit its liability without offering a greater liability for a greater charge, subject only to the requirement that the limitation be not so obscured (as, for example a baggage check not in usual contract form) as to make it probable that it would escape plaintiffs' attention. Here the type in which the contract was printed is uniform in size and contained entirely on the face of one sheet of paper, and there are no paragraph headings or subtitles that could mislead a reader. If plaintiffs read the contract at all they were aware of the limitation, and the law's teaching since *Pimpinello v. Swift & Co.* (170 N.E. 530) has been that if they *could* read it, the fact that they did not is immaterial, absent evidence of fraud.

In this commercial setting, where the language of the limitation is clear, there is no necessity to "resort to a magnifying glass and lexicon", *no* governing statute and no special relationship between the parties that would warrant relieving plaintiffs of their contract. The Appellate Division's direction of summary judgment for plaintiffs in the amount of $50 was, therefore, correct.

Order affirmed.

5

Alarms

Alarms are an integral part of the overall loss prevention plan implemented by the private security manager. In today's electronic world, there are alarms for myriad situations, locations, and conditions. And in today's litigious society, there are countless lawsuits concerning the nonperformance of, or malfunctioning of, alarms or alarm systems counted on to prevent loss.

Cases in this chapter examine several areas of alarm law that should be of interest to the security manager who either has, or is interested in getting, an alarm system. Limitation of liability clauses, or disclaimers, are usually inserted in the alarm contract and favor the vendor. In this situation, one party to the contract relieves themselves of liability in the event of negligence or failure of performance. These limitations are usually upheld under normal negligence situations, absent special conditions such as gross negligence or willful or wanton conduct on the part of the vendor. One jurisdiction, which had held that gross negligence could be the subject of a limitation of liability clause, has abandoned that position in favor of public policy precluding exemption from liability for grossly negligent acts. Needless to say, willful and wanton misconduct is different than negligence. Thus a lawsuit may not be barred via the usual exculpatory language.

Having an alarm system adequate to do the job is the goal of the security director. Intentionally recommending and installing an alarm system known to be inadequate for the job subjects the vendor, whose expertise is relied on, to a cause of action. Likewise, intentionally misrepresenting particular features and capabilities of an alarm system renders void an exculpatory cause. One cannot benefit from one's own fraud.

Alarm companies are expected to exercise reasonable care in supervising their employees. This is to prevent employees from disconnecting the system and then stealing goods from the supposedly protected area. The employer's duty to supervise attaches when employees are privileged by their employment to enter another's property. Liability may also attach to the alarm company when a terminated employee returns to an area he has worked on and steals possessions, if that employee was negligently employed. The intervening criminal act of burglary may not relieve the alarm company of its contractual obligation to repair and maintain the alarm system.

Not to be overlooked as vehicles for legal redress are consumer protection acts, deceptive and unfair trade practice laws, and warranties. A sample false alarm ordinance can be found in Appendix 5.

LIMITATION OF LIABILITY CLAUSES

Contracts which provide alarm system services may contain limitation of liability clauses on the part of the provider or lessor. These exculpatory clauses, or disclaimers, have been for the most part valid and enforceable, and claims for the breach of these contracts have been dismissed.

New England Watch Corp. v. Honeywell, Inc., 416 N.E.2d 1010 (1981) and *Florence v. Merchants Central Alarm Co., Inc.*, 412 N.E.2d 1317 (1980) examine the limitations of liability for negligence. They are found in the Disclaimer section of Chapter 4, page 159.

Exculpatory clauses, or limitations on liability, relieve one party to the contract of major damages. Alarm companies are not insurers. If they were, they would have to charge a great deal more. For plain negligence, these limiting clauses are generally valid where the public interest is not adversely affected or where a higher degree of negligence is involved.

GROSS NEGLIGENCE

In the following case, an alarm system installation, service, and monitoring contract was executed. The contract contained a typical limitation of liability clause. Included in the services to be provided was "guard response." The court, upon reflection, felt compelled to preclude gross negligence as a subject for a limitation of liability clause.

HANOVER INSURANCE COMPANY v. D & W CENTRAL STATION
ALARM, CO., INC.
560 N.Y.S.2D 293 (1990)

KASSAL, Justice.

This appeal calls upon the Court to clarify the law with respect to limitation of liability clauses in contracts for the provision of burglary alarm services and related protection. For the reasons that follow, defendant-appellant may not rely upon such a contractual provision to limit its liability for acts of alleged gross negligence, and the IAS part properly denied its motion for summary judgment.

Plaintiff, Hanover Insurance Company ("Hanover"), brings this action as subrogee and/ or assignee of NBK Company Manufacturing Jewelers ("NBK") which, on February 18, 1986, entered into a written agreement with defendant-appellant D& W Central Station Alarm Co., Inc. ("D&W"), pursuant to which D & W agreed to install, service, and monitor a burglary alarm system at NBK's premises. Included in the services to be provided under the contract was "guard response".

Subsequent to D & W's installation of the burglary alarm equipment in NBK's premises, and at some point between the evening of December 26 and the morning of December 27, 1986, NBK's premises were burglarized. The record establishes that D & W received an alarm signal from the subject premises on December 26, 1986 at 10:47 p.m., and that a second alarm signal was received at 12:38 a.m. on December 27. The record further establishes that a guard dispatched from D & W's central office in response to the alarm signals arrived at NBK's premises at 1:54 a.m. and departed therefrom at 2:15 a.m. on December 27. In a handwritten and signed report, that guard stated that the reason he left without investigating the alarm condition or otherwise acting upon it was that he could not gain entry into the building and, when he called D & W to so inform them, he was told to "forget that assignment and go on another guard run".

The earliest report of police notification was recorded by Sergeant Jeffrey Miller who received a call at 5:02 a.m. on December 27, 1986. Also contained in the record is a report prepared by North Atlantic Security Alarm, Inc. ("NASA"), which monitored NBK's premises on television equipment, stating that the burglars were viewed on camera at approximately 4:44 a.m. on the morning of the 27th, and that NASA notified the police. By the time that Sergeant Miller arrived at the premises at approximately 5:03 a.m., the burglars had escaped, and they have not been apprehended to date. NBK, plaintiff Hanover's subrogor, sustained losses totalling $243,000.

The contract governing D & W's provision of burglary alarm services to NBK contained a limitation of liability clause stating as follows:

> The parties agree that the alarm system is not designed or guaranteed to prevent loss by burglary, theft, and other illegal acts of third parties, or loss by fire. If, notwithstanding the terms of this agreement, there should arise any liability on the part of the lessor, as a result of burglary, theft, hold-up, equipment failure, fire, smoke, or any cause whatsoever, regardless of whether or not such loss, damage or personal injury was caused by or contributed to by lessor's negligent performance or failure to perform any obligation under this agreement, such liability shall be limited to an amount equal to six (6) times the monthly payment by lessee at the time such liability is fixed, or to the sum of $250.00, whichever is greater.

It is well settled that exculpatory clauses in security alarm contracts "have been repeatedly enforced by the courts of this State, and claims for breach of these contracts have been dismissed, where the plaintiff has sought to recover damages for losses sustained as a result of crimes such as burglaries. However, to the extent that such agreements "purport to grant exemption for liability for willful or grossly negligent acts, they have been viewed as wholly void".

This Court, relying upon dictum in *Feldman Furs, Inc. v. Jewelers Protection Services, Ltd.*, 134 A.D.2d 171, held that gross negligence could properly be the subject of a limitation of liability clause. Further reflection compels us to abandon this course in favor of sound public policy grounds which preclude exemption from liability for grossly negligent acts.

In contrast to *Feldman Furs, Inc. v. Jewelers Protection Services, Ltd., supra*, the record before us establishes that triable issues of fact exist regarding whether D & W was grossly negligent in its response or failure to respond to alarm signals transmitted from NBK's premises. Among the matters to be considered in this regard are D & W's failure to notify the police upon receipt of three alarm signals in the span of four hours, and the decision by a member of the D & W staff to direct the guard who responded to "forget the assignment" because he encountered difficulty in entering the building.

Accordingly, the order, Supreme Court, New York County (Harold Baer, J.), entered October 22, 1989, which granted defendant's motion to reargue and, upon reargument, adhered to its prior determination denying defendant's motion for summary judgment, should be affirmed, without costs.

Order, Supreme Court, New York County, (Harold Baer, Jr., J.), entered on October 22, 1989, unanimously affirmed, without costs and without disbursements.

CASE COMMENT

In this case, the court considered the alarm company's failure to respond to alarm signals, its failure to notify the police upon receipt of these alarm signals, and the decision by a staff member to direct the responding guard to forget the assignment. The court felt that sound public policy precludes exemption from liability for grossly negligent acts.

WILLFUL OR WANTON MISCONDUCT

The previous case showed a distinction between negligence and gross negligence. The difference is one of degree. The following case discusses the difference between willful and wanton misconduct and negligence. In this case, the defendant installed sensitive listening devices in various parts of the plaintiff's shop. The defendant was to provide continuous central station monitoring during off hours so it could detect any sounds of a break-in and immediately alert the plaintiff and police. Evidence at the trial showed that although the burglars engaged in a great deal of noisy activity, it took the defendant about one and a half hours to recognize and report it. The monitoring employee had turned the sound down and was finally alerted by an independent perimeter alarm.

TESSLER AND SON, INC. v. SONITROL SECURITY SYSTEMS OF NORTHERN
NEW JERSEY, INC.
497 A.2D 530 (1985)

COHEN, J.A.D.

Plaintiff operates an auto body repair shop in Newark. Defendant installs and services burglar alarm systems. One of its systems was installed in plaintiff's premises. After an undetected break-in, plaintiff sued defendant for its losses, charging breach of contract, negligence and "gross and wanton negligence." A second count was abandoned at trial.

The break-in occurred during the term of the third annual contract between the parties. At the beginning of the first contract, defendant sold and installed sensitive listening equipment in various parts of plaintiff's shop at a cost to plaintiff of $800. Defendant then provided continuous central station monitoring of the listening equipment during plaintiff's off hours so that it could detect any sounds of a break-in and immediately alert plaintiff and the police. The monitoring charge was $50 per month. Plaintiff additionally paid the telephone company's charges for a trunk line connecting its premises with the monitoring station.

The evidence at trial permitted the conclusion that the break-in occurred about one and a half hours before defendant recognized and reported it; that the burglars first broke a substantial amount of sky-light glass and then gained entry by smashing through a block wall with a sledge hammer; that a wall of metal shelves holding paint cans was thrown over and that a good deal of noisy activity took place over a long period of time in the shop. Defendant's monitoring employee failed to detect the break-in because she turned down the sound volume on the listening equipment to avoid hearing sounds she considered non hostile, including the barking of plaintiff's guard dog, which defendant's employees had previously adjudged overexcitable. She was finally awakened to the true situation only when an independent perimeter alarm was set off by the burglars' raising on overhead door to drive away a customer's Cadillac.

In answer to the court's special verdict questions, the jury found that defendant failed to perform its contract obligations reasonably, diligently and competently; that losses of the nature incurred by plaintiff were foreseeable as a result of a contract breach, and that losses were incurred by plaintiff as a result of defendant's failure to perform. The jury was not asked if defendant was guilty of the complaint's charge of "gross and wanton negligence." The jury was not asked to fix the quantum of damages. Instead, the court entered judgment of $250, for reasons which occasion plaintiff's appeal.

Each of the three yearly contracts between the parties contained a provision limiting defendant's liability to $250. Among other things, they said:

> If Sonitrol should be found liable for loss or damage due to the failure of its services in any respect, even if due to Sonitrol's negligence, its liability shall be limited to a sum equal to ten percent of the annual monitoring charge for the premises or $250 whichever is greater, as liquidated damages and not as a penalty. . . .

The first two yearly contracts were accompanied, however, by a separate guarantee. It promised that, if there was an undetected and unreported forcible entry, defendant would make good plaintiff's losses and damages up to $5,000. Partway through the second contract, defendant revoked the guarantee. When it came time to sign the third contract, plaintiff asked for the elimination of the provision limiting defendant's liability in view of the withdrawal of the $5,000 guarantee. Defendant declined to remove the provision, and plaintiff nevertheless signed the contract. It was satisfied with defendant's services and was mindful of its own $800 investment in equipment, which it was afraid would be rendered useless by ending defendant's services.

The clause purports to be a liquidated damage clause, justified, according to its own language, by the parties agreement that Sonitrol is not an insurer. . . that the amounts payable to Sonitrol . . . are based on the value of the services and. . . it is impractical, if not impossible, to fix the actual damages. . . .

In real effect, however, it is an exculpatory clause, because it denies liability for all but a nominal amount of damages. The limit of $250 is obviously not the result of an effort to fairly estimate plaintiff's likely damages from a break-in. Defendant's service cost $800 at the outset and $600 per year plus telephone company charges. It is unlikely that a business would spend those amounts to protect $250.

The trial court held that the contractual limitation on liability was enforceable and, in the circumstances revealed by the proofs, limited plaintiff's damages. We agree. Exculpatory clauses like this one are valid where they do not adversely affect the public interest, where the exculpated party is not under a public duty to perform, as in the case of a public utility or common carrier, and where the contract does not grow out of unequal bargaining power or is otherwise unconscionable. These principles have grown out of cases involving burglar alarms, fire alarms, and lease provisions assigning to an industrial or commercial tenant the risk of loss of its goods however caused. Such a clause will not be enforced in the case of a residential apartment lease where suitable living quarters are at a premium and unequal bargaining power results, *Kuzmiak v. Brookchester*, 111 A.2d 425, or where the limitation clause is hidden in a provision ostensibly conferring a benefit on the buyer of fire protection equipment.

Plaintiff charged defendant, not only with breach of contract and negligence, but also with "gross and wanton negligence." The present contract clause limits damages recoverable for its failures "in any respect, even if due to Sonitrol's negligence." The clause thus applies to a default in any aspect of Sonitrol's service, and it is not rendered inoperative if the default was negligently caused. The clause does not purport to limit liability for willful and wanton misconduct. Although plaintiff's complaint is inarticulately drawn, we read it to charge willful and wanton misconduct in addition to a high degree of negligence.

We hold that an exculpatory clause may expressly excuse or limit liability for negligent contract performance, but that such a clause does not operate to bar a claim of willful and wanton misconduct.

In *Kuzmiak v. Brookchester*, 111 A.2d 425, this court stated in *dictum* that, although a promise not to sue for simple negligence may be valid, an attempted exemption from liability for intentional tort or willful act or gross negligence is generally declared to be void. In *Swisscraft Novelty Co. v. Alad Realty Corp.*, 274 A.2d 59, this court quoted the *Kuzmiak dictum* and held that an exculpatory lease clause that was sufficient to bar damage suit for lessor negligence would not bar a complaint alleging willful and wanton misconduct or gross negligence.

Willful and wanton misconduct is different in kind from negligence. It is defined in *McLaughlin v. Rova Farms, Inc.*, 266 A.2d 284:

> It must appear that the defendant with knowledge of existing conditions, and conscious from such knowledge that injury will probably or likely result from his conduct, and with reckless indifference to the consequences, consciously and intentionally does some wrongful act or omits to discharge some duty which produces the injurious result.

Thus, a contract clause that bars suit for negligent failure to perform contract responsibilities does not bar suit for willful and wanton misconduct. Gross negligence, however, is different from negligence only in degree. There is no reason why that difference should have an operative effect in the circumstances of this case. The difference has no vitality under the comparative negligence statute.

We hold that an exculpatory clause which bars suit for negligent performance of contractual duties also bars suit for very negligent or grossly negligent performance.

In other jurisdictions, the better authorities support our views. In *Peacock's, Inc. v. South Central Bell*, 455 So.2d 694, a telephone company tariff which limited liability for negligent performance did not bar suit charging the company with willful misconduct in connecting a burglar alarm system. In *Morgan Co. v. Minnesota Min. & Mfg. Co.*, 246 N.W.2d 443, an exculpatory clause in a burglar alarm contract which excused negligent nonperformance did not bar suit charging intentional misconduct and "willful and wanton negligence." The court did not define the latter term. In *Shaer Shoe Corp. v. Granite State Alarm, Inc.*, 262 A.2d 285, a sprinkler system contract which limited liability for "willful default or negligence" was held effective to bar suit for both causes of action.

In *Lenny's Inc. v. Allied Sign Erectors, Inc.*, 318 S.E.2d 140, a provision in a lease of a fire detection system limited damages for negligent performance. The provision was held ineffective in a case of willful and wanton conduct. In *Carriage Meat Co., Inc. v. Honeywell, Inc.*, 442 So.2d 796, a contract to monitor the temperature of a commercial freezer limited liability for negligent nonperformance. The clause was held not to apply to willful failure to perform or other deliberate disregard of duty.

Florida has held that an exculpatory clause in a burglar alarm contract barring suit for negligent performance also bars suit charging gross negligence, but not intentional tort. One federal court, applying Pennsylvania law, has ruled the other way in a case factually like this one. *Douglas W. Randall, Inc. v. AFA Protective Systems*, 516 F.Supp. 1122, aff'd 688 F.2d 820.

The trial court ruled that plaintiff's evidence, viewed most favorably and indulgently, was insufficient to show "reckless disregard of consequences." We agree that there was insufficient evidence for the jury reasonably to have found willful and wanton misconduct. Defendant's conduct was, at worst, negligent misjudgment in interpreting the sounds emanating from plaintiff's premises during the break-in. For that reason, the trial court was correct in limiting plaintiff's recovery to the amount permitted by the contract in cases of defendant's negligence.

Affirmed.

CASE COMMENT

The appellate court affirmed the trial court's holding that the defendant's limitation on liability was enforceable, but such a clause does not operate to bar a claim 0of willful and wanton misconduct. The trial court ruled that the plaintiff's evidence was insufficient to show willful and wanton misconduct, and the defendant's conduct was, at worst, negligent misjudgment in interpreting sounds.

INADEQUATE ALARM SYSTEMS

The purchaser or lessee of an alarm system spends money to detect a problem and have an adequate response that prevents or limits loss. Each location has its own particular problems and situations. In the following case, the alarm company was made aware of a previous fire caused by an electric sign. The alarm company installed a fire detection system and represented that it was adequate and would work sufficiently to prevent damage like that suffered in the previous fire. On numerous occasions, the smoke sensor alarm malfunctioned and the alarm company was called to make repairs. Each time a repair was made, the manager was assured that the system would work to detect a fire before substantial damage occurred. A new fire occurred and caused extensive damage before fire fighting equipment arrived.

LENNY'S, INC. v. ALLIED SIGN ERECTORS, INC.
318 S.E.2d 140 (1984)

SHULMAN, Presiding Judge.

Appellant Lenny's, Inc., leased a fire detection system from appellee Rollins Protective Services Company ("Rollins"). Thereafter, an electric sign purchased from defendant Allied Sign Erectors, Inc. (not a party to this appeal) caught fire and, in spite of the new fire detection system, caused extensive damage to Lenny's premises before fire fighting units could arrive. Appellant Early American Insurance Company paid Lenny's approximately $500,000 for a portion of the fire loss. Lenny's also suffered business losses for which it had no insurance coverage. Appellants filed suit against Rollins and Allied Sign Erectors , Inc., seeking damages alternatively for breach of contract, breach of warranty, and negligence. In an amendment to the complaint, appellants alleged that Rollins willfully and wantonly installed a system at Lenny's that they knew was inadequate and that such action constituted gross negligence on the part of Rollins. Rollins filed a motion for summary judgment seeking to limit its liability to $250 pursuant to a liquidated damages clause in the lease agreement. This appeal is from the grant of that motion.

Appellants submitted the affidavit of Leonard Odom, the manager of Lenny's, who averred that Rollins' agent was made well aware of a previous fire that had been caused by the electric sign purchased from Allied Sign Erectors. Odom stated that the agent represented that the fire detection system Rollins installed at Lenny's was adequate and would work sufficiently to prevent damage like that suffered in the earlier fire. The smoke sensor alarm malfunctioned on numerous occasions and Rollins was continually called upon to make repairs. Each time a repair was made, Odom was assured that the system would work to detect a fire before substantial damage to the premises occurred.

Appellants also submitted a certified copy of the affidavit of a former Rollins employee, which affidavit was given in a case other than the one before this court on appeal. The former employee averred that Rollins taught its salesmen to "sell" the protective service that provided a minimal level of protection and to make the sale "no matter what." He further averred that the bulk of Rollins' profit comes from the installation fee charge to each customer when the system is delivered and that this fee is substantially the same no matter what type of system is installed.

Appellants claim that representatives of Rollins fraudulently induced Lenny's representatives to sign the lease agreement by misrepresenting the system's capabilities in general and its suitability for Lenny's in particular. Rollins directs our attention to the following clause in its lease agreement with Lenny's: "This Agreement and Exhibit 'a' contain the entire understanding of the parties and may not be modified or amended except in writing signed by the President of Rollins in Atlanta, Georgia." Rollins argues that this "integration clause" prevents Lenny's from relying on oral representations made by Rollins' agent. However, such a clause "can have no bearing in a case where fraud in procuring the signing of the instrument is the issue." *Williams v. Toomey* 159 S.E. 866. See also *Chestnut v. Al Means Ford, Inc.*, 149 S.E.2d 410. "Where the purchaser of personal property has been injured by the false and fraudulent representations of the seller as to the subject matter thereof, he ordinarily has an election whether to rescind the contract, return the article and sue in tort for fraud and deceit, or whether to affirm the contract, retain the article and seek damages resulting from the fraudulent misrepresentation." *Bob Maddox Dodge v. McKie*, 270 S.E.2d 690. "'Fraud may not be presumed, but, being in itself subtle, slight circumstances may be sufficient to carry conviction of its existence.'"

Therefore, we hold that the evidence in the record is sufficient to establish a question of fact with regard to Lenny's allegation that its representative was fraudulently induced by Rollins' agent to sign the lease agreement in question. It follows that the trial court erred in granting summary judgment in favor of Rollins, thereby precluding consideration of this issue by a jury.

Rollins successfully argued at the trial level that appellants had no cause of action based on the contract itself for any amount exceeding $250 because of a clause in the lease agreement limiting Rollins' liability to $250 in case of loss or damage resulting from the failure of operation, defective operation, or the improper installation or servicing of the system. However, appellants have alleged that Rollins acted willfully and wantonly in failing to fully inform Lenny's of the nature of the protection afforded by the system that was leased and that Rollins knew the system was inadequate for Lenny's needs. Appellants further claim that that action on the part of Rollins demonstrated a willful disregard for the safety of persons and property. A clause in a contract limiting one's liability for negligent acts does not serve to limit one's liability for willful or wanton conduct.

Therefore, appellants' "allegations charging the defendant with willful and wanton conduct resulting in damage to Lenny's premises are sufficient to carry the case to a jury. Accordingly, the trial court erred in granting Rollins' motion for summary judgment with regard to the foregoing issue.

Finally, appellants attempted to sustain a count against Rollins sounding in tort separate from the fraud and gross negligence counts that were based on the lease agreement itself.

A single act or course of conduct may constitute not only a breach of contract but an independent tort as well, if in addition to violating a contract obligation it also violates a duty owed to plaintiff independent of contract to avoid harming it. Such an independent harm may be found because of the relationship between the parties, or because of defendant's calling or because of the nature of the harm . . . However, not all breaches of contract are also independent torts: 'where defendant's negligence ends merely in nonperformance of the contract and where defendant is not under any recognized duty to act apart from contract, the courts generally still see no duty to act affirmatively except the duty based on—and limited by—defendant's consent.'. . . Even this formulation, however, is limited by the rule that where nonperformance or inaction is of such a type as to create an unreasonable risk of harm to others, even nonperformance of a contract duty—nonfeasance—may give rise to a tort action. *Orkin Exterminating Co. v. Stevens.* 203 S.E.2d 587.

In the present case it is alleged that the agent from Rollins knew of the previous fire caused by the electric sign but that he intentionally recommended a fire system he knew to be inadequate for Lenny's while representing to Lenny's representative that the premises were fully protected. These allegations, combined with Rollins' expertise in this field, may give rise to an independent tort. Whether such a relationship existed between the parties such as that which would authorize the finding of an independent harm is a question of fact to be resolved by a jury. Additional issues for a jury's determination are whether Rollins' conduct amounted to "nonfeasance" or "misfeasance" and if it was nonfeasance, whether it was of such magnitude as to create an unreasonable risk of harm to others. Thus, appellant's count sounding in tort cannot be summarily dismissed.

Inasmuch as questions of fact remain for consideration by a jury, it was error for the trial court to summarily limit Rollins' liability to $250 and to grant its motion for summary judgment.

Judgment reversed.

CASE COMMENT

In this case, fraudulent inducement, willful and wanton failure to inform of the nature of the protection provided, and knowledge that the system was inadequate for the needs, precluded summary judgment. A limitation of liability clause for negligent acts did not limit liability for willful and wanton conduct. In this case, the allegations that the alarm company representative knew of the previous fire, intentionally recommended an inadequate system, and represented that the premises were fully protected, coupled with the company's expertise, allowed for the matter to be considered by a jury.

INTENTIONAL MISREPRESENTATION

In the following case, the trial court granted summary judgment for the defendant on all three counts of plaintiff's complaint seeking damages for loss resulting from the failure of the burglar alarm system. Summary judgment was based on the exculpatory clause even though contracts which relieve a party of liability for their own negligence are generally looked upon with disfavor. Note that the first count alleged intentional misrepresentation in that the security system would meet the Underwriter's Laboratory AA requirements.

MANKAP ENTERPRISES, INC. v. WELLS FARGO ALARM SERVICES
427 So.2d 332 (1983)

FERGUSON, Judge.

Appellant filed a three-count complaint seeking to recover damages for loss resulting from failure of a burglar alarm system. The first count was based on intentional misrepresentation as to a particular feature or capability of the system; count two was based on negligence; the third count alleged unconscionability of an exculpatory clause in the contract. After filing an answer generally denying the complaint, appellee, relying on a line of recently decided cases, moved for and was granted a summary judgment. Appellant's affidavit,[1] filed in opposition to the motion, was uncontroverted.

We affirm the summary judgment as to count two on authority of *L. Luria & Sons, Inc. v. Alarmtec International Corp.*, 384 So.2d 947 and *Ace Formal Wear, Inc. v. Baker Protective Service*, 416 So.2d 8 which hold that although exculpatory contracts which relieve a party of liability for his own negligence are generally looked upon with disfavor, they will be upheld where the intention (of one who installs burglar alarm systems) is clear and unequivocal.

We also affirm the summary judgment as to count three on authority of *Continental Video Corp. v. Honeywell, Inc.*, 422 So.2d 35, which holds that an exculpatory clause of a contract for installation of burglar alarms which provides that installer would be held harmless for losses caused by improper operation of the system was not invalid and unenforceable on grounds of inequity in bargaining positions between the parties.

As to count one, we reverse. The authorities cited in appellee's brief, and apparently relied upon by the trial court, are not controlling. None of the cited burglar alarm cases dealt with intentional misrepresentation on the part of the seller. The law is settled that a party cannot contract against liability for his own fraud in order to exempt him from liability for an intentional tort, and any such exculpatory clauses are void as against public policy.

Because there are material issues of fact on the issue of misrepresentation, summary judgment was inappropriate.

Affirmed in part, reversed in part, and remanded for further proceedings.

CASE COMMENT

The appellate court reversed the summary judgment granted by the trial court for count one because there were material issues of fact on the issue of misrepresentation. The court pointed out that the law is settled. One cannot contract against liability for one's own fraud. Any such exculpatory language is void as against public policy.

NEGLIGENT SUPERVISION

In the case of *International Distributing Corporation v. American District Telegraph Company*, 569 F.2d 136 (1977) (discussed in Chapter 1), the alarm company provided burglar alarm service to the distributing company. The allegations were that two of the alarm company's employees stole thousands of dollars worth of liquor. The alarm company was to provide central monitoring and an employee response; the distributing company provided keys to the building. In discussing negligent supervision, the court noted that employers have the duty to supervise those employees who are privileged

---

[1] The affidavit, containing declarations of appellant's president, stated that appellant was assured by Wells Fargo that the installed security system would meet the Underwriter's Laboratory AA requirements and standards, a grade designed specifically for premises which require a higher degree of security (banks, jewelry stores). Attached thereto was a copy of two Underwriter's Laboratory Certificates issued to appellant by Wells Fargo.

to enter another's property, and the alarm company may not have exercised reasonable care in supervising its employees.

CRIMINAL ACT OF FORMER EMPLOYEE

In this case, the alarm company contracted to install a burglar alarm system in the plaintiff's home. The employee who did the installation was either a wanted felon or a person with a long felony record. When the work was done and the employment terminated, the former employee returned to the house, disconnected the alarm, and stole the possessions of the plaintiff. Should the alarm company be held liable for the plaintiff's loss as a result of a criminal act committed by the alarm company's former employee? The court believed that there might be liability.

McGUIRE v. ARIZONA PROTECTION AGENCY

609 P.2d 1080 (1980)

MATTHEW W. BOROWIEC, Judge.

The sole issue to be decided in this case is whether defendant, Arizona Protection Agency, Inc., can be held liable for plaintiff's loss as a result of a criminal act of defendant's former employee, committed after termination of the employment. We believe there may be liability.

The facts sufficient for our purposes, pieced together from the pleadings, the affidavit of defendant's vice-president accompanying the motion to dismiss, and plaintiff's opposition to the motion, are: Defendant contracted to install a burglar alarm system in plaintiff's home; the person defendant employed to do the work was either a wanted felon or a person with a long felony record; and after the work was completed and the employment terminated, the former employee returned to plaintiff's home, disconnected the alarm system and stole plaintiff's possessions, damaging plaintiff in the claimed sum of $371,800.00. Plaintiff alleges defendant was negligent in the ". . . employment and maintaining . . ." of this employee.

We find no case in point or a different rule pronounced by our appellate courts or legislature; therefore we look to the Restatement of Law.

An act or an omission may be negligent if the actor realizes or should realize that it involves an unreasonable risk of harm to another through the conduct of the other or a third person which is intended to cause harm, even though such conduct is criminal. Restatement 2d of Torts, § 302B.

The fact that the felon was at one time the employee of defendant does not prevent the application of the Restatement principle, supra. Comments to Restatement 2d of Torts, § 302B deal both with the conduct of employees of and strangers to the party found to be negligent.

In light of the sensitive nature of the work and the temptations and opportunity attendant thereto, defendant owed a duty to plaintiff to employ a responsible and trustworthy person, without a criminal proclivity that could reasonably be determined, to install the alarm system.

"An especial temptation and opportunity for criminal misconduct, brought about by the defendant, will call upon him to take precautions against it." Prosser on Torts, Fourth Edition, § 33, Page 174.

A case of like hue and not so dissimilar to ours that we cannot gain therefrom is this court's decision in *Central Alarm of Tucson v. Ganem*, 567 P.2d 1203. In that case, defendant Central Alarm was held to be negligent for the burglary loss at plaintiff's pawn shop as a result of the criminal conduct of a third person unknown to defendant, who gained access to plaintiff's pawn shop and deactivated the alarm system installed by defendant. This was made possible by defendant leaving a key to the alarm system "... where an unauthorized person could obtain access to the controls of the system and deactivate it ..." The burglar in Central Alarm was not a former employee of defendant, but this is of little moment. In our case, defendant may have provided the key to the burglar by employing one of his character and propensity, and giving him access to plaintiff's home.

Unquestionably, defendant may be found negligent in knowingly employing a wanted felon or a felon with a long record to install the burglar alarm. If it could be negligence to employ such a person, then it could be negligence where this is not known to the employer but should have been known, especially in light of the sensitive nature of the work, the temptations inherent therein and the opportunities presented. The risk is there and the possible loss is certainly foreseeable.

It remains to be seen in the development of the facts whether the surreptitious entry and theft was the result of the employment of the felon; whether the felon's background projected the risk; and whether defendant had any knowledge of this background or could have acquired such knowledge. It remains to be determined whether defendant took the precautions a reasonable man would be required to take under the circumstances.

Reversed and remanded.

CASE COMMENT

In reversing this case, the court took note of the sensitive nature of the work and the temptations and opportunities attendant with the work. The court discussed the duty of the defendant to employ a responsible and trustworthy person to install an alarm system when it brings about an especial temptation and opportunity for criminal misconduct. An alarm company should take reasonable steps to determine the criminal proclivity of its employees. The court also pointed out that it could be negligence not to know the background of an employee, if it should have been known, especially in light of the sensitive nature of the work.

UNFORESEEABLE INTERVENING CRIMINAL ACT

In this case, a shop owner's burglar alarm was damaged by lightning. He contracted to have the alarm repaired and maintained. The owner claims the repairs were negligently made leaving him with a defective alarm system, including a test light indicating the system was working and operative when it was not. A burglary occurred during this malfunction, and the owner claimed he would not have suffered the loss but for the defective alarm. The alarm company challenged this under the theory that burglary is an unforeseeable intervening act which breaks the chain of causation. The cause of the loss is not the negligence but the burglary.

McCORD v. SENTRY PROTECTION, INC.
427 So.2d 1132 (1983)

COWART, Judge.

Can an owner who suffers a loss by burglary while a burglar alarm is malfunctioning recover the loss from the burglar alarm company whose negligence in performing an agreement to repair and maintain caused the malfunction of the alarm, or was the burglary an unforeseeable intervening criminal act breaking the chain of causation?

Plaintiff-appellant appeals a final order dismissing an action after plaintiff's second amended complaint was dismissed with prejudice. The dismissed complaint is in four counts: breach of contract, negligent repair, breach of implied warranty of fitness and breach of express warranty. The complaint alleges that plaintiff, owner of a lapidary shop having a burglar alarm that had been damaged by lightning, contracted with the defendant burglar alarm company to repair and maintain the burglar alarm; that in performance of such contract the defendant negligently made repairs leaving the alarm system defective and with a test light indicating that the alarm system was operational when, in fact, it was not; that while the burglar alarm system was so defective plaintiff suffered a loss and damages as the result of a burglary that would not have occurred, or that would not have resulted in plaintiff's loss, but for the defective burglar alarm. The defendant challenged the sufficiency of the complaint to state a cause of action citing *Nicholas v. Miami Burglar Alarm Co.*, 339 So.2d 175, and *Singer v. I.A. Durbin, Inc.*, 348 So.2d 370.

Both *Nicholas* and *Singer* involved claims by an owner against a security or burglar alarm company for damages resulting from a burglary but neither case involved a defect in the burglar alarm system alleged to have been the direct result of a breach of contract to repair and maintain the system. In *Nicholas*, the alarm company's agent allegedly failed, contrary to an alleged agreement, to notify the police when the alarm system functioned and relayed a "trouble signal." In *Singer*, it was alleged that the alarm company contracted to, but negligently failed to, wire into the alarm system all windows of a home and the home was burglarized through an unwired window. In both *Nicholas* and *Singer*, complaints were held to state a cause of action as against a motion to dismiss based on an argument that there is a general rule of law that a burglar alarm company whose system fails to function properly is not liable for a burglary loss. *Nicholas* and *Singer* refer to this "rule of law" but both held it inapplicable to the facts in those cases. The theory for the rule is given to be that a burglary is an unforeseeable intervening act breaking the chain of causation because the occurrence of the burglary at a particular time is unforeseeable and the defendant's negligence is purely speculative and dependent on several contingencies, and the proximate cause of the loss is not the negligence but the burglary. In short, the rule is based on the theory that the defendant's negligence or breach of contract is not the proximate cause of the loss because the particular burglary that occurred is unforeseeable. The courts in *Nicholas* and in *Singer* recognized that the general rule that an intervening criminal act breaks the chain of causation is based on the premise that a person usually has no reason to foresee the criminal acts of another and both cases qualify the rule by saying that when the intervening criminal act, or the loss therefrom, is foreseeable, a defendant may be liable notwithstanding the intervening criminal act, citing *Cooper v. I.B.I. Security Service of Florida, Inc.*, 281 So.2d 524. Neither *Nicholas* nor *Singer* stopped there but both went on to hold that the burglary in question was foreseeable. *Nicholas* said that the burglary and loss in that case was foreseeable as a result of the receipt of the ignored trouble signal while *Singer* found foreseeability more generally based on statistics showing the great increase in burglaries in Florida from 1973 to 1977.

Whatever the state of the development of the law and of burglar alarm equipment in Pennsylvania in 1914, this court has held that a specific violent criminal assault is foreseeable merely because prior criminal acts have occurred in the community and has upheld the liability of those who were not in the business of foreseeing criminal activity and protecting against it. In statements of the supposed general rule of law that a burglar alarm company is not liable for a burglary if its equipment malfunctions, there is some indication that what was contemplated were "spontaneous" or unforeseeable malfunctions and not, as here, defects in the system alleged to have been directly caused by negligence or the breach of an agreement to repair and maintain the burglar alarm system. In any event, we hold that as between owners of property and burglar alarm companies who contract with them to provide, repair or maintain burglar alarms, the possibility of a successful burglary, and of loss resulting therefrom resulting from the negligent breach of a contractual obligation to provide, repair or maintain a burglar alarm, is reasonably foreseeable.

REVERSED.

CASE COMMENT

In reversing the trial court's dismissal of the complaint, the appellate court noted there appeared to be a rule of law that a burglar alarm company whose system fails to function properly is not liable for a burglary loss. The theory for this rule was given to be that a burglary is an unforeseeable intervening criminal act which breaks the chain of causation. The occurrence of a burglary at a particular time is thus unforeseeable. The rule continues that the proximate cause of the loss is not the negligence but the unforeseeable burglary. After discussing foreseeability through criminal statistics, prior criminal acts, and ignored trouble signals, the court focused on alarm company equipment malfunctions. The court noted there was some indication that what was contemplated were spontaneous or unforeseeable equipment malfunctions and not system defects directly caused by negligence or breach of agreement. The court held that the possibility of a successful burglary is reasonably foreseeable when it results from the negligent breach of a contractual obligation to provide, repair, or maintain a burglar alarm.

CONSUMER PROTECTION ACT

The purchaser of a fire alarm system warned the alarm company about her ill husband's smoking habits. The alarm company represented to her that the system was virtually foolproof and that it was designed to monitor the house and automatically notify the proper authorities in the event of a fire. The alarm company failed to install fire or smoke detectors in the area where the ill husband spent most of his time. The house burned because of a fire started by careless smoking in that area. The fire alarm failed to call the authorities, the inside alarm failed to sound, and the inside lights failed to operate. There was no record of an alarm sent from the house on the night of the fire. While the Consumer Protection Act exculpates a supplier if a misrepresentation is made despite the supplier's best efforts to prevent such an occurrence, evidence in this case showed that certain representations were untrue.

GILL v. ROLLINS PROTECTIVE SERVICE COMPANY
836 F.2d 194 (1987)

ERVIN, Circuit Judge:

In July 1981, Mrs. Gill brought this diversity suit against Rollins Protective Services Company ("Rollins") on behalf of herself and her husband for damages arising from the burning of her house in which Rollins had installed a fire alarm system. The case was submitted to the jury on theories of common law negligence and violations of Virginia's Consumer Protection Act, Va. Code Ann. § 59.1-196 et seq. The jury returned a general verdict in favor of Mrs. Gill for $238,032.78 and Rollins appealed. Because the contract signed by Mrs. Gill limited any negligence recovery to $250.00, and because the verdict did not reveal upon which theory the recovery was premised, this court vacated the judgement and remanded the case for a new trial. *Gill v. Rollins Protective Services*, 722 F.2d 55.

The jury in the second trial returned a verdict for Rollins on the statutory claim alone. The district court, Judge Williams, denied Gill's motion for a new trial and Gill appealed. This court ruled that the district court applied the wrong standard in ruling on the new trial motion, and remanded the case a second time for reconsideration of the motion under the proper standard. *Gill v. Rollins Protective Services*, 773 F.2d 592.

On remand, Judge Williams ordered a new trial. In the third full jury trial of this case, before Judge Hilton, Mrs. Gill again prevailed on the statutory claim. At the conclusion of the case the district court instructed the jury that it could award prejudgment interest to Mrs. Gill and it could pick the date upon which the running of the interest would commence. The jury returned a verdict in favor of Mrs. Gill in the amount of $244,238.17 and awarded prejudgment interest commencing from the date of the fire. This sum was calculated to be $192,819.68. Rollins filed this appeal, asserting that errors were made by both district court judges. Specifically, Rollins argues that Judge Williams abused his discretion by granting the third trial because the jury's verdict in the second trial was not against the clear weight of the evidence. Rollins also argues that since the third trial concerned only the statutory claims, Judge Hilton erred by admitting evidence of the improper placement of smoke detectors. Finally, Rollins argues that the award of prejudgment interest is improper under the facts of this case. Because we believe that Judge Williams did not abuse his discretion in granting a new trial, and because we find no reversible error in the proceedings of the third trial, we affirm the decisions below.

The facts of this case have been elaborately set forth in our prior opinions. We note here only that Mrs. Gill purchased a fire alarm system from Rollins in August of 1978. Rollins represented to her that the system was virtually foolproof. The system was designed to monitor the house and automatically notify the proper authorities using the existing telephone system in the event of fire. Mrs. Gill purchased the system because her husband, who was suffering from Alzheimer's disease at the time, was careless in his smoking habits. Despite Mrs. Gill's warnings about her husband's smoking habits, Rollins failed to install fire or smoke detectors in his basement study, the place where General Gill spent most of his time.

The Gill's house burned on April 11, 1979. A fire investigation revealed that the fire started because of careless smoking in the basement study. The fire alarm system failed to call the authorities; the inside alarm failed to sound; and the inside lights failed to operate. Mrs. Gill did not call the fire department, relying on her fire alarm system to place the call for her. Neither Rollins nor the Emergency Communications Center had any record of an alarm sent from the Gill house on the night of the fire.

Rollins argues that the jury in the second trial could have ruled against the Gills for a number of reasons. The alarm company argues first that the jury could have believed that the alarm system was inadvertently placed on the "sentinel" setting rather than the "instant-alert" setting. The sentinel setting would not have notified the fire station, but would trigger only local alarms in the event of an emergency.

Mrs. Gill testified that the setting on the alarm stayed in the "instant-alert" position at all times. She said that she checked the alarm almost daily and that it was always on the proper setting. Rollins tried to show that General Gill could have moved the setting and prevented the system from calling the emergency center. There was no testimony that the General had ever touched the alarm. In fact there was testimony by Mrs. Gill that the General did not even know that the system was in the house. Even if the General had altered the setting on the alarm on his way to bed on the night of April 11, 1979, thereby disabling the dialing out function of the system, the sirens inside the house should have sounded and the lights should have switched on. Mrs. Gill testified that only the sirens on the outside of the house worked. The other features of the alarm system malfunctioned.

Rollins next argues that the jury in the second trial could have reasonably found that the statements contained in the Rollins brochure were not misrepresentations. The brochure said the system would "automatically call the fire department" through a "central emergency station." The "wireless" system was said to be "virtually foolproof." Mrs. Gill refrained from calling the fire department in reliance on these statements.

The testimony at trial revealed that the system was actually designed to dial an answering service, not a fire station or an emergency station. The answering service would, in turn, place a call to the proper authorities. There was testimony that the answering service employees sometimes had difficulties in convincing the relevant authorities to respond to an emergency. Furthermore, the Gills' alarm system was connected to the telephone lines in the house and when those lines burned, the Gills' "wireless" system became inoperative. Because the system never sounded the sirens located inside the house, never switched on any emergency lights, and never dialed the answering service, we find it hard to believe that the system was "virtually foolproof."

Finally, Rollins argues that the jury could have ruled in its favor on an "unintentional violation" theory. The Virginia Consumer Protection Act exculpates a supplier if a misrepresentation was made despite the supplier's best efforts to prevent such an occurrence. Rollins says that it put before the jury evidence on training procedures and technical programs designed to assure customer satisfaction. Rollins argues that the jury could have believed this evidence, that a salesperson made a mistake despite Rollins' best training efforts, and voted against the Gills.

While we agree that the defense was properly before the jury, we believe that certain objective factors render it unlikely that the jury based its decision on this defense. First, the evidence on training procedures, as presented, goes to the issue of whether there was a violation of the Act, not whether the violation was an innocent one. Second, the Gills' primary claims of misrepresentation flow from the language of the brochure and the quality of the installation of the system, not the comments that a salesperson made.[3] As a result, Rollins' testimony on effective employee training does not contradict her claim. Finally, no one argued this defense to the jury. The trial court instructed the jury as to the existence of this defense but none of the attorneys told the jury that the evidence on training procedures was designed to support an argument in the alternative; i.e., that there was no violation, but if there was it was an innocent one. With only the trial court's minimal instruction as guidance, we cannot infer that the jury made the counterintuitive leap to arguments in the alternative.

Even a cursory review of the record reveals that Mrs. Gills' testimony that she believed the representations made to her were true, that she told Rollins of her husband's special needs, and that the alarm system failed to switch on inside lights and sirens, is wholly uncontradicted.[4] The trial judge has the discretion to order a new trial if he believes that the verdict, even if supported by substantial evidence, is against the clear weight of the evidence. In this case, we are not persuaded that Judge Williams abused his discretion in ordering a new trial.

Rollins begins its attack on the rulings of Judge Hilton by arguing that the judge's decision to admit evidence of the improper placement of the smoke detectors in the Gill household is reversible error. The company argues that the placement of the smoke detectors is

[3] Mrs. Gill does argue that a telephone salesperson contacted her with the "ideal" system for her, but testimony at trial primarily centered around the representations made in the brochure.

[4] Rollins called the installer of the alarm system who testified that he would have installed a heat rise indicator in the General's basement study if he had been told by Rollins of the special fire hazard. Rollins called the author of its training manuals. He testified similarly. Rollins' other witness testified as to how the system is designed to operate, not how it may have operated in the Gill home.

important only as to whether a standard of care for fire safety was met: i.e., the number and placement of the smoke detectors is relevant only to the abandoned negligence issue. We believe the evidence is also relevant to the misrepresentations alleged under the Consumer Protection Act.

Evidence concerning the number and placement of smoke detectors is relevant to both the statutory and the abandoned negligence claims. Mrs. Gill argued at trial that Rollins' virtually foolproof fire alarm system, when installed, did not possess the features represented to her. Steven Swab, the plaintiff's expert, testified that the Gill house had too few smoke detectors, and those that were installed were poorly located. Swab also testified that a rate of rise heat detector should have been installed in the General's study.[6] Finally, Swab testified that the fire burned for twenty to forty minutes undetected by the fire alarm system. Such testimony certainly tends to show that the representations contained in the brochure; to wit, that the system's "sensitive fire detectors can detect fire conditions before there is flame," were untrue.

We have reviewed carefully Rollins' other exceptions and find them without merit. Because we find no abuse of discretion in the grant of a new trial, and because we find no error in the course of that trial, we affirm the judgment of the district court.

AFFIRMED.

CASE COMMENT

In affirming the judgment of the lower court, the appellate court relied on misrepresentation in the language of the brochure and the quality of the installation of the system. The brochure said the system would automatically call the fire department through a central emergency station and that the wireless system was virtually foolproof. Testimony revealed the system was designed to dial an answering service and not a fire or emergency station. Because of other testimony, the court found it hard to believe the system was virtually foolproof. Also expert testimony was introduced that there were not enough smoke detectors and those installed were poorly placed. All-in-all, the testimony tended to show that the representations contained in the brochure were untrue, and that the evidence in the case was relevant to the misrepresentations alleged under the Consumer Protection Act.

DECEPTIVE AND UNFAIR TRADE PRACTICES

A burglar system was installed and allegedly serviced for more than two years by a subsidiary of the defendant. The alarm system did not work at the time of the burglary, and the plaintiff suffered a loss in excess of one million dollars. Key provisions in the Deceptive and Unfair Trade Practices Act make unlawful unfair methods of competition and unfair or deceptive acts or practices in the conduct of any trade or commerce. This phrase was legislatively weighted in favor of the Federal Trade Commission Act's judicial interpretation that the false, unfair, or deceptive acts need not be such as would constitute fraud. Having found that the supplier violated the Deceptive and Unfair Trade Practices Act, the question of awarding actual and punitive damages arose. Should the legally guilty supplier pay for the value of items stolen or should it be only responsible for the cost of the alarm system and services it agreed to provide?

---

[6] Such a device would trigger the alarm system but would not activate simply because of the General's heavy smoking.

ROLLINS, INC. v. HELLER
454 So. 2d 580 (1984)

NESBITT, Judge.

Rollins appeals a final judgment finding it liable for gross negligence and deceptive and unfair trade practices in connection with the installation and servicing of a burglar alarm system and granting an award of compensatory and punitive damages totalling $228,487. We reverse as to the award of damages.

The Hellers entered a contract with Rollins Protective Services Company (RPS) to install and maintain a burglar alarm system in their home. RPS is a subsidiary corporation of Rollins, Inc., the defendant below. The Hellers believed themselves to be dealing with Rollins, Inc. and were unaware of the separate corporate identities. The system was installed and then allegedly "serviced" regularly for more than two years, up until the time the Hellers' residence was burglarized. The alarm system did not work at the time of the burglary and property belonging to the Hellers, valued in excess of one million dollars, was stolen. Subsequently, through investigation and paying of ransom monies, about ninety per cent (in dollar value) of the stolen property was recovered.

The Hellers commenced an action claiming negligence, breach of express and implied warranties, fraud and deceit, misleading advertising, gross negligence and deceptive and unfair trade practices on the part of Rollins. The Hellers voluntarily abandoned their claims based upon ordinary negligence and warranties. The trial court found that the Hellers failed to establish their claims based upon fraud and deceit and misleading advertising. The Hellers have not challenged these findings. The court, however, found Rollins liable for gross negligence and deceptive and unfair trade practices under Section 501.201 *et. seq.*, Florida Statutes (1981). The court awarded $128,487 in compensatory damages (based upon the value of the unrecovered stolen items) and $100,000 in punitive damages. Rollins thereupon instituted this appeal challenging its liability as found by the trial court and the damages awarded.

We now turn to the trial court's finding that Rollins violated the Florida Deceptive and Unfair Trade Practices Act (FDUTPA). The applicable provision makes unlawful "[u]nfair methods of competition and unfair or deceptive acts or practices in the conduct of any trade or commerce." Although the trial court found no fraud on Rollins' part, such a finding is not necessary to sustain a violation under the FDUTPA. The legislature specifically provided that great weight was to be given to the federal courts' interpretations of the Federal Trade Commission Act. In *D.D.D. Corp. v. Federal Trade Commission*, 125 F.2d 679, the court held "that the false, unfair or deceptive acts defined in the Federal Trade Commission Act need not be such as would constitute fraud." Reviewing the record, we find that there was competent substantial evidence presented to support the court's finding that Rollins violated the FDUTPA.

Having upheld the trial court's finding on the FDUTPA violation, we now must determine what damages are allowed by the act. The Act specifically provides that an "individual may recover actual damages, plus attorney's fees and court costs." The Act, however, only allows recovery of damages related to the property which was the subject of the consumer transaction. We find that the subject of the consumer transaction in the present case was the installation of the burglar alarm system and the services performed thereon, rather than the items stolen from the Hellers' house. A company which installs and services burglar alarms does not assume the responsibility of insuring all the items intended to be protected by the system.[4] *Central Alarm of Tucson v. Ganem*, 567 P.2d 1203. This immunity was made

---

[4] Any such holding would in effect convert burglar alarm companies into insurance companies. It is most likely that the majority of persons obtain a burglar alarm system to deter by threat

clear in the present case by the provision in the contract stating that "Rollins is not an insurer of the Customer's property." Therefore, the damages awarded pursuant to the violation of the FDUTPA must be limited to the actual damages related to the system and services Rollins contracted to provide.

While the FDUTPA does not define "actual damages", courts of other jurisdictions have had occasion to define the term within similar statutes. In interpreting Texas' Deceptive Trade Practices Act, the Texas supreme court held that actual damages are those damages recoverable at common law.

In determining the measure of actual damages, the court in *Raye v. Fred Oakley Motors, Inc.*, 646 S.W.2d 288, 290, held:

> Generally, the measure of actual damages is the difference in the market value of the product or service in the condition in which it was delivered and its market value in the condition in which it should have been delivered according to the contract of the parties. A notable exception to the rule may exist when the product is rendered valueless as a result of the defect — then the purchase price is the appropriate measure of actual damages.

We hold that Florida's statutes should be interpreted, and actual damages measured, in a similar manner. Therefore, the actual damages awardable to the Hellers pursuant to the FDUTPA violation should be measured in accordance with formula set out in *Raye*.

The recovery of actual damages pursuant to this violation, however, is not limited by the limitation of damages provision in the contract. The provision, literally read, does not attempt to cover this situation.

Further, any attempt to limit one's liability for deceptive or unfair trade practices would be contrary to public policy. *John's Pass Seafood Co. v. Weber*, 369 So.2d 616 (it would be contrary to public policy to enforce an exculpatory clause that attempts to immunize one from liability for breach of a positive statutory duty); *Mankap* (exculpatory clauses relating to fraud or intentional misrepresentation are contrary to public policy and unenforceable). Therefore, actual damages are recoverable in full for the FDUTPA violation notwithstanding Rollins' attempt to limit its liability in the contract.

We now must determine whether an award of punitive damages is allowable pursuant to an FDUTPA violation. The Act specifically provides for the recovery of actual damages, but makes no provision for punitive damages. A claim for punitive damages is outside the scope of chapter 501 and the FDUTPA. Accordingly, any award of punitive damages based upon a violation of FDUPTA would be improper absent some independent basis such as fraud.

In the present case, the trial court specifically found in favor of Rollins on the Hellers' claim of fraud. Since no basis existed in the present case upon which punitive damages could be assessed beyond the amount stated in the limitation of damages provision, it was error for the trial court to award $100,000 in punitive damages.

CONCLUSION

In sum, we hold that the record supports the trial court's findings that Rollins is liable for its gross negligence and for violating the FDUTPA. We find, however, that the damages awarded were improper. Any damage award, including an award of punitive damages, based upon liability for gross negligence is limited by the limitation of damages provision in the contract. Although this provision does not apply to an award of damages pursuant to

of detection some would-be thieves. Having such a system would probably result in lower insurance premiums, but it should not be used as an alternative to insurance. It is apparent in the present case that the Hellers had underinsured the unrecovered stolen property. There is no sound reason why Rollins should bear the burden of this oversight by the Hellers.

the FDUTPA violation, any such award must be limited to "actual" damages. The actual damages in the present case should be computed based upon the alarm system and the services Rollins agreed to provide, and not with regard to the value of the items stolen during the burglary. The trial court, of course, will ensure that the Hellers do not recover twice for the same element of damages.

Following our determination of the above issues, we find that the other points raised by Rollins do not merit discussion and that the Hellers' points on cross-appeal are hereby rendered moot. Reversed and remanded for a new trial on damages.

CASE COMMENT

Although the Act specifically provides for the recovery of actual damages, it only allows for the recovery of damages related to the property subject to the consumer transaction — in this case, the alarm system and services rather than the items stolen. The court noted that the installer and servicer of burglar alarm systems does not assume the responsibility of insuring all the items intended to be protected by the system. To hold otherwise would in effect convert burglar alarm companies into insurance companies. Having an alarm system may result in lower premiums, but it should not be an alternative to having insurance. Thus, the actual damages in this case are based on the alarm system and services and not with regard to the items stolen in the burglary.

WARRANTY

A resort hotel contracted for the installation and maintenance of a fire alarm system. The hotel relied on the supplier's expertise in recommending an affordable system that would provide reliable protection for the hotel's property and guests. The supplier was obligated to inspect the system every six months. The supplier warranted that the system was the best system for the hotel. One fire broke out causing damage. The fire detection system failed to activate the alarm. The supplier was notified but took no action to identify or correct any problem. Subsequently, another fire destroyed a room and endangered the entire hotel. The alarm system did not work, and the hotel sued the supplier, claiming the system failed to meet all the warranties.

A warranty is a promise that a proposition of fact is true. It is a voucher for the condition and quality of the thing sold, that the thing sold is fit for the particular purpose for which the seller has reason to know it is required. The buyer trusts and relies on the seller's skill, experience, and judgment to furnish goods suitable and applicable for the purpose. An implied warranty is where the law derives it by implication or inference from the nature of the transaction or the relative situation or circumstances, or of the acts of the parties. Note the different reasons the court found that the system was not the best system as expressly warranted, and that the system was neither merchantable nor fit for the purpose for which it was intended.

FIRE SUPPLY & SERVICE, INC. v. CHICO HOT SPRINGS
639 P. 2d 1160 (1982)

SHEA, Justice.

On July 24, 1979, the plaintiff, Fire Supply & Service, Inc. filed an action against the defendant, Chico Hot Springs, in Park County District Court to recover delinquent payments under the terms of a lease the parties had made for the installation and maintenance of a fire alarm system at the Chico Hot Springs resort hotel. Chico Hot Springs counterclaimed for the return of all monies paid under the lease, arguing that Fire Supply had installed a system which failed to meet all expressed and implied warranties. Chico Hot Springs also sought damages resulting from the system's alleged failure to operate as warranted. Trial without jury was held December 15, 1980, and judgment was entered for Chico Hot Springs in the amount of $5,776. Fire Supply appeals.

In 1976, Chico Hot Springs, through its president, Michael Art, approached Fire Supply for the purchase of a fire alarm system for the Chico Hot Springs resort hotel, and relied upon Fire Supply's expertise in recommending an affordable system that would provide reliable protection for the hotel's property and guests. Near the end of November 1976, Fire Supply installed an automatic fire alarm system consisting of several heat detection devices wired to a large and complicated control panel. Fire Supply also installed manual "pull" alarm stations throughout the hotel. On November 26, 1976, the parties signed a "Lease Agreement" which provided that Chico Hot Springs would lease the system for $178.25 per month for a five-year term. Fire Supply was obligated to inspect the system at least once every six months. Upon expiration of the five-year term, Chico Hot Springs had the option to either renew the lease for another five-year term or to purchase the system for one dollar, in which event Fire Supply's duty to service the system was terminated.

On July 14, 1979, a fire destroyed one of the hotel's guest rooms and endangered the entire hotel. The system did not sound an alarm, either automatically or after an employee pulled the manual alarm. Although the system's control panel had been routinely observed by hotel employees, there was no indication that the system was malfunctioning. It was later determined by Fire Supply that the control panel light which indicates a system malfunction had burned out, but that this would not prevent the alarm from sounding.

Fire Supply obtained a court order to prevent Chico Hot Springs from interfering with the removal of the system, and the system was finally removed from the hotel in November 1979. Fire Supply then filed this action to recover the payments due it under the agreement, contending that Chico Hot Springs breached the agreement by not making the required monthly payments. Chico Hot Springs counterclaimed, contending that the system did not work properly after it was installed.

The record reveals that Chico Hot Springs called Fire Supply several times after the system was installed to indicate there were problems with the system. In December 1978, a substantial fire had broken out in the resort's snack bar, causing several thousand dollars worth of damage. The fire detection system failed to activate the hotel's alarm, but the fire was discovered by a night watchman. Chico Hot Springs notified Fire Supply of the system's failure, but Fire Supply took no action to identify or correct any problems. Chico Hot Springs also contends that the June 24, 1979 letter it received constituted a breach of the parties' agreement, which entitles it to damages.

The trial court found that Chico Hot Springs relied upon Fire Supply's expertise to furnish a system that would afford reliable protection; that the parties' agreement was actually a sales contract rather than a lease agreement; that Fire Supply had tolerated for three years a schedule whereby Chico Hot Springs made no payments during the winter and then caught up in the summer, and that there appeared to have been a tacit agreement to that payment schedule. The court also found that the system was not the "best" system for the hotel as expressly warranted by Fire Supply and that the system was neither merchantable nor fit for the purpose for which it was intended. The court ordered Fire Supply to return to Chico Hot Springs all monies paid under the agreement ($5,526) and awarded $250 damages for repairs to the fire-damaged guest room.

Fire Supply appeals to this Court to determine whether the trial court's judgment was correct. We affirm that judgment, but do not consider the measure of damages because it has not been challenged in this appeal.

The trial court also concluded that the fire alarm system failed to meet Fire Supply's express warranty that it was the "best" system for the hotel, and that it failed to meet both the implied warranty of merchantability and the implied warranty of fitness for a particular purpose.

To recover damages for a breach of warranty, the buyer must plead and prove that he gave the seller notice of the breach within a reasonable time after it was discovered or be barred from any remedy. The trial court accepted Chico Hot Springs' contention that it advised Fire Supply of the system's failure after the December 1978 fire in the resort's snack bar. In addition, the record reveals that from August 1977 through June 1978, Chico Hot Springs repeatedly notified Fire Supply that the system's alarm, control panel, and heat detectors weren't working as they were supposed to. This was sufficient to inform Fire Supply that the system was troublesome and should have been watched.

Where the seller is aware that the buyer is relying upon the seller's judgment to select suitable goods, an implied warranty that the goods are fit for that particular purpose arises. The trial court found that Fire Supply was aware that Chico Hot Springs was relying on it to recommend and install a fire alarm system which would be suitable for use in the large, old, woodframe resort. Fire Supply installed a system which was complicated and difficult to use, and which often required Fire Supply to service it. The alarm bells frequently sounded when there was no fire, and did not sound when there were fires. The control panel did not work properly; its "trouble" light continually malfunctioned and then burned out entirely. Fire Supply's own records show that the system was troublesome to operate.

Because we hold that the trial court correctly found that Fire Supply breached the parties' agreement by installing a fire alarm system which failed to meet the implied warranty of fitness for a particular purpose, we need not consider whether any other warranty was breached. Under the breach of warranty, Chico Hot Springs is entitled to recover any loss in value of the goods because of the breach, plus consequential and incidental damages, where proper. Chico Hot Springs prayed for the return of all monies it had expended under the agreement ($5,526), and the trial court awarded it that amount. Fire Supply has not challenged the validity of that measure of damages.

The trial court's award of consequential damages for the fire damage to the hotel's guest room was also proper. The judgment is affirmed.

CASE COMMENT

The court accepted the hotel's contention that it had repeatedly notified the supplier that the alarm, control panel, and heat detectors were not working as they were supposed to. It also found that the hotel relied on the supplier to recommend and install a system suitable for a large, old, woodframe resort; that the system installed was complicated and difficult to use and often required servicing; that alarm bells frequently sounded when there was no fire and did not sound when there were fires; that the control panel did not work properly; and that the trouble light continually malfunctioned and then burned out entirely. In addition, the court found that the hotel relied on the supplier's expertise to furnish a system that would afford reliable protection. The system, however, was not the best system for the hotel as expressly warranted by the supplier. Also, the supplier failed to meet both the implied warranty of merchantability and the implied warranty of fitness for the particular purpose.

FALSE ALARM ORDINANCE

A sample false alarm ordinance can be found in Appendix D.

6

Damages

Damages are a financial compensation which may be recovered in court by a person who has suffered a loss, detriment, or injury whether to his person, property, or rights through the unlawful act or omission or negligence of another. It is an award of money to a person injured by the tortious act or breach of contract by another. The purpose of the award is to make the person or property whole and be put in the same position he was prior to the tortious act or breach of contract. Normally, the plaintiff cannot be made more than whole, make a profit, or receive more than one recovery for the same harm. A discussion of the two types of damages, compensatory and punitive, follows. Damages may be sought for circumstances such as:

- personal and property injury,
- permanent physical and mental disability,
- past physical and mental pain and anguish,
- future physical and mental pain and anguish,
- loss of consortium, earnings, and enjoyment of life,
- past and future medical and hospital expenses,
- diminution in earning capacity,
- expenses to repair damage,
- future expenses and disability,
- subsequent disease or complication of injury,
- aggravation of a pre-existing condition, and
- deprivation of the use of property.

COMPENSATORY OR ACTUAL DAMAGES

Compensatory or actual damages are the natural, necessary, and usual result of a wrongful act. Compensatory damages compensate the injured party for injury sustained and nothing more. Compensatory damages make good or replace the loss caused by the wrong or injury. In the following case, a 68-year-old woman was "karated" to the floor by two security guards. She received $60,000 in compensatory damages for physical and mental suffering. Some of

185

the pain suffered because of the assault continued "intermittently" over four years between the time of the incident and the time of trial.

INTERNATIONAL SECURITY CORPORATION OF VIRGINIA v. McQUEEN
497 A.2d 1076(1985)

FERREN, Associate Judge.

In this civil action for assault and battery, the jury found for plaintiff-appellee and awarded $60,000 in compensatory damages for physical and mental suffering. Defendant-appellant contends on appeal that the trial court acted improperly when, *sua sponte*, it vacated the new trial order it had entered shortly after trial and reinstated the jury verdict. Because we conclude that the trial court did not err in reversing itself, that all the issues were properly submitted to the jury, and that the jury verdict was not excessive, we affirm.

The underlying facts are essentially uncontested. On April 7, 1979, at about 11:45 p.m., plaintiff Butterfly McQueen, who had come to the District of Columbia to receive an award from the District of Columbia Department of Recreation, was waiting in the Greyhound bus station for a bus to Tampa, Florida. McQueen, then a 68-year-old woman, was in the ladies' lounge when two security guards employed by defendant, International Security Corporation of Virginia (ISCV), approached and asked to see her bus ticket, apparently thinking she was a thief. McQueen refused to show the guards her ticket unless they displayed their badges and gave their names. At this point, McQueen testified, one of the guards "pushed me back into the room, . . . karated me to the floor and I banged my ribs against the metal bench against the wall." McQueen elaborated: "I fell down. My left leg doubled under me, and my right leg went under. My right buttock hit the cement floor, . . . and this rib hit the metal bench, banged up against the bench." The guards then detained McQueen and took her upstairs where she was questioned by the police before being released.

Other persons were present during McQueen's assault and apprehension, and she testified that she was "embarrassed" in their presence. McQueen also testified that, after the assault, she suffered from a radiating pain in her left shoulder and a swelling under her left knee. She further testified that she had never had either kind of pain before the assault, and that thereafter it had continued "intermittently" over the "four years" between the incident and trial.

Neither side presented any medical testimony at trial. McQueen, who testified that she did not consult a doctor until two or three years after the assault, explained why she did not do so earlier: "Because I'm ashamed of being ill. I don't believe in sickness. . . . I didn't want to go and talk about how I was hurt."

The trial court submitted to the jury the issues of ISCV's liability and of compensatory damages for assault and battery. The jury returned a verdict in McQueen's favor and awarded her $60,000 in damages. It appears from the authorities that a jury may reasonably infer permanence of injury without supporting expert medical testimony when the effects of such injury according to the testimony of the plaintiff have persisted for a long period of time and there is no uncontradicted medical testimony that the injury is temporary.

In every personal injury case, the plaintiff carries the burden of proving not only that he or she was injured but also that the defendant's tortious conduct caused the injury. In the absence of "complicated medical questions," *Jones V. Miller*, 290 A.2d 587, the plaintiff's own testimony, without need for supporting expert medical testimony, will suffice to prove causation of injury. "No complicated medical question" arises when: (1) the injury "'develops coincidentally with, or within a reasonable time after, the negligent act,'" or (2) "'the causal connection is clearly apparent from the illness or injury itself and the circumstances surrounding it,'" or (3) "'the cause of the injury relates to matters of common experience, knowledge, or observation of laymen.'"

In this case, the second *Jones* rationale applies. McQueen suffered from a radiating pain in the left shoulder and a swelling under the left knee—injuries which by their very nature, reflect the causes evidenced by McQueen's sworn testimony: "a karate thrust (demonstrating) like that, and the person goes down," followed by a doubling of the left leg (plus the banging of a rib against a metal bench and the striking of the right buttock against a cement floor). Thereafter, McQueen suffered intermittent pain in her shoulder and knee, which she never had suffered before. In accordance with *Jones*, therefore, a jury properly could find that the assault caused McQueen's injuries, without need for medical testimony.

Once the issue of causation was properly before the jury, McQueen's testimony also sufficed for the jury to consider the permanence of her injuries as well. "When the bad effects of an injury have continued for years, laymen may reasonably infer permanence," even in the absence of expert medical testimony, if there is no contrary testimony that the injuries are temporary. McQueen testified that, after the pain began, she felt it "intermittently" and continually to the time of trial, four years after the assault. No evidence to the contrary was offered. On the basis of McQueen's testimony, therefore, the jury could infer permanence.

Appellant also contends that the trial court improperly reinstated the jury verdict because the verdict was excessive. The trial court, in determining whether a verdict is excessive, "must consider whether the verdict resulted from passion, prejudice, mistake, oversight, or consideration of improper elements." *Vassiliddes*, 492 A.2d at 594. It should allow that verdict to stand unless it is " 'beyond all reason' " or " 'so great as to shock the conscience.' " Here, the trial court stated in its July 3, 1984 order: "based upon the uncontroverted proof of damages respecting her injuries adduced by plaintiff, the Court is of the view that the jury award was generous but not generous to a fault or outside the bounds of legal appropriateness.' "

This court must accord great deference to the trial court's decision to grant or deny a motion for new trial based on excessiveness of the verdict and may reverse that decision only for an abuse of discretion. We perceive no such abuse here.

In arriving at its award of compensatory damages, the jury could properly consider the physical pain of the assault itself and any lasting physical injuries that McQueen may have suffered. The jury also could properly consider the embarrassment and humiliation that McQueen suffered at the time of the assault.

Under the circumstances, the jury's award of $60,000 was not so great as to "shock the conscience."

EXEMPLARY OR PUNITIVE DAMAGES

Exemplary or punitive damages are over and above compensatory damages. They are in addition to or an enhancement of the actual damages. They may be awarded where the wrong done was aggravated by violence, recklessness, malice, oppression, fraud, or wicked, evil, or wanton conduct. They are intended to punish the defendant for his evil behavior, to make an example of him, to warn others, and to act as a deterrent of future like conduct. They are sometimes called smart-money or vindictive damages. These damages, for gross misconduct, are based on a different public policy consideration, which is the punishing of the defendant or the setting of an example. Awarding punitive damages in the following case demonstrates that the actions of the guard in pulling on a customer's colostomy bag from under his shirt exceeded the ordinary and reasonable standard of care required. The second case shows that an employer can be vicariously liable for punitive damages for an employee's misconduct. The third case sets forth some of the criteria of what would "smart" or "pinch" the defendant.

CANTY v. WACKENHUT CORPORATION
311 So. 2d 808 (1975)

Per Curiam.

Plaintiff-appellant seeks review of the trial court's order granting the motion of defendant-appellees for a new trial.

Plaintiff-appellant, Richard Canty, at the time of the events giving rise to the instant action as a result of stomach surgery had a colostomy bag protruding from his body. On October 26, 1972, plaintiff went to an Eagle Family Discount Store to purchase a few items. In order to cover the colostomy bag, plaintiff was wearing his shirt outside of his trousers. Appellant paid for his purchases and started toward the front door at which time he was stopped by Eduardo A. Fernandez, a security guard employed by the defendant-appellee, The Wackenhut Corporation, and assigned to the store. Fernandez demanded to see what the plaintiff was carrying under his shirt. Plaintiff-appellant attempted to explain that it was a colostomy bag. Fernandez, having failed to understand due to an inability to understand English, reached under the appellant's shirt, grabbed the colostomy bag, and pulled on it until it was practically ripped off resulting in a prolapse of a portion of the colon protruding from the skin. Eventually surgery was necessary to remove that portion of plaintiff's colon.

Thereafter, plaintiff Canty filed suit against defendant Wackenhut Corporation and its liability insurer, Aetna Casualty and Surety Company. The cause came on for jury trial and ultimately was submitted to the jury on one count of battery and two counts of negligence. The jury returned a verdict in favor of the plaintiff in the sum of $50,000 as compensatory damages and in the sum of $180,000 as punitive damages. Thereupon, appellees filed a motion for new trial and after a hearing thereon, the trial judge entered the following order:

> ORDER GRANTING NEW TRIAL
> ... The court is of the opinion that the compensatory damages awarded are adequately sustained by the evidence but that the amount of punitive damages is so grossly excessive and contrary to the evidence as to shock the conscience of the court, and that a remittitur to the verdict should be made by the plaintiff to the extent of $130,000. The Court having ordered such a remittitur and the plaintiff, through his counsel, having indicated in open court, upon the Court's announcement of said ruling, that he would not accept the remittitur; therefore, in lieu thereof, the Court will grant a new trial to the defendants on all issues as to damages, both compensatory and punitive.
> It is thereupon,
> ORDERED AND ADJUDGED that a new trial is hereby granted as to compensatory and punitive damages only upon the sole ground that the punitive damage verdict is contrary to the evidence and so grossly excessive as to shock the conscience of the court. In all other respects the motion for new trial is denied.

Plaintiff appeals therefrom. We reverse.

Basically, there are three situations wherein the courts in this state have determined that the amount of a verdict for punitive damages is excessive. First, where the punitive damages awarded bears no relation to the amount the defendant is able to pay and results in economic castigation. Second, where the tort committed is lacking the degree of maliciousness and/or outrageous disregard for the plaintiff's rights required to sustain the amount of the verdict. Third and last, where the amount of punitive damages fixed by the jury bears no reasonable relation to the compensatory damages awarded and which is excessively out of relation to compensatory damages.

After a careful review of the record on appeal, we cannot say that the amount of the punitive damages fixed by the jury in the case sub judice falls into any of the hereinabove categories. For punitive damages are "peculiarly left to the discretion of the jury as the degree of punishment to be inflicted must always be dependent on the circumstances of each case, as well as upon the demonstrated degree of malice, wantonness, oppression or outrage found by the jury from the evidence."

We also have considered defendant Wackenhut's interlocutory appeal involving the issue of Wachenhut's liability and plaintiff's cross-appeal directed thereto, and find the points raised therein to be without merit.

There being competent substantial evidence contained in the record in support of the jury's verdict, we hereby reverse the order granting a new trial and remand the cause to the trial court with directions to reinstate the jury's verdict and enter judgment thereon.

It is so ordered.

CASE COMMENT

McQueen received $60,000 in compensatory damages and Canty received $50,000 in compensatory damages and $180,000 in punitive damages. The question of excessiveness arose in both cases. The deference of the court to the discretion of the jury should be noted, especially in today's atmosphere of high awards. In McQueen's case, the verdict, although generous, did not result from passion, prejudice, oversight or consideration of improper elements and was allowed to stand because it was not beyond all reason, nor did it shock the conscience of the court. Canty's compensatory award was not challenged and his punitive award stood as it bore no relation to the defendant's ability to pay. There was sufficient outrageous disregard for his rights to sustain the amount, and the amount was not excessively out of relation to his compensatory award. Damages in these two cases totaled $290,000. Additional costs might include legal fees and time used preparing for the trial, and appeals. A higher degree of professionalism in each case might have precluded or lessened these losses.

K-MART CORPORATION v. MARTINEZ
761 S.W. 2d 522(1988)

NYE, Chief Justice.

Appellees, Minerva Martinez, Elsa Nichols, and Marta Mata, brought suit against appellants, K-Mart Corporation and Nathan Christian, for actual and exemplary damages for slander, assault, false imprisonment, and negligent hiring. The trial court, pursuant to jury answers, rendered judgment for the appellees. By three points of error the appellants complain of an award of exemplary damages to each appellee, plaintiffs below, in the amount of $30,000.00 each.

The plaintiffs/appellees were employees of K-Mart Corporation. Appellant Christian worked for K-Mart as a loss prevention district manager.

K-Mart and Christian were found to be jointly and severally liable to the appellees in the following amounts for Christian's slanderous statements:

Martinez - $37,000 in compensatory damages
Nichols - $35,000 in compensatory damages
Mata - $36,000 in compensatory damages

Although the jury found Christian acted maliciously in making the slanderous statements, it assessed zero exemplary damages against Christian for the slander.

The jury, finding that appellant Christian did not assault the appellees, did not award any damages for assault. K-Mart and Christian were found to be jointly and severally liable to the appellees in the following amounts for Christian's false imprisonment of each appellee:

> Martinez - $10,000 in compensatory damages
> Nichols - $10,000 in compensatory damages
> Mata - $10,000 in compensatory damages

Again, the jury found Christian acted maliciously and willfully, but assessed zero exemplary damages against Christian for his acts of false imprisonment.

After finding that K-Mart ratified the acts of Christian, and that K-Mart negligently hired Christian, the jury assessed exemplary damages against K-Mart for slander, false imprisonment, and negligent hiring as to each appellee.

In Special Issue 21 (the only issue challenged by the appellants on appeal), the jury found that K-Mart was liable for exemplary damages as follows:

> *For appellee Martinez*
> $15,000 for Christian's slanderous statements
> $ 0 for assault
> $10,000 for Christian's act of false imprisonment
> $30,000 for K-Mart's failure to use ordinary care in hiring defendant Christian.
> *For appellee Nichols*
> $15,000 for Christian's slanderous statements
> $ 0 for assault
> $10,000 for Christian's act of false imprisonment
> $30,000 for K-Mart's failure to use ordinary care in hiring defendant Christian.
> *For appellee Mata:*
> $15,000 for Christian's slanderous statements
> $ 0 for assault
> $10,000 for Christian's act of false imprisonment
> $30,000 for K-Mart's failure to use ordinary care in hiring defendant Christian.

By the first point of error, the appellants contend the trial court erred in permitting the submission of Special Issue 21 because it allowed double recovery for each appellee. The trial objection was very long and rambling. Trial objections to special issues must clearly designate the error and explain the grounds for the complaint to provide the trial court an opportunity to correct the errors in the charge. After careful scrutiny of the appellants' objection at trial, we fail to see how the trial court could have been apprised of the appellants' complaint that the submission regarding negligent hiring allowed double recovery. Appellants' first point of error is overruled.

By two points two and three, the appellants contend the trial court erred in denying appellants' motion for judgment notwithstanding the verdict and in rendering judgment. The appellants complained in a "Motion for Judgment Notwithstanding the Verdict and to Disregard the Jury Answers" that the award for exemplary damages against K-Mart resulted in a double recovery of monies for the same act, transaction, and occurrence. On appeal, the appellants contend the $30,000.00 exemplary award (in Special Issue 21) for negligent hiring of Christian should be reversed as to each appellee because it constituted a double recovery for the same injury already compensated by the award of exemplary damages for false imprisonment ($10,000), and slander ($15,000).

There were two different theories of recovery for exemplary damages against K-Mart. An employer can be vicariously liable for punitive damages for the employee's misconduct if one of the following is shown:

1) the employer authorized the doing and the manner of the act;
2) the employee was unfit and the employer was reckless in employing him;
3) the employee was employed in a managerial capacity and was acting in the scope of employment; or
4) the employer or a manager ratified or approved the act.

In this sense, the theory of negligent hiring is used as a method to recover exemplary damages under the theory of respondeat superior.

Since the jury found that K-Mart ratified the acts of Christian and that K-Mart was reckless in employing Christian, the appellees were entitled to recover for Christian's reckless and malicious conduct.

An employer can also be directly liable for exemplary damages for its own act of negligently hiring an employee. Since the jury found that K-Mart acted with reckless disregard in hiring Christian, and the negligent hiring was the proximate cause of appellee's actual damages, K-Mart could be assessed exemplary damages for its own tortious act of negligently hiring Christian.

The issue is whether each appellee can recover exemplary damages against K-Mart for both the malicious acts of its employee (i.e., $15,000 for Christian's slanderous statements, and $10,000 for Christian's act of false imprisonment) and for K-Mart's act of negligently hiring the employee (i.e., $30,000). We hold that to allow recovery under both theories allows for double recovery because 1) K-Mart's derivative and direct liability is based on K-Mart's single act of negligently hiring the employee, Christian; and 2) both theories of exemplary damages are predicated upon the same findings of actual damages.

Appellant requested that we render the judgment to disallow the $30,000 exemplary damage finding to each appellee for K-Mart's negligent hiring of Christian. However, the appellees were entitled to elect between the amount of exemplary damages for the negligent hiring of Christian ($30,000) and the slander and false imprisonment ($25,000).

When the prevailing party fails to elect between alternative measures of damages, the court is to utilize the findings affording the greater recovery and render judgment accordingly. Therefore, we reverse and render that part of the judgment of the trial court regarding exemplary damages against K-Mart in the amount of $15,000 and $10,000 respectfully as to each appellee and render judgment as follows:

K-Mart Corporation is liable for exemplary damages, plus post-judgment interest thereon at ten percent per annum, as follows:
(1) to Minerva Martinez...$30,000.00
(2) to Elsa Nichols.............$30,000.00
(3) to Marta Mata...............$30,000.00

The costs are assessed against appellants. The remainder of the judgment is AF-FIRMED.

KEEFE v. GIMBEL'S
478 N.Y.S.2d 745 (1984)

LORRAINE S. MILLER, Judge.

The New York State Legislature in 1960 enacted General Business Law sections 217 and 218, clearly "special-interest" protective legislation for retail mercantile establishments where "goods, wares or merchandise are offered to the public for sale" (L.1960, ch. 1005, 6/1/60). It provided that in any action for false arrest, false imprisonment, unlawful detention, defamation of character, assault, trespass or invasion of civil rights, an authorized agent of the store may detain a person to question the ownership of merchandise as long as the detention is done in a reasonable manner and for a reasonable time and the agent had reasonable grounds to believe that the person detained was committing or attempting to commit larceny on the premises. This protective shield, unique because of its grant to only a segment of our commercial community, i.e., retail mercantile establishments, was designed to stem an acknowledged tide of "shoplifting"; it has also led to many abuses imposed upon innocent shoppers by negligent storekeepers and their ill-trained and often uncaring employees. Wooed and courted by attractive, extensive and costly newspaper, TV and magazine advertising, members of the public are invited and urged daily to enter through the doorways of vast commercial emporiums, deposit earnings and savings for goods, leaving behind a profit for the merchant, and frequently their dignity, pride and health in addition. While "shoplifters" have admittedly proliferated in recent years, unwary legitimate shoppers have also been increasingly ensnared, not by the "reasonable stop" contemplated by GBL 218, but by the careless and cavalier negligence of store personnel, as illustrated by the within case. The special legislation enacted for the unique problems of retail establishments was never intended by the Legislature to confer a license to embarrass, humiliate and harm innocent business invitees and consumers.

Helen Keefe, a 65-year-old diminutive, snow-capped, gentle woman with a background that included three years in a religious order, piano teaching and studies at the New York Art Students League, had been coming to Gimbel's main store from her New Jersey residence for more than 30 years. She had also been attending the adjacent St. Francis of Assisi church for approximately the same length of time except for a period when she was hospitalized for a spleenectomy after a serious auto mishap.

On January 9, 1981 she responded to an advertisement by defendant offering men's outerwear, and after buying a hat for herself, she went to the store's popular lower level. She purchased a corduroy jacket and a down coat for her husband. Payment was made by check and each garment was separately packaged. The receipt was handed to her but not stapled by the store's employee to the outside of either coat box in contravention of the alleged store policy. When she attempted to leave the store, she testified that red lights began to flash and a "bell like a fire engine" went off, that a red-jacketed man "grabbed her by the arm"; that another "tore the boxes out of her hand" and loudly commanded she accompany them; that the boxes were thrown to the floor; that a large crowd gathered, some of whom she knew from her St. Francis Church attendance; that her efforts to display her paid receipt were refused and rejected until it was finally discovered that a large white plastic sensomatic device had been left on one of the coats by the defendant's employee at the time of her purchase. Both garments were then repacked. Plaintiff was crying and upset and security personnel testified she kept asking, "How could this be happening to me?" Feeling ill and shaken, plaintiff asked for aspirin and was taken to the office of the Chief of Security from which calls were placed to her family. Apologies (but no aspirins) were offered by Chief Bradley. When she was eventually recomposed, she was accompanied by security personnel to the employees' exit, and once more, as she attempted to exit, the bells lights, etc. were activated a *second* time, again in the presence of numerous people. Another white sensomatic device was found, this time in the pocket of one of the garments she had purchased. Security personnel admitted they laughed at this second occurrence. Chief Bradley testified that similar erroneous "stops" happen 20 times a day (and the "door monitor" estimated 100 erroneous "stops" a week). Bradley also admitted that the store knew that shoplifters frequently detach these devices and place them in pockets of garments still on the racks rather than throw them on the floor or carry them out on their own persons. Yet, despite the knowledge of responsible store executives and alleged instructions to cashiers and packers of this known practice, they had clearly failed to inspect the garments when plaintiff first paid for them, and had again failed to inspect even when the boxes had been opened upon the first wrongful stop of plaintiff. He testified that often "they are too busy." Both he and defendant's counsel's summation admitted they had made "mistakes" in regard to plaintiff, Helen Keefe.

The trial herein extended over a period of several days. At the conclusion of the testimony and summations the court determined, as a matter of law, that defendant was negligent and so advised the jury, predicated upon the admissions by the Chief of Security and other witnesses, and the summation of defendant's counsel. The jury thereafter awarded plaintiff $100,000 in compensatory damages for injuries, conscious pain and suffering, and mental anguish that resulted from defendant's negligence.

The jury was charged that if they found defendant's acts went beyond ordinary negligence, were so wanton and reckless as to constitute extreme or gross negligence, they might, but were not required to allow plaintiff exemplary or punitive in addition to compensatory damages. (It was clearly explained to them that if any amount was so awarded by them in the exercise of their sound judgment and discretion it would be to punish the defendant and deter others from similar acts.) Their verdict was $500,000 exemplary damages. Defendant moves herein to set aside the jury's verdict as to both sums.

The jury also determined there was no assault or battery or wrongful detention. The plaintiff cross-moves herein to set aside that part of the verdict.

At the conclusion of the entire trial, this court stated that the amount of the verdict was excessive and urged parties and counsel to meet and negotiate a mutually acceptable reduced settlement. When their efforts were unsuccessful the court held several post-verdict conferences. The plaintiff was both reasonable and realistic citing her age, state of health and the trauma of the trial as motivation for accepting the court's recommendation of a settlement at a substantially reduced sum from the jury's verdict of $600,000. The defendant and its carrier remained adamant at $40,000, however, (admitting they would prefer to disburse considerable funds for an appeal than give the cost thereof to the plaintiff to resolve the matter).

This court has carefully reviewed many, many cases in which verdicts were declared to be excessive and the pronouncements by several courts that the verdict in a case would be set aside unless the *plaintiff* agreed to a reduction to a more reasonable sum. The court could find no cases, however, where, as here, the plaintiff acceded to the court's suggestion of a substantial reduction, but the defendant, while admitting its culpability, remained inflexible and intransigent. To set aside the verdict, in toto, under those circumstances and compel this plaintiff to expend further funds to commence an appeal would be compounding the wrong that has already been done to her by this defendant. Ordering an entire new trial would severely prejudice plaintiff for the additional reason that defendant's employees and counsel will surely never again admit their series of mistakes before a new jury and another judge, necessitating the purchase by plaintiff of voluminous minutes of the first trial—and a trial on damages only would deprive the new jury of the facts that are intimately interwoven into the damages.

The court denies the defendant's motion to set aside the jury's verdict of compensatory damages in the sum of $100,000. There was nothing unconscionable or unfair in light of plaintiff's uncontradicted testimony of headaches, sleeplessness, incontinence, mental suffering including depression, anxiety, ridicule, embarrassment, and restricted physical, occupational and social activities, etc. Plaintiff had had a serious auto accident sometime prior to the within incident necessitating the removal of her spleen and had been under continuous treatment at a hospital as an out-patient since that time. Her earlier physical problems were exacerbated by the within occurrence. Defendant must "take the plaintiff as he finds her." In view of all of the foregoing, the compensatory damages were commensurate with the injury done.

Clearly the jury found and decided that the admitted negligence of defendant was misconduct which transgressed *mere ordinary* negligence and constituted a reckless, willful and wanton disregard of both the rights of the plaintiff, to whom it happened twice within a space of an hour, and the public to whom a mistaken "stop" occurs 20 times a day. The defendant was and is duty-bound to take appropriate measures to stop the mishandling of customers who unwarily come onto defendant's premises, expecting a pleasant shopping trip but who experience something quite traumatic at least 100 times a week.

When one who operates a retail premises opens his doors to consumers and invites them in to inspect his wares and spend their funds, he has a duty to provide, at the very least, not only a physically safe place, but one in which they will not come to emotional harm, embarrassment, humiliation and mental anguish because of his negligent operation of the premises. Should a legitimate consumer have to assume a risk because there are others on the premises who may be a detriment to the vendor's business? Must they assume the risk now of being stopped, being physically "pushed around" to the accompaniment of bells and flashing lights, detention and possible arrest simply because the store and its employees are mindful only of the store's own interests? The law has long required a property owner, a storekeeper, etc., to keep the physical premises in a reasonably safe condition without hidden "traps." Is this any less a trap? Should a lesser degree of care be required when it is within the total control of the financially benefitted defendant to prevent harm of this kind to the consumer? It is inconceivable that the Legislature enacted GBL 217 and 218 to confer a "sword" into the hands of negligent mercantile establishments, and it is significant that while the GBL enumerates the types of actions in which the defense may be raised, it does not include actions for negligence and/or gross negligence. *Expressio unius est exclusio alterius!*

The jury herein made a "statement." By their verdict and the size thereof they issued a warning to the mammoth chains whose wealth they were entitled to consider that they deemed it an affront to invite this plaintiff in and then inflict such oppressive conduct upon her by the reckless and admittedly negligent conduct of employees who were "too busy." The court construes their verdict as one designed to prevent similar injurious impact to other consumers at large and as a deterrent to defendant and other stores who daily engage in the same offensive conduct resulting from a system *they* have authorized, initiated, adopted and installed for their benefit without regard for the innocent who are negligently brought into the net they have woven.

While it might be said by some that the amount of the verdict herein indicates prejudice or passion against the defendant by members of the public sitting on this jury, the court sees this instead as a pointed expression by the community which has a right to rebuke defendant for its system by way of punitive damages to insure the protection of the innocent. The wealth and resources of a defendant are appropriate considerations for a jury in determining the amount of punitive damages, for what would be a punishment to the "mom and pop" corner grocery store would scarcely be a deterrent for the affluent multi-store chain such as the defendant herein. As one court reasons, "Would we deter the commission of malicious acts by the wealthy if they were punished the same as the poor?" Would we deter reckless conduct or conduct that evidenced a sheer disregard for a consumer-plaintiff's rights without making the aforesaid distinction? This court and others have held that a defendant's financial status is surely a factor in determining a punitive damage award. The court should not substitute its judgment for that of the jury but is bound to view the evidence in the light most favorable to the prevailing party and to give it the benefit of all inferences which the evidence fairly supports. Precise ascertainment of damages is not always possible with regard to a defendant's tortious conduct. A just and reasonable estimate by a jury sitting in a quasi-judicial capacity must suffice and they are vested with a broad discretion in assessing punitive damages.

There is no yardstick in measuring what amount will deter repetition of grossly negligent acts and lack of supervision as in the instant case. Cases speak of an award being excessive that "shocks the conscience" of the court—or an award that results from "passion or prejudice." This court believes that the criteria should be what amount will "smart" or "pinch" the defendant sufficiently, and others in the same business or similarly situated, to motivate more careful training and supervision of employees, the hiring of more employees to properly handle the volume of work without being "too busy" to remove the tags and search for those already illicitly removed. In short, a relation to reality is required as long as it is consonant with the jury's intention, since the trial court is in the best position to evaluate the reactions of the jury.

As Mr. Justice Kassal formerly of this court once said: "Regarding the amount of such punitive damages the jury has determined what it feels will set an example and establish guidelines to avoid recurrence. The jury, as such, represents the voice of the community and it is not the province of the Trial Judge to substitute his judgment for the jury's unless it is so excessive as to shock the conscience of the court."

The court determines that punitive damages in the sum of $75,000 will serve as a sufficient deterrent to prevent repetition by the within defendant and others similarly situated, and will encourage better training and supervision of employees and the hiring of more employees, if necessary, to accord innocent shoppers the care and courtesy they are entitled to. It may also motivate the introduction of a better system that will not entrap the innocent consumer.

Accordingly, the motion to set aside the verdict of $600,000 herein is granted unless plaintiff files a written stipulation agreeing to the reduction of the verdict herein to the total sum of $175,000 (representing compensatory damages of $100,000 and punitive damages of $75,000) within 15 days from the filing of this decision, in which event a judgment for the reduced amount may be entered by the plaintiff. Should the defendant thereafter decide to pursue an appeal from this decision and the aforesaid reduced sum, the court also determines that the plaintiff's cross-motion re causes of action for assault, battery and wrongful detention should be and they hereby are reinstated so that all causes of action may be before any reviewing court.

CASE COMMENT

The court in discussing the criteria of what would "smart" or "pinch" the defendant also gave a focus or sense of direction that the defendant:

- was duty-bound to take appropriate measures to stop mishandling customers;
- had a duty to provide a place where customers would not come to emotional harm, embarrassment, humiliation and mental anguish;
- should have more careful training and supervision of its employees;
- should hire more employees to handle the volume of work; and
- should not repeat the grossly negligent acts or lack of supervision.

CORPORATE PARENT OR SUBSIDIARY OWNER

A subsidiary corporation is owned or controlled by a parent corporation. In this sense, it is affiliated or associated with, or auxiliary to, the corporate parent. The corporate parent usually owns a majority of shares in the subsidiary and thus has control over it and has a voice in its management. While each appears to have an independent existence, liability may attach to the corporate parent for intentional torts committed by the subsidiary's employees at the subsidiary's location. In the past decade, there has been a tremendous number of corporate acquisitions and mergers. The security director of the parent corporation should be cognizant of the potential liability which could accrue from security problems of the subsidiary. Although the activity in the following case took place in the subsidiary department store, the parent corporation was the object of the suit. The security practices of the parent corporation were entitled to be decided by the jury. Judicial notice was taken of the corporate parent revenues in determining the damage award.

GARDNER v. FEDERATED DEPARTMENT STORES, INC.
717 F. Supp. 136 (1989)

WHITMAN KNAPP, District Judge.

Jason Gardner brought suit against Federated Department Stores, Inc. ("Federated"), the corporate parent of Bloomingdale's department store, alleging false imprisonment, false arrest, battery, malicious prosecution and abuse of process. After a four-day trial, the jury awarded damages totalling $2.3 million—$150,000 for the deprivation of liberty, $150,000 for pain and suffering up to the date of the verdict, $500,000 for future pain and suffering and $1,500,000 in punitive damages. Defendant moves to set aside the verdict as excessive and contrary to the weight of the evidence.

For reasons which follow, we deny defendant's motion except to the extent that we direct plaintiff to remit $490,000 of the amount he was awarded for future pain and suffering. If plaintiff declines to remit that amount, we shall order a new trial limited to the issue of future pain and suffering.

BACKGROUND

For approximately five years before the events giving rise to this lawsuit, plaintiff worked, primarily at Bloomingdale's in Manhattan, as a free-lance promotional model, displaying and selling perfume. On April 16, 1984, he returned to Bloomingdale's a gray jacket that he had purchased a few days earlier. Although he did not have a receipt for the jacket, the supervisor at the return desk agreed to process the return using a receipt for the same amount of money for a black jacket plaintiff had also purchased.

Three days later, on April 19, 1984, plaintiff, wearing the black jacket, returned to the store, this time to visit his friend Arielle Stern. Ms. Stern, who also worked as a free-lance promotional model, gave him some free samples and agreed to meet him for dinner after she finished her shift. As plaintiff waited for her outside the store, James Boyce, a security executive who was second in command for internal corporate investigations and responsible for internal investigations and security audits in Bloomingdale's stores nationwide, and a second unidentified security officer accosted plaintiff. They twisted his hands behind his back, handcuffed him, picked him up and dragged him back into the store. In full view of customers and employees, they dragged him across the selling floor and pushed him through the swinging doors that opened onto the stairs leading to the security office, causing him to fall and bruise himself. They then picked him up and pulled him up the stairs.

Once in the security office, they put him in a cell and searched through his belongings. Other unidentified security officers taunted him, calling him a "blond faggot."

After plaintiff was unable to produce any document of identification, Boyce told him that it was illegal not to carry identification. He then read plaintiff his *Miranda* warnings and began to interrogate him, demanding that he reveal who had given him the samples. He threw a bag of clothes at plaintiff, and asked him if he had earlier returned a jacket for credit. Plaintiff refused to answer.

Boyce placed a printed "confession" form in front of plaintiff and directed him to sign it. The form stated that plaintiff admitted that he had stolen merchandise from Bloomingdale's and agreed not to enter the store for seven years. Plaintiff, denying that he had stolen anything, refused to sign the form and asked to speak with a lawyer. Boyce refused this request.

Plaintiff then asked to go to the bathroom, a request that was at first similarly denied. Then, after a time, another security officer (also unidentified) escorted him to the bathroom and removed the handcuffs. When that officer put the handcuffs back on plaintiff's wrists to return him to the cell, he fastened them so tightly that they cut him. Later, plaintiff was taken from the cell back to Boyce's office. When plaintiff again refused to sign the confession form, Boyce came around his desk to where plaintiff, handcuffed and defenseless, was sitting and repeatedly punched him very hard in the ear.

The security officers conversed with one another within the plaintiff's earshot, saying that they "didn't have anything on him" and that "American Express won't do anything." They nevertheless turned him over to the police at about 10:30 p.m. He had been in Bloomingdale's custody for almost two hours.

The police transported him to Central Booking, fingerprinted and photographed him. He was put into a cell with about thirty-five other prisoners, many of whom, plaintiff learned, had been apprehended on charges of drug dealing or rape. Some of them menaced plaintiff, demanding candy and money and trying to take his watch.

At about 4:30 a.m., Ms. Stern, the coworker with whom he had planned to dine the night before, and her husband secured plaintiff's release by posting $1000 bail. After a few hours, plaintiff went to court to wait for his case to be called. He spent the entire day there and returned on each of the next three days, waiting from early morning to late at night until on the fourth day he was permitted to enter his plea of not guilty. Over the next several months, he was required to make several court appearances until his case was finally dismissed.

After continuing to work in various department stores—including Abraham & Straus which was owned by defendant Federated—for a year after the incident, plaintiff moved to California to try to escape his memories. Unemployed for a time, he now works with Ms. Stern at a catering concern.

Dr. Gerald Appelle, an expert dental witness retained by defendant, examined plaintiff four years after the incident. According to his report, which plaintiff offered in evidence, plaintiff suffers from symptoms consistent with temporo-mandibular joint syndrome, a malady commonly know as "TMJ". His symptoms, which plaintiff testified still continue, include tenderness in his front mandibular joint and left masseter muscle, an inability completely to open his mouth, a jaw that periodically goes out of joint or locks causing a cramp-like pain, and a clogging and buzzing sensation in his ear when he swims or, sometimes, when he showers. According to plaintiff, he can no longer swim, which up until the incident was his favorite means of recreation. Nor can he eat certain foods or bite down hard. Dr. Appelle was of the opinion that it was "possible that the blow received to the jaw could have resulted in the condition described." He found it "difficult to evaluate the degree of permanency especially since very little therapy has been received to date." Dr. Appelle's report was the only medical evidence on plaintiff's dental condition.

Plaintiff testified that since the incident he has experienced severe anxiety when entering a department store or watching a police or courtroom drama on television, has changed from an outgoing person into a "loner", suffers from low self-esteem, finds it difficult to control his eating and has recurring stomach cramps and diarrhea. He often relives the incident, suffering great emotional pain each time. He worries that he might again be arrested. According to Ms. Stern, he continually washes his hands and appears worried about leaving fingerprints. Plaintiff admitted that he had not made any effort to seek psychiatric treatment. The psychiatric experts retained by plaintiff and defendant agreed that plaintiff suffered from extreme anxiety and avoidance behavior, but that his condition might improve if he saw a psychiatrist. Dr. Peter Schiffman, the expert retained by plaintiff, pointed out, however, that the longer plaintiff delays, the less likely it will be that he will respond to psychiatric treatment. After considerable hemming and hawing, Dr. Schiffman opined that, without treatment, the condition would probably be permanent. Dr. Morton Marks, the expert retained by defendant, on the other hand, was of the view that plaintiff could resume his normal occupational activities.

Although the testimony suggested that, for plaintiff, the events of April 19, 1984 were pivotal, defendant apparently did not deem them of any significance. John Harden, Bloomingdale's director of security, testified at his deposition that he did not learn of the incident until three and one half years after its occurrence and two and one half years after this lawsuit had been filed. He further testified that neither Federated nor Bloomingdale's had any practice of reviewing allegations of wrongdoing by the security staff, and that there existed no procedure for bringing such complaints to the attention of any executive.

During more than three years of discovery, defendant insisted that it had no way of identifying a single one of the security officers—other than Boyce—who had been directly involved in plaintiff's detention. It further claimed that Boyce had left Bloomingdale's employ and that it was wholly impossible to locate him. It also claimed throughout the entire period of discovery that it was impossible to ascertain the whereabouts of Tom Hayden, a sales clerk who had been involved in processing the return of plaintiff's jacket.

The trial started on Tuesday, April 25, 1989. Defense counsel told us that he had not been retained until the previous Friday and that his investigator would be, as the trial proceeded, trying to locate witnesses. Defendant did not present a single witness who contradicted or in any way questioned plaintiff's account of the circumstances surrounding his apprehension. After both sides had rested, however, defense counsel informed us that his investigator had, in only three days, succeeded in finding the elusive Mr. Hayden.

Defendant's sole defense seemed to be that plaintiff's arrest was somehow justified by some sort of fraud surrounding plaintiff's return of the gray jacket some days previously. We ultimately rejected that defense as a matter of law and directed a verdict on the false arrest and false imprisonment claims.[1] Concluding that any damages the jury might award for malicious prosecution or abuse of process would duplicate those awarded for false arrest and false imprisonment, we submitted only the battery claim to the jury. After a short period of deliberation, the jury returned with a finding that plaintiff had established his claim for battery. As above stated, the jury awarded $150,000 to compensate plaintiff for the time he was deprived of his liberty as a result of the security officers' actions, $150,000 for his pain and suffering up to the date of the verdict, $500,000 for his future pain and suffering and $1,500,000 in punitive damages.

As the law requires, we here discuss not what might have been the situation had the case

[1] G.B.L. § 218 renders privileged detention by store security officers when they observe someone stealing or trying to steal merchandise and for only so long as is reasonably necessary to investigate. The statute did not authorize the officers to detain plaintiff nearly two hours on the unsubstantiated suspicion that he had committed some sort of fraud three days earlier.

been properly defended but what inferences the jury was entitled to draw from the evidence actually before it. We look to see whether—in that view of the situation-the compensatory or punitive awards were so high as to shock our conscience or to constitute a denial of justice.

We first turn to compensatory damages. Based on the evidence detailed above, our conscience is by no means shocked by the award of a total of $300,000 for the deprivation of liberty and for pain and suffering up to the date of the verdict. Although it seems probable, however, that plaintiff is entitled to some damages for future pain and suffering, our conscience is shocked by the award of $500,000. Because neither party seemed to have fully developed the issues crucial to ascertaining future damages, the record is replete with unanswered questions. For example, why did plaintiff, who claimed to have been morbidly frightened of even entering a department store, continue to work in such stores for approximately a year after the incident? Why, if each visit to a department store caused plaintiff such pain, was he unable to remember on what days or for how many days he had worked in each of several department stores during that year? Why did not plaintiff at least try to find out whether psychological counselling within his budget was available? Is it likely, given that plaintiff's career path mirrored that of his friend, Ms. Stern, who never seems to have had any problem with any employer, that plaintiff's leaving department store work in New York for catering in California was a result of this incident? Why did not the plaintiff consult a doctor—or even a swimming coach—to see if earplugs or some other simple remedy would allow him to continue swimming, allegedly his favorite pastime? Why, if in fact "TMJ" subjects plaintiff to such misery, has he not aggressively pursued treatment? Indeed, Dr. Appelle, the only dental expert whose opinion was before the jury, declined to speculate on the permanency of plaintiff's condition "since very little therapy has been received to date." As above indicated, we direct plaintiff remit $490,000 of the $500,000 he was awarded for future pain and suffering or face a trial limited to that issue. If plaintiff chooses a new trial, we shall reopen discovery to allow the parties to develop a fuller record on future damages and plaintiff's efforts, if any, to mitigate those damages.

We now turn to punitive damages. Punitive damages may be imposed on a corporation for the intentional wrongdoing of its employees "where management has authorized, participated in, consented to or ratified the conduct giving rise to such damages or has deliberately retained the unfit servant . . . or the wrong was in the pursuance of a recognized business system of the entity." In *Stevens*, a woman was falsely imprisoned on suspicion of stealing a watch. The court upheld the jury's award of punitive damages, observing (51 A.D. at 368, 64 N.Y.S. at 666):

> Although there was no evidence of any express malice against this plaintiff individually, the act was done in pursuance of a system which had been adopted in that store; and if this system was such as to place an innocent customer in the position in which plaintiff's evidence showed she was placed, the jury had the right to say that the results of this system were of such a character as to require rebuke by way of punitive damages in order that innocent people should not be placed in the position in which plaintiff was placed without fault on her part.

A corporate defendant's failure to investigate the wrongful conduct of its employees can also justify punitive damages. *Brink's Inc. v. City of New York* 546 F.Supp. 403.

We have no doubt that the punitive damages award was warranted on at least three theories. First, Boyce, a high ranking manager responsible for internal security, not only acted without legal justification but also with gratuitous brutality. Second, the fact that Boyce tolerated and, it could be reasonably inferred from the evidence, encouraged by example his subordinates' abusive behavior, supported the conclusion that it was Bloomingdale's "recognized business system" to improperly apprehend, harass and physically abuse persons it suspected of stealing. Third, the jury was entitled to decide, based on Federated's practice of never investigating complaints or even maintaining any facilities for such investigation, that outrageous conduct by the security staff was knowingly tolerated at the highest level of the corporation.[5]

Nor do we see a reason to reduce the award. Although there is no precise formula for arriving at a figure that will punish defendant for its misconduct, the jury is to consider the bad acts of the defendant and the underlying purposes of punitive damages. As Judge Weinfeld observed, if punitive damages are to deter defendant from engaging in similar outrageous conduct in the future and to serve as an object lesson to other corporations, it must be large enough to "smart" a little. *Id.* at 413. Defendant offered no evidence that its financial circumstances were such that a large punitive damage award would be unduly harsh. Perhaps this was a wise decision. We take judicial notice that Federated's revenues in 1987, the last year before it was acquired by Campeau Corporation, exceeded $11 billion. Given defendant's atrocious conduct and its significant wealth, we cannot say that the punitive damages award in any way shocks our conscience.

CONCLUSION

We deny defendant's motion to reduce or set aside the verdict, except to the extent that we direct plaintiff to remit $490,000 for his award for future pain and suffering.

SO ORDERED.

ON MOTION FOR RECONSIDERATION

Our memorandum and order of June 26, 1989, familiarity with which is here assumed, has prompted both sides to make further motions. Plaintiff moves for reconsideration of our order directing that he remit $490,000 of the $500,000 jury award for future pain and suffering or submit to a new trial on that issue. Defendant, taking issue with our observation that its counsel neglected properly to prepare the defense, moves to reargue its motion to set aside the verdict for punitive and past compensatory damages. In the alternative, defendant moves to supplement the record. For reasons which follow, we deny both motions for reconsideration, but grant defendant's motion to supplement the record.

DISCUSSION

Plaintiff argues that in our memorandum and order we improperly imposed on him the burden of proof on the issue of whether or not he took appropriate steps to mitigate his pain and suffering. He also purports to have unearthed in the record answers to several of the "unanswered questions" about extent of his future pain and suffering and his efforts to mitigate.

Plaintiff's contentions ignore two simple facts. First, plaintiff's testimony made it abundantly clear that he had failed to take any of the steps that a sensible person would have taken to mitigate his supposed future pain and suffering. Plaintiff's failure was so obvious that defendant could have borne its burden without introducing any evidence on the issue. Second, our decision was based on the fact that our conscience was shocked, not by the wholly ephemeral nature of the evidence introduced by both sides, but by the enormity of the verdict in relation to that evidence. Accordingly, we deny plaintiff's motion for reconsideration.

---

[5] Although the matter was not brought to the jury's attention, we cannot help but be ionfluenced by defendant''s conduct in falsely asserting during three years of discovery that it could not locate Boyce or any other of the persons involved. Aside from being ridiculous on its face, this assertion is belied by the ultimately retained counsel's ability to locate Mr. Hayden in just three days.

We grant defendant's motion to supplement the record. We deny both motions for reconsideration.

SO ORDERED.

CASE COMMENT

Punitive damages have been imposed on a corporation for the intentional wrongdoing of its employees where management authorized, participated in, consented to, or ratified the conduct giving rise to such damages; where it deliberately retained unfit servants; where the wrong was in pursuance of a recognized business system; or where it failed to investigate the wrongful conduct of its employees. Lending support for the court's decision was the situation where a high-ranking manager responsible for internal security acted without legal justification, gratuitous brutality, and tolerated and encouraged by example a subordinate's abusive behavior. Also the court noted that the corporate parent's practice of never investigating complaints, or maintaining facilities for such an investigation was outrageous conduct by the security staff and was knowingly tolerated at the highest corporate level. Even with a remittitur of $490,000, the loss, not prevented by security, totaled $1,810,000. Note: This case has since been modified. See 907 F.2d 1348.

COMPARATIVE/CONTRIBUTORY NEGLIGENCE

Simply put, negligence is the absence of due diligence. It is the doing of something that a reasonable and prudent person would not do, or it is the failure of doing something that a reasonable person would do. When a legal duty is breached in this fashion and the breach is the proximate cause of another's injury or harm, the possibility of legal action ensues with the injured party as the plaintiff. If the plaintiff's actions or failure to act amount to a want of ordinary care, and concurs with the negligence of the defendant, it is also a proximate cause of the injury. The notion here is that the conduct of the plaintiff is below the standard of care to which he is legally required to conform for his own protection. The plaintiff's contribution to the proximate cause of his own injury coincides with or happens at the same time as the defendant's. The law imposes a duty upon people to protect themselves from injury. If a breach of this duty acts together with the defendant's actionable negligence, the plaintiff contributes to his own injury or harm. Comparative negligence can be considered to be equivalent or similar in meaning. If contributory negligence is found on the part of the plaintiff, the question then arises as to what amount or percentage did the plaintiff contribute to his own injury. The defendant's costs will then be reduced by the percentage assessed against the plaintiff.

The following case has an excellent discussion of the evolution of this doctrine, comments on many factors to be taken into consideration, and shows how the law changes as society marches on. In this case the defendant's share was assessed at only 3 percent.

WASSELL v. ADAMS
865 F.2d 849 (1989)

POSNER, Circuit Judge.

The plaintiff, born Susan Marisconish, grew up on Macaroni Street in a small town in a poor coal-mining region of Pennsylvania—a town so small and obscure that it has no name. She was the ninth of ten children, and as a child was sexually abused by her stepfather. After graduating from high school she worked briefly as a nurse's aide, then became engaged to Michael Wassell, also from Pennsylvania. Michael joined the Navy in 1985 and was sent to Great Lakes Naval Training Station, just north of Chicago, for basic training. He and Susan had decided to get married as soon as he completed basic training. The graduation was scheduled for a Friday. Susan, who by now was 21 years old, traveled to Chicago with Michael's parents for the graduation. The three checked into a double room at the Ron-Ric motel, near the base, on the Thursday (September 22, 1985) before graduation. The Ron-Ric is a small and inexpensive motel that caters to the families of sailors at the Great Lakes Naval Training Station a few blocks to the east. The motel has 14 rooms and charges a maximum of $36 a night for a double room. The motel was owned by Wilbur and Florena Adams, the defendants in the case.

Four blocks to the west of the Ron-Ric motel is a high crime area: murder, prostitution, robbery, drugs—the works. The Adamses occasionally warned women guests not to walk alone in the neighborhood at night. They did not warn the Wassells or Susan.

Susan spent Friday night with Michael at another motel. On Saturday the Wassells checked out and left for Pennsylvania, and at the Wassells' suggestion Susan moved from the double room that she had shared with them to a single room in the Ron-Ric. Michael spent Saturday night with her but had to return to the base on Sunday for several days. She remained to look for an apartment where they could live after they were married (for he was scheduled to remain at the base after completing basic training). She spent most of Sunday in her room reading the newspaper and watching television. In the evening she went to look at an apartment.

Upon returning to her room at the motel, she locked the door, fastened the chain, and went to bed. She fell into a deep sleep, from which she was awakened by a knock on the door. She turned on a light and saw by the clock built into the television set that it was 1:00 a.m. She went to the door and looked through the peephole but saw no one. Next to the door was a pane of clear glass. She did not look through it. The door had two locks plus a chain. She unlocked the door and opened it all the way, thinking that Michael had come from the base and, not wanting to wake her, was en route to the Adamses' apartment to fetch a key to the room. It was not Michael at the door. It was a respectably dressed black man whom Susan had never seen before. He asked for "Cindy" (maybe "Sidney", she thought later). She told him there was no Cindy there. Then he asked for a glass of water. She went to the bathroom, which was at the other end of the room, about 25 feet from the door (seems far—but that was the testimony), to fetch the glass of water. When she came out of the bathroom, the man was sitting at the table in the room. (The room had a screen door as well as a solid door, but the screen door had not been latched.) He took the water but said it wasn't cold enough. He also said he had no money, and Susan remarked that she had $20 in her car. The man went into the bathroom to get a colder glass of water. Susan began to get nervous. She was standing between the bathroom and the door of her room. She hid her purse, which contained her car keys and $800 in cash that Michael had given her. There was no telephone in the room. There was an alarm attached to the television set, which would be activated if someone tried to remove the set, but she had not been told and did not know about the alarm, although a notice of the alarm was posted by the set. The parking lot on which the motel rooms opened was brightly lit by floodlights.

A few tense minutes passed after the man entered the bathroom. He poked his head out of the doorway and asked Susan to join him in the bathroom, he wanted to show her something. She refused. After a while he emerged from the bathroom—naked from the waist down. Susan fled from the room, and beat on the door of the adjacent room. There was no response. The man ran after her and grabbed her. She screamed, but no one appeared. The motel had no security guard; the Adamses lived in a basement apartment at the other end of the motel and did not hear her screams.

The man covered Susan's mouth and dragged her back to her room. There he gagged her with a wash cloth. He raped her at least twice (once anally). These outrages occupied more than an hour. Eventually Susan persuaded the rapist to take a shower with her. After the shower, she managed to get out of the bathroom before he did, dress, and flee in her car. To save herself after the rapes, she had tried to convince him that she liked him, and had succeeded at least to the extent that his guard was down. The Adamses' lawyer tried halfheartedly to show that she had consented to the rapes, but backed off from this position in closing argument.

The rapist was never prosecuted; a suspect was caught but Susan was too upset to identify him. There had been a rape at the motel several years previously (a sailor had opened the door of his room to two men who said they were "the management", and the men raped his wife). There had also been a robbery, and an incident in which an intruder kicked in the door to one of the rooms. These were the only serious crimes committed during the seven years that the Adamses owned the motel.

Susan married Michael, but the rape had induced posttrauma stress that has, according to her testimony and that of a psychologist testifying as her expert witness, blighted her life. She brought this suit against the Adamses on January 21, 1986. It is a diversity suit that charges the Adamses with negligence in failing to warn Susan or take other precautions to protect her against the assault. The substantive issues are governed by the law of Illinois. A jury composed of four women and three men found that the Adamses had indeed been negligent and that their negligence had been a proximate cause of the assault, and the jury assessed Susan's damages at $850,000, which was the figure her lawyer had requested in closing argument. But in addition the jury found that Susan had been negligent too—and indeed that her negligence had been 97 percent to blame for the attack and the Adamses' only 3 percent. So, following the approach to comparative negligence laid down in *Alvis v. Ribar*, 421 N.E.2d 886—the decision in which the Supreme Court of Illinois abolished the common law rule that contributory negligence is a complete bar to a negligence suit-the jury awarded Susan only $25,500 in damages. This happens to be approximately the midpoint of the psychologist's estimate—$20,000 to $30,000—of the expense of the therapy that the psychologist believes Susan may need for her post-traumatic stress.

Susan's lawyer asked the district judge to grant judgment in her favor notwithstanding the verdict, on the ground either that she had been nonnegligent as a matter of law or that her negligence was immaterial because the Adamses had been not merely negligent but willful and wanton in their disregard for her safety. In the alternative, counsel asked the judge to grant a new trial on the ground that the jury's apportionment of negligence was contrary to the manifest weight of the evidence. There were other grounds for the motion, but they have been abandoned. The judge denied the motion, and Susan appeals.

Had she filed her suit after November 25, 1986, she could not have recovered any damages, assuming the jury would have made the same apportionment of responsibility between her and the Adamses. Illinois' new comparative negligence statue (Ill.Rev.Stat. ch. 110, ¶ 2-1116; see also ¶ 2- 1107.1) bars recovery in negligence (or strict liability product) cases in which the plaintiff's "fault . . . is more than 50% of the proximate cause of the injury or damage for which recovery is sought." But as her suit was filed before that date, the new statute is inapplicable. See Ill.Rev.Stat. ch. 34, ¶ 429.7 Historical Note.

Susan Wassell's counsel argues that the jury's verdict "reflected a chastened, hardened, urban mentality—that lurking behind every door is evil and danger, even if the guest is from a small town unfamiliar with the area." He takes umbrage at the defendants' argument that

Susan's "antennae" should have been alerted when she didn't see anyone through the peephole. He rejects the metaphor, remarking unexceptionably that human beings do not have antennae and that this case is not a Kafka story about a person who turned into an insect (i.e., is not *The Metamorphosis*). He points out that a person awakened from a deep sleep is not apt to be thinking clearly and that once Susan opened the door the fat was in the fire— if she had slammed the door in the rapist's face he might have kicked the door in, as had happened once before at this motel, although she didn't know that at the time. The Adamses' counsel argued to the jury (perhaps with the wisdom of hindsight) that Susan's "tragic mistake" was failing to flee when the man entered the bathroom. Susan's counsel insists that Susan was not negligent at all but that, if she was, she was at most 5 percent responsible for the catastrophe, which, he argues, could have been averted costlessly by a simple warning from the Adamses. To this the Adamses' counsel replies absurdly that a warning *would* have been costly—it might have scared guests away! The loss of business from telling the truth is not a social loss; it is a social gain.

The common law refused to compare the plaintiff's and the defendant's negligence. See 4 Harper, James & Gray, The Law of Torts § 22.1 (1986). The negligent plaintiff could recover nothing, unless the defendant's culpability was of a higher degree than simple negligence. See *id.*, §§ 22.5, 22.6, and the discussion of "degrees" of negligence in *Alvis v. Ribar, supra*. Susan argues that the defendants were willful and wanton, which, she says, would make her negligence as irrelevant under a regime of comparative negligence as it would be in a jurisdiction in which contributory negligence was still a complete defense.

Both the premise (that the Adamses were willful and wanton) and the conclusion (that if so, her own negligence was irrelevant) are wrong. As we guessed in *Davis v. United States*, 716 F.2d 418 that it would, Illinois appears to be lining up with the states that allow the plaintiff's simple negligence to be compared with the defendant's "willful and wanton conduct," see *State Farm Mutual Automobile Ins. Co. v. Mendenhall*, 517 N.E.2d 341; see also *Bofman v. Material Service Corp.*, 466 N.E.2d 1064; *Soucie v. Drago Amusements Co.*, 495 N.E.2d 997. We say "appears to be" because only *Mendenhall* discusses the issue and it is not a decision of the Illinois Supreme Court, and because a critical premise of the decision may be shaky. That is the proposition that "willful and wanton" under Illinois law denotes merely a heightened form of negligence, so that there is only a small difference between simple negligence and willful and wanton misconduct despite the ominous sound of the words "willful" and "wanton." As we noted in *Davis*, there are two lines of "willful and wanton" decisions in Illinois. One, which seemed to be in the ascendancy when we wrote *Davis*, and is the position taken in section 342 of the Second Restatement of Torts (1965), indeed regards "willful and wanton" as merely a heightened form of "negligent." Section 342 requires only that the defendant "knows *or has to reason to know* of the dangerous condition of his premises and *should* realize that it involves an unreasonable risk of harm". But the cases since *Davis* appear to have swung round to the narrower concept, under which willful and wanton conduct denotes "conscious disregard for. . .the safety of others," or "knowledge that the defendant's conduct posed a high probability of serious physical harm to others."

These formulations come close to—perhaps duplicate—the standard of recklessness that we limned in *Duckworth v. Franzen*, 780 F.2d 645, a prisoners' suit involving a claim that reckless disregard for prisoners' safety violates the Eighth Amendment's prohibition against cruel and unusual punishments. *Bresland v. Ideal Roller & Graphics Co.*, 501 N.E.2d 830, describes willful and wanton misconduct as "so close to . . . intentional misconduct that a party found liable on that basis should not be able to obtain contribution from his joint tortfeasors."

If the more recent formulations are authoritative, this would undermine the argument in

Davis and *Mendenhall* for allowing a plaintiff's simple negligence to be compared with a defendant's willful and wanton misconduct. But it would not help Susan Wassell win her case. No rational jury could find that the Adamses *consciously* disregarded a *high* probability of serious physical harm. If the laxer version of "willful and wanton" is used, Susan's argument against permitting the jury to compare her culpability with that of the Adamses falls, yet she might seem in that event to have a powerful fallback position. The laxer the standard for "willful and wanton," the stronger the inference that the Adamses *were* willful and wanton—and if so, surely Susan's own negligence was not so great as to outweigh theirs by a factor of more than 30. But as we shall see in a moment, the defendants' negligence in this case was at most simple, not aggravated, negligence. Indeed, the jury may not have thought the defendants negligent at all.

The old common law rule barring the contributorily negligent plaintiff from recovering *any* damages came eventually to seem too harsh. That is why it has been changed in most jurisdictions, including Illinois. It was harsh, all right, at least if one focuses narrowly on the plight of individual plaintiffs, but it was also simple and therefore cheap to administer. The same cannot be said for comparative negligence, which, far from being simple, requires a formless, unguided inquiry, because there is no methodology for comparing the causal contributions of the plaintiff's and of the defendant's negligence to the plaintiff's injury. In this case, either the plaintiff or the defendants could have avoided that injury. It is hard to say more, but the statute requires more—yet without giving the finder of facts any guidance as to how to make the apportionment.

We have suggested in previous cases, such as *Davis v. United States, supra,* that one way to make sense of comparative negligence is to assume that the required comparison is between the respective costs to the plaintiff and to the defendant of avoiding the injury. If each could have avoided it at the same cost, they are each 50 percent responsible for it. According to this method of comparing negligence, the jury found that Susan could have avoided the attack at a cost of less than one thirty-second the cost to the Adamses. Is this possible?

It is careless to open a motel or hotel door in the middle of the night without trying to find out who is knocking. Still, people aren't at their most alert when they are awakened in the middle of the night, and it wasn't crazy for Susan to assume that Michael had returned without telling her, even though he had said he would be spending the night at the base. So it cannot be assumed that the cost—not to her (although her testimony suggests that she is not so naive or provincial as her lawyer tried to convince the jury she was), but to the reasonable person who found himself or herself in her position, for that is the benchmark in determining plaintiff's as well as defendant's negligence—was zero, or even that it was slight. As innkeepers (in the increasingly quaint legal term), the Adamses had a duty to exercise a high degree of care to protect their guests from assaults on the motel premises. And the cost to the Adamses of warning all their female guests of the dangers of the neighborhood would have been negligible. Surely a warning to Susan would not have cost the Adamses 32 times the cost to her of schooling herself to greater vigilance.

But this analysis is incomplete. It is unlikely that a warning would have averted the attack. Susan testified that she thought the man who had knocked on the door was her fiance. Thinking this, she would have opened the door no matter how dangerous she believed the neighborhood to be. The warning that was not given might have deterred her from walking alone in the neighborhood. But that was not the pertinent danger. Of course, if the Adamses had told her not to open her door in the middle of the night under any circumstances without carefully ascertaining who was trying to enter the room, this would have been a pertinent warning and might have had an effect. But it is absurd to think that hoteliers are required to give so *obvious* a warning, any more than they must warn guests not to stick their fingers into the electrical outlets. Everyone, or at least the average person, knows better than to open his or her door to a stranger in the middle of the night. The problem was not that Susan thought that she *should* open her bedroom door in the middle of the night to anyone who knocked, but that she wasn't thinking clearly. A warning would not have availed against a temporary, sleep-induced lapse.

Giving the jury every benefit of the doubt, as we are required to do especially in a case such as this where the jury was not asked to render either a special verdict or a general verdict with answers to written interrogatories, we must assume that the jury was not so muddle-headed as to believe that the Adamses' negligence consisted in failing to give a futile warning. Rather, we must assume that the jury thought the Adamses' negligence consisted in failing to have a security guard, or telephones in each room, or alarms designed to protect the motel's patrons rather than just the owners' televisions sets. (The Adamses did, however, have an informal agreement with the local police that the police would cruise through the parking lot of the Ron-Ric whenever they drove down the street at night—and this was maybe three or four times a night.) The only one of these omitted precautions for which there is a cost figure in the record was the security guard. A guard would have cost $50 a night. That is almost $20,000 a year. This is not an enormous number. The plaintiff suggests that it would have been even lower because the guard would have been needed only on busy nights. But the evidence was in conflict on whether the Sunday night after a Friday graduation, which is the night that Susan was attacked, was a busy night. And the need for a security guard would seem to be greater, the less busy rather than the busier the motel; if there had been someone in the room adjacent to Susan's she might have been saved from her ordeal. In any event the cost of the security guard, whether on all nights or just on busy nights—or just on unbusy nights—might be much greater than the monetary equivalent of the greater vigilance on the part of Susan that would have averted the attack.

The assumption that the jury was clear-thinking and instruction-abiding is artificial, of course. During its deliberations, the jury sent the judge a question about the duty to warn (the judge did not answer it). This is some indication that the jury thought that the Adamses' negligence consisted in failing to warn Susan. But it is equally plausible that the jury didn't think the Adamses were negligent at all toward Susan, but, persuaded that she had suffered terribly, wanted to give her a token recovery. Concern with sympathy verdicts appears to lie behind Illinois' new statute barring the plaintiff from recovering any damages if he is more than 50 percent negligent. "The adoption of the pure comparative negligence doctrine (the doctrine, adopted in *Alvis v. Ribar*, that allows the plaintiff to recover something however great his negligence was relative to the defendant's) was thought to have increased a plaintiff's chances for winning at trial from about 50% to 60%, even though at the same time it tended to reduce the amount of the damage awards made at trial." It may be more than coincidence that the jury awarded Susan just enough money to allow her to undertake the recommended course of psychological therapy. We are not supposed to speculate about the jury's reasoning process, and we have just seen that it would not necessarily strengthen Susan's case if we did. The issue for us is not whether this jury was rational and law-abiding but whether a rational jury could, consistently with the evidence, have returned the verdict that this jury did.

If we were the trier of fact, persuaded that both parties were negligent and forced to guess about the relative costs to the plaintiff and to the defendants of averting the assault, we would assess the defendants' share at more than 3 percent. But we are not the trier of fact, and are authorized to upset the jury's apportionment only if persuaded that the trial judge abused his discretion in determining that the jury's verdict was not against the clear weight of the evidence. We are not so persuaded. It seems probably wrong to us, but we have suggested an interpretation of the evidence under which the verdict was consistent with the evidence and the law. And that is enough to require us to uphold the district judge's refusal to set aside the verdict.

AFFIRMED.

CASE COMMENT

Notice how the law in this jurisdiction was changed in 1981 by a State Supreme Court decision which abolished the common law rule that contributory negligence was a complete bar to a negligence suit. It changed again in 1986 when a new comparative negligence statute became operable which bars recovery in negligence cases in which the plaintiff's fault is more than 50 percent of the proximate cause of the injury or damages for which recovery is sought. The adoption of the new statute appeared to the court to be because of concern with sympathy verdicts as opposed to the 1981 court adoption of the pure comparative negligence doctrine. One should be familiar with the rules in their own particular jurisdiction since an award may be lessened if the plaintiff was contributorily negligent.

MITIGATION OF DAMAGES

Sometimes a plaintiff may not recover all the damages due for the effects of harm or injury which could have reasonably been avoided. The limitation on recovery in these cases is known as mitigation of damages or avoidance of consequences. This arises only after the injury-producing event has occurred. The law imposes a duty on an injured person to exercise reasonable, prudent, and ordinary diligence and care in attempting to lessen, moderate, or minimize damages after the injury has been inflicted. The care, prudence, and reasonableness required is the same as would be used by a person of ordinary prudence under like circumstances. This doctrine applies when the plaintiff fails to take reasonable action to lessen, moderate, or mitigate injuries. In *Cappo v. Vinson Guard Service, Inc.* (discussed in Chapter 2 page 56) plaintiff Cappo, who had been drinking and who hurled an epithet at the guard, was struck by the guard, causing Cappo to fall and injure a bone in his left wrist. The trial court awarded him $13,490 but reduced it to $7,500 for two mitigating reasons. Cappo played a part in provoking the incident and he failed to submit to reasonable medical treatment to minimize his injuries through surgery.

ETHICS, PROFESSIONALISM, LACK OF JURISDICTION

For many years, the private security industry has been involved in many activities to become more professional. Professionalism includes being engaged in, or worthy of, the high standards of the profession. *Private Security: Report of the Task Force on Private Security* (Appendix C) in 1976 set a goal that a code of ethics should be adopted and enforced for private security personnel and employers. In its commentary on this subject, the report stated that a code of ethics is a statement that incorporates moral and ethical principles and philosophies, that it is necessary for any profession, and that it would provide guidance to its members so that their activities could be measured against a standard of behavior. The Task Force felt that the need for a code of ethics was apparent and called upon employers, private security personnel, and professional organizations to adopt and publish a code, to enforce the code to the best of their ability through peer pressure, disciplinary procedures, and, as appropriate, criminal and civil actions. The report also suggested that a combined effort of all parties involved would be required if the code were to truly represent a standard of excellence for the industry, that employers should insist on compliance with the code by all employees, and that peer pressure should be exerted by employees against their colleagues who do not abide by the code. In the following case, look carefully to see if the private security employees conducted themselves professionally and in a manner that reflects credit on themselves, their employer, and the private security industry.

TURNER v. GENERAL MOTORS CORP.
750 S.W.2d 76 (1988)

KAROHL, Presiding Judge.

This is an appeal from a jury verdict in an action for negligent infliction of emotional distress. Following judgment based on a jury award of actual and punitive damages in favor of plaintiff, Jerry Turner, Sr., defendant General Motors appealed.

To have the right to maintain an action, plaintiff must be shown to have a justiciable interest in the subject matter of the action. In order to have standing as a party, the prospective plaintiff must have an actual and justiciable interest capable of protection through litigation. Any doubt concerning the jurisdiction of the trial court over the subject matter is a jurisdictional question which we must raise *sua sponte* if not presented at the trial court. The circumstances surrounding this case are unfortunate. However, the pleadings and the evidence make it clear that the trial court lacked and this court lacks subject matter jurisdiction.

Plaintiff, an employee of General Motors, brought suit against two defendants, Eugene Hadley, chief security officer at the General Motors Hazelwood Plant, and General Motors Corporation. Plaintiff filed a three count petition in the circuit court alleging: (I) intentional infliction of emotional distress; (II) outrageous conduct; and (III) negligent infliction of emotional distress. The case was tried by a jury and the only claim submitted was Count III, negligent infliction of emotional distress. The jury found in favor of plaintiff Turner and against defendant General Motors Corporation. Defendant Eugene Hadley was absolved of liability. Plaintiff has not cross-appealed.

Plaintiff's reliance on the negligent infliction of emotional distress cause of action was based on the following facts. On January 26, 1981, Jerry Turner, Sr., was an employee at the General Motors Parts Division Plant in Hazelwood, Missouri. That day he was working the second shift which ran from 4:00 p.m. until 12:30 a.m. His son, Jerry Turner, Jr., drove onto the company parking lot at approximately 11:30 p.m. to provide his father a ride home.

Surveillance cameras had been installed on the grounds by General Motors as a protection against theft and vandalism on the parking lot. While plaintiff's son was waiting for his father, the surveillance camera taped him in an act of masturbation. The security guard who taped the occurrence, Glenn Tompkins, thereafter approached Turner's vehicle where the subject identified himself as Jerry Turner's son and stated that he was waiting to pick up his father. Tompkins did not tell plaintiff's son what he had seen, nor that he had preserved the act on tape. When plaintiff got off work he passed by Tompkins at the exit door, but Tompkins did not mention to him what had just transpired.

The next day, the videotape of plaintiff's son was exhibited to numerous employees at the General Motors Plant. The film was shown by the defendant Eugene Hadley and by other security guards with the knowledge and consent of the plant manager. The film was exhibited in the security office to anyone interested.

Plaintiff became the target of ridicule, humiliation and insults during the entire shift, some of it by fellow workers who had not seen the tape, but had been told about it. Plaintiff endured daily harassment for three to four months and then with lessened frequency until time of trial.

Plaintiff was very emotionally distraught over the entire incident. He sought medical advice complaining of chest pains, upset stomach, nervousness and sleeplessness. His doctor prescribed Valium in increased dosages and when this did not suffice he prescribed a stronger medication. Plaintiff missed work over the incident, but had to return out of the necessity of supporting his family. Jerry Turner came to hate his job, never knowing when he would be ridiculed about his son.

There are basically two elements required for a negligent infliction of emotional distress cause of action: (1) that "the defendant should have realized that his conduct involved an unreasonable risk of causing distress", and (2) that "the emotional distress or mental injury must be medically diagnosable and must be of sufficient severity so as to be medically significant." Looking solely at these factors one may assume, as evidently all concerned assumed, that plaintiff pleaded and proved a submissible case.

However, an even more basic requirement essential to any tort cause of action is the infringement of a legally cognizable right and the corresponding breach of a legally recognized duty. The existence of a cause of action presupposes the presence as a matter of law of a right and corresponding duty as elements of a justiciable claim.

Those rights which are recognized and protected by the law encompass property rights, including contractual and business relations, and personal rights, including the right to enjoyment of one's reputation, and the right to privacy. Plaintiff's claim that General Motors owed him a duty not to cause emotional distress does not involve any of these rights or interests.

We emphasize, however, that there is no necessary nexus between a legal right or duty and a moral or humane right or duty. The former are the accepted bases for an action in tort. The latter are principles which are dictated by good morals and conscience but are not necessarily within the boundaries of the law.

The events which transpired at the General Motors Plant and the ridicule to which Jerry Turner was subjected were tragic and devoid of any semblance of good judgment. The conduct and remarks were callous, cruel and contemptible. Likewise, the actions of General Motors' supervisors, in allowing its security officers to exhibit with impunity to plant personnel the tape depicting plaintiff's son in a very private act, was reprehensible. The widespread showing was unjustified even to demonstrate the need of plant security. We note, however, the acts were not performed in plaintiff's presence and he was never directly a participant.

Moreover, the theory of plaintiff's submitted case was negligent infliction of emotional distress—not intentional infliction, not invasion of privacy and not defamation. Plaintiff sought to recover damages for the emotional distress he suffered upon discovering that General Motors personnel had exhibited and seen the film depicting acts of his son. In essence, plaintiff tried to expand the typical negligent infliction of emotional distress cause of action wherein the mental disturbance and its consequences are not caused by any fear for plaintiff's own safety, or by distress at witnessing some peril or harm to another person.

Here, however, plaintiff never viewed the film, and thus cannot claim physical harm through fright or upset as a direct result thereof. Similarly, and perhaps more pertinent, General Motors never placed Turner's son in any danger, harm or peril by virtue of any negligent acts. Plaintiff seeks to rely on an act or acts of employees of General Motors which were not negligent in relation to plaintiff's son. The son was on another's private property, had no reasonable expectation of privacy for acts he commited thereon,[1] and apparently would have no basis for claiming General Motors owed him a duty not to exhibit videos of his own conduct or misconduct taped while he was on the premises. Where plaintiff's son has no cause of action against General Motors for the acts of its employees then those same acts will not support plaintiff-father's claim.

Affirmatively, where plaintiff was not personally or directly present during the alleged negligent acts (i.e., the showing and viewing of the film by General Motors' personnel), then those acts will not support a cause of action for negligent infliction of emotional distress unless they involve a breach of some duty owed the son. This is true because without the relationship, attachment, and affection of plaintiff-father for his son, there would have been no emotional distress. In the absence of a duty, a breach and a resulting actionable injury by defendant to plaintiff's son, the acts of defendant, although reprehensible, do not give rise to the tort of negligent infliction of emotional distress.

A fundamental test of whether an individual has a cause of action in tort against another is:

> Did the person, sought to be held liable, owe to the person, seeking to recover, any duty, to do something he did not do, or not to do something he did do? If so, his failure to do what he ought to have done or his doing what he ought not to have done constitutes a legal wrong, whether it be intentional or merely negligent, for which the person injured thereby can recover. . . .

Here, however, plaintiff does not and cannot contend and we cannot find that General Motors had any *legal* duty not to publish the contents of the videotape. It would be an unreasonable burden on human activity if a defendant who has embarrassed one person by conduct which is not actionable were to be compelled to pay for the lacerated feelings of every person disturbed by reason of it, including every bystander, relative, and friend shocked by such actions. Consequently the trial court and this court are without subject-matter jurisdiction.

We reverse and remand with direction that the trial court dismiss the cause for lack of subject matter jurisdiction.

SMITH, Judge, concurring.

I concur on a slightly different basis. The embarrassment suffered by plaintiff arose from the actions of his son. Those actions arose on defendant's premises on which the son had no expectation of privacy. Plaintiff seeks to impose upon defendants a duty of non-disclosure of the son's activities. I am unaware of the existence of any such legal duty. Frequently persons in this society are embarrassed by the actions of their relatives. The potential of such embarrassment does not create a legal duty upon other members of the society to refrain from disclosing such embarrassing conduct. Human nature being what it is, such conduct will likely be revealed if known. As tasteless as I find the conduct of defendants to be, I find no legal basis for imposing upon them, or anyone else, an obligation to keep secret, information which is true and not covered by the tort of invasion of privacy. Plaintiff has failed to plead a cause of action.

---

[1] A sign visible to all who entered the GM premises stated that the grounds, including the parking lot, were subject to surveillance.

CASE COMMENT

Although the jury's award of actual and punitive damages was overturned for lack of jurisdiction, it appears that some loss occurred. How much employee time and productivity was lost when the tape was exhibited to numerous employees at the plant and in the Security Office to anyone who was interested? How much time was lost by employees going to court? And what were the legal expenses for trial and appeal? The very idea of security is to prevent loss, not perpetrate it. Other considerations for the security manager are professionalism as it pertains to the security industry, ethics as promulgated by the American Society for Industrial Security or other professional organization, and supervision of the security officers which was described by the court as reprehensible. The security manager should provide a code of ethics to those being supervised and attempt to enforce the code as recommended by the Task Force on Private Security. Appendix C contains codes of ethics for the American Society for Industrial Security, Private Security Management; and Private Security Employees.

PART II

Authority, Probable Cause, Arrest, Search and Seizure, Interrogation, Use of Force, Deprivation of Rights, Entrapment

7

Authority of Private Citizen

Security directors should be aware of the various state laws in their jurisdictions and the interpretations thereof, so that they can determine if their employees are acting as private citizens or governmental agents. Different standards apply to the two different classes of employee. Is the off-duty, moonlighting uniformed police officer working as a private citizen or a sworn police officer? Does the licensing, commissioning, or deputizing of the security employee convert that employee into a governmental agent? And if the authority of the security employee is derived from the state, what is the extent of that authority, and what is the potential liability if the actions of that employee are illegal? State laws and court interpretations differ and vary from state to state, therefore it is of primary importance that the employer know precisely under what authority the employee is working.

STANDS IN SHOES

Virtually all states regulate some aspect of the private security industry. The security manager should be familiar with the state's regulatory and licensing laws and its constitution and legal interpretations through such mediums as opinions of the attorney general and court decisions. A private security employee may be considered to be a private citizen or a law enforcement officer. If the private security employee is classified as private citizen, federal constitutional sanctions and statutes may not attach. If the employee is classified as a law enforcement officer, then his or her action may be state action if sufficient trappings of state authority exist, which in turn may trigger federal sanctions.

The following two cases show the opposite ends of the private citizen/law enforcement officer spectrum. In the first case (*Brant*), a security guard licensed by the state was clearly a *law enforcement officer.* The state supreme court interpreted the law to find that security guards licensed by the State Law Enforcement Division stand in the shoes of sheriffs for purposes of arrest while they are on the property they were hired to protect. In the second case (*Waters*) the security guard licensed by the state seized some cocaine.

In a suppression hearing, the defendant claimed that state action was involved, likening security guards to special police officers. Here the appellate court found that, although licensed by the state police, security guards are not vested with police powers. Without governmental powers, security guards are acting as private citizens. Note the opinion of the attorney general in this case—to the effect that, since security guards act on the authorization of their employers, authorization can be no broader than that the employer possesses, namely, the authority of a private citizen.

STATE v. BRANT
293 S.E.2d 703 (1982)

NESS, Justice:

Appellant Betty Brant was convicted of resisting arrest pursuant to § 16–9–320, S.C. Code of Laws, (1976). Brant asserts the indictment here was defective and that the arresting security guard was not a law enforcement officer within the meaning of the statute. We disagree and affirm.

Ronald Sturkie, a security guard, observed appellant shoplifting in the Richway Store where he was employed. Sturkie followed appellant out to the store's parking lot where he arrested her for shoplifting. When placed under arrest, appellant and two of her relatives beat Mr. Sturkie in the head and face causing him serious injuries. Appellant was indicted for resisting arrest.

Appellant contends the indictment was fatally defective because it charged the common law crime of resisting arrest which had been codified as S.C.Code of Laws § 16–9–320 prior to appellant's arrest. The indictment charged as follows:

"That Betty A. Brant did in Richland County on or about the 15th Day of December, 1980, resist with force the efforts of Russell Sturkie, a peace officer of this State, to make a lawful arrest of the said Betty A. Brant."

An indictment is sufficient if the offense is stated with sufficient certainty and particularity to enable the court to know what judgement to pronounce, the defendant to know what he is called upon to answer, and so that an acquittal or conviction will sufficiently bar any subsequent prosecution.

The language of the indictment clearly charged the crime of resisting arrest with force and provided appellant with adequate notice of the offense. This issue has no merit.

Appellant further alleges the security guard Sturkie was not a law enforcement officer under the statute and thus the charge and arrest was invalid.

The term "law enforcement officer" is defined in S.C.Code of Laws, § 16–9–310:

"For purposes of this article 'law enforcement officer' shall mean any duly appointed or commissioned law enforcement officer of the State, a county or municipality."

The State Law Enforcement Division (SLED) has the authority to license and regulate private security agencies under § 40–17–10, S.C.Code, et seq. Security guards licensed by SLED, as was the security guard in this case, are granted powers identical to those of a sheriff on the property he is hired to protect. See S.C.Code of Laws § 40–17–130.

In determining the meaning of one statute, it is proper to consider other statutory provisions relating to the same subject matter. Section 40–17–130 of the Code provides:

"Any person covered by the provisions of § 40-17-90 or properly registered or licensed under this chapter who is hired or employed to patrol, guard or render a similar service on certain property *shall be granted the authority and power which sheriffs have to make arrest of any persons violating or charged with violating any of the criminal statutes of this State,* but shall have such powers of arrest only on the aforementioned property." (Emphasis added).

According to this provision, a security guard licensed by SLED stands in the shoes of the sheriff for purposes of arrest while he is on the property he is hired to protect.

Thus the SLED-licensed security guard here was clearly a "law enforcement officer" within the meaning of the statute. Appellant's conviction is affirmed.

AFFIRMED.

STATE COMMISSION/LICENSURE

WATERS v. STATE
575 A.2d 1244 (1990)

MURPHY, Chief Judge.

At a nonjury trial in the Circuit Court for Anne Arundel County, DeWayne Waters was convicted of possession of cocaine and sentenced to a term of imprisonment. During the pendency of his appeal before the Court of Special Appeals, we granted certiorari on our own motion to decide whether, as Waters claimed, the Fourth Amendment prohibition against unreasonable searches and seizures was applicable in the circumstances of this case.

On the evening of May 16, 1988, Paul Madden was employed as a security guard at Wayson's Corner in Anne Arundel County. He accosted Waters as he leaned against a vehicle in the parking lot. Observing that Waters appeared to have a large object in his pocket, Madden reached into Waters's pocket and extracted a beer can and a plastic bag containing a whitish substance. Madden then called the Anne Arundel County Police Department and Waters was arrested and charged with possessing cocaine.

Upon Waters's motion to suppress the seized cocaine, Madden testified that he was a plainclothes security guard licensed by the Maryland State Police and working in that capacity on the night of Waters's arrest. Asked whether he was a "special police officer," Madden replied, "No, I was just a plainclothes security officer for Wayson's." He testified that he did not have the general arrest powers of a policeman but believed that he had the power to detain a felony. He said that he had attended two security schools in the early 1980's for training. He now stated that he had been involved in about seventeen "drug busts" over a one-year period; his involvement had been as "eyewitness, spotting people, pointing them out, identifying them." Madden said that he was wearing a suit and tie with his "security officer" badge clipped to his belt on the night of Waters's arrest.

Waters testified at the suppression hearing that at the time of the search, he was standing next to his friends' car when Madden drove up, jumped out of his car, drew a gun and forced him to lean against the car. Waters said Madden had "lost his grip" and was "out of control." He said Madden pulled the plastic bag from his pocket without asking permission.

Waters argued that Madden was a state agent by reason of his employment and that the search and seizure conducted by him was in violation of the Fourth Amendment. Waters conceded that Madden was a private security guard employed by a private detective agency regulated by what is now Maryland Code §§ 13–101 through 13–801 of the Business Occupations and Professions Article. But Waters maintained that security guards are like special police officers who are commissioned by the Governor and exercise general police powers in the protection of their employer's property. Waters suggested that both security guards and special policemen are agents of the State because their duties are similar to those of regular police officers; they are both regulated by the State and authorized to wear badges and to obtain permits to carry guns. Thus, Waters urged the trial judge to conclude that Madden's seizure of the plastic bag involved state action, and because it was unreasonable, the evidence should be suppressed.

Judge Goudy found that Madden's security guard employment did not make him an agent of the State. In denying the motion to suppress, he said:

> "The Court finds from the evidence . . . that the witness in the case was not a police officer, not an agent of the State. The witness was licensed by the State, but merely being licensed . . . does not show enough control to be an agent.
>
> "The witness was an employee of a private enterprise. . . . The prohibition against search and seizure is a sanction against the State not against private citizens, which is what the witness was in this case. The search, while it could very well have been a trespass in this case, a trespass to the person, is not inadmissible . . . by the State against the Defendant."

Before us, Waters renews his argument that because private security guards employed by private detective agencies, and special police officers commissioned by the Governor, perform duties similar to those of regular police officers, Madden's seizure of the plastic bag constituted illegal state action. Alternatively, Waters suggests that notwithstanding his concession at trial that Madden was a private security guard, reversal of his conviction is nevertheless mandated because the trial judge made no factual findings as to whether Madden was a security guard or a special policeman. As to this, he argues that Madden's use of the phrase "security officer" or "security guard," in describing his employment, was inconclusive as to his actual status.

The Fourth Amendment of the United States Constitution guarantees the right of individuals to be secure against unreasonable searches and seizures. It applies to actions by the State, *Mapp v. Ohio,* 367 U.S. 643, but generally does not apply to actions by private individuals. *Burdeau v. McDowell,* 256 U.S. 465. Thus when a private individual obtains incriminatory matter from an accused, no matter how improperly, and such matter comes into the possession of the government without a violation of the accused's rights by governmental authority, the exclusionary rule does not prohibit its use at trial. A private search or seizure may, however, trigger Fourth Amendment protections if the private individual whose actions are in question, "in light of all the circumstances of the case, must be regarded as having acted as an 'instrument' or agent of the state."

Maryland Code Article 41, §§ 4–901 through 4–913 (entitled "Special Policemen"), authorizes the Governor to "appoint and deputize as special policemen persons he deems qualified for special police commissions." § 4–901. Section 4–902 provides that applications for a commission shall be made to the Superintendent of the Maryland State Police by governmental agencies, political subdivisions, colleges or universities, or by private business entities for the purpose of protecting their properties. Once commissioned, a special police officer "has, and may exercise, the powers of a police officer upon the property," including the power to preserve the "peace and good order" of the property and to make arrests. § 4–905. A special police officer is considered the employee of the applicant for the commission, § 4–909, and is generally limited to exercising police powers on the property. Nevertheless, the police power itself is not so limited since the words "peace and good order," contained in the statute, " 'permit a special policeman, when on his employer's property, to enforce the criminal law generally.' "

When special police officers are enforcing the criminal law, they are exercising governmental powers which involve state action. *See, e.g., Griffin v. Maryland,* 378 U.S. 130, (holding that "if an individual is possessed of state authority and purports to act under that authority, his action is state action"). *Griffin* involved special deputy sheriffs, employed by a private park, who were deputized pursuant to the provisions of a county ordinance which invested them with powers similar to those exercised by a special policeman commissioned by the Governor. The Court said that the arrests made by these special deputies constituted state action. *See also United States v. Lima,* 424 A.2d 113, (where security guard has powers akin to regular police officer, and is appointed by government official even though privately employed, sufficient trappings of state authority exist to trigger Fourth Amendment restrictions). Thus, had Madden been a special police officer commissioned by the Governor under § 4–901, his seizure of the plastic bag would have been subject to the Fourth Amendment.

Unlike special policemen commissioned by the Governor, security guards are not vested with arrest or other police powers. They are employed by private detective agencies which are licensed by the Superintendent of the Maryland State Police under Code, Title 13 of the Business Occupations Article. Section 13–101(k) of the Article defines a "Security guard" as an individual "who provides security guard services"; these services are defined in subsection (1) to include "any activity that is performed for compensation as a security guard to protect any individual or property, except the activities of an individual while performing as . . . (2) a special police officer commissioned by the Governor under Article 41 of the Code." As employees of detective agencies engaged to guard the property of their employer's clients, security guards have not been granted police powers by statute and therefore are not state agents in any traditional sense for purposes of the Fourth Amendment. Without governmental powers, security guards are acting as private citizens when protecting property, and their private status is not altered because their interest in protecting property coincides with the public's interest in preventing crime generally. The Attorney General of Maryland has also recognized that licensed security guards are not state agents. *See* 50 Op. Att'y Gen. 309 (1965) (holding that since security guards act upon the authorization of their employer, that authorization can be no broader than that which the employer possesses, namely, the authority of a private citizen). *See Stevenson v. State,* 413 A.2d 1340 (defining a citizen's power to arrest); *Great Atlantic & Pacific Tea Co. v. Paul,* 261 A.2d 731 (shopkeeper's authority to arrest or detain is limited to the authority of a private citizen). Moreover, mere state licensing of a private individual's occupation, without more, does not constitute sufficient state control to make the individual a state agent. Nor does extensive state regulation of itself convert the actions of those regulated into state action.

The burden was upon Waters, as the proponent of the motion to suppress, to establish that his Fourth Amendment rights were violated by the challenged search and seizure. In the same vein, the burden of establishing government involvement in a private search rests on the party objecting to the admissibility of the evidence.

The only evidence in the case was that Madden was a licensed security guard at the time he seized the plastic bags, and the trial judge so held. Water's argument that Madden was a state agent is wholly unconvincing. Consequently, Judge Goudy correctly determined that the seized cocaine was admissible in evidence, there being no showing (or even an allegation) that Madden was working in collusion with the police at the time of the search, or otherwise acted as an instrument of the State in the performance of his duties.

JUDGEMENT AFFIRMED.

CASE COMMENT

In both cases the security officer was licensed by the state. One state considered the security officer clearly a *law enforcement officer* while the other did not. In the state where the guard stands in the shoes of the sheriff, the security manager and employee should be cognizant of federal restrictions and guidelines related to their activity.

LIMITATION ON STATE AUTHORITY

CHILES v. CROOKS
708 F. Supp. 127 (1989)

Once it has been determined that the authority of a security guard is derived from the state, the question then arises as to the extent of that authority. In this case, it was contended that security guard Crooks was licensed by the state and that he was acting under color of state law. The statutory scheme for the licensing of security guards in this state granted them the power to arrest and detain persons on the premises they were hired to protect. However, a limitation on the authority of a security guard was given in an opinion of the state Attorney General. The Attorney General concluded that while a security guard is empowered to affect an arrest as a public law enforcement agent might, the guard is empowered to do no more and that the state law does not raise the private security guard to the level of a public law enforcement official. Also that the state legislation does not provide for any investigatory authority on the part of security guards. The court rationalized that private security guards are neither educated in the techniques of criminal investigation, that they are not authorized by statute to conduct any such investigations, and therefore must defer to the appropriate law enforcement agency. For a broader treatment of this aspect see this case in another Chapter.

POLICE MOONLIGHTING—PRIMARY RESPONSIBILITY

Another area of interest to the security manager is related to the authority and duties of an off-duty police officer who moonlights as a security guard. If this employee is injured while on security duty for a private employer, who will be responsible for compensation for the injuries—the private employer or the municipality? Under what conditions does the police officer's authority cease and that officer become a private citizen for purposes of injury compensation?

In the following case, an off-duty city police officer was injured while moonlighting as a security officer at a hospital. The hospital contended that the off-duty officer was under the direction and control of the city and was acting as a police officer at the time of the injury. The compensation commission found the hospital liable, and it appealed. The answer in this case was found in a recently passed statute and the identity of the compensator depended on whether the officer was discharging his or her *primary responsibility* (prevention or detection of crime or enforcement of law) and was not engaged in services paid for by a private employer and on whether the officer and the public employer had no agreement providing for worker's compensation coverage for that private employment.

MOUNT SINAI HOSPITAL v. CITY OF MIAMI BEACH
523 So.2d 722 (1988)

BARFIELD, Judge.
Mount Sinai Hospital appeals a workers' compensation order finding it liable for injuries sustained by an off-duty City of Miami Beach policeman who fell while performing security guard duties at the Hospital. We affirm.

Gary Lehman worked a ten hour shift four days a week for the City police department. He also worked at the Hospital several times a month as an alternate security guard, filling in for the officer who regularly worked this permanent off-duty job. He was paid $14/hour by the Hospital, which deducted withholding and social security from his checks but did not provide pension or group insurance benefits. His supervisor, who worked out of a security trailer behind the Hospital, was not a City police officer, but an employee of the Hospital. Lehman's job duties included keeping family members or other people from restricted areas of the emergency room, and keeping the reserved spaces in the parking lot outside the emergency room free for ambulances.

Competent, substantial evidence supports the deputy commissioner's finding that Lehman was exiting the emergency room door to check on the parking lot when he slipped and his right knee gave way, and that he was in the course and scope of his employment with the Hospital at the time of the accident. We reject the contention of both the Hospital and the City, that because Lehman had injured his right knee in several previous accidents, and because the medical and accident reports failed to mention a "slip", the deputy commissioner was required to find that Lehman suffered an idiopathic fall unrelated to his employment. This was a factual determination to be made by the deputy commissioner, based upon the competence and credibility of all the evidence before him. Lehman's testimony, which the deputy commissioner accepted, indicates that his fall was not attributable solely to his pre-existing condition, but that he slipped as he exited the emergency room door while performing his security guard duties for the Hospital. This court will not reweigh the evidence and substitute its judgment for that of the deputy commissioner.

The Hospital contends that even if the accident is found to be compensable, the evidence establishes that Lehman was under the direction and control of the City and was acting as a police officer at the time of his injury, so that the deputy commissioner erred in ruling that the Hospital was his employer. It relies upon *City of Hialeah v. Weber,* 491 So.2d 1204, in which this court held that an off-duty police officer working as a security guard for a lounge, who was injured in the process of apprehending persons slashing car tires at a business across the street from the lounge, was an employee of the city police department at the time of his injury. The court indicated in that opinion that there might be circumstances in which an off-duty police officer would be considered the employee of the off-duty employer. Such a circumstance exists in this case.

Section 440.091, Florida Statutes, provides that an injured law enforcement officer "shall be deemed to have been acting within the course of employment" at the time of the injury if he was discharging his "primary responsibility" (prevention or detection of crime or enforcement of law) *and* "was not engaged in services for which he was paid by a private employer, and he and his public employer had no agreement providing for workers' compensation coverage for that private employment." The statute indicates a legislative intent that the public employer be responsible for injuries sustained by a police officer acting "in the line of duty," i.e., in fulfillment of his primary responsibility, so long as his actions do not also constitute a service for which he is paid by a private employer, unless the public employer had agreed to provide workers' compensation coverage for the private employment.

Weber presents one end of the spectrum of situations in which the applicability of this statute must be determined. In that case, the claimant was unequivocally performing a police function, responding to his duty as a police officer to investigate a crime in his presence, and was not performing a service for which he was hired by the private employer. Under those circumstances, section 440.091 provides that he should be deemed to have been acting within the course of his employment with the City of Hialeah at the time of his injury.

At the other end of the spectrum, in the case at issue Lehman was performing a service for which he was paid by the Hospital, checking the emergency room parking lot to see that the spaces reserved for ambulances were not being used by other vehicles, and testified that he was not performing a police function at the time he was injured. Under these circumstances, section 440.091 provides that he should not be deemed to have been acting within the course of his employment with the City of Miami Beach at the time of his injury.

Even if it could be said that Lehman was performing both a police function and a service for which he was paid by the private employer, no evidence was presented that the City had agreed to provide workers' compensation coverage for injuries sustained by off-duty officers performing services for private employers. The portion of the City's police department manual which was presented to the deputy commissioner speaks only to the reporting procedures for off-duty accidents, and Lehman testified that he was not aware of any agreement between the City and the Hospital specifically covering injuries while performing the off-duty job. No other evidence directly addressing the question was presented.

Under the evidence presented in this case, the deputy commissioner did not abuse his discretion in finding the Hospital, and not the City, to be the employer at the time of this accident. The order is AFFIRMED, the claimant's motion for appellate attorney fees is granted, and the case is REMANDED to the deputy commissioner for determination of the amount of the appellate attorney fee.

CASE COMMENT

Since the officer was not acting *in the line of duty* (primary responsibility or police function) and was paid by a private employer, the ruling of the compensation commission was upheld. Note the court's citation of a case where an off-duty police officer working as a security guard was injured in the process of apprehending persons engaged in crime across the street from where he was employed. Here the court held that he was an employee of the police at the time he was injured.

CATCH 22

In the next case, a bank employed an off-duty police officer as a part-time teller. He had a higher hourly pay rate than did full-time tellers, and there was evidence the bank valued the extra protection through his presence. An armed robbery took place. Bank rules instructed employees to do nothing to provoke an armed robber and police department rules did not permit discharging a weapon when innocent persons might be endangered. The off-duty officer identified himself as a police officer and fired shots, missing the robber but hitting a customer. The bank attempted to avoid liability contending that, as soon as the off-duty officer identified himself as a police officer, he was no longer a servant of the bank and was acting solely in the role of a police officer.

SHAW v. MANUFACTURER'S HANOVER TRUST COMPANY
464 N.Y.S.2d 172 (1983)

MEMORANDUM DECISION.

Judgment of the Supreme Court, New York County, entered on January 15, 1982, which dismissed the complaint after a jury verdict on written interrogatories finding an absence of negligence attributable to any of the defendants, unanimously reversed, on the law and the facts and in the exercise of discretion and the matter remanded for a new trial, with costs to abide the event.

Plantiff-appellant Leonard Shaw allegedly suffered permanent and debilitating spinal injuries when he was accidentally shot by defendant Donald Sommers, an off-duty New York City Police officer who was working as a part-time teller in a Manufacturer's Hanover branch office when an armed robbery occurred on June 12, 1978.

Appellant Shaw was waiting to transact business at a teller's counter when two armed robbers entered the bank and demanded money from a bank officer seated at a desk. The officer then entered the tellers' area, obtained the money, and delivered it to one of the robbers who then escaped. The other robber was standing with his gun pointed at the defendant Sommers when Sommers identified himself as a police officer, ordered the robber to drop his gun, and directed everybody else in the bank to get down on the floor. From a protected position behind a pillar, Sommers fired two shots at the remaining robber who did not return fire but merely stood there staring at Sommers. Both shots missed the robber, one narrowly missing a bank officer who was lying on the floor behind another pillar.

At that point, the robber began moving toward the main entrance. On the way, he grabbed hold of Shaw, who had been crouching in the customers' waiting area, and attempted to use him as a shield as he successfully completed his escape. As the bandit, with appellant in tow, approached the entryway, Sommers, from his position behind the pillar with a partially obstructed view, fired two more shots in rapid succession. The last shot fired by Sommers struck appellant, whom Sommers testified he had not seen.

The bank is not entitled to the emergency instruction because the possibility of a bank robbery cannot be said to be one that is not anticipated. In the words of Prosser, "a further qualification which must be made is that some 'emergencies' must be anticipated, and the actor must be prepared to meet them when he engages in an activity in which they are likely to arise." Prosser, *Law of Torts*.

In the present case, the employees of the bank were instructed on what to do in the event of an armed robbery. Sommers testified that he was instructed to do nothing that would provoke an armed robber. Sommers testified further that he was aware that there were customers in the bank at the time of the robbery. Thus, Sommers' response to the robbery was in direct contravention of both the rule of the bank not to provoke an armed robber and the Police Department regulation against discharging a weapon when innocent persons may be endangered.

Throughout the trial, counsel for Manufacturer's Hanover advanced the dubious contention that as soon as Sommers announced that he was a police officer he was no longer a servant of the bank but was acting solely in his role as a police officer. In light of the testimony that Sommers was paid for part-time work at a higher hourly rate than full-time tellers earned, and evidence that the bank valued the "extra protection" Sommers' presence at the bank afforded, liability cannot be avoided by this argument. If, as the bank argues, Sommers was in a "Catch 22" position between the bank's no provocation rule and his duty as a police officer, he was placed in that situation by his employer, the bank.

A further limitation on the availability of the emergency rule charge is that the actor did not aggravate or create the emergency situation by his own conduct. Sommers' conduct, in direct contravention of the bank's no provocation rule, increased the danger inherent in the situation. Bank officer Smith testified that the robber at whom Sommers fired the shots recognized Sommers as a police officer and stated, before the other robber had been handed the money, "I know he's a cop. If he touch the gun, I'll shoot him." Thus, when Sommers took cover behind the pillar, announced he was a police officer and ordered everyone in the bank to get down, he aggravated the already existing emergency situation. Accordingly, defendants were not entitled to the emergency charge.

Had Sommers abided by the bank's instruction not to provoke armed robbers, it is possible that both robbers, who never returned fire, would have left the bank without harming anyone.

In view of the foregoing, we consider it unnecessary to reach the question as to whether the verdict was against the weight of the evidence.

CASE COMMENT

The court held that a bank robbery cannot be said to be an emergency that is not anticipated and that the off-duty officer contravened both bank policy against provoking armed robbers and police department policy against discharging weapons when innocent persons may be endangered. The court described as dubious the bank's contention that he was no longer a servant of the bank and was acting solely as a police officer. The court took into consideration his higher pay scale and value as extra protection. Whatever "Catch 22" situation the officer was in was created by the bank. In holding that the bank could not avoid liability on these grounds, the court also pointed out that the officer increased the danger inherent in the situation. When hiring police officers, the security manager may desire to be aware of police regulations so as not to create this type of potential loss situation.

8

Probable Cause

Security managers and employees should be aware of the probable cause standard in the event they make an arrest. In the event the employee is a sworn officer, Fourth Amendment standards will apply. They may also apply if the employee is commissioned, deputized, or licensed. Normally Fourth Amendment proscriptions do not attach to the activities of the private citizen. Appendix H defines the statutory arrest authority for private citizens. In some states, the knowledge requirement is higher than probable cause in that a felony has been committed in fact. Having the degree of knowledge required is a necessity in order to make a valid arrest. Probable cause is also a defense to a false arrest/imprisonment tort lawsuit.

STANDARDS OF PROBABLE CAUSE

The point of law to be learned in the following case is what constitutes probable cause for arrest. Probable cause for arrest means that, at the time of arrest, the officer must possess knowledge of facts sufficient for a prudent person to believe that the subject committed, or was committing, an offense. Probable cause, or reasonable grounds to believe, rests on the reasonable belief of the officer. Probable cause is an affirmative defense to false arrest charges. Anything with less certainty than reasonable belief such as "may have committed" or suspicion, does not satisfy the probable cause requirement. Probable cause is the law enforcement standard for arrest. In this case, this standard was conferred on private officers by the Board of Police Commissioners for exercise on property assigned to the private officers for protection.

PALCHER v. J.C. NICHOLS COMPANY
783 S.W.2d 166 (1990)

SHANGLER, Presiding Judge.
The plaintiff Palcher brought suit against the J.C. Nichols Company for false arrest and malicious prosecution as a result of an incident on the Kansas City Country Club Plaza on

October 13, 1985. The claims were submitted to the jury, and verdicts were returned in favor of the defendant J.C. Nichols Company on both counts. The plaintiff appeals from the judgment entered on those verdicts.

The plaintiff Palcher and two male friends, John Kostelac and Dan Dumovich, drove to the Kansas City Country Club Plaza and parked on the second level of the Bonwit Teller garage. Kostelac walked down the ramp for exit onto the street. Palcher and Dumovich lingered next to the car to discuss where they were going. As they were so engaged, a Plaza patrol vehicle came by slowly and the driver, Plaza security officer Karney, surveilled them. The incidence of car burglary is a common problem on the Country Club Plaza, he explained, so that his attention was captured by the two men—Palcher and Dumovich—who, as he observed, were peering into a vehicle parked next to them. He was concerned that a car burglary was underway. They were in the same posture on the return patrol down the ramp of the parking lot, so Karney parked the vehicle on the street, came up the stairwell and approached them. Karney testified that he saw Palcher "exposing himself urinating against the south wall." He actually saw the head of the penis and a flow of urine. Karney advised Palcher that what he did was a violation of the law. Palcher denied that he was urinating. Dumovich also protested that his friend was innocent. Karney then advised them: "I will let you go this time. If you come back to the Plaza for 2 or 3 weeks, I will arrest you for trespassing." Dumovich again insisted Palcher did not do anything wrong, and Karney thereupon arrested Dumovich.

Karney then frisked Palcher, cuffed the hands behind the back, and led him away. Dumovich continued to protest, and Karney radioed for assistance. Soon Officer Rishel arrived in the company of Ratterman, onduty supervisor of security guards. Rishel, an off-duty detective with the Kansas City, Missouri, Police Department, was in the uniform of a police officer. She worked the Plaza Security duty as a second job. Karney told her that he observed Palcher urinating against a wall in a parking stall, and so placed him in arrest and in handcuffs. Karney explained that he called for assistance because Dumovich was interfering with the movement of Palcher to a detention area. The officer placed Dumovich in arrest for disorderly conduct on the complaint of Karney. They were both taken to the Plaza Security Office, and thence to the police station. There they remained in a holding cell for about an hour and then were released on bond.

Palcher engaged an attorney to defend against the ordinance charge of indecent exposure, and upon a trial was acquitted.

The claims of false arrest and malicious prosecution were submitted to the jury and found against the plaintiff. Instructions on punitive damages were also tendered by the plaintiff, but refused by the court. On this appeal, Palcher complains only of instructions given, not of those withheld. The plaintiff contends that the affirmative defense instruction submitted by the defendant to the false arrest claim was prejudicially erroneous, as was the converse to the malicious prosecution theory.

False arrest was submitted by Instruction Number 7 and the common law affirmative defense of justification for arrest was submitted by Instruction Number 8.

INSTRUCTION NUMBER 7:
Your verdict must be for plaintiff if you believe:

Defendant intentionally restrained or intentionally instigated the restraint of plaintiff against his will unless you believe plaintiff is not entitled to recover by reason of Instruction Number 8.

INSTRUCTION NUMBER 8:
Your verdict must be for defendant under Instruction Number 7 if you believe:

that defendant, in restraining plaintiff, had a *reasonable suspicion* that plaintiff had indecently exposed himself in violation of Kansas City, Missouri, ordinance.

The phrase *"reasonable suspicion"* as used in this instruction means a *suspicion* based upon facts which would warrant an ordinarily cautious and prudent person in believing plaintiff Dennis Palcher was guilty of the offense charged.

Justification for detention and arrest of a person based on *reasonable cause* may be pleaded by the defendant and then submitted to the jury by instruction where the evidence supports the defense. The defendant fashioned affirmative defense Instruction Number 8 after the text of § 84.710, RSMo 1986, which defines the powers of members of the police force of Kansas City to stop and arrest:

They shall have power within the city or on public property of the city beyond the corporate limits thereof to arrest, on view, any person they see violating or whom they have reason to suspect of having violated any law of the state or ordinance of the city .... They shall also have the power to stop any person abroad whenever there is reasonable ground to suspect that he is committing, has committed or is about to commit a crime and demand of him his name, address, business abroad and whither he is going.[3]

The plaintiff argues that the proper standard to justify the exercise by the police of the power to arrest is probable cause, and not suspicion—however reasonable. The defendant asserts the text of the statute to validate the affirmative defense.

The argument the defendant makes is literal and without resort to the judicial gloss that informs the text of the statute. Those decisions discredit the instruction. It has been made explicit by repeated opinions of this court that § 84.710 and § 84.440 empowers a Kansas City police officer to effect a lawful warrantless arrest upon *reasonable ground to believe* that the person committed a felony or misdemeanor or violated an ordinance of the city, or was in the commission of such an offense. The *reasonable ground to suspect* component of § 84.710, validates the detention of a person on less than probable cause for arrest. That sanction to stop on reasonable suspicion within the constitutional principle of *Terry v. Ohio,* 392 U.S. 1, however, does not empower arrest on less than probable cause. In the absence of a *reason to believe* that a person committed or was in the commission of a violation of the law, a Kansas City police officer has no power to arrest under § 84.710. The construction a court gives to statutory language becomes a part of the text of the statute as if it had been so amended by the legislature. Accordingly, § 84.710 is to be read to empower a Kansas City police officer to arrest only upon probable cause.

The meaning of *probable cause* for arrest is fixed: At the time of arrest, the officer must have known facts sufficient for a prudent person to believe that the subject committed, or was committing, an offense. *Beck v. Ohio,* 379 U.S. 89. *Probable cause* for arrest and *reasonable ground* for arrest both rest on the reasonable *belief* of the officer who acts that the person arrested committed or was in the commission of a crime. An instruction that submits the affirmative defense of justification for arrest with less certainty than *belief,* therefore, misstates the premise of the defense. An instruction that dilutes that belief by "may have committed" or justifies an arrest by suspicion of guilt does not satisfy the requirement of probable cause.

Instruction Number 8 justifies the arrest by the security officer on the *reasonable suspicion* that Palcher indecently exposed himself in violation of the ordinance. It is palpably in error. That the instruction defines *reasonable suspicion* in terms of *believing* does not expunge the

---

[3]This statute in terms applies only to police officers. The police power is also conferred by commission on private officers by the Kansas City Board of Police Commissioners under 17 C.S.R. 10-2.010(3) for exercise on the property assigned to them for protection.

error or redress the misdirection to the jury. It defines doubt in terms of belief and so introduces an ambivalence in the essential component of the affirmative defense that cannot be reconciled by the finder of the fact. It was prejudicial for that reason. The false arrest claim requires a new trial.

The judgment on the false arrest claim is reversed and remanded for a new trial.

CASE COMMENT

The security manager needs to be aware of the particular standards necessary for making a litigation-proof arrest. In this case, the law enforcement standard of probable cause was applicable because it was conferred on private officers by the police commission. In arrests by private citizens, a felony in fact must usually have been committed or the offense must be a breach-of-peace type misdemeanor. Appendix H lists statutory arrest requirements for private citizen arrests. Loss from a false arrest suit can be avoided or diminished by utilizing the correct standard for making an arrest.

REASONABLE CAUSE v. PROBABLE CAUSE

In the next case, two women were detained by a store manager because a purse had not been paid for. A police officer responded and, after talking to the two women and store employees, placed them under arrest. One woman pleaded guilty. The other, the plaintiff in this matter, did not, and the charges against her were later dropped. She then sued the store for damages stemming from her detention and arrest. The trial court judgement was in her favor and against the store. The appellate court reversed finding that the store did have reasonable cause to detain her.

JOHNSON v. WAL–MART STORES, INC.
574 So. 2d 502 (1991)

LABORDE, Judge.

Plaintiff, Andrea Johnson, brought this suit against defendant, Wal-Mart Stores, Inc. (Wal-Mart), for damages stemming from her detention and subsequent arrest for shoplifting on December 13, 1984. After a trial on the merits, the trial court rendered judgment on February 25, 1987, in favor of plaintiff and against defendant for the sum of One Thousand and no/100 ($1,000.00) Dollars with legal interest from the date of judicial demand until paid and for all costs of the proceedings. From this judgment defendant appeals. We reverse.

Facts

The salient facts as found in the Joint Stipulation are as follows. Plaintiff went to Wal-Mart on December 13, 1984, with her mother, Theresa Johnson, and a friend, Beverly Johnson. The three of them started using one cart but plaintiff's mother left to shop elsewhere. Plaintiff and Beverly went to look at some purses which were on sale and they each picked up a purse and put it in their basket. Plaintiff then left the buggy to get a package from layaway and subsequently returned to the buggy. After plaintiff got some washing powder and the two women looked at some Christmas stockings, they proceeded to a checkout line. Both purchased purses. Plaintiff checked out first, leaving Beverly with the buggy. After being checked out, plaintiff went back to the check-out line in order to purchase a calculator. At this time Beverly was in the aisle between the check-out counter and the front of the store, leaning on the buggy. Plaintiff then saw a Wal-Mart employee point at her.

An employee of Wal–Mart at that time, Ruth Price, observed the actions of plaintiff and Beverly at the check-out counter facing hers. She saw plaintiff pick up a black purse and place it in the return merchandise buggy. Plaintiff then walked over to the layaway counter. Beverly concealed the purse under other packages in the return merchandise buggy. Plaintiff returned to the buggy and Mrs. Price saw her take the black purse out of the return merchandise buggy and put it back in their buggy. When Mrs. Price ascertained that the black purse had not been paid for, she called her manager. The store manager stopped both women and asked them to accompany him to the back of the store.

Officer Allen McBride of the Alexandria Police Department was dispatched to the scene in response to a call from Wal-Mart. He spoke to the two women and to Wal-Mart employees. Based on the information he obtained, he placed the two under arrest. Plaintiff and Beverly were taken to city jail and charged. Plaintiff pled not guilty at City Court and the charges against her were later dropped. Beverly pled guilty to the charge. Plaintiff then brought the present civil suit against Wal-Mart.

Reasonableness of the Detention

On appeal, defendant, Wal-Mart, contends that the trial court erred in finding it liable for the illegal detention, false imprisonment and false arrest of the plaintiff.

A merchant will be immune from civil liability if he can meet the requirements of an authorized detention. At the time of the incident an authorized detention was defined in LSA–C.Cr.P. art. 215(A)(1) as follows:

> "A. (1) A peace officer, merchant, or a specifically authorized employee or agent of a merchant, may use reasonable force to detain a person for questioning on the merchant's premises, for a length of time, not to exceed sixty minutes, when he has reasonable cause to believe that the person has committed a theft of goods held for sale by the merchant, regardless of the actual value of the goods. The merchant or his employee or agent may also detain such a person for arrest by a peace officer. The detention shall not constitute an arrest."

Thus, it must be shown that: 1) the person effecting the detention is a peace officer, merchant, or specifically authorized employee or agent of a merchant; 2) the party making the detention has reasonable cause to believe that the detained person has committed a theft; 3) unreasonable force is not used in detaining the suspect for interrogation; 4) the detention occurs on the merchant's premises; 5) the detention does not last longer than sixty minutes.

Defendant argues that the trial court erred in finding that it did not have reasonable cause to detain plaintiff for suspicion of shoplifting.

"Reasonable Cause" under LSA–C.Cr.P. art. 215 is not synonymous with probable cause. Reasonable cause for an investigatory detention is something less than probable cause. It requires that the detaining officer have articulable knowledge of particular facts sufficiently reasonable to suspect the detained person of criminal authority.

The test of liability is not based on the store patron's actual guilt or innocence, but rather on the reasonableness of the store employee's action under all the circumstances. Furthermore, the determination of whether there was reasonable cause to detain a person is a factual question to be decided by the trier of fact and his determination will not be reversed in the absence of a manifest abuse of discretion.

In its written Reasons for Judgment the trial court emphasized the fact that plaintiff did not attempt to hide her actions, but rather executed them in full view of two Wal–Mart employees. It stated:

"The first question to be answered is 'Did the employees of Wal–Mart have reasonable grounds to detain Andrea Johnson?' The answer to that is very easy and simple. No! All of the acts committed in the presence of and observed by Ruth Price and Jessica Howell (Wal–Mart Store employees) clearly established that Andrea Johnson did nothing that would even tend to suggest that she was attempting to steal the purse. Upon seeing it in the 'check out basket,' she removed it and placed it in the 'return merchandise basket.'

The return of the purse to the 'check out basket' was not done in a surreptitious manner. To the contrary it was done in the full view of the two check out ladies and only after being requested to do so by Beverly Johnson. There was no reason for any of the employees to detain Andrea in connection with the attempted theft of the purse. The facts related by Mrs. Price and Mrs. Howell establish the absence of 'reasonable cause' for detention of Andrea Johnson. It necessarily follows that there were no facts or circumstances present on the day in question that would lead any of the employees of Wal–Mart to believe that Andrea Johnson had committed or was attempting to commit a theft."

We must disagree with the learned trial judge. Our review of the stipulated facts convinces us that it was reasonable for Wal–Mart store employees to believe that plaintiff and Beverly Johnson were trying to avoid paying for the purse. Mrs. Price certainly had sufficient knowledge through personal observation to lead her to suspect the plaintiff of criminal activity. She saw plaintiff pick up a black purse and place it in the return merchandise buggy. She also saw Beverly Johnson conceal the purse under other packages in the return merchandise buggy. Mrs. Price then witnessed plaintiff take the purse out of the return merchandise buggy and place it in their common buggy. Jessica Howell, the cashier who checked out the women, confirmed that the black purse that was found in the shared buggy had not been paid for when the women checked out of her line. At no time did plaintiff state that she intended to pay for the purse. Thus, the mere fact that plaintiff's actions were conducted in open view does not mean that the store's employees lacked reasonable grounds to suspect plaintiff of shoplifting.

Accordingly, we are compelled to find that the trial court was manifestly erroneous in failing to find that defendant had reasonable cause to detain the plaintiff. Further, there was absolutely no evidence presented of any unreasonable force used at any time during the detention or that the detention lasted longer than sixty minutes. Nor do we find that defendant acted unreasonably after plaintiff's initial detention and questioning so as to cause her arrest by the Alexandria police.

Thus, we find that the defendant's actions met the requirements of an authorized detention under LSA–C.CR.P. art. 215 and that defendant is immune from civil liability in the present case.[1]

Accordingly, the judgment of the trial court is reversed. All costs are to be borne by plaintiff.

REVERSED.

[1] We note that the terms *illegal detention* and *false imprisonment* used by the trial court are synonymous.

CASE COMMENT

In this case, state law authorizes a merchant to detain a person if certain requirements are met. One of the requirements here is that the merchant, his agent or specifically authorized employee, or a peace officer, must have reasonable cause to believe that the person has committed a theft of goods held for sale by the merchant. Note that by state law, a detention in this situation does not constitute an arrest. The court pointed out that reasonable cause is not synonymous with probable cause and that reasonable cause for an investigatory detention is something less than probable cause. Reasonable cause requires that the detaining officer have articulable knowledge of particular facts sufficiently reasonable to suspect the detained person of criminal authority. Detention, while restraining freedom of movement, is on a lower order than is an arrest. In this situation, there is a time, location, and force limitation. The time cannot exceed 60 minutes, the location is on the merchant's premises, and unreasonable force cannot be used for the detention. Since there was no evidence that unreasonable force was used, the detention did not last longer than 60 minutes, the interrogation took place on the store's premises, and there was reasonable cause, the appellate court reversed.

PROBABLE CAUSE AS AN AFFIRMATIVE DEFENSE

In the following case, a security guard requested a female shopper to go to a room in the back of the store at which time he accused her of shoplifting. She was interrogated, threatened with police action, and strip-searched. When incriminatory efforts failed, she was released with apologies after which she sued the store alleging false imprisonment and assault and battery. Probable cause, or reasonable grounds to believe that a crime has been committed or is being committed, is an affirmative defense to the charges brought here. The store failed to present any evidence to establish its affirmative defense. Note that while the decision states the store denied that the incident occurred, it also states that the store contended that the plaintiff's son gave consent to the search of his mother. It is axiomatic that the son could not give consent for the search of his mother so long as she retained the capacity to do so.

HERNANDEZ v. K–MART CORPORATION
497 So. 2d 1259 (1986)

NESBITT, Judge.

There being an absence of any evidence to support K–Mart's affirmative defenses of probable cause and consent, we find that the trial court erred in submitting these issues to the jury. Therefore, we reverse the judgment below.

A security guard, working for K–Mart, approached Dany Hernandez in the parking lot of the K–Mart store. At the guard's request, she accompanied him to a room in the back of the store where she was accused of shoplifting. Though she denied the accusation, she was interrogated, threatened with police action, and strip-searched. When the K–Mart employees' efforts to inculpate her proved fruitless, they released her with their apologies. Dany filed a lawsuit alleging false imprisonment, assault and battery. She also alleged that K–Mart had negligently hired, trained, supervised, and retained the employees involved in the incident.

Miguel, Dany's husband, filed a claim for loss of consortium. In its answer, K–Mart denied that the incident occurred, and, in the alternative, set forth the affirmative defenses of probable cause and consent.

At trial, the only evidence of the incident was presented by the Hernandezes. Dany testified that she went to K–Mart with her thirteen-year-old daughter, Marlene, to price washing machines. Marlene brought a shirt over to Dany and requested that Dany purchase it. After Dany declined to do so, they both left the store. Dany further testified that after she was accused, the guard told her he was calling the police, but that the police never arrived. She was told to strip so that she could be searched, and she complied. Dany's son Miguel, Jr., testified that he was telephoned by either Dany or Marlene and went to the store, arriving while his mother was being interrogated.

It was upon this evidence, and over the Hernandezes' objections, that the court instructed the jury as to K–Mart's affirmative defenses, and submitted the issues to the jury. The jury returned a verdict finding that, although K–Mart was the legal cause of any injuries which might have been suffered, it had probable cause to believe that Dany had shoplifted. The jury mistakenly left the question of consent unanswered.

K–Mart had the burden of proving probable cause, (defendant has burden of proving its affirmative defense, and plaintiff may counter with other evidence).

Though the standard of proving probable cause for a merchant to detain a suspected shoplifter is less than the probable cause required to support a later prosecution, K–Mart failed to come forward with any evidence showing probable cause and, in fact, denied the occurrence of the incident. This, as a matter of law, was insufficient to carry its burden of presenting evidence of its affirmative defense. K–Mart contends that Miguel, Jr. gave consent to the search of his mother when he said, "If you don't believe her, why don't you search her?". Not only does this quotation not appear in the record, but even if it did, Miguel Jr. was not capable of giving consent for Dany where she had the capacity to give her own consent and Miguel Jr. was unauthorized to do so.

K–Mart failed to present any evidence establishing its affirmative defenses; therefore, the trial court erred in submitting the issues of probable cause and consent to the jury over objection of the Hernandezes' counsel.

Accordingly, we reverse the judgment under review and remand to the trial court with directions to enter a directed verdict in favor of the Hernandezes on the issues of probable cause and consent; and to enter a judgment in accordance with the jury's verdict finding K–Mart's false imprisonment assault and battery to be the proximate cause of the injuries allegedly suffered by the Hernandezes. Finally, upon remand, the trial court is directed to grant a new trial as to compensatory and punitive damages. Having so ruled, we find that it is unnecessary to address the remainder of the contentions advanced by the plaintiff.

It is so ordered.

On Motion for Rehearing

We agree with K–Mart's contention on rehearing that "in order for an employer to be held vicariously liable in punitive damages for the tort of an employee under the doctrine of respondeat superior, there must be proof of some fault on the part of the principal."

As we recognized in the panel opinion, Hernandez failed to present any evidence of fault on the part of K–Mart. Consequently, the jury's verdict finding that K–Mart was not liable for punitive damages is supported by the evidence.

Accordingly, we amend the final paragraph of page 3 to read:

Accordingly, we reverse the judgment under review and remand to the trial court with directions to enter a directed verdict in favor of the Hernandezes on the issues of probable cause and consent; and to enter a judgment in accordance with the jury's verdict finding 1) K–Mart's false imprisonment and assault and battery to be the proximate cause of the injuries allegedly suffered by the Hernandezes, and 2) that K–Mart acted without malice, moral turpitude, wantonness, wilfulness or reckless indifference to the rights of Dany Hernandez. Finally, upon remand, the trial court is directed to grant a new trial as to compensatory damages. Having so ruled, we find it is unnecessary to address the remainder of the contentions advanced by the plaintiff.

It is so ordered.

CASE COMMENT

Probable cause is an affirmative defense to the charge of false imprisonment and must be raised in the responsive pleading to the lawsuit. The defendant store did so in this case. The store had the burden of proving its affirmative defense yet denied that the incident occurred and offered no evidence. This was insufficient, as a matter of law, to carry the burden forward. The security manager should be aware that if probable cause is to be used as an affirmative defense, evidence of probable cause needs to be available for possible introduction in court.

9

Arrest by Private Citizens

Private citizens may make arrests under certain and varying conditions in specific jurisdictions. Fourth Amendment sanctions apply to sworn police and may apply to those who are commissioned, deputized, or licensed. Normal requirements for police to make an arrest is probable cause, that is, reasonable grounds that a crime has been, or is being, committed. Appendix G contains a state recap of statutory citizen arrest authority. Note that the requirements for some states include the restriction that a felony in fact has been committed. This requirement is more stringent than are probable cause or reasonable grounds. Appendix G contains the type of knowledge required to make arrests for minor and major offenses. Note the differences in the various jurisdictions. Presence is a requirement in most jurisdictions. Making an unreasonable arrest or invalid detention subjects the arrestor or detainor to intentional tort lawsuits such as false arrest/imprisonment and assault and battery. Knowledge of the exact arrest requirements to prevent loss from lawsuit, is a necessity for security employees. Appendix F contains the private citizen requirements for one state.

BACKGROUND

Private persons have long had the authority to make *citizens arrests*. The questions are: For what crimes can a private person make an arrest? Under what conditions can the arrest be made? What are the requirements for making the arrest good? The following case gives an excellent historical treatment of the derivation of this authority and how it applies in one jurisdiction today. The authority is derived in some states by statute and in other states by common law. While the same general theme applies on a nationwide basis, the reader should remember that different states may have their own "spin" on the general theme. A list of statutory requirements of various states can be found in Appendix G. One should also be familiar with the various state interpretations of the statutes. Note how English common law was made into a statute in this case and how case law interpreted the phrase "certain information" that came from the statute.

STATE v. NALL
404 S.E. 2d 202 (1991)

BELL, Judge:

From the earliest times, the English common law placed a duty on every person who encountered another in the commission of a felony to apprehend him or to make outcry calling the community to pursue and take him.[1] This duty has remained an important feature of Anglo-American law into modern times. Under the modern common law, any person who views a felony being committed has a duty to endeavor to arrest the felon either personally or by calling others to his aid or by seeking out an officer of the peace.

The law also permits a private person to arrest for a felony not committed in his presence if (1) the felony was actually committed and (2) the private person has reasonable cause to believe the one he is arresting committed the felony for which the arrest is made. Both requirements must be met. If it later appears that the felony for which arrest has been made was not in fact committed, the arrest is unlawful.[4] Likewise, if there was no reason in fact to believe the person arrested committed the felony, the arrest is unlawful. On the other hand, if the felony was committed, but it later appears the person arrested did not commit it, the arrest is still lawful if there was reasonable cause to suspect him.

Finally, the law permits a private person to arrest for a misdemeanor committed in his presence, if it constitutes a breach of the peace. A private person has no lawful authority to arrest for misdemeanors not committed in his presence.

Except when made upon view of the felony, a private person making an arrest must give reasonable notice of his purpose to arrest and the cause for the arrest, together with a demand that the suspect submit to arrest. No particular form of words must be used. What constitutes a reasonable notice depends on the circumstances of each case.

Once notice is given, it is the duty of the suspect to submit peaceably to the arrest without resistance or disturbance of the peace. If after notice of arrest, the suspect attempts to flee or forcibly to resist arrest, the person making the arrest may use reasonable means to effect it. On the other hand, if the person making the arrest fails to make known his purpose, he may be treated as a trespasser.

---

[1]*See, e.g.,* Dooms of Canute, c. 29 (1020): "And if anyone encounters a thief and wilfully lets him go without making outcry, he shall pay the thief's wergeld as compensation, or shall clear himself by a full oath, that he did not know [whom he let go] to be guilty of anything. And if any one hears the outcry and neglects it, he shall pay the king's *oferhyrnesse* or clear himself by a full oath." C. Stephenson and F. Marcham, SOURCES OF ENGLISH CONSTITUTIONAL HISTORY, 23–24 (1937). (The *oferhyrnesse* was a special fine of 120 shillings for violation of a royal command.) At the time of Canute, the institution of private arrest was already centuries old in England. *See* Laws of Ine, 36 (circa 690 A.D.), in W. Stubbs, SELECT CHARTERS AND OTHER ILLUSTRATIONS OF ENGLISH CONSTITUTIONAL HISTORY, 68 (9th ed.1913); Ordinance of the Hundred, c. 2, (959 A.D.) Private arrest is also a feature of other ancient legal systems. For example, the Code of Hammurabi (circa 2150 B.C.) made citizens of the locality where a homicide or theft was committed liable for compensation if they failed to apprehend the offender. *See* C. Edwards, THE HAMMURABI CODE, secs. 23–24, at 31, and comment, at 94 (1971).

[4]*Samuel v. Payne* (1780) 1 Dougl.K.B. 359, 99 Eng. Rep. 230. The common law is different for peace officers. They are authorized to arrest upon probable cause that a felony has been committed, even if it has not. Arrest by a private person following the hue and cry was likewise valid even though no felony had been committed. This exception flowed from the premise that the hue and cry created probable cause that a felony had been committed. Thus, any person under a duty to follow the hue and cry could make the arrest without personally knowing whether a felony had in fact taken place. *See* M. Dalton, THE COUNTREY JUSTICE, 308 (1622); M. Hale, PLEAS OF THE CROWN: A METHODICAL SUMMARY, 91 (1678).

The English common law of private arrest was received as the common law of South Carolina in 1712 and remained essentially unchanged until 1865.[13] In that year, the General Assembly passed a statute that is now codified as Section 17-13-10, Code of Laws of South Carolina, 1976.[14] The statute provides:

> Upon (a) view of a felony committed, (b) certain information that a felony has been committed or (c) view of a larceny committed, any person may arrest the felon or thief and take him to a judge or magistrate, to be dealt with according to law.[15]

Subsection (b) changed the common law rule that a citizen's arrest was unlawful if no felony had been committed. *State v. Griffin,* 54 S.E. 603. Under this provision a private person is authorized to arrest upon information that a felony has been committed. *Id.*[16] An arrest upon "certain information," is lawful even though no felony has been committed. "Certain information" is that which is positive, credible, reliable, and trustworthy. The statute does not change the common law requirement that the person making the arrest must have reasonable cause to believe the person he is arresting is the culprit.

In this case, the State's evidence failed to establish a lawful citizen's arrest for two reasons. First, Mr. Moore arrested Emmett Nall on information from his daughter, not upon viewing the crime being committed. In order, therefore, for his arrest to be lawful the crime had to be a felony. As it was, the crime for which he arrested Nall—cutting the canvas top of his daughter's automobile—was a misdemeanor. *See* S.C.Code Ann. §§ 16-1-10 to -20. Mr. Moore had no lawful authority to arrest for a misdemeanor not committed in his presence. He is supposed to have acted with a knowledge of the law on this point. *See State v. Griffin, supra.*[17] Second, Mr. Moore effected the arrest by grabbing Nall without any prior warning. In other words, he failed to give notice that he was making a citizen's arrest. As a result, the arrest was not lawful.[18]

Accordingly, the trial judge committed error when he refused to direct a verdict for the Nalls on the charge of assault and battery of a high and aggravated nature. We reverse the judgment on this charge.

---

[13] In 1712 the General Assembly enacted a reception statute declaring the common law of England to be the law of South Carolina. *See* 2 Stat. at Large of South Carolina 401, 413-14 (Cooper ed. 1837). The common law of England ordinarily is presumed to govern if there is no South Carolina authority to the contrary.

[14] *See An Act to Amend the Criminal Law,* sec. XXXI, 13 Stat. at Large of South Carolina 253 (1865).

[15] Subsection (c) was added in 1898. *See An Act to Amend Section 1 of the Criminal Statutes of South Carolina,* 22 Stat. at Large of South Carolina 809 (1898). It is declaratory of the common law, since at common law grand larceny is a felony and petty larceny is a breach of the peace.

[16] The statutory rule is similar to the common law rule that an arrest made upon the hue and cry was valid even if no felony had been committed. The hue and cry constituted probable cause *per se* and those responding to it were protected from the rigor of the normal rule that the felony must actually have been committed for the arrest to be lawful. *See* Dalton, COUNTREY JUSTICE, *supra,* 308-09; 2 Hale, P.C., *supra,* 81.

[17] Mr. Moore may well agree with Mr. Bumble: "If the law supposes that, the law is a ass, a idiot." C. Dickens, THE ADVENTURES OF OLIVER TWIST, 197 (1837-38 ed.). The State's attorney, however, should have known better when it charged the Nalls with assault and battery with intent to kill on the theory that Moore made a lawful arrest.

[18] Our holding that the arrest was unlawful does not imply any moral criticism of Mr. Moore. One might easily conclude that a citizen who arose in the middle of the night and left the safety of his home, unarmed, to apprehend a criminal who could reasonably be presumed to be armed with a deadly weapon acted with unusual courage and civic spirit.

D.

In light of our reversal on the charge of assault and battery of a high and aggravated nature, we need not reach the question of the requested jury charges.

AFFIRMED IN PART, REVERSED IN PART.

CASE COMMENT

From the earliest times citizens have had authority to make arrests—normally for felonies being committed in their presence and for breach of peace misdemeanors also committed in their presence. Note the lack of authority to arrest for misdemeanors not committed in one's presence. Notice of the purpose of the arrest should be given and reasonable force may be used to effect the arrest. Once the arrest is made, the person arrested should be presented to the appropriate judicial or law enforcement officer, and of course, one should have the requisite probable cause to believe that the crime is being committed and reasonable cause that the person being arrested is the culprit. A note of caution: Be particularly knowledgable of the specific requirements of the state in which you or your employees may possibly make a *citizens arrest.*

RATIONALE OF CITIZENS ARREST

Two security guards stopped several men on private property, and pursuant to a consent search, found drugs. The guards transported two of them to a security station, called the police, and detained the men until the police arrived. The police searched the appellant and ultimately charged him with possession of LSD for sale and possession of marijuana. The appellant, claiming the search by the security guards was illegal, appealed from the denial of his motion to suppress the evidence. He also claimed that the guards were not acting in a purely private capacity since they were carrying out a police function and that, since they were licensed by the state, their conduct must be imputed to the state. If the guards were serving in a private, rather than a public, interest, the Fourth Amendment would not attach. Note the change in the state constitution relative to the exclusion of evidence. This state now relies on the federal standard.

PEOPLE v. TAYLOR
271 Cal. Rptr. 785 (1990)

PREMO, Associate Justice.

Asserting that a search by private security guards which yielded LSD and marijuana was illegal, Adam Jason Taylor appeals from the denial of his motion to suppress evidence. We affirm.

On April 10, 1989, at 9:25 p.m., two security guards employed by the Seaside Security Company, the corporate security department of the Seaside Land Company, owner of the Santa Cruz Beach Boardwalk, encountered appellant and three others on a small path under the boardwalk leading from a parking lot to the beach. The four had open containers of beer. One, a Mr. Light, was smoking a marijuana cigarette. Appellant had a baggie containing a green substance on his lap.

Officer Kerr asked appellant for the baggie and identification. Appellant handed him the baggie, but said he had no identification. Kerr then asked Light, who had turned over both his cigarette and identification, if he had more drugs or contraband on his person. Light said that he did not, and agreed to a search which yielded no additional drugs.

Kerr then asked appellant if he had more drugs on his person and if he could search him. Appellant began to tremble and shake. He denied he had drugs, agreed to a search, and opened and handed over his pouch, known as a "fannypack."[2] After finding no contraband in it, Kerr patted down appellant's pants. As his hand touched appellant's left pocket, he felt a baggie and heard a rustling or crumpling sound. He partially removed four similar baggies of marijuana and two individually wrapped baggies containing several sheets of colored perforated paper which he thought contained LSD. Kerr pushed the items back into appellant's pocket and handcuffed him. He finished the patdown for weapons, found none, and transported both appellant and Light to a security station operated by Seaside Security Company where the Santa Cruz police were called.

Police Officer Carr responded. Kerr told him that appellant and Light were detained on narcotics charges, and that he believed appellant had marijuana and LSD in his pocket. Carr then searched appellant and removed the drugs from appellant's pocket. Appellant was ultimately charged with possession of LSD for sale and possession of marijuana.

Appellant's motion to suppress the evidence was denied. He then pled guilty to a violation of possession of LSD, conditioned on no prison commitment. The marijuana charge was dismissed. The court placed appellant on probation for five years, and ordered him to serve six months in the county jail. This appeal ensued.

Appellant asserts that since private individuals may not search each other for contraband under California law, the evidence was illegally seized and should be excluded. Second, he contends that since the security guards were private individuals who arrested him without complying with statutes defining how private citizens may exercise the power to arrest, this court should refuse to give binding legal effect to his consent.

Alternatively, he claims that the guards were not acting in a purely private capacity, since they were carrying out a police function properly reserved to the state, and because the guards were acting jointly with the police. Furthermore, he claims that the conduct of the guards must be imputed to the state because they were subject to the state's licensing and regulatory scheme. Therefore, a Fourth Amendment analysis is required.

Appellant has withdrawn his final claim, that the state exceeded the scope of the initial private search and of any consent when the contents of his pockets were tested later without the authorization of a search warrant.

Appellant contends that if the search by the security guard was a private search, it violated section 846, which strictly limits private citizen searches to removing offensive weapons on the person of the arrestee.

"An arrest is taking a person into custody, in a case and in the manner authorized by law. An arrest may be made by a peace officer or by a private person." A private person may arrest another for a public offense committed or attempted in his presence; for a felony, although not committed in his presence; or when a felony has been in fact committed and the private person has reasonable cause for believing the person arrested to have committed it. A private person has the duty to take the person arrested before a magistrate or deliver him to a peace officer without unnecessary delay.

Our courts have repeatedly held that a citizen is not authorized by section 846 to conduct a search for contraband "incidental" to the arrest, or to seize such contraband upon recovering it. "Absent statutory authorization, private citizens are not and should not be permitted to take property from other private citizens." *People v. Zelinski* 594 P.2d 1000.

---

[2]Appellant claims that he consented to a search of the fannypack only.

Therefore, appellant argues that although Kerr had cause to arrest "for a public offense (possession of marijuana committed . . . in his presence) he was not justified in seizing and examining the baggies.

Appellant suggests exclusion of the evidence as a proper remedy for an unlawful search by a private citizen. However, "the exclusionary rules were fashioned 'to prevent, not to repair,' and their target is official misconduct. They are 'to compel respect for the constitutional guaranty in the only effectively available way—by removing the incentive to disregard it.' But it is no part of the policy underlying the Fourth and Fourteenth Amendments to discourage citizens from aiding to the utmost of their ability in the apprehension of criminals. If, then, the exclusionary rule is properly applicable . . . , it must be upon the basis that some type of unconstitutional police conduct occurred."

Therefore, the protection of the Fourth Amendment does not extend to searches carried out by private persons. Appellants remedy is civil in nature and can be pursued, as appropriate, as in any other action involving civil wrongs.

Next, appellant contends that "finding consent would abrogate California's statutory scheme which strictly defines when private citizens may exercise full powers of arrest," and that this court "should refuse to give binding legal effect to his consent."

Appellant relies on *People v. Martin* 36 Cal.Rptr. 924, for the proposition that consent given in submission to express or implied authority cannot be said to be free and voluntary and the fruits must be deemed to be inadmissible. In *Martin,* two Los Angeles Police Department narcotics officers made an arrest beyond the city limits, and sought and received consent to search. At that time, a police officer for one geographical district had no official power to arrest outside that district. The court of appeal therefore held that the officers merely had the powers of private citizens and no authority to search beyond removal of all offensive weapons from the person of the arrestee. The court excluded the evidence.

However, in that case, the police officers were asserting the power of the state when they identified themselves as police officers, arrested Martin, immediately questioned him about his "scabs," ordered him to remove his jacket so they could see his tracks, and then asked for and received permission and his cooperation in searching his hotel room.

Here, if the security guards were acting in a private capacity, the exclusionary rule does not apply. In a case where private investigators, hired by a father to discover what happened to his two missing sons, stopped and searched the automobile of a defendant later convicted of the sons' murder, the court said: "although their conduct was outrageous, unquestionably tortious, and no doubt violative of several penal statutes, those are not the questions here. The question we confront is whether substantial evidence supports the trial court's findings that the investigators were serving a private . . . rather than a public interest . . . ." (*People v. De Juan* 217 Cal. Rptr. 642.)

Next, appellant contends that the state is involved in the security guards' actions because they were operating jointly with the police and because they acted solely for a public purpose.

The guards' duties were to patrol the boardwalk, and not to generally enforce laws. However, he asserts that when the guards questioned him, searched him for contraband, and then arrested him, they were acting for a public purpose.

Appellant relies on *People v. Zelinski,* in which the Supreme Court held that if private security personnel were not acting in a purely private capacity but were fulfilling a public function in bringing violators of the law to public justice, they were asserting the power of the state, and were therefore subject to the constitutional proscriptions that secure an individuals' right to privacy.

In *Zelinski,* the court relied on *United States v. Price* 383 U.S. 787, for the proposition that "a person does not need to be an officer of the state to act under color of law and therefore be responsible, along with such officers, for actions prohibited to state officials when such actions are engaged under color of law.

However, the court held that "exclusion of the illegally seized evidence is required by article 1, section 13 of the California Constitution."

Zelinski is a pre-Proposition 8 case. This court recently wrote: "The enactment of California Constitution, article I, section 28, subdivision (d) (Proposition 8) on June 8, 1982, permits us to suppress evidence only if that result is compelled by the United States Constitution; a violation of the California Constitution is no longer a basis for exclusion. In interpreting the United States Constitution, as in the case of all federal law, we are bound by the decisions of the United States Supreme Court and find persuasive authority in the decisions of other federal courts. We are also bound by the decisions of the California Supreme Court." (*People v. Brouillette,* 258 Cal.Rptr. 635.) Only if this search may be fairly characterized as state action does the exclusionary rule apply.

The Ninth Circuit recently held: "to the extent *Zelinski* expanded the concept of state action under the California Constitution beyond federal law, it was abrogated by Proposition 8." (*Collins v. Womancare* 878 F.2d 1145. "*Zelinski* directly conflicts with and is superseded by *Lugar v. Edmondson Oil Co.* 457 U.S. 922.

Under federal law, searches and seizures by private security employees have traditionally been viewed as those of a private citizen and consequently not subject to Fourth Amendment proscriptions. *United States v. Lima* 424 A.2d 113. Although the United States Supreme Court has not considered the constitutional status of private police forces (*Collins v. Womancare*), *Lugar v. Edmondson Oil Co., Inc.,* 457 U.S. 922, mandates a two-prong test to determine whether state action is involved in the deprivation of a federal right.

First, the deprivation must be caused by the exercise of some right or privilege created by the state or by a rule of conduct imposed by the state or by a person for whom the state is responsible. Second, the party charged with the deprivation must be a person who may fairly be said to be a state actor. *Lugar* explains that "this may be because he is a state official, because he has acted together with or has obtained significant aid from state officials, or because his conduct is otherwise chargeable to the State."

Turning to this case, the first question is whether the deprivation of appellant's right to be free from unreasonable searches and seizure resulted from the exercise of a right or privilege created by the state and which was traditionally exclusive to the state.

In *Zelinski*, the California Supreme Court said: "the store employees arrested defendant pursuant to the authorization contained in Penal Code section 837, and the search which yielded the narcotics was conducted incident to that arrest. Their acts, engaged in pursuant to the statute, were not those of a private citizen acting in a purely private capacity. Although the search exceeded lawful authority, *it was nevertheless an integral part of the exercise of sovereignty allowed by the state to private citizens.* In arresting the offender, the store employees were utilizing the coercive power of the state to further a state interest. Had the security guards sought only the vindication of the merchant's private interests they would have simply exercised self-help and demanded the return of the stolen merchandise. Upon satisfaction of the merchant's interests, the offender would have been released. By holding defendant for criminal process and searching her, they went beyond their employer's private interests."

For the first prong of the *Lugar* test, it is important to determine whether the state, in enacting statutes describing the circumstances in which citizens may arrest, was creating in citizens a right or privilege which was traditionally exclusive to the state.

Federal courts have not so held. "Arrest has never been an exclusively governmental function. Not all state-authorized coercion is governmental action." (*Spencer v. Lee* 864 F.2d 1376),

"There have been citizen arrests for as long as there have been public police—indeed much longer. In ancient Greece and Rome, and in England until the nineteenth century, most arrests and prosecutions were by private individuals."

In *United States v. Lima,* in discussing a District of Columbia citizen's arrest statute, the court said: "Neither can it be argued that Congress intended to make the citizen an agent of the state for the purposes of making arrests by enacting a statue codifying the citizens common law power of arrest.

Congress' intent by enacting this statute was to define and restrict the private citizens' common law right to arrest . . . . By so limiting the citizen's power of arrest, Congress recognized that 'law enforcement should generally be carried out by professionals.' A citizen's arrest power presumes that a law abiding citizen for his own personal purposes may desire to stop criminal activity just as a merchant has a personal interest in deterring theft of his goods. Consequently, Congress has recognized these legitimate private interests of apprehending persons committing certain crimes within their presence. The fact that a private person makes a citizen's arrest does not automatically transform that individual into an agent of the state. His conduct is not actionable for any deprivation under color of law of rights, privileges or immunities secured by the Constitution."

Since the issue of what constitutes action under color of state law is ultimately one of federal, not state law (*Gorenc v. Salt River Project Agr. Imp. & Power* 869 F.2d 503), it appears that appellant has not satisfied the first prong of the *Lugar* test by showing that the right to arrest was traditionally exclusive to the state.

Appellant's next contention is that the security guards were operating jointly with the police, and that their action should be imputed to the state.

Appellant refers us to our analysis in *Brouillette* (distinguishing *Zelinski*), where we stated that "the security guards here did not make an arrest or in any other way assert the power of the state. They merely inspected lost property finding marijuana and cocaine and called the police. The decision reached by the trial court suppressing the evidence required an implicit finding that the security guards asserted the power of the state when they took the particular action of inspecting the wallet, but that is not supported by substantial evidence. There was evidence to support the findings that the security guards dressed like police and are looked upon by others as representing police authority, and that they assisted the police by calling the deputy sheriff to the mall and allowing Brouillette to come to the mall office to be arrested when she perhaps thought that she was coming to collect her wallet. There was nothing to show that they made the inspection of the wallet as agents of the state."

Therefore, appellant contends, if we consider the same factors that we did in *Brouillette,* we should come to the conclusion that the security guards in the instant case were asserting the power of the state.

First, he asserts, the security guards acted jointly with the local police in that the private police maintained "Station 2," the detention center, but the public police used it also. In addition, appellant charges that since the guards had access to police radios, they should have used them and called the police, rather than "doing the dirty work of the invasive search" first.

Second, the guards exercised the authority of the State by arresting appellant, handcuffing him, and searching him. Third, the officers were clothed in the indicia of state authority. They looked like state-authorized police officers. They wore uniforms of light green pants, "duty belts," and tan shirts with badges and shoulder patches reading "Security, Santa Cruz Beach Boardwalk." They carried handcuffs, batons, and two-way radios. They also carried police radios. Furthermore, they patrolled an area used by the public which was not posted with "no trespassing" signs, and which provided access to a public beach. When these guards accosted appellant, they did not identify themselves as private security guards.

Finally, the guards did not act for a purely private purpose. Appellant and his companions were not harming Seaside Land Company's property. The officers were not afraid of appellant. Rather than protecting their employer's property by telling appellant and his companions to leave, since the Boardwalk was closed for business, they acted for the sole purpose of law enforcement: to get evidence of crime. "They wanted to find contraband: all their questions to Mr. Taylor were directed to that end. Since the Officer's sole purpose was to act in a law enforcement capacity, the Fourth Amendment must apply to their activities."

" 'The joint action inquiry focuses on whether the state has "so far insinuated itself into a position of interdependence with the private entity that it must be recognized as a joint participant in the challenged activity . . . ." ' Joint action therefore requires a substantial degree of cooperative action." (*Collins v. Womancare*). "Merely complaining to the police does not convert a private party into a state actor. Nor is execution by a private party of a sworn complaint which forms the basis of an arrest enough to convert the private party's acts into state action. There was no joint action where a private party, besides effecting the citizens' arrest, also transported the arrestee to the police station, attempted to persuade police to file charges, and swore out a complaint against the arrested party.

In light of the foregoing cases, the facts presented by appellant fail to establish that the state has " ' "so far insinuated itself into a position of interdependence with Seaside Security employees that it must be recognized as a joint participant in the challenged activity." '

First, the impetus for the arrests came from the security guards. The evidence showed that the actions of the security guards sprang solely from their observations at the time. Next, appellant presented no evidence that the Seaside Security Company had contracts or agreements with the city, the county, or the state. There was no evidence from which this court can infer a "prearranged plan, customary procedure, or policy that substituted the judgment of a private party for that of the police . . . ."

In short, there was no indication in the record that the state agents failed to use independent judgment or in any way coerced or encouraged the security guards to effect the citizen's arrest.

Furthermore, there is no evidence in the record to establish that the security guards' uniform was in any way similar in color to that of the Santa Cruz police department. The guards wore badges and shoulder patches marked "security." They did not carry guns. Although they did not identify themselves verbally as security guards, they did not verbally claim to be police officers. The evidence showed that their private purpose was to patrol Seaside Land Company's property. There was no evidence either establishing or negating specific instructions. Thus, there is no reason to conclude that their duties were limited to deterring crimes against property such as vandalism, littering, or trespass.

Although the security guards made an arrest, federal cases cited *ante* disagree with *Zelinski's* assertion "that store detectives *when they make an arrest* do not act in a purely private capacity but 'assert the power of the state.' " The *Lugar* test, requiring a showing of deprivation of a state created right by persons who can be shown to be state actors, was not satisfied.

Finally, the mere fact that California licenses security guards and regulates their conduct does not transform them into state agents. Security guards are required to take a course in exercise of power to arrest. (Bus. & Prof. Code, §§ 7545.1, 7545.2.) The state emphasizes, in its pamphlet Powers to Arrest, Security Guard Training (1987 Rev.) Department of Consumer Affairs, Bureau of Collection and Investigative Services, page 8, "A security guard is *not* a police officer. Guards do not have the same job duties as police officers; they do not have the same training; and they do not have the same powers according to law." A security guard arrests with the same power as any other citizen.

Substantial evidence in the record supports the finding of the trial court.

The judgment is affirmed.

CASE COMMENT

In this state, arrests may be made by private persons for public offenses committed or attempted in the private individual's presence. Arrests may also be made for felonies not committed in the arrestor's presence or when a felony has been in fact committed and with reasonable cause to believe the person arrested committed it. Private persons have the duty to take the persons arrested before a magistrate or deliver them to peace officers without unnecessary delay. The protection of the Fourth Amendment does not extend to searches carried out by private persons, thus the exclusionary rule does not apply. The court, because of a recent change in the state constitution, is permitted to suppress evidence only if that result is compelled by the U.S. constitution. Historically, arrest has never been an exclusive governmental function. Codifying common law, citizen arrest power does not make the citizen an agent of the state, the intent being to define, restrict, and limit the power of arrest. While Congress has recognized that law enforcement should generally be carried out by professionals, it has also recognized legitimate private interests of apprehending persons committing certain crimes. There was no joint operation in this case between security and police as there was no substantial degree of cooperation. The mere state licensing and regulation of the security guards did not transform them into state agents. The court noted that a state pamphlet informs that a security guard is not a police officer and does not have the same job duties, training, and powers. Security managers should be constantly aware of changes in the law as happened in this case and in doing so will then be able to know what standards of legal care personnel will be subject to.

PRESENCE—ACTUAL

In the next case, a private citizen hotel security guard arrested a woman for criminal trespass and then turned her over to city police. Cocaine was found in her make-up kit, and she attempted to get the evidence suppressed. The legality, or lawfulness, of this arrest depended on whether the offense was committed in the guard's presence or within his immediate knowledge. The test for the validity of this warrantless arrest was the knowledge of the guard and not that of the police who assumed custody of her. Appendix G contains a compilation of statutory citizen arrest authority for misdemeanors and felonies. Presence is a statutory requirement in a number of states and may be a common law requirement in states that do not have statutes.

WALKER v. STATE
242 S.E.2d 753 (1978)

SMITH, Judge.

Walker appeals her conviction for criminal trespass and possession of cocaine, enumerating error on the court's refusal (1) to grant a writ of habeas corpus following her preliminary hearing, (2) to grant her motion to suppress evidence, and (3) to direct a verdict in her favor. We find no error and affirm.

An Atlanta police officer arrested the appellant inside the Peachtree Plaza Hotel on charges of prostitution. At that time, security personnel acting as agents for the Hotel photographed the appellant, warning her that her photograph would be on file and if she were again found on the Hotel's premises she would be subject to arrest for criminal trespass. At a later date, a Hotel security guard spotted the appellant, verified her identity with the file photograph, then approached her and, after obtaining verbal verification of her identity, told her she was being arrested. Atlanta police officers were called to the scene and took custody of the appellant. As they escorted her from the hotel, she attempted to pass certain of her personal belongings to an acquaintance standing nearby, but this transaction was prevented. After she was placed in a patrol car, her purse and makeup kit were removed from her possession, and a search of the makeup kit revealed a vial containing cocaine.

An analysis of the arrest and search here shows that the arrest was lawful and the search was properly incident to the lawful arrest. The evidence shows clearly that the arrest was made by the Hotel security guard, a private citizen, and not, as the appellant contends, by the Atlanta police officer who subsequently appeared on the scene. Whether this arrest by a private citizen was lawful depends on whether the offense was committed in his presence or within his immediate knowledge. Here, the criminal trespass took place in the presence of and within the knowledge of the security guard, and it was he who arrested the appellant. When Atlanta police came onto the scene, the appellant was not "rearrested" by them; her arrest status did not change, only her custody. Thus, it does not matter whether the police officers had sufficient personal knowledge of the crime to give them cause for a warrantless arrest, for they did not consummate the arrest, and their knowledge is not the test for the validity of this warrantless arrest.

The arrest itself being lawful, there can be no question that the subsequent search of the appellant's personal effects, on her person and within her immediate control and possession, was likewise lawful. The cocaine was properly discovered, seized, and introduced into evidence.

Competent evidence supported a finding of guilty as to both counts. Thus, denial of the motion for directed verdict was correct.

Judgment affirmed.

CASE COMMENT

Presence is a specific requirement for certain arrests in a number of jurisdictions as is indicated in Appendix G. There are two types of presence: actual and constructive. *Actual presence* means within sight or view and comes about when the person making the arrest sees the act committed. It can be at a distance. *Constructive presence* may be acceptable in some jurisdictions and is found through the other senses, for example, hearing and/or smell. Here the person making the arrest does not see the crime committed but is so close, or near enough via the senses, to allow immediate knowledge that the person committed the act. Since jurisdictions may vary in degree and scope of the presence requirement, security managers should be well versed in interpretations of this requirement that apply to the area in which they serve.

PRESENCE—CONSTRUCTIVE

A security guard with 15 years of experience observed a shopper conceal items on hangers, go into a fitting room with a specific number of items that the sales clerk could not observe, and leave the fitting room with fewer items than she went in with. The guard heard the clerk's instructions to the shopper, checked the fitting room immediately after the shopper left, and found nothing. The penal code allows for a private citizen arrest for a public offense committed or attempted "in his presence." The guard obviously did not see the shopper place any items in her purse. Physical proximity and sight are not essential for constructive presence. Presence may be constructed when circumstances exist that would cause reasonable persons to believe that a crime had been committed in their presence.

PEOPLE v. LEE

204 Cal. Rptr. 667 (1984)

SIMMONS, Judge.

Appellant, Marcia Ann Lee, hereinafter referred to as Lee, entered a plea of no contest to charges of petty theft following a denial of a motion to suppress heard on July 19, 1983. This appeal followed.

Factual Setting

Diane Paul, hereinafter referred to as Paul, a security guard with 15 years employment, was working for the GEMCO store in Victorville on March 15, 1983. She saw Lee in the women's clothing section of the store select two items, removing them from hangers. Thereafter Paul observed Lee select an additional four items, leaving them on the hangers. She further observed Lee place the two unhung items underneath the items on hangers and proceed to the fitting room area. At that point a clerk in the department instructed Lee to take only three items into the fitting room, whereupon Lee removed one of the items on a hanger and left it outside the fitting room, entering with three items on hangers and two items underneath which the clerk could not observe. Paul was close enough to the conversation to be able to see Lee's conduct and hear the clerk give her the instructions. Paul remained close to the fitting area, observing the room which Lee had entered. Emerging from the fitting room Lee returned three items to the racks and Paul immediately checked the fitting room and found no additional clothing therein. Lee shortly thereafter returned to the room with three additional items and after a brief period within the fitting room again emerged and returned three items to the clothing racks. Thereupon Paul immediately checked the fitting room area and discovered no additional clothing therein. Lee subsequently exited the store without paying for the unaccounted for two items of clothing, whereupon she was stopped by Paul and arrested for petty theft. When they were back inside an office in the store Paul asked if she could recover the items from her purse. Lee replied "No" but thereafter removed two items of apparel herself and handed them to Paul.

Contention on Appeal

The trial court should have suppressed the merchandise and Lee's statement because the security guard had no authority to arrest and the consent to search was, therefore, invalid.

Discussion

Penal Code Section 837, subdivision 1 provides that a private citizen may arrest another for a public offense committed or attempted "in his presence." The evidence clearly disclosed that the offense had, in fact, been committed. Therefore, the only question remaining is whether the offense was committed "in the presence" of Paul. The term "in his presence" has historically been liberally construed in this state. Neither physical proximity nor sight is essential. In *People v. Burgess,* 338 P.2d 524 the court held that a private citizen may arrest another when circumstances exist which would cause a reasonable person to believe that a crime had been committed in his presence.

In the instant case the circumstances clearly suggest to any reasonable person that an offense had been committed in the presence of the security guard. Paul, with 15 years experience, observed the collection of the clothing items and concealment of two of those pieces of clothing. In addition, she heard the clerk's instruction to Lee and her obvious circumvention of those orders. Thereafter, the replacement of the items as set forth above together with the absence of additional clothing in the dressing room could only lead to the conclusion that Lee had concealed merchandise with the intent to steal the same. The separation of Lee from Paul's observations by the closing of the fitting room door cannot be deemed such a removal of Lee from the "presence" of Paul so as to strip her of authority to make the arrest.

Cervantez v. J.C. Penney Company, 595 P.2d 975 does not address itself to the determination of what constitutes "presence" within the meaning of Penal Code section 837, subdivision 1. The jury instruction in *Cervantez* given at trial had directed the jury to consider only whether there was probable cause to arrest, and, hence, did not require that the jury find that the offense had been committed in the presence of the security guard in order to avoid civil liability. *Cervantez* is, therefore, inapposite to the present inquiry. For the reasons indicated above we find that the arrest was lawful in this case.

Moreover, the security guard did have the right to detain Lee without arresting her. Under Penal Code Section 490.5 a merchant may detain a person whom he has reasonable cause to believe has shoplifted from him. He may also request that person to voluntarily surrender the merchandise taken. If refused, the merchant may make a limited search of packages, shopping bags, handbags, etc. It would be illogical to conclude that a merchant has less authority when he places the shoplifting suspect under arrest so that in the latter situation he would be prohibited from requesting return of his merchandise or a consent to search. This case does not conflict with *People v. Zelinski,* 594 P.2d 1000, where the Supreme Court held that an unlawful search by private security personnel violated the California Constitution's search and seizure prohibition so that evidence seized thereby should have been suppressed. The opinion noted that the private security guard could either detain a suspect, recover the merchandise, and then release him, or it could arrest him and hold him for the police. In *Zelinski*, after making the arrest, the guards had gone beyond both the permissible scope of a search incident to a citizens' arrest and the limits of the merchant's authority to search under Penal Code Section 490.5.

Here, the issue is only whether the private security guard has the authority to ask for return of the merchandise or consent to search. There appears to be no compelling policy reason to allow him to do so in one situation and not in the other.

We cannot conclude from the facts in this case that the consent given by Lee was the result of any illegal act by Paul. This case is a far cry from *People v. Leib,* 548 P.2d 1105, cited by Lee, where the defendant had requested the police to take him to his apartment only after being illegally arrested and detained for hours in a holding cell without being given the opportunity to call an attorney. Here, there was a simple request for the merchandise after a short detention, and a lawful arrest.

Disposition

For the reasons set forth above we hold that the evidence obtained was admissible and the judgment below is affirmed.

CASE COMMENT

The court felt that the separation of the shopper from the guard's observations by closing the door of the fitting room was not such a removal of the shopper from the presence of the guard. This was so because the guard had 15 years' experience, observed the concealment of two items of clothing, heard the sales clerk's instructions to the shopper, and saw the obvious circumvention of those instructions. To the court, this clearly suggested that, under circumstances such as these, any reasonable person may have believed an offense had been committed in their presence.

LEGITIMATING THE CITIZEN ARREST

In the following case, a security guard, after receiving some information on his radio, observed a man run out of a store. Once the man was outside, the guard saw a gun in the man's hand and observed him putting the gun in his jacket pocket. Another security guard helped arrest the man who was then taken to the store detention room. The gun and a wallet from a wounded robbery victim were taken from the man. The arrestee wanted to suppress the evidence obtained as a result of the arrest by saying the arrest was illegal, lacking probable cause. If the arrest lacked the type of probable cause necessary for a citizen's arrest, the arrest would be illegal and the evidentiary fruits of the arrest would be suppressed. Private citizen arrest powers in this state operate through common (not statutory) law as interpreted and modified by the courts. The court held that one making a citizen's arrest is acting under the authority of the state and the legitimating factor is state recognition and sanction of the act. Note the court's statement that in citizen arrest cases, "the requisite standard of probable cause is considerably higher than that for arrests made by the police." The court did not feel there was adequate probable cause for a felony arrest but allowed a personally observed breach of peace misdemeanor arrest as immediate apprehension was necessary to preserve or restore public order.

COMMONWEALTH v. CORLEY
462 A.2d 1374 (1983)

BROSKY, Judge:

This appeal is from the denial of a Post Conviction Hearing Act (PCHA) petition. Appellant argues that his arrest by security officers was illegal and that, consequently, the evidentiary fruits of that arrest would have been suppressed had the issue been raised pre-trial. His PCHA petition requested either discharge or a new trial on the grounds that he was denied ineffective assistance of counsel in that trial counsel withdrew a suppression motion. The PCHA petition was denied and we affirm.

Facts

The factual situation of appellant's arrest is as follows. Appellant robbed an individual at gunpoint in the men's room of a department store and then shot the victim in the cheek. Robert Greer, a security investigator for the store, received some information[1] over his radio and then observed appellant running toward the main escalator. Greer followed appellant out of the store. He saw appellant with a gun in his hand and observed appellant put it in his jacket pocket. Appellant was then arrested by Greer and a security guard from a second department store.[2] The jacket and the gun which it contained was taken from appellant. Greer took appellant to a detention room in the security office of his department store. In the detention room, a store detective removed a wallet from appellant, which was later identified as the victim's. After all of the above events, Philadelphia police arrived and took appellant into custody.

Prior to the trial, counsel filed a motion to suppress the evidence obtained as a result of the arrest. The motion alleged that the arrest was illegal, lacking probable cause. However, at the suppression hearing, counsel withdrew the motion and stipulated that there had been probable cause for the arrest. At the PCHA hearing, trial counsel testified that he had withdrawn the motion and stipulated that there was probable cause because he knew what information the arresting person was given over his radio. By the time of the PCHA hearing, three and a half years later, trial counsel could not recall what that information was.

PCHA Petition

The issue abandoned with the suppression motion withdrawal and revived in the PCHA petition is the same: whether there was lacking the type of probable cause necessary for a citizen's arrest. If the arrest was illegal, then the evidentiary fruits of that arrest must be suppressed. *Wong Sun v. U.S.*, 371 U.S. 471.

In pursuing this enquiry, we will engage in a two-step analysis. First, are there any legal consequences to a finding that this citizen's arrest was illegal? (We hold that there are.) Second, was this arrest illegal? (We find that it was not.)

Legal Consequences of an Illegal Arrest

It is long-established law that the fruits of an illegal search made by an individual who was not acting for the state are not suppressible under the exclusionary rule. *Burdeau v. McDowell*, 256 U.S. 465.[6]

Unlike the private searcher who can be acting for his own ends, one making a citizen's arrest[8] is, definitionally, acting under the authority of the state. The legitimating factor which distinguishes his actions from an unprivileged battery or kidnapping is the state recognition and sanction of this act.[9] Of course, in any case which would come before the criminal courts,

[1]The information received by Greer is not established by the record.

[2]After leaving Greer's store, appellant briefly entered a second department store.

[6]The wisdom of this rule has been called into question. See Burkoff, Not So Private Searches and the Constitution, 66 Cornell L.Rev. 627.

[8]The arrest of appellant occurred in a citizen's arrest context.

[9]As will be seen in the next section, in Pennsylvania this operates through the common law tradition as interpreted and modified by the courts of this Commonwealth.

the police and prosecution would also have ratified the citizen's arrest by taking the arrestee into custody and by seeking to use any evidence that was the fruit of that arrest. Since the very occurrence of the act is freighted with the authority of the state, if that act is committed improperly, the fruits of that arrest must be suppressed.

A case recently decided by the U.S. Supreme Court reviews and restates the elements necessary for "state action." Our cases have accordingly insisted that the conduct allegedly causing the deprivation of a federal right to be fairly attributable to the state. These cases reflect a two-part approach to the question of "fair attribution." First, the deprivation must be caused by the exercise of some right or privilege created by the state . . . Second, the party charged with the deprivation must be a person who may fairly be said to be a state actor. This may be because . . . his conduct is otherwise chargeable to the state. *Lugar v. Edmondson Oil Co., Inc.,* 102 S.Ct. 2744.

These conditions are met here.

The test has also been set out by the U.S. Supreme Court in a criminal context.

The critical factor, as the United States Supreme Court has stated, "is whether the private individual in light of all the circumstances of the case, must be regarded as having acted as an 'instrument' or agent of the state . . ." *Coolidge v. New Hampshire,* 403 U.S. 443.

Again, it is clear that in a citizen's arrest, legitimated by state law, and ratified by the police and prosecution, the arresting person is an "instrument" of the state.

To hold, as we do here, that the fruits of an illegal arrest by an individual must be suppressed, is not inconsistent with the rule stating that fruits of an illegal search and seizure of things by an individual are not suppressible. This is so because an arrest by an individual is necessarily undertaken under the authority of the state; while a search and seizure of things may, of course, be carried out for personal purposes, without such authority.

This holding acts to fill a gap in the law, rather than to contradict established law. The usual case dealing with private actors and the Fourth Amendment involves searches and seizures of things; not the seizure of a person. A few cases have dealt with the suppressibility of the fruits of an illegal citizen's arrest.

A 1949 case out of Kentucky, *Thacker v. Commonwealth,* 221 S.W.2d 682, held that a person making a citizen's arrest "is acting for and on behalf of the sovereignty." Therefore it followed that he would be subject to Kentucky's constitutional provision which is parallel to the Fourth Amendment of the Federal Constitution.

The legality of a citizen's arrest was examined by this court recently. *Commonwealth v. Andrews,* 426 A.2d 1160.[11] The arrest was found to have been legal; but there would have been no purpose to that enquiry and finding if legal consequences did not flow from the finding. The only apparent legal consequence of illegality of the arrest would have been the suppression of the fruits of the arrest. This was not made explicit in *Andrews,* but here we make it so.

We hold, as a matter of federal constitutional law, that the fruits of an illegal citizen's arrest are subject to the full action of the Fourth Amendment and to the exclusionary rule. On

---

[11]See also *U.S. v. Fannon,* 556 F.2d 961 (reversed by that Circuit *en banc* on an interpretation of the facts, not on a repudiation of the statement of law).

separate, independent and adequate state grounds, applying Article 1, Section 8 of the Constitution of this Commonwealth, we hold that the same results also obtain.[12]

Illegality of Arrest

We now turn to the core requirement of appellant's case, the illegality of the arrest. Such illegality would be due to not meeting the requirements of a proper arrest by an individual. In citizen's arrest cases, the requisite standard of probable cause is considerably higher than that for arrests made by the police.

The standard of probable cause to be met in a citizen's arrest for a felony cannot be met here. Greer neither observed the commission of a felony nor does the record establish that he knew of the commission of a felony.[13] The only potentially criminal act he had knowledge of was that appellant was holding a handgun. Possession of a gun does not, in itself, rise to the level of a felony. 18 Pa.C.S.A. § 6108. If, in addition to this observation, Greer had learned other facts about the robbery it is possible that an arrest for that felony would have been proper. But we cannot decide that as there is no evidence on the record regarding what information Greer received on his radio.

The only other basis for legitimating the citizen's arrest made by Greer is a citizen's arrest for a misdemeanor. It is uncontradicted that Greer did see appellant holding a gun in his hand on a center city Philadelphia street. There is no doubt that this could constitute a misdemeanor, a breach of the peace. What is not clear is whether a citizen's arrest can be made for a misdemeanor.

The proper focus here is on Pennsylvania state law regarding citizen's arrests.

> If the arrest is legal under state standards and not violative of federal constitutional rights the arrest and the search incidental thereto is valid. And in the absence of an applicable federal statute the law of the state where an arrest without warrant takes place determines its validity.

There is a difference of opinion within this state on the propriety of a citizen's arrest for a non-felony. The common law rule would allow an arrest such as the one made here.

> Arrest for a misdemeanor constituting a breach of the peace was also permitted at common law when immediate apprehension was necessary to preserve or restore public order.

This traditional, common law view was repeated, albeit in *dicta,* in *Samuel v. Blackwell,* 76 Pa.Super. 540, (1921). Later, a Common Pleas Court held that under this rule a private citizen could make a citizen's arrest for driving under the influence on a public highway if such a breach of the peace occurred in his presence. *Commonwealth v. Giles,* 14 Adams L.J. 34, 57 D & C2d 13 (1972).

However, this line of cases was contradicted, again in *dicta,* by a 1964 Superior Court opinion, *In re Stanley,* 201 A.2d 287 (1964). "A constable's authority to . . . arrest on sight for breach of the peace . . . is not conferred upon private citizens . . ."

---

[12]Of course, states can choose to accord greater protection to the individual than is mandated under federal law.

[13]We do not hold, either impliedly or in *dicta,* that knowledge of a felony he hadn't witnessed would legitimate a citizen's arrest. We simply do not reach this as such knowledge was not established to have been present here.

This statement from *Stanley* was quoted, yet again in *dicta,* in *Commonwealth v. Gregg,* 396 A.2d 797, (1979). The opinion added that, "A lay person, i.e., a person lacking police powers, can only effectuate an arrest when the same citizen personally observes a felony." In neither *Stanley* nor *Gregg* was this statement necessary for the disposition of the case. Nor was there any indication that the courts were emphasizing felony as opposed to a misdemeanor. Indeed, to the contrary, the facts in each case related more to the personal observation element than to the felony/misdemeanor distinction.

Thus, except for one Common Pleas case on point, and contradictory Superior Court *dicta,* there is no Pennsylvania law on this issue. We are, therefore, free to address the issue, free from binding precedential encumbrance.[14]

In view of the foregoing, we hold that a citizen's arrest can be made for a breach of the peace that is personally observed by the arrestor. Two policy considerations support this. First, it is desirable that citizens be encouraged to stop breaches of the peace. Second, it is unreasonable to put citizens at their peril in deciding, on the spur of the excited moment, which violations they observe are breach of the peace misdemeanors and which are felonies. Such an exercise might well tax the abilities of a learned member of the criminal bar or bench—it is certainly an unreasonable task to impose upon our citizenry. The citizen's arrest of appellant was, therefore, not illegal.

Conclusion

Having found that appellant's arrest was lawful, it follows that appellant's suppression motion, based as it was on the illegality of the arrest, was meritless. Since appellant would not have prevailed on this issue even if the suppression motion had not been withdrawn, counsel cannot be said to have been ineffective for not proceeding with it.

The denial of the PCHA petition is consequently affirmed.

CASE COMMENT

The court determined that the elements necessary for "state action" as pertains to a citizen's arrest had been met in this case. The court made it clear that in a citizen's arrest, legitimated by state law and ratified by police and prosecution, the arresting person is an "instrument" of the state. If one is an instrument of the state, federal constitutional sanctions apply, and in this case, the exclusionary rule applies in particular. The court felt that the standard of probable cause to be met in a citizen's arrest was not met in that the guard did not observe the commission of a felony and the record did not establish that he knew of one. Had the guard learned of other facts about the robbery, it is possible that a felony arrest would have been proper. Having disposed of the felony arrest situation, the court turned its attention to whether a citizen could make an arrest for a misdemeanor

---

[14]A recent case of this Court treated a related, but distinct, issue: the validity of a citizen's arrest for a summary offense. *Commonwealth v. Stahl,* 442 A.2d 1166 (1982). Judge O'Kicki wrote that a citizen's arrest could not be made for a summary offense. Involving, as it does, a summary offense, *Stahl* is not on point with the issue before us—the validity of a citizen's arrest for a breach of the peace misdemeanor.

and noted that there was a difference of opinion in the state on the propriety of a citizen arrest for a nonfelony. In holding that a citizen's arrest can be made for a personally observed breach of peace, the court gave two policy considerations to support this. They are the desirability that citizens be encouraged to stop breaches of peace and the unreasonableness of putting citizens at their peril in deciding, on the spur of the excited moment, which violations they observe are breach of peace misdemeanors and which are felonies. The court also noted that such decision making might well tax the abilities of learned members of the criminal bar or bench. This last point demonstrates the necessity of the security manager to be well versed and of security personnel to be well trained as to legal rules in the jurisdiction they are charged to protect.

FELONY IN FACT COMMITTED

The next case deals with an arrest and with the statutory requirement in most jurisdictions that a felony in fact has been committed. The danger to security personnel who make an arrest when a felony in fact has not been committed is the potential civil lawsuit and/or criminal charges for false arrest or imprisonment. The case also discusses probable cause that is a law enforcement requirement to make an arrest. A more stringent requirement for the private citizen to make a felony arrest is that a felony in fact has been committed. This can be likened to *positive cause* as opposed to the probable cause standard for police. The judge in the suppression hearing found that the citizens had acted on the basis of probable cause rather than on actual knowledge (positive cause) and concluded that the arrest and search were illegal. While the case was saved because the judge found, on the Commonwealth's motion for reconsideration of the suppression order, that the police made or directed the defendant's arrest, the point is that security personnel should be well versed in the intricacies, requirements, and potential problems of making a felony arrest. Footnote 4 in the case shows how complicated these situations can become where the court "would conclude that the defendant's arrest was 'technically a citizens arrest made by police officers.'"

COMMONWEALTH v. COLITZ
431 N. E. 2d 600 (1982)

PERRETTA, Justice.

Pursuant to Mass.R.Crim.P. 15(a)(2), the Commonwealth appeals from a decision of a District Court judge allowing the defendant's motion to suppress two checks and $800 in marked bills taken from his person at the time of his arrest. Citizens acting with probable cause to believe, but without actual knowledge, that the defendant had taken over $100 from Osco Drug, Inc., requested the police to arrest the defendant. The judge found that "the arrest was made by or at the direction of the police" but that they had acted without probable cause. We hold that the arrest and the search were valid, and we reverse the order allowing the motion to suppress.

In 1980, the defendant was a manager of the Osco store in Medford, where one Donna Maloney was also employed. She testified that she worked in the cash room office. Included among her daily responsibilities were the tasks of giving cashiers fifty dollars with which to open their registers and the preparation of "end-of-the-day" reports. These were itemizations of all the checks, charges, and cash transactions for the day. Maloney would then balance the total amount of actual cash received against the cash transactions shown on the report. In addition, Maloney would also perform "picks" throughout the day: whenever there was over $200 in a register till, the cashier would band the money, place it in a box beneath the register, and Maloney would periodically pick it up. By hitting a certain button on the register terminal located in the cash room office, Maloney could see and record the amount of cash in each register on the store floor at any given time. She would get these figures just before going to the registers to pick up the bands of money which she would bring to the cash room. Maloney would next count the money and record the amount on a tally sheet as well as on her register terminal. She would then place the money on a shelf in the safe in the cash room. There were about five or six managers at the store, including the defendant, who had access to the cash room and to the register terminal in the manager's office.

On December 3, 1980, after doing her second "pick" of the day, Maloney discovered that the amount of cash she had retrieved on the two "picks" was $400 less than the amount reflected on her tally sheet. She was unable to discover the cause for this discrepancy that day. The next morning she was rechecking her records when her attention was attracted to her register terminal. Whenever a "void" is entered on any register in the store, the transaction is reflected on her register terminal. It was then indicating that a $400 void was being entered on the register terminal located in the manager's office. That register was used to monitor sales taking place throughout the store, no money was kept in that register, and it was not authorized for use for void transactions. Maloney related her observations to a co-worker, one Cindy Gianquitto. Gianquitto had knowledge of the cash room procedures, and Maloney, whenever leaving the room to do her "picks," would advise Gianquitto as to how much money was in the room. On December 10, 1980, her suspicions aroused, Maloney reported the incident to two men employed in Osco's loss prevention unit, Tom Gender and Ted Lorentzen. She reviewed the records of all void transactions for the previous three weeks, and these records indicated that during that time period, approximately $10,000 in void transactions had been entered at the store. The next day she met with Gender and Lorentzen, and she brought these records with her.

About 11:45 A.M. on December 12, 1980, Maloney saw that her register terminal was reflecting that a $400 void was being entered on the register terminal in the manager's office. She immediately hit the button on her terminal to obtain and to record a reading of the amount of cash in each register on the floor. As she did this, she also telephoned to an upstairs office, but no one answered. She then called the manager's office, the location of the register terminal on which the $400 void was entered, and the defendant answered the phone. She reported the incident to Gender at his Cambridge office. At about 1:30 P.M., that day, Maloney saw on her register terminal that another $400 void was being entered on the register terminal in the manager's office. She notified Gender of this fact, and the vice-president of the loss prevention unit, one Ron Green, decided that the money in the cash room safe should be marked. Maloney and Gianquitto marked between four and six thousand dollars with a red pen, recorded the amounts, returned the money to the safe, and left the cash room. Maloney stated it was then about 2:30 P.M. At about 3:20 P.M., to her best estimate, Maloney was on the store floor by the cash registers waiting for a cashier to arrive so that Maloney could give her $50 with which to open her register before she (Maloney) left for the day. The defendant approached and asked Maloney what she was doing. She told him, and he informed her that he had already seen the cashier and that he had given her the money.

Gianquitto testified that about ten minutes after marking the bills and leaving the cash room, she saw that one of the cashiers had arrived and that she had her fifty dollar "till" with which to open her register. Gianquitto knew that neither she nor Maloney had given any money to this cashier. She returned to the cash room, counted the marked bills in the safe, discovered that $800 was missing, and proceeded to the front of the store to speak with Maloney.

Lorentzen testified that after analyzing the void transactions information provided by Maloney, he, Green, and Gender met with her at about 3:00 P.M., on December 12, 1980, at the Osco parking lot. Maloney informed them that money was missing from the safe. Gender and Green entered the store, met the defendant, and they proceeded to a security office. Green told the defendant about the void transactions and the missing money. He told the defendant that he believed that the defendant had the missing money on his person. When the defendant asked Green what he was talking about, Green asked him and Gender to leave the security office so that he could telephone an Osco official. As the two men turned and left the office, Green saw the defendant "shuffling" with the back pocket of his trousers, and Green saw "something like a lump" in that pocket. He yelled to Gender, "He's got it with him," and Gender brought the defendant back into the office. Green again asked the defendant to cooperate with them, but the defendant denied knowing what they were talking about. The Medford police were then called.

Officer Alpers testified that he and Officer Chiampi arrived at the Osco store some time after 3:30 P.M. but before 5:00 P.M. They were met by Gender who "explained a situation" to them, and Alpers immediately called his supervisor, Sergeant Padula.

Padula testified that when he arrived, Gender informed him that he believed that the defendant had on his person $800 in marked bills which the defendant had taken from the cash room. Padula further testified that he asked Gender for the basis of his belief, and Gender told him "something to do with cash register receipts and refunds and shortages in the money room on a daily basis that they were investigating." Padula related that "most of the information that Gender was providing me at the time was of a bookkeeping or accounting nature, and was a little over my head." Indeed, Padula stated that Gender explained the "bookkeeping matters" to him, but he doubted whether he could "relate the information to having probable cause to make an arrest." Padula suggested to Green and Gender that they could make a citizen's arrest.

The testimony of Green, Gender, Alpers, and Padula varies as to the specifics of the defendant's arrest, but there is testimony which supports the judge's finding, contained in his memorandum of decision on the Commonwealth's motion for reconsideration, that the arrest was made by or at the direction of the police. After Padula suggested that a citizen's arrest could be made, Green asked Padula to place the defendant under citizen's arrest for larceny. The testimony is consistent on the point that after Green stated that he wished the defendant to be arrested, Alpers advised the defendant that he was under arrest, and he read him his *Miranda* rights. Alpers searched the defendant and found $800. Padula testified that when he saw that each of the bills found in the defendant's pocket was marked in the fashion that Gender had previously described to him, he (Padula) ordered Alpers to place the defendant under arrest and read him his *Miranda* rights.

As the defendant was about to be escorted from the office and the store, he indicated that he would like his coat which was in his office. Gender contacted an assistant store manager and asked him to get the defendant's coat. When the assistant store manager brought the coat to the security office, Padula took it and searched the pockets. He found a large white envelope which he opened. The envelope contained two certified checks, both payable to the defendant, in a total amount of $16,000.

The judge's finding that the citizens had knowledge of facts constituting probable cause to believe that the defendant had taken money from Osco is supported by the recited evidence. "These facts and circumstances amply warranted the police in concluding that it was 'more probable than not' that the defendant had committed the offense." In Massachusetts "a private person may lawfully arrest one who in fact had committed a felony."

"Generally, the person arrested must be convicted of a felony before the 'in fact committed' element is satisfied and the arrest validated. If the citizen is in error in making the arrest, he may be liable in tort for false arrest or false imprisonment." It was also noted that "as a practical matter, the 'in fact committed' requirement cannot be met when the propriety of a citizen's arrest is questioned on a motion to suppress because there has been no validating conviction." At the hearing on the motion to suppress the Commonwealth introduced evidence to show that the defendant had in fact committed the felony with which he was charged; the judge construed the phrase "in fact committed" as meaning that the citizens had to have had actual knowledge of the defendant's felonious act at the time of his arrest. At the conclusion of the hearing, the judge made an oral finding that the citizens had acted on the basis of probable cause rather than actual knowledge; he concluded that the arrest and search were illegal and he allowed the motion to suppress.

In urging us to uphold the citizen's arrest, the Commonwealth argues that when such an arrest is questioned at a pretrial stage of the criminal proceedings, probable cause is the applicable standard. In the alternative, it contends that it sufficiently demonstrated that the defendant had in fact committed a felony. It is unnecessary for us to consider these issues, because the judge found, upon the Commonwealth's motion for reconsideration of the order allowing the motion to suppress, that the police made or directed the defendant's arrest. There is no basis for disturbing this finding, and the key question becomes whether the conduct of the police was such as to violate the Fourth Amendment to the United States Constitution and to require suppression of the checks and the money. "If, then, the exclusionary rule is properly applicable to the evidence taken from the defendant, it must be upon the basis that some type of unconstitutional police conduct occurred."[4]

In concluding that the arrest and the search of the defendant were illegal, the judge found that the police had promoted the defendant's arrest without having probable cause to do so. No subsidiary findings in support of this ultimate finding were made. The defendant argues that it rests upon the testimony of Gender and Alpers showing that even if Gender and Green had knowledge of facts and circumstances constituting probable cause, they did not communicate that information to the police.[5] However, the defendant overlooks Sergeant Padula's testimony which consistently expands that given by Gender and Alpers. Padula related that Gender told him about "cash register receipts and refunds and shortages in the money room on a daily basis," that Gender provided him with the "bookkeeping or accounting" information but it was "a little over my head," and that Gender described the markings that had been made on the money in the safe. At the conclusion of the hearing on the motion to suppress, the judge considered aloud the Commonwealth's evidence, and we find nothing in his statements to indicate a disbelief or rejection of Padula's testimony.[6] If the judge's finding is based

---

[4]Even if the judge's finding that the police arrested the defendant is erroneous, we would conclude that the defendant's arrest was "technically a citizen's arrest made by the police officers," and the controlling issue would remain whether "the police had probable cause to believe that a felony had been committed and that the person arrested had committed it." *Commonwealth v. Harris,* 415 N.E.2d 216.

[5]Gender stated that when the police arrived, he "abreasted them of the situation as it prevailed" and that he "informed them of what had transpired and what we, Osco Drug, had reasons to believe—a felony was committed." Alpers testified that Gender "explained the situation to us."

[6]As we try to follow the judge's train of thought, we see two statements which are relevant to this question: (1) "We are also in agreement that the police officer, when he was summoned, after having been given all of the pertinent facts on the ongoing investigation—and that's all you can call it—felt that in his mind (not that it was binding upon the Court) that he did not have reason to arrest;" (2) "You mean to tell me that an ordinary . . . forget a police officer . . . any ordinary, intelligent person says that we have had a terminal which has been isolated under observation, and

upon a subsidiary determination that Gender did not sufficiently relate his information to the police, it is clearly erroneous.

The evidence shows that Gender explained the sophisticated and technical method of the larceny to the police who were admittedly unable to comprehend it. On the other hand, if the judge's finding that the police lacked probable cause was based on the officers' inability to recognize that the register terminal's data showed probable cause, we conclude that the judge was in error. The record shows that Padula's doubt as to the existence of probable cause was not because he lacked faith or belief in the reliability or credibility of the citizens, nor was the doubt due to a faulty assessment of facts ascertainable from common knowledge and experience. Rather, Padula's concern was the result of his erroneous determination of the legal significance of intricate but highly probative information which called for immediate action. The distinction is major because courts are not concerned with an officer's subjective judgment in the latter situation. See *United States v. Day,* 455 F.2d 454, ("We would not consider ourselves bound by a police officer's inability to articulate his conclusions if the facts clearly demonstrated the existence of probable cause"); *United States ex rel. Senk v. Brierley,* 381 F.Supp. 447, ("Since the courts have never hesitated to overrrule an officer's determination of probable cause when none exists, consistency suggests that a court may also find probable cause in spite of an officer's judgment that none exists"). *United States v. McCambridge,* 551 F.2d 865, ("The validity of an arrest is normally gauged by an objective standard rather than by inquiry into the officer's presumed motives").

We conclude that there is no support in the record for the judge's ultimate finding that the police made or directed the defendant's arrest without probable cause. Because the judge correctly found that the citizens had information constituting probable cause and because the evidence shows that that information was related to the police, it follows that the police had probable cause to arrest the defendant. We see no police misconduct which requires the exclusion of the money or the checks taken from the defendant.

The order allowing the motion to suppress is reversed, and the matter is remanded to the District Court for further proceedings.

CASE COMMENT

Probable cause, reasonable grounds to believe that a person has committed, is committing, or will commit a crime, is a law enforcement requirement for making an arrest. The officer should have reasonably trustworthy information and knowledge of facts and circumstances that would warrant a reasonably prudent man to believe that a crime has been, or is being, committed. Put another way, the officer has more evidence favoring the belief than not favoring it, and this leaves room for some doubt. As the court put it in this case, the police were amply warranted in concluding that it was more probable than not that the defendant had committed the offense. There is not less room for doubt with the private citizen requirement that a felony in fact has been committed. Police arrest

the only person who had access to that terminal was so-and-so, and while I was watching it, I saw two voids totaling $800 check in; I immediately picked up the phone, called that terminal, and so-and-so answered. You mean to tell me the police officer wouldn't be able to understand that type of dialogue?" The prosecutor responded, "I find it hard to believe that that is true. But the officer . . . you know, we have to stand by what the officer said." The judge replied, "And I have to go on facts that I hear." We would point out that the judge's description of the accounting procedure is a simplified summary of over 360 pages of transcript and register tapes introduced in evidence.

activity is governed by the Fourth Amendment, which does not apply to private citizens unless there was a nexus with the police. An arrest deprives a person of liberty and, if it is done illegally, presents a most serious situation. For private citizen security personnel, the potential for loss is great and defeats the notion of loss prevention. This risk can be reduced or eliminated by knowledgeable and appropriately trained personnel.

UNREASONABLE DETENTION

Restricting a person's locomotion or freedom of movement is a most serious action. The identity of the detaining person (store security guard) and the reason or purpose for the detention should be signalled or announced to the person being detained. In the following case, the plaintiff was not informed of the identity of the security officers until after he was forced to his stomach in the parking lot, handcuffed, and had had his face held to the surface by a club or baton. Who wouldn't fear an assault when identity and purpose are not announced? There was a protest of innocence and a demand to be searched. No attention, however, was paid to these protests, and when the correct suspect was apprehended, the plaintiff was kept handcuffed for an additional 15 to 20 minutes.

LATEK v. K MART CORPORATION
401 N.W. 2d 503 (1987)

WHITE, Justice.

This is an appeal by the plaintiff below from a jury verdict in favor of appellees, K Mart Corporation and others, on a cause of action for false imprisonment. The jury found for appellant on a separate cause of action for assault and battery and returned a verdict in the amount of $15,000. No appeal was taken by K Mart from that verdict, and the disposition of that cause will not be discussed here.

Two principal errors are assigned. First, the trial court erred in refusing to direct a verdict for appellant on the false imprisonment count, and second, the court erred in sustaining an objection to the testimony of Dr. Jerome Sherman, an economist, concerning appellant's diminished capacity to earn in the future.

A review of the facts is necessary. Henry R. Latek was, on November 23, 1982, a self-employed builder and carpenter. After completing a remodeling project and collecting from the owner, Latek drove first to a banking outlet and then to a K Mart store at 50th and L Streets in Omaha, Douglas County, Nebraska, arriving at 6:45 p.m. He parked his van near the entrance and went immediately to an area of the store in which cassette tapes were offered for sale. As the tape case was secured, he requested assistance. After ascertaining that the desired tape was not available, he left the store.

The K Mart store has a vestibule consisting of a space, on opposite sides of which are inner and outside doors. As he was leaving through the outer doors he heard one of two men say, "Let's get him," whereupon Latek, fearing an assault and conscious of some $500 in his possession, started to run toward his van. Before reaching the van he was tackled, forced to the parking lot surface on his stomach, his arms forced behind his back, and handcuffed. At the same time his face was held to the surface by means of a baton or club held to the back of his neck.

Latek was lifted to his feet and was informed that the two men were security guards. They escorted Latek through the store, handcuffed, to a second-story office, where he was held for a period of 15 to 20 minutes until he was released, a suspected offender having been apprehended in the meantime. Latek claims injuries to his neck, arm, and leg as a result of the incident. At the time of the incident Latek was dressed in denim jeans and a denim jacket, wore a full beard and mustache, and had nearly shoulder-length hair. He was about 5 feet 7 inches tall.

Charles Gurzick and Joseph Costello were, at the time of these events, observing customers of K Mart from a window overlooking the selling area. It was to this area that Latek was later removed. Gurzick observed a man approximately 5 feet 7 inches in height. The man had a full beard, mustache, and long hair, and was wearing blue jean trousers, and bright blue vest, and a long-sleeved red shirt. Gurzick observed this male tearing the plastic covering from packs of two batteries each and placing the batteries in his trouser pockets or down the front of the trousers. Gurzick dispatched Costello to the sales floor to observe the suspect. He shortly followed. Gurzick and Costello did not obtain a clear front view of the suspect, but saw him from the rear, and had a fleeting view of the side and front when he passed from their view.

Gurzick and Costello then adjourned to the outside of K Mart and engaged in a conversation. Costello had forgotten what the suspect looked like, and Gurzick reminded him that the suspect resembled a neighbor of Gurzick's. It was at this point Latek walked out of the store and was pursued and apprehended. Before pursuing Latek, Gurzick informed Costello, "I don't think that's him, Joe." According to Gurzick, Costello replied, "That's him, man, that's him." After a further protest by Gurzick, Costello said, "It is damn it."

At all times Latek was protesting his innocence and demanding to be searched. No search was made, and no attention was paid to Latek's protests.

As Latek was being escorted through the vestibule, Gurzick's attention was diverted to the checkout lanes immediately in front of the inner doors: "At this time . . . I glanced over at the check-out lanes; and at this point I noticed Mr. Roberts, who was the actual shoplifter. I noticed him going through the check-out lines." Without informing Costello, who held Latek near the door, Gurzick left to apprehend the actual shoplifter. When asked, "Is there a reason why at that time you did not let Mr. Latek go?" Gurzick responded, "At that point I figured it would have caused a lot more trouble and harm if we would have explained the situation in the midst of the floor . . . and stuff." Gurzick was further asked, "Now, by this time you knew Mr. Latek was not the individual that you initially were after?" to which he responded, "Yes."

The actual shoplifter was apprehended, asked to accompany Gurzick to the office, and did so. He was not handcuffed, though Latek, whom Gurzick now knew to be innocent, was led handcuffed through the store to the office, where he was held an additional 15 to 20 minutes, and finally released from the handcuffs and allowed to leave.

Neb.Rev.Stat. § 29–402.01 states:

> A peace officer, a merchant, or a merchant's employee who has probable cause for believing that goods held for sale by the merchant have been unlawfully taken by a person and that he can recover them by taking the person into custody may, for the purpose of attempting to effect such recovery, take the person into custody and detain him in a reasonable manner for a reasonable length of time. Such taking into custody and detention by a peace officer, merchant, or merchant's employee shall not render such peace officer, merchant, or merchant's employee criminally or civilly liable for slander, libel, false arrest, false imprisonment, or unlawful detention.

Assuming, as we must do for the purposes of this case, that the statements of Gurzick and Costello constituted probable cause for the detention of Latek, we are faced with the acknowledged fact that Gurzick knew that he had apprehended and detained an innocent person. Nevertheless, he did not inform Costello of that fact, and detained Latek for a substantial period of time, handcuffed.

The record establishes clearly that a detention arguably lawfully made was continued for an unreasonable time, i.e., after the detainers knew that their suspicions were groundless and the apprehension a mistake. Such further detention was clearly unreasonable, and the judge was in error in not so holding.

We reverse and remand for further proceedings in conformity with this opinion.

CASE COMMENT

The statute in this case requires *probable cause* to take a person into custody and detain that person in a reasonable manner for a reasonable length of time. It does not allow for a lesser standard such as reasonable suspicion. One security officer protested more than once to the other security officer that he did not think plaintiff was the right person. Neither security officer had a clear front view of the suspect. The suspect's red shirt might have been a critical identifier. While the court assumed probable cause (arguably) and remand was for the unreasonably lengthy detention, scrupulous attention should be paid to the standard that allows for the restriction of a person's freedom of movement.

OUTRAGEOUS CONDUCT

A female shopper, who was wearing shorts and a T-shirt, complied with the store security officer's request to accompany him to his office at the back of the store. She immediately dumped the contents of her purse on the desk and said she hadn't stolen anything. Over a 35-minute period she was restrained against her will, badgered, insulted, pressured to confess, made to give personal information, and forced to sign a release. She was unlawfully detained after determination that no offense had been committed. The court felt that there was sufficient evidence of outrageous conduct and that the evidentiary forecast revealed willful and wanton conduct on the part of the security officer that manifested a reckless disregard for the plaintiff's rights. Punitive damages, designed to punish the wrongdoer and deter others from acting similarly, is the potential consequence of outrageous conduct.

ROGERS v. T.J.X. COMPANIES, INC.
404 S.E.2d 664 (1991)

MARTIN, Justice.

This action was filed on 12 August 1988 by the plaintiff for compensatory and punitive damages for false imprisonment and intentional infliction of emotional distress. Summary judgment for defendants was granted by Judge Henry W. Hight, Jr., on 3 October 1989. The Court of Appeals reversed the trial court on all claims except the punitive damages issue. Judge Phillips dissented in part, reasoning that the plaintiff's forecast of the evidence was sufficient to survive summary judgment with respect to punitive damages. The only issue before this Court is whether there is a genuine issue of material fact on the plaintiff's claim for punitive damages. We hold that the trial court erred in granting summary judgment for the defendants on that issue and therefore reverse the Court of Appeals.

The action arose out of events occurring on 17 July 1988 at the T.J. Maxx department store in Cary, North Carolina, owned by defendant T.J.X. Companies, Inc. Taken in the light most favorable to the plaintiff, as we must for summary judgment purposes, the evidence tends to show the following. Plaintiff entered T.J. Maxx, hereinafter "the store," about 4:30 P.M. shopping for linens. She wore bermuda shorts and a T-shirt and carried a pocketbook, approximately twelve inches by twelve inches. The purse contained two cosmetic bags, a wallet, two pens, a glasses' case, and a ziploc bag containing material and wallpaper samples. Plaintiff went first to the cosmetics area and then to the linens department. After leaving the linens department, she walked around a counter containing dishes and crystal and then left the store without making a purchase. Plaintiff never entered the lingerie department and never examined any items of lingerie.

As plaintiff exited the store, Michael Nourse stopped her, identified himself as a store security officer, and asked her to return to the store because he wished to talk with her about some merchandise. Nourse carried a badge of his own design and an identification card issued by the company; he showed these items to plaintiff. Plaintiff told him he was making a mistake, but complied with his request and accompanied Nourse to his office at the back of the store. Plaintiff testified that she did not feel that she had a choice about accompanying Nourse because "he was the law of the store" and she had to obey him. On the way to the office, Nourse asked another store employee, Sheri Steffens, to join them and act as a witness.

Once inside the small office, plaintiff immediately dumped the contents of her purse onto the desk. Nourse told plaintiff to take a seat, but she refused, saying that this would not take long because she was a good customer and had not stolen anything. Nourse responded, "Good customers will steal," and again directed her to have a seat. Telling her he would soon return, he then left the office for five to fifteen minutes. Plaintiff testified that she believed that he might have gone to call the police, and she stepped out of the office to look for them. Seeing no one, she gathered up her belongings, but did not feel free to leave because Nourse had told her he would return. Steffens paged Nourse, who returned momentarily. He said to plaintiff, "Ma'am, all we want is our merchandise. What did you do with it? You were in our lingerie department." Plaintiff denied wrongdoing, again dumped her purse on the desk, and told him that he must have seen her putting the packet of material samples in her purse. As she reached to gather her belongings, Nourse instructed her not to touch anything.

Nourse pulled down a clipboard hanging on the wall and showed her a card which said that the store employees had the right to detain her if they had reason to believe she had been shoplifting. Nourse repeatedly questioned plaintiff about the location of the missing merchandise as she tried to read the card. Plaintiff told him to "shut up" so that she could concentrate. Nourse remarked to Steffens, "Usually the dog that barks the loudest is guilty." Nourse then told plaintiff that he could call the police if she wanted them to settle it; that he could handcuff her to a chair; and that he would call the police and have them put her in jail. Plaintiff continued to deny the allegations and asked if he wanted her to take her clothes off to prove that she had not done anything, even though she was a very modest person. Steffens testified that plaintiff was very upset throughout the incident and that Nourse's attitude and demeanor toward plaintiff was sarcastic.

Nourse instructed plaintiff to sign two forms, one of which was a waiver of Miranda rights. The other form released T.J. Maxx from liability for any claims arising out of the incident. Neither of the papers had been filled out when plaintiff signed. Plaintiff testified that she signed the release form only because she believed that she would not be allowed to leave the store and go home if she did not sign it. Nourse refused to give plaintiff copies of the forms, because it was not company policy. After signing the papers, plaintiff left the store and drove home. She had been in the security office approximately 35 minutes. About one-half hour after plaintiff left the store, Nourse announced to Steffens that he had found the missing merchandise, a beige brassiere.

Plaintiff's evidence showed that she became sick, nervous and upset as a result of the incident. She had difficulty sleeping and took sleeping pills for two weeks as prescribed by her doctor. In addition, she testified that she no longer went shopping, because she felt as if someone was always looking over her shoulder.

False imprisonment is the illegal restraint of the person of any one against his or her will. The tort may be committed by words or acts; therefore, actual force is not required. Restraint of the person is essential, whether by threats, express or implied, or by conduct. The Court of Appeals held that plaintiff had established facts sufficient to support her claim for false imprisonment; however, the false imprisonment issue is not before us. The sole basis for the dissent was the issue of whether plaintiff's claim for punitive damages should survive summary judgment.

The purpose of punitive damages, sometimes denominated as exemplary damages or smart money, is two-fold: to punish the wrongdoing of the defendant and to deter others from engaging in similar conduct. The tort in question must be accompanied by additional aggravating or outrageous conduct in order to justify the award of punitive damages. To constitute outrageous behavior, there must exist evidence of " 'insult, indignity, malice, oppression or bad motive.' " *Hinson v. Dawson,* 92 S.E.2d 393 (quoting *Swinton v. Realty Co.,* 73 S.E.2d 785).

> Actual ill will or vindictiveness of purpose is not as a rule required, and exemplary damages have been frequently awarded when the imprisonment was accompanied by circumstances of fraud, recklessness, wantonness, . . . bad faith, circumstances of oppression, . . . insult or outrage, willful injury, or a wrongful act without a reasonable excuse, . . . or in known violation of law.

35 C.J.S. *False Imprisonment* § 67; *see also Robinson v. Duszynski,* 243 S.E.2d 148 (aggravation shown where the wrong is done willfully or under circumstances of rudeness or oppression, or in a manner evincing a wanton and reckless disregard for plaintiff's rights). Willful conduct is done purposefully in violation of law, or knowingly of set purpose, or without yielding to reason. Wanton conduct is done wickedly or needlessly, manifesting a reckless indifference to the rights of others. *See also Hinson v. Dawson,* 92 S.E.2d 393 ("Conduct is wanton when in conscious and intentional disregard of and indifference to the rights and safety of others").

Whether the evidence of outrageous conduct is sufficient to carry the issue of punitive damages to the jury is a question for the court. Punitive damages are recoverable only where the jury determines plaintiff is entitled to compensatory or nominal damages. However, if a punitive damage issue is submitted, the decision of whether punitive damages are warranted, and in what amount, is one for the jury in its discretion.

Defendants analogize *Ayscue v. Mullen,* 336 S.E.2d 863, a case in which a false imprisonment was accompanied by an assault and battery. In that case, the defendant store owners required customers who did not make a purchase to obtain a "no sale slip" before leaving each department. When two shoppers, who were apparently unaware of the store policy, attempted to leave the store without such a slip, defendant barred the door and refused to allow them to leave. When one plaintiff pushed one of the defendants in an attempt to leave, that defendant pushed her back to prevent her exit. The entire incident lasted about three to five minutes. The Court of Appeals held, without elaboration, that the facts in that case did not support the award of punitive damages by the jury. We find the analogy here unpersuasive. The assault and battery committed by defendant in *Ayscue* was precipitated by a similar assault and battery by the plaintiff. Further, that incident was considerably shorter than the detention in the instant case.

The rules governing summary judgment are now familiar learning and we need not repeat them here. Taken in the light most favorable to the plaintiff, the evidence tends to show that (1) defendant Nourse impersonated a police officer by using a badge of his own design; (2) plaintiff was restrained against her will in the store security office for approximately one-half hour; (3) plaintiff was badgered, insulted and pressured to confess by defendant Nourse despite her efforts to prove her innocence; (4) plaintiff was frightened and upset and asked if she could leave; (5) defendant unlawfully detained plaintiff after determination that no offense had been committed, N.C.G.S. § 15A-404(d); (6) plaintiff was made to give up personal information including her driver's license number, telephone number, and social security number; and (7) plaintiff was forced to sign a release of liability as a condition to her release from Nourse's custody. We are unable to conclude, as a matter of law, that these facts justify an order of summary judgment in the defendant's favor.

We hold that there was sufficient evidence of outrageous conduct, in addition to that conduct constituting the false imprisonment, to survive defendants' motion for summary judgment. Plaintiff's forecast of the evidence reveals both willful and wanton conduct on the part of Nourse, manifesting a reckless disregard for plaintiff's rights. Nourse continued to detain plaintiff even after it became obvious that she did not have the merchandise in her possession. There is also plenary evidence of unnecessary insult and indignity heaped upon plaintiff by one with superior power and authority. Plaintiff was threatened with handcuffing and arrest. That plaintiff was forced to sign a release is also evidence of aggravation. The evidence demonstrates sufficient aggravation of the tort of false imprisonment to survive defendants' motion for summary judgment on the punitive damages issue. Accordingly, we reverse in part the decision of the Court of Appeals and remand the case to them for further proceedings not inconsistent with this opinion.

REVERSED IN PART AND REMANDED.

CASE COMMENT

False imprisonment (false arrest) is the illegal restraint of the person against their will. It may be accomplished by words or acts—actual force is not required. Restraint of the person is essential, whether by threats (express or implied) or by conduct. Punitive or exemplary damages, designed to punish the wrongdoer and deter others from engaging in similar conduct, are recoverable where compensatory or actual damages have been found. To justify an award of punitive damages, aggravating or outrageous conduct must accompany the tort in question. Insult, indignity, malice, oppression, or bad motive is evidence of outrageous conduct or aggravation. Willful conduct is done purposely in violation of law and conduct is wanton when it is in conscious and intentional disregard of, and indifference to, the rights and safety of others.

10

Search and Seizure by Private Citizen

Fourth Amendment sanctions apply to sworn law enforcement officers and not to private citizens generally speaking. If members of your security staff are commissioned, deputized, or licensed, they may be state actors. If the private citizen acts in concert with, or at the behest of, police, sanctions of the Fourth Amendment may attach. Searches by private citizens might be permissible in one of the following situations.

- Actual consent
- Implied consent
- In some instances, and then limited, as incidental to a valid arrest or detention

If a consent is obtained, it must be given freely, voluntarily, and knowingly. Implied consent may come through union or employment contract or by adequate warnings. Stemming the flow of stolen property and protecting life and property are important tasks for the security staff. Searches may be a tool in accomplishing this task. They must be done, however, within the constraints of law.

FOURTH AMENDMENT AND PRIVATE CITIZENS

The originative or seminal case in the search and seizure field as it pertains to private citizens follows and sets forth the basic Fourth Amendment standard that continues to exist today. The U.S. Supreme Court said the Fourth Amendment gives protection against unlawful search and seizure, and as is here shown, its protection applies to governmental action. Its origin and history clearly show that it was intended as a restraint on activities of the sovereign government, and it was not intended to be a limitation on other than governmental agencies. No governmental official had anything to do with the wrongful seizure in this case. It was several months after the property had been taken that the government first learned of it. Note the court's assumption that the petitioner had an unquestionable right of redress against those who illegally and wrongfully took his private property.

BURDEAU v. McDOWELL

256 U.S. 465, 41 S. Ct. 574, 65 L. Ed. 1048 (1921)

Mr. Justice Day delivered the opinion of the court:

J. C. McDowell, hereinafter called the petitioner, filed a petition in the United States district court for the western district of Pennsylvania, asking for an order for the return to him of certain books, papers, memoranda, correspondence, and other data in the possession of Joseph A. Burdeau, appellant herein, Special Assistant to the Attorney General of the United States.

In the petition it is stated that Burdeau and his associates intended to present to the grand jury in and for the western district of Pennsylvania a charge against petitioner of an alleged violation of § 215 of the Criminal Code of the United States for the fraudulent use of the mails; that it was the intention of Burdeau and his associates, including certain postoffice inspectors cooperating with him, to present to the grand jury certain private books, papers, memoranda, etc., which were the private property of the petitioner; that the papers had been in the possession and exclusive control of the petitioner in the Farmers' Bank Building, in Pittsburgh. It is alleged that during the spring and summer of 1920 these papers were unlawfully seized and stolen from petitioner by certain persons participating in and furthering the proposed investigation so to be made by the grand jury, under the direction and control of Burdeau as Special Assistant to the Attorney General, and that such books, papers, memoranda, etc., were being held in the possession and control of Burdeau and his assistants; that in the taking of the personal private books and papers, the person who purloined and stole the same drilled the petitioner's private safes, broke the locks upon his private desk, and broke into and abstracted from the files in his offices his private papers; that the possession of the books, papers, etc., by Burdeau and his assistants, was unlawful and in violation of the legal and constitutional rights of the petitioner. It is charged that the presentation to the grand jury of the same, or any secondary or other evidence secured through or by them, would work a deprivation of petitioner's constitutional rights secured to him by the 4th and 5th Amendments to the Constitution of the United States.

An answer was filed, claiming the right to hold and use the papers. A hearing was had before the district judge, who made an order requiring the delivery of the papers to the clerk of the court, together with all copies, memoranda, and data taken therefrom, which the court found had been stolen from the offices of the petitioner at rooms numbered 1320 and 1321 in the Farmers' Bank Building, in the city of Pittsburgh. The order further provided that, upon delivery of the books, papers, etc., to the clerk of the court, the same should be sealed and impounded for the period of ten days, at the end of which period they should be delivered to the petitioner or his attorney unless an appeal were taken from the order of the court, in which event, the books, papers, etc., should be impounded until the determination of the appeal. An order was made restraining Burdeau, Special Assistant Attorney General, the Department of Justice, its officers and agents, and the United States Attorney, from presenting to the United States Commissioner, the grand jury, or any official tribunal, any of the books, papers, memoranda, letters, copies of letters, correspondence, etc., or any evidence of any nature whatsoever secured by or coming into their possession as a result of the knowledge obtained from the inspection of such books, papers, memoranda, etc.

In his opinion the district judge stated that it was the intention of the Department of Justice, through Burdeau and his assistants, to present the books, papers, etc., to the grand jury with a view to having the petitioner indicted for the alleged violation of § 215 of the Criminal Code of the United States, and the court held that the evidence offered by the petitioner showed that the papers had been stolen from him, and that he was entitled to the return of the same. In this connection the district judge stated that it did not appear that

Burdeau, or any official or agent of the United States, or any of the Departments, had anything to do with the search of the petitioner's safe, files, and desk, or the abstraction therefrom of any of the writings referred to in the petition, and added that "the order made in this case is not made because of any unlawful act on the part of anybody representing the United States or any of its Departments, but solely upon the ground that the government should not use stolen property for any purpose after demand made for its return." Expressing his views, at the close of the testimony, the judge said that there had been a gross violation of the 4th and 5th Amendments to the Federal Constitution; that the government had not been a party to any illegal seizure; that those Amendments, in the understanding of the court, were passed for the benefit of the states against action by the United States—forbidden by those Amendments, and that the court was satisfied that the papers were illegally and wrongfully taken from the possession of the petitioner, and were then in the hands of the government.

So far as is necessary for our consideration, certain facts from the record may be stated. Henry L. Doherty & Company of New York were operating managers of the Cities Service Company, which company is a holding company, having control of various oil and gas companies. Petitioner was a director in the Cities Service Company and a director in the Quapaw Gas Company, a subsidiary company, and occupied an office room in the building owned by the Farmers' Bank of Pittsburgh. The rooms were leased by the Quapaw Gas Company. McDowell occupied one room for his private office. He was employed by Doherty & Company as the head of the natural gas division of the Cities Service Company. Doherty & Company discharged McDowell for alleged unlawful and fraudulent conduct in the course of the business. An officer of Doherty & Company and the Cities Service Company went to Pittsburgh in March, 1920, with authority of the president of the Quapaw Gas Company, to take possession of the company's office. He took possession of room 1320; that room and the adjoining room had McDowell's name on the door. At various times papers were taken from the safe and desk in the rooms, and the rooms were placed in charge of detectives. A large quantity of papers were taken and shipped to the auditor of the Cities Service Company at 60 Wall Street, New York, which was the office of that company, Doherty & Company, and the Quapaw Gas Company. The secretary of McDowell testified that room 1320 was his private office; that practically all the furniture in both rooms belonged to him; that there was a large safe belonging to the Farmers' Bank and a small safe belonging to McDowell: that on March 23, 1920, a representative of the company and a detective came to the offices; that the detective was placed in charge of room 1320; that the large safe was opened with a view to selecting papers belonging to the company, and that the representative of the company took private papers of McDowell's also. While the rooms were in charge of detectives both safes were blown open. In the small safe nothing of consequence was found, but in the large safe papers belonging to McDowell were found. The desk was forced open, and all the papers taken from it. The papers were placed in cases, and shipped to Doherty & Company, 60 Wall Street, New York.

In June, 1920, following, Doherty & Company, after communication with the Department of Justice, turned over a letter, found in McDowell's desk, to the Department's representative. Burdeau admitted at the hearing that, as the representative of the United States in the Department of Justice, he had papers which he assumed were taken from the office of McDowell. The communication to the Attorney General stated that McDowell had violated the laws of the United States in the use of the mail in the transmission of various letters to parties who owned the properties which were sold by or offered to the Cities Service Company; that some of such letters, or copies of them, taken from McDowell's file, were in the possession of the Cities Service Company; that the company also had in its possession portions of a diary of McDowell in which he had jotted down the commissions which he had received from a number of the transactions, and other data which, it is stated, would be useful in the investigation of the matter before the grand jury and subsequent prosecution should an indictment be returned.

We do not question the authority of the court to control the disposition of the papers, and come directly to the contention that the constitutional rights of the petitioner were violated by their seizure, and that having subsequently come into the possession of the prosecuting officers of the government, he was entitled to their return. The Amendments involved are the 4th and 5th, protecting a citizen against unreasonable searches and seizures, and compulsory testimony against himself. An extended consideration of the origin and purposes of these Amendments would be superfluous in view of the fact that this court has had occasion to deal with those subjects in a series of cases.

The 4th Amendment gives protection against unlawful searches and seizures, and, as shown in the previous cases, its protection applies to governmental action. Its origin and history clearly show that it was intended as a restraint upon the activities of sovereign authority, and was not intended to be a limitation upon other than governmental agencies; as against such authority it was the purpose of the 4th Amendment to secure the citizen in the right of unmolested occupation of his dwelling and the possession of his property, subject to the right of seizure by process duly issued.

In the present case the record clearly shows that no official of the Federal government had anything to do with the wrongful seizure of the petitioner's property, or any knowledge thereof until several months after the property had been taken from him and was in the possession of the Cities Service Company. It is manifest that there was no invasion of the security afforded by the 4th Amendment against unreasonable search and seizure, as whatever wrong was done was the act of individuals in taking the property of another. A portion of the property so taken and held was turned over to the prosecuting officers of the Federal government. We assume that petitioner has an unquestionable right of redress against those who illegally and wrongfully took his private property under the circumstances herein disclosed, but with such remedies we are not now concerned.

The 5th Amendment, as its terms import, is intended to secure the citizen from compulsory testimony against himself. It protects from extorted confessions, or examinations in court proceedings by compulsory methods.

The exact question to be decided here is: May the government retain incriminating papers, coming to it in the manner described, with a view to their use in a subsequent investigation by a grand jury, where such papers will be part of the evidence against the accused, and may be used against him upon trial should an indictment be returned?

We know of no constitutional principle which requires the government to surrender the papers under such circumstances. Had it learned that such incriminatory papers, tending to show a violation of Federal law, were in the hands of a person other than the accused, it having had no part in wrongfully obtaining them, we know of no reason why a subpoena might not issue for the production of the papers as evidence. Such production would require no unreasonable search or seizure, nor would it amount to compelling the accused to testify against himself.

The papers having come into the possession of the government without a violation of petitioner's rights by governmental authority, we see no reason why the fact that individuals, unconnected with the government, may have wrongfully taken them should prevent them from being held for use in prosecuting an offense where the documents are of an incriminatory character.

It follows that the District Court erred in making the order appealed from, and the same is reversed.

Mr. Justice Brandeis dissenting, with whom Mr. Justice Holmes concurs:

Plaintiff's private papers were stolen. The thief, to further his own ends, delivered them to the law officer of the United States. He, knowing them to have been stolen, retains them for use against the plaintiff. Should the court permit him to do so?

That the court would restore the papers to plaintiff if they were still in the thief's possession is not questioned. That it has power to control the disposition of these stolen papers, although they have passed into the possession of the law officer, is also not questioned. But it is said that no provision of the Constitution requires their surrender, and that the papers could have been subpoenaed. This may be true. Still I cannot believe that action of a public official is necessarily lawful because it does not violate constitutional prohibitions, and because the same result might have been attained by other and proper means. At the foundation of our civil liberty lies the principle which denies to government officials an exceptional position before the law, and which subjects them to the same rules of conduct that are commands to the citizen. And in the development of our liberty insistence upon procedural regularity has been a large factor. Respect for law will not be advanced by resort, in its enforcement, to means which shock the common man's sense of decency and fair play.

CASE COMMENT

McDowell alleged that Burdeau, a U. S. Special Assistant Attorney General, intended to use his private property against him in a criminal case, that his private property had been in his possession and exclusive control, and that his property was unlawfully seized and stolen. The trial judge stated it did not appear that any government agent had anything to do with the illegal search and seizure. The Supreme Court held that the record clearly showed that no government official had anything to do with the wrongful seizure and that there was no invasion of the security afforded by the Fourth Amendment. It was obvious to the court that the taking of the property was illegally and wrongfully done, and the court suggested that McDowell had an unquestionable right of redress. While the Fourth Amendment applies to governmental actions and not to those of private citizens if the government had no hand in it, the security manager should be cautious in searching and seizing private property so as not to do it illegally, unethically, or unprofessionally.

GUIDELINES

The following case raised the question of whether a special police officer privately employed as a security guard is affected by the Fourth Amendment as to the admissibility of evidence he discovered. The case hinges on whether the officer's private function affects the constitutionality of his conduct.

The officer searched the sleeping compartment of a contract truck that made regular trips between plants and found a gun in a travel bag that was later determined to have been stolen from a city police officer. The job of the officer was checking persons entering and leaving the plant, inspecting vehicles, and ensuring that any company materials leaving the property were authorized to do so. Gate inspections of vehicles, their contents, and their drivers personal bags were routine. Company regulations, in a booklet provided to employees and contractors, recognized the authority of guards to examine all company property and to inspect all items or vehicles being taken into, on, or from the premises.

COMMONWEALTH v. LEONE
435 N.E. 2d 1036 (1982)

HENNESSEY, Chief Justice,

This is an interlocutory appeal by the Commonwealth, which objects to the suppression of certain evidence in a criminal proceeding in a District Court. The issues posed are whether the Fourth Amendment to the United States Constitution affects the admissibility of evidence discovered by a special police officer privately employed as a plant security guard, and if so, whether the officer's conduct constituted an unreasonable search and seizure. We conclude that the Fourth Amendment does apply, but that the officer's private function may affect the constitutionality of his conduct. Further, because of the incomplete record before us, we vacate the judge's ruling suppressing the evidence, and we direct that further proceedings be held.

The defendant is charged with possession of a firearm and receipt of stolen goods (the firearm). At the time of his arrest, he was employed as a truck driver by an independent contractor which leased his services to General Electric Company. He drove exclusively for General Electric, and regularly traveled between General Electric plants in Lynn, Massachusetts, and Durham, North Carolina. On these trips the defendant used a truck bearing General Electric insignia and leased by General Electric from a truck rental company. Inside the cab of the truck was a sleeping compartment, which the defendant used as his personal living quarters while driving between Lynn and Durham.

On January 29, 1981, John Vousboukis, a General Electric security guard, stopped the defendant at the gate of General Electric's Lynn plant to determine whether the defendant's cargo was properly authorized to leave the plant. Vousboukis first inspected the cargo section of the truck, checking the cargo against a description on the defendant's gate pass. Then, over the defendant's objection, he entered the cab of the truck.[1] On the bed in the defendant's sleeping quarters was a travel bag. It appears that the bag was closed, but not secured. Vousboukis picked up the bag, and discovered a gun within.

After questioning the defendant concerning firearms identification (the defendant stated that he had no Massachusetts identification card but had a North Carolina card at his home), Vousboukis took custody of the gun. He then contacted another security officer, who came to the gate and questioned the defendant further. The second officer contacted the Lynn police, and learned that the gun had been stolen from a Lynn police officer. Vousboukis turned over the gun to the police when they arrived.

The defendant moved to suppress the gun on the ground that Vousboukis had conducted an unreasonable search and seizure in violation of the United States and Massachusetts constitutions. At a hearing on the defendant's motion, Vousboukis testified that he was a "special police officer" for the city of Lynn, employed by General Electric to patrol its Lynn plant. His duties at General Electric included checking persons entering or leaving the plant to determine whether they were company personnel, and inspecting vehicles, to ensure that any "company materials" leaving the property were authorized to leave. There was no evidence explaining his status and duties as a special police officer.

Vousboukis stated that gate inspections of vehicles and their contents, including the drivers' personal bags, were routine practice. He also mentioned a company regulation providing that security plant guards could inspect any items brought onto or taken away from

---

[1] Vousboukis testified that the defendant had told him angrily that he "did not want him in the cab." Vousboukis also stated that he had noticed the defendant holding first a wooden club and later a tire iron, and had feared that the defendant would hit him. He added, however, that the defendant had explained that he wished to check the tires, and had relinquished both items upon request.

company property. According to Vousboukis, all employees and contractors were provided with a copy of the company regulations.[4] The defendant testified that security guards had never inspected his truck or belongings during the eight years in which he had driven to and from the Lynn plant. He also stated that he had not received a copy of the company regulations, and had no knowledge of the provision for inspections.

The judge assumed that the Fourth Amendment governed the admissibility of the gun. He found that Vousboukis had acted in accordance with plant custom in stopping the defendant at the gate, but did not state whether he believed that further inspection was customary. He ruled that Vousboukis "had the right and duty to inspect the cargo, and the inside of the cab, but had no right to handle the travel bag," and that Vousboukis' conduct had "violated the reasonable expectation of privacy held by the defendant." On this ground, he suppressed the evidence.

There is no suggestion that, before stopping the defendant's truck, Vousboukis had probable cause to search the truck, or even reason to suspect that the defendant was involved in crime. Under the standards applied to ordinary police officers, he was not entitled to conduct even a cursory search.

Therefore, the admissibility of the evidence he discovered depends on whether and in what manner the Fourth Amendment applies to privately employed special police officers such as Officer Vousboukis.

The Fourth Amendment, and the accompanying rule of exclusion, apply only to government action. Evidence discovered and seized by private parties is admissible without regard to the methods used, unless State officials have instigated or participated in the search.

This rule follows from the origins and design of the Fourth Amendment as a restraint against arbitrary or lawless use of sovereign power, with its great potential for intrusion upon the privacy of individuals. Limitation of Fourth Amendment sanctions to government action is also consistent with a major objective of the rule of exclusion—deterrence of unreasonable searches and seizures. Private persons are not regularly involved in law enforcement, and those who undertake searches generally do so for reasons other than to secure criminal conviction. Therefore, exclusion of the fruits of their activities will not have a significant deterrent effect.

Privately employed security forces pose a difficult problem of distinction between State and private action. Most courts have held that the Fourth Amendment does not apply to private security personnel who hold no special authority under State law. In reaching this conclusion, they have reasoned that the primary function and concern of privately employed security officers is protection of their employers' property, rather than conviction of wrongdoers. Several courts and commentators have taken a different view, pointing out that private security forces have come into increasing use as supplements to police protection, and perform functions much like those of ordinary police. Private security personnel investigate criminal activity on a regular basis, and may well have an interest in the outcome of criminal actions against persons who pose a threat to the employer's property.

A different rule prevails when an officer possesses additional status as a special or deputy police officer. Specially commissioned officers are formally affiliated with the sovereign and generally possess authority beyond that of an ordinary citizen in matters such as arrest and the

---

[4]The Commonwealth offered as evidence a booklet entitled "Code of Plant Conduct," addressed to plant employees. Appearing on the third page of the booklet was the statement: "We recognize that plant guards have authority to examine all company property and to inspect all items or vehicles being taken into, on, or . . . from the premises." The judge marked the booklet for identification, but refused to allow it as an exhibit in the absence of any evidence that the defendant had knowledge of it.

use of weapons. Therefore, they are treated as agents of the State, subject to the constraints of the Fourth Amendment.

We agree that a State officer privately employed as a security guard is bound to comply with the Fourth Amendment when performing investigatory duties, and that evidence he discovers through methods in violation of the Fourth Amendment is subject to the rule of exclusion. But this does not mean that the bounds of permissible conduct are the same for the privately employed special officer as they would be for an ordinary police officer. The guard's private function adds a new aspect to his activities, which we believe is relevant to the proper application of the Fourth Amendment. The action he takes on behalf of his employer may be a lawful and necessary means of protecting the employer's property, although it would be impermissible if taken on behalf of the State in pursuit of evidence. Restatement (Second) of Torts § 260 (privilege to interfere with another's property in defense of actor's property). When the guard's conduct is justified by his legitimate private duties, it should not be treated as lawless, or "unreasonable," search and seizure.

Established principles support the conclusion that the existence of a lawful private purpose should be taken into account in applying the Fourth Amendment. The guard's position is similar to that of a police officer who intrudes by lawful means upon an individual's privacy, and then discovers unanticipated evidence. The subject of the search, for his part, has reason to expect some scrutiny or interference by the agents of the private party whose property he uses or handles. Moreover, when the guard takes legitimate steps for the protection of his employer's property, there is no cause for the deterrent sanction of the exclusionary rule. Exclusion would serve only to frustrate prosecution of those whose crimes happen to come to light in the course of a routine inspection by a security guard. For these reasons, we conclude that an investigation by a special police officer privately employed as a security guard does not violate the Fourth Amendment when it is conducted on behalf of the private employer, in a manner that is reasonable and necessary for protection of the employer's property. If, on the other hand, the officer steps outside this sphere of legitimate private action, the exclusionary rule applies as it would to any State officer. The burden of establishing the constitutionality of the officer's conduct rests with the Commonwealth.

The present record does not afford sufficient basis for applying the principle we have outlined. We have no information concerning Vousboukis' duties as a special police officer in the city of Lynn. Nor does the record reveal the nature of the private property he purported to protect. Neither the judge nor the parties could have anticipated the requirements of our decision, and a new hearing is necessary.

At the new hearing, the propriety of the guard's action should be determined in light of the reasons for special treatment of a privately employed special police officer acting on his employer's behalf. These reasons are the private nature and purpose of his conduct, the legitimacy of the specific action he takes as a means of protecting private property, and the diminished expectations of privacy of the subject of the investigation. Several definite requirements follow from these foundations.

First, the guard must have acted under the control of his private employer. If the investigation exceeded his private duties or authorization, he must be considered to have acted in his official capacity. Similarly, if the guard has received instructions from State authorities, on a regular basis or in regard to the particular investigation at issue, his conduct is not protected by his private role.

Second, the guard's action must be clearly related to his employer's private purposes. An investigation that goes beyond the employer's needs cannot be justified as an incident of the guard's private function. If, for example, none of the General Electric property to which the defendant had access could have been concealed in a travel bag or sleeping compartment, Vousboukis was not entitled to search these areas.

Third, the investigation must be a legitimate means of protecting the employer's property, and so must be reasonable in light of the circumstances surrounding it. Restatement (Second) of Torts § 278. Reasonableness depends in part on the expectations engendered by the particular setting. If the employer has maintained the private character of his property, those who use it must anticipate and accept supervision. But if the employer has exposed his premises and chattels to semi-public use, the sense of private prerogative to control its users is much diminished. Custom or advance warning may bear upon the propriety of an investigation, but should not be determinative.

Finally, the judge should consider the methods chosen and the manner in which they are carried out. Failure to employ available, less intrusive alternatives may suggest that the methods employed were unwarranted, and an offense to individual dignity is impermissible in almost any circumstances.

Accordingly, we vacate the judge's decision. Further evidence on the motion to suppress the gun from evidence is to be received in the judge's discretion, and further proceedings shall be in accord with this opinion.

So ordered.

CASE COMMENT

The court concluded that an investigation by a special police officer privately employed as a security guard does not violate the Fourth Amendment when it is conducted on behalf of the private employer in a manner that is reasonable and necessary for the protection of the employer's property. It also concluded that, if the officer steps outside the sphere of legitimate private action, the Fourth Amendment exclusion would apply. Some of the court-stated reasons for special treatment of a privately employed special police officer acting on his employer's behalf are: the private nature and purpose of his conduct, the legitimacy of the specific action taken as a means of protecting private property, and the diminished expectations of privacy of the subject of the investigation. Three requirements follow from these foundations: the guard must have acted under control of the private employer, the guard's actions must be clearly related to the employer's private purposes, and the investigation must be a legitimate means of protecting the employer's property and must be reasonable in light of the circumstances surrounding it. The security manager should also consider the consent, real or implied, of all the parties involved. In this case, employees and contractors were provided with a copy of company regulations as described in footnote 4. Ensuring that all involved—employees, contractors, and so on—understand the regulations would be advantageous.

JOINT OPERATION

In the following case, the private citizen credit card company special agent worked with the police in locating and effecting the arrest of the plaintiff. The private citizen special agent subsequently searched the plaintiff's car, which was parked some distance down the street. While looking in the car for credit cards and merchandise the special agent discovered tear gas like cannisters. The plaintiff was subsequently charged with possession of these cannisters in violation of the criminal code. The plaintiff moved to suppress the cannisters as evidence. While the Fourth Amendment normally does not apply to private citizens, it may attach if private citizens are part of a joint operation with law enforcement officers. Official participation in the planning and implementation of the overall operation is sufficient, without any more activity, to taint the subsequent acts of private citizens with state action.

STAPLETON v. SUPERIOR COURT OF LOS ANGELES COUNTY
447 P. 2d 967 (1969)

TOBRINER, Justice.

Petitioner seeks a writ of prohibition to compel the Superior Court of Los Angeles County to grant his motion pursuant to section 1538.5 of the Penal Code to suppress certain evidence seized from his automobile. The People contend that a private citizen conducted the search and the search therefore does not fall within the purview of the Fourth Amendment. Because of police involvement in the search we have concluded that petitioner's motion to suppress the evidence should have been granted.

On the night of November 23, 1967, Lee Bradford, a special agent for the Carte Blanche credit card corporation, together with agents from two other credit card corporations, went to the Highland Park police station in Los Angeles to aid in the arrest of petitioner, for whom the police had an outstanding arrest warrant for credit card fraud. The agents and the police agreed to meet near petitioner's home. After arriving at petitioner's home around midnight, the officers instructed Bradford and another agent to cover the rear of the house to prevent an escape while the two officers and the third agent went to the front door with the warrant. Bradford testified that he was armed at the time.

Bradford further testified to the following effect. Bradford entered petitioner's house after one of the officers requested him to do so and let him in through the back door. Bradford and the officers arrested and handcuffed defendant. Bradford then started searching the house; the officers were also engaged in searching the premises and Bradford assisted them. He shortly asked whether anyone had searched petitioner's car which, he remembered, he had seen parked some distance down the street. Bradford could not recall who had answered his question negatively. Bradford then asked where the keys were and someone indicated the keys lying on a table. Another agent handed the keys to Bradford, who then went outside to the car. In response to the question why he went out to the car, Bradford answered: "Well, it's one of those things that we have done in making arrests, searching incidental to the arrest." He also stated that he was looking for credit cards or merchandise which may have been purchased with cards, and admitted that he had no search warrant and that the petitioner had not given permission for the search.

Bradford searched inside the car, which was not locked, and then unlocked the trunk. In the trunk he discovered 60 canisters containing a tear gas-like substance. In order not to disturb the "evidence," Bradford closed the trunk and reported his discovery to the officers. One of the officers returned to the car with Bradford, opened the trunk, and retrieved the canisters.

Petitioner was subsequently charged with possessing a "shell, cartridge, or bomb containing or capable of emitting tear gas" in violation of Penal Code, section 12420. Petitioner moved to suppress the canisters under section 1538.5 of the Penal Code, and, following a hearing pursuant to that section, the motion was denied. This petition for a writ of prohibition followed.

I

The Fourth Amendment's prohibition against unreasonable searches and seizures applies to the states, and evidence obtained in violation of that amendment is inadmissible in state courts. Mapp v. Ohio (1961) 367 U.S. 643. The Fourth Amendment does not apply, however, to searches by private individuals. Burdeau v. McDowell (1921) 256 U.S. 465.

The search of petitioner's car was clearly part of a joint operation by police and the credit card agents aimed at arresting petitioner and obtaining evidence against him. This official participation in the planning and implementation of the overall operation is sufficient without more to taint with state action the subsequent acts of such credit card agents.

In Byars v. United States (1927) 273 U.S. 28, city police, then not subject to the Fourth Amendment, obtained a warrant—invalid by constitutional standards—to search the defendant's home for intoxicating liquors. After obtaining the warrant, but before commencing the search, Police Officer Densmore asked a federal prohibition agent, Mr. Adams, to join the group making the search. Upon reaching the defendant's home Densmore assigned each member of the party to search a particular room of the house. Both Adams and a police officer named Taylor found counterfeit whiskey stamps. Although Adams had not initiated the search and had not directed the actions of Taylor or any other police officers, the Supreme Court excluded the stamps, including those found by Taylor. Justice Sutherland, speaking for the court, noted that Adams participated under the color of his federal office, and thus rendered the search in substance a "joint operation" of local and federal authorities, and concluded that the legal significance of such a search was "the same as though he (Adams) had engaged in the undertaking as one exclusively his own."

United States v. Price, 383 U.S. 787, illustrates the minimal extent of official participation needed to bring such group action within the purview of the Constitution. In Price the court held that the alleged murder of two civil rights workers by 18 men, including three Mississippi policemen, constituted "state action" (which the court equated with action "under color of law") in violation of 18 U.S.C. section 242. "Private persons, jointly engaged with state officials in the prohibited action, are acting 'under color' of law * * *. To act 'under color' of law does not require that the accused be an officer of the State. It is enough that he is a willful participant in joint activity with the State or its agents." (See also Weeks v. United States (1914) 232 U.S. 383, (evidence barred which was taken from the house of the accused by a federal official acting "under color of his office.")

The well-coordinated joint operation conducted in the instant case by the police and the agents clearly falls under the rule laid down in Byars and Price. Bradford joined the operation and entered petitioner's house at the request and as an agent of the police. The agency did not end nor Bradford revert to private status when as part of that operation, although without a specific instruction from the police, Bradford searched petitioner's car. Accordingly, even though police officers did not direct Bradford to search the car, just as Adams had not directed Taylor to search the defendant's house in Byars, the evidence discovered by Bradford during that joint operation is inadmissible.

The instant case also resembles that dealt with in Moody v. United States 163 A.2d 337. In Moody a Willie Johnson, after a series of thefts from his apartment, recognized some of the stolen goods in the apartment of defendant Moody. Johnson chased Moody into the street and held him until police arrived. Following Moody's arrest Johnson and a police officer returned to Moody's apartment. Johnson entered the apartment and handed the stolen articles to the police officer who remained in the hallway.

The court noted, "there was no indication in the record that the officer did anything to induce Johnson's actions or that he made an effort to deter him." Applying the silver platter standards laid down by Lustig v. United States 338 U.S. 74, the court concluded "that there was a participation by the arresting officer and that the complaining witness (Johnson) acted as an arm of the police in reducing the articles to possession. The construction to be attached to the Fourth Amendment *** may be violated just as effectively through the intervening agency of one not a policeman. While no objection can be raised to the propriety of the arresting officer's conduct in merely viewing the articles from the adjacent hallway, we cannot characterize him as a willing but innocent beneficiary in *standing silently by* while the appropriation was taking place." (Italics added.)

In the instant case the Highland Park police, by allowing Bradford to join in the search and arrest operation, put Bradford in a position which gave him access to the car keys and thus to the trunk of petitioner's car. Thereafter the police stood silently by while Bradford made the obviously illegal search. Contrary to the assumption of the respondent court, the police need not have requested or directed the search in order to be guilty of "standing idly by"; knowledge of the illegal search coupled with a failure to protect the petitioner's rights against such a search suffices. Here police permitted action by Bradford which probably constituted both a misdemeanor (Veh. Code, § 10852, tampering with a vehicle or the contents thereof) and a trespass to petitioner's personal property. The circumstances closely parallel those in *Moody*, and the evidence thus obtained must be excluded.

Neither the agent who searched the car nor the police officers possessed a search warrant.

Let a peremptory writ of mandate issue directing the respondent superior court to grant petitioner's motion to suppress the evidence consisting of the canisters found by agent Bradford.

CASE COMMENT

The court felt that the activities engaged in by the credit card company special agent and the police were well coordinated. Although Bradford searched Stapleton's car without specific instructions from the police, the agency link or connection did not end. Thus the Fourth Amendment applied, and lacking a search warrant, consent, or other constitutionally acceptable method, the search of the vehicle was illegal. Also since the vehicle was some distance from the scene of the arrest, the search could not be classified as incidental thereto. The court also called attention to the fact that Bradford's actions probably constituted both a misdemeanor and a trespass. If private security officers are found to have violated constitutional prohibitions and/or are convicted of crimes while they are engaged in security activity, it may be difficult, if not impossible, to prevent loss from civil litigation. This is an example of why the security manager should be fully cognizant of laws pertaining to the activities of the private security industry.

STOP-&-FRISK

This case involves the claim of right of a security guard to a pat-down search while investigating a crime and a right of privacy claim by the one who was arrested. The bulge in the arrestee's jacket, which the guard thought might be a weapon, turned out to be coins, tie tacks, and jewelry. The trial court held that the guard's action had to be measured against constitutional standards, that there was nothing to suggest there had been a full custodial arrest, and that the search had been reasonable. The arrestee moved to suppress the evidence seized by the security guard in a *stop-&-frisk* during an investigation of possible trespass and theft as violative of the state constitution. The court noted the similarity of the *Terry* case, which set standards for police situations. This case contains a good discussion of reasonable suspicion and probable cause and of what factual information linked the suspects to the crimes. This is a case of first impression in this state, and security managers should keep the court's rationale in mind to see whether it might apply in their jurisdictions in a situation with similar facts.

STATE v. BRADFORD
683 P. 2d 924 (1984)

GULBRANDSON, Justice.

James Andrew Bradford and David Allen Oppelt were convicted of criminal mischief, criminal trespass to vehicles, attempt, and felony theft by a jury in the District Court of the Eighth Judicial District, Cascade County. Only defendant Oppelt appeals his conviction. We affirm.

At approximately 5:00 a.m. on August 9, 1982, the night clerk at the Heritage Inn in Great Falls received a phone call from a guest who had just observed two persons breaking into a vehicle located on the Inn's parking lot. The clerk immediately notified Roy Cisneros, a private security guard employed by the Inn, and the two men went to Cisneros' truck and drove around the hotel to the southwest parking lot. Cisneros parked the truck and both he and the clerk approached the area just outside the room of the guest who had reported the break-in.

Cisneros and the clerk observed a man later identified as Robert Ruiz standing next to a vehicle in the lot. They approached Ruiz and questioned him about his presence in the lot. Ruiz told them that he was preparing to jog, and was waiting for a friend to join him. Cisneros was suspicious, and asked Ruiz to position himself for a pat-down search. In the course of that search, Cisneros discovered a .22 caliber semiautomatic pistol in Ruiz's front waistband, and removed it. At that point, Cisneros observed a second individual, later identified as James Andrew Bradford, lying under a vehicle approximately forty-five feet away. Bradford apparently realized that Cisneros had seen him, and tried to roll away.

Cisneros asked the clerk to hold Ruiz while he went after Bradford. He told Bradford to stop. Bradford then began to reach for his back pocket. Cisneros gave a second command to stop, and unsnapped the holster to his service weapon. Bradford froze, and Cisneros approached him, ordering him to assume the position for a pat-down. In the frisk, Cisneros seized a five inch hunting knife and scabbard from Bradford's back pocket. He placed Bradford in handcuffs, and took him back to the area where the clerk was holding Ruiz.

Cisneros called his dispatcher for assistance. A few minutes later he noticed a third individual, later identified as the appellant, David Allen Oppelt, inside the glass-enclosed section of the Inn, about to come down the stairway leading to the parking lot. (The guest who made the phone call testified at trial that he had seen a third man in the parking lot during the break-in. This third man, who apparently disappeared before Cisneros and the clerk arrived on the scene, had a physical appearance matching Oppelt's.) Oppelt was coming down the steps until both he and Cisneros established mutual eye contact. At this point, Oppelt turned and proceeded to run back up the stairs. Cisneros instructed the clerk to follow Oppelt and ask him to come to the parking lot for questioning

The clerk followed Oppelt up the stairs and down the hallways of the Inn. Oppelt was either running or taking long strides down the hallways. After Oppelt had traversed a distance of about two city blocks, the clerk caught up with Oppelt and told him that Cisneros wanted to question him. Oppelt voluntarily accompanied the clerk back to the lot where Cisneros was waiting.

As Oppelt approached, Cisneros asked him if he had any identification, and Oppelt responded that he had none. Cisneros noticed that the left front pocket of Oppelt's brown vinyl jacket was "full" and "bulged to the side." Concerned that Oppelt might be armed, Cisneros told him to place his hands on a nearby vehicle so that Cisneros could conduct a search. Oppelt said, "no," but Cisneros repeated his order to have him place his hands on the vehicle. At this point Oppelt complied and Cisneros patted him down to see if he had a knife or other weapon. Cisneros discovered that the bulge was created by several coins, tie tacks, and pieces of jewelry. Cisneros handcuffed Oppelt and notified police to come and make an arrest.

When the police arrived to arrest Ruiz, Bradford and Oppelt, they also looked into the vehicle that the hotel guest had seen the suspects looking into prior to the investigation by Cisneros and the clerk. Officer Wayne Doeden of the Great Falls Police Department observed that the wing window had been entered and the glove box had been opened. Various items from the box had been spilled on the floor of the car. When looking up and away from the car, Doeden saw another vehicle which he had seen Oppelt in previously. Doeden looked in this car as well, and spotted in plain view a knife, tools and what appeared to be either a holster or a handgun on the car floor. The vehicle was impounded and a search warrant was obtained. Officers discovered a watch, a ring, several guns and knives, jewelry and a mobile phone. These items were eventually identified as property stolen from several parked cars in the lots of the Village Motor Inn and the Holiday Inn, both in Great Falls. Most of the victims of these robberies lived out of state.

Investigators also found wallets belonging to Bradford and Oppelt in the impounded vehicle. The auto was registered in the name of Oppelt's half-sister. An investigation was also authorized for the first vehicle, in which police lifted fingerprints matching those of Bradford.

On August 19, 1982, Bradford and Oppelt were charged with three counts of criminal trespass to vehicles, two counts of felony theft, two counts of misdemeanor theft, and one count of felony criminal mischief. Both men, represented by separate counsel, plead not guilty to all counts. Ruiz, a juvenile, was apparently not charged. Oppelt moved to dismiss six of the eight counts against him, and to suppress the evidence seized from his person during the pat-down search, alleging that his right to privacy had been violated by the search. After a hearing and upon submission of briefs, the trial court denied the motion. Judge Coder concluded that, while Cisneros' action had to be measured against constitutional standards, there was nothing to suggest that Oppelt had been under a full custodial arrest or that he had been the victim of an unreasonable search.

In the meantime, the State had given notice that it was preparing to file an amended information and supporting affidavit. The new information revised the charges against both Bradford and Oppelt. They were now charged with five counts of misdemeanor criminal trespass to vehicles, one consolidated count of felony theft, one of attempt, and one of felony criminal mischief. The parties went to trial on these charges.

At the conclusion of the State's case-in-chief, Oppelt's attorney moved to dismiss the charges against him. The motion was denied. The court did dismiss, without objection by the State, one charge of criminal trespass to vehicles. The court also reduced the felony criminal mischief charge to a misdemeanor, again without objection by the State. The other charges were allowed to stand.

The defendant's case revolved almost exclusively around an alibi defense supplied by Robert Ruiz. Ruiz insisted that he alone was responsible for the thefts, and that Bradford and Oppelt had been called around 5 a.m. to come to the Heritage Inn and help him start his stalled car. Ruiz had no explanation for Oppelt's presence in the hotel.

The jury returned guilty verdicts on all charges. Oppelt was sentenced to twenty years in prison and was designated a persistent felony offender. Bradford received a similar sentence, but he has not appealed his conviction.

Oppelt raises the following issues:

1. Whether the trial court erred in denying Oppelt's motion to suppress evidence seized from his person by a private security guard in a "stop-and-frisk" during an investigation of possible trespass and theft on hotel property patrolled by the security guard?
2. Whether the amended information charging Oppelt with criminal trespass to vehicles, criminal mischief, attempt and felony theft was supported by a showing of probable cause in the State's affidavit?

The gist of Oppelt's argument on the first issue is that the constitutional right to privacy, Mont. Const. art. II, sec. 10, as construed in this Court's decisions in *State v. Van Haele* 649 P. 2d 1311; *State v. Hyem* 630 P.2d 202; *Duran v. Buttery Food, Inc.* 616 P.2d 327; bars the kind of stop and search involved in his case, therefore mandating suppression of the evidence seized from his person.

This is the first time that a stop-and-frisk operation by a private security guard in Montana has been challenged. The search and seizure involved here is very similar to the one held lawful for police to perform. See *Terry v. Ohio* 392 U.S. 1. Oppelt maintains that the issue of whether a *Terry* stop-and-frisk can be conducted by a private security guard must be settled by reference to this Court's line of cases extending the protections of the exclusionary rule to private searches. We disagree. Regardless of any argument supporting the possible relevance of our earlier decisions respecting private searches, we hold that a private security guard may conduct the kind of "stop-and-frisk" involved in the instant case during an investigation of possible trespass and theft on property patrolled and protected by the security guard.

In the immediate case, the search of Oppelt is justified as action taken to protect the hotel and its occupants against trespassers in the process of committing an offense. A person has a right to use "any necessary force" to protect himself or his employer, or his or her employer's property, from wrongful injury. Section 49–1–103, MCA. See also Mont. Const. art II, sec. 3 (constitutional right to protect self and property); Section 45–3–102, MCA (authorization to use reasonable force to defend self); Section 45–3–104, MCA (authorization to use reasonable force to defend property). A reasonable construction of these constitutional and statutory provisions compels the conclusion that Cisneros had legal authority to protect the hotel property, to investigate the circumstances surrounding Oppelt's presence there, and to use "reasonable force" to protect himself during the course of his investigation. "Reasonable force" under the facts of this case includes the right of the security guard to conduct a *Terry* "stop-and-frisk."

Oppelt responds that Cisneros did not have "probable cause" to believe that he was trespassing or committing some other offense, so as to justify the search. "Probable cause" is not the correct standard. All Cisneros needed to have was a "reasonable suspicion" that something illegal was taking place and that Oppelt might be armed. Given that he had just seized two armed individuals lurking around a hotel parking lot at five o'clock in the morning, and that Oppelt was heading toward the lot until he saw Cisneros, the night clerk, and the two detainees, after which time he turned and walked or ran in the opposite direction, and that Oppelt's jacket pocket bulged to the side, we find that Cisneros had a reasonable suspicion to investigate Oppelt's presence and conduct a pat-down search for weapons.

Oppelt's challenge to the amended information and supporting affidavit appears to flow from a narrow conception of probable cause. Whether this conception is justified depends on the nature of the facts cited in the affidavit in support of the information and case law construing the scope of probable cause.

Oppelt challenges the criminal trespass charges on the grounds that the various stolen items do not link him to the crimes. His theory is that there is no proof that he entered the vehicles, even if his co-defendant, Bradford, or the juvenile, Ruiz, did so enter. He further challenges the felony theft charge on the grounds that most of the items were not "connected" to his presence at the hotel when he was seized. The remaining items were allegedly not valued, thus making proof of a felony theft impossible. Similarly, Oppelt insists that the attempt and criminal mischief charges are tied to damage to a mobile telephone in one vehicle and that there is no necessary connection between him and the vehicle.

An affidavit in support of a motion to file an information need not make out a prima facie case that a defendant committed on offense. A mere probability that he committed the offense is sufficient. Similarly, evidence to establish probable cause need not be as complete as the evidence necessary to establish guilt. In *State v. Riley* 649 P.2d 1273, this Court observed that the determination whether a motion to file an information is supported by probable cause is left to the sound discretion of the trial court. Thus, the scope of review is one of detecting abuse in the exercise of that discretion.

The first criminal trespass charge was connected to the fact that the items stolen from the first car were found on Oppelt's person during the search. This is clearly a basis for probable cause that Oppelt was in that vehicle. Although the remaining trespass charges involve evidence found in the suspect's car, but not on Oppelt's person, the State alleged in its affidavit that Oppelt and the other suspects had participated and assisted each other in a common criminal scheme. This Court has held that more than a mere presence at the scene of a crime is necessary to establish criminal responsibility. In the instant case, however, the State was able to establish Oppelt's presence, the stolen articles on his person, his unusual behavior, and his connection to the other suspects. At this stage of the criminal proceedings, this was all that was necessary for a valid showing of probable cause.

Oppelt cites *State ex rel. Wilson v. District Court* 498 P.2d 1217, in support of his argument that he cannot be charged without a more positive connection to the evidence. Although arguably close on some facts, *Wilson* is nevertheless distinguishable. In that case, the trial court found probable cause to link a suspect to a burglary of a beer distributer's business. The evidence, however, was found in a car belonging to another individual. Although that individual and the suspect had been charged with another burglary at a lumber yard, this Court held that this was not enough to establish probable cause on the beer theft. In the instant case, there is more evidence than the fact that Oppelt was arrested with Bradford and Ruiz. His suspicious behavior at the scene, the presence of his wallet in the impounded car with most of the stolen items, his identification with the car on a previous occasion, and his familial relationship to Bradford and Ruiz offer enough evidence to warrant a finding that Oppelt probably was a participant in a common scheme of thefts.

Probable cause for theft also was sufficiently established. The items found on Oppelt's person alone were reported to have a value of more than $150, clearly establishing sufficient grounds for a charge of felony theft. There was also a fair probability of attempt and criminal mischief shown on Oppelt's part, given the simultaneous presence of defendants at the crime scene and the evidence of other thefts.

From the facts and controlling case law, we conclude that the affidavit of probable cause is sound. The trial court did not abuse its discretion in denying Oppelt's motion to dismiss.

Having failed to convince the trial court that the State lacked probable cause to charge Oppelt, defense counsel still had the opportunity to challenge the State's evidence at trial. The following discussion essentially summarizes the facts and issues developed during the trial.

A guest at the Heritage Inn testified that he had seen two individuals, later identified as Bradford and Ruiz, breaking into cars in the Inn's parking lot. He also had seen another individual walking around the cars. His testimony at trial indicated that the physical description of this third individual matched that of Oppelt. The security guard had apprehended Ruiz, who had been standing by a car, and then had retrieved Bradford, who had been hiding under another car and trying to roll away. The security guard had seen Oppelt inside the glass enclosure of the motel. After Oppelt had spotted the guard with Ruiz and Bradford, he had withdrawn in the opposite direction. After Oppelt had been apprehended and patted down, his pockets were found to contain what were believed to be stolen articles. Indeed, these articles had been taken that same night from a vehicle parked at the Holiday Inn. Four vehicles in two motel parking lots had been forcibly entered and various items had been stolen from three of the cars. Most of the items were found in an automobile parked at the Heritage Inn. This car was registered to Oppelt's sister-in-law, and Oppelt had been observed using the car on a previous occasion. The car also contained wallets belonging to Bradford and Oppelt. It was established that Oppelt, Bradford and Ruiz are related. There was testimony even from defense witnesses that Bradford and Oppelt were together during the time of the break-ins. Defendant Bradford's fingerprints had been found in one of the burglarized vehicles. The record also discloses that the break-ins had been similar in all significant aspects and followed one another, evidencing a continuing criminal design: they had taken place the same night and early morning at motels in Great Falls, the vehicles had been forced open through the wing windows, and items had been taken, with firearms having been removed from at least two vehicles. All the vehicles were from out of town, and the items stolen were either on the three suspects or in the car that was used by Ruiz and Oppelt at different times.

The orders denying Oppelt's motion to suppress evidence are affirmed. The convictions on the aforementioned charges of criminal mischief, criminal trespass to vehicles, attempt, and felony theft are likewise affirmed.

CASE COMMENT

The court held that a private security guard may conduct the kind of "stop-&-frisk" involved in this type of case. The search was justified to protect the hotel, the occupants of the hotel, and the security guard. The court noted the State constitutional right to protect a person's own self and property and to use reasonable force to do so. Reasonable force under the facts of this case included the right of the guard to conduct a *Terry* "stop-&-frisk." The court pointed out that "probable cause" was not the correct standard to justify the search and that all that the guard needed was "reasonable suspicion." It is important for the security manager to be aware of the conditions by which security employees can protect themselves and the property they are guarding.

EMERGENCY DOCTRINE

What does a security guard do when complaints are received that an offending odor emanates from space under their protective jurisdiction? Must security guards stand idly by or can they check the complaints out in their quest to ensure the safety of persons in the offending area? In this case, the room complained about had been aired out for a day, yet the noxious order remained and permeated the room strongly. The solution to the problem resulted in the arrest and conviction of the defendant for possession of marijuana for sale, which was upheld by the state supreme court (*En banc*). The court felt that a "compelling urgency" had been shown and that it was reasonable to undertake a prompt inspection for the purpose of discovering and abating the nuisance.

PEOPLE v. LANTHIER
488 P.2d 625 (1971)

MOSK, Justice.

Defendant was charged with possession of marijuana for sale. His motions to dismiss the information and to suppress the evidence on the ground of illegal search and seizure were denied, and he entered a plea of guilty. The court placed him on probation for a period of three years on the condition that he serve 60 days in the county jail. Defendant appeals from the order denying the motion to suppress the evidence and from the order granting probation.

The motions were submitted on the transcript of the preliminary examination. Defendant, a student at Stanford University, had been assigned a "carrel"—i.e., a desk with attached bookcase and small locker—in a study hall in a university library building. On the morning of Monday, January 13, 1969, Joseph Riley, supervisor of maintenance services and security guards at the library, received a complaint of a noxious order emanating from somewhere in the study hall. He was informed that "it smelled as if someone had vomited in the room," and it had been necessary to prop the doors open to air out the room throughout the previous day. That remedy had not cured the situation, however, and Riley was asked to check the room "and see if there was something causing the smell coming from the lockers." To Riley, the odor resembled that of sweet apples; he was not able to determine its source by smelling the outside of the lockers, however, as it "permeated the room so strongly that you could smell any locker and think it was coming from any locker." Using his master key, he therefore began opening each of the lockers in turn, "looking for anything that would put off the smell that was complained about in the area."

When Riley opened the locker used by defendant—the last of 42 in the room—the odor grew noticeably stronger. A briefcase occupied virtually the entire inside space. Riley removed it in order to examine the rest of the locker, and then realized the odor was emanating directly from the briefcase. On the basis of that smell, Riley testified, "I though it was bad food that was in the briefcase. *** So I opened the briefcase to see if it was bad food and then I saw all these small packets of material there." The contents were 38 packets of marijuana, each in a transparent plastic wrapping of the size of a sandwich bag; the odor, also described in the transcript as resembling that of sour wine, apparently came from a preservative added to the marijuana.

Although he did not know what marijuana looked or smelled like, Riley "suspected it might be something like marijuana." He informed the director of the undergraduate library, Mr. Golter, that he had found the substance which had been causing the smell, and was told to bring it to the latter's office. There he opened the briefcase and showed its contents to Golter, who said, "We'll have to find out what it is." Other Stanford officials were consulted, during which time the briefcase was held in the basement because "It was giving off a very strong odor." Finally it was turned over to a university police officer, who contacted the Santa Clara Sheriff's Department.

Deputy Richard Saldivar responded to the call. He testified he was advised there was "a possible narcotics violation" and that "a briefcase was found in a locker at Meyers Library at Stanford University and that a strong odor was emanating from this briefcase. It was turned over *** by the officials at the university, and they asked me to inspect it to determine if I could identify the contents." The university police officer unfastened the catch on the briefcase, opened it, and exposed its contents; Deputy Saldivar removed one of the packets, and by sight and smell recognized the material to be marijuana. Defendant was subsequently arrested when he returned to his locker to reclaim the briefcase.

Riley testified that it was part of his job to periodically check the lockers in the study room. Once a month he opened each locker to see if it contained any overdue library books; at the end of each quarter, when the carrel permits expired, he reopened the lockers and removed their entire remaining contents, storing the latter in a utility closet until claimed by the owners; and whenever he received complaints of offensive odors he promptly examined the inside of the lockers for rotten food, explaining that "Occasionally, you find someone may leave a sandwich in there for weeks." He conceded he had not previously found it necessary to open a student's briefcase, but also testified that at least once before he had had dealings with this particular defendant when he had emptied the contents of the defendant's locker at the end of a quarter.

The defense consisted primarily of testimony bearing on the size, facilities, services, and financing of Stanford University, offered in support of defendant's contention that Riley and his fellow university officers and employees were acting as governmental agents throughout the events in question.

In overruling defendant's objections to the evidence on the ground of illegal search and seizure, the magistrate at the preliminary examination made two findings: First, he found that "the initial search by Mr. Riley in this case was a reasonable search. Mr. Riley was merely seeking to locate the source of an unpleasant odor in a part of the library that was under his control and supervision. He was not looking for contraband or illicit or stolen property or any form of evidence of guilt of any crime or other offense and, under the law, such a search is not unreasonable and it did not become unreasonable even when Mr. Riley opened the briefcase from which that odor apparently was emanating."[2] Secondly, the magistrate ruled that governmental involvement in the operations of Stanford University was not so pervasive as to render that institution subject to the limitations placed upon "state action" by the Fourteenth Amendment.

We need not reach the latter issue. Even if Stanford University were a "public" rather than a "private" institution, the search here challenged would be reasonable within the meaning of the Fourth Amendment. It is true the search was conducted without a warrant, and the burden therefore rested upon the People to show justification. But that burden was sustained in the case at bar by a compelling showing of facts bringing the search within the "emergency" exception to the warrant requirement.

In Camara v. Municipal Court, 387 U.S. 523, the United States Supreme Court held that routine administrative searches of private property for violations of local health or safety codes must be made with a warrant; among other objections, the court dismissed the claim that the delay attendant upon obtaining a warrant would frustrate the governmental purpose behind the search. But in authorizing such warrants to be based on area-wide conditions rather than on probable cause to believe that a particular dwelling contains code violations, the court recognized that "the public interest demands that all dangerous conditions be prevented or abated." Finally, the court was careful to emphasize that "since our holding emphasizes the controlling standard of reasonableness, nothing we say today is intended to foreclose prompt inspections, even without a warrant, that the law has traditionally upheld in emergency situations. The court distinguished the routine administrative searches before it as presenting "no compelling urgency," and concluded that "warrants should normally be sought only after entry is refused unless there has been a citizen complaint or there is other satisfactory reason for securing immediate entry."

---

[2]Earlier in the hearing the court overruled defendant's motion to strike the testimony of Riley and Deputy Saldivar on the same ground, stating that "Mr. Riley I feel had a perfect right to ascertain the source of this unusual odor. *** And, having located the locker finally and then the immediate source as the bag and having looked in there and having at least aroused his curiosity, I think the original finding of this and observing of it was perfectly proper. And *** the fact that the odor of course remained there, just finding it didn't eliminate the problem that the library was having. So that reporting it to the superior and indicating—apparently some clue as to what he thought it might be, and from thereon, I feel all of this is perfectly proper."

In the case at bar such a "compelling urgency" was clearly shown. There had indeed been a "citizen complaint" about the malodorous smell permeating the entire study hall, and the smell was no less noticeable to Riley when he arrived to investigate. It was therefore reasonable for him to undertake, in his capacity of maintenance supervisor, a "prompt inspection" of the carrel area for the purpose of discovering and abating the nuisance. And inasmuch as the students entitled to use the room had already been disturbed by this offensive odor throughout the preceding day, further delay in suppressing it would have been unjustifiable.

Once the defendant's briefcase was discovered and opened, its contents were in plain sight. In distinction to the closed brown-paper bag containing the marijuana seized in People v. Marshall 442 P.2d 665, here the contraband was packaged only in transparent plastic bags. An observation from a lawful vantage point of contraband in plain sight is not, of course, a "search" in the constitutional sense (Harris v. United States 390 U.S. 234), and evidence obtained by this means is admissible without offending the Fourth Amendment.

Defendant concedes that Riley had the right, acting on his own initiative and in the discharge of his duties, to open the locker and remove the offending briefcase. He contends, however, that once Riley had thus pinpointed the source of the odor he should have refrained from opening the briefcase and should instead have stored it in the utility closet where unclaimed student belongings are kept. Secondly, defendant contends that even if it was reasonable for Riley to open the briefcase at that time, he closed it after doing so and its contents were therefore no longer "in plain sight" when Deputy Saldivar arrived on the scene. The emergency permitting a warrantless search of defendant's locker did not end with the discovery that the noxious odor was emanating from the briefcase contained therein. To have stored the briefcase, unopened, in a utility closet would not have eliminated the odor but would merely have transferred it to another part of the library building. Having reasonably assumed control of the briefcase under the emergency doctrine, it was equally reasonable for the university officials to open it and determine the precise cause of the smell so as to permit a proper disposition of the offending object. If, as appeared likely from past experience, the cause had simply been a piece of rotting food, it could have been removed and disposed of without further ado; the trial court, indeed, emphasized this very possibility in ruling that Riley "did what any normal person would have done under those circumstances, having the same duties to perform as he had."

It is true that upon opening the briefcase Riley did not immediately recognize the contents, although he suspected it was marijuana. But it remained a reasonable course of action for the university officials to seek to identify the substance thus exposed to view. If, for example, the substance had presented an immediate health hazard, its summary destruction might well have been justified (North American Cold Storage Co. v. City of Chicago, supra, 211 U.S. 306); on the other hand, if the substance had been wholly innocuous apart from its odor it would have been proper to return it to the owner, albeit with directions to store it in a different location. Such a decision could be made only with knowledge of the precise nature of the material involved.

In their effort to identify the contents of defendant's briefcase, finally, it was reasonable for the university officials to secure professional advice by enlisting the aid of campus and local police. A single consultation by such officials with a police expert on narcotics falls far short, for example, of a general police-instigated exploratory search of student housing or belongings in the hope of turning up contraband. Rather, the officials' conduct in the case at bar is analogous to that of "the landlord or bailee who innocently discovers the suspicious circumstances, and seeks expert advice as to the nature of the use to which his premises or facilities are being appropriated. The latter would be no more than an extension of the plain-sight rule, by augmenting the observations of the layman with the expertise of the police." (People v. Baker 96 Cal.Rptr. 760).

Viewed in this light, the question of who opened or closed defendant's briefcase pales into insignificance.[4] What matters here is that until Deputy Saldivar was asked to examine the briefcase, its contents remained a mystery to the officials who bore the responsibility of properly disposing of it. The deputy's inspection therefore does not require justification over and above that of the continuing emergency which authorized the original warrantless search of defendant's locker.

We conclude there was substantial evidence to support the trial court's ruling that the contraband here in issue was not the product of an illegal search and seizure.

The appeal from the order denying the motion to suppress the evidence is dismissed as nonappealable, and the order granting probation is affirmed.

CASE COMMENT

Note that security had a master key to the lockers and that they were checked monthly for overdue books and quarterly when the permits expired. The purpose of this inspection was to locate the source of the noxious odor and not to search for evidence of crime. Justification for the search was sustained by a compelling showing of facts about the emergency situation. The holding emphasized the standard of reasonableness and nothing the court said was intended to foreclose prompt inspections in emergency situations. It was reasonable to undertake a prompt inspection for the purpose of discovering and abating the nuisance, and further delay in suppressing it would have been unjustifiable

PLAIN VIEW

The following case points out that a search, with legal constraints, is not conducted every time a person sees something. If, for example, an employee leaves a bicycle in the middle of the sidewalk between the employee parking lot and the company plant, it might be considered to be a safety hazard. Security is called. A security official goes to the area and observes the bicycle. This object is in plain view, and the observation of it is not a search. The bicycle may or may not have been stolen. The purpose of the observation is to check a safety hazard. In the case below, a guard, made aware of certain stolen articles, observed them in a locker that was open. Thus the court held that the articles were in plain view.

---

[4]In any event, the fact that the briefcase was closed when it was carried to the university offices or to the campus police department appears to have been merely a matter of convenience compelled by the design of the briefcase itself. We infer from certain testimony on the point that the briefcase was of the commonplace type having a hinged opening at the top and a handle on each lip of the opening. When such a briefcase is picked up in the normal manner—i.e., in one hand, grasping both handles together—the opening automatically closes.

COMMONWEALTH v. BORNHOLZ
446 N.E. 2d 1085 (1983)

Before BROWN, CUTTER and SMITH, JJ.
RESCRIPT.

The defendant appeals from his conviction on a complaint charging larceny. The case was tried before a jury of six. (The defendant was also found guilty on two complaints charging breaking and entering, but findings of not guilty were subsequently entered on those complaints at the prosecutor's request.) Prior to trial the defendant moved to suppress certain evidence. The judge denied the motion after hearing, but made no findings. The only issue on appeal is the correctness of the denial of the defendant's motion to suppress.

We would have been greatly helped had the trial judge made findings. We cannot stress too strongly the need for appropriate findings in circumstances such as those presented here.

Notwithstanding the absence of findings, on our review of the evidence adduced at the suppression hearing, we are able to conclude that the judge did not err.

The defendant's argument completely misses the point. There was no search, either unlawful or otherwise. The locker tags and stolen money were observed by the school employee acting lawfully in his capacity as a guard of the premises and in that capacity he seized the articles at a place to which this defendant had no proper claim to access.

Even if we were to assume that a State law enforcement official was involved here, the motion to suppress properly could have been denied for the reason, if no other, that it is clear from the evidence that the school gymnasium locker was open and that the articles seized therein were in plain view.

"The guard could recognize the articles in combination with the statements received, 'to be . . . related as proof to criminal activity of which he was already aware.'" *Commonwealth v. Meehan*, 387 N.E.2d 527. The guard certainly was "already aware" of recent criminal activity in the locker room because immediately prior to the seizure of the articles from the locker, a student had told him that "his (the student's) wallet was just taken from his locker."

Judgment affirmed.

CASE COMMENT

Observing items in plain view cannot always be said to be a search with attendant legal constraints. While this case deals with a guard who was "already aware" of recent criminal activity, the purpose of a search should not be overlooked. If the purpose of a search is other than for seeking evidence of criminal activity such as a safety or hazard situation, there may be no legal constraints.

FOUND PROPERTY

In the case that follows, a shopping mall patron found a wallet in a common area. The patron turned the wallet over to a uniformed security officer. To protect the mall from liability the wallet was inventoried by two employees and then logged into the lost-and-found property locker. Among the items found in the wallet were what appeared to be marijuana and cocaine. The police were called. The owner of the wallet called to retrieve her wallet, and she was escorted to the security office because it was hard to find. After being *Mirandized* by the police, she waived her rights and admitted that the wallet and contents were hers. After being charged with possession of marijuana and cocaine, she challenged the legality of the search of her wallet. The court concluded that she had a reasonable expectation of privacy in her inadvertently misplaced wallet and ordered the exclusion of the evidence as being illegally seized. The appellate court reversed as there was nothing to show the security guards were acting as agents of the state.

PEOPLE v. BROUILLETTE
258 Cal. Rptr. 635 (1989)

COTTLE, Associate Justice.

Defendant Robin Brouillette was charged with possession of cocaine and possession of marijuana. At the preliminary examination, the magistrate heard testimony and denied a motion to suppress the drugs found in Brouillette's wallet. In superior court, Brouillette, again challenged the legality of the search of her wallet. After an in camera hearing and additional testimony, the superior court issued a detailed decision and order in which it concluded that Brouillette had a reasonable expectation of privacy with regard to the contraband contents of the wallet even though the wallet had been inadvertently misplaced. In reliance on *People v. Zelinski*, 594 P.2d 1000, it determined that the cocaine and marijuana should be excluded as illegally seized evidence.

The People appeal from the dismissal of the charges pursuant to Penal Code section 1385. We reverse.

Facts

The following facts are taken from the written decision and order of the superior court:

> "A Vallco Park Shopping Mall patron gave Cheryl Stern, a uniformed private security officer working for the mall, a wallet found in one of the mall's common areas. Stern took the wallet to the mall's security office. To protect itself from liability for valuable items, the mall requires its employees to go through lost property with another person to verify valuables and identification, then log the property into the lost and found property locker. Stern first found a wad of money. She then inventoried the wallet's contents and found a driver's license with Brouillette's name on it, a fishing license, a home video club card, checks, some of which were imprinted with Brouillette's name, a partial marijuana joint, and a paper bindle which, after being opened, yielded a powder that resembled cocaine. Although Stern equivocated about the order in which she found the items, it is established that she found the money and driver's license before she found the bindle and joint. Thinking the bindle contained drugs, Stern's supervisor, Lt. Sanders, called the County Sheriff. Deputy Mecir responded, looked at Brouillette's driver's license, examined the powder, and concluded it was cocaine.
>
> "While Mecir was at the office, Brouillette called to retrieve her wallet. Mecir asked Sanders to have someone escort Brouillette to the security office because it was hard to find. After Mecir *Mirandized* Brouillette, she waived her rights and admitted the wallet and bindle was hers.
>
> "At the hearing, Stern acknowledged (1) she could have inventoried the entire green bindle without looking inside; and (2) Vallco Park makes its offices available to the Sheriff to make shoplifting and other kinds of arrests."

The superior court stated also that the mall's private security officers "operate like police—they wear uniforms and organize themselves in a para-military style," that they "helped to apprehend Brouillette," that the mall had a "regular policy to make its offices available to the sheriff" suggesting "an ongoing mutuality of interest between police and the security people which, if not creating an agency, comes very close" and that "although privately retained, mall security hold themselves out to be and are looked upon by others as police authority." Finally, it added that the inspection of the contents of the wallet by the private security guard was not in fact done to protect the interests of the guard's employer but "was an investigation."

Discussion

Standard of Review
"On appeal, we review the evidence in a light favorable to the trial court's ruling on the suppression motion. . . . We uphold those express or implicit findings of fact by the trial court which are supported by substantial evidence. . . . Insofar as the evidence is uncontradicted, we do not engage in substantial evidence review, but face pure questions of law. . . . We must independently determine whether the facts support the court's legal conclusions."

The enactment of California Constitution, article I, section 28, subdivision (d) (Proposition 8) on June 8, 1982, permits us to suppress evidence only if that result is compelled by the United States Constitution; a violation of the California Constitution is no longer a basis for exclusion. In interpreting the United State Constitution, as in the case of all federal law, we are bound by the decisions of the United States Supreme Court and find persuasive authority in the decisions of other federal courts. We are also bound by the decisions of the California Supreme Court.

Expectation of Privacy
"A 'search' occurs when an expectation of privacy that society is prepared to consider reasonable is infringed." We shall assume, without deciding, that Brouillette had a reasonable expectation of privacy in the contents of her wallet in the circumstances of this case.

The Search by Mall Security Guards
In acting as they did, the mall security guards acted in a purely private capacity and did not assert the power of the state, so the Fourth Amendment does not apply.

The protection of the Fourth Amendment against an unreasonable search generally applies only to government actions and does not extend to searches carried out by private persons. Brouillette claims the exclusionary rule applies to the conduct of the mall's private security guards, relying upon the reasoning of the California Supreme Court in *People v. Zelinski, supra,* a case decided on the basis of an interpretation of the California Constitution at a time when that constitution provided an independent ground for the exclusion of evidence. We shall assume, without deciding, that *Zelinski* is a correct construction of the federal exclusionary rule.

In *Zelinski*, department store detectives saw the defendant shoplifting, made a citizen's arrest and conducted a search which led to the discovery of illegal drugs. The trial court denied the motion to suppress; the California Supreme Court reversed. First, the

Court recognized that conduct of private security personnel "poses a threat to privacy rights of Californians that is comparable to that which may be posed by the unlawful conduct of police officers." Second, it determined that the exclusionary rule would be an effective deterrent since private security guards, like police but unlike ordinary citizens, regularly perform "quasi-law enforcement activities." Those points are equally applicable here.

But there was a third point that distinguishes this case from *Zelinski*. The Supreme Court there held that store detectives *when they make an arrest* do not act in a purely private capacity but "assert the power of the state." It stated that it was not deciding that "all of the varied activities of private security personnel" are governed by the restraints of the exclusionary rule. The security guards here did not make an arrest or in any other way assert the power of the state. They merely inspected lost property and called the police. The decision reached by the trial court required an implicit finding that the security guards asserted the power of the state when they took the particular action of inspecting the wallet, but that is not supported by substantial evidence. There was evidence to support the findings that the security guards dressed like police and are looked upon by others as representing police authority, and that they assisted the police by calling the deputy sheriff to the mall and allowing Brouillette to come to the mall office to be arrested when she perhaps thought that she was coming to collect her wallet. There was nothing to show that they made the inspection of the wallet as agents of the state.

In *People v. De Juan*, 217 Cal.Rptr. 642, a case in which the search occurred before the enactment of Proposition 8, the court treated the requirements of state and federal exclusionary rules as coextensive and cited *Zelinski* for the rule that is consistent with our decision: "The constitutional proscriptions will be applied and suppression will be ordered when the search or seizure was conducted by a member of a private security force in furtherance, not of a private interest, but a public or governmental interest so that, in essence, it constituted performance of a law enforcement function."

The Later Search

Since the private security guards had inspected the wallet and discovered both the marijuana and the cocaine before the deputy sheriff arrived, the later actions of the police in repeating the inspection of the contents of the wallet "did not infringe any constitutionally protected privacy interest that had not already been frustrated as the result of private conduct." (*United States v. Jacobsen, supra,* 466 U.S. 109).

In *Jacobsen*, employees of a freight carrier discovered bags of white powder (later shown to be cocaine) while inspecting a damaged package that was in their care. They reclosed the package and called in federal agents. The court found that this was not an illegal search even if the motive of the employees who carried out the inspection was a suspicion of illegality. "Whether those invasions were accidental or deliberate, and whether they were reasonable or unreasonable, they did not violate the Fourth Amendment because of their private character." When the federal agents arrived, they reopened the package, finding those same bags of cocaine. This was held not to be an unlawful search since the private inspection had already occurred.

Disposition

We reverse the decision of the superior court. We order that it vacate its order suppressing evidence and its order of dismissal, and we remand for further proceedings consistent with this order.

CASE COMMENT

In reversing this case, the appellate court took note of the superior court's decision that mall security officers operate like police, that they wear uniforms and organize themselves in a paramilitary style, that the mall has a regular policy to make its offices available to the police, and that mall security hold themselves out to be and are looked on by others as police authority. In this state, by a change of its constitution, courts can only suppress evidence if that result is compelled by the U.S. Constitution. Thus the courts in the state interpret via federal law as far as searches go. Here the private security guards acted in a purely private capacity and did not assert the power of the state. Fourth Amendment protection does not extend to searches carried out by private persons. The court also commented on the applicability of private security guards performing "quasi-law enforcement activities." The court further stated that, in making an *arrest*, store detectives do not act in a purely private capacity but "assert the power of the state." The furtherance of private or public interests is conspicuous to the court insofar as application of proscriptions is concerned. While this decision held that private security did not act as agents of the state, it suggests that security managers may desire to review their operations so as to be able to distinguish and clarify private and public interests.

LOCKER—INVENTORY

In the following case, a woman was arrested at her place of employment, a public safety department at a university, for a first-degree murder that occurred at another location. Following her arrest, her locker at her place of employment was inventoried by her supervisor. Police were present during the inventorying of the locker, and evidence found during that inventory was turned over to them. This evidence was later found to be consistent with evidence found at the crime scene. The defendant argued that the trial court erred by denying her motion to suppress the evidence obtained during the inventory of her locker. Her claim was that the inventory by her supervisor, a private citizen, was a *de facto* governmental search, thereby bringing it within the purview of the Fourth Amendment. In affirming her conviction, the court found the purpose of the search was to inventory the locker so that the defendant could not later claim something was missing and was not for the purpose of discovering evidence of crime.

STATE v. BEMBENEK
331 N.W.2d 616 (1983)

MOSER, Presiding Judge.

Lawrencia Bembenek (Bembenek) appeals from a judgment of conviction entered March 9, 1982, following a jury trial in which she was found guilty of first degree murder, contrary to sec. 940.01, Stats. We affirm.

Bembenek was convicted for the first-degree murder of Christine Schultz (Christine). Christine was the former wife of Milwaukee Police Detective Elfred Schultz (Schultz). Following his divorce from Christine, Schultz married Bembenek. At the time of her murder, Christine resided at 1701 West Ramsey Street in the city of Milwaukee with her two children, Sean and Shannon.

In the early morning hours of May 28, 1981, an intruder entered Christine's home. The intruder went into the boys' bedroom and placed a gloved hand around the face of Sean and attempted to tie something around his neck. Sean screamed and the intruder left and went into Christine's bedroom. Sean testified that he then heard a loud bang which sounded like a firecracker. He then saw the intruder flee down the stairs.

Sean went to his mother's bedroom and telephoned Stuart Honeck (Honeck), Christine's boyfriend. Honeck telephoned the police and told them to send a squad car and the paramedics to Christine's home.

Upon arriving at the scene, the police discovered Christine's body on the bed in her bedroom. Her left wrist was bound with clothesline and there was a bandana-type handkerchief tied about her face in a gag fashion. After examining the body, the police discovered a single strand of reddish-brown hair-like material on her right calf. The police also recovered other hairs from the bandanna gag.

The medical examiner testified that Christine died from a single gunshot wound which passed through her heart. The medical examiner concluded that the weapon which fired the fatal shot was either touching or extremely close to Christine's body when it was fired.

At the time of the murder, Schultz was on duty. When he was informed of his former wife's murder, he proceeded to the scene with his partner. Following this, he went to his residence with Detective Michael Durfee (Durfee). Detective Lieutenant Richard Abrams told Durfee to take Schultz home and check his offduty revolver. Durfee examined the revolver and concluded that it had not been recently fired. Durfee returned the revolver to Schultz. On June 18, 1981, Schultz's offduty revolver was examined by ballistics experts at the state crime laboratory, who determined that the bullet which killed Christine was fired by this revolver.

On June 10, 1981, a plumber was sent to the apartment of the former neighbors of Schultz and Bembenek to alleviate overflow problems with their toilet. The plumber discovered that a wig was caught in a drainage pipe into which the plumbing from both Schultz's and Bembenek's former apartment and their neighbors' apartment flowed. The fibers from this wig were analyzed by experts at the state crime laboratory, who found that these fibers were consistent with fibers found on Christine's right calf.

Bembenek was arrested on June 24, 1981, at Marquette University, where she was employed by the Public Safety Department. Following her arrest, her locker at the Public Safety Department was inventoried by her supervisor, Thomas Conway (Conway). Milwaukee Police Department Detectives Thomas Repischak and Michael Jankowski were present during the inventorying of the locker. A hairbrush belonging to Bembenek, found during the inventory, was turned over to these detectives. The hair found in the brush was tested by experts at the state crime laboratory, who found that these hairs were consistent with the hairs found in the bandanna used to gag Christine.

A jury found Bembenek guilty of first degree murder on March 9, 1982. Judgment of conviction was entered the same day and Bembenek was sentenced to life imprisonment. Bembenek appeals from this judgment.

Further facts will be delineated as are necessary during the discussion of the issues.

Bembenek raises the following issues on appeal:

(3) whether the trial court erred by denying her motion to suppress the evidence found during the inventory of her locker at Marquette University;

Exhibit N establishes that a wig was found in a drainage pipe into which the plumbing from both Schultz's and Bembenek's former apartment and their neighbors' flowed. This exhibit also establishes that the wig could only have been flushed down the toilet of the Schultz/ Bembenek apartment or their neighbors' apartment. Exhibit R establishes that the fibers from the wig were consistent with the hair-like fiber found on Christine's right calf.

A review of the transcript of the preliminary hearing establishes that the following evidence was adduced at the preliminary hearing:

(1) that the wig found in the drainage pipe could have come only from the Schultz/Bembenek apartment or their neighbors' apartment;

Suppression of Evidence

Bembenek next argues that the trial court erred when it denied her motion to suppress the evidence obtained during the inventory of her locker at the Public Safety Department of Marquette University. We disagree.

On review of an order granting or denying a motion to suppress evidence, the findings of fact, if any, by the trial court will be sustained unless they are contrary to the great weight and clear preponderance of the evidence. However, appellate courts will independently examine the circumstances of the case to determine whether the constitutional requirements of reasonableness are satisfied.

Bembenek contends that the inventory of her locker by the Marquette Public Safety Department, which resulted in the discovery of a hairbrush containing her hairs, was a *de facto* governmental search, thereby bringing the search within the purview of the fourth amendment. We disagree.

It is a long-established rule that the constitutional guarantee against unlawful searches and seizures applies only to actions of government agents and not private individuals.[12] A private search is beyond the reach of the exclusionary rule. One of the reasons for the exclusionary rule is to deter the police from illegal searches by denying them convictions based on the fruits of illegal searches. The policy behind not applying the exclusionary rule in private searches is that private individuals will not be so deterred, because they have less knowledge of criminal procedure and are not interested in getting convictions.

There is no question that Conway, the Marquette University public safety officer who conducted the inventory, was a private person within the meaning of the fourth amendment limitations. The record reflects that Conway was not searching the locker to discover evidence relating to the crime for which Bembenek had been arrested. Conway testified that he was merely inventorying the locker because he wanted to ascertain whether Bembenek had any Marquette public safety equipment in her locker. Conway also stated that he wanted to list Bembenek's personal property so that she could not later claim that something was

[12]*Burdeau v. McDowell*, 256 U.S. 465, 475, 41 S.Ct. 574, 576, 65 L.Ed. 1048 (1921).

missing. Conway stated that he would have inventoried the locker even if the police had not been present. The evidence in question was discovered in a purse belonging to Bembenek. Conway testified that he searched the purse only to see if it contained any money, not to discover evidence of a crime.

Bembenek cites this court to *United States v. Mekjian*[15] and *United States v. Clegg*,[16] and argues that, because the police had preknowledge of the search, Conway became a *de facto* agent of the police. We disagree.

In *Clegg*, the fifth circuit stated, "It is only when the government has preknowledge of and yet acquiesces in a private party's conducting a search and seizure which the government itself, under the circumstances, could not have undertaken" that the problem discussed in *Mekjian* arises. That court held that the search there was not a governmental search because the government did not have any knowledge that the private search being conducted was the type which would be a violation of the fourth amendment if it would have been undertaken by the government. In *Mekjian*, the government had knowledge that a private individual was copying records which established that the defendant was committing medicare fraud and they tacitly acquiesced to her conduct.

The *Mekjian* rule is not applicable to this case. Here, the police could not have had any knowledge that Conway was engaging in a search which, if conducted by them, would be violative of the fourth amendment, because Conway was merely inventorying the locker and not searching for evidence of a crime.

In *United States v. Gomez*,[19] the ninth circuit rejected a contention that the mere presence of law enforcement officials at the search of a suitcase by an airline's employee converted the search into a governmental search. The airline's employee in *Gomez* merely searched the suitcase to ascertain the identity of the owner. The court held that, based on this motivation for the search, even slight participation by officers did not convert it from a private search to a governmental one.

Here, as in *Gomez*, the search was not done in order to discover evidence of a crime to be used to obtain a conviction. The police officers did not initiate, encourage or participate in any way in the inventory. The police officers did not remove any property from Bembenek's locker. The hairbrush, which was eventually seized, was removed from the purse by Conway. Only after it was placed on a bench in the locker room did the police seize it. Accordingly, we hold that the trial court's finding that this was a private search and not subject to the fourth amendment protections was not contrary to the great weight and clear preponderance of the evidence.

Judgment affirmed.

CASE COMMENT

The court noted the long-established rule that the constitutional guarantee against unlawful searches and seizures applies only to actions of governmental agents and not to private individuals and that the policy behind not applying the exclusionary rule to private searches is that private individuals will not be so deterred as are the police who will be denied convictions based on the fruits of illegal searches. The court felt that private individuals have less knowledge of criminal procedure and are not interested in

[15]505 F.2d 1320.
[16]509 F.2d 605.
[19]614 F.2d 643.

getting convictions. The court held further that the supervisor was a private person, that he was merely inventorying her locker for public safety equipment and personal property (so as to avoid a later claim), and that he was not searching to discover evidence of crime. The court also noted that he would have inventoried the locker even if the police had not been present.

Since the supervisor was merely inventorying the locker, the court disagreed with the defendant's argument that because the police had preknowledge of the search, the supervisor became a *de facto* agent of the police. The mere presence of police at a search by a private person, if they do not initiate, encourage, or participate in that search in any way, may not always convert that private search to a governmental one.

LOCKER—INVASION OF PRIVACY

In the following case, employees of the store were provided lockers for the storage of personal effects during working hours. Those employees who provided their own locks were not required to provide the manager with either a combination or duplicate key. This was the case with Trotti, the appellee. Security personnel raised the suspicion that an unidentified employee, not the appellee, had stolen a watch. The appellee recalled locking her locker and on her later return discovered the lock hanging open. She discovered personal items in her locker and purse in considerable disarray; nothing, however was missing. She asked her manager if he had searched the locker and purse, and after a month of denials he admitted searching the locker and purse. The manager testified that all prospective employees received verbal notification that it was store policy to conduct unannounced locker searches. Other supervisory personnel testified that, although locker searches occurred regularly, prospective employees were not apprised of this policy. The appellee demonstrated a legitimate right of privacy in the locker and contents by having placed a lock on the locker at her own expense and with the consent of the store. The search was an unwarranted invasion of privacy. The point to note here is who had control over the locker. Also note that exemplary damages discussed in Chapter 6 can be awarded for wrongful, malicious conduct.

K-MART CORPORATION STORE NO. 7441 v. TROTTI
677 S.W.2d 632 (1984)

BULLOCK, Justice.

K-Mart Corporation appeals from a judgment awarding the appellee, Trotti, $8,000.00 in actual damages and $100,000.00 in exemplary damages for invasion of privacy.

We reverse and remand.

The appellee was an employee in the hosiery department at the appellants' store number 7441. Her supervisors had never indicated any dissatisfaction with her work nor any suspicion of her honesty.

The appellants provided their employees with lockers for the storage of personal effects during working hours. There was no assignment of any given locker to any individual employee. The employees could, on request, receive locks for the lockers from the appellants, and if the appellants provided the lock to an employee they would keep either a copy of the lock's combination or a master key for padlocks. Testimony indicated that there was some problem in providing a sufficient number of locks to employees, and, as a result, the store's administrative personnel permitted employees to purchase and use their own locks on the lockers, but in these instances, the appellants did not require the employee to provide the manager with either a combination or duplicate key. The appellee, with appellants' knowledge, used one of these lockers and provided her own combination lock.

On October 31, 1981, the appellee placed her purse in her locker when she arrived for work. She testified that she snapped the lock closed and then pulled on it to make sure it was locked. When she returned to her locker during her afternoon break, she discovered the lock hanging open. Searching through her locker, the appellee further discovered her personal items in her purse in considerable disorder. Nothing was missing from either the locker or the purse. The store manager testified that, in the company of three junior administrators at the store, he had that afternoon searched the lockers because of a suspicion raised by the appellant's security personnel that an unidentified employee, not the appellee, had stolen a watch. The manager and his assistants were also searching for missing price-marking guns. The appellee further testified that, as she left the employee's locker area after discovering her locker open, she heard the manager suggest to his assistants, "Let's get busy again." The manager testified that none of the parties searched through employees' personal effects.

The appellee approached the manager later that day and asked if he had searched employees' lockers and/or her purse. The manager initially denied either kind of search and maintained this denial for approximately one month. At that time, the manager then admitted having searched the employees' lockers and further mentioned that they had, in fact, searched the appellee's purse, later saying that he meant that they had searched only her locker and not her purse.

The manager testified that during the initial hiring interviews, all prospective employees received verbal notification from personnel supervisors that it was the appellants' policy to conduct ingress-egress searches of employees and also to conduct unannounced searches of lockers. A personnel supervisor and an assistant manager, however, testified that, although locker searches did regularly occur, the personnel supervisors did not apprise prospective employees of this policy.

The fundamental and basic right to be left alone constitutes the essence of the right to privacy.

The right of privacy has been defined as the right of an individual to be left alone, to live a life of seclusion, to be free from unwarranted publicity. This right to privacy is so important that the United States Supreme Court has repeatedly deemed it to stem implicitly from the Bill of Rights. Our State courts have long recognized a civil cause of action for the invasion of the right to privacy and have defined such an invasion in many ways: As an intentional intrusion upon the solitude or seclusion of another that is highly offensive to a reasonable person and as the right to be free from the wrongful intrusion into one's private activities in such manner as to outrage or cause mental suffering, shame or humiliation to a person of ordinary sensibilities.

The appellants requested the trial court to define an "invasion of privacy" as "the intentional intrusion upon the solitude or seclusion of another that is highly offensive to a reasonable person." The court refused to include the part of the requested instruction, ". . . that is highly offensive to a reasonable person." The appellants argue that this refusal constituted an abuse of discretion because the Rules of Civil Procedure require such an instruction. Tex.R. Civ.P. 273 and 277. The appellee alleges that the record establishes that the intrusion was highly offensive as a matter of law, and that, therefore, the instruction was unnecessary.

The definition of "invasion of privacy" that the appellant requested is one widely and repeatedly accepted. Although the Texas Supreme Court has not adopted a verbatim rendition of this definition, it is clear that, in Texas, an actionable invasion of privacy by intrusion must consist of an unjustified intrusion of the plaintiff's solitude or seclusion of such magnitude as to cause an ordinary individual to feel severely offended, humiliated, or outraged.

The appellants correctly point out that no Texas case yet reported has ever declined to include a requirement that the intrusion complained of be highly offensive to a reasonable person, and the appellee agrees with this statement. Nevertheless, the appellee urges that since the facts of this case established the highly objectionable nature of the intrusion as a matter of law, the requested instruction was unnecessary, and thus the trial court properly refused to include it.

We disagree with the appellee's contention. The record does indicate the appellee's outrage upon discovering the appellant's activities but fails to demonstrate that there could be no dispute as to the severity of the offensiveness of the intrusion, thereby making it impossible for us to conclude that the facts established the disputed portion of the instruction as a matter of law.

Moreover, we note that the result of accepting this contention would be to raise the legal theory of invasion of privacy from the realm of intentional torts into the sphere of strict liability. It would make any wrongful intrusion actionable, requiring a plaintiff to establish merely that the intrusion occurred and that the plaintiff did not consent to it. Because of the stern form of liability which already stems from an invasion of privacy, accepting a definition of invasion of privacy which lacked a standard of high offensiveness would result in fundamentally unfair assessments against defendants who offended unreasonably sensitive plaintiffs, but whose transgressions would not realistically fill either an ordinary person or the general society with any sense of outrage. A business executive, for example, could find himself liable for entering an associate's office without express permission; so could a beautician who opened a co-worker's drawer in order to find some supplies needed for a customer.

We hold that the element of a highly offensive intrusion is a fundamental part of the definition of an invasion of privacy, and that the term "invasion of privacy" is a highly technical, legal term, requiring, under Rule 277, an explanation to the jury. In the instant case, the definition of an invasion of privacy necessarily required the inclusion of the requested standard of offensiveness.

The lockers undisputably were the appellants' property, and in their unlocked state, a jury could reasonably infer that those lockers were subject to legitimate, reasonable searches by the appellants. This would also be true where the employee used a lock provided by the appellants, because in retaining the lock's combination or master key, it could be inferred that the appellants manifested an interest both in maintaining control over the locker and in conducting legitimate, reasonable searches. Where, as in the instant case, however, the employee purchases and uses his own lock on the lockers, with the employer's knowledge, the fact finder is justified in concluding that the employee manifested, and the employer recognized, an expectation that the locker and its contents would be free from intrusion and interference.

In the present case, there is evidence that appellee locked the locker with her own lock; that when the appellee returned from a break, the lock was lying open; that upon searching her locker, the appellee discovered that someone had rifled her purse; that the appellants' managerial personnel initially denied making the search but subsequently admitted searching her locker and her purse. We find this is far more evidence than a "mere scintilla," and we hold that there is some evidence to support the jury's finding.

As to the "insufficiency" point, after examining the record as a whole, we find it indicates all of the above. The appellee remembers having locked the locker and having seen the lock closed before starting work that day. The record indicates that the searching personnel denied having gone through any employee's purses, yet nothing in the record directly challenges the appellee's testimony as to the disruption of her personal effects inside her purse, and, therefore, the jury could make a reasonable inference that the managerial personnel had, in fact, gone through her personal effects. The record also establishes that other employees knew these searches were going on. The store manager testified that all employees received notification of these sporadic searches during their hiring interviews; however, two administrators, including a former personnel supervisor, denied that employees ever received this notification. We hold that the weight of the evidence indicates that the appellants' employees came upon a locker with a lock provided by an employee, disregarded the appellee's demonstration of her expectation of privacy, opened and searched the locker, and probably opened and searched her purse as well; and, in so holding, we consider it is immaterial whether the appellee actually securely locked her locker or not. It is sufficient that an employee in this situation, by having placed a lock on the locker at the employee's own expense and with the appellants' consent, has demonstrated a legitimate expectation to a right of privacy in both the locker itself and those personal effects within it.

The appellants argue that the trial court erred in failing to instruct the jury to consider questions of causation in fact and proximate cause, and, further, erred in failing to instruct the jury to consider whether the appellee actually suffered any injury at all.

The appellants urged the trial court to adopt concepts of negligence in submitting an intentional tort to the jury and now ask this court to require such concepts in all disputes involving an invasion of privacy. The appellants cite considerable authority applying negligence concepts to cases involving intentional civil assaults and batteries.

These concepts are inapplicable, and the appellants' authorities are distinguishable on two grounds. First, the circumstances of those assault and battery cases raised questions of causation not usually encountered in intentional torts. Here, however, there is no question that the appellants invaded the appellee's privacy by opening the locked locker and by opening and investigating her purse. This unwarranted invasion of privacy alone demonstrates that the single act of opening and inspecting the locker, and certainly the purse, was sufficient to justify the jury's findings. We overrule the appellant's eighteenth through twenty-first points of error.

The appellants further argue that any physical effects of the intrusion were merely effects stemming from an earlier health problem the appellee had suffered. The record does support these facts, and it would be reasonable to conclude that the unwarranted intrusion of the locker and purse at best exacerbated an earlier physical ailment. This contention, however, is immaterial in this kind of case.

The basis of a cause of action for invasion of privacy is that the defendant has violated the plaintiff's rights to be left alone. This intrusion itself is actionable, and the plaintiff can receive at least nominal damages for that actionable intrusion without demonstrating physical detriment. The appellants' improper intrusion of an area where the appellee had manifested an expectation of privacy alone raised her right to recover. We overrule the appellants' fifteenth point of error.

Appellants' sixth through tenth points of error pertain to the trial court's instructions to the jury regarding mental anguish and comprise two basic arguments. The first is that the trial court improperly refused to submit the appellants' definition of "mental anguish" to the jury; the second, that the trial court improperly allowed the jury to consider mere embarrassment in determining the appellee's damages.

In evaluating the appellants' first argument under these points of error, we find that the trial court failed to act in accordance with Tex.R.Civ.P. 273 and 277, by failing to provide the jury with any definition of "mental anguish," despite a requested definition offered by appellants. "Mental anguish" requires a plaintiff to show more than mere worry, anxiety, vexation, or anger. The term "mental anguish" implies a relatively high degree of mental pain and distress. It is more than mere disappointment, anger, resentment, or embarrassment, although it may include all of these. It includes a mental sensation of pain resulting from such painful emotion as grief, severe disappointment, indignation, wounded pride, shame, despair and/or public humiliation.

It is clear, therefore, that "mental anguish" is a technical, legal term, and that the trial court should have defined that term for the jury in accordance with Rule 277.

The special issue dealing with mental anguish reads:

What sum of money, if paid now in cash, do you find from a preponderance of the evidence would fairly and reasonably compensate Billie Trotti for the damages she suffered from the occurrence in question?

In answering this issue you shall take into account the following elements of damage and none other:

(a) Mental suffering or anguish

(b) Physical pain

(c) Embarrassment

You are to consider each element of damage separately, so as not to include damages for one element in any other element.

Answer in dollars and cents.

We hold that this instruction was improper, because it allowed the jury to assess damages against the appellants for any embarrassment the appellee suffered from the intrusion. The foregoing cases make it clear that, while mental anguish and physical suffering are compensable, mere embarrassment is not. In addition, the instruction clearly required the jury to consider embarrassment separately from mental anguish. We cannot, therefore, find that the instruction merely defined embarrassment as a factor or element of mental anguish, which would have been proper.

We sustain appellants' sixth through tenth points of error.

The jury awarded $8,000.00 as actual damages and $100,000.00 as exemplary damages to the appellee. The appellants contend that this award of exemplary damages was improper because: (1) no evidence, or insufficient evidence, exists of malice; and (2) the 12.5 to 1 ratio of exemplary to actual damages is excessive because it is disproportionate.

Any award of damages must have support in the record. An award of exemplary damages will be improper where the defendant acted in good faith.

A mere wrongful act is insufficient to justify the award of exemplary damages. An award of exemplary damages requires a preliminary finding that the defendant behaved maliciously or with wanton disregard for the plaintiff. Malice is an unlawful act done intentionally and without justification or excuse.

The appellants argue that no malice exists in this case because: (1) the appellants acted correctly and lawfully in opening and searching the lockers; and (2) even if the appellants wrongfully searched the lockers, they did so in a good faith belief that they had the right to do so. Neither of the appellants' allegations has merit.

First, the record establishes, and we have held herein, that the appellant's search of the appellee's locker and purse was wrongful. The mere suspicion either that another employee had stolen watches, or that unidentified employees may have stolen price-marking guns was insufficient to justify the appellants' search of appellee's locker and personal possessions without her consent. The record also demonstrates that the appellants lied to appellee and concealed the truth of their wrongful search for approximately one month.

The record indicates, particularly through the appellants' subsequent denial of their activities, that there was sufficient evidence from which the jury could reasonably conclude that the appellants acted with malicious disregard for both the appellee's rights of privacy and the rights of privacy of her co-workers. We find that there was sufficient evidence to support the jury's finding of malice.

It is the general rule in Texas that the amount of the award is uniquely within the jury's discretion.

> An appellate court should not substitute its verdict on damages for that of the jury unless the record indicates that the jury was influenced by passion, prejudice, improper motive, or something other than conscientious conviction. . . . The mere fact that a verdict is large is no indication of passion, prejudice, sympathy, or other circumstances not in evidence.

Therefore, the question of damages, if not excessive, is properly left for the jury to determine. . . . In the absence of a clear showing that passion, prejudice, or other improper matters influenced the jury, the amount assessed will not be set aside in this court as excessive.

The appellants argue that the exemplary damages in the instant case are excessive because the ratio of exemplary damages to actual damages is 12.5 to 1. They cite several cases with the implicit conclusion that any ratio other than 3 to 1 creates a presumption of excessive damages. It is true that ratios are indicators which a court may consider in determining whether the jury's award was an excessive one; however, they are nothing more than indicators. A holistic view of the entire situation is necessary when determining the propriety of exemplary damages, a view that recognizes both the purpose of exemplary damages and the special considerations of the dispute at bar.

Exemplary damages exist to promote the protection of an important public interest by making an example of the defendant for particular wrongful, malicious conduct. In determining whether the award will effectively yet fairly make such an example of a wrongful defendant, we should consider many factors. These factors include, but may encompass more than: (1) the nature of the wrong; (2) the character of the conduct involved; (3) the degree of the wrongdoer's culpability; (4) the situation and sensibilities of the parties; and (5) the extent to which the defendant's conduct offends a public sense of justice and propriety.

The appellants intentionally intruded upon the area where the appellee had a legitimate expectation of privacy. The evidence supports a further finding that the appellants wrongfully intruded upon the appellee's personal property. The conduct of this inspection, and the appellants' subsequent denial and ultimate admission support the conclusion that they were aware that their actions constituted a covert intrusion. The appellants clearly made this wrongful intrusion with neither the appellee's permission nor justifiable suspicion that the appellee had stolen any store inventory. Sufficient factors exist to enable this court to conclude that the jury's award of exemplary damages was the result of proper motivations. We disagree with the appellant that any set ratio of exemplary to actual damages constitutes a ceiling beyond which a greater award would be excessive, and even were we to agree with appellants, we do not find that the exemplary damages in the instant case exceed that ceiling.

The evidence supports the jury's award of exemplary damages from the factors cited. There is no evidence to support a conclusion that the jury acted as a result of passion or prejudice.

The judgment is reversed, and the case is remanded for new trial.

CASE COMMENT

The appellee in this case demonstrated a legitimate expectation of privacy by maintaining control over the locker and had the consent of the store. As the store did not maintain control, the search was an unwarranted invasion of privacy. If a business deems it necessary to have a policy of searching lockers, it should notify all the employees involved and get an acknowledgment in writing. This is best done at the time they are hired. The essence of the right to privacy is the basic and fundamental right to be left alone. This right to privacy is extremely important, and courts have long recognized a cause of action for an invasion of this right. To be actionable, the invasion by unjustified intrusion must be of such magnitude to cause an ordinary individual to feel severely offended, humiliated, or outraged. That is to say, it must outrage or cause mental suffering, shame, or humiliation to a person of ordinary sensibilities. The reason for a standard is to avoid unfair assessments against defendants by unreasonably sensitive plaintiffs. Exemplary damages will not be awarded if a defendant acted in good faith, but will be awarded if the defendant is found to have behaved maliciously or with wanton disregard. It is recognized that mistakes, accidents, and wrongful acts happen. But mere wrongful acts are insufficient to justify exemplary damages. The security manager should train and supervise his personnel to avoid exemplary or punitive damages.

SEARCH OF A FEMALE BY A MALE

The next case deals with the search of a female shopper by a uniformed male security guard regarding nail polish, which eventually cost the company $27,500. The search took place behind doors marked "Employees Only." During the course of the trial, the female testified that the guard, in checking her blouse pockets, placed both hands on her breasts and squeezed. The female testified that she felt offended, repulsed, embarrassed, violated, and terrified. The $20,000 award for battery speaks for itself. Loss from litigation because of a security employee's action should be a primary concern of the security manager.

CLARK v. SKAGGS COMPANIES, INC.
724 S.W. 2d 545 (1986)

MANFORD, Judge.
This is a civil action for false imprisonment and battery. The judgment is affirmed.
The pertinent facts are as follows:
On December 18, 1984, respondent, Joy Clark, was shopping at appellant's (defendant) store at 10th and Minnesota in Kansas City, Kansas. While browsing in the cosmetics aisle, Clark encountered a uniformed security guard, one Johnny Rogers. Clark continued shopping and picked up some nail polish and carried it to another area of the cosmetics section to compare with some lipstick. Clark decided not to purchase the cosmetics and left the nail polish where she was comparing it with the lipsticks. After about fifteen minutes, Clark attempted to exit the store without making any purchases. She noticed the security guard was following her and she turned to him and asked if he knew her from somewhere. Rogers stated, "No, but I was wondering where you put that nail polish." Clark stated that it was somewhere back in the store. Rogers then asked Clark to take him to find the nail polish.
Clark testified that at that point she realized Rogers thought she was shoplifting and she felt that she had no choice but to accompany Rogers back into the store. Clark led Rogers into the cosmetics aisle but Rogers pointed to some doors that said "Employees Only" and stated, "Why don't we go through those doors and see if it's in your purse." Once inside the doors, Clark dumped the contents of her purse onto the top of some boxes. The nail polish was not there.
Clark was wearing blue jeans, a plaid blouse and a sweater-jacket. She removed the jacket and handed it to Rogers and said, "It's not in my sweater pockets either." Rogers did not search the sweater. Clark patted her jeans pockets saying, "It's not in these pockets either."

Rogers did not search the jeans pockets. Clark then said, "It's not in my shirt pockets," indicating toward the breast pockets of her blouse. Clark testified that it was obvious there was nothing in her blouse pockets because there was no lump or bulge of any package or container. Clark unbuttoned the blouse pocket buttons and said, "See," and Rogers stated, "Well, let me check," whereupon he stepped forward and reached out, placing both hands upon Clark's breasts and squeezed. Clark told Rogers that she didn't think that was legal. Clark testified that she felt offended, repulsed, embarrassed, violated and terrified.

Rogers apologized and asked Clark to accompany him into the store to find the nail polish. While walking through the store they were joined by a store clerk. Eventually, Clark led them back to the cosmetics aisle and found the nail polish with the lipsticks. The clerk stated, "Well, I guess we have to take your word for it." Clark said, "Well here it is and I had to be searched for this." The clerk asked, "Did you empty your purse?" When Clark stated that she did, the clerk responded, "Well, then he didn't search you." Clark asked if she could leave but got no response. Rogers apologized again and Clark repeated her request to leave. The clerk said, "Yeah, go on, get out of here."

Clark testified that during the time she was with the security guard, approximately fifteen minutes, she felt that she could not leave. Clark stated that she no longer feels free to browse through stores, she feels paranoid when shopping, and she no longer picks up little objects to examine them while shopping. Clark testified that she did not see a doctor about her problems, but that she had spoken with her father who is a doctor.

The jury awarded Clark $7,500 for the false imprisonment and $20,000 for the battery.

One seeking to recover for false arrest or false imprisonment must prove that he or she was unlawfully caused to be arrested by the defendant, and, though it is not necessary that the arrest be directly ordered by defendant, it must appear that defendant either instigated it, assisted in the arrest, or by some means directed, countenanced or encouraged it.

Appellant's own evidence established that Rogers was an employee of defendant[2] and that he had been instructed to conduct surveillance and to detain and/or apprehend suspected shoplifters. Although physical restraint is not essential, there must, in absence of such restraint, be words or conduct that induce the reasonable belief that resistance or attempted flight would be futile.

In the present case, respondent testified that she was approached by a uniformed security guard and she realized that he (the guard) was accusing her of shoplifting. She stated that at that point, she felt that she could not leave; that she had no choice but to accompany the guard back into the store. Appellant argues that there was no evidence that the guard used force or threats, or that he accused respondent of shoplifting, and that, in fact, respondent voluntarily accompanied the guard back into the store, wishing to cooperate.

Viewing the evidence as stated, reasonable minds may infer from the evidence that respondent was intimidated and/or coerced by the presence of the uniformed security guard and that upon his request that she accompany him, respondent reasonably believed that flight would in fact be futile. Such an inference may be drawn from respondent's testimony that she realized the guard thought she was shoplifting and that she felt she had no choice but to cooperate with him. Furthermore, respondent stated that she asked permission to leave and in fact did not leave until said request was granted. The fact that she did so cooperate does not negate the conclusion that her actions were involuntary. An employer is liable for the assaults committed by his employee upon a third party where such assaults are committed by the

[2]Although the security guard was actually an employee of Advance Security, which does contract security for appellant, both parties agreed to try the case as though the guard was employed by Skaggs, and, as an accommodation to both parties, Advance Security assumed the defense of the case.

employee while acting within the scope of his employment. Under the doctrine of respondeat superior, an employer may be vicariously liable for the act of his employee because there is a relationship between the act done and the employer's business, to wit: the employee in acting is benefiting the employer in the furtherance of his (the employer's) business.

It is not disputed that Johnny Rogers was a security guard for appellant and that he was on duty on December 18, 1984. Two witnesses testified on behalf of appellant, both of whom were familiar with the security policies of Skaggs stores and Advance Security. Both witnesses stated Rogers had been instructed on security policies, and that Rogers was instructed to attempt to apprehend and detain possible shoplifters and, if the suspect is cooperative, to "follow through with whatever is necessary". Furthermore, both witnesses stated that it was against policy for security personnel to make sexual advances to a suspected shoplifter and that if such incident should occur and be brought to the attention of the management, the employment would be terminated.

Appellant does not deny that Rogers put his hands upon Clark's breasts and squeezed. Rather, appellant argues that in so doing, Rogers was acting outside the scope and course of his employment. Appellant states that, the evidence, as testified to by respondent that "it was obvious" that there was nothing inside her breast pockets, establishes that Rogers acted for his own gratification and was in no way acting to benefit his employer's business. Appellant concludes that there was no evidence that Rogers acted within the scope and course of his employment and that the evidence and legitimate inferences therefrom were such that reasonable minds could not differ on this.

The evidence was such that would support an inference that it was within the scope of Roger's employment to "search" a suspected shoplifter, and that, in so doing, Rogers would be acting to benefit his employer's business. The questions then become: Was Rogers attempting a search of respondent's breast pockets at the time he touched her breasts? Does the fact that Rogers' actions were outside the scope of decency and good taste take his actions outside the bounds of what might otherwise be classified as a search? Respondent testified that she felt humiliated and embarrassed that she had to accompany the uniformed security guard through the store and into the "Employees Only" room in full view of other shoppers and Skaggs employees.

In any event, this court cannot say that the jury award of $7,500 for false imprisonment wherein the plaintiff was detained within the store for a period of approximately fifteen minutes, where during such time she suffered embarrassment and humiliation, is against the weight of the evidence. Therefore, the trial court did not err in entering judgment in conformity with the verdict and in overruling appellant's motion for new trial on the count of false imprisonment.

In regard to the battery, appellant again argues that the award was excessive and against the weight of the evidence because plaintiff suffered no physical injury, lost no income, and had no medical expenses.

Damages for mental suffering may be recovered where such suffering is the proximate and natural result of the assault even though no bodily injury was inflicted. In the present case, respondent testified that when the guard put his hands on her breasts she felt offended, repulsed, terrified and violated. This court holds that the award of $20,000 on the battery count was not against the weight of the evidence. The trial court did not err in entering its judgment in conformity with the verdict or in overruling appellant's motion for new trial.

CASE COMMENT

Supervision, training, adequate screening, an understanding of the law, and professionalism will go a long way to prevent loss from litigation because of an incident like this.

NONCOERCIVE SEARCH TACTICS/ALTERNATIVE PROCEDURES

In an effort to reduce pilferage, a large urban hospital instituted a package control system together with random spot inspections. Prior to doing this, the hospital advertised the policy for several weeks on walls in corridors, elevators, departments, and laboratories. They also created three parcel "check" locations that stored packages, bags, and parcels until the owner was ready to leave. The contents of these packages were never inspected at any time nor were women's pocketbooks. The plaintiff in the following case lost one week's wages for being "insubordinate" in willfully failing to comply with the requirements of the package control system.

CHENKIN v. BELLEVUE HOSPITAL CENTER, NEW YORK CITY HEALTH & HOSPITALS CORPORATION
479 F. Supp. 207 (1979)

EDWARD WEINFELD, District Judge.

This action challenges the legality of a regulation issued by a large urban municipal hospital in an effort to prevent or reduce pilferage of hospital property, whereby bags, packages and large parcels carried by employees leaving the hospital are subject to random spot inspection. The question for decision is whether such inspections are violative of the Fourth Amendment, made applicable to the States through the Fourteenth Amendment.

Plaintiff is an assistant chemist employed by Bellevue Hospital Center ("Bellevue"). He instituted this action for a declaratory judgment that Bellevue's "pilferage control-package pass system" (the "package control system," or "the system") is unconstitutional, and to enjoin its continued enforcement. In addition, he seeks reimbursement for one week's lost wages, which amount was deducted from his salary after a hearing officer had determined that he was "insubordinate" in willfully failing to comply with the requirements of the package control system. The defendants contend that the system is fair and reasonable and a valid condition of employment, and, therefore, that it is constitutional.

The material questions of fact are undisputed. The parties agree that the matter is ripe for summary judgment disposition and that the sole issue for determination is the constitutionality of the package control system.

Bellevue is a municipal medical complex of enormous size. It is the largest municipal hospital in Manhattan and the second largest in the City of New York. It covers four entire city blocks, stretching from 26th to 30th Streets and from First Avenue to the East River. It employs approximately 5,600 people and has 22 exists through which those employees, as well as visitors, may leave.

In March 1978, Bellevue officials determined to stem what they perceived to be a rising tide of pilferage of hospital property including, but not limited to, medical equipment, sheets, towels, flatware and foodstuffs, all of which were readily available throughout the hospital. Accordingly, on March 17, 1978, they issued a memorandum that was posted on elevators, corridors, walls and various departments and laboratories throughout the hospital announcing the adoption of the package control system effective on April 3, 1978. Under the system employees leaving the hospital with packages may be asked by guards of the hospital's security division to permit inspection of those packages. The system requires all staff and employees carrying "shopping bags, brown paper bags, boxes, tote bags, wrapped packages, suitcases, etc." when leaving the hospital to use either of two designated exits. At each of these exits security guards are intermittently placed and are authorized at random intervals to stop persons carrying parcels from the hospital and to inspect those parcels for the sole purpose of determining whether they contain pilfered hospital property. Because of the volume of the traffic in and out of the facility, and the limited size of the security force, not all persons carrying such packages are stopped. Instead, the officers randomly select packages for inspection. Persons whose packages are selected are required to open them and exhibit their contents. When packages are inspected only a minimal examination is undertaken. The security guards making these inspections are not authorized to confiscate personal property or examine personal papers, and there is no claim that they ever did so. Nor do they ever conduct "frisks" or "pat downs" or any other contact searches. Moreover, women's pocketbooks are never inspected.

An important feature of the system announced at its inception is an alternative procedure whereby employees may entirely avoid having their packages searched. Upon entering the hospital those who wish to do so may "check" their packages at one of three locations where they are stored until the owner is ready to leave the building. Checked packages are not inspected at any time. Thus, hospital personnel who avail themselves of this procedure may enter and leave without having their packages inspected by anyone.

Bellevue maintains that the system reduces the amount of pilferage of hospital property in two ways: it provides a means of detecting theft of hospital property and constitutes a general deterrent to those who might otherwise be inclined to pilfer hospital property. While no precise statistical data has been submitted, Bellevue's officers swear that pilferers have been apprehended on "numerous occasions" since the system was implemented and that the system has been an effective deterrent.

The origin of the present controversy stems from an incident on June 28, 1978, when security guards stopped the plaintiff Chenkin while he was on his way out of the hospital and attempted to inspect the contents of the knapsack he was carrying with him. The officers chose Mr. Chenkin's bag at random as the object of their search; it is undisputed that they had no probable cause to believe, or even an articulable suspicion supporting an inference, that plaintiff's bag in particular contained any hospital property. The plaintiff has never denied that he had received due notice of the existence of the regulation, which included notice of the availability of the alternate procedure. In the absence of such a denial, it may be assumed that at the time of the incident, he was aware of the package control system, which had already been in effect for more than twelve weeks.[2]

When asked by security guards to exhibit the contents of his knapsack, plaintiff refused to do so. Upon presenting his identification to a security guard, his name was noted, and he was permitted to leave the hospital without being searched. No immediate action was taken against plaintiff as a result of this incident.[3]

─────

[2]Plaintiff does claim, however, that at the time of the incident, he was unaware that those who failed to comply with the security regulations were subject to fines or even dismissal from employment. The only notice that clearly prescribed the penalties for failure to comply was posted for the first time on July 20, or *after* plaintiff had been stopped. Nevertheless, the language of the original notice is clearly obligatory. Employees were informed, beginning on April 3, that security was regarded as "everyone's responsibility"; that the package control system "required full cooperation for its success"; and that "compliance with this procedure is essential." In light of these statements, it may be assumed that plaintiff realized that these directives, if valid, were enforceable by appropriate sanctions, including fines.

[3]The June 28 incident, however, was mentioned in the letter of reprimand sent by Bellevue to the plaintiff after his second failure to comply. It is not clear whether the hospital would have taken disciplinary action against the plaintiff had he subsequently chosen to comply. It is, of course, clear beyond question that the plaintiff had actual notice of the hospital's policy as a result of the June 28 incident.

On July 14, 1978, security guards again stopped plaintiff while he was leaving the building. Again, the stop was made randomly, as part of the "spot-check" program. No suspicion of unauthorized activity was directed at plaintiff; nor is there any evidence that the security guards who stopped him on the second occasion remembered him from the first. A scenario ensued similar to that which had transpired on the first occasion The guards requested that the plaintiff open his knapsack, and he refused. His name was once more taken, and he was allowed to leave with his bag uninspected. Plaintiff was never subjected to any coercion, physical or mental abuse.

Following the second incident, the plaintiff was summarily suspended without pay for a five-day period, from July 24 to July 28, 1978, for his refusal to comply with "instructions for inspection of bags he was carrying out of the hospital." Thereafter and pursuant to New York law, a hearing was conducted on October 5, 1978, before a neutral hearing officer. Plaintiff appeared, with counsel, and testified on his own behalf. The only issue raised in defense of plaintiff's conduct was the claim that the system was unconstitutional. The hearing officer found that the plaintiff had "knowingly violated, after due notice, an official regulation of the Corporation and therefore is guilty of insubordination." He found the package control system to be a "fair and reasonable means of coping with the serious problem" of pilferage and "a reasonable condition of employment." He recommended that the suspension of plaintiff for five days without pay be upheld. After a final appeal, the recommendation of the hearing officer was accepted and implemented; the penalty was imposed by Bellevue's Director of Personnel Management, who is named in her official capacity as a defendant in this suit.

Upon these facts the plaintiff claims that, as a matter of law, Bellevue's policy is violative of the Fourth Amendment to the United States Constitution. He claims that the system authorized unreasonable intrusions into his privacy, that are made without compelling justification and that achieve no discernible reduction of pilferage. With equal vigor Bellevue asserts that employees have no reasonable expectation of privacy in the packages they bring to work; that, when viewed in the totality of circumstances its regulation is reasonable; and that in any event the plaintiff impliedly consented to be searched. Each of these contentions will be examined in turn.

A. Plaintiff's Expectation of Privacy

Counsel for the parties cite leading Supreme Court cases in support of their respective positions, but none of these is dispositive of the issues here presented.[8] While those cases

---

[8]Some of the cases cited are quite wide of the mark. For example, much of the argument in the briefs concerns whether the decision to stop a particular individual for inspection of his bag should be made by a neutral hearing officer, and whether it should be supported by probable cause. Not only would the requirements of a warrant and probable cause be unworkable in this context, but they are singularly inappropriate in situations in which the authorities have no suspicion that a particular individual has engaged in wrongful conduct. As the Supreme Court has said:

> In analyzing the issue of reasonableness *vel non*, the courts have not sought to determine whether a protective inventory was justified by "probable cause." The standard of probable cause is peculiarly related to criminal investigations, not routine, noncriminal procedures. . . . The probable-cause approach is unhelpful when analysis centers upon the reasonableness of routine administrative caretaking functions, particularly when no claim is made that the protective procedures are a subterfuge for criminal investigations.

Equally inapplicable is that line of cases, cited by the parties, requiring government regulatory agencies
(continued)

give direction to the general principles to be applied when an issue is raised as to whether a particular action constitutes a "search" within the meaning of the Fourth Amendment, and if so, whether it is "reasonable," each case must turn on its own individual facts. Thus, we turn to an examination of each of the parties' contentions.

The plaintiff's essential contention, no matter how conceptualized, is that the hospital's policy of subjecting the contents of his bag to inspection, upon his leaving the place of his employment, constitutes an invasion of his right to privacy. He relies principally upon the "lodestar" case, *Katz v. United States,* in which the Supreme Court held that the Fourth Amendment protects people, not places, from unreasonable intrusions into their privacy by the government. However, subsequent decisions have made clear that not all privacy interests which a person asserts are constitutionally protected. As the Court recently reiterated: "The application of the Fourth Amendment depends on whether the person invoking its protection can claim a 'justifiable,' a 'reasonable,' or 'legitimate expectation of privacy' that has been invaded by government action. This, in turn, involves a dual inquiry into whether the individual's conduct evinces an actual, subjective expectation of privacy; and second, whether that expectation, when viewed objectively, is justifiable under the circumstances.

Here it may be acknowledged that the plaintiff entertained an expectation of privacy with respect to his belongings contained within his bag. By his conduct in refusing to permit an inspection of his bag, he has "exhibited an actual (subjective) expectation of privacy" and has shown that he "seeks to preserve its contents as private."

Plaintiff's belief cannot be dismissed as wholly unreasonable. The item that he asserts is protected—a closed bag, containing personal effects, and carried on his person—is the type of item that traditionally has been accorded protection under the Fourth Amendment. Numerous cases have recognized a legitimate expectation of privacy in objects not nearly so intimately connected with the individual's person as are the contents of a knapsack carried on the back. Certainly the plaintiff did not lose that protection in that he did not "knowingly expose to the public" the contents of his bag. Nor did he relinquish control over his bag, or release its contents into the public domain. He took affirmative steps to shield the bag's contents from public view and to protect their privacy.

Nevertheless, Bellevue claims that plaintiff's subjective belief was unreasonable. It points to the gigantic size of the institution and the enormous number of people who traverse its portals daily; from these facts, it contends that the hospital was so "public" in character that no one in it could reasonably expect to enjoy the benefits of privacy. But this argument, if accepted, would strip individuals who ventured from their homes of most of the protection of the Fourth Amendment. The Fourth Amendment protects people, both in their homes and in public places. Indeed, even when people venture into areas which, for compelling reasons, are accorded a lesser degree of Fourth Amendment protection, such as airport lobbies, they still retain some justifiable expectation of privacy in their belongings.

Bellevue also contends that the warning posters it displayed announcing the package control system apprised employees that they could not justifiably harbor subjective expectations of privacy in the contents of the packages they carried into the building. That argument, however, is also unavailing. The mere announcement by Bellevue that packages are

to obtain warrants before inspecting places of employment for safety hazards, *Marshall v. Barlow's Inc.,* 436 U.S. 307 or commercial buildings and dwellings for fire and health code violations. *See v. City of Seattle,* 387 U.S. 541; *Camara v. Municipal Court,* 387 U.S. 523.

The violations that the government sought to uncover in those cases involved fixed conditions, existing in a confined area and unchanged over a period of time long enough to permit government agents to make the requisite showing of need before a neutral hearing officer. The instant case involves manifestly different conditions. Any requirement that Bellevue's security officers appear in front of a neutral officer before making inspections would emasculate the hospital's efforts to control pilferage.

subject to search is not enough either to change the plaintiff's expectations or to legitimate the inspection system. If this argument were accepted, the government and quasi-public institutions would gain broad power to refashion the contours of the Fourth Amendment merely by proclamation. Plainly, this is not the case, and no court has so held.

We hold that the plaintiff exhibited an actual, subjective expectation of privacy in his bag and in its contents, and that that expectation was not rendered unreasonable either by the size and public character of the hospital or by the announcement of the hospital's inspection policy. These conclusions, however, are not the end of the inquiry. The crucial question is whether the plaintiff's expectations, viewed objectively, were "reasonable" in light of the hospital's interest in controlling pilferage.

B. Reasonableness

It is axiomatic that the Fourth Amendment forbids only those warrantless searches deemed "unreasonable." The process of determining which particular searches are forbidden requires a balancing of "the public interest against the Fourth Amendment interest of the individual." Three factors are crucial to that analysis: the strength of the public necessity for the search; the efficacy of the search; and the degree and nature of the intrusion upon the individual. On the basis of these factors, plaintiff seeks to distinguish his case from those cases involving "unique circumstances," such as searches conducted at airport boarding gates or at the courthouse doors, in which the courts have relaxed the strictures of the Fourth Amendment in order to protect the public from the threat of grave physical harm. Plaintiff argues that, by comparison, the situation at Bellevue required no extraordinary measures. The argument has some force. Certainly the harm to the public occasioned by even rampant pilferage of public property, though not insignificant, is not on the same scale as that posed by airport terrorism. There is dramatic evidence, as well, that airport and courthouse searches have effectively curtailed the danger against which they are directed. Nonetheless, the comparison that plaintiff offers proves only that in the airport and courthouse cases, the balance of interests points more strongly in favor of the public interest than it does in the case at bar; those cases are not dispositive.

Plaintiff also urges that this case is directly analogous to those "public arena" cases, in which courts have struck down search procedures instituted at the entrance to public events, particularly rock music concerts, for the purposes of apprehending suspected drug offenders and controlling the flow of dangerous projectiles into the performance area. Those cases also rest upon their own particular facts. In them the courts made clear that, although the dangers of drug abuse and of public riot were real, the means adopted by the authorities to check these dangers were largely ineffectual. More importantly, the tactics employed, which were directed principally against minors, created an atmosphere of fear and coercion. The concert patrons were "grabbed" without warning by police officers. They were subjected to intrusive and humiliating searches, including "patdowns" of their garments, and searches of their pockets, coats, shirttails, and pocketbooks. Moreover, they were given either inadequate warning, or no warning at all, of the possibility of a search. Nor were they informed of their right to refuse the search and to have their ticket money refunded. In these circumstances, where the public interest is only moderate, the searches are degrading and largely ineffectual, and the victims are often uninformed minors, the courts have appropriately concluded that such security measures are unreasonable.

The facts of the instant case are discernibly different. Although not overwhelming, the public's interest in controlling pilferage from public institutions is nevertheless substantial and legitimate. The problem is fueled by Bellevue's sheer size. With hospital personnel concerned essentially with the ill and the maimed, as they should be, protection of hospital property becomes increasingly difficult. The aggregate value of property lost through theft in a facility as large as Bellevue, employing 5,600 people and utilized by countless visitors is likely to be substantial, and the cost is borne by the community. According to the uncontested affidavits of hospital personnel, the measures adopted by Bellevue have served to alleviate the problem. In other words, the searches have been efficacious.

Moreover, the search tactics adopted at Bellevue are reasonable. The hospital's methods have none of the coercive and offensive impact of those used at rock concerts. Plaintiff was forewarned of the possibility of a search, and thus was not intimidated by the element of surprise. He was an adult employee, familiar with the area in which he was stopped. He was not "grabbed" by the security guards; indeed, no one attempted either to touch or to search his person. Because he was chosen at random, he was not stigmatized by the suspicion of wrongdoing. The scope of the intended search was limited by the sole objective of locating unauthorized hospital property; there is no indication that the searching officers were looking for, or intended to confiscate any other property, even if illicit, that their search might have revealed. No compulsion or threats were invoked, even after the plaintiff refused to comply with the officers' request. Upon identifying himself, the plaintiff was permitted to leave without undergoing any inspection. The intrusion contemplated by the inspection policy would have been minimal, and the examination, brief. It has not been suggested, and cannot be contended, that any other, less restrictive measures could have been utilized to accomplish the hospital's purposes. If firms trading on the stock exchange may require their employees to submit to fingerprinting in an effort to curb the problem of thievery, no reason appears why hospitals functioning in the public interest should not be permitted the lesser intrusion caused by inspection of bags.

The reasonableness of the hospital's package control system is underscored by the availability of the alternative procedure.[33] It would have been a simple matter, that in no way would have inconvenienced him, for plaintiff to have checked his bag upon entry into the building; he thereby would have avoided all risk of a random spot check. He freely chose not to pursue this alternative; instead, he insisted and continues to insist, upon a right to carry his bag into the building without accepting the concomitant obligation of submitting its contents to an appropriate examination when requested to do so.

After viewing the totality of the circumstances and balancing all of the aforementioned factors, it is this Court's considered judgment that the package control system adopted by Bellevue Hospital Center constitutes a fair, reasonable, and minimally intrusive method of efficaciously coping with a serious public problem. Accordingly, it is not prohibited by the Fourth Amendment.

Plaintiff has raised two other arguments that require brief attention. First, he contends that the hospital's policy violates the principle of equal protection because it expressly exempts women's pocketbooks from the inspection requirement. If the heart of this claim is that the system accords women an undeserved exemption, then this constitutes a benefit, not a detriment, and the claim does not state a cause of action. On the other hand, if plaintiff is contending that Bellevue's system irrationally classifies pocketbooks as different from knapsacks, we hold that Bellevue might rationally conclude both that pilfered

---

[33]In two of the cases upon which the plaintiff most heavily relies, the courts have stated, in dicta, that they would have upheld security systems similar to the one used at Bellevue, provided that the systems were adequately publicized and that they offered some means, such as the use of a "check room," by which people could avoid having their packages inspected. *See Wheaton v. Hagan*, 435 F.Supp. 1134; *Collier v. Miller*, 414 F.Supp. 1357.

items could more readily be concealed in a knapsack than in a pocketbook, and that a search into the former would be less intrusive than one into the latter. Finally, the policy reflects a sensitivity for Fourth Amendment rights and underscores the reasonableness of the regulation.

Furthermore, plaintiff urges that even though he was informed about the system, the general public who visit the hospital are not adequately informed about it, and thus, the searches are unreasonable at least with respect to them. Plaintiff, however, has no standing to assert claims on behalf of other employees, and even less with respect to claims that might be raised by the general public. In any event, nothing has been presented on this motion as to an inspection of the property of any persons other than employees.

Bellevue has also urged us to conclude that by his actions plaintiff has impliedly consented to the inspection policy. In light of our disposition of the other issues, it is unnecessary to reach this contention.

The motion of the defendant Bellevue Hospital Center for summary judgment is granted.

CASE COMMENT

In granting the hospital's motion for summary judgment, the court noted some of the factors that contributed to the fairness, reasonableness, and minimal intrusiveness of the package control system. The hospital announced and warned of the adoption of the package control system for several weeks. Security guards were intermittently placed and inspections were made at random intervals. The sole purpose of the inspection was to determine if parcels contained pilfered hospital property. Only a minimal examination of the inspected packages was undertaken. The guards were not authorized to confiscate personal property or examine personal papers. They did not conduct "frisks," "pat downs," or other contact searches. An important feature of the system was an alternative procedure whereby employees might entirely avoid having their packages searched by checking them in one of three locations. Random search selection does not stigmatize the person chosen by a suspicion of wrongdoing.

In this case, the plaintiff was forewarned of the possibility of a search and thus was not intimidated by the element of surprise. The plaintiff, when he was asked by guards to exhibit the contents of his knapsack, refused to do so. The guards did not search his bag; they merely took his name. He was never subjected to any coercion or physical or mental abuse. He chose freely not to avail himself of the alternative procedure.

FOURTH AMENDMENT—NON-APPLICATION TO PRIVATE PROPERTY

The question raised in the following case is whether conduct by security personnel in a privately-operated amusement park can be equated with governmental action that would thrust into play Fourth Amendment protections. While Francoeur was being detained by park security, certain incriminating items were obtained and identification procedures were performed. The claim was made that the amusement park was wide open to public access and contained all of the necessary adjuncts and amenities of an ordinary town, thus triggering constitutional rights guarantees. Security managers should determine if any or all of the property under their jurisdiction comes under the public principle. If so, there are two sets of legal rules: one encompassing constitutional guarantees, the other encompassing private citizen law.

UNITED STATES v. FRANCOEUR
547 F. 2d 891 (1977)

TUTTLE, Circuit Judge:

This appeal of the three appellants, each on several counts of an indictment charging them with having passed counterfeit $50 bills at Disney World in Florida, and having conspired to do so, raises principally the question whether the conduct of the security personnel of the privately-operated amusement park is to be equated with, and to be given the same effect as, actions by Government officials in the application of Fourth Amendment protection.

There is no issue on this appeal as to the sufficiency of the evidence for the conviction of the three defendants. The grounds of the appeal relate to the appellants' claim that they were detained, questioned, and viewed for identification purposes in a manner which, if carried on by either state or federal officials, would have amounted to a violation of their Fourth Amendment rights.

Briefly stated, a Disney World employee alerted a Mr. Morgan to the fact that several $50 counterfeit bills had been cashed on the morning in question. Morgan promptly sought to notify various outlets for merchandise, separately run throughout the park. He personally saw a transaction in which Francoeur took an article from the China Shop at a time when he observed a $50 bill with the critical serial number lying on the counter in his immediate presence. Morgan followed Francoeur and observed him meet appellant Pacheco in what was known as Artist's Alleyway. He followed the two on to the Main Street where they made a couple of moves that increased Morgan's suspicions, turning and retracing their steps toward the alleyway. Morgan then stopped long enough to call a Mr. Schmidt, a Walt Disney World security officer, at about which time appellant Pizio joined Pacheco and Francoeur. Schmidt followed the defendants until they reached the Train Station. There, they were stopped by Schmidt who identified himself and showed his badge (the insignia of Walt Disney World, a design of a globe with Mickey Mouse ears on top). He told them to keep their hands out of their pockets; that he wanted to talk with them; that they should not run; and that they should follow him to the Disney Security Office. Without objection, Schmidt testified at the trial at about this time, Pacheco went through some motions which Schmidt "assumed" represented an effort by Pacheco to hand a folded Disney World guidebook to Pizio but that Pizio moved away "like he didn't want to have anything to do with it."

After the three defendants were moved to a room in the Disney Security Office, Schmidt examined the Disney guidebook obtained from Pacheco and found that between the pages were nine crisp $50 counterfeit bills all with the critical serial number. He asked the three men to empty their pockets, which they did. Among the articles turned over were three Eastern Airline tickets, carbon copies dated the same day from Boston to Orlando, in the names of Kramer, Sullivan and Sousa, the names that the three men gave to the security officers when they were being questioned. Pacheco also gave up the key to Room No. 1220 in one of the hotels in the compound serving Disney World and the receipts for the payment for the room in the names of Sousa, Creamer and Sullivan. Pacheco also had nine packets of genuine currency, each packet containing bills folded just once and each containing less than $50. Without objection, Schmidt testified: "It was in nine little packets. It was all together like if you went in and got change for a larger bill and you kept all of that change in one pocket. The stacks weren't taken out in your tens or your twenties or whatever, and put together. It was just packets of money like change from a bill."

While in custody, which we may assume for the purpose of this issue, would have amounted to forcible detention if the defendants had sought to leave over the protest of the security officials, they were placed before a one-way mirror and groups of sales persons were permitted to look at each of them individually in an effort to identify any or all of them as persons who had passed $50 bills to such sales persons during the day. Some one or other of the sales persons identified each of the three defendants as having passed such a bill or more. Thereupon, the Secret Service officials took over and filed formal charges, and obtained a search warrant for the search of the hotel room. There, or in the security office, they found a key which fit a suitcase found in the hotel room, which contained some $48,000 in counterfeit $50 bills with the same serial number.

All of the activities through the identification procedures were performed by Disney World security personnel and before special agents of the Secret Service arrived at the scene.

The appellants do not contest the validity of the arrest or of the issuance of the search warrant except to the extent that they were the result of the actions of the Disney World security personnel which we may assume, for the purpose of this discussion, would have violated the defendants' constitutional rights if carried out by governmental officials.

As has been recognized since *Burdeau v. McDowell,* 256 U.S. 465, the Fourth Amendment gives protection only against unlawful governmental action. In that case, the Supreme Court said:

"The Fourth Amendment gives protection against unlawful searches and seizures, and as shown in the previous cases, its protection applies to governmental action. Its origin and history clearly show that it was intended as a restraint upon the activities of sovereign authority, and was not intended to be a limitation upon other than governmental agencies; as against such authority it was the purpose of the Fourth Amendment to secure the citizen in the right of unmolested occupation of his dwelling and the possession of his property, subject to the right of seizure by process duly issued."

In *United States v. Mekjian,* we said: "Where no official of the federal government has any connection with a wrongful seizure, or any knowledge of it until after the fact, the evidence is admissible. (Citations omitted)." 505 F.2d 1320.

This same principle has been announced in *United States of America v. Lamar & Aaron,* 545 F.2d 488: "Thus, if a search is conducted by a private individual, for purely private reasons, it does not fall within the protective ambit of the Fourth Amendment."

Recognizing this principle, appellants say that, nevertheless, the security personnel of Disney World in this case are in truth and in fact "government" officials. This they seek to do under some such principle as announced by the Supreme Court in *Marsh v. Alabama,* 326 U.S. 501. In *Marsh,* the Court held that even though the town in question was totally a company-owned town, the fact that it was wide open to public access, and contained all of the necessary adjuncts and amenities of an ordinary town, a person could not be denied the right guaranteed under the First Amendment of freedom of speech on the streets of the company town. Of course, the most obvious difference between this case and *Marsh* is that Disney World is not an open town fully accessible and available to all commerce. This private property is an amusement park to which admission is charged. Moreover, there is no showing that it has all of the facilities ordinarily identified with a community in which persons live and carry on their business. No one is permitted into the outer gates of Disney World except by consent of the owners.

If the owners of this amusement park impose in an illegal manner on their clientele, such imposition, if in violation of statutes forbidding trespass, assault, false arrest, or any other offense, would subject the owners to a civil suit on behalf of the injured person. Such illegal conduct would not, however, give them the protection of the Fourth Amendment and the exclusionary rule which has developed from it. The exclusionary rule, itself, was adopted by the courts because it was recognized that it was only by preventing the use of evidence illegally obtained by public officials that a curb should be put on over-zealous activities of such officials. The Supreme Court has in no instance indicated that it would apply the exclusionary rule to cases in which evidence has been obtained by private individuals in a manner not countenanced if they were acting for state or federal government.

We have considered the further objection that the trial court erred in not suppressing testimony of identification from the several witnesses because of what the appellants alleged to have been a suggestive presentation of photographs to the witnesses by the Secret Service agents. The trial court ruled on the evidence that the method by which several witnesses were shown the nine photographs containing those of the three defendants was "not suggestive, much less impermissibly suggestive." We do not find that determination by the trial court clearly erroneous.

The judgments are AFFIRMED.

CASE COMMENT

The court held that the amusement park was not an open town fully accessible and available to all commerce. The property was private because admission was charged, because there was no showing that it had all of the facilities ordinarily identified with a community in which persons live and carry on business, and because no one was permitted into the outer gates except by consent of the owners. The court also pointed out that should the owners of the park impose illegalities on their clientele, such as trespass, assault, or false arrest, they would be subject to civil suit, and this illegal conduct would not give those injured protection of the Fourth Amendment. The court reiterated the longstanding principle that constitutional sanctions are meant to curb public officials. Also note that when the security officer detained the men he identified himself and displayed his badge.

FOURTH AMENDMENT—APPLICATION TO PRIVATE SECURITY

The next case is somewhat unusual in that the court activated safeguards provided by the Fourth Amendment and made them applicable to private security suggesting that there are exceptions to the general rule that evidence obtained by a private individual pursuant to unlawful means need not be excluded. The rationale of the decision, while binding only in one county in one state, is what should be of interest to the security practitioner. Given the growth of the private security industry, the trend toward privatization of governmental activities, the gradual transfer of police tasks to private security, and continuing governmental budgetary problems, might not this decision be a forerunner of things to come? Security managers may want to determine if their security forces are solely in control and if, therefore, routine police patrols are not necessary, if citizens' privacy rights are increasingly jeopardized because their security staffs replace local law enforcement authorities, and if the security force is engaged in a public function.

PEOPLE v. STORMER
518 N.Y.S. 2d 351 (Co. Ct. 1987)

MOYNIHAN, Judge:

The defendant, is charged in a one count indictment with grand larceny in the third degree in violation of former subdivision 1 of Section 155.30 of the Penal Law, a class E felony. A "probable cause" hearing was scheduled to be held on July 7, 1987, before this Court. However, the defendant waived her right to said hearing and entered into a stipulation with the District Attorney by which it was agreed that the Court would determine whether certain evidence should be suppressed based solely upon its consideration of the minutes of the preliminary hearing, the minutes of the Grand Jury proceeding and other additional facts which were stipulated to orally on the scheduled hearing date.

Upon a review of all of the foregoing, this Court finds as follows: the defendant was at the time of the incident set forth in the indictment employed by the Sagamore Hotel (here-inafter "Sagamore") to perform essentially chambermaid-type duties. The Sagamore is a large resort hotel located on an island in Lake George known as Green Island which is in the Town of Bolton, and County of Warren. The only connection with the main land is a causeway between the Village of Bolton Landing and the Sagamore property on Green Island.

At the time of the incident in question, security personnel employed by the Sagamore were involved in an investigation of a series of thefts from guest rooms at the hotel. In an attempt to apprehend the individual or individuals involved, two members of the Sagamore security force placed the sum of $260.00 in a room to which this defendant was assigned for purposes of housekeeping. It is alleged that the defendant was seen entering the room in question. Subsequently, a check of the room revealed the money to be missing, and members of the Sagamore security force searched the defendant's automobile in her absence and without her knowledge or consent. As a result of the search, the $260.00 previously placed in the room was discovered in a paper bag. When confronted with this fact the defendant denied taking the money and further denied ever entering the room in question. She was detained by the Sagamore security officers until such time as she was placed in the custody of the Warren County Sheriff's Department. Of particular importance to this decision, this Court also finds that the Sagamore security force had, previous to this incident, advised personnel of the Warren County Sheriff's Department that routine patrols by them on Green Island were unnecessary and further that their presence on the island would be required only upon a special request. It is clear to this Court that the matter of hotel and island security was solely within the control of the hotel's private security force.

The defendant's attorney has moved to suppress the money which was allegedly discov-ered in the automobile on the grounds that the discovery was as a direct of an unreasonable search and seizure (U.S. Const., 4th Amend.; N.Y. Const., Art. I, Section 12), notwithstanding that it was made by a "private" security force. The People contend that the prohibitions regarding unlawful search and seizure "do not require exclusion of evidence because a private individual has gathered it by unlawful means" (*People v. Horman*, 239 N.E.2d 625; *People v. Gleeson*, 330 N.E.2d 72).

Despite considerable research the Court has been unable to find any precedent which deals specifically with the facts and circumstances present herein. However, given the proliferation in this country of privately-employed security personnel as a supplement to or, as in this case, a replacement for local law enforcement authorities, the privacy rights of a citizen of this State may be increasingly jeopardized.

As is suggested in a leading treatise on the subject of the exclusionary rule (LaFave, Search and Seizure, 1987 ed., Vol. 1, Section 1.8(d), p. 200), *Marsh v. Alabama*, 326 U.S. 501, supplies "a basis for holding that private investigators and police are subject to the Fourth Amendment because they are with some regularity engaged in the 'public function' of law enforcement." *Marsh* involved a company-owned town which had "all the characteristics of any other American town." It appears to this Court that there are considerable similarities between *Marsh* and the Sagamore insofar as the latter is also a self-contained and otherwise autonomous entity, the "operation of which is essentially a public function."

Professor LaFave further noted that it is necessary not only to make a threshold determination as to whether private police are engaged in a "public function" but also that "exclusion can be an effective deterrent only if two conditions are met: (i) 'the searcher must have a strong interest in obtaining convictions'; and (ii) 'the searcher must commit searches and seizures regularly in order to be familiar enough with the rules to adopt his methods to conform to them'" (quoting Stanford Law Review, Vol. 19, pp. 614–615). This Court finds that the Sagamore's private security force not only performs a "public function" but that said force falls within the parameters of the two criteria above-listed.

In a relatively recent case decided by the Supreme Court of California (*People v. Zelinski,* 594 P.2d 1000), which this Court finds particularly compelling, it was stated that "in any case where private security personnel assert the power of the state to make an arrest or to detain another person for transfer to custody of the state, the state involvement is sufficient for the court to enforce the proper exercise of that power by excluding the fruits of illegal abuse thereof." The *Zelinski* case involved department store detectives who performed a search of a suspected shoplifter. The court found that if "the security guards sought only vindication of the merchant's private interests they would have simply exercised self-help and demanded the return of the stolen merchandise [and that upon] satisfaction of the merchant's interest, the offender would have been released." By analogy to the facts herein, the Sagamore's interests could have been vindicated by the confiscation of the $260.00 from the defendant and the termination of her services. By going further and detaining her for eventual criminal process the Sagamore's security personnel were promoting society's interest and, as such, the safeguards provided by the Fourth Amendment were activated.

In *People v. Adler,* 409 N.E.2d 888, it was held that "private conduct may be so imbued with governmental involvement that it loses its character as such and calls into play the full panoply of Fourth Amendment protections". Furthermore, it has been held that merely "because a search was not conducted with police involvement, however, does not mean that the exclusionary rule arising from the Fourth Amendment does not apply" (*People v. Haskins,* 369 N.Y.S.2d 869). While this Court readily concedes that these two cases involved somewhat different circumstances, it suggests that there are exceptions to the general rule that evidence obtained by a private individual pursuant to unlawful means need not be excluded.

In conclusion, given the unique nature of the facts and circumstances present at the Sagamore, i.e., the operation of what amounts to a "public function", and the performance of their private security force in a manner which amounts to a "public function" (especially insofar as local law enforcement agencies are excluded except upon request), it is the carefully considered judgment of this Court that the seizure of the money was from the defendant's automobile was unlawful and, as such, is thus suppressed as unconstitutionally seized (U.S. Const., 4th Amend.; N.Y.Const., Art. 1, Section 12).

CASE COMMENT

The court found that the private security force not only performed a "public function" but also had a strong interest in obtaining convictions and committed searches and seizures regularly in order to be familiar enough with the rules to adopt methods to conform to them. By detaining the defendant for eventual criminal prosecution, security personnel were promoting society's interest that activated Fourth Amendment safeguards. As noted at the beginning of this case, the decision is binding only in one county. Is it not the job of the security manager, however, to look ahead and prognosticate what the future may hold so as to limit or prevent loss?

11

Interrogation by Private Citizen

The constitutional sanctions imposed by the Fifth Amendment (and the Miranda rule) against self-incrimination apply to sworn police officers and not to private citizens. They may also apply to those persons who are commissioned, deputized, or licensed. Information obtained in an interrogation by a private citizen security employee must be freely and voluntarily given. No pressures, force, duress, and/or coercion should be applied in an attempt to obtain information. If a confession is obtained by private security personnel in a custodial situation with more than minimal or peripheral police participation, the security personnel may be found to have acted as an extension of the police, and the confession could be suppressed. The security manager should also be aware that, in some instances, an employee has the right to union representation if that employee is called in for an interview where the employee reasonably believes the investigation will result in disciplinary action.

MANTLE OF STATE AUTHORITY

An important principle of law is brought out in the following case in what appears to be a simple shoplifting case. A private security guard observed a shopper place several items in his pocket and did not see the shopper present or pay for the items. After identifying herself to the shopper as a security guard, she accompanied the shopper inside to the security office. She ordered him to remove the items from his pocket. She then read him his rights from a form and asked him to sign a waiver. The shopper refused to sign the waiver and said that he wanted the assistance of his lawyer. The security guard refused the request and called the state police. Later, and before he was taken into custody by the state police, he signed the waiver and completed a questionnaire, which elicited incriminating statements. The shopper was convicted at a jury trial. The security manager must be concerned with not only federal sanctions, but also with state constitutional sanctions. Under this state's constitution, once a person has exercised his state constitutional rights, those in whose custody he is held must scrupulously honor that priviledge.

STATE v. MUEGGE
360 S.E. 2d 216 (1987)

McGRAW, Chief Justice:

This is an appeal by William Hubert Muegge from a final judgment order entered in the Circuit Court of Marshall County following a jury verdict finding him guilty of shoplifting in violation of West Virginia Code § 61–3A–3(a)(1). We reverse the conviction and remand the case to the circuit court because evidence obtained from the appellant and used against him at trial was improperly admitted.

On September 29, 1984, the appellant, who was then the mayor of Wheeling, West Virginia, was shopping at Rink's Department Store in Benwood, a town located a few miles south of Wheeling. The private security guard employed by the store noticed the appellant placing several items of merchandise in his pockets during the course of his shopping. She continued to observe him as he went through the checkout aisle and did not see him present or pay for those items. The security guard approached the appellant as he left the store, identified herself, and asked to speak with the appellant inside the store, adding, "I will do things for you the easy way or the hard way."

The appellant accompanied the security guard and the assistant store manager to the security office just before three o'clock in the afternoon. That office is a windowless room measuring about four feet by ten feet, and does not contain a telephone. The security guard ordered the appellant to empty his pockets, which contained several unpaid for items valued at a total of $10.65. She then informed the appellant that she was going to read him his rights and proceeded to read aloud from a prepared form labeled "constitutional rights." She then asked the appellant to sign a waiver of his constitutional rights.

The appellant refused to sign the proffered waiver form and told the security guard that he wanted the assistance of his lawyer. The security guard refused the appellant's request and instead said, "I will call the state police. We will wait until they get here and we will take care of it from there." The appellant asked her not to call the state police and asked to see the store manager so that something could be worked out. The security guard refused to allow the appellant to talk to the store manager and went into an adjacent office to summon a member of the state police.

At this point, the evidence presented at trial is in conflict. The security guard's testimony was to the effect that nothing else occurred until the state police trooper arrived. She said that she informed the trooper that the appellant was not cooperating by refusing to answer any of her questions. She testified that the appellant then changed his mind and agreed to sign the waiver. She said she again read the appellant his rights, in the presence of the trooper. After signing the waiver, the appellant completed a "questionnaire" which elicited various incriminating statements from the appellant.[1] The security guard, with appellant's assistance, also completed an "apprehension report."

The state trooper's testimony varied significantly from the security guard's. He testified that the waiver was already signed and the questionnaire completed before he arrived at 3:18 p.m. He denied that the security guard ever told him that the appellant was refusing to

---

[1]For example, one question asked that an x be placed at the appropriate answer:

I took the merchandise without paying because:

I thought I could get away with it	_____
The value seemed small	_____
I didn't have sufficient money	_____
Others have done it	_____
Other reason(s)	_____

cooperate and he denied that the security guard read the constitutional rights form in his presence. He did, however, testify that he never explained these rights to the appellant, relying on his understanding that the security guard had already done so. The trooper left with the appellant in custody at 3:41 p.m.

At trial, the unpaid for items were admitted without objection while the questionnaire was read aloud to the jury and entered into evidence over the defendant's objection. The jury returned a guilty verdict and this appeal is from the ensuing sentence imposing a fine on the appellant and assessing a civil penalty in favor of the department store.

The appellant's primary contention before this Court is that his detention by the security guard was of such a nature as to require application of federal and state constitutional protections against compelled self-incrimination. The appellee responds that the appellant's detention did not trigger any constitutional safeguards and, alternatively, argues that the appellant waived any applicable privileges.

I.

In detaining the appellant, the security guard acted pursuant to West Virginia Code § 61–3A–4. That statute reads, in its entirety:

> An act of shoplifting as defined herein, is hereby declared to constitute a breach of peace and any owner of merchandise, his agent or employee, or any law-enforcement officer who has reasonable ground to believe that a person has committed shoplifting, may detain such person in a reasonable manner and for a reasonable length of time not to exceed thirty minutes, for the purpose of investigating whether or not such person has committed or attempted to commit shoplifting. Such reasonable detention shall not constitute an arrest nor shall it render the owner of merchandise, his agent or employee, liable to the person detained.

The primary purpose of this statute is to temper the common law's harsh rule of civil liability in actions for false imprisonment. At common law, a merchant detaining someone he suspected of stealing his goods was subject to liability if it turned out the accused party was not guilty. Numerous legislatures and courts have modified the original rule so as to protect the merchant from liability so long as he acts on reasonable grounds and in a reasonable fashion. Thus, the propriety of a West Virginia merchant's detention of a possible shoplifter is no longer dependent on a finding that the suspect was actually guilty.

In the context of this case, an arrest is the "detaining of the person of another . . . by any act or speech that indicates an intention to take him into custody and that subjects him to the actual control and will of the person making the arrest." Under the common law, a private citizen is authorized to arrest another who commits a misdemeanor in his presence when that misdemeanor constitutes a breach of the peace. 5 Am. Jur. 2d *Arrest* § 34. The impact of the West Virginia statute is to modify the common law rule regarding any subsequent liability, however, the statute cannot make an arrest into something else by refusing to call it an arrest.[2]

The question presented us is whether the appellant's arrest by the security guard activates constitutional protections. We initially examine the appellant's right, under article three, section six of the West Virginia Constitution, to be free from unreasonable searches

---

[2]"The distinction between the merchant's power to 'detain,' the terminology used in most statutes, and his power to arrest is artificial." Wm. Ringel, *Searches & Seizures, Arrests and Confessions* § 23.8(c) (1986).

and seizures. Next, our analysis concentrates on article three, section five of our constitution and appellant's right not to be compelled to be a witness against himself.

This Court has held that the proscription on unreasonable searches and seizures does not apply to private individuals unless they are acting as instruments or agents of the state. In the instant case, however, we find that the security guard was not acting in a purely private fashion, but under the mantle of state authority and that, therefore, the protections of article three, section six of the West Virginia Constitution apply to her dealings with the appellant.

While we recognize that some jurisdictions have refused to invoke constitutional protections in searches by privately employed security officers, we think the better rule is that such protections apply when the security officers act pursuant to statutory authority.

Private security forces today play an increasing role in the enforcement of our criminal laws, a traditional state function. A federal study shows that about one-half of the persons employed fighting crime in this country, or more than one million persons, are employed by the private sector. Private security police regularly investigate criminal activity and often play a role which goes beyond the protection of their employer's property interests.

The unfettered conduct of private security personnel presents a threat to the rights of our citizens which is equivalent to any unlawful conduct of public police officers, and the application of constitutional protections to their conduct should have a deterrent effect on the unlawful practices of these security personnel. *Zelinski*, 594 P.2d at 1005. Therefore we hold that the proscription against unreasonable searches and seizures found in article three, section six of the West Virginia Constitution applies when a citizen has been detained pursuant to statutory authority, as in this case.

The rule is clearly established in West Virginia that

> Searches conducted outside the judicial process, without prior approval by judge or magistrate, are *per se* unreasonable under the Fourth Amendment and Article III, Section 6 of the West Virginia Constitution—subject only to a few specifically established and well-delineated exceptions. The exceptions are jealously and carefully drawn, and there must be a showing by those who seek exemption that the exingencies of the situation made that course imperative.

State v. Moore, 272 S.E.2d 804. Further, "the burden rests on the State to show by a preponderance of the evidence that the warrantless search falls within an authorized exception."

When the security guard ordered the appellant to empty his pockets, she conducted a search, because a demand to disclose or produce concealed objects is treated as a search for purposes of constitutional analysis. A warrantless search of the person and the immediate area under his control is authorized incident to a valid arrest, *Moore*, 272 S.E.2d 804, but such a search is only permissible when it is necessary to uncover weapons that might be used against the arresting officer or to prevent destruction of evidence by the arrested party. *State v. Cook*, 332 S.E.2d 147. No showing has been made by the State that the search by the security guard was necessary for either of these reasons, or that the evidence should have been admitted under any other exception to the warrantless search prohibition. On remand, the items taken from the appellant should be admitted only if the state can meet its burden of proving the security guard's search falls within an authorized exception to the general rule.

III.

We next turn to the appellant's contention that the circuit court erred when it admitted into evidence the incriminating statements made by the appellant on the questionnaire. As noted earlier, article three, section five of the West Virginia Constitution provides that no person may be compelled to be a witness against himself in any criminal case. We have held that this constitutional section provides at least co-equal coverage as does the fifth amendment to the United States Constitution, and its scope is to be liberally interpreted. *State v. Burton*, 254 S.E.2d 129.

In the landmark case of *Miranda v. Arizona*, 384 U.S. 436, the United States Supreme Court held that, whenever a person is subject to custodial interrogation, certain procedural safeguards must be employed to protect the privilege against self-incrimination. Thus, a suspect must be warned of his constitutional rights and the "opportunity to exercise these rights must be afforded to him throughout the interrogation." This Court has adopted the reasoning of *Miranda* and has gone on to expand its protections. *State v. Hamrick*, 236 S.E.2d 247. It is clear that once a person has exercised his rights under article three, section five of the West Virginia Constitution, those in whose custody he is held must scrupulously honor that privilege.

While no constitutional warnings are required to establish the admissibility of purely private conversations,[3] for the reasons analogous to those expressed in part II of this opinion, we hold that the procedural safeguards protecting the constitutional right not to be compelled to be a witness against oneself in a criminal case apply whenever a citizen is subject to custodial interrogation pursuant to statutory authority. Thus, it was error for the circuit court to admit the questionnaire over the appellant's objection, because that evidence was obtained after the appellant had refused to waive his constitutional rights and had clearly stated his desire for legal counsel. Contrary to the assertion by the appellee that the appellant voluntarily waived any constitutional rights, it is clear that only the security guard's refusal to allow the appellant to exercise his rights resulted in the appellant's subsequent admissions. This is precisely the sort of abuse this Court was concerned about. On remand, the questionnaire should not be admitted into evidence.

IV.

Appellant's assignment of error regarding the circuit court's failure to direct a verdict of not guilty is summarily made and may be summarily disposed of. We have refused to adopt the appellee's contention that the appellant waived his constitutional rights, and the appellant has not made a showing that he was entitled to a directed verdict based on the sufficiency of the evidence.

Because evidence obtained from the appellant and used against him at trial was improperly admitted, the appellant's conviction is reversed and the case remanded to the circuit court.

Reversed and remanded.

CASE COMMENT

The security guard acted pursuant to the state code in detaining the shopper for the purpose of investigating the alleged shoplifting. The statute authorizing *detention* did not make the arrest into something else by refusing to call it an arrest. The distinction in the terminology between power to detain and power to arrest is artificial. The state constitution provides that no person may be compelled to be a witness against himself in any criminal prosecution. The appellate courts in this state have held that the state

---

[3]Defendants may, however, raise the issue of whether a statement made to a private party was voluntary.

constitutional protection provides at least co-equal coverage as the Fifth Amendment and that its scope is to be liberally interpreted. Since it was a custodial interrogation it was error for the trial court to admit the questionnaire as it was obtained from the shopper after he refused to waive his rights and had clearly stated his desire for legal counsel. The abuse was the guard's refusal to allow the shopper to exercise his rights. The liberal interpretation of the state constitution includes the scrupulous honoring of the procedural safeguards.

JOINT OPERATION

Normally private security personnel are not subject to *Miranda* warning requirements (Fifth Amendment). But there are circumstances when *Miranda* applies to private security such as in the following case. Store security personnel, suspecting a shoplifting incident, alerted police who watched the suspect for a short time and then left. Later, store security watched the suspect take six coats and leave the store at which time they stopped him and notified the police. Store security recovered the coats and one of the arriving police officers identified himself as a police officer. All accompanied the suspect back to the store security office. The police stayed outside while the store detectives questioned him. The suspect signed a form confession, and he was turned over to the police for prosecution. It was conceded that neither the police or the store detectives informed him he had a right to remain silent or to consult with an attorney. The Court of Appeals suppressed the confession because it was obtained without advising the defendant of his rights even though the police were not inside the store security office. This case discusses the amount or degree of joint security–police participation required which will cause Fifth Amendment requirements to be attached to private security activity.

PEOPLE v. JONES
393 N.E. 2d 443 (1979)

WACHTLER, Judge.

The question on this appeal concerns the admissibility of a confession obtained without *Miranda* warnings by private store detectives who took the defendant into custody, with assistance from county police officers, and questioned him in the store's security office while the police officers waited outside. The County Court held the statement was admissible and, following a jury trial, the defendant was convicted of grand larceny in the third degree. But a majority at the Appellate Division reversed, suppressed the confession and ordered a new trial. The prosecutor now appeals to our court.

On the afternoon of August 28, 1975 two Nassau County police officers, who were assigned to patrol a Valley Stream shopping center in plainclothes, entered Gimbel's Department Store. They were informed by the store's security personnel that a man was then under observation in the men's clothing department. Security officers in the men's department pointed out the defendant to the police but indicated that they did not "have anything yet". The police officers watched the defendant for 5 or 10 minutes without incident and then left the store.

Soon after the defendant took a pair of wire clippers, cut the chains that ran through the sleeves of six leather coats, placed the coats in a plastic bag and proceeded to leave the store. This was observed by members of the store's security staff who followed the defendant while one of the security guards went to find the police officers. The guard informed the police officers that store personnel were about to stop someone and that their assistance was needed.

The defendant was stopped outside the store by security officers who identified themselves and took the coats. When the police arrived one of the security officers was holding the defendant against the wall attempting to handcuff him. As the defendant stepped away from the wall one of the police officers placed his hand on the defendant's shoulder, showed the defendant his badge, identified himself as a police officer and told the defendant to stand there or keep his hands on the wall. The defendant was then handcuffed and brought back to the store's security office by the police and the store personnel. The policemen left the defendant at the security office and waited outside the door while the store detectives questioned him. This apparently was the "normal procedure".

Inside the office the defendant was handcuffed to a desk, by one hand, and was asked to sign various items by the security officers. He was given a form confession with his name, address, a description of the stolen property and the date added and was asked to sign it if he understood it. He signed this form and another one by which he agreed not to enter the store for a three-year period. He also signed photographs of the stolen coats and the wire clippers. When this paper work was completed, the store detectives turned the defendant over to the police officers for criminal prosecution. It is conceded that neither the police nor the store detectives had previously informed the defendant that he had a right to remain silent or to consult with an attorney.

In *Miranda v. Arizona*, 384 U.S. 436, the Supreme Court held that "the prosecution may not use statements, whether exculpatory or inculpatory, stemming from custodial interrogation of the defendant unless it demonstrates the use of procedural safeguards effective to secure the privilege against self-incrimination." The court defined custodial interrogation as "questioning initiated by law enforcement officers after a person has been taken into custody or otherwise deprived of his freedom of action in any significant way." The People contend that in this case it was not necessary to advise the defendant of his rights or to employ other procedural safeguards because the defendant was taken into custody and questioned by private store detectives, and not by police officers.

By statute, store detectives and other employees of retail stores are empowered to arrest or detain individuals suspected of shoplifting (General Business Law, § 218). Like police officers they are relieved of civil liability for false arrest if they can show reasonable grounds for the suspicion (*Jacques v. Sears, Roebuck & Co.*, 285 N.E.2d 871). Nevertheless in exercising this authority store employees are generally held to act as private individuals and not as police officers or State officials (*People v. Horman*, 239 N.E.2d 625; but see *People v. Smith*, 368 N.Y.S.2d 954, holding that store detectives in New York City who are appointed by municipal officials as "special patrolmen" are governmental agents for Fourth Amendment purposes).

It is settled that an unauthorized search or seizure by private individuals, including store detectives, does not render the evidence inadmissible at subsequent civil or criminal proceedings (*Burdeau v. McDowell*, 256 U.S. 465). This is so, the cases hold, because the Fourth Amendment is meant to regulate government activity; the unauthorized act of a private person does not violate the constitutional limitations. That, at least, has been the rule when the individual has acted entirely on his own "without the participation or knowledge of any governmental official."

The government, of course, cannot avoid constitutional restrictions by using a private individual as its agent (see, e.g., *People v. Esposito*, 332 N.E.2d 863; CPL 710.20, subd. 2), nor can it claim that only a private act is involved when government officers, subject to constitutional limitations, have participated in the act (see, e.g., *Lustig v. United States*, 338 U.S. 74). Under such circumstances the constitutional restrictions on governmental activity cannot be said to be inapplicable.

In this case the People recognize that the store detectives did not act entirely on their own. The People claim however that there was no need to advise the defendant of his rights because the police participation was "minimal" or "peripheral".

In order to properly assess the significance of the police participation in this case it must be borne in mind that the purpose of the *Miranda* rule—the requirement that the defendant be advised of his rights before being questioned—is "to dispel the compulsion inherent in custodial surroundings." It is, of course, intended to regulate police conduct and here the People note that the defendant was "initially" taken into custody by the store detectives, and that the police did not take an active part in obtaining the confession or the defendant's signature on the photographs. But the police were not merely anonymous observers. They actively participated in the arrest, one of them clearly identified himself to the defendant and both of them escorted the defendant to the place where he was interrogated while they awaited the outcome of the questioning. Although the store detectives who actually obtained the confession and other items may not have acted as police agents, the participation by the police was sufficient to create the type of custodial atmosphere which the *Miranda* rule was intended to alleviate.[2] Thus the confession and the signed photographs, obtained without advising the defendant of his rights, should be suppressed.

The People argue, in the alternative, that the confession and the photographs, if erroneously admitted, were harmless beyond a reasonable doubt. They claim that even without the confession, the eyewitness testimony of the security officers presented "overwhelming and conclusive" evidence of the defendant's guilt. Undoubtedly the People's case was strong, but apparently not so strong that they felt they could do without the defendant's confession at the trial. Indeed nothing could be more conclusive evidence of the defendant's guilt than a signed confession, significantly, during summation the prosecutor argued that the confession corroborated the eyewitness accounts. And while deliberating the jury made an inquiry concerning the confession. Thus on the record it cannot be said that "there is no reasonable possibility that the error in admitting the confession might have contributed to defendant's conviction."

Accordingly, the order of the Appellate Division should be affirmed.

CASE COMMENT

Private security store personnel are generally not held to act as police officers or state officials unless appointed by government as governmental agents. The Fourth and Fifth Amendments are meant to regulate government activity. The government cannot avoid constitutional restrictions by using private individuals as its agents, nor can it claim an act as private when government officers have participated in the act. Minimal or peripheral police participation, not merely anonymous observation, may trigger constitutional sanctions. Here police identification and escorting to the store security office was sufficient participation to create the type of custodial atmosphere which the *Miranda* rule was intended to alleviate. The security manager should be aware of the amount, type, and degree of police participation, if any, with members of the security staff so as to insure that appropriate safeguards are invoked.

---

[2]In light of this disposition there is no need to consider the defendant's alternative arguments (1) that store security officers should be considered police officers where they exercise their special powers to *interrogate* those suspected of shoplifting (General Business Law, § 218) or (2) that the presence of the police at the scene would be sufficient State action even if they were only standing idly by.

PUBLIC INTEREST/PUBLIC FUNCTION/
PUBLIC ACCOMMODATION

In this case a hospital security officer was instructed by his supervisor to go to the hospital parking lot and locate a certain auto reportedly containing a handgun. He was also told the police had been notified and would arrive shortly. The security officer located the car and gun inside the car and radioed his supervisor who told him the police would be on the scene. The security officer checked the door to the auto and found it locked. The defendant, also a hospital security officer, arrived and saw the responding security officer standing by his auto. The security officer asked the defendant if the auto was his; the defendant replied that it was. The defendant voluntarily unlocked his auto, handed the gun to the responding security officer, and left the scene. The police arrived and the security officer reported his findings and gave them the gun. The defendant returned and was arrested by the police for possessing a handgun without a permit. The question in this case is whether the hospital security officer was acting in a private capacity or as an operative of the police (coordinated venture). Note the sympathy of the court to the early warning decisions placing security guards within the ambit of constitutional sanctions. The court was of the opinion that there was a private-public law enforcement investigation of a crime incident that triggered the application of the public accommodation test.

PEOPLE v. ELLIOTT
501 N.Y.S.2d 265 (1986)

WILLIAM D. FRIEDMANN, Justice.

Defendant, charged with possession of a handgun without a permit, seeks suppression of that gun seized by a private hospital security officer, and certain inculpatory statements made to the security officer and later to the New York City Police.

A so-called *Mapp-Huntley* hearing, conducted on November 13, 1985, places into focus seldom considered but critical questions as to whether the seizure of the gun in the hospital parking lot by the private security officer was subject to federal-state constitutional scrutiny, and whether the verbal and non-verbal encounter between the defendant (also a hospital security officer), the responding security officer and the New York City Police Officers, took place in a custodial environment requiring the administration of *Miranda* safeguards (warnings) *(Miranda v. Arizona*, 384 U.S. 436).

Relevant Facts

Fiore Papa, a security officer (this court takes judicial notice that Papa was a retired member of the New York City Police Department) at the Long Island Jewish Hospital, was instructed by his security supervisor, via radio transmission, to proceed to the Schneider's Children's Hospital parking lot (also part of the same hospital complex). He was told to locate a certain auto reportedly containing a handgun. He was also informed that the New York City Police Department had been notified and would arrive shortly. When he located the auto, he observed the handgun in a holster on the front seat. He immediately radioed his supervisor who replied, "the police will be on the scene." The security officer checked the auto door and found it locked. The defendant, Charles Elliott, himself a security officer at Schneider's Children's Hospital, arrived on the scene and saw the responding uniformed security officer standing by his auto. Defendant, without prodding, told the security officer that the auto was his. He then opened the auto door and gave the gun to the security officer. Defendant then left the scene. The New York City police arrived within minutes, and the responding security officer reported his findings and handed the gun to the police. Defendant then returned to the scene. New York City Police Officer Richard Rudakiewich asked defendant if the auto was his; defendant replied affirmatively. Rudakiewich then asked defendant if he had a permit for the gun. Defendant replied he did not. The police officer then placed the defendant under arrest. While in a police car on the way to the police station defendant was read his *Miranda* warnings. He then told Officer Rudakiewich that he had gotten the gun down south.

Contentions of the Parties

The prosecution contends that any action by the hospital security officer is not subject to constitutional scrutiny under either the United States or New York State Constitutions. It is further contended that even if the action of the security officer was subject to constitutional scrutiny, that the result should still be a denial of suppression of the gun and statements made to the private security officer and to the New York City Police (both before and after *Miranda* warnings).

Defendant, in support of his suppression application, contends that the seizure of the gun by the hospital security officer, and the pre-*Miranda* statements made by him to the security officer, and to the New York City Police were made while he was under custodial restraint. That the post *Miranda* statement to the city police was improperly obtained, as it was not proceeded by probable cause to arrest.

Are the Actions of the Private Security Officer Subject to Constitutional Restraints?

In order to determine the propriety of the seizure of the gun by the hospital security officer and the reception of the statements made in connection therewith (in the hospital parking lot), this court must initially address whether the hospital security officer was acting in a private capacity or as an operative of the Police Department. This preliminary inquiry is necessary as generally statements made to private individuals, or an unauthorized search or seizure by such persons, does not render that evidence inadmissible, at a subsequent law enforcement proceeding.

Modern Development of Private Security

The modern development of private security challenges some of our most fundamental legal and constitutional concepts. Such concern is illustrated by the increasing number of businesses, governmental agencies, neighborhoods and individuals that are giving private security entities a new role that spills over into public law enforcement areas.

In a recent New York Times article, "Private Guards Get New Role in Public Law Enforcement" (November 29, 1985, p. 1 col. 4), we are acquainted with the fact that in the United States approximately 1.1 million private security guards are not only performing traditional security functions, i.e., the protection of property, but also assuming traditional police functions for private entities as well as for federal, state and local government authorities around the country.

According to the National Institute of Justice, the number of security guards has increased by 50 percent over the last ten years, and there are indications projecting an even further expansion, for example, there exists grave concern about the ability of many police departments to competently investigate the technical complexities of corporate crime, computer crime, as well as commercial bribery and/or industrial espionage, etc.

In summary, officials of the private security industry say their services save money and get around "red tape." However, critics of this rapid extension of private security into both the private and public sectors point to less strict training programs for those in private security, as compared to those for official police officers, the general nonexistence of regulation of the private security industry, and the fact that private security officers and personnel are not subject to the same constitutional scrutiny and control as public officers.

The popular press, as well as legal periodicals, are now discussing the problems posed by the fear of crime, the proliferation of private forms of security measure to protect against crime, and the fact that society has a legitimate interest in being safeguarded from potential abuses posed by private protectors or enforcers. In spite of this growing interest, very few courts to date have addressed the question whether private security personnel must give *Miranda* warnings to suspects whom they are questioning, and/or must they observe other constitutional restraints with respect to identification, search and seizure, etc. (Safe Customers Now Duty of Security Guards, Los Angeles Daily Journal, December 4, 1984, p. 1, col. 3; No Warning Needed From Guards, Los Angeles Daily Journal, November 6, 1981, p. 1 col. 1; Reality and Illusion: Defining Private Security Law in Ohio, 13 Toledo Law Review 377 [Winter-1982]; the *Miranda* Policies and Requirements as They Relate to Department Store Detectives, 9 Pepperdine Law Review, vol. 9, No. 4 [1982] 1015; The Quiet Revolution: The Nature, Development and General Legal Implications of Private Security in Canada [Stenning and Shearing] Criminal Law Quarterly 220 [March, 1980]; *People v. Zelinski:* State Action and Constraints on Store Detectives, 3 Criminal Justice Journal 489 [Spring, 1980]).

Miranda Safeguards

No decision more rightly deserves the label "Landmark" than *Miranda v. Arizona (supra).* Its name echoes daily in almost every criminal courtroom across the United States. It has, without question, drastically impacted law enforcement for the past 20 years. In summary, it was intended to place realistic teeth into the Fifth Amendment privilege against compulsory self-incrimination.

Miranda's main thrust was directed at the use by law enforcement agencies of statements, whether exculpatory or inculpatory, which stem from the custodial interrogation of a defendant, unless there be a demonstration that effective procedural safeguards were used to secure a defendant's privilege against self-incrimination.

Application of *Miranda* to Private Law Enforcement Personnel

The Fifth Amendment privilege against compulsory self-incrimination, which the *Miranda* safeguards were designed to protect, has been very cautiously applied to situations not involving interrogation by official law enforcement personnel.

The majority of state courts, which have considered the application of *Miranda* to private security personnel, have held that *Miranda* only applies to official law enforcement agents, and does not apply to interrogations by private security personnel. In the view of this court, this position grants to these privately employed, and often illtrained individuals, great and undoubtedly unsupervised powers.

Recently, however, a few courts have acknowledged the real impact upon the public interest of private security employees, and the potential dangers which can result from their rising importance in crime prevention and detection (see *People v. Zelinski*, 594 P.2d 1000, rev'd by *People v. Geary*, 219 Cal. Rptr. 557, California Grand District Court of Appeals, Los Angeles Daily Journal, October 31, 1985, p. 19, col. 1; *United States v. Lima*, 47 U.S.L.W. 2696 (holding store security guard subject to Fourth Amendment exclusionary rule because of its deterrent effect on guard abuses of authority and because store guards perform a public function), rev'd, 424 A.2d 113; *State v. Brecht*, 485 P.2d 47, (Fourth Amendment protects a person's right to privacy and is violated whether the intrusion is governmental or private).

As a result of these early warning decisions, there are already predictions within the private security industry that similar rulings will be adopted in other jurisdictions. Some members of the security industry have even recommended that private security employees act as if these rules were already in effect in their jurisdiction, to assure that the evidence they obtain is admissible in court.

This court finds itself in sympathy with those courts which have expressed concern. It has previously held private security guards subject to constitutional scrutiny. Such has been decision of this court in a case where the issue was private lineup identification (*People v. Martinez*, N.Y. L.J., July 6, 1984, p. 15, col. 1). These few concerned courts have fashioned a realistic "public function or acting in the public interest test" which maintains that where organized and structured private security entities or agents assert the power of the state to investigate or make an arrest, or detain persons for subsequest transfer of custody to the state, or subsequent state law enforcement and the state has acquiesced or allowed such use of public power, such private organized action, in contemplation of state involvement, is sufficient to enable a court to apply constitutional restraints as called for by *Miranda*, etc. no extended coverage would affect truly private actions of private individuals acting in private capacities.

The New York Court of Appeals has, on several recent occasions, outlined its views concerning the sufficiency of state-private involvement necessary to triggering the observance of *Miranda* safeguards. That court has set down what may be termed a public accommodation test which must be applied here.

In *People v. Ray*, 480 N.E.2d 1065 the status of the law in New York was succinctly digested:

> "The avowed purpose of *Miranda* was to secure the privilage against self-incrimination from encroachment by governmental action. In the absence of active governmental participation in a private investigation, no *Miranda* warnings need be administered. Private conduct, however, may become so pervaded by governmental involvement that it loses its character as such and invokes the full panoply of constitutional protections. (*People v. Jones*, 393 N.E.2d 443). Relevant indicia of State involvement which may transform private conduct into State action, include: a clear connection between the police and the private investigation; completion of the private act at the instigation of the police; close supervision of the private conduct by the police; and a private act undertaken on behalf of the police to further a police objective."

Here, there was, in the opinion of this court, coordinated private-public law enforcement involving the investigation of a crime incident. The parking lot investigation and response here, by the hospital security officer, did accommodate police objectives. It should be contrasted with the traditional role of protecting hospital property or keeping order within the hospital, etc. A gun was sighted in an auto in the hospital parking lot. The hospital security department was notified and it, in turn, notified the city police. The security supervisor radioed a security officer to investigate the scene. The investigating officer was told that the New York City police had already been notified and would arrive shortly. Upon finding the gun in the auto, the security officer was informed again by his supervisor that "the police will be on the scene." Further investigation by the security officer revealed that the auto door was locked. The defendant arrived around that time, and the security officer asked defendant if the auto was his. Defendant replied that it was. Defendant then voluntarily unlocked the auto and handed the security officer the gun. Moments later the police arrived and the security officer turned over the gun.

Application of *Miranda* Tests to the Parking Lot Confrontation

Having found that this encounter constitutes coordinated law enforcement, which accommodated and furthered police objectives, it becomes necessary to apply *Miranda* standards to this parking lot confrontation.

The following inquiries must be made: Was the parking lot setting that kind of custodial environment proscribed by *Miranda?* Was the security officer's single question about the auto's ownership, and defendant's verbal and nonverbal response thereto, exempted from the necessity of *Miranda* safeguards? Were the limited on-the-scene questions by the New York City Police as to auto ownership and gun permit exempted from *Miranda?* Was the post-*Miranda* question and response contaminated?

Before such exploration, it would be useful to recall that *Miranda* was clearly directed at custodial interrogation, that is, on a case-by-case analysis, where one is in custody, where he is deprived of his freedom of action in any significant way. *Miranda* was not meant to preclude police from carrying out their traditional investigatory function of investigating crime, including general on-the-scene questioning as to the facts surrounding a crime, and *Miranda* did not in any way bar volunteered statements of any kind.

The sole question asked by the hospital security officer regarding the auto's ownership was made openly in an on-the-scene setting, i.e., a hospital parking lot open to the public. Such type of confrontation does not approach the custodial environment or atmosphere envisioned by *Miranda*.

Further, the limited routine questions, although having the potential of producing an incriminating statement from a suspect, does not appear to be "interrogation" as that term was addressed in *Miranda*.

Defendant's affirmative response concerning the auto's ownership and his opening of the car and his turning the gun over to the security officer, for whatever assigned reason, whether defendant was naive or trying to curry favor or understanding, etc., appears to have been voluntarily made and thereby exempted from *Miranda* requirements.

In concluding (1) that the parking lot setting was not of a custodial character, and (2) that the security officer's inquiry was of a routine investigatory nature, and (3) that defendant's response was voluntarily made, this court notes that the defendant himself was a security guard at the same hospital. He should have been aware of the lack of custodial restraint concerning the confrontation in the parking lot, as he was allowed to leave the parking lot scene prior to the arrival of the city police. For the purpose of determining when *Miranda* safeguards are required, i.e., when a custodial setting is in effect, which deprives freedom of action in any significant way, it is not a suspect's objective belief that is determinative, but rather that of the perverbial reasonable man, innocent of any crime; what he would have thought had he been in the suspect's shoes. In applying this test, this court concludes that defendant's contention of being under custodial restraint was not substantiated by the facts, nor by what a reasonable man, innocent of any crime, would have thought.

Pre-*Miranda* Statements to Police

With respect to defendant's parking lot statements to the New York City Police, this court, for the reasons stated above, with respect to statements made to the private security officer, also finds that these limited and routine inquiries and responses thereto are exempt from the necessity of *Miranda* safeguards.

When the New York City police arrived on the scene, they were handed the gun by the security officer. The New York City Police Officer asked the defendant the following questions: Was the auto his? Was this his handgun? Did he have a permit for the gun? This questioning represents routine investigative inquiries necessary in ascertaining facts. According to this court, these inquiries are specifically exempted from *Miranda* requirements. *Miranda* excludes "general on-the-scene questioning as to facts surrounding a crime or other questioning of citizens in the fact-finding process." Defendant's responsive on-the-scene statements were the product of a routine on-the-scene fact-finding inquiry. Until defendant's responses were made, he was not in custody and any of his statements were voluntarily made. The court notes that when the officer received affirmative replies to his routine inquiries, he arrested the defendant, placed him in the police car and read him his *Miranda* safeguards.

Defendant's statement, after receiving his *Miranda* warnings, about having gotten the gun down south, does not seem improper or contaminated in any way as it was proceeded by probable cause to arrest.

Seizure of Gun by Private Security Officer

Having determined that the hospital security officer was involved in a coordinated law enforcement objective with the New York City Police, and therefore his behavior must stand the muster of constitutional scrutiny, we now must examine the defendant's turning over of the gun to him.

Based upon the *Miranda* discussion concerning voluntarily made statements, etc., this court concludes that the seizure of the gun from the auto in the parking lot after the car was opened by defendant, was made with defendant's full consent. That the consent to the search and seizure by the security officer was given fully and voluntarily in all respects, and the seizure by the security officer was made incidental to defendant's lawful arrest by the police.

Conclusions

Under circumstances evidencing a simple and brief but coordinated police-private investigation venture, involving hospital security officers and the New York City Police Department, this court concludes that the action by the hospital security officer should be subject to federal-state constitutional scrutiny.

Even though this action is found subject to constitutional scrutiny, it is determined by a showing of clear and convincing evidence, that the seizure of the gun by the hospital security officer was not improper, but rested upon defendant's consent freely and voluntarily made, and was incidental to a lawful arrest made shortly after seizure by the New York City Police. It is further determined, beyond a reasonable doubt, that the limited on-the-scene investigatory questions (one by the security officer and three by the New York City Police) and defendant's responses thereto, were voluntarily made within the meaning of CPL 60.45 and were not made in a custodial setting or under other circumstances requiring the administration of *Miranda* warnings. Further, that the post-*Miranda* question and response was properly made and was proceeded by probable cause to arrest.

Accordingly, the motions to suppress physical evidence and statement are hereby denied.

CASE COMMENT

This case placed into focus the critical question of whether the hospital private security officer was subject to constitutional scrutiny regarding the seizure of the gun and the verbal and non-verbal encounter with the defendant in an alleged custodial environment. Before making a determination, the court took note of the development of, and the new role of, private security that spills over into the area of public law enforcement. Private security not only performs traditional security functions but is also assuming traditional police functions. Of concern to the court was the general nonexistence of regulation of the private security industry and the fact that private security personnel are not subject to the same constitutional scrutiny as are public officers. Decisions such as *Miranda* were intended to put realistic teeth into the Fifth Amendment privilege against compulsory self-incrimination and have been cautiously applied to situations not involving law enforcement personnel. This court found itself in sympathy with those few courts that have held private security subject to constitutional scrutiny where they have asserted the power of the state or where the state has acquiesed or allowed the use of such power. In this state-private involvement, private security functions as does the public, acts in public interests, or accommodates the public. Private conduct may become so pervaded by governmental involvement that it loses its character as such and invokes the full panoply of constitutional protections. Indicia of state involvement that may transform private conduct into state action include:

   A clear connection between the police and the private investigation
   Completion of the private act at the instigation of the police
   Close supervision of the private conduct by the police
   A private act undertaken on behalf of the police to further a police objective

While the court found that there was no custodial character in the parking lot, that the defendant's response was voluntary, and that the seizure of the gun was made with the defendant's full and voluntary consent, it opined that there was a coordinated private-public law enforcement investigation of a crime incident thus subjecting the actions to constitutional scrutiny. See *People v. Stormer* for another "public function" case in which it was held that a private security search of an automobile was unlawful, and therefore the evidence was suppressed as being unconstitutionally seized. The security manager should be aware of any joint or coordinated venture with law enforcement or any public interest, public function, or public accommodation action by his personnel. If so, constitutional and other sanctions may apply.

OUTRAGEOUS CONDUCT

The concern for the security manager in the following case is the method or style of interrogation and investigation and the potentiality of lawsuit if these are not done correctly. Also note that investigative and interrogation parameters or limits may be set according to a collective bargaining agreement. Plaintiff McCann brought a tort lawsuit in state court, and defendant Alaska Airlines succeeded in removing the case to federal court a short time later claiming that the Railway Labor Act preempted state law. After hearing the matter, the federal court remanded the case back to the state court for resolution stating that there was no preemption. Also note the court's use of the words "outrageous conduct" relative to the style of interrogation.

T. M. McCANN v. ALASKA AIRLINES, INC.
758 F. Supp. 559 (1991)

THELTON E. HENDERSON, Chief Judge.

At the time of the events here at issue, Catherine McCann was employed by the defendant, Alaska Airlines, Inc. ("Alaska"), as a customer service agent. McCann's employment is governed by a collective bargaining agreement (CBA) entered into by Alaska and her union. Alaska and its employees are covered by the Railway Labor Act (RLA). The following are the facts as alleged by the plaintiff.

Patrick Partridge, a security representative employed by Alaska, was assigned to investigate a report that $95 had been taken from a cash drawer at Alaska's Oakland facility. Toward the end of McCann's shift on August 1, 1990, her supervisor, Vern Organ, asked her to enter a private room on Alaska's premises. McCann there encountered Partridge for the first time. Partridge identified himself as a law enforcement officer and began to interrogate McCann. Partridge detained McCann for a total of over three hours, and for one hour beyond the end of her shift. Despite McCann's request, Partridge refused to allow her to leave the room for this period, even to use the restroom.

Partridge told McCann that she was soon to be arrested for unspecified crimes and would be taken to Alameda County Jail and incarcerated. He told her that she had been under the surveillance of a video camera with a lens "the size of the tip of a ball point pen," and that he had a videotape showing McCann engaged in crimes and improper conduct. Partridge told McCann that she would lose her job regardless of her guilt or innocence. Partridge repeatedly left the room to telephone a high ranking Alaska executive named Ray Vecci concerning the matter, and for instructions on whether to detain McCann further. Many of Partridge's questions were of a personal nature, wholly unrelated to McCann's employment.

McCann denied any improprieties, and asked to see the videotape. Partridge said she would only see the videotape when it was shown to the jury. No videotape is now alleged to exist.

Upon McCann's return to work on August 6, 1990, her supervisor, Vern Organ, ordered her to leave the premises and not to return until she was treated by a psychiatrist. Much of this exchange was observed by McCann's co-workers.

To date, McCann remains employed by Alaska in the same position.

On October 22, 1990, McCann commenced this action in Alameda County Superior Court, naming Alaska, Partridge, and 20 Does as defendants, and alleging state law claims for: (1) false imprisonment; (2) intentional infliction of emotional distress; (3) assault; (4) slander; and (5) conspiracy.

On November 6, 1990, Alaska removed to federal court, claiming that the state law claims are preempted by the RLA.

We find that the state claims are not preempted and therefore order the case remanded back to state court on two independent grounds: (1) the resolution of the state law claims is not "inextricably intertwined" with the grievance machinery of the collective bargaining agreement (CBA); (2) the state claims are based upon "outrageous conduct" of "merely peripheral concern to federal law," and the conduct affects "interests which were deeply rooted in local feelings and responsibility."

We find that under any of the articulations of the Ninth Circuit standard, McCann's claims are not preempted by the RLA. There are no provisions in McCann's CBA which even "arguably govern" the dispute here at issue, and the dispute therefore has an "obviously insubstantial relationship" with the CBA. Also, we find that the "matrix of facts" here involved are not "inextricably intertwined with the grievance machinery of the collective bargaining agreement or of the R.L.A."

The untenable nature of Alaska's position was revealed in oral argument when Alaska's attorney admitted that under his interpretation of governing law, even claims for employer torture of employees would be preempted by the RLA. Alaska's position was that even if detective Partridge had administered "thirty lashes" to Ms. McCann during the investigation, McCann would have been preempted from bringing any state tort claim for any permanent scars or injuries sustained from the abuse. Certainly it was not Congress' intent in enacting the RLA to allow employers free reign to inflict such abuse upon their employees.

RLA preemption does not swallow all matters which fall into its path. To say that all employee-employer actions are preempted by the RLA would be to say that the RLA employee effectively leaves her non-contractual rights at her employer's door. The defendant can direct us to no binding authority which compels such a result. For these reasons, Alaska's reliance on the above provision is of little moment.

Alaska also notes that the CBA prohibits theft, and argues that the CBA "contemplates that employees suspected of theft will be subject to an investigation." Reply Memorandum in Support of Def's Mtn to Dismiss, at 18. However, the provisions relied upon state only that an employee may be removed from Alaska's premises "until an investigation of a possible rule infraction can be completed." System Regs. § 2.120, and that "Before taking disciplinary action, a supervisor should complete an Investigation Report."

These provisions and other provisions cited allow discipline and removal from the workplace, but discipline and removal are not an issue here. The activities at issue here were investigation and interrogation. The contract provisions do not purport to allow or to even govern the type of investigation which occurred to Ms. McCann. Nowhere does the CBA grant to Alaska the right to detain at length, falsely accuse, and interrogate its employees in the manner which allegedly occurred in this case.

The state tort claims raised by Ms. McCann in this case can be resolved wholly independently from the CBA, are not inextricably intertwined with the CBA, and are not substantially related to the CBA. The state court would not find it necessary to interpret the CBA or the RLA since no contract provisions apply here. Thus, the action poses no threat to federal labor policy. We therefore find that the state law claims here at issue are not preempted by the RLA; were therefore improperly removed; and that the case should be remanded to the state court from which it was removed. Alaska's CBA nowhere gives the employer a right to investigate or interrogate its employees. Alaska cannot claim to have followed CBA procedures in conducting the investigation, since the CBA nowhere establishes procedures to follow in such circumstances. Therefore, unlike in the cases cited by the defendant, the state court will be able to resolve the tort issues raised without reference to the CBA.

In *Farmer v. United Brotherhood of Carpenters*, 430 U.S. 290, the Supreme Court held that an exception to federal preemption exists for "outrageous conduct," especially when the "conduct was a merely peripheral concern of federal law," and when the conduct affects "interests which were deeply rooted in local feelings and responsibility." The outrageous conduct exception applies even to a claim which would otherwise be preempted, and so provides an independent grounds to find this action not preempted.

In *Balzeit v. Southern Pacific Trans.*, 569 F.Supp. 986, Judge Williams of this Court followed *Farmer* to find state claims for emotional distress and violation of "fundamental public policy" to be not preempted by the RLA.

The conduct at issue in McCann's case seems at least as outrageous as that in *Farmer* and *Balzeit* and fits squarely within the "outrageous conduct" exception. The state certainly has a strong interest in protecting its citizens from false imprisonment, verbal abuse, emotional distress, slander and assault. These are interests which are "deeply rooted in local feeling." Citizens should not be denied these rights without compelling reasons, such as their interference with federal policy. However, in our case, as in *Farmer* and *Balzeit*, there is nothing in either the CBA at issue, or in the RLA which purports to protect such outrageous conduct. Allowing the suit will in no way interfere with the statutory scheme established by the RLA. In fact, it appears that the dispute would not even be arbitrable under the CBA since no CBA terms govern the matters at issue, and that therefore, the action does not even "peripherally" concern the CBA or the RLA.

Therefore, the "outrageous conduct" exception to RLA preemption provides an independent ground for finding the plaintiff's state law claims to be not preempted by the RLA. Since the claims are not preempted, they were improperly removed and should be remanded to the state court in which they were filed.

CASE COMMENT

The security officer identified himself as a law enforcement officer. If he was not one, there may be a criminal violation on his part. The plaintiff was not allowed to use the rest room and there was no mention of her being paid for the time she was detained beyond the end of her shift. She was told she would be arrested for unspecified crimes and jailed, that she would lose her job regardless of guilt or innocence, and that there was a videotape showing her engagement in crimes and improper conduct. She was also asked questions of a personal nature, wholly unrelated to her employment. The court pointed out that it was not the intent of Congress in enacting the Railway Labor Act to allow employers free reign to inflict such abuse on employees. Provisions in the collective bargaining agreement allowed discipline and removal, which were not at issue in this case. The issues were interrogation and investigation neither of which were addressed in the contract provisions. The court pointed out that nowhere does the collective bargaining agreement grant to the defendant the right to detain at length, falsely accuse, and interrogate its employees in the manner that allegedly occurred in this case. Loss from litigation can be minimized or prevented by proper conduct on the part of the security staff.

PUBLIC PLACE

The plaintiff, in the following case, sued for, among other things, battery and false imprisonment. She alleged that, after she was outside the store, a security guard came up from behind, tapped her on the shoulder, moved around in front of her, and ordered her to return to the store. Of concern to the jury was whether the guard was within his legal rights to question anyone outside the store. The opinion of the three-judge federal appellate court was that the guard *was* within his legal rights.

COBB v. STANDARD DRUG COMPANY, INC.
453 A. 2d 110 (1982)

TERRY, Associate Judge:

This is an appeal from a judgment for the defendants in an action for battery, false imprisonment, and defamation. Appellant alleged in her amended complaint that she purchased two items of merchandise in a drug store and was about to leave the store when she was accosted by a security guard, who asked her if the goods she was carrying had been paid for; she said that they had been and showed him the sales slip, then continued out the door. She further asserted that after she was outside on the public sidewalk, the security guard came up from behind and tapped her on the shoulder, then moved around in front of her and ordered her to return to the store. There the manager, in the presence of other customers, allegedly announced that the cashier had told him that appellant had not paid for the merchandise. Appellant sued the corporation that owned the drug store and the corporate employer of the security guard, seeking compensatory and punitive damages. The jury returned a verdict for both defendants, and on that verdict the trial court entered a judgment, which we affirm.

Appellant makes two arguments here. First, she contends that the trial court erred in failing to strike a juror whom she allegedly challenged for cause. Second, she contends that the trial court committed error in responding to a note from the jury, and that the error was magnified by the "inadequate, unfair and confusing" verdict form by which the court submitted the case to the jury. The first claim of error fails for lack of an adequate record; the second we reject for other reasons.

II

Some time after it began its deliberations, the jury sent the following note to the court:

Question: Was the guard within his legal rights to question anyone outside the store?

After an extended discussion with all counsel, the court sent a written response back to the jury, saying, "The answer to the question asked is yes." Appellant now contends that the court erred in failing to amplify its answer by instructing the jury on the limited law enforcement powers of security guards.[3] Because none of the testimony has been transcribed, we do not know the facts surrounding the guard's questioning of appellant outside the store; consequently, we can only determine whether the court's answer to the jury note was correct in the abstract as a matter of law. We conclude that it was.

In *United States v. Burrell*, 286 A.2d 845, *rehearing en banc denied*, 288 A.2d 248, a police officer noticed the defendant acting suspiciously on a downtown street. After watching him for a few moments, the officer walked up to him, placed his hand on the defendant's arm, and said, "Hold it, sir, could I speak with you a second?" An incriminating answer led to a search and the discovery of a concealed pistol. We held that the officer's question, accompanied by the touch on the arm, did not amount to an intrusion on the defendant's constitutionally

[5]Although the record does not disclose whether the guard in this case was commissioned as a special police officer under D.C.Code § 4–114 (1981), our disposition of this case does not depend on whether he was or was not.

protected rights. *Burrell* simply illustrates a basic proposition which the courts have long recognized: that "there is nothing in the Constitution which prevents a policeman from addressing questions to anyone on the streets." *Terry v. Ohio*, 392 U.S. 1; see *United States v. Wylie*, 569 F.2d 62, cert. denied, 435 U.S. 944, (distinguishing between mere police-citizen "contacts" and investigative stops). The right of a police officer to ask anyone on the street a question does not depend on his status as an officer; on the contrary, "every citizen" has the right "to address questions to other persons, for ordinarily the person addressed has an equal right to ignore his interrogator and walk away. . . ." *Terry v. Ohio*, supra. In other words, a police officer—or the security guard in this case—has the same right that "every citizen" has to question another person in a public place because the other person has an "equal right" to pay no attention to the question. Since the jury's note dealt only with the guard's right to ask a question, we cannot say that the trial court erred in answering the note as it did.

There being no discernible error on the record, the judgment of the Superior Court is *Affirmed*.

CASE COMMENT

The court made the point that there is nothing in the Constitution that prevents a policeman from addressing questions to anyone on the streets and analogized that "every citizen" has the right to address questions to other persons in public places. On the other hand, the person addressed has the right to ignore or pay no attention to the question and walk away. Note that this decision was made in the abstract as there was no transcription of testimony. The security manager should give great care and consideration to this type of situation. Restraint constituting false imprisonment may arise out of words, acts, or gestures. Tapping on the shoulder, in the sense of offensive touching, may constitute an illegal application of force (battery).

INVESTIGATORY INTERVIEW—UNION REPRESENTATION

Absent a nexus with law enforcement, a private citizen is not usually concerned with the proscriptions of the Fifth and Sixth Amendments. There may be times, however, when the private citizen security agent needs to be aware of an employee's statutory right to union representation at an investigatory interview that the employee reasonably believes might result in disciplinary action. This may constitute an unfair labor practice in violation of the National Labor Relations Act. Representation must be requested by the employee and is limited to situations where the employee reasonably believes the investigation will result in disciplinary action. On the other hand, the employee may forgo this guaranteed right and participate in an interview unaccompanied by his union representative.

NATIONAL LABOR RELATIONS BOARD v. J. WEINGARTEN, INC.
420 U.S. 251 (1975)

Mr. Justice **Brennan** delivered the opinion of the Court.

The National Labor Relations Board held in this case that respondent employer's denial of an employee's request that her union representative be present at an investigatory interview which the employee reasonably believed might result in disciplinary action constituted an unfair labor practice in violation of § 8(a)(1) of the National Labor Relations Act, as amended, 61 Stat 140,[1] because it interfered with, restrained, and coerced the individual right of the employee, protected by § 7 of the Act, "to engage in . . . concerted activities for . . . mutual aid or protection. . . ."[2] 202 NLRB 446.

The Court of Appeals for the Fifth Circuit held that this was an impermissible construction of § 7 and refused to enforce the Board's order that directed respondent to cease and desist from requiring any employee to take part in an investigatory interview without union representation if the employee requests representation and reasonably fears disciplinary action. 485 F2d 1135. We granted certiorari and set the case for oral argument with Garment Workers v Quality Mfg. Co. 420 US 276. We reverse

I

Respondent operates a chain of some 100 retail stores with lunch counters at some, and so-called lobby food operations at others, dispensing food to take out or eat on the premises. Respondent's sales personnel are represented for collective-bargaining purposes by Retail Clerks Union, Local 455. Leura Collins, one of the sales personnel, worked at the lunch counter at Store No. 2 from 1961 to 1970 when she was transferred to the lobby operation at store No. 98. Respondent maintains a companywide security department staffed by "Loss Prevention Specialists" who work undercover in all stores to guard against loss from shoplifting and employee dishonesty. In June 1972, "Specialist" Hardy, without the knowledge of the store manager, spent two days observing the lobby operation at Store No. 98 investigating a report that Collins was taking money from a cash register. When Hardy's surveillance of Collins at work turned up no evidence to support the report, Hardy disclosed his presence to the store manager and reported that he could find nothing wrong. The store manager then told him that a fellow lobby employee of Collins had just reported that Collins had purchased a box of chicken that sold for $2.98, but had placed only $1 in the cash register. Collins was summoned to an interview with Specialist Hardy and the store manager, and Hardy questioned her. The Board found that several times during the questioning she asked the store manager to call the union shop steward or some other union representative to the interview, and that her requests were denied. Collins admitted that she had purchased some chicken, a loaf of bread and some cake which she said she paid for and donated to her church for a church dinner. She explained that she purchased four pieces of chicken for which the price was $1, but that because the lobby department was out of the small-size boxes in which such purchases were usually packaged she put the chicken into the larger box normally used for packaging larger quantities. Specialist Hardy left the interview to check Collins' explanation with the fellow employee who had reported Collins. This employee confirmed that the lobby department had run out of small boxes and also said that she did not know how many pieces

---

[1] Section 8(a)(1), 29 USCS § 158(a)(1) [29 USCS § 158(a)(1)] provides that it is an unfair labor practice for an employer "to interfere with, restrain, or coerce employees in the exercise of the rights guaranteed in section 157 of this title."

[2] Section 7, 29 USC § 157 [29 USCS § 157], provides:
"Employees shall have the right to self-organization, to form, join, or assist labor organizations, to bargain collectively through representatives of their own choosing, and to engage in other concerted activities for the purpose of collective bargaining or other mutual aid or protection, and shall also have the right to refrain from any or all of such activities except to the extent that such right may be affected by an agreement requiring membership in a labor organization as a condition of employment as authorized in section 158(a)(3) of this title."

of chicken Collins had put in the larger box. Specialist Hardy returned to the interview, told Collins that her explanation had checked out, that he was sorry if he had inconvenienced her, and that the matter was closed.

Collins thereupon burst into tears and blurted out that the only thing she had ever gotten from the store without paying for it was her free lunch. This revelation surprised the store manager and Hardy because, although free lunches had been provided at Store No. 2 when Collins worked at the lunch counter there, company policy was not to provide free lunches at stores operating lobby departments. In consequence, the store manager and Specialist Hardy closely interrogated Collins about violations of the policy in the lobby department at Store No. 98. Collins again asked that a shop steward be called to the interview, but the store manager denied her request. Based on her answers to his questions, Specialist Hardy prepared a written statement which included a computation that Collins owed the store approximately $160 for lunches. Collins refused to sign the statement. The Board found that Collins, as well as most, if not all, employees in the lobby department of Store No. 98, including the manager of that department, took lunch from the lobby without paying for it, apparently because no contrary policy was ever made known to them. Indeed, when company headquarters advised Specialist Hardy by telephone during the interview that headquarters itself was uncertain whether the policy against providing free lunches at lobby departments was in effect at Store No. 98, he terminated his interrogation of Collins. The store manager asked Collins not to discuss the matter with anyone because he considered it a private matter between her and the company, of no concern to others. Collins, however, reported the details of the interview fully to her shop steward and other union representatives, and this unfair labor practice proceeding resulted.

II

The Board's construction that § 7 creates a statutory right in an employee to refuse to submit without union representation to an interview which he reasonably fears may result in his discipline was announced in its decision and order of January 28, 1972, in Quality Mfg. Co. 195 NLRB 197, considered in Garment Workers v Quality Mfg. Co. 420 US 276. In its opinions in that case and in Mobil Oil Corp. 196 NLRB 1052, decided May 12, 1972, three months later, the Board shaped the contours and limits of the statutory rights.

First, the right inheres in § 7's guarantee of the right of employees to act in concert for mutual aid and protection. In Mobil Oil, the Board stated:

> "An employee's right to union representation upon request is based on Section 7 of the Act which guarantees the right of employees to act in concert for 'mutual aid and protection.' The denial of this right has a reasonable tendency to interfere with, restrain, and coerce employees in violation of Section 8(a)(1) of the Act. Thus, it is a serious violation of the employee's individual right to engage in concerted activity by seeking the assistance of his statutory representative if the employer denies the employee's request and compels the employee to appear unassisted at an interview which may put his job security in jeopardy. Such a dilution of the employee's right to act collectively to protect his job interests is, in our view, unwarranted interference with his right to insist on concerted protection, rather than individual self-protection, against possible adverse employer action."

Second, the right arises only in situations where the employee requests representation. In other words, the employee may forgo his guaranteed right and, if he prefers, participate in an interview unaccompanied by his union representative.

Third, the employee's right to request representation as a condition of participation in an interview is limited to situations where the employee reasonably believes the investigation will result in disciplinary action.[5] Thus the Board stated in Quality:

> "We would not apply the rule to such run-of-the-mill shop-floor conversations as, for example, the giving of instruction for training or needed corrections of work techniques. In such cases there cannot normally be any reasonable basis for an employee to fear that any adverse impact may result from the interview, and thus we would then see no reasonable basis for him to seek the assistance of his representative." 195 NLRB, at 199.

Fourth, exercise of the right may not interfere with legitimate employer prerogatives. The employer has no obligation to justify his refusal to allow union representation, and despite refusal, the employer is free to carry on his inquiry without interviewing the employee, and thus leave to the employee the choice between having an interview unaccompanied by his representative, or having no interview and forgoing any benefits that might be derived from one. As stated in Mobil Oil:

> "The employer may, if it wishes, advise the employee that it will not proceed with the interview unless the employee is willing to enter the interview unaccompanied by his representative. The employee may then refrain from participating in the interview, thereby protecting his right to representation, but at the same time relinquishing any benefit which might be derived from the interview. The employer would then be free to act on the basis of information obtained from other sources." 196 NLRB, at 1052.

The Board explained in Quality:

> "This seems to us to be the only course consistent with all of the provisions of our Act. It permits the employer to reject a collective course in situations such as investigative interviews where a collective course is not required but protects the employee's right to protection by his chosen agents. Participation in the interview is then voluntary, and, if the employee has reasonable ground to fear that the interview will adversely affect his continued employment, or even his working conditions, he may choose to forego it unless he is afforded the safeguard of his representative's presence. He would then also forego whatever benefit might come from the interview. And, in that event, the employer would, of course, be free to act on the basis of whatever information he had and without such additional facts as might have been gleaned through the interview." 195 NLRB, at 198.

Fifth, the employer has no duty to bargain with any union representative who may be permitted to attend the investigatory interview. The Board said in Mobil, "we are not giving the Union any particular rights with the respect to predisciplinary discussions which it otherwise was not able to secure during collective bargaining negotiations." 196 NLRB, at 1052. The Board thus adhered to its decisions distinguishing between disciplinary and investigatory interviews, imposing a mandatory affirmative obligation to meet with the union representative only in the case of the disciplinary interview. Texaco, Inc., Houston Producing Division, 168 NLRB 361; Chevron Oil Co. 168 NLRB 574; Jacobe-Pearson Ford, Inc. 172 NLRB 594. The employer has no duty to bargain with the union representative at an investigatory interview. "The representative is present to assist the employee, and may attempt

[5] ... The key objective fact in this case is that the only exception to the requirement in the collective-bargaining agreement that the employer give a warning notice prior to discharge is "if the cause of such discharge is dishonesty." Accordingly, had respondent been satisfied, based on its investigatory interview, that Collins was guilty of dishonesty, Collins could have been discharged without further notice. That she might reasonably believe that the interview might result in disciplinary action is thus clear.

to clarify the facts or suggest other employees who may have knowledge of them. The employer, however, is free to insist that he is only interested, at that time, in hearing the employee's own account of the matter under investigation." Brief for Petitioner 22.

III

The Board's holding is a permissible construction of "concerted activities for . . . mutual aid or protection" by the agency charged by Congress with enforcement of the Act, and should have been sustained.

The action of an employee in seeking to have the assistance of his union representative at a confrontation with his employer clearly falls within the literal wording of § 7 that "employees shall have the right . . . to engage in . . . concerted activities for the purpose of . . . mutual aid or protection." Mobil Oil Corp. v NLRB, 482 F2d 842. This is true even though the employee alone may have an immediate stake in the outcome; he seeks "aid or protection" against a perceived threat to his employment security. The union representative whose participation he seeks is, however, safeguarding not only the particular employee's interest, but also the interests of the entire bargaining unit by exercising vigilance to make certain that the employer does not initiate or continue a practice of imposing punishment unjustly.[6] The representative's presence is an assurance to other employees in the bargaining unit that they, too, can obtain his aid and protection if called upon to attend a like interview. Concerted activity for mutual aid or protection is therefore as present here as it was held to be in NLRB v Peter Cailler Kohler Swiss Chocolates Co. 130 F2d 503, cited with approval by this Court in Houston Contractors Assn. v NLRB, 386 US 664:

> "When all the other workmen in a shop make common cause with a fellow workman over his separate grievance, and go out on strike in his support, they engage in a "concerted activity" for "mutual aid or protection," although the aggrieved workman is the only one of them who has any immediate stake in the outcome. The rest know that by their action each of them assures himself, in case his turn ever comes, of the support of the one whom they are all then helping; and the solidarity so established is "mutual aid" in the most literal sense, as nobody doubts.'"

The Board's construction plainly effectuates the most fundamental purposes of the Act. In § 1, 29 USC § 151, the Act declares that it is a goal of national labor policy to protect "the exercise by workers of full freedom of association, self-organization, and designation of representatives of their own choosing, for the purpose of . . . mutual aid or protection." To that end the Act is designed to eliminate the "inequality of bargaining power between employees . . . and employers." Ibid. Requiring a lone employee to attend an investigatory interview which he reasonably believes may result in the imposition of discipline perpetuates the inequality the Act was designed to eliminate, and bars recourse to the safeguards the Act provided "to redress the perceived imbalance of economic power between labor and management." American Ship Building Co. v NLRB, 380 US 300. Viewed in this light, the Board's recognition that § 7 guarantees an employee's right to the presence of a union representative

---

[6]"The quantum of proof that the employer considers sufficient to support disciplinary action is of concern to the entire bargaining unit. A slow accretion of custom and practice may come to control the handling of disciplinary disputes. If, for example, the employer adopts a practice of considering a foreman's unsubstantiated statements sufficient to support disciplinary action, employee protection against unwarranted punishment is affected. The presence of a union steward allows protection of this interest by the bargaining representative." Comment, Union Presence in Disciplinary Meetings, 41 U Chi L Rev 329.

at an investigatory interview in which the risk of discipline reasonably inheres is within the protective ambit of the section "'read in the light of the mischief to be corrected and the end to be attained.'" NLRB v Hearst Publications, Inc. 322 US 111.

The Board's construction also gives recognition to the right when it is most useful to both employee and employer.[7] A single employee confronted by an employer investigating whether certain conduct deserves discipline may be too fearful or inarticulate to relate accurately the incident being investigated, or too ignorant to raise extenuating factors. A knowledgeable union representative could assist the employer by eliciting favorable facts, and save the employer production time by getting to the bottom of the incident occasioning the interview. Certainly his presence need not transform the interview into an adversary contest. Respondent suggests nonetheless that union representation at this stage is unnecessary because a decision as to employee culpability or disciplinary action can be corrected after the decision to impose discipline has become final. In other words, respondent would defer representation until the filing of a formal grievance challenging the employer's determination of guilt after the employee has been discharged or otherwise disciplined. At that point, however, it becomes increasingly difficult for the employee to vindicate himself, and the value of representation is correspondingly diminished. The employer may then be more concerned with justifying his actions than re-examining them.

IV

The Court of Appeals rejected the Board's construction as foreclosed by that court's decision four years earlier in Texaco, Inc. Houston Producing Division v NLRB, 408 F2d 142, and by "a long line of Board decisions, each of which indicates—either directly or indirectly—that no union representative need be present" at an investigatory interview. 485 F2d, at 1137.

The Board distinguishes Texaco as presenting not the question whether the refusal to allow the employee to have his union representative present constituted a violation of § 8(a)(1) but rather the question whether § 8(a)(5) precluded the employer from refusing to

---

[7]See, e.g., Independent Lock Co. 30 Lab Arb 744:
"Participation by the union representative might reasonably be designed to clarify the issues at this first stage of the existence of a question, to bring out the facts and the policies concerned at this stage, to give assistance to employees who may lack the ability to express themselves in their cases, and who, when their livelihood is at stake, might in fact need the more experienced kind of counsel which their union steward might represent. The foreman, himself, may benefit from the presence of the steward by seeing the issue, the problem, the implications of the facts, and the collective bargaining clause in question more clearly. Indeed, good faith discussion at this level may solve many problems, and prevent needless hard feelings from arising. . . . It can be advantageous to both parties if they both act in good faith and seek to discuss the question at this stage with as much intelligence as they are capable of bringing to bear on the problem."
See also Caterpillar Tractor Co. 44 Lab Arb 647,
"The procedure . . . contemplates that the steward will exercise his responsibility and authority to discourage grievances where the action on the part of management appears to be justified. Similarly, there exists the responsibility upon management to withhold disciplinary action, or other decisions affecting employees, where it can be demonstrated at the outset that such action is unwarranted. The presence of the union steward is regarded as a factor conducive to the avoidance of formal grievances through the medium of discussion and persuasion conducted at the threshold of an impending grievance. It is entirely logical that the steward will employ his office in appropriate cases so as to limit formal grievances to those which involve differences of substantial merit. Whether this objective is accomplished will depend on the good faith of the parties, and whether they are amenable to reason and persuasion."

deal with the union. We need not determine whether Texaco is distinguishable. Insofar as the Court of Appeals there held that an employer does not violate § 8(a)(1) if he denies an employee's request for union representation at an investigative interview, and requires him to attend the interview alone, our decision today reversing the Court of Appeals' judgment based upon Texaco supersedes that holding.

In respect of its own precedents, the Board asserts that even though some "may be read as reaching a contrary conclusion," they should not be treated as impairing the validity of the Board's construction, because "these decisions do not reflect a considered analysis of the issue." Brief for Petitioner 25. In that circumstance, and in the light of significant developments in industrial life believed by the Board to have warranted a reappraisal of the question,[10] the Board argues that the case is one where "the nature of the problem, as revealed by unfolding variant situations, inevitably involves an evolutionary process for its rational response, not a quick, definitive formula as a comprehensive answer. And so, it is not surprising that the Board has more or less felt its way . . . and has modified and reformed its standards on the basis of accumulating experience." Electrical Workers v NLRB, 366 US 667.

We agree that its earlier precedents do not impair the validity of the Board's construction. That construction in no wise exceeds the reach of § 7, but falls well within the scope of the rights created by that section. The use by an administrative agency of the evolutional approach is particularly fitting. To hold that the Board's earlier decisions froze the development of this important aspect of the national labor law would misconceive the nature of administrative decisionmaking. "'Cumulative experience' begets understanding and insight by which judgments . . . are validated or qualified or invalidated. The constant process of trail and error, on a wider and fuller scale than a single adversary litigation permits, differentiates perhaps more than anything else the administrative from the judicial process." NLRB v Seven-Up Co. 344 US 344.

The responsibility to adapt the Act to changing patterns of industrial life is entrusted to the Board. The Court of Appeals impermissibly encroached upon the Board's function in determining for itself that an employee has no "need" for union assistance at an investigatory interview. "While a basic purpose of section 7 is to allow employees to engage in concerted activities for their mutual aid and protection, such a need does not arise at an investigatory interview." 485 F2d, at 1138. It is the province of the Board, not the courts, to determine whether or not the "need" exists in light of changing industrial practices and the Board's cumulative experience in dealing with labor management relations. For the Board has the "special function of applying the general provisions of the Act to the complexities of industrial life," NLRB v Erie Resistor Corp. 373 US 221; see Republic Aviation Corp. v NLRB, 324 US 793; Phelps Dodge Corp. v NLRB, 313 US 177, and its special competence in this field is the justification for the deference accorded its determination. American Ship Building Co. v NLRB, 380 US, at 316, 13 L Ed 2d 855. Reviewing courts are of course not "to stand aside and rubber stamp" Board determinations that run contrary to the language or tenor of the Act, NLRB v Brown, 380 US 278. But the Board's construction here, while it may not be required

---

[10]"There has been a recent growth in the use of sophisticated techniques—such as closed circuit television, undercover security agents, and lie detectors—to monitor and investigate the employee's conduct at their place of work. See, e.g., Warwick Electronics, Inc. 46 LA 95; Bowman Transportation, Inc. 56 LA 283; FMC Corp. 46 LA 335. These techniques increase not only the employees' feelings of apprehension, but also their need for experienced assistance in dealing with them. Thus, often, as here and in Mobil, supra, an investigative interview is conducted by security specialists; the employee does not confront a supervisor who is known or familiar to him, but a stranger trained in interrogation techniques. These developments in industrial life warrant a concomitant reappraisal by the Board of their impact on statutory rights. Boys Markets, Inc. v Retail Clerks, Local 770, 398 US 235."

by the Act, is at least permissible under it, and insofar as the Board's application of that meaning engages in the "difficult and delicate responsibility" of reconciling conflicting interests of labor and management, the balance struck by the Board is "subject to limited judicial review." NLRB v Truck Drivers, 353 US 87. In sum, the Board has reached a fair and reasoned balance upon a question within its special competence, its newly arrived at construction of § 7 does not exceed the reach of that section, and the Board has adequately explicated the basis of its interpretation.

The statutory right confirmed today is in full harmony with actual industrial practice. Many important collective-bargaining agreements have provisions that accord employees rights of union representation at investigatory interviews. Even where such a right is not explicitly provided in the agreement a "well-established current of arbitral authority" sustains the right of union representation at investigatory interviews which the employee reasonably believes may result in disciplinary action against him. Chevron Chemical Co. 60 Lab Arb 1066, (1973).[12]

The judgment is reversed and the case is remanded with direction to enter a judgment enforcing the Board's order.

It is so ordered.

CASE COMMENT

Legitimate employer prerogatives such as the giving of instruction, training, or correction of work techniques are not involved. The employee must request representation and reasonably believe the investigatory interview will result in disciplinary action. The employer is free to carry out the inquiry without interviewing the employee and many advise the employee that it will not proceed with the interview unless the employee is willing to enter the interview unaccompanied by the employees representative. The employee may refrain from participating in the interview thereby protecting his right to representation, and the employer is free to act on the basis of information obtained from other sources. The union representative at the investigatory interview is present only to assist the employee in clarifying facts or to suggest other employees who may know of them. Note the court's concern (footnote 10) about the employee's need for assistance because of the growth of sophisticated security techniques.

INVESTIGATORY INTERVIEWS—PREINTERVIEW CONFERENCE

Since the statutory right of an employee to union representation at any investigatory interview conducted by an employer that the employee fears may result in his or her discipline has been established, two more questions need be addressed. (1) Does the *Weingarten* right include the right to be informed prior to the interview of the subject matter of the interview, the nature of any charge of impropriety it may encompass, and the right to a

[12]See also Universal Oil Products Co. 60 Lab Arb 832:
"An employee is entitled to the presence of a Committeeman at an investigatory interview if he requests one and if the employee has reasonable grounds to fear that the interview may be used to support disciplinary action against him."

preinterview conference with a union representative? (2) Must the request for a conference come from a union representative or must it come from the employee himself? This court held that, without information and conference prior to the interview, union representation would be effectively diminished and that either the union representative or the employee may make the request for a preinterview conference.

PACIFIC TELEPHONE AND TELEGRAPH COMPANY
v. NATIONAL LABOR RELATIONS BOARD
711 F.2d 134 (1983)

MERRILL, Circuit Judge:

In consolidated cases Pacific Telephone and Telegraph Company petitions for review of orders issued by the National Labor Relations Board holding the company guilty of unfair labor practices in violation of § 8(a)(1) of the National Labor Relations Act, 29 U.S.C. § 158(a)(1). The Board ruled that Pacific Telephone had deprived employees of rights guaranteed by § 7 of the Act, 29 U.S.C. § 157, in holding investigatory interviews regarding improper employee conduct without first informing the employees of the subject matter of the interviews and allowing them time for a pre-interview conference with a union representative. The Board cross-applies for enforcement of its orders.

One of the consolidated cases involves conduct in 1978 by employees Ebojo and Flores, two installer repairmen. By independent investigation Pacific Telephone had secured evidence that on company time Flores had installed unauthorized telephone equipment in Ebojo's home. Company supervisors summoned Ebojo and Flores to interviews and also summoned union steward Robert Green to act as the employees' representative. Ebojo, Flores and Green all inquired as to the purpose of the interview but received no information. Flores was interviewed first and after being told of the evidence in the possession of the company, admitted having installed unauthorized equipment in Ebojo's home. Discrepancies in Flores's timesheets were also discussed. When Ebojo was summoned for an interview, Green requested an opportunity to confer with him prior to the interview but this request was refused.[2] Ebojo denied possession of the sort of equipment the company believed he had but did admit possession of other unauthorized equipment. Both Ebojo and Flores were subsequently discharged. The company discharged Flores for timesheet falsification and for the unauthorized installation of equipment in Ebojo's home. The company discharged Ebojo for timesheet falsification and for having unauthorized equipment installed in his home.

In the other case (262 N.L.R.B. No. 125), Pacific Telephone, by independent investigation, obtained information in 1980 that two of its long-distance operators, Revada and Martinez, had used company equipment to place lengthy long-distance calls from their homes while taking steps to avoid billing. In this case, the company investigating officer did advise the employees and their union representative of the subject matter of the interview, but refused a request of the representative to a pre-interview conference with the employees. The employees refused to give any information and were subsequently discharged for misuse of company time and equipment.

---

[2]Substantial evidence supports the Board's finding that Green made the request to meet with Ebojo and that the request was not withdrawn. Likewise, substantial evidence supports the Board's finding that the company gave no responsive answer to the inquiries of Ebojo, Flores and Green regarding the nature of the interviews.

Ebojo and Flores filed charges with the Board, as did the union on behalf of Revada and Martinez. In both cases the Board found that the employer had violated § 8(a)(1) by refusing to grant pre-interview conferences to Ebojo, Revada and Martinez and to inform Flores and Ebojo as to the subject matter of the investigation. It entered cease and desist orders and also ordered Flores and Ebojo reinstated with back pay.

In *NLRB v. J. Weingarten, Inc.*, 420 U.S. 251, the Supreme Court, accepting the position taken by the Board, held that § 7 of the National Labor Relations Act created a statutory right of an employee to union representation at any investigatory interview conducted by the employer which the employee reasonably fears may result in his discipline.

The questions, presented on this petition are: (1) whether the Board permissibly construed the *Weingarten* right to include the right to be informed prior to the interview of the subject matter of the interview and the nature of any charge of impropriety it may encompass and the right to a pre-interview conference with a union representative; (2) whether the request for a conference may come from the union representative or must come from the employee himself; and (3) whether the grant to Flores and Ebojo of reinstatement and back pay was within the Board's statutory authority. The first two questions require an examination of the Board's construction of § 7 and its view of the nature of the employee's right to act in concert as approved and accepted by the court in *Weingarten*. This Court will uphold the Board's construction of the National Labor Relations Act if it is reasonable or permissible. *Ford Motor Co. v. NLRB*, 441 U.S. 488.

I.

Answer to the first question depends upon the nature of the employee's right to act in concert. In *Weingarten*, the Court quoted with approval from the Board's decision in *Mobil Oil Corp*, 196 N.L.R.B. 1052. The Board in *Mobil Oil Corp*. held it to be a violation of § 8(a)(1) to compel the employee to "appear unassisted at an interview which may put his job security in jeopardy". The Board regarded this as "a dilution of the employee's right under § 7 of the Act to act collectively to protect his job interests" and an "unwarranted interference with his right to insist on concerted protection rather than individual self-protection against possible adverse employer action."[3]

The *Weingarten* Court held that "the Board's holding is a permissible construction of 'concerted activities for . . . mutual aid or protection' by the agency charged by Congress with enforcement of the Act, and should have been sustained."

If the right to insist on concerted protection against possible adverse employer action encompasses union representation at interviews such as those here involved, then in our view the securing of information as to the subject matter of the interview and a pre-interview conference with a union representative are no less within the scope of that right. The Board's order that failure to provide such information and grant such pre-interview conferences

[3]The *Weingarten* Court noted in several other respects "the contours and limits of the statutory right" as shaped by the Board in *Mobil Oil* and other decisions: the employee must request representation; his right is limited to situations where he reasonably believes the investigatory interview may result in disciplinary action; "the employer is free to carry on his inquiry without interviewing the employee and thus leave to the employee the choice between having an interview unaccompanied by his representative or having no interview and foregoing any benefits that might be derived from one"; and the employer is under no duty to bargain with the attending union representative.

constituted unfair labor practices is as permissible a construction of § 7 as was the construction upheld in *Weingarten*. Without such information and such conference, the ability of the union representative effectively to give the aid and protection sought by the employee would be seriously diminished.[4]

II.

The second question presented by the petition is whether the request for a conference must come from the employee himself. Here, in the case of Ebojo, Revada and Martinez, the request came from the union representative. As we note in footnote 3, the Supreme Court has stated that the right to union representation at an investigatory interview as defined by the Board is a right which must be requested by the employee and which the employee may choose to forego. We read this to mean that the employer need not suggest that the employee have union representation and not, as Pacific Telephone argues, that only the employee himself may so request. In our judgment, once union representation has been afforded, the representative may speak for the employee he represents and either the union representative or the employee may make the request for pre-interview conference.

We affirm the decision of the Board holding that Pacific Telephone violated § 8(a)(1) by failing to inform Flores and Ebojo as to the subject matter of the interview and failing to grant Ebojo, Revada and Martinez pre-interview conferences with their union representatives. Save in the respect hereinafter noted the Board's order is entitled to enforcement. IT IS SO ORDERED.

CASE COMMENT

Compelling employees to appear unassisted at an interview that may put their job security in jeopardy is regarded as a dilution of the employees' right to act collectively to protect their job interests and is an unwarranted interference with their right to insist on concerted protection against possible employer adverse action. Therefore if the right to insist on concerted protection encompasses union representation, the securing of the subject matter of the interview and a pre-interview conference lie within that scope. The ability of the union representative to give aid and protection effectively would seriously be diminished without such information and conference. While the employer need not suggest that the employee have union representation, once this representation has been afforded, either the employee or the union representative may make the request for the pre-interview conference.

---

[4]In *Climax Molybdenum Co. v. NLRB*, 584 F.2d 360, the court "decline d" to extend *Weingarten* to a pre-interview conference under the facts of that case. *Id*. at 365. There, however, ample time had been provided after notice and before the interview to allow the employee to arrange a conference. Under the circumstances it was held that refusal to delay the interview to allow further time for conference did not amount to a denial of a conference or constitute an unfair labor practice. In the cases before us, no time at all had been allowed for a conference.

12

Use of Force by Private Citizens

On occasion, private citizens, including security personnel, use either deadly or non-deadly physical force. This is done to protect themselves and others, to protect or recover their property, or to prevent crime. This should be of great concern to security managers, as they will hire others to protect corporate property. The user of force, and potentially the security manager and corporation, must justify not only the use of force but also the degree used in each particular instance. The key to using force lies in what is a reasonable response under the circumstances presented by the threat. One must take into consideration the seriousness, danger present, and kind and degree of the threatened misconduct. The more serious threat allows for the use of a higher degree of force than does a lesser threat, and, of course no security person should actually cause an escalation in the degree of force being used. Also there is no need for any force to be used when the threat has subsided, except to make the apprehension.

One should consider that generally speaking life is worth more than property is worth; that the law does not condone the use of unnecessary violence, and that one should use no more force than is necessary to accomplish one's purpose under the circumstances. Other considerations to think about before using force include determining: whether the threat is real, imminent, or pressing and accompanied by the ability to carry it out; whether there are other alternatives to using force; how much time has elapsed since the incident occurred; whether force to be used is for retaliatory purposes only; and who actually is the provocateur or aggressor. Remember that the amount of force used by an employee may be measured at a much later date by others—namely by a jury. Also note that many states have statutes covering the permissible limits on the use of force. One such state statute can be found in Appendix I.

CONFRONTATION—AGGRESSION

In the following case a guard was licensed to carry a gun and had extensive training in the use of it. At the initial confrontation inside the store, the guard took a defensive position with his nightstick. The guard obeyed the gunpoint command of the would-be customer and put the nightstick away. After the would-be customer left the store, the guard went out to find a policeman to report a man with a gun. Outside the store the guard asked the would-be customer if he was a policeman. There was no response, and the would-be customer headed back toward the guard drawing his gun while he walked. The guard told the man to freeze. This order was ignored. The man kept coming at the guard, and the guard yelled "freeze" a second time. At about a four- to five-foot distance, the guard went into a combat stance, aimed, and fired his weapon, killing the man. The trial court held that the guard was the aggressor, and that the deceased, who was the initial aggressor, had effectively withdrawn from the encounter. Thus the guard initiated the second confrontation and could not claim self-defense. The appellate court reversed the trial court's conviction of the guard for criminally negligent homicide holding that the guard had reasonable apprehension that he was about to be shot and had not been negligent in the use of his weapon. The court also held that the guard was entitled to make a citizen's arrest as an offense had been committed in his presence, which is what he left the store to do. Also discussed is the doctrine of retreat when the other party is using or is about to use deadly physical force. It is interesting to note that the court felt that perhaps, in hindsight, the guard could have handled the situation differently. He would have been remiss, however, had he simply ignored what the accused had done and gone about his business as if he had never encountered the deceased.

PEOPLE v. BORRERO
504 N.Y.S.2d 654 (1986)

MILONAS, Justice.

This case involves an incident which occurred in the Bronx on May 8, 1982 and resulted in the shooting death of John Johnson, a retired police officer. Defendant herein was indicted for manslaughter in the second degree and, following a nonjury trial, was convicted of criminally negligent homicide as a lesser included offense. On appeal, defendant urges that the People failed to meet their burden of disproving beyond a reasonable doubt that he was justified in firing his gun at Johnson. Moreover, he contends that there was no reasonable view of the evidence which would support a finding that he acted with sufficient recklessness or negligence to be convicted of criminally negligent homicide. Since both arguments are meritorious, defendant is entitled to a reversal of his conviction and dismissal of the indictment against him.

On the date in question, defendant herein, who was licensed to carry a handgun and had extensive training in its use, was working as a security guard in a drugstore located at 1500 Metropolitan Avenue. When Johnson entered the store at approximately 4:30 P.M. with a brown paper bag in his hand, he was requested to check his package. He did so but then inquired about a claim ticket. Defendant replied that although he did not have any tickets, Johnson's parcel was the only one being held so there would be no difficulty in retrieving it. Johnson thereupon exploded, declaring, "Give me the fucking bag. I'm not going to shop in this store anymore." Defendant returned the bag to Johnson who, still dissatisfied, stated, "I ought to punch you in the mouth." Defendant stepped back and took out his nightstick, holding it in a defensive position with both hands at waist level.

At that point, Johnson pulled out a gun and told defendant to put the stick away, asserting, "You're not fucking with no kid." Defendant complied. Johnson subsequently threatened to kill defendant if the latter made another sound. Valente Silva, one of the employees of the store, then interceded and endeavored to calm Johnson. He succeeded in getting Johnson to leave the premises. This incident was also witnessed by Ely Krellenstein, the owner of the business, and Jennine Catania, another employee. After Johnson's departure, defendant attempted to follow him but was initially delayed by the pleas of those inside. However, defendant explained that it was his duty to find a policeman (he had recently seen one pass by) and notify him that there was a man with a gun walking the streets. He also apparently did not want Johnson to disappear before the police arrived. Defendant did not believe that his leaving the store would provoke any further confrontation or lead to the use of firearms. Krellenstein contacted the police and activated the silent alarm system.

Once outside, defendant, failing to see a police officer, looked in the direction in which Johnson had gone and called out loudly to him, "Hold it, are you a police officer?" Johnson did not respond to the question, but instead turned and headed back to defendant, drawing his gun from his waistband. Defendant told him to "Freeze." Johnson ignored the directive and continued approaching defendant. Defendant, crouching for protection behind a car situated near the drugstore, drew his own gun and again yelled "Freeze." Johnson, however, kept coming toward defendant. When Johnson was some four to five feet from defendant, he went into a combat stance and aimed his weapon at defendant's head. Defendant fired his own gun once, hitting Johnson in the head. He observed Johnson fall, then went over to the body and picked up Johnson's gun by inserting a pen through its muzzle. He placed the gun on the hood of the vehicle behind which he had taken cover.

The street altercation was witnessed by a number of people. Michael Lyden, a former legislative aide to a state assemblyman and now assistant director of Neighborhood Emergency Telephone Systems, Inc., testified that defendant was empty-handed when he emerged from the store and only reached for his gun after Johnson was at the opposite side of the car from him. He heard defendant ask the other man if he was a police officer and order him to stop. Johnson did not respond. Roy Grundmann also heard defendant ask Johnson if he was a cop. According to Grundmann, Johnson was waving his gun around and did not react to defendant's question. Frank Rios, a corrections officer, was sitting in his automobile across the street from the drugstore when he heard someone shout. He glanced up and saw a man walking toward the store. That person held a gun in his hand which was aimed at the front of the store. After Johnson was shot, Rios ran over, identified himself and offered to secure the scene while defendant summoned an ambulance. He noticed the gun lying on the hood of the car but did not see any holster.

Police Officer Israel Larracuente was about one and one-half blocks away from the drugstore when he was informed by a pedestrian that an officer required assistance. He was heading toward the store when he heard a shot. Upon arriving at the scene, he saw a black male lying face up with a wound in his left temple. On the trunk of a nearby car there was a holstered gun loaded with five rounds of ammunition, a pipe and some bloodstains. Officer Larracuente also asserted that some minutes prior to the incident, he had passed by the drugstore and exchanged waves of the hand with defendant.

At the end of the People's case, the parties entered into several stipulations. First, it was agreed that if the ballistics expert were to testify, he would state that defendant's gun was operable and that one shell had been discharged. He would also state that the gun recovered from Johnson was operable but showed no evidence of discharge. Second, it was stipulated that if a witness from the Department of Licensing were called, he would testify that John Johnson was a retired New York City police officer with a permit to carry a weapon within city limits. Third, on the basis of testimony before the Grand Jury, if one David Rivera were called to the stand, he would say that while he was crossing the street on the day of the shooting, he heard a man dressed in blue calling to another man to identify himself and asking whether he was a police officer. Without replying, the second man pulled out a gun and began to walk toward defendant, who also had his gun out. The former then leaned over a car and aimed his unholstered pistol at the man in blue, who knelt down and fired one shot. Finally, it was agreed that an autopsy performed upon Johnson's body showed the cause of death to be a gunshot wound to the head. A supplementary toxicology report indicated the presence of .07% ethyl alcohol in Johnson's brain.

Defendant moved to dismiss the indictment following the admissions of the stipulations. The trial court denied the motion, and the defense introduced its case. After both sides had rested and concluded their summations, the court, acting as the trier of the facts, found that all of the testimony, including that of defendant, was credible. However, the judge determined that defendant had drawn his gun as soon as he left the store. Thus, while Johnson was the initial aggressor, he had effectively withdrawn from the encounter. When defendant left the store to go after Johnson, he, therefore, initiated the second confrontation and could not now claim self-defense. Since defendant had created a grave risk of death to Johnson, he was guilty of criminally negligent homicide, the lesser included offense of manslaughter in the second degree. The court subsequently sentenced defendant to five years' probation.

It should be noted that virtually every facet of defendant's account of what transpired was corroborated by other witnesses. The proof at trial clearly reveals that Johnson entered the drugstore and began a confrontation with defendant during which he displayed a weapon and behaved in a generally menacing manner. The fact that a simple dispute over a claim check was transformed into an extremely dangerous situation can only be indicative of Johnson's instability.

Pursuant to section 35.30 of the Penal Law, which sets forth the situations under which a person is justified in using physical force to make an arrest or to prevent an escape:

4. A private person acting on his own account may use physical force, other than deadly physical force, upon such person when and to the extent that he reasonably believes such to be necessary to effect an arrest or to prevent the escape from custody of a person whom he reasonably believes to have committed an offense and who in fact has committed such offense; and he may use deadly physical force for such purpose when he reasonably believes such to be necessary to:

    (a) Defend himself or a third person from what he reasonably believes to be the use or imminent use of deadly physical force. . . .

In the drugstore in which defendant was a security guard, Johnson drew his gun and threatened defendant with it, and he did so solely because he was not presented with a claim ticket for his checked package. The druggist and several employees observed Johnson's menacing behavior for which he was subject to prosecution for a variety of crimes. The fact that Johnson turned out to be a retired police officer with a permit to carry a gun would not have absolved him for liability for his conduct. Since it is evident that Johnson had committed an offense in his presence, defendant was entitled, purely as a private citizen and without consideration of his status as a security guard, to follow Johnson out of the drugstore and make a citizen's arrest. Certainly, the evidence is more than adequate to satisfy the mandates of Penal Law 35.30(4).

The record further demonstrates that defendant left the store for the specific purpose of effecting Johnson's arrest. According to defendant, he had seen a policeman pass by only a few minutes earlier (and Officer Larracuente recalled exchanging waves of the hand with defendant). Therefore, when defendant went outside, it was his intention to find the police officer or else to detain Johnson until the arrival of the police summoned by the druggist. Under section 35.30(4) of the Penal Law, defendant had the authority to use ordinary physical force to the extent necessary to arrest Johnson or to prevent his escape. Yet, defendant made no attempt to use force. Rather, he repeatedly called out to Johnson to stop and identify himself. Instead of responding, Johnson simply pulled out his gun and advanced upon defendant, who was still standing near the drugstore. Although defendant crouched behind a parked car for cover, Johnson kept coming at him. It was not until Johnson assumed a combat stance and took aim at defendant's head that defendant fired at Johnson.

Although section 35.30(4) does not require that an individual who is contemplating making a valid citizen's arrest retreat in the face of imminent deadly physical force, subdivision (2) of

Penal Law section 35.15, which encompasses the most common "self-defense" claim, does state that:

> A person may not use deadly physical force upon another person under circumstances specified in subdivision one unless:
>
> (a) He reasonably believes that such other person is using or about to use deadly physical force. Even in such case, however, the actor may not use deadly physical force if he knows that he can with complete safety as to himself and others avoid the necessity of so doing by retreating....

Even assuming the defendant did have a duty to retreat, the People have failed to establish beyond a reasonable doubt that defendant knew that he could with complete safety retreat from a man advancing at him with a pointed gun. Further, the fact that defendant came out of the drugstore to locate a policeman clearly did not constitute an attempt to start a second confrontation. Defendant acted entirely reasonably and within statutory parameters in endeavoring to stop Johnson from possibly continuing his aggressive behavior and injuring someone. In all respects, defendant's conduct was that of a responsible citizen. Contrary to the trial court's determination, the proof overwhelmingly shows that defendant did not draw his gun as soon as he walked out of the store but did so only after Johnson's threat to his safety and/or life had become immediate and unavoidable. He did not demonstrate anger or personal animosity toward Johnson. He merely requested that Johnson identify himself and then tried to back away in the face of Johnson's hostile reaction. At any rate, under the circumstances herein, defendant's subjective belief as to the imminence and gravity of danger was clearly reasonable.

As for defendant's second argument, there is no reasonable view of the evidence to support a finding that he was guilty of criminally negligent homicide because he acted in a reckless or negligent way. The trial court apparently concluded that defendant negligently disregarded the danger of death to Johnson. However, defendant, an armed security guard and a marksman skilled in the use of firearms, in the course of attempting to make a valid citizen's arrest of Johnson or to detain him until the police could arrive on the scene, was threatened with deadly physical force when Johnson crouched down and took aim at him. Defendant, under a reasonable apprehension that he was about to be shot, responded by aiming back at Johnson and firing a single bullet at the latter's head. He never claimed that his intention was to scare the victim rather than to kill him, that the gun discharged by accident, that he believed the gun to be unloaded, or that he was unfamiliar with its use. On the contrary, defendant's act was a deliberate one, and he was aware at all times of what he was doing and the precise consequences of his actions. There was thus nothing reckless, negligent or accidental in the shooting.

Defendant was originally indicted for manslaughter in the second degree in that it was alleged that he recklessly caused the death of John Johnson. Under Penal Law 15.05(3), a person acts recklessly when "he is aware of and consciously disregards a substantial and unjustifiable risk" that a particular result will take place—in this instance, the death of Johnson. The lesser included offense of which defendant was convicted, criminally negligent homicide (Penal Law 125.10) is defined as causing the death of another person with criminal negligence—that is, negligently failing to perceive the risk at all.

Since defendant was justified in following Johnson out of the drugstore in order to ensure the safety of people in the street against the peril posed by Johnson, and no evidence was introduced at trial that defendant was not completely cognizant that if he aimed and fired his gun at Johnson from a close distance, death might ensue, there is no basis for a determination that defendant was guilty of criminally negligent homicide. The fact that defendant may have failed to anticipate Johnson's violent behavior is scarcely sufficient reason to hold that defendant acted in a negligent (or reckless) manner by leaving the store. Perhaps, in hindsight, the defendant could have handled the situation differently but his conduct was certainly in no way criminal. Defendant, however, would have been remiss had he simply ignored what had occurred and gone about his business as if he had never encountered Johnson.

Therefore, the judgment of the Supreme Court, Bronx County (Peggy Bernheim, J.), rendered on July 6, 1983, which convicted defendant, following a trial without jury, of criminally negligent homicide and sentenced him to a period of probation for five years, is reversed on the law and the facts, the conviction vacated and the indictment dismissed.

Judgment, Supreme Court, Bronx County (Peggy Bernheim, J.), rendered on July 6, 1983, unanimously reversed, on the law and the facts, the conviction vacated and the indictment dismissed.

All concur.

CASE COMMENT

There were two confrontations in this case. The initial one was in the store where the deceased displayed a weapon and behaved in a generally menacing manner. The second one was outside the store in the street where the deceased again drew his weapon. The security manager should be well versed in the use of deadly and nondeadly physical force as the amount and degree of force used by the security staff needs to be justified. A question to be asked is: "What is a reasonable response under the circumstances?" The more serious threat allows a higher degree of force to be used. Conversely the lesser threat calls for a lesser degree of force. One should try not to escalate the degree of force used and should remember that when the aggression ceases and the threat thus subsides, there may well be no reason to use deadly or nondeadly physical force except for the reasonable amount of (nondeadly) force necessary to make an arrest. State statutes on the use of force, together with appropriate interpretations, should be examined for each particular jurisdiction.

In this case, the threat subsided in the first confrontation, when the aggressor withdrew and left the store. It would be hard to claim self-defense at this point as there was no threat of imminent harm. In the second confrontation in the street, the aggressor kept coming at the guard with his weapon drawn. What should the guard have done? Use deadly physical force to defend himself or retreat? By statute in this state, one may not use deadly physical force if he knows that he can, with *complete safety* to himself and others, avoid the necessity of doing so by retreating. This concerns the doctrine of retreat. The idea behind this doctrine is that one should try to use a reasonable avenue of escape to avoid the danger to his person and preclude the necessity of having to kill the aggressor. In this case, the court pointed out that the prosecutor failed to establish that the guard could have retreated in complete safety from a man advancing at him with a pointed weapon. Knowledge of the situations where force is allowed and the limitations thereof is a most important and critical consideration for the security manager.

SELF-DEFENSE

The following case involves a guard who was legally on duty and who was legally authorized to carry a gun. He had experience with weapons in the military. The guard was grabbed by two persons; his glasses were knocked off; his arms were pinned; and he was being beaten with his own billyclub. As the attackers wrestled him to the ground, he fired one shot that killed one of the attackers. This case involves the use of deadly physical force and the concept of self-defense. Under what circumstances can such force be used? The guard repelled force by force and the question is whether it was reasonable under the circumstances.

PRICE v. GRAY'S GUARD SERVICE, INC.
298 So.2d 461 (1974)

BOYER, Judge.

Plaintiff in the trial court has appealed a summary final judgment in favor of the defendants.

The facts are not in substantial dispute but must, of course, be construed most favorably to the plaintiff in our review of a summary judgment in favor of the defendants.

Gray's Guard Service was in charge of security at the Greater Jacksonville Fair held in 1969 at the Gator Bowl. The guards employed by Gray's Guard Service were authorized by the sheriff of Duval County to carry a gun but they enjoyed no arrest powers. On October 20, 1969 one Petty, a guard employed by Gray's Guard Service, was stationed at Gate No. 5, which gate was not open to the general public but was reserved for exhibitors and other persons connected with the fair. There was no facility at that gate for the sale or collection of tickets.

Petty was a career navy man having there received training in firearms and having experienced guard duty, shore patrol duty and sentry duty. He had been employed by Gray's Guard Service for a little over a year.

On the night of October 20, 1969 one James R. Price accompanied by Billy Frank Motes arrived at the Greater Jacksonville Fair at some time between 10:00 and 11:00 p.m. Both Price and Motes were big, strong young men, each approximately five feet eleven inches tall and weighed approximately 170 pounds. Price had been a high school football player.

Price and Motes attempted to enter the fair at Gate No. 5 but were informed by Petty that that gate was not open to the general public and that they could not there enter. A rather brisk conversation ensued, culminating in an exchange of curse words but no altercation. Price and Motes finally entered the fair through an appropriate gate where there was a booth for the sale and collection of tickets. They remained at the fair where they met and chatted with various acquaintances until the fair closed, which was approximately one hour after their arrival. While there they took in the rides, sideshows and other attractions, walking the entire midway while stopping occasionally to talk with friends. They did not, during that period, discuss with any of their friends the prior incident with Petty.

When the fair closed Price and Motes left through the gate by which they had entered and proceeded to walk toward their car. Price then began to talk about the earlier incident with Petty, telling Motes that he was going "to whip his ass." Motes admonished Price that "you ought to leave him alone." They then discussed the fact that Petty was armed with a pistol but Price insisted that he "wanted to jump on the guy" and to "knock him down," saying "to hell with him." As they approached Gate No. 5 Price said to Motes "let's get him." Thereupon Price grabbed Petty from the blind side and Motes immediately grabbed him from the other side, both hitting him, one getting a slug into Petty's jaw. Motes managed to wrench Petty's billyclub away from him and commenced hitting him with it. Petty's glasses and his uniform cap were knocked off. Petty did not know who his assailants were, but although both arms were pinned to his body by Price and Motes as they attempted to wrestle him to the ground Petty managed to draw his pistol and fire. The first shot found its mark in Price, and Motes discontinued the attack and fled.

Motes testified that his best approximation of the time that the assault and beating of Petty had been in progress before Petty drew his pistol was approximately 30 seconds. Price was pronounced dead upon arrival at the hospital.

Price's administrator filed suit against Gray's Guard Service, Inc. and its bonding company. After permitting several amended complaints the trial judge granted a motion for summary judgment in favor of both defendants.

The briefs of the parties filed here address themselves primarily to the doctrine of respondeat superior. We do not find it necessary to reach that point since our examination of the record simply reveals that plaintiff has no cause of action. Indeed, under the facts of the case, we are amazed that suit was ever filed. The record does not reveal one iota of evidence of negligence on the part of Petty. This is not a case of "hot blood." Price had ample opportunity to "cool down" assuming, arguendo, that the initial encounter with Petty was sufficient to raise his ire. Price and Motes deliberately attacked Petty while he was in uniform, knowing him to be armed. Petty did not even know who his assailants were or that he was about to be attacked until he was grabbed from "the blind side." What, we ask rhetorically, was Petty supposed to do upon being suddenly attacked from behind by two young men who gave every indication that they intended "to do him in." Petty acted as would have any reasonable prudent person under the circumstances. He was legally on duty as a guard. He was legally authorized to carry a gun. For all practical purposes he was a police officer. Guns are not worn by officers of the law merely as decorations. Petty's arms were pinned beside him and he was being beaten with his own club. He had no opportunity to retreat initially and no opportunity, after being attacked, to cogitate as to his next move. Price and Motes neglected to inform Petty in advance that they really intended to do him no harm but simply wanted to afford themselves an opportunity to vent their anger. Petty's action under such assault was that of an individual who was fighting to protect his own life and body from what he reasonably believed to be imminent peril and, indeed, death. The attack upon Petty was sudden, unprovoked and without warning. A person unlawfully assaulted may repel force by force to the extent which to him seems reasonably necessary under the circumstances to protect himself from injury. A person who has no reason to believe that he can with safety avoid the necessity of defending himself is privileged to defend himself against another by force intended or likely to cause death or serious bodily harm, when he himself reasonably believes that the other is about to inflict upon him an intentional bodily harm or death. The conduct of a person acting in self defense is measured by an objective standard, but the standard must be applied to the facts and circumstances as they appeared at the time of the altercation to the one acting in self defense. A person acting in self defense is not held to the same course of conduct which might have been expected had he been afforded an opportunity of cool thought as to possibilities, probabilities and alternatives.

Petty, under the circumstances, could most certainly not retreat because he was being held and wrestled to the ground by two overpowering young men. Once upon the ground, with Motes swinging the billyclub and Price intent upon "whipping his ass" the superior force of his attackers may well have resulted in Petty's demise. A person simply is not required to docilely acquiesce while under such vicious and sudden attack. The 30 seconds which elapsed between the commencement of the attack and the time that Petty fired afforded no opportunity for meditation nor deliberation. A quick decision had to be made and we are not prepared to say that, under the circumstances, Petty acted rashly. Certainly he did not act negligently.

Neither the parties' briefs nor our independent research have revealed any cases involving such bizarre circumstances. The reason is obvious: Never before has anyone had the intestinal fortitude to bring suit under such circumstances. If they did, they did not take an appeal when they lost.

According to the philosopher Jean-Jacques Rousseau (French, 1712-1778) men were originally wild and free, accountable to no one. A man's possessions, including freedom and indeed his very life, depended entirely upon his mental and physical prowess. Every man was the law unto himself, responsible to no one. (See also Holy Bible, Judges 21:25)

The English philosophers, Thomas Hobbes (1588–1679) and John Locke (1632–1704) philosophized that men, in order to protect themselves from aggression, greed, violence, disorder and strife, consciously banded together, sacrificing some of their unfettered rights and freedom in order to secure unto themselves the exercise of their remaining rights within a legally defined social system. (See also Holy Bible, 1 Samuel 8:19–20)

The responsibility for maintaining order in civilized societies originally rested in the military, which exercised the absolute authority of the crown. The word "police" comes from the Latin word *politia* which means "the state." In ancient times a trespass against a soldier, or the police, while discharging his duties was an affront to the crown, usually punishable by death. Modern civil police, as distinguished from the military, had their genesis in Great Britain by the establishment in 1829 of the metropolitan police in the sprawling urban and suburban areas surrounding the City of London by the home secretary, Sir Robert Peel. (Thus the popular term "bobby" to denote a policeman in England.) (Encyclopedia Brittanica, Police)

We are living in an era in which it is popular to challenge established authority. Numerous institutions and firms are finding it necessary to retain the services of guard companies, there simply being insufficient police protection. There are those, we are informed, who consider it a mark of distinction to physically attack, without provocation, uniformed guards and policemen. We hope that Petty's action, the trial judge's summary judgment, and our affirmance, might serve as some deterrence to such a dangerous (both to society and to the attacker) practice.

Affirmed.

McCORD, J., and DREW, E. HARRIS, (Ret.), Associate Judge, concur.

CASE COMMENT

The court pointed out that the guard was legally on duty and that he was legally authorized to carry a firearm. He did not know who his assailants were; his arms were pinned; and he was being beaten with his own club. Due to the rapidity of the event he had no opportunity to retreat nor even time to think about it. He fought to protect his life from what he reasonably believed to be imminent peril. There appeared no reason to believe he could with safety avoid the necessity of defending himself. This court also pointed out that a person unlawfully assaulted may repel force by force to the extent that to him seems reasonably necessary under the circumstances to protect himself from injury. Here the guard acted reasonably and prudently under the circumstances.

DEFENSE OF PROPERTY

Generally speaking, in our society today, life is worth more than property is, and the law does not condone the use of unnecessary force. In the next case, a proprietor was attempting to protect his property, which had been burglarized in the past. In order to do this, he booby-trapped the target cigarette machine with dynamite. A teenager committing theft of the machine was killed. While the mother of the deceased was awarded a civil judgment, the court noted that the defendant proprietor might be guilty of a crime, either murder or some degree of manslaughter. Clearly the use of deadly physical force to prevent loss from petty theft was excessive.

McKINSEY v. WADE
220 S.E. 2d 30 (1975)

EVANS, Judge.

This case is an action for wrongful death. Robert Joel McKinsey, aged 16, was killed by a dynamite charge exploding in a *booby-trapped* cigarette vending machine on the premises of A. C. Wade, a liquor store operator in Cordele, Georgia. Ella Christine McKinsey, his mother, sued Wade for the wrongful death of her minor son.

Defendant admitted booby-trapping the vending machine with dynamite, but contended it was not for the purpose of killing the deceased. He contended the machine had been burglarized in the past, and he was merely attempting to scare the vandals. He made no test to determine what damage would be inflicted by activating the dynamite while in the vending machine.

Plaintiff admitted her minor son was in the act of committing a theft immediately before he was killed. She moved for summary judgment as to liability. The motion was denied, and plaintiff appeals. *Held:*

1. The duty of the property owner is not to wilfully or intentionally injure a trespasser.
2. The defendant may be guilty of a crime, either murder or some degree of manslaughter in this instance, but that question is not before us in a criminal prosecution as this is a civil action.
3. The wrongful death statute (Code Ch. 105-13) clearly provides for the recovery for the full value of the life of a human being resulting from a crime or criminal negligence. The law does not provide that if the human being is killed while in the performance of an unlawful act there shall be no recovery.
4. Both the facts and the law in this case are simple and uncomplicated. The defendant set a booby-trap by loading a vending machine with dynamite to protect his property. He probably reasoned that a thief who sought to take a few dollars out of a vending machine forfeited all rights, including the right to live. He must have believed that the law afforded him the right of protection of his dollars and placed him in the superior position of killing one or a hundred people if it became necessary so to do in protecting his property. If he himself was a lawful citizen, selling liquor during the daytime and going home at night, those who came upon his premises for an evil purpose must suffer the consequences, no matter how severe, so he must have reasoned. It is significant that in placing dynamite into the vending machine, whereby it would be triggered and exploded upon tampering with the machine, he did not make one single test to determine how severe the resulting explosion might be. In other words, he deliberately set a booby-trap, or man-trap, or death trap, and left it where it might work its destructive forces upon trespassers or wrongdoers on his property, and even an innocent person who might be nearby, even 100 or 200 yards away.
5. What is a mantrap? *Crosby v. Savannah Electric Co.*, 150 S.E. 2d 563, held: "The doctrine of mantrap or pitfall is rested upon the theory that the owner is expecting a trespasser or a licensee and has prepared the premises to do him injury. A typical example is the setting of a spring or trap gun to stop or prevent depredations by animals or humans. In that situation the owner expects that a trespasser will come, and deliberately sets a trap designed to do injury. It may result from the knowledge on the part of the owner of the existence of a dangerous or hazardous condition coupled with a conscious indifference to the consequences, so that a deliberate intent to inflict injury is inferable, or from a

dangerous condition hidden with sufficient cover to obscure it or to render it unobservable to one who approaches it. The hazard is latent or concealed. In *Kahn v. Graper,* 152 S.E.2d 10, this court, speaking through Judge Eberhardt, holds: " 'The general rule supported by the authorities is that, while a landowner cannot intentionally injure or lay traps for a trespasser or a licensee upon his land, he owes no other duty to him.'

Also, the court holds: "The doctrine of mantrap or pitfall . . . may result from a knowledge of the owner of the existence of the dangerous condition coupled with a conscious indifference to the consequences, so that an intent to inflict injury is inferable."

In *Central of Georgia R. Co. v. Ledbetter,* 168 S.E. 81, it is held: "To the licensee, *as to the trespasser,* no duty arises of keeping the usual condition of the premises up to any given standard of safety, *except that they must not contain pitfalls, mantraps, and things of that character."* (Emphasis supplied.)

The foregoing authorities are sufficient to show that defendant set up a mantrap, or deathtrap; that he had no right to do so, even as against a wrongdoer, and that where injury results therefrom, even to a wrongdoer, he is liable.

6. But let us set forth one additional principle of law which leaves it beyond peradventure that defendant had no right to defend his wrongful, unconscionable, and destructive conduct by showing that the minor son of plaintiff was engaged in theft of his vending machine. What negligence did the minor son commit? He was a trespasser and engaged in petty theft. What wrong did the defendant commit? He had an abandoned and malignant heart; he set a deathtrap with dynamite, never testing it to determine how many innocent persons might be killed if within 100 to 200 yards of it, and thus sought to protect his several dollars in the vending machine. *He had a conscious indifference to consequences, and by all the tried-and-tested rules of our laws, he was guilty of wilful and wanton negligence.* There need be no actual intent by defendant; his conscious indifference to consequences is all that is required to characterize his negligence as *wilful and wanton conduct.*

7. Where a party's negligence is wilful and wanton, he is debarred from pleading that the other party was a trespasser, or was negligent or was a wrongdoer. These are not defenses to the one who is wilfully and wantonly negligent. There is no duty of a plaintiff to exercise ordinary care to avoid the injury as against a defendant who commits wilful and wanton negligence. A deaf person who walks down a railroad track commits a high degree of negligence. But if he is struck by a train that approaches him from the rear, and the engineer is guilty of wilful and wanton negligence, the negligence of the plaintiff is immaterial. *Central Railroad & Banking Co. v. Denson,* 11 S.E. 1039; and it is held that *although plaintiff by exercise of ordinary care could have avoided the defendant's negligence, yet if defendant's negligence is so gross as to amount to wanton and wilful negligence, the want of ordinary care by plaintiff would be no bar to a recovery for the injury received.*

8. In this case, the plaintiff moved for summary judgment as to liability, which motion was denied. Under the facts and circumstances in this case, that judgment is erroneous and is reversed and remanded with direction that summary judgment as to liability be entered up on behalf of plaintiff.

Judgment reversed.

CASE COMMENT

The security manager, in attempting to deter crime and prevent loss, should test mechanisms to determine if damage or injury will be inflicted if the mechanism is activated. Property owners have a duty not to wilfully or intentionally injure trespassers and, if they do, may be guilty of a crime. One should have a conscious difference to the consequences of what is being done and not have a conscious indifference, which can be characterized as wilful and wanton negligence.

TO RECOVER PROPERTY

In the following case a store security guard observed the plaintiff put items of clothing in her purse. When the guard approached and identified himself, the plaintiff attempted to flee. A scuffle ensued; the plaintiff pummeled the guard with her purse; and then discarded the purse under a display rack. The purse was retrieved and searched by store personnel, disclosing the items of clothing. The plaintiff, who was convicted of concealing merchandise, contended that the trial court was in error by failing to suppress the items of clothing in that they were illegally seized in violation of both state and federal constitutions. Can a store recover its own property and how much force can be used to do so?

JACKSON v. STATE
657 P. 2d 407 (1983)

SINGLETON, Judge.

Carol Jackson was convicted of concealment of merchandise, AS 11.46.220, and assault in the fourth degree, AS 11.41.230(a)(1). She appeals contending that the trial court erred in failing to suppress the property which she allegedly concealed. She argues that the property in question was illegally seized from her purse by a store security guard in violation of the state and federal constitutions. We affirm.

Christian Martin, a security guard employed by Nordstrom Department Store, was engaged in his duties on April 26, when he observed Andrew Walker and Carol Jackson concealing merchandise on their persons. Specifically, he saw Jackson put a women's blazer and skirt in her purse and Walker put two dresses in his pants. Martin approached Walker and Jackson and identified himself as a store security guard. When Jackson and Walker attempted to flee, Martin took Walker by the arm and a scuffle ensued. Jackson jumped on Martin's back and began to pummel him with her purse and then discarded her purse under a display rack. Martin summoned assistance and Jackson and Walker were subdued. During the scuffle, the two dresses were removed from Walker's pants. Subsequently, Jackson's purse was retrieved by store personnel and searched, disclosing the blazer and skirt.

Jackson argues that Martin, while an employee of Nordstrom, a private business, was acting under color of state law in searching her purse and retrieving property from Walker's pants. Since he had no warrant, she continues, the search violated her right to be free from unreasonable searches and seizures under the state and federal constitutions requiring the suppression of the evidence in question. She relies on *People v. Zelinski*, 594 P.2d 1000 (1979).

It is not necessary for us to decide the extent to which the respective constitutions limit searches by private security guards since, if Jackson is correct that Martin should be treated as a peace officer, the concealed property was properly retrieved from Jackson's purse in a search incident to an arrest. Martin observed Jackson and Walker conceal property belonging to Nordstrom on their persons. He thus had probable cause to believe that they were violating AS 11.46.220 and Anchorage Municipal Ordinance 8.05.550(B) in his presence. AS 12–25.030(a)(1). *See Smith v. Municipality of Anchorage,* 652 P.2d 499 (setting out the elements of these offenses). Assuming that we treat him as a peace officer, authorization to arrest where an arrest actually is made carries with it permission to search for evidence of the offense. *See Hinkel v. Anchorage,* 618 P.2d 1069. In *Hinkel,* permission to search was expressly extended to Hinkel's purse even though it had been seized and was therefore beyond her power to retrieve any weapon or destroy any evidence contained within it. Martin saw the defendants conceal property in Jackson's purse. Under these facts, his search was not unreasonable.

We recognize that the Supreme Court of California in *Zelinski* held that while store security guards acted under color of state law and were therefore subject to constitutional limitations on searches and seizures, they were not police officers and therefore could not search a person detained for contraband without express statutory authority. The *Zelinski* court noted that California law expressly authorizes those making citizen's arrests to search for weapons but was silent regarding searches for evidence.

We need not decide the extent of a private person's authority to search incident to a citizen's arrest under Alaska law in order to decide this case. *People v. Zelinski* is distinguishable. In *Zelinski,* the store detective searched the defendant and discovered illegal drugs. Zelinski was prosecuted for the possession of those drugs. Here the store detective searched for his employer's merchandise and recovered it. Jackson was prosecuted for the theft of the merchandise. No applicable Alaska statute purports to regulate searches by private persons. AS 11.46.230 (authorized reasonable detention) and AS 12.25.030 (authorizes arrests without a warrant). Thus, the common law would appear applicable. *See* AS 01.10.010. At common law, a merchant has the right to retrieve, by nondeadly force, property illegally obtained from him by force or fraud. *See* Restatement (Second) of Torts, § 100–111. See AS 11.81.350(a) (use of nondeadly force permitted in defense of property). Thus, even if we were to follow *Zelinski,* and hold that an arrest and subsequent search by a store security guard of a suspected shoplifter is partly state action and partly private action, we would find Martin's actions, in recovering his employer's property, legal and reasonable and therefore permissible under the state and federal constitutions. Consequently, the merchandise taken from Jackson's purse was admissible in evidence against her. We note that a California appellate court reached the same conclusion on similar facts distinguishing *Zelinski* in this way. *People v. Carter,* 181 Cal. Rptr. 867. Consequently, we need not decide whether a violation of any statutory or common law limitations on searches of suspected shoplifters by merchants would require application of an exclusionary rule. Alaska Rule of Evidence 412, which bars illegally obtained evidence, applies to evidence seized in violation of constitutional protections. Whether to suppress evidence seized in violation of statute which does not constitute a violation of the constitution as well will be determined on a case-by-case basis.

The judgement of the superior court is AFFIRMED.

CASE COMMENT

The court noted that no state statute purported to regulate searches by private persons. Thus the common law appeared to be applicable. In common law, merchants have the right to retrieve, by nondeadly force, property illegally obtained from them by force or fraud. The court distinguished this case from one in another state where a search by store guards discovered contraband (drugs) for which that person was prosecuted. In that state, guards acted under color of state law and were subject to certain limitations regarding searches for contraband. Note that there is a difference in searching for weapons (protection) and one's own property as opposed to searching for evidence of other crime. In this case, only the store's property was used in evidence against the plaintiff. The guard observed the plaintiff conceal the store's property, had probable cause of a violation in his presence, and his actions in recovering his employer's property was reasonable, legal, and therefore permissible.

EJECTION FROM PREMISES

Occasionally a person may come on to a business premises by either implied or express invitation and become abusive, rude, profane, provocative, offensive, or threatening. If that person remains on the premises after being properly warned, cautioned, and re-quested to leave, the business has several choices: to endure that person's presence and subject the business to further offensive conduct, to attempt to forcibly eject or expel that person from the premises, or to notify the appropriate law enforcement agency. If the business elects to eject or expel that person, which after issuing proper cautionarys it has the right to do, the expulsion may be accomplished by reasonable (not excessive) force. The following case is an example of the use of excessive, therefore unreasonable, force.

TOMBLINSON v. NOBILE
229 P. 2d 97 (1951)

MUSSELL, Justice.
Action for damages for personal injuries.
Plaintiff received serious injury to his right eye from a blow struck by defendant John Nobile with a "blackjack" (a leather bag full of shot). He recovered damages therefor against defendant Nobile and his employer Frank Stielow, individually and doing business as "Frank's Detective Service." These defendants appeal from the judgment and submit as reasons for reversal that (1) The evidence does not support the verdict and judgment; (2) The jury was erroneously instructed; and (3) Plaintiff committed prejudicial error in the voir dire examination of jurors.
The evidence is here briefly summarized and stated in accordance with the rules that it must be construed most strongly against the party against whom the judgment is rendered; that every favorable inference which may fairly be deduced from the evidence should be resolved in favor of the prevailing party and that the prevailing party's evidence must ordinarily be accepted as true and the evidence which contradicts it must be disregarded.

Evidence

Plaintiff and two male companions, during the evening of February 5, 1949, visited "Johnny's Place," a combination restaurant, bar and dance hall in Fresno. They secured a table near the dance floor and while plaintiff was sitting at the table drinking beer, Robert Welch (one of his companions) became somewhat hilarious and noisy. Defendant Nobile, who was employed by Frank's Detective Service and instructed to watch plaintiff's table by one of the proprietors of the cafe, approached Welch, told him he was creating too much disturbance and that he would have to leave. Nobile accompanied Welch to the door. Plaintiff got up from the table and followed. When he was outside, he asked Nobile why they were throwing Welch out. Nobile replied that Welch was making too much noise and he had to leave. Plaintiff then stated that he was going back inside and see "Cecil" (one of the proprietors of the cafe) and see if he could get Welch back in, if he would be quiet. As plaintiff started through the door, Nobile "grabbed him by the hair" and pulled him back.

One witness, Eugene O'Neal testified as follows: "He pulled Marion (plaintiff) back, threw him off balance, and I don't know whether he swung a blow or not, but it looked like it to me. The cop swung a blow and Marion came up fighting. He hit the cop and backed away. He hit him and knocked the cop down and Marion commenced to backing up, and both cops started circling him." In this connection plaintiff testified that after stating that he was going back inside to see "Cecil," he "turned around, went back toward the crowd, which had already gathered there, started in the door, and somebody grabbed me and pulled me; they had ahold of my hair and ahold of my shoulder. I don't know who it was. I just turned around and more or less shook or hit whoever it was to keep them off of me * * *." He further testified as follows: "After I hit the officer, I hit him in the face some place, I don't know where, I backed into the crowd. When I did that somebody grabbed me ahold of my arms and I was trying to get loose from who had ahold of me. I don't know who it was and as I was shaking my head and wiggling my body * * *. I saw a fist and a club or blackjack coming down, and it hit me in the face. I fell to the ground—rolled over on my face—and somebody either kicked me or stepped on me, on my back, and the officers picked me up."

Another witness, Joyce O'Neal, testified that she accompanied her husband to the door and heard the "officer" call the plaintiff a vile name and saw the "officer" pull plaintiff back and hit him in the face.

According to the testimony of defendant Nobile, plaintiff, in the presence of the crowd which had gathered in the door of the cafe, used profane language and was told that he was under arrest; that he then took "ahold" of plaintiff's left arm and he jerked it away; that he "grabbed" plaintiff the second time and told him he was under arrest and that then the plaintiff struck him with his right hand, knocking him back against the car, where he went down; that as he was coming up off the ground, he swung his blackjack and struck plaintiff, who then fell to the ground; that he placed plaintiff under arrest because of the language he was using; that he struck the plaintiff because he (Nobile) thought he was about to be assaulted again.

There was a sharp conflict in the evidence as to whether plaintiff did use profane language and as to whether the defendant Nobile informed plaintiff that he was under arrest. The foregoing evidence is ample to support the verdict and judgment.

The contention that the court erroneously instructed the jury is without merit. At the request of the plaintiff, the jury was instructed in the following language: "You are instructed that the defendant John Nobile is not a peace officer but is a private detective operating under the provisions of Division 3, Chapter 11 of the Business and Professions Code, and that said John Nobile has the same authority and no more authority to make arrests and preserve the peace than any other private citizen." And a further instruction, as follows: "Mere words however threatening or profane will not amount to an assault."

It is defendant's contention that by the first of these instructions the court erroneously limited Nobile's authority to that of a private citizen. However, as stated in the instruction, Nobile was not a peace officer as defined by Penal Code section 817 and the definition of a peace officer under that section was given in the instruction immediately preceding the one complained of and at the request of the defendants. The jury was instructed as follows: "You are instructed that any person, be he a police officer or private citizen, may arrest another for the commission of a misdemeanor in his presence. In this connection, if you find that the plaintiff, Marion Tomblinson, committed either a felony or a misdemeanor in the presence of the defendant, John Nobile, that the defendant, John Nobile, had the right to arrest the plaintiff, Marion Tomblinson, for the commission of such felony or misdemeanor." The jury was further instructed fully as to the rights of defendant Nobile to repel force by force in the defense of his person under the circumstances here shown. It is true that Nobile had the right to eject trespassers from the premises involved, if the circumstances warranted such action. However, he had authority to use only such force as was reasonably necessary and the brutal use of a "blackjack" was clearly without justification. The instructions properly covered the authority of the defendant John Nobile in making an arrest, whether he was a peace officer or not. The second instruction is a correct statement of the law and while its application to the facts presented may be somewhat obscure, no prejudicial error was occasioned by it or by the first instruction. Especially is this true when defendant Nobile himself testified that he struck the plaintiff to prevent a further assault upon himself and the apparent fact that the injury to plaintiff was not incurred while he was being ejected from the premises.

Under the circumstances here presented, we conclude that there was no showing of bad faith and that the questions asked the prospective jurors were not prejudicially erroneous, where, as here, there was no contention that the judgment awarded was excessive and the liability was established by abundant evidence.

Judgment affirmed.

CASE COMMENT

A business proprietor has the right to expel or eject persons who persist in abusive conduct. Appropriate warnings must be given, and if force is used to eject that person, it must be justifiable. The force used must be reasonably commensurate to the task at hand, and only enough force may be used to accomplish that task. The use of excessive force overcomes the justification.

PUSHING

The use of force, however slight, can be expensive as can be seen in the following case. The fact that compensatory damages were awarded indicates that the force used was unreasonable. The award of punitive damages indicates that some type of wanton, malicious, evil, or wicked behavior was involved.

RAMADA INNS, INC. v. SHARP
711 P. 2d 1 (1985)

PER CURIAM:

This appeal arises out of an altercation between respondent and two security guards employed by appellant hotel. Following a trial on the merits, the jury awarded $15,000 in compensatory damages and $10,000 in punitive damages to respondent. For the reasons set forth below, we affirm the award of compensatory and punitive damages.

Respondent was employed by an escort service. According to her, it was her job to visit potential clients and arrange an escort for them if possible. In order to see these potential clients, respondent claimed she often had to go to their hotel rooms. At the time of the incident, respondent was preparing to leave appellant's hotel after having just completed one such "run." Respondent was approached by a hotel security guard as she was waiting for an elevator to return to the casino. The parties' versions of respondent's fall differ greatly;

however, the jury accepted the respondent's contention that she had been pushed down a flight of stairs by security guards employed by appellant. The jury ordered appellant to pay respondent compensatory damages of $15,000 for intentional infliction of emotional distress and battery and $10,000 as punitive damages.

Appellant hotel contends that punitive damages may not be assessed against an employer for an act of his employee unless the employer either (1) authorized the act or (2) ratified or approved of the act resulting in an award of punitive damages. *See* Restatement (Second) of Torts § 909 (1979). This is otherwise known as the "complicity theory." Respondent, on the other hand, maintains that an employer is vicariously liable for acts of an employee which give rise to an award of punitive damages if the employee was acting within the scope of his employment. This is known as the "vicarious liability rule."

Appellant asked for and received, over objection, a jury instruction predicated on the complicity theory; therefore, the jury was instructed in accordance with appellant's view of the law. There was evidence in the record indicating that appellant gave its security guards wide latitude in dealing with unescorted females who were not registered guests. Because there was substantial evidence to support the jury's verdict under either the complicity theory or the vicarious liability rule, we will not overturn the judgment on appeal.

A plaintiff is never entitled to punitive damages as a matter of right; their allowance or denial rests entirely in the discretion of the trier of fact. Therefore, the amount of punitive damages to be awarded cannot be ascertained until the trier of fact has heard all the evidence. Because the amount of punitive damages to be awarded is not known until the judgment is rendered, we hold that prejudgment interest may not be granted by a trial court on punitive damage awards.

Accordingly, we affirm the judgment of the trial court with respect to the award of compensatory and punitive damages.

CASE COMMENT

Both compensatory and punitive damages were awarded to the respondent: $15,000 for intentional infliction of emotional distress and battery and $10,000 as punitive damages. There was evidence that the security guards were given wide latitude in dealing with unescorted females who were not registered as guests. Closer supervision and less latitude may have obviated this $25,000 award.

RETREAT

In the following case a 5-foot 4-inch, 139-pound, armed security guard, got into an altercation with a 6-foot 3-inch, 175-pound, "strong as a bull," theater patron. The situation developed from the patron's displeasure with the sanitariness of a salt dispenser for a $0.68 order of popcorn. While the facts of the scuffle are controverted, the security guard killed the patron with one shot in the chest. The issue in the guard's appeal of a sentence of life imprisonment involves retreat when one is faced with deadly assault in one's place of business. Should a security guard, assigned to protect theater patrons, be required to flee when confronted with a deadly attack thereby disregarding the possibility that such a withdrawal might permit the aggressor to vent his anger on the patrons?

Or, should the security guard, hired to protect business invitees and maintain order, not be obligated to retreat and meet deadly force with deadly force? And does the proprietor of a place of amusement have a duty to maintain order and, if so, under what circumstances?

PEOPLE v. JOHNSON
254 N.W. 2d 667 (1977)

RILEY, Judge.

Following a jury trial and conviction on a charge of second-degree murder, the trial court meted out a sentence of life imprisonment to defendant Joeseype Johnson. Defendant now appeals raising four claims of error. We reverse on one and refrain from addressing the others since they are unlikely to recur on retrial.

The facts surrounding the death of George Peaks were hotly contested at trial. Undisputed testimony reveals, however, that on August 12, 1974 Mr. Peaks entered the Colonial Theater in Detroit accompanied by a man and two women at approximately 2:30 a.m. Mr. Peaks approached the concession stand, purchased a container of popcorn and asked the attendant, Ms. Gladys Campbell, for some salt. Ms. Campbell pointed to a red plastic container designed to dispense catsup and informed Mr. Peaks that the salt was in the catsup container. Mr. Peaks balked at the idea of using the catsup container, claiming it was unsanitary, and demanded that he be given a regular salt shaker. Ms. Campbell explained that prior patrons had taken the theater's salt shakers and that the catsup container was the only available dispenser of salt.

Unmollified, Mr. Peaks continued to protest loudly. The theater manager, Mr. Frederick Kregear, hearing the disturbance, approached Mr. Peaks and discussed the problem for two or three minutes. Being unable to satisfy Mr. Peaks, the manager then summoned the defendant who was stationed at the theater as a private guard in the employ of the Gardner Security Agency. The manager then withdrew as defendant attempted to ascertain what was wrong. After learning of Mr. Peaks's complaint, defendant asked Ms. Campbell to return the purchase price of the popcorn; she complied by placing 68 cents on the counter.

In the meantime, a number of theater patrons, variously estimated at 15 to 30 persons, sensed the dispute, left their seats and entered the lobby apparently to satisfy their curiosity.

At this point the facts are controverted. Defendant claimed that Mr. Peaks refused the money, spoke derisively of defendant, punched defendant in the jaw and then reached into his coat pocket, at which time defendant out of mortal fear pulled his gun, while falling backward from the punch, and shot Mr. Peaks once in the chest. Others testified that defendant poked Mr. Peaks two or more times in the chest with a flashlight as defendant was returning the coins, that Mr. Peaks attempted merely to ward off the jabs of the flashlight but did not otherwise resist, and that Mr. Peaks stumbled backward and was then shot by defendant. It is unclear when defendant pulled his gun. Some said defendant had drawn his weapon at the start of the affray; others testified that he pulled it only a moment before the shot was fired; and still others were unsure when the gun was drawn. Mr. Peaks was later found to have been unarmed.

The testimony of the medical examiner provided support for both defense and prosecution theories of the incident. The examiner testified that the bullet entered Mr. Peaks's chest, traveled upward, and lodged in the muscles of the neck. Such a wound would result if, as defendant contended, he were falling backward as he shot, or if as the People's witnesses suggested, Mr. Peaks stumbled backward from the jabs of defendant's flashlight.

Abundant testimony was presented showing that Mr. Peaks had been drinking and appeared inebriated. In addition, it was established that Mr. Peaks weighed 175 pounds and stood 6 feet 3 inches tall; he was described by one of the women accompanying him to the theater, who had known him for several years, as being "strong as a bull." Defendant weighs 139 pounds and stands 5 feet 4 inches tall.

Defendant submits that, even absent objection, the lower court erred in instructing the jury that defendant, a private guard, was under a duty to retreat, if possible, to a safe haven when attacked on business premises. Citing *People v. Lenkevich*, 229 N.W.2d 298 (1975), defendant contends that his failure to object or to request a different instruction is no bar to appellate review. Without attempting to reconcile the apparent conflict between *Lenkevich* and GCR 1963, 516.2, we proceed to the merits because of the importance of the question involved.

Admittedly, a majority of jurisdictions considering the question have held with defendant that one faced with a deadly assault in his place of business may respond in kind without the necessity of first retreating to a place of safety. See, *e.g., Commonwealth v. Johnston*, 263 A.2d 376, 41 A.L.R.3d 576; *State v. McNamara*, 104 N.W.2d 568; *State v. Feltovic*, 147 A. 801, and cases cited in 41 A.L.R.3d 584. This rule, however, is not without its critics. See *Wilson v. State*, 69 Ga. 224 (1882); *Hall v. Commonwealth*, 22 S.W. 333 (1893); *Commonwealth v. Gagne*, Mass., 326 N.E.2d 907 (1975), and *Commonwealth v. Johnston, supra*, 263 A.2d 376.

For purposes of the present appeal, however, we need not and hence do not decide whether to expand the "no-retreat" exception to cover all persons who encounter deadly force in their places of business.[1] We approach with caution a decision to enlarge an exception that has grown but little since its original Michigan enunciation in *Pond v. People*, 8 Mich. 150, 177 (1860). Especially is this so where extending the "no-retreat" exception might heighten the prospect that an individual will choose to shed another's blood rather than avoid a conflict.

On the other hand, the virtue of the common law is its resilience, its willingness to yield in the face of reason and common understanding. The choice is not whether to be for or against unnecessary killing. As with most of the law, the alternatives are neither so polar nor simplistic. To hold that a security guard, assigned to protect theater patrons, must flee to a place of safety when confronted by a deadly attack is to disregard the possibility that such a withdrawal might permit an aggressor to vent his anger on those patrons remaining in the crowded lobby.

This is not to suggest that we accept defendant's view of the conflagration. We do not. Nor do we accept the contrary versions, for the jury's verdict tells us little. It may be that the jury believed the account of defendant and his corroborative witnesses but were nonetheless compelled to convict because defendant did not retreat. Then again, the jury might have concluded that, irrespective of the duty-to-retreat issue, defendant's response to decedent's request for a salt shaker far exceeded the force required to subdue a noisy patron. In any event, given this indeterminate state of the record, there exists the significant possibility that the question of retreat was decisive. Hence, we confront it squarely. We hold as a matter of law that under the circumstances of this case a private security guard hired to maintain order and protect business invitees has no obligation to retreat when acting in the course of his employment, but may meet deadly force with deadly force. It is incongruous to expect defendant to retire to safety when his job commands that he remain. It is illogical to demand that he flee when by so doing he, as well as his employer and the theater owner, may arguably be held civilly accountable for the havoc wreaked in his absence.[2] It is unrealistic for this

---

[1]Moreover, we express no opinion regarding the retreat issue *vis à vis* a security guard employed to protect property.

[2]*See* 2 Restatement Torts, 2d, § 344, pp. 223–224, Comment f:

"f. *Duty to police premises.* Since the possessor of premises open to the public for business purposes is not an insurer of the visitor's safety, he is ordinarily under no duty to exercise any care until he knows or has reason to know that the acts of the third person are occurring, or are about to occur. He may, however, know or have reason to know, from past experience, that there is a likelihood of conduct on

Court, safely isolated in its appellate aerie, to enforce a rule whose practical application in the instant setting denies common sense.

The testimony adduced below manifests that noisy disturbances often necessitating police assistance were common occurrences at the Colonial, a 24-hour theater located near downtown Detroit. The defendant's job was to maintain order there within the bounds of the law. Whether in fact he exceeded those limits is for a properly instructed jury, not this Court, to decide.

We do not intend to intimate by this opinion that private security guards may now kill noisome patrons with carefree abandon. The decision to take life can only be countenanced in the most extreme and compelling circumstances. Thus, to make the defense of self-defense available, evidence on the other requisite elements must still appear. Specifically, defendant must produce evidence (a) that his own aggressive acts did not precipitate the conflict;[3] (b) that he entertained an honest belief at the time that he was in imminent danger of death or serious bodily harm; and (c) that his only recourse lay in physically repelling the attack. See *People v. Bright*, 50 Mich. App. 401, 406, 213 N.W.2d 279 (1973).

That a man died because of his insistence on using a salt shaker is a tragedy we do not condone. That another man may be incarcerated for life for a crime he may not have committed is an evil equally as lamentable.

Reversed and remanded.

ALLEN, Presiding Judge (concurring).

I concur in the decision to reverse because of the possibility that the jury may have felt that the defendant's failure to retreat automatically required his conviction. For the reasons so eloquently expressed by Judge Riley, I agree that the law should take into account the fact that

---

the part of third persons in general which is likely to endanger the safety of the visitor, even though he has no reason to expect it on the part of any particular individual. If the place or character of his business, or his past experience, is such that he should reasonably anticipate careless or criminal conduct on the part of third persons, either generally or at some particular time, he may be under a duty to take precautions against it, *and to provide a reasonably sufficient number of servants to afford a reasonable protection.*" (Emphasis added.)

[3] On remand, the following observation from 4 Am.Jur.2d, Amusements and Exhibitions, § 9, p. 120 should prove helpful to the lower court in fashioning its instruction on self-defense.

"The proprietor of a place of public amusement has a duty to maintain proper quiet and good order in and about his place during the performance and while persons are assembling and leaving. He may, where he believes a patron's conduct justifies it, request the latter to be quiet and orderly, but he must do so quietly, politely, and without unnecessarily humiliating the patron. If that is not enough, he may take such additional reasonable steps as he deems necessary to end the noise or disturbance, as by summoning a police officer to act in quieting the patron, *or he may request the patron to leave, or, if it seems necessary, may use necessary and reasonable force to eject one who refuses to leave and persists in noise or disorder or in violating proper and reasonable regulations adopted to secure quiet and good order, if he exercises the right of ejection within the limitations of good order and without insult, abuse, or defamation, or, it has been said, not arbitrarily, or without just reason or cause.*" (Emphasis added. Footnotes omitted.) Hence, with regard to the element of self defense requiring that the accused be without fault or non-aggressive, defendant would be entitled, upon request, to an instruction that defendant is not the aggressor "if it seemed necessary" that defendant "use *necessary and reasonable* force to eject one who refuses to leave and persists in noise or disorder." (Emphasis added.)

Moreover, to allay confusion, it should be noted that even an aggressor may justifiably defend himself in two situations:

"(1) A nondeadly aggressor (*i.e.*, one who begins an encounter, using only his fists or some nondeadly weapon) who is met with deadly force in defense may justifiably defend himself against the deadly attack. This is so because the aggressor's victim, by using deadly force against nondeadly aggression, uses unlawful force. (2) So too, an aggressor who in good faith effectively withdraws from any further encounter with his victim (and to make an effective withdrawal he must notify the victim, or at least take reasonable steps to notify him) is restored to his right of self-defense." Thus if the evidence warrants it, appropriate instructions should issue incorporating the foregoing qualifications.

other lives may be lost if a security guard retreats in order to save his own life. Therefore, even if retreat is possible, I agree that it should not be absolutely required in all cases.

However, I am afraid that the opinion may be interpreted as establishing a rule that a security guard is entitled to stand and fight even if he could retreat without immediately jeopardizing anyone's safety.

I prefer the approach adopted by the proposed new Michigan Criminal Jury Instructions which state that a failure to retreat when retreat is possible is a circumstance which the jury may consider in determining whether the defendant was justified in using deadly force.

CASE COMMENT

The court held that as a matter of law under the circumstances of this case that a private security guard hired to maintain order and protect business invitees has no obligation to retreat when he is acting in the scope of his employment and may meet deadly force with deadly force. While the court went along with the majority of jurisdictions on this rule, it noted that the rule was not without critics. The court pointed out that while possessors of business premises open to the public are not insurers of the visitor's safety, they may be under a duty of care if they know or have reason to know certain types of acts of a third party may occur. If the place, the character of the business, or experience is such that they should anticipate careless or criminal conduct, they may be under a duty to provide servants to afford reasonable protection. The court did not intend to intimate that security guards could kill noisome patrons as the decision to take life can only be countenanced in the most compelling and extreme circumstances. The defense of self-defense must include evidence that one's own aggressive acts did not precipitate the conflict, that he entertained an honest belief at the time that he was in imminent danger of death or serious bodily injury, and that his only recourse lay in physically repelling the attack.

WHOLLY WITHOUT JUSTIFICATION

Plaintiff, in the next case, was a patently mentally retarded man who entered a store, purchased a soft drink, and sat down at a table with his drink. A security guard and others teased and taunted him. He asked that the group not bother him. After a few minutes the security guard punched him to the extent that blood was pouring down his face. He was handcuffed and thrown into a booth. The store manager did not require written reports and admonished the guard that he should "cover" himself. Note the punitive damage award due to malicious action and the extension of this award to the corporation by ratification due to the manager's reprehensible action and inaction.

O'DONNELL v. K–MART CORPORATION
474 N.Y.S. 2d 344 (1984)

DILLON, Presiding Justice:

At the time of the event giving rise to this suit, plaintiff was 23 years of age and patently mentally retarded. On the trial of his causes of action for assault and battery and false imprisonment, there was overwhelming credible evidence, upon which the jury apparently relied, that the conduct of defendant Philip McCarthy, security officer for defendant K-Mart Corporation (K-Mart) in assaulting, striking, seizing, handcuffing and unlawfully detaining plaintiff on the premises of K-Mart, was wholly without justification, and was wanton and malicious. The jury awarded plaintiff $35,000 in compensatory damages against both defendants and $70,000 in punitive damages against defendant K-Mart only, and we affirm.

On the evening of August 17, 1979 plaintiff went into the snack bar of K-Mart's downtown store in the City of Syracuse, ordered Coca Cola and sat down at a table. Seated at a nearby table was a group of four K-Mart employees, including defendant McCarthy and two assistant store managers, Anthony Kozak and Robert Perhacs. Kozak was in charge of the store that evening. According to plaintiff, McCarthy said "look at the guy with the goofy looking glasses" and plaintiff asked that the group not bother him. McCarthy told plaintiff to leave the store but plaintiff refused because he had not finished consuming his drink. After passage of a few minutes, during which it appears that McCarthy teased and taunted plaintiff without objection from either Kozak or Perhacs, McCarthy again asked plaintiff to leave and when plaintiff refused, McCarthy, according to both plaintiff and Perhacs, "punched" plaintiff in the mouth and Perhacs observed blood "pour down O'Donnell's face." At some point during the altercation, McCarthy asked another employee to "get a camera." Plaintiff was crying "and hysterical" and Kozak joined with McCarthy in putting handcuffs on plaintiff, who was then thrown into a booth where he was detained until the arrival of police. On orders of Police Sergeant Henry Burns, who had come to know plaintiff from having observed him hundreds of times in the downtown area, the handcuffs were removed from plaintiff by McCarthy. Indeed, Burns threatened McCarthy with arrest if plaintiff was not immediately freed. Burns testified that plaintiff was upset and crying as he was taken in the police car by Burns to plaintiff's parents' home where, according to his mother, he continued crying.

The incident was reported to George Halter, the store manager, by Perhacs and McCarthy, if not also by Kozak. Significantly, Halter did not require that written incident reports be filed, and not only did he perpetuate McCarthy's employment but, quoting McCarthy's testimony, Halter said that "I should cover myself."[1] Even though Halter was still in the employ of K-Mart, he was not called as a witness.

K-Mart contends that the award of punitive damages against it cannot stand in the absence of an award of punitive damages against McCarthy. We disagree. The necessary predicate for assessing punitive damages against K-Mart is that defendant McCarthy acted maliciously and, as previously stated, the evidence fully supports a finding that he did. Additionally, in this regard, K-Mart made no objection to the court's charge and thus the charge was the law of the case. It freely allowed the jury to make a punitive award against K-Mart without making such an award against McCarthy.

We turn next to the preserved issue of whether there was a sufficient showing of culpability on the part of K-Mart to justify the award of punitive damages. K-Mart interposed a precharge objection that there had been no showing by plaintiff that K-Mart had "condoned," authorized or ratified McCarthy's acts. The argument is repeated on appeal and we reject it, as did the trial court.

The rule for employer liability in this State requires more than a mere showing that the employee was acting within the scope of his employment; there must be some degree of wrongdoing on the employer's part (Prosser, Torts, 4th ed, p. 12; Restatement, Torts 2d, § 909, comment b). Corporations, of course, may act only through human beings and, as

---

[1]To add insult, indignity and separate injury to those already suffered by plaintiff, defendants in their answer pleaded the totally unfounded "shoplifting" defense provided by section 218 of the General Business Law.

expressed in the Restatement, the corporate employer may be held punitively liable for the act of an employee if the act was authorized, ratified, approved or performed by a managerial agent.

In determining whether an employee is a managerial agent of such rank as to bind the employer, we examine the function of the managerial employee in relation to the nature and operation of the employer's business. K-Mart operates an interstate chain of retail stores, each of which functions under the day-to-day direction of a store manager who oversees the conduct of the store's employees. In the case of this retail operation, in the manager's absence, an assistant was in charge. These managerial employees were the principal representatives of the corporation at this store. Their acts can only be viewed as acts of the corporation for which the corporation must be held responsible. The assistant manager, Kozak, at least passively participated in ridiculing plaintiff and affirmatively participated in restraining, handcuffing and detaining plaintiff. His superior, Halter, took no action against him or McCarthy, and Halter's admonition to McCarthy that he should "cover" himself was so reprehensible that the jury could have viewed it as ratifying or approving McCarthy's conduct. In that connection, the jury was properly charged on the permissible inferences which could be drawn from the failure of defendants to produce Halter's testimony.

In all of the circumstances we see here there was more than an adequate basis for the jury to conclude that the employees in charge of this store had sufficient managerial authority upon which to impose liability against K-Mart for punitive damages for their actions, and we further conclude that the jury was justified in finding authorization or ratification by K-Mart of McCarthy's malicious acts.

On the causes of action alleged and proved, plaintiff was entitled to recover damages for his physical injuries, pain and suffering, and also for his mental suffering and injury to his reputation. While there was no proof that his physical injuries were permanent, they were not insubstantial, and the duration of his conscious pain and suffering is not itself all-controlling. The principal element of his damage, however, was mental suffering. He was subjected to gross indignity and public humiliation. While it is difficult, in view of his handicap, to assess the amount and degree of fear instilled in plaintiff, it cannot be gainsaid that he was exposed to a terrifying experience. We do not find the award of compensatory damages to be so high as to shock the conscience of the court.

Nor do we find that the award of punitive damages should be reduced. The jury was properly charged that the purpose of a punitive damage award is to punish and deter defendant, and to deter and warn others against committing similar acts. The propriety of a punitive award is not generally susceptible to precise measurement, but any such award should not be reduced by an appellate court unless it is grossly excessive. The deterrent effect of a punitive damage award is to some extent dependent upon the wealth of the defendant, and no claim is made here that K-Mart is less than a substantial business entity.

Accordingly, the judgment and order denying defendants' motions to set aside the verdicts should be affirmed.

Order and Judgment unanimously affirmed with costs.

CASE COMMENT

The court took note of the overwhelming credible evidence as to the conduct of the security guard in assaulting, striking, seizing, handcuffing, and unlawfully detaining the plaintiff. The court found that this was wholly without justification and was wanton and malicious. Punitive damages were awarded against the corporation even though they were not awarded against the guard. The subjecting of a customer to gross indignity, public humiliation, assault, seizure by handcuffs, and detention without justification hardly fits into the aegis of loss prevention.

INEXCUSABLE ACTS

In the next case, a casino patron found a wallet and attempted several times through casino security to get some assurance that the wallet would be returned to its owner or that an announcement be made. For his troubles he was harassed, threatened, imprisoned, and manacled after being physically assaulted. He spent time in a locked office with numerous security guards in it. He was taken "downtown" and booked by city police for disorderly conduct and obstructing a public officer. The patron was acquitted after a two-day trial.

HALE v. RIVERBOAT CASINO, INC.
682 P.2d 190 (1984)

MOWBRAY, Justice:

This is an appeal from an order granting a new trial. Appellant, James R. Hale (Hale), brought suit to recover damages caused by respondent Riverboat Casino, Inc. (Riverboat). The jury favored him with its verdict following a four-day trial. Riverboat moved for a new trial, alleging juror misconduct and excessive punitive damages. The district court initially ordered a new trial unless Hale accepted a reduction in the amount of damages. Before Hale could accept the remittitur, the district court *sua sponte* ordered an unconditional new trial.

Hale appeals this order arguing that there was no juror misconduct and that the damages were not excessive. We agree and reverse, reinstating the jury verdict.

The Facts

On May 23, 1977, Hale was in Las Vegas attending a Far West Regional Conference sponsored by the National Teacher Corporation. Hale came with a group from Portland, Oregon. He holds a doctoral degree, and had been a professor at Portland State University for more than twenty-one years, where he was administrator of the teacher education program. The following narrative is drawn from the testimony in support of the jury's verdict.

On the evening of May 23, 1977, Hale and three members of his regional group played keno at the Holiday Casino, owned by respondent Riverboat. Someone nearby noticed a wallet next to Hale's chair, and pointed it out. Hale saw the wallet on the floor next to his foot, and a man standing beside him reached down and handed it to him. Hale inquired of his companions, but none of them owned the wallet. Hale searched for identification. He found no identification, but did discover several hundred dollars in United States and Canadian currency, a shopping list and a monogram on the wallet itself. The wallet appeared to be a woman's wallet.

Hale reported his discovery to the keno window. A security guard soon appeared in the keno lounge area, and Hale waved him over. Hale explained what had occurred. The guard simply said: "Okay, give me the billfold." Hale reiterated his story, suggesting that perhaps the guard could make an announcement and have the owner come and identify it. According to Hale, the guard simply said: "I can't do that;" then he stuck out his hand and said: "Give me the wallet," or "Give me the money." The guard left after Hale refused to hand over the wallet and Hale resumed playing keno. Sometime later, Hale repeated the story to a second security officer, again asking whether an announcement could be made. The security officer merely responded that he'd "better give it to Fitzgerald," the first guard. Hale expressed concern over dealing with the first guard, whom he described as acting in an ugly and threatening manner.

Sometime later, Fitzgerald returned to where Hale was playing keno and demanded that Hale move to the perimeter of the lounge area. After a joking response, Hale complied. Once they were separated from the keno lounge by a bank of slot machines, Hale testified that the guard backed him into the slot machines and demanded: "Give me the money." Hale asked for some assurance that the wallet would be returned to the owner, or that an announcement be made. According to Hale "he got his finger down in my face and he called me stupid-ass boy, and he told me I was going to get myself in a lot of trouble if I didn't give him that money and said he was going to call Metro." Hale refused to surrender the wallet without assurances, and he rejoined his friends.

Soon Hale was introduced to a new officer, who was a member of the Las Vegas Metropolitan Police Department. Hale repeated his story and his concern. The officer suggested that Hale give the wallet to him, or turn it over to the first guard. When Hale refused to do so, without assurances, the officer read him the Trespass Act, while the first guard said he had "better not try to leave." It was then suggested that they all go upstairs and settle the matter. Hale consented, so long as his friends could accompany him.

The guards surrounded Hale and proceeded upstairs to an office. They entered the office and the door was slammed shut and locked with Hale's friends outside, banging on the door and attempting to talk to the guards. Hale was ordered to sit. The wallet was again demanded, and Hale again requested assurance that it would be returned to its rightful owner. Hale testified that someone said: "Get up," so he stood, and was told to put his hands behind his back. He did not know how many guards were in the room, but at least four of them came toward him and one of them said: "Let's teach this guy a lesson." They grabbed his wrists and took his glasses out of his pocket. Then Hale testified that the guards yanked him out of the corner, pulled his arms over his head, handcuffed him and threw him back into the chair. They then took the billfold out of his pocket and sat down and began counting the money.

Hale asked to see a manager. He testified at this point that a man wearing a suit came forward, leaned down and said: "I am the manager and you are going to get just what you deserve," and walked out of the office. Hale pleaded with the guards to take the handcuffs off. One of the guards leaned down and said that Hale had called him a name, and "no one has ever gotten away with that."

Meanwhile, one of Hale's colleagues was rapping on the office window, calling out that the woman who had lost the wallet was there. Some of the guards left the office, apparently to return the wallet. The others got Hale up, saying: "Come on, we are going downtown." As Hale passed out of the office with the guards he saw a woman, crying, and expressed his gratification that she had her wallet back. Then Hale and the guards proceeded downstairs, and through the casino, Hale handcuffed and surrounded. The police officer put Hale in a car and drove him downtown. He informed Hale that Fitzgerald had made a citizen's arrest at the casino.

Hale was booked for disorderly conduct and obstructing a public officer. Despite his offer of cash bail, he was stripped, body searched, sprayed for lice and placed into a crowded holding cell. He was fingerprinted and photographed in jail coveralls. Several hours later he was released onto the street, with a check in place of the cash that had been in his wallet. Fortunately, he met his friends, and returned with them to his hotel.

Knowledge of his arrest became widespread among participants in the conference. He was called upon to give an explanation to the entire group from Oregon, but faltered so from humiliation that a colleague had to intercede and explain.

When Hale returned to Portland he was required to seek medical attention for a back sprain which had occurred when the guards had pulled his arms. The pain persisted for two to three months thereafter. Hale also testified that his standing and reputation had been injured and that his educational consulting business had declined dramatically since the arrest.

Respondent pursued prosecution of Hale, and until the charges were resolved he felt unable to attend other conferences where he might encounter persons from the Las Vegas conference. Hale had to return to Las Vegas to defend the charges in a two-day trial. This required retaining counsel and borrowing money to pay witnesses for flying to Las Vegas from various parts of the country. He was acquitted after a two-day trial.

Hale brought the instant suit against Riverboat, acting through its agents and employees, for negligence, assault and battery, false imprisonment, malicious prosecution, defamation, and negligent and/or intentional infliction of emotional distress. In his Amended Complaint Hale sought punitive, as well as compensatory damages.

After a four-day trial and approximately two hours of deliberations, a unanimous jury verdict was reached in favor of Hale and against Riverboat as follows: compensatory damages were awarded in the amount of $2,100 and punitive damages in the amount of $97,900 for a total assessment of $100,000.

Thereafter, Riverboat brought motions to "Recall Jurors to Order Background Checks on the Jury Panel," and for "New Trial and/or Remittitur." Opposition to these motions was filed by Hale. Approximately five months later the district judge denied Riverboat's Motion to Recall Jurors and ordered that Riverboat be granted a new trial if, within twenty days, Hale did not consent to the following: increasing the compensatory damage award from $2,100 to $8,000, and reducing the punitive damage award assessment from $97,900 to $30,000; *i.e.,* modifying the total jury assessment from $100,000 to $38,000. Later, on the nineteenth day after this decision, the trial judge informed counsel for both parties that he was going to vacate his order reducing the jury verdict and granted Riverboat a new trial. This appeal followed. The trial court abused its discretion in granting a new trial under the circumstances presented in this case.

Damages

In support of its motion for a new trial, Riverboat argued that the punitive damages were excessive. Hale contends on appeal that the punitive damage award of $97,900 was not so excessive as to justify a new trial. We agree.

Recently, we reiterated the general rule regarding the award of excessive punitive damages:

> Heretofore, we have recognized the subjective nature of punitive damages and the absence of workable standards by which to evaluate the propriety of such an award. Accordingly, we have allowed that determination to rest with the discretion of the trier of the fact unless the evidence introduced at trial shows that the amount awarded by the jury would financially destroy or annihilate the defendant in which event we would attempt an appropriate adjustment of the award.

The award should be not be disturbed unless it is so large as to appear "to have been given under the influence of passion or prejudice." A large award alone does not conclusively indicate that passion and prejudice influenced the trier of fact. The amount of an award need not be proportional to the amount of compensatory damages. Rather, punitive damages are authorized "for the sake of example and by way of punishing the defendant."

In the case at bar the facts regarding Riverboat's culpability are essentially undisputed. The security guards' acts were inexcusable. Hale conscientiously attempted to assure the return of the lost wallet. For his concern he was harassed, threatened, imprisoned and manacled after being physically assaulted. Hale was then escorted to jail in handcuffs, booked and held in jail for a good portion of the night. Riverboat's employees participated in Hale's prosecution, causing him not only the ignominy of a criminal trial, but also the incurrence of substantial expense.

The award in this case at the time of the jury verdict amounted to less than 1.5% of Riverboat's annual net profit, and less than ½ percent of its net worth. It is clear that the award will not financially destroy or annihilate Riverboat. The amount of damages was not large nor excessive, in view of Riverboat's net worth. Our judicial conscience is not shocked. For these reasons we find that the trial judge abused his discretion in ordering a new trial.

We accordingly reverse the order for a new trial and we reinstate the jury verdict.

CASE COMMENT

The plaintiff did not consent to remittitur of the damages award, and the Supreme Court upheld the original compensatory and punitive damages award against the defendant corporation. The court held the acts of the security guards inexcusable, noting that for his concern in attempting to assure return of the wallet he was harassed, threatened, imprisoned, and manacled after being physically assaulted. He was also booked and jailed, which caused him not only ignominy but also considerable expense. The court pointed out that punitive damages are authorized for sake of example and by way of punishing the defendant.

STANDARD OF PROOF—CIVIL/CRIMINAL

This next case, a civil case, is related to *People v. Borrero,* a criminal case, located earlier in this chapter. Both cases deal with negligence: criminal and civil. The standard of proof in a criminal case is *beyond a reasonable doubt,* and the standard of proof in a civil case is a *fair preponderance of evidence.* While the security guard's conviction for criminally negligent homicide was vacated and the indictment dismissed, the civil negligence award against the guard and his employer was reinstated. Thus an acquittal on criminal negligence charges does not necessarily mean that this higher standard of proof can be used in a civil matter.

JOHNSON v. OVAL PHARMACY
569 N.Y.S. 2d 49 (1991)

KASSAL, Justice.

This lawsuit arises from a tragic incident in which a minor dispute between plaintiff's deceased, John T. Johnson, and defendant Georgino Borrero, a part-time armed security guard employed by defendant Epic Security Protection & Intelligence Systems, Limited (Epic Security), assigned to work at defendant Oval Pharmacy Drug Store (Oval Pharmacy), escalated into a confrontation that ultimately resulted in Johnson's death. Following a jury verdict in plaintiff's favor against Borrero and Oval Pharmacy, the trial court granted said defendants' motions to set aside the verdict pursuant to CPLR § 4404, and dismissed the complaint. Upon examination of this record, we modify the court's ruling to the extent of reinstating the verdict with respect to defendant Borrero, and directing entry of judgment thereon against Borrero and defendant Epic Security.

As relevant to this appeal, the trial testimony established that at approximately 4:55 p.m. on May 8, 1982, Johnson, a 63-year-old retired narcotics detective, who was then employed by the Legal Aid Society as a supervisor of investigators, and who was licensed to carry a gun, entered Oval Pharmacy and, as required by the store, checked his shopping bag with defendant Borrero. A dispute arose when Johnson requested a receipt for the bag and was told by Borrero that he had run out of receipts, but that Johnson would have no trouble reclaiming his package because not many items had been checked. As this trivial matter quickly developed into a heated argument, Johnson angrily demanded the return of his shopping bag, saying that he was not going to shop in the store any more and that he "ought to punch (Borrero) in the mouth." At this point, Borrero took out his night stick, prompting Johnson to draw his gun and direct the guard to put the stick away, while admonishing that he would not be treated "like a kid." Another store employee asked Johnson to put his gun away, and Johnson complied. He then left the store, shopping bag in hand and a pipe in his mouth.

The record further reveals that the pharmacist-president of Oval Pharmacy, Eli Krellenstein, attempted to prevent Borrero from following Johnson out of the store, but that the guard nevertheless did so, an act which he testified was for the purpose of looking for a police officer who had passed the store minutes earlier. Upon failing to see the officer, Borrero began to move in the direction of Johnson, who had crossed two traffic lanes of Metropolitan Avenue, on which the pharmacy was located, and was standing on its center island with his back toward Borrero. Johnson still carried his shopping bag and had a pipe in his mouth.

Calling out from the sidewalk, Borrero demanded to know whether Johnson was a police officer, but Johnson ignored him and continued to walk away. Borrero, however, persisted in his calls and Johnson ultimately turned around. According to Borrero's testimony, Johnson turned with an unholstered gun in his hand, causing Borrero to take cover behind a car, pull his own gun, and order Johnson to "freeze." This testimony conflicted with that of a non-party witness, Roy Grundmann, who had been crossing Metropolitan Avenue in the same direction and at the same time as Johnson. Grundmann testified that he heard a voice yell "halt" and turned around to see Borrero standing with his gun drawn and pointed in his and Johnson's direction. Grundmann next heard Borrero call out, while still pointing his gun, "Are you a cop?," and observed Johnson remove his own gun, still in its holster, and move behind the other side of the parked vehicle from which Borrero was aiming his gun. When Grundmann turned to escape from what he correctly perceived to be a potentially dangerous situation, he heard a shot and turned back in time to observe Johnson falling on top of the parked car and sliding down onto the street. At no time had this witness ever seen Johnson with his gun outside of its holster.

Borrero's version of the shooting was that Johnson had continued to come toward him from the other side of the car behind which he had taken cover, holding an unholstered gun in one hand and his shopping bag in the other. Borrero further testified that Johnson put his bag on top of the car and assumed a combat stance, holding the gun with both hands and pointing it at Borrero. It was then, the security guard testified, that he fired the fatal shot into Johnson's head.

The first police officer to arrive, Israel Larracuente, was about approximately one block from the scene when a passing motorist told him that he was needed. As Officer Larracuente was on his way, he heard the shot and, arriving within 20 seconds thereof, found Johnson lying face up between two parked cars with a gunshot wound to the left side of his temple. Larracuente recovered Johnson's gun, which was holstered and contained five unspent rounds. The holster latch guarding the gun's hammer was closed and the muzzle of the gun was similarly secured within the holster.

The jury unanimously found in plaintiff's favor against defendants Borrero and Oval Pharmacy, apportioning liability at 60% against Borrero and 20% against Oval Pharmacy, and attributing 20% comparative negligence to the decedent. Although Epic Security was found negligent in its supervision and training of Borrero, the jury held this negligence not to be the proximate cause of Johnson's death. Damages were assessed in the sum of $160,000.

Following the verdict, defendants Borrero and Oval Pharmacy moved, pursuant to CPLR § 4404, to set aside the verdict on the grounds that it was against the weight of the evidence and insufficient as a matter of law. This motion was granted by the trial court, which found that no negligence by these defendants had been established. Upon examination of this record, we modify to reinstate the jury's verdict as against defendant Borrero, and direct entry of judgment thereon against Borrero and his employer, defendant Epic Security.

At the outset, it should be noted that the factual determinations and principles of law applicable to the criminal prosecution of Georgino Borrero, which preceded this civil suit, are neither binding nor dispositive of the issues currently before this Court. Borrero, who was indicted for manslaughter in the second degree and convicted, after a bench trial, of criminally negligent homicide, successfully appealed the judgment of conviction to this Court, which predicated its reversal on the ground that "there was no reasonable view of the evidence to support a finding that he was guilty of criminally negligent homicide." *People v. Borrero,* 504 N.Y.S.2d 654.

In light of the lack of identity of parties in the two proceedings, neither issue preclusion nor collateral estoppel is applicable to the civil proceeding. Moreover, the criminal action, in which the state bore the burden of establishing beyond a reasonable doubt that Borrero had committed the crime of criminally negligent homicide, was necessarily subjected to an entirely different standard of proof than that applicable here. It is for this very reason that acquittal on criminal charges is inadmissible in a subsequent civil action. With respect to whether the jury's verdict was insufficient as a matter of law or against the weight of the evidence, we first note that it is well established that the evidence must be viewed in the light most favorable to the prevailing party. Bearing this in mind, we have reviewed the record and conclude that the verdict determining that Borrero was negligent cannot be said to have been based upon legally insufficient evidence. Such a determination requires a finding that "there is simply no valid line of reasoning and permissible inferences which could possibly lead rational men to the conclusion reached by the jury on the basis of the evidence presented at trial." That Borrero's testimony conflicted with that of non-party witness Grundmann, merely raises an issue of credibility for the jury to resolve, and does not constitute a ground for dismissal of the complaint on grounds of legal insufficiency. Furthermore, a plaintiff is held to a lesser standard of proof in a wrongful death action, where the deceased is unavailable to recount his version of the events. Nor does this record yield any support for the claim that there is no valid line of reasoning which could rationally lead a jury to conclude that Borrero was negligent. Rather, the jury was entitled to conclude, from the evidence presented, that Borrero's act of following an armed man—and, specifically, one with whom he had just had a heated dispute—out into the street, was not consistent with the exercise of reasonable care. The jury was further entitled to accept, and interpret as evidence of negligence, the testimony of eyewitness Grundmann, to the effect that Borrero called out to Johnson (who was walking way from the store and posing no threat to anyone) while holding a drawn gun. This undoubtedly caused Johnson, who turned and saw Borrero aiming the weapon at him, to take out his own gun. That the first arriving police officer found Johnson's gun still in its holster lends support to Grundmann's testimony that Borrero was the first to draw his weapon, and further supports a finding that Borrero prematurely resorted to deadly force. In short, the evidence amply supports the verdict—Borrero did not undertake his self-imposed duty of capturing an armed and potentially dangerous person in a manner consistent with a reasonable person's standard of care.

In this regard, we note that the trial court improperly substituted its own factual determination to supplant that of the jury in finding that it was Johnson who first drew a gun. With respect to the setting aside of the verdict as against the weight of the evidence, a court may only exercise its discretion to do so where the verdict is "palpably wrong and it can be plainly seen that the preponderance is so great that the jury could not have reached its conclusion upon any fair interpretation of the evidence." As with the claim of legal insufficiency, this determination relies heavily upon the resolution of factual controversy. As such, the jury's fact-finding role must not be unnecessarily interfered with or usurped. For the very reasons noted with respect to defendants' claims of legal insufficiency, we hold that it was improper for the verdict to have been set aside as against the weight of the evidence.

Inasmuch as Epic Security, Borrero's employer, is vicariously liable for the guard's acts of negligence committed within the scope of his employment, we direct that judgment be entered as a matter of law against that defendant. In so doing, we note that it was undisputed that any negligence on the part of Borrero would be imputed to Epic Security as his employer and, indeed, the court so charged the jury. The record establishes that the court specifically acknowledged that counsel for Epic Security had conceded that Borrero was acting within the scope of his employment and that Epic Security was therefore vicariously liable for his negligence under the doctrine of *respondeat superior.* Of course, vicarious liability does not require that the employer foresee the precise act or manner in which the injury occurred, but only that the general type of conduct may reasonably have been expected. However, we discern no negligence, vicarious or direct on the part of Oval Pharmacy, which merely contracted with Epic Security for the assignment of an unspecified armed security guard to its store. This defendant was neither involved in Borrero's training nor aware of any deficiencies or behavioral problems in the part-time guard assigned by Epic Security.

Moreover, the owner of Oval Pharmacy had attempted to restrain Borrero when he insisted on leaving the store in pursuit of Johnson. In light of all these circumstances, we conclude that Oval Pharmacy was not negligent and that the complaint as to this defendant was properly dismissed.

Accordingly, the order, Supreme Court, Bronx County (Philip C. Modesto, J.), entered July 12, 1989, which set aside the jury's verdict in favor of plaintiff and dismissed the complaint, should be modified, on the law and facts, to reinstate the verdict with respect to defendant Georgino Borrero and direct entry of judgment thereon against defendants Borrero and Epic Security, and otherwise affirmed, without costs.

Order, Supreme Court, Bronx County (Philip C. Modesto, J.), entered on July 12, 1989, modified, on the law and facts, to reinstate the verdict with respect to defendant Georgino Borrero and direct entry of judgment thereon against defendants Borrero and Epic Security, and otherwise affirmed, without costs.

CASE COMMENT

The court noted that it was undisputed that any negligence on the part of the guard was imputed to his employer and that the guard was acting within the scope of his employment. Therefore the security company was vicariously liable for the negligence of the guard under the doctrine of *respondeat superior.* For a more in-depth treatment of vicarious liability and scope of employment, see Part I of this book.

13

Deprivation of Rights

Two federal statutes regarding the deprivation of rights sometimes attach to private citizens. They are Title 42, United States Code (USC), Section 1983 (civil sanctions) and Title 18, United States Code, Section 242 (criminal sanctions). Normally liability only attaches to governmental actors. A private citizen, however, can be transformed into a governmental actor under certain circumstances. The cases in this chapter examine conditions and situations under which actions of a private citizen can transform that private citizen into a governmental actor.

Of great concern to the security manager is the notion that a private corporation may be vicariously liable under Section 1983 for the acts of its employees. With this in mind, security managers should be knowledgeable about whether their employees are acting under color of law by ordinance or statute, through joint action or significant involvement with governmental agents, as a public function, or because a nexus exists between the state and the challenged activity.

COLOR OF LAW—STATUTORY PROVISION

Plaintiff Roby, in the next case, brought a civil rights action under 42 USC, Section 1983 against defendant Skupien as an officer of the Conrailroad Police Department. To sustain a Section 1983 action the plaintiff must show that the defendant acted under color of state law and that, while he was acting in such manner, he deprived the plaintiff of constitutional rights. The defendant claimed he was a private individual employed by a private corporation and denied that he was a state actor. Generally speaking, employees of a private company cannot be charged with exercising state action. In this case, however, the defendant employee of a private corporation was found to be exercising state action via statutory provision. Security managers should be knowledgeable about whether their employees are acting under color of state law. If they are so acting, constitutional sanctions apply. Note the discussion regarding lineups and probable cause for arrest.

ROBY v. SKUPIEN
758 F. Supp. 471 (1991)

BUA, District Judge.

Plaintiff Isaac Roby has filed a complaint charging defendant Officer George Skupien with violating Roby's constitutional rights. Officer Skupien has responded by moving to dismiss the complaint. Plaintiff, in turn, has filed a motion for judgment. For the reasons stated below, Officer Skupien's motion to dismiss is denied. Plaintiff's motion for judgment is also denied.

Roby's complaint consists of two counts. Count One refers to an incident which occurred on May 24, 1990. Plaintiff alleges that, on May 24, 1990, Chicago police detectives entered his home because they "had a complaint by defendant Officer George Skupien Badge No. 721 of the Conrailroad Police Department that Plaintiff had committed a theft . . . on May 19, 1990." Complaint at 2. Subsequently, Roby was brought to the police station where " 'alone' in a chair, (not in a line-up)" Roby was identified by Officer Skupien. Complaint at 2. In Count Two, Roby claims that substantially the same events occurred on June 21, 1990. Chicago police officers entered plaintiff's home and took him to the police station where he was identified by Officer Skupien. Plaintiff claims that these actions violated his first and fourteenth amendment rights. He brings his charges as a civil rights action under 42 U.S.C. § 1983.

To sustain a § 1983 action, Roby must show that (1) Officer Skupien was acting under color of state law and that (2) while acting under color of state law, Officer Skupien deprived Roby of constitutional rights. Demonstrating that Officer Skupien acted under color of state law requires a showing of state action. State action exists where plaintiff's rights have been deprived by the exercise of some right or privilege created by the state or by a rule of conduct imposed by the state, and the party charged with the deprivation is said to be a state actor.

In his motion to dismiss, Officer Skupien denies that he is a state actor. He claims that he is a private individual employed by a private corporation. Generally, employees of a private company cannot be charged with exercising state action. Yet, the private corporation in this case is a railroad. Officer Skupien is employed as a police officer in the railroad's police force. In operating a police force, the railroad is acting under a right conferred by the State. Railroads are given the power to appoint and maintain a police force through a statutory provision. When Officer Skupien acts as a member of the railroad police force, then, he is acting pursuant to a statutorily conferred right.

Moreover, railroad police officers can be said to be state actors. "When private individuals or groups are endowed by the State with powers or functions governmental in nature, they become agencies or instrumentalities of the State and subject to its constitutional limitations." The railroad police force is designed to "aid and supplement the police forces of any municipality . . . While engaged in the conduct of their employment, the members of such railroad police force have and may exercise like police powers as those conferred upon the police of cities." These considerations led the Seventh Circuit to conclude in a case involving railroad police officers that acts performed by the railroad police under authority granted them as railroad policemen are acts performed while the railroad policemen are "cloaked with the authority of the state."

Here, plaintiff has sufficiently alleged that Officer Skupien was acting in his railroad police capacity. Since plaintiff identified Officer Skupien by his badge number, Officer Skupien must have been wearing the badge at some time during his contact with plaintiff or the Chicago police officers. According to the complaint, Officer Skupien was investigating a theft of Conrail property. It follows that Officer Skupien would have furnished any information to the police and participated in an identification of plaintiff during the course of that investigation. From these allegations, the court can conclude that Officer Skupien performed the claimed actions in his railroad police capacity and, therefore, under color of state law.

Roby must also show that, while acting under color of state law, Officer Skupien deprived him of his constitutional rights. In his complaint, Roby claims violations of his first and fourteenth amendment rights. Even liberally construing plaintiff's arguments, the court cannot find evidence of a violation of first amendment rights. The fourteenth amendment claims are a different story. While it is difficult to determine the extent of Officer Skupien's involvement in the events alleged in the complaint, plaintiff does supply sufficient facts to state a claim. Roby's first claim is that his arrest was false. Count One alleges that the Chicago police officers "had" a complaint from Officer Skupien. It seems that Roby is claiming that his arrest was based on false information provided by Officer Skupien. In addition, plaintiff alludes to an overly suggestive lineup procedure. He talks of the lack of a lineup—an identification made while Roby was alone in a chair. Such a show-up could constitute a violation of Roby's rights if Roby went to trial and the pretrial show-up identification was proven so "unreliable that Roby's due process right to fair judicial procedures should have precluded an identification at trial." Both these claims, then, could be the bases for allegations of fourteenth amendment violations.

Whether Officer Skupien's actions rise to the level of a constitutional violation is a question of fact. At this stage in the proceedings, the court cannot make that determination. The court assumes that such questions will be resolved once plaintiff's complaint is supplemented by further information. Since it does not appear "beyond doubt that plaintiff can prove no set of facts in support of his claim which would entitle him to relief," the court will not dismiss Roby's complaint. Officer Skupien's motion to dismiss is denied.

Plaintiff Roby has also filed a motion for judgment. Roby appears to be asking the court to render judgment in his favor because the criminal charges upon which he was originally arrested have been dropped. Dismissal of those charges, though, does not *per se* prove a false arrest. Nor does dismissal conclusively establish an infringement of plaintiff's constitutional rights. To secure a conviction, criminal charges must be proved beyond a reasonable doubt. In contrast, actions taken during the investigative stage can be supported by a lesser standard of proof. For instance, an arrest need only be supported by probable cause—facts which would warrant a prudent person in believing that the individual in question had committed or was committing an offense. *Beck v. Ohio,* 379 U.S. 89. Therefore, even though the criminal charges could not be proved at trial, the officer could still have been acting constitutionally, pursuant to his lesser burden, when he performed his actions during the investigation. Further, far from establishing a constitutional violation, dismissal of the charges would eliminate the second of plaintiff's claims involving a suggestive show-up. Any allegations of a constitutional violation connected to the show-up could only be raised during trial. If no charges remain, no trial will occur. A constitutional claim regarding the show-up would never come up. Accordingly, plaintiff's motion for judgment is denied.

CASE COMMENT

Here the court held that the defendant Skupien, a railroad police officer, was a state actor. In operating a police force, the railroad acted under a right conferred by state statute to appoint and maintain a police force. The railroad police force was designed to aid and supplement the police of any municipality. Members of the railroad police have and may exercise like police powers to those conferred on police of the cities. Thus in some instances, private individuals or groups who are endowed by the state with powers or functions governmental in nature, become agencies or instrumentalities of the state *and subject to its constitutional limitations.*

JOINT ACTION—PRIVATE SECURITY/POLICE

In this next case, the question is whether the private security guard was acting as a private citizen or whether his activities transformed him into a governmental actor "acting under color of state law." If so, one of the two essential elements of a Section 1983 action has been met. Private citizens can come within the reach of Section 1983 liability if they are willful participants in joint action with the state or its agents (police). Joint action can be found where there is an agreement on a joint course of action in which the private party and state have a common goal and act in furtherance of that goal. Note the application of vicarious liability to the private corporation (employer of the security guard).

CARR v. CITY OF CHICAGO
669 F. Supp. 1418 (1987)

BUA, District Judge.

Before this court is a motion brought by the Palmer House Company and James Lindsey to dismiss them from plaintiff's First Amended Complaint. Plaintiff's claim is based on the deprivation of various constitutional rights, and is brought pursuant to 42 U.S.C. § 1983. This court denies defendants' motion for the reasons stated below.

Facts

On January 14, 1983, plaintiff was exiting a restaurant in the Palmer House Hotel in Chicago. Several hotel security guards took plaintiff into custody. One of the security guards, defendant Lindsey, called the Chicago Police and signed a complaint against plaintiff.

Plaintiff was transported by the police officers to police headquarters for the First District. One of the officers informed plaintiff that "every time he came into the First District and they saw him, he would be arrested." Plaintiff was detained at the station lockup for five to six hours before being released. Plaintiff alleges he was arrested, detained and charged in a similar fashion at least twenty times since May 1982. Finally, plaintiff filed this suit on August 29, 1985.

Discussion

A. Security Guard James Lindsey

Plaintiff brought a 42 U.S.C. § 1983 action against James Lindsey who is a security guard employed by the Palmer House. The Supreme Court has articulated the two essential elements of a § 1983 action: that plaintiff was deprived of a federally protected right, and the person who deprived plaintiff of the federally protected right acted under the color of state law. *Gomez v. Toledo,* 446 U.S. 635.

The threshold issue before this court is whether James Lindsey was "acting under the color of state law" when he detained plaintiff and signed a complaint against plaintiff. This court believes Lindsey was acting under the color of state law. This court rules Lindsey was not acting as a private citizen in his capacity as a private security guard when he detained plaintiff and signed a complaint against him.

Section 1983 liability can attach only to governmental actors. A private citizen can be transformed into a governmental actor under special circumstances. A private citizen comes within the reach of § 1983 liability only when "he is a willful participant in joint action with the state or its agents." *Gramenos v. Jewel Companies, Inc.,* 797 F.2d 432. Joint action can be defined as an agreement on a joint course of action in which the private party and the state have a common goal and act in furtherance of that goal. *See also Adickes v. S.H. Kress & Co.,* 398 U.S. 144.

Private security guards are engaged in "state action" when they enter into agreements with police pursuant to which the security guards carry out the policemen's directions. Security guards who carry out such directions are exercising the state's function and are treated as if they were state officials. But if a security guard is acting independently, his conduct is judged under state tort law principles (*e.g.,* false arrest, malicious prosecution, and battery) rather than being judged under the Fourth Amendment principles.

In the instant case, plaintiff alleges defendant Lindsey arrested and detained plaintiff while he notified the police. Two police officers arrived at the Palmer House Company and allegedly "had" Lindsey sign a complaint against plaintiff. Paragraph 25 of the complaint alleges the charge against plaintiff, and the arrest and detention of plaintiff were carried out by the Palmer House pursuant to a policy, practice or custom of the City of Chicago. These allegations were reiterated with a slight modification in paragraph 27. Finally, the complaint suggests Lindsey's cooperation with the police amounts to a conspiracy.

In evaluating plaintiff's pro se complaint, this court construes plaintiff's allegations liberally. This court applies substantially less stringent standards than those applied to complaints drafted by professional counsel. This complaint will not be dismissed because it does not appear beyond doubt that the plaintiff can prove no set of facts in support of his claim that would entitle him to the requested relief.

Although plaintiff's complaint is not a model of clarity, it tugs at the root of state action. For example, plaintiff alleged the police officers "had" Lindsey sign a complaint against plaintiff. Such an allegation suggests the police officers had some control over Lindsey or that Lindsey was acting in cooperation with the police. In addition, the word "had" connotes control, authority or influence that the police held over Lindsey. A more sophisticated counsel may have phrased the relationship differently between Lindsey and the police. Nevertheless, plaintiff can prove a set of facts sufficient to support his claim. This court will not dismiss this pro se plaintiff's claim merely because he was not schooled in the art of proper pleading.

Now that this court has held that Lindsey was acting under the color of state law, this court must also determine whether Lindsey's actions deprive plaintiff of a constitutional right. After careful consideration, this court finds that plaintiff's constitutional rights were violated. Plaintiff was clearly deprived of his Fourteenth Amendment right to liberty when he was arrested and detained by plaintiff and two Chicago police officers. In sum, this court denies defendant Lindsey's motions to dismiss and for summary judgment.

This court may not be so liberal if it is confronted by a proper motion for summary judgment. Plaintiff may be required to offer some evidence of some concerted effort or plan between Lindsey and the police officers. Otherwise, plaintiff will have failed to establish a question of fact about whether Lindsey violated plaintiff's constitutional rights while acting under the color of state law.

The defendants are in tune with this court's logic and have attempted to defeat plaintiff by moving in the alternative for summary judgment. However, defendant fails to comply with local General Rule 12(e) of the U.S. District Court for the Northern District of Illinois. Under Local Rule 12(e), a party moving for summary judgment must serve and file, in addition to affidavits and other materials referred to in Fed.R.Civ.P. 56(e), a statement of the material facts which the moving party contends there is no genuine issue and those facts that entitle the moving party to judgment as a matter of law. Local Rule 12(e) also states that failure to submit such a statement constitutes grounds for denial of the summary judgment motion. Defendant failed to file a statement of material facts. Consequently, this court denies defendant's motion for summary judgment for its failure to comply with Local Rule 12(e).

B. Palmer House Corporation

The Palmer House Corporation also moves to dismiss the amended complaint. The Palmer House claims it cannot be held liable under § 1983 based on vicarious liability for acts of its security guards.

This argument was raised and rejected by Judge Shadur of the United States District Court for the Northern District of Illinois. *Carr v. City of Chicago,* 85 C 6521 (N.D.Ill. Aug. 11, 1986). In *Carr,* Judge Shadur was confronted by a plaintiff who had brought suit against the Plitt Theatres, Inc. in response to the allegedly wrongful conduct committed by its employees. Employees of the Plitt Theatres allegedly arrested and detained plaintiff and filed a false complaint against plaintiff. Plitt Theatres moved to dismiss claiming liability cannot be based upon the theory of respondeat superior. Judge Shadur denied the motion stating that private corporations may be vicariously liable under § 1983 for acts of its employees.

This court is confronted by a factually identical case. The instant plaintiff brought the claims before both this court and Judge Shadur. Moreover, the plaintiff in both cases was detained and arrested by private security employees of a private corporation. In addition, these employees filed complaints against plaintiff. Since the instant case is legally and factually identical to the case before Judge Shadur, this court will adopt the holding presented by Judge Shadur. Accordingly, this court denies the Palmer House's motion to dismiss.

Conclusion

This court denies defendant Lindsey's motions for summary judgment and to dismiss plaintiff's Second Amended Complaint. In addition, the Palmer House's motion to dismiss is also denied.

IT IS SO ORDERED.

CASE COMMENT

The court held that private security guards are engaged in "state action" when they enter into agreements with police pursuant to which the security guards carry out the directions of the police. Guards who carry out such directions are exercising the state's functions and are treated as if they were state officials. The court felt that the police allegedly had the guard sign the complaint in this case. The connotation arose that the police had control, authority, or influence over the security guard. Also to be noted is the Section 1983 vicarious liability attachment to the employer of the security guard.

SIGNIFICANT INVOLVEMENT/PUBLIC FUNCTION/NEXUS TESTS

The plaintiff in the following case brought in a Section 1983 action against the Pennsylvania Security Officers Training Academy claiming the academy's lethal weapons training program was a public function. In deciding the case, the court looked at various criteria pursuant to which state action can be imputed to the challenged activity of the private person or entity. An activity does not constitute a public function merely because the state also engages in the activity or because the activity is made necessary by state statute. Significant state involvement may be found when the state and the entity are joint participants in a symbiotic relationship or where the entity is pervasively regulated by the state and a sufficient nexus exists between the state and the challenged activity. The significant involvement—joint participant analysis—requires the state to so far insinuate itself into a position of interdependence that it must be recognized as a joint participant in the challenged activity.

LOWELL v. WANTZ
85 F.R.D. 286 (1980)

HUYETT, District Judge.

Plaintiff Joseph E. Lowell (Lowell), formerly an instructor at the defendant Pennsylvania Security Officers Training Academy, Inc. (The Academy), was dismissed from that position allegedly pursuant to a conspiracy between The Academy and defendant Russell L. Wantz, Jr. (Wantz) to prevent Lowell from teaching his course in accordance with Pennsylvania law.[1] Charging violation of his First Amendment rights, Lowell brought suit against Wantz and The Academy pursuant to 42 U.S.C. § 1983. The Academy has moved for summary judgment, arguing that its activities do not constitute state action. Because 42 U.S.C. § 1983 does not authorize relief absent state action,[2] and because the facts of this case do not support a finding of state action, The Academy's motion will be granted.

---

[1]Specifically, Lowell contends that he told his students, as he claims he was required by law, that they could not lawfully carry a lethal weapon in connection with their employment unless they possessed a valid certificate issued by the state police evidencing successful completion of a state-certified training program, that the defendants did not want this information given to particular students at the academy, and that he was dismissed to prevent him from giving that information to those students.

[2]42 U.S.C. § 1983 provides:

> Every person who, under color of any statute, ordinance, regulation, custom, or usage, of any State or Territory, subjects, or causes to be subjected, any citizen of the United States or other person within the jurisdiction thereof to the deprivation of any rights, privileges, or immunities secured by the Constitution and laws, shall be liable to the party injured in an action at law, suit in equity, or other proper proceeding for redress.

In *Magill v. Avonworth Baseball Conference,* 516 F.2d 1328, the Third Circuit set forth three criteria pursuant to which state action can be imputed to private persons or entities. Lowell invokes two of them, arguing that state action is present in that (1) The Academy is performing a public function and (2) the state has significantly involved itself with The Academy. In *Brenner v. Oswald,* 592 F.2d 174, the Third Circuit noted that state action may be found under the "significant involvement" category "either (1) when the state and the entity whose activities were challenged are joint participants in a symbiotic relationship or (2) where the entity is pervasively regulated by the state and a sufficient nexus exists between the state and the challenged activity." None of these support a finding of state action in this case.

Lowell argues that The Academy's lethal weapons training program is a public function because the Pennsylvania Lethal Weapons Training Act, 22 P.S. § 41 *et seq.,* requires special training before a person can be licensed to carry a lethal weapon in connection with his business, and because that act authorizes only two types of entities to conduct the requisite training, the state police and private institutions such as The Academy. In essence, Lowell argues that because the state police conduct the same type of training as does The Academy, The Academy performs a public function. In support of this argument Lowell cites *Parks v. "Mr. Ford,"* 556 F.2d 132, in which the Third Circuit applied the public function doctrine to the Pennsylvania garagemen's lien statute and concluded that statutorily authorized retention of a vehicle does not constitute state action while statutorily authorized sale of a vehicle does. The distinction rested upon the proposition that retention is a traditional common law right of suppliers of services, while sale has traditionally been performed exclusively by constables and sheriffs. This case is clearly distinguishable from *Parks,* however, because state action was found there where private persons were given powers traditionally reserved to state officials. The operation of a lethal weapons training program can not be characterized as a function traditionally reserved by the state. The supplemental affidavit of Leonard Capuzzi submitted in support of The Academy's motion shows that numerous private institutions provided such instruction prior to the promulgation of the Pennsylvania Lethal Weapons Training Act. Furthermore, the Third Circuit has declined to find state action where a private entity provides free library services, an activity far more "traditionally associated with sovereignty" than lethal weapons training. *Hollenbaugh v. Carnegie Free Library,* 545 F.2d 382. Further, the Supreme Court has made it clear that an activity does not constitute a public function merely because the state also engages in that activity, or because that activity is necessitated by a state statute. *Jackson v. Metropolitan Edison Co.,* 419 U.S. 345. Finally, the Supreme Court's recent decision in *Flagg Brothers, Inc. v. Brooks,* 436 U.S. 149, makes it clear that the public function test is not met unless the activity in question has been "*exclusively* reserved to the State." As the uncontradicted supplemental affidavit of Leonard Capuzzi makes clear, lethal weapons training has not been within the exclusive province of the state of Pennsylvania. Thus The Academy's activities can not be viewed as constituting state action pursuant to the public function doctrine.

The "significant involvement-joint participants" analysis of state action is based on *Burton v. Wilmington Parking Authority,* 365 U.S. 715. This analysis requires a review of the specific facts of each case to determine whether "the State has so far insinuated itself into a position of interdependence . . . that it must be recognized as a joint participant in the challenged activity." Lowell argues that the following constitutes the requisite interdependence:

1.   The Academy is certified by the Pennsylvania State Police;
2.   The Schaad Detective Agency operates as a private detective agency with court approval;
3.   The teachers at the Academy are all certified by the Pennsylvania State Police;

4. The transfer of ownership of the Academy was subject to State Police control;
5. The students at the Academy are cleared for entrance to the classes by the Pennsylvania State Police;
6. The firing range scores of the students are forwarded to the Pennsylvania State Police;
7. Upon successful completion of the program, the Academy assists the students in getting the certification to carry a lethal weapon as a private security agent;
8. The classes at the Academy are monitored by State Policemen;
9. The license of the Academy was once suspended by the Pennsylvania State Police;
10. The State Police inspect on an annual basis the operation of the Academy; and
11. Without the Lethal Weapons Training Act, there would be no need for the Academy's lethal weapons program.

I do not believe that these activities render the state and The Academy "joint participants" in lethal weapons training. The state does not participate in The Academy's program's directly; indeed, The Academy is free to offer any curriculum it desires. The activities listed above merely constitute regulation, albeit extensive regulation. However, "the mere fact that a business is subject to state regulation does not by itself convert its action into that of the State for purposes of the Fourteenth Amendment . . . Nor does the fact that the regulation is extensive and detailed, as in the case of most public utilities, do so." *Jackson v. Metropolitan Edison Co., supra,* 419 U.S. at 350, citing *Moose Lodge No. 107 v. Irvis,* 407 U.S. 163, and *Public Utilities Comm'n v. Pollack,* 343 U.S. 451. My review of all of the materials submitted in opposition to The Academy's motion fails to disclose any facts which would establish the type of interdependence found in *Burton.* These facts show a lower level of interdependence than found in *Metropolitan Edison.* Thus Lowell has failed to establish state action pursuant to the "significant involvement-joint participants" analysis.

The Third Circuit has specifically differentiated the third test, "significant involvement-nexus," from that discussed above. *See, e.g., Brenner v. Oswald, supra.* Under the nexus test, two requirements must be met: the private entity must be pervasively regulated, and a nexus must exist between the state and the challenged activity. While it is questionable whether the extensive regulation of The Academy can be regarded as "pervasive," that issue is irrelevant because it is clear from the record that there is no nexus between the state and the challenged activity. The challenged activity here is the discharge of plaintiff Lowell. Aside from the requirement that The Academy employ teachers certified by the state police, the state has no involvement in The Academy's hiring and firing practices. Other state involvement is limited to regulation of the subject matter and manner of presentation of the curriculum. Thus, while the state excludes from employment a class of noncertified persons, it does not in any way dictate which persons within the class of certified instructors should or should not be employed by The Academy. For this reason the requisite nexus between the state and the hiring practices of The Academy is not present in this case. *Moose Lodge No. 107 v. Irvis, supra* (licensing of lodge by Liquor Control Board does not constitute involvement with lodge's racially discriminatory guest policy); *Flagg Brothers, Inc. v. Brooks, supra* (mere acquiescence to challenged activity not enough). Lowell also argues that the nexus test is met by the following breach of a state-imposed duty:

The Academy, as a private institution, was performing the governmental function of preparing students for state certification to carry a lethal weapon as private security guards and was required by law to keep Schaad Detective Agency from participatiang, directly or indirectly, in the administration of the program. Yet, despite this explicit restriction, the Academy conspired with the Schaad Detective Agency to terminate the plaintiff's employment because Schaad and the Academy wanted persons who were not otherwise qualified to carry weapons on the job.

Plaintiff's Supplemental Brief at 19–20. This does not establish a nexus, however, because the cited activity occurred in violation of, rather than in accordance with, a state statute. As Justice Stevens has stated:

> It is only what the State itself has enacted that plaintiff may ask the federal court to review in a § 1983 case. If there should be a deviation from the state statute . . . the defect could be remedied by a state court and there would be no occasion for § 1983 relief.

Flagg Brothers, Inc. v. Brooks, supra, 436 U.S. at 176. Indeed, the Supreme Court has stated that "a State is responsible for a discriminatory act of a private party when the State, by its law, has *compelled* the act." *Adickes v. Kress & Co.,* 398 U.S. 144. Here the state has attempted to do just the opposite. Thus Lowell's argument that The Academy's activities constitute state action under the third test fails as well.

Because the activities of The Academy do not constitute state action under any legally cognizable analysis, and because the statute under which Lowell claims entitlement to relief, 42 U.S.C. § 1983, requires state action as a prerequisite to that relief, The Academy's motion for summary judgment is granted.

CASE COMMENT

The plaintiff was dismissed from his instructor's position at the academy. He claimed a First Amendment violation and brought the Section 1983 suit against the defendant and the academy. Citing 11 factors of interdependence with the state, the plaintiff argued that the lethal weapons training program was a public function. The court held that even though there was extensive regulation by the state, the activities of the academy could not be viewed as constituting state action. Also the state was not in a joint participant-symbiotic relationship, and a sufficient nexus between the state and the challenged activity did not exist. The state had no involvement in the academy's hiring and firing practices. The academy was free to offer any curriculum it desired, and the state did not dictate which instructors should or should not be employed.

MERE FURNISHING OF INFORMATION TO POLICE

The security guard in the following case observed what he suspected to be a criminal act (auto tampering) in the parking lot of the company he was hired to protect. He reported the suspected criminal act to the police and also to the employee who owned the car. The plaintiff, who was arrested by the police and whose case was later dropped, alleged in a Section 1983 action that the security guard deprived him of his federal constitutional and statutory rights. Some factors to consider in making joint action with police are a conspiracy or meeting of the minds, a previously agreed upon or prearranged plan, or willful participation with a state official. Although empowered to make arrests by the state, the guard did not do so. He merely reported suspected criminal activity to the police and therefore was not acting under color of state law.

CHILES v. CROOKS
708-F. Supp. 127 (1989)

HAMILTON, District Judge.

Plaintiffs, Ronald A. Chiles and Patrick R. Hollis, instituted this action under 42 U.S.C. §§ 1981 and 1983 alleging that defendant Louis Crooks deprived them of their federal constitutional and statutory rights. Plaintiffs' complaint also raises the pendent state law claims of malicious prosecution and intentional infliction of emotional distress against Crooks and Crooks' employer, Security Group, Inc., d/b/a Wells Fargo Guard Services (hereinafter "Security Group"). Defendant Crooks has moved to dismiss the federal claims for lack of subject matter jurisdiction, and for failure to state a claim upon which relief can be granted. Both defendants have moved to dismiss the pendent state law claims for resolution in state court.

Background Facts

On November 5, 1987, plaintiffs drove to Colonial Life and Accident Insurance Company's Columbia office, where Chiles' wife was employed. Plaintiffs alleged that they entered the parking lot so that Chiles could pick up his wife's car. According to plaintiffs, Mrs. Chiles' car was not in its assigned spot so they left the lot without getting out of Hollis' car.

When plaintiffs left the parking lot, Crooks, then working as a security guard at Colonial Life and employed by Security Group, followed them and recorded their license plate number. Crooks then returned to Colonial Life and reported a suspected criminal act to the Columbia Police Department. Crooks told the police that, while in Colonial Life's parking lot, Chiles had gotten out of Hollis' car and had tampered with a car belonging to another Colonial Life employee. Crooks also called the victim and informed her that her car had been tampered with.

As a result of Crooks' alleged false report, Chiles was arrested for auto tampering under S.C.Code Ann. § 16-21-90. Hollis was later interviewed by Columbia police regarding the incident. After Hollis told the interviewing officer that neither he nor Chiles got out of his car in the Colonial Life parking lot, Hollis was arrested and charged with giving false information to a police officer under S.C.Ann. § 16-17-725. The charges against both plaintiffs were dropped after they agreed to sign covenants not to sue the City of Columbia or its employees.

Plaintiffs' first cause of action seeks damages under 42 U.S.C. § 1983 against Crooks for allegedly causing the Columbia City Police Deparment to arrest them illegally, in violation of their rights under the Fourth, Fifth, and Fourteenth Amendments to the United States Constitution. Plaintiffs' second cause of action against Crooks is for a denial of equal rights under 42 U.S.C. § 1981 for allegedly accusing plaintiff Chiles of committing a crime simply because he is black. Plaintiffs' third cause of action for malicious prosecution and their fourth cause of action for intentional affliction of emotional distress are pendent state claims which apply to both defendants. Defendants have moved to dismiss all claims.

Analysis

Crooks has moved to dismiss plaintiffs' federal claims for lack of subject matter jurisdiction, Rule 12(b)(1), Fed.R.Civ. Proc., and for failure to state a claim upon which relief can be granted, Rule 12(b)(6), Fed.R.Civ.Proc. Where, as here, a defendant's challenge to the court's jurisdiction is also a challenge to the existence of a federal cause of action, the proper procedure for the district court is to find that jurisdiction exists and to determine the merits of the claim pursuant to Rule 12(b)(6) or Rule 56.

In ruling on defendants' 12(b)(6) motion, this court must follow the accepted rule that "a complaint should not be dismissed for failure to state a claim unless it appears beyond doubt that the plaintiff can prove no set of facts in support of his claim which entitle him to relief." The complaint must be construed liberally and all doubts must be resolved in favor of the nonmoving party.

Even after accepting plaintiffs' allegations as true, their complaint fails to state a federal cause of action. Consequently, the court must dismiss plaintiffs' federal claims under Rule 12(b)(6), Fed.R.Civ.Proc. The court dismisses without prejudice plaintiffs' pendent state law claims for resolution in state court.

Section 1983 Claim

In order to state a claim under 42 U.S.C. § 1983,[1] plaintiffs must show: (1) that Crooks caused them to be deprived of a right secured by the Constitution or laws of the United States; and (2) that in doing so he acted under color of state law. Where, as here, plaintiffs attempt to state a claim under § 1983 for violation of constitutional rights guaranteed them by the Fourteenth Amendment, they must show sufficient "state action" to make out a constitutional violation.[2]

The Court in *Lugar v. Edmondson Oil Co.*, 457 U.S. 922, announced a two-part test for determining the existence of state action:

First, the deprivation must be caused by the exercise of some right or privilege created by the State or by a rule of conduct imposed by the State or by a person for whom the State is responsible . . . *Second,* the party charged with the deprivation must be a person who may fairly be said to be a state actor.

The first prong is satisfied here because officers of the Columbia police force—"persons for whom the state is responsible"—made the alleged unconstitutional arrests. But plaintiffs cannot satisfy the second prong of the *Lugar* test because they failed to allege sufficient facts to show that Crooks, the party they have charged in this lawsuit with their constitutional deprivations, "may fairly be said to be a state actor."

Courts have set forth a number of tests for determining when the circumstances of a case convert a private individual into a state actor. *See, e.g., Terry v. Adams,* 345 U.S. 461; *Marsh v. Alabama,* 326 U.S. 501 ("public function" test); *Jackson v. Metropolitan Edison Co.,* 419 U.S. 345; *Burton v. Wilmington Parking Authority,* 365 U.S. 715 ("nexus" test); *Lugar,* 457 U.S. at 941; *Daniel v. Ferguson,* 839 F.2d 1124 ("joint action" test). In this case, plaintiffs, proceeding under the "joint action" test, contend that Crooks is a state actor because "he was a willful participant in joint action with officers of Columbia Police Department, agents of the State of South Carolina." Notably, if plaintiffs could prove that Crooks willfully participated in a joint action with police, they would not only meet the Fourteenth Amendment's state-action

---

[1]42 U.S.C. § 1983 provides, in relevant part: Every person who, under color of any statute, ordinance, regulation, custom, or usage, of any State or Territory or the District of Columbia, subjects, or causes to be subjected, any citizen of the United States or other person within the jurisdiction thereof to the deprivation of any rights, privileges, or immunities secured by the Constitution and laws, shall be liable to the party injured in an action at law, suit in equity, or other proceeding for redress.

[2]The Fourteenth Amendment of the United States Constitution provides, in relevant part: "No State shall make or enforce any law which shall abridge the privileges or immunities of citizens of the United States; nor shall any State deprive any person of life, liberty, or property without due process of law; nor deny to any person within its jurisdiction the equal protection of the laws." U.S. Const. Amend. 14. Because the Fourteenth Amendment is directed at the states, it can be violated only by conduct that may be characterized fairly as "state action."

requirement, but the "under color of state law" requirement of § 1983 as well. Plaintiffs' complaint, however, is devoid of any factual allegations from which a jury could reasonably infer that Crooks acted jointly with officers of the Columbia Police Department.

Plaintiff's allegations, if proven, would only establish that Crooks recorded Hollis' license plate number, alerted the victim that Chiles had tampered with her car, reported the crime to the police, and gave a written statement, upon which the police took action. As the authorities discussed below make clear, plaintiffs' failure to allege a conspiracy, a prearranged plan, or a meeting of the minds between Crooks and the police is fatal to their "joint action" theory.

The Court in *Adickes v. S.H. Kress & Co.*, 398 U.S. 144, found that state agents and Kress employees acted jointly because their conduct constituted a *conspiracy* or *meeting of the minds*. Likewise, the Court in *United States v. Price*, 383 U.S. 787, found joint action because the government agent and the private party laying in wait for the victims carried out a *previously agreed upon plan. See also Dennis v. Sparks*, 449 U.S. 24 (private parties who corruptly *conspired* with the judge were acting under color of law within the meaning of § 1983). But in cases, such as this, where a plaintiff relies upon the "joint action" theory without alleging a conspiracy, a prearranged plan, or a meeting of the minds, courts have dismissed at the pretrial stage those claim(s) requiring state action. *See, e.g., Daniel*, 839 F.2d at 1130–31 (plaintiff's allegation that private defendants willfully participated in joint action with a state official properly dismissed on 12(b)(6) motion because record lacked evidence of conspiracy between private defendants and state actor); *Dahlberg v. Becker*, 748 F.2d 85, *cert. denied*, 470 U.S. 1084 (complaint properly dismissed on 12(b)(6) motion where no claim was made that the state judges actually entered into a conspiracy or had a meeting of the minds, as in *Price* and *Adickes*, with the attorney defendants to deprive plaintiff of his liberty.); *Cruz v. Donnelly*, 727 F.2d 79 (where complaint failed to allege the existence of a prearranged plan by which the police substituted the judgment of private parties for their own official authority, private store owner cannot be said to have engaged in concerted or joint action with police).

Contrary to their contentions, plaintiffs cannot establish joint action here simply by proving their allegation that Columbia police officers based their decision to arrest Chiles on Crooks' accusations alone. It is well-settled that "police reliance in making an arrest on the information given by the private party does not make the private party a state actor." *Daniel*, 839 F.2d at 130; *see also Lugar*, 457 U.S. at 939 ("We do not hold today that 'a private party's mere invocation of state legal procedures constitutes joint participation or conspiracy with state officials satisfying the § 1983 requirement of action under color of state law.' "); *Sims v. Jefferson Downs Racing Association*, 778 F.2d 1068, ("The execution by a private party of a sworn complaint, which forms the basis for an arrest, is, without more, not sufficient to make the party's acts state action."); *Benavidez v. Gunnell*, 722 F.2d 615 (held that the mere furnishing of information to police officers who take action thereon does not constitute joint action); *Tarkowski v. Robert Barlett Realty Co.*, 644 F.2d 1204 ("A private person does not conspire with a state official merely by invoking an exercise of the state's official authority.").

In sum, the court concludes that even if plaintiffs proved every factual allegation contained in their complaint, they would not establish joint action so as to satisfy the Fourteenth Amendment's state-action requirement or § 1983's "color of state law" requirement.

Plaintiffs next contend that Crooks acted under the color of state law in this case because: (1) he was licensed under the South Carolina Private Detective and Private Security Agencies Act, S.C.Code Ann. § 40-17-10 (hereinafter "the Act"); and (2) he investigated and reported criminal behavior while on the job. The Act sets forth a statutory scheme for the licensing of security guards and grants them the power to arrest and detain persons on the premises they have been hired to protect. S.C.Code Ann. § 40-17-130. If Crooks had arrested plaintiff on Colonial Life's premises in exercise of rights granted him under § 40-17-130 of the Act, he clearly would have been acting under the color of state law. *See, e.g., Thompson v. McCoy*, 425 F.Supp. 407 (security guard found to have acted under color of state law when he allegedly arrested and assaulted the plaintiff on premises he was hired to protect); *see also State v. Brant,* 293 S.E.2d 703 ("According to this provision § 40–17–130, a security guard licensed by SLED stands in the shoes of the sheriff *for purposes of arrest* while he is on the property he is hired to protect." But in this case, Crooks never arrested plaintiffs, nor did he act pursuant to any other authority that might have been granted to him by the Act.

Based upon the plaintiffs' allegations, Crooks merely investigated and reported alleged criminal behavior. In so doing, he was not acting pursuant to any provision of the Act. According to a South Carolina Attorney General Opinion issued on February 7, 1980, the Act does not authorize security guards to conduct criminal investigations. In this particular opinion, the Attorney General concluded that:

> Section 40–17–130 . . . merely empowers the private security guard to effect an arrest as a public law enforcement official might. It empowers him to do no more. The South Carolina Detective and Private Security Agency Act does not raise the private security guard to the level of that of a public law enforcement official . . . The legislation (the Private Security Act) does not provide for any investigatory authority on the part of security guards; and there is no apparent intention to give security guards these powers. The ostensible purpose of the Act was to provide security guards with the powers of arrest and assistance to local law enforcement who are charged with the responsibility of conducting criminal investigations. Therefore, it can be said that private security guards are neither educated in the techniques of criminal investigation nor are they authorized by statute to conduct any such investigations, and therefore must defer to the appropriate law enforcement agency.

1980 Op.Att'y Gen., No. 80–20, p. 47. Therefore, the court must conclude that Crooks did not act under color of state law simply because: (1) he was licensed under the Act; and (2) he investigated and reported criminal behavior while on the job.[3]

Conclusion

Based upon the foregoing reasoning and cited authorities, this court grants Crooks' motion to dismiss plaintiffs' causes of action under 42 U.S.C. §§ 1981 and 1983 for failure to state a claim upon which relief can be granted. The court dismisses plaintiffs' pendent state claims of malicious prosecution and intentional infliction of emotional distress without prejudice for disposition in state court.

IT IS SO ORDERED.

---

[3]To be distinguished are those cases finding action under color of law in which security guards or off-duty police officers acted, or purported to act, pursuant to some authority granted to them by the state. *See, e.g., Lusby v. T.G. & Y. Stores, Inc.,* 749 F.2d 1423 (off-duty police officer working as security guard found to have acted under color of law in *arresting* plaintiff; court noted that defendant acted as an on-duty officer, *e.g.,* flashing his badge), *vacated on other grounds,* 474 U.S. 805; *Traver v. Meshriy,* 627 F.2d 934 (action under color of law found where bank guard responded to problem as police officer by identifying himself as such, showing police identification, and pulling his gun); *Davis v. Murphy,* 559 F.2d 1098 (action under color of law when Milwaukee statute provided that police officers were always subject to duty; officers in question identified themselves as police and showed their badges and guns during brawl they started); *Thompson v. McCoy,* 425 F.Supp. 407 (discussed above).

CASE COMMENT

The test for determining the existence of state action is that the deprivation must be caused by the exercise of some right or privilege created by the state or by a rule of conduct imposed by the state or by a person for whom the state is responsible and that the party charged with the deprivation must be a person who may fairly be said to be a state actor.

A police arrest on information given by a private party does not make the private party a state actor. The mere invocation of state legal procedures does not satisfy the acting under color of law requirements. The execution by a private party of a sworn complaint that forms the basis for an arrest, without more, is not sufficient to make the party's acts state action. Had the guard made an arrest there may have been subject matter jurisdiction based on state legislative empowerment.

NOT ACTING IN CONCERT

The plaintiff in the next case alleged he was accused by a store detective of trying to steal a box of glue. He also alleged that if he did not sign a store form, the manager would have called the police and had him and his wife arrested. And also if he did sign the release, the form would not leave the manager's desk. The next day he was fired from his job because of the incident at the store. The plaintiff claimed, in a Section 1983 action, that store employees acted in concert with local police according to a customary plan and under color of law when they detained and searched him. The court in finding that the store's employees did not act under color of law, distinguished the shopkeeper's detention authority for purely private interests (the recovery of concealed unpurchased goods) from an arrest.

Taking advantage of state-recognized self-help remedies for purely private purposes does not of itself convert one into a state actor. Two exceptions noted by the court are (1) when the store detective is authorized to actually make arrests and (2) when the merchant acts in concert with the police in accordance with a preconceived, customary plan.

GIPSON V. SUPERMARKETS GENERAL CORPORATION
564 F. Supp. 50 (1983)

ANNE E. THOMPSON, District Judge.

I. Facts

The relevant facts and procedural posture of this case are as follows. The plaintiffs are Leroy C. Gipson, Sr. and his wife Peggy Gipson. On December 20, 1979, the Gipsons were grocery shopping at the Linden, New Jersey, Pathmark store which is owned by Supermarkets General Corporation. Gipson alleges that while they were already at the checkout counter, his wife sent him back into the store to get a different brand of glue. At the same time he picked up a jar of deodorant. Gipson states in his affidavit submitted in opposition to this motion that he placed the deodorant in his overcoat pocket so that he could hold the box of glue up to the light with both hands to read the fine print. As he was returning to the checkout counter with the two items, Gipson was stopped by Detective Guerrero, a store security guard, and accused of trying to steal the glue by placing it up his sleeve. Gipson and Detective Guerrero were then accompanied by Store Manager Zirkel to an area near the store office. Gipson claims that he denied trying to steal anything. Also, he claims that when he was alone with Zirkel, Gipson explained that he was employed by Realty Maintenance, Inc. ("Realty") as a maintenance man at the SGC warehouse in Woodbridge, New Jersey. Gipson was very concerned that any accusation of shoplifting would affect his job.

Gipson was then presented with a form stating that he released SGC, its officers and employees from any liability in connection with the transaction. The names of the parties and the statement that Gipson was stopped and questioned about the two items were added on the form. Gipson states in his affidavit that he was told that if he did not sign the form, Zirkel would call the Linden policeman in the store and have Gipson and his wife arrested. He claims that he was also told that if he did sign the release form, it would not leave Zirkel's desk.

Gipson signed the release form. He then returned to the checkout counter and purchased the glue and deodorant. The following day, Gipson reported to work at the SGC Woodbridge warehouse. That afternoon the SGC supervisor told Gipson that due to the incident at the Linden Pathmark he received orders from SGC security to fire him.

The Gipsons filed suit against SGC, Service Employees International Union Local 389 AFL–CIO and Realty on September 4, 1981. An amended complaint was filed on October 26, 1981. On March 18, 1982, arbitration proceedings were held. The arbitrator ruled in an opinion dated May 6, 1982, that Gipson was to be reinstated to his former or comparable position with seniority unimpaired and that he was to receive three months back pay. Following the May 6, 1982 award, a stipulation of dismissal was filed as to defendant Local 389.

II. Discussion

The Gipsons' federal claims against SGC are brought under 42 U.S.C. § 1983 with jurisdiction pursuant to 28 U.S.C. § 1343 and under § 301 of the Labor Management Relations Act of 1947 ("LMRA"), 29 U.S.C. § 185(a). This motion concerns only the § 1983 claims. In the complaint, Gipson alleges that SGC violated his constitutional right not to be deprived of liberty, privacy or property or to be punished without due process of law. More specifically, the complaint states that SGC's employees and agents were acting in concert with the local police, according to a customary plan and under color of law, when Gipson was detained, searched and deprived of his liberty against his will in the Pathmark Linden store. The complaint asserts that SGC's employees and agents acted under color of state law when they detained Gipson. In addition, the complaint asserts that SGC exercised control over the employment policies of Realty causing Gipson to be summarily discharged from his employment with Realty. The complaint also states that by this termination Gipson was deprived of his property rights without due process of law in direct contravention of the Fifth, Eighth, Ninth and Fourteenth Amendments to the United States Constitution and provisions of the LMRA. In support of this assertion, the complaint goes on to state that pursuant to Article I, Paragraph 1 of the Constitution of the State of New Jersey and case law thereunder, the right to employment is a constitutional right protected by state law. (Count 1, §§ 21–24).

SGC filed the instant motion to dismiss returnable April 5, 1982. The long delay in deciding this motion has been due in part to the plaintiffs' request to adjourn the motion until they had received sufficient answers to their interrogatories. On January 4, 1983, Magistrate John W. Devine ordered SGC to provide more specific answers. The plaintiffs' brief in opposition to SGC's motion was received January 24, 1983. The plaintiffs submitted with their brief an affidavit of Leroy Gipson, Sr., the opinion and award of arbitration, a copy of the release form which also accompanied the complaint and an excerpt from Pathmark's "Store Security and Loss Prevention Guide."

A suit pursuant to § 1983[1] must satisfy two criteria. The plaintiff must show that the defendant deprived him of a right "secured by the Constitution and the laws" of the United States and the plaintiff must show that the defendant deprived him of this right while acting "under color of any statute . . . ." "It is clear that these two elements denote two separate areas of inquiry." *Flagg Brothers, Inc. v. Brooks,* 436 U.S. 149, citing *Adickes v. S.H. Kress & Co.,* 398 U.S. 144.

The court finds that as a matter of law SGC's employees and agents did not act under color of state law. In addition, the court finds that as a matter of law Gipson was not deprived of any constitutional right by the actions of SGC's agents.

A. State Action

In New Jersey, a merchant's right to detain persons suspected of shoplifting is stated in N.J.S.A. 2C:20–11.[2] The issue of whether a merchant or an employee who detains a customer pursuant to this statute is acting under color of state law appears to be one of first impression in New Jersey.

Generally, courts which have considered similar detentions by store personnel and store detectives have held that they were not acting under color of state law and have dismissed the plaintiff's § 1983 claim. In *Weyandt v. Mason's Stores, Inc.,* 279 F.Supp. 283, the plaintiff alleged that while she was a customer in a department store, store employees took her to a private office; slapped and beat her; refused her request to contact an attorney; forcibly restrained her from leaving the office; forcibly searched her and then took her to the justice of the peace where she was charged with shoplifting. This charge was later dismissed. In reviewing the plaintiff's later § 1983 suit, the federal district court found that the Pennsylvania statute which authorized detention of suspected shoplifters by merchants was intended to license a qualified right of self-help. This permitted detention by a shopkeeper distinguished from an arrest since it furthered purely private

---

[1]42 U.S.C. § 1983 provides in relevant part:

> Every person who, under color of any statute, ordinance, regulation, custom, or usage, of any State or Territory or the District of Columbia, subjects, or causes to be subjected, any citizen of the United States or other person within the jurisdiction thereof to the deprivation of any rights, privileges, or immunities secured by the Constitution and laws, shall be liable to the party injured in an action at law, suit in equity, or other proper proceeding for redress . . . . laws, shall be liable to the party injured in an action at law, suit in equity, or other proper proceeding for redress. . . .

[2]N.J.S.A. 2C:20–11 provides in pertinent part:

> A law enforcement officer, or a special officer, or a merchant, who has probable cause for believing that a person has wilfully concealed unpurchased merchandise and that he can recover the merchandise by taking the person into custody, may, for the purpose of attempting to effect recovery thereof, take the person into custody and detain him in a reasonable manner for not more than a reasonable time, and the taking into custody by a law enforcement officer or special officer or merchant shall not render such person criminally or civilly liable in any manner or to any extent whatsoever.
> Any law enforcement officer may arrest without warrant any person he has probable cause for believing has committed the offense of shoplifting as defined in this section. A merchant who causes the arrest of a person for shoplifting, as provided for in this section, shall not be criminally or civilly liable in any manner or to any extent whatsoever where the merchant has probable cause for believing that the person arrested committed the offense of shoplifting.

interests—*i.e.,* the recovery of concealed unpurchased goods. The *Weyandt* court thus viewed the defendants as acting under license of state law rather than under authority of state law and dismissed the plaintiff's § 1983 suit.

The *Weyandt* opinion was relied on by the court in *Battle v. Dayton-Hudson Corp.,* 399 F.Supp. 900. In that case, the plaintiff was held in accordance with a statute which allowed a merchant to detain a customer for the "sole purpose of delivering him to a peace officer . . . ." The court dismissed the plaintiff's § 1983 claim after finding that the statute licensed self-help, had a limited purpose and did not permit the merchant to make an arrest. Significantly, the court noted that "the defendants were in pursuit oif their own personal interests when they confronted the plaintiffs" rather than acting as an extension of the state. A similar holding was reached by the court in *Warren v. Cummings,* 303 F.Supp. 803; *accord, Estate of Iodice v. Gimbels, Inc.,* 416 F.Supp. 1054.

The cases discussed above were decided prior to the Supreme Court's decision in *Flagg Brothers, Inc. v. Brooks,* 436 U.S. 149. In *Flagg Brothers,* the Supreme Court held that a warehouseman was not acting under color of state law when he sold goods that he was storing in order to pay past-due storage fees as provided by a New York statute. In reaching this holding, the court rejected the argument that the warehouseman was performing a public function. Rather, the court limited the finding that a private party was performing a public function to the situation when the activity was "exclusively reserved to the state." The court offered the holding of elections and the municipal functions of a company town as examples of when a private party would be performing a public function. The *Flagg Brothers* decision noted that there was no state participation in the warehouse sale which distinguished its facts from *North Georgia Finishing, Inc. v. Di-Chem, Inc.,* 419 U.S. 601; *Fuentes v. Shevin,* 407 U.S. 67; and *Sniadach v. Family Finance Corp.,* 395 U.S. 337, in which state action was found. In addition, the court rejected the argument that the warehouseman's actions should be attributed to the state since the state adopted the warehouseman's statute. The court stated that the statute permitted these sales, but did not compel them.

The court in *White v. Scrivner,* 594 F.2d 140, relied on *Flagg Brothers* in determining whether store employees acted under color of state law when they detained the plaintiffs, searched their purses and, after finding a gun, called the police who arrested the plaintiffs. The court in *Scrivner* found that as in *Flagg Brothers,* the merchant did not perform any functions exclusively reserved to the state. "A storekeeper's central motivation in detaining a person whom he believes is stealing his property is self-protection not altruism." *Scrivner, supra,* at 142. The court also rejected the argument that state acaction could be found since the merchants acted under a Louisiana statute which insulated merchants from liability for detention of persons reasonably believed to be shoplifting. Rahter, relying on *Flagg Brothers,* the court found that the "Louisiana provision does not compel merchants to detain shoplifters, but merely permits them to do so under certain circumstances. Absent some compulsion or some overt state involvement, no state action can be found because of mere existence of the statute."

The United States Court of Appeals for the Third Circuit has not specifically reviewed whether a merchant self-help statute authorizes action under color of state law. However, the Court of Appeals recently considered whether the concept of state action should be extended to private persons acting under a state statute in *Luria Brothers & Co., Inc. v. Allen,* 672 F.2d 347. In *Luria Brothers,* the court reviewed whether a private landlord's posting of a notice of distraint under the Pennsylvania Landlord & Tenant Act constitutes state action. In determining whether the landlord was acting under color of state law, the court noted that as in *Flagg Brothers,* no public official was named as defendant in the complaint and that there was an absence of "overt official involvement." Moreover, "the Commonwealth's authorization of procedures for obtaining relief does not of itself convert into a state actor one who avails himself of those procedures." Thus, the court found that "Pennsylvania law permitted, but did not compel" the landlord's actions. The court held that "when a private person merely takes advantage of a self-help remedy recognized by the state, his actions are not attributable to the state."

Thus, under *Flagg Brothers, Luria Brothers, Scrivner* and in light of the federal district cases discussed above, this court holds that a merchant and his agent and employees are not acting under color of state law when a customer is detained as provided by N.J.S.A. 2C:20–11. The statute permits detention in a reasonable manner for the purpose of recovering unpurchased merchandise. The statute permits the merchant to act for his own benefit, but it does not compel the merchant to detain a suspected shoplifter and does not make the merchant an arm of the state concerned generally with enforcing the state's laws.

There are two exceptions in the case law to the finding that there is no state action. One exception is when the store detective is given authority to actually make arrests. The other exception is when there is a finding that the merchant is acting in concert with the police in accordance with a preconceived, customary plan.

In *DeCarlo v. Joseph Horne Co.,* 251 F.Supp. 935, the store detective was given authority to make a legal arrest under the Pennsylvania Professional Thieves Act of 1939. It was this state-given authority which determined the court's finding that the detective acted under color of state law. *Id.* at 937.[3] Similarly, in *Thompson v. McCoy,* 425 F.Supp. 407, there was a finding that private security guards acted under color of state law based on the intensive regulation by the state *plus* the statutory grant of police authority to make arrests. *See also Williams v. U.S.,* 341 U.S. 97 (state action found when private detective took an oath and qualified as a special police officer and flashed a special police officer card issued by the Miami police).

The *Weyandt* court distinguished *DeCarlo* and *Williams* as inapplicable to the situation in which there was no allegation that the store detective had any state-given authority to make arrests or act as a police officer. Similarly, in the instant case, there is no suggestion that Detective Guerrero had authority to arrest Gipson or otherwise had state-given authority to display police power.

Gipson argues that the SGC personnel were acting in concert with the local police and according to a customary plan when he was detained at the Pathmark store. There are cases in which courts have found that merchants were acting under color of state law due to the close, pre-arranged association with the police department. *El Fundi v. DeRoche,* 625 F.2d 195; *Duriso v. K-Mart,* 559 F.2d 1274; *Smith v. Brookshire Brothers,* 519 F.2d 93; *Classon v. Shopko Stores, Inc.,* 435 F.Supp. 1186. *But see White v. Scrivner,* 594 F.2d 140; *Davis v. Carson Pirie Scott & Co.,* 530 F.Supp. 799. The court finds, however, that this precedent is not on point with the facts of Gipson's case. The police never became

---

[3]Mere licensing of detectives by the state has been found insufficient to place their actions under color of state law. *Jenkins v. White Castle Systems, Inc.,* 510 F.Supp. 981.

involved in any way with the events at the store. They were never called and Gipson was never arrested. Gipson does assert in his affidavit that the store manager threatened to call a policeman in the store to arrest Gipson and his wife if he did not sign the release form. However, assuming for the purpose of this motion that this threat was made, this fact alone does not establish any *police* involvement with the case which would permit the court to make a finding that the Pathmark personnel were acting in concert with the police in a preconceived, customary manner.

Finally, Gipson argues that while the SGC personnel may have acted under a constitutional statute, they went beyond the scope of the statute by informing Gipson's supervisor of the detention. He asserts that it was this abuse of the statute which gives rise to a cause of action for damages under § 1983. In support of this argument, Gipson relies on *Hollis v. Itawamba County Loans,* 657 F.2d 746. The court finds this argument unavailing for two reasons. Firstly, as will be discussed, there was no constitutional deprivation as a result of SGC's actions. Secondly, *Hollis* concerns a situation in which abuse of a statutory procedure for replevin invoked state power. However, in the instant case, even if the SGC personnel acted beyond the scope of N.J.S.A. 2C:20–11, that alleged abuse is not sufficient to place the actions under color of state law. *Cf. Weyandt, supra,* (plaintiff allegedly was slapped, beaten, forcibly restrained and searched).

B. Constitutional Deprivation

Gipson asserts that he was deprived of his constitutional right to property when the actions of SGC led to the termination of his job. Property interests are not created by the federal constitution. They are created and defined by an independent source such as state law. *Board of Regents v. Roth,* 408 U.S. 564. A property interest is more than a mere expectation. It is a "legitimate claim of entitlement" which is protected by the due process clause of the Fourteenth Amendment. *Id.*

Gipson cites Article I, Section 1 of the New Jersey Constitution and cases interpreting this section as guaranteeing his property interest in his job.[4] However, the court finds that this section of the New Jersey Constitution does not guarantee a person's expectation in holding a particular job. It is true that *Carroll v. Local No. 269, International Brotherhood of Electrical Workers,* 31 A.2d 223, states in dicta that "the right to earn a livelihood is a property right which is guaranteed in our country by the Fifth and Fourteenth Amendments of the Federal Constitution, and by the State Constitution." In *Peper v. Princeton University Board of Trustees,* 389 A.2d 465, the court states that in "New Jersey, the right to obtain gainful employment and to use the fruits of such labor to acquire property has traditionally been considered basic." However, these are very general statements of a protected right to earn a livelihood as opposed to providing a property interest in any one particular job.

In summary, the court finds that as a matter of law, SGC did not act under color of state law and did not violate Gipson's constitutional rights. Consequently, the court grants summary judgment to SGC on Gipson's claims under § 1983. However, since the

---

[4]Article I, Paragraph 1 of the New Jersey Constitution provides:

All persons are by nature free and independent and have certain natural and unalienable rights, among which are those of enjoying and defending life and liberty, of acquiring, possessing, and protecting property, and of pursuing and obtaining safety and happiness.

plaintiffs also assert federal claims against SGC and Realty under § 301 of the LMRA, the court will not grant summary judgment or dismiss as to any other claims against SGC or Realty at this time.

CASE COMMENT

Summary judgement was granted to the store as the court found the store did not act under color of state law. The police were never called, and the plaintiff was never arrested. The alleged threat by the store manager to call the police did not establish police involvement. Absent overt official involvement the obtaining of state-recognized relief does not convert that party into a state actor. State action cannot be found because of the mere existence of a state statute. Pursuing one's own personal interests, limited purpose, and absence of other factors does not make one an extension of the state.

SECTION 242—CRIMINAL SANCTIONS

Defendants were convicted and sentenced to prison for inflicting summary punishment under color of law and willfully intending to deprive the victims of due process of law. The punishment inflicted were beatings and brutal assaults. The thrust of this violation is the misuse of power made possible because the wrongdoers are clothed with the authority of state law. Note the somewhat confusing status of the defendants' authority. Their appointments in 1960 and 1966 were renewed in 1973. The appointments expired within one year with option for renewal. Yet they weren't required to be commissioned at all, and their territoriality was limited.

UNITED STATES v. HOFFMAN
498 F.2d 879 (1974)

CUMMINGS, Circuit Judge.

Defendant railroad police officers were named in a 13-count indictment. The first count charged that they and Chester Garelli, an unindicted co-conspirator, conspired to deprive seven named individuals of their constitutional rights in violation of 18 U.S.C. § 241. The twelve substantive counts charged violations of twelve individuals' constitutional rights in violation of 18 U.S.C. §§ 242 and 2 over a time period ranging from early October 1971 to April 1972. A jury found the defendants guilty on all counts. They received concurrent sentences of two years on the conspiracy count and one year on each of the remaining counts.

A 1968 Illinois statute gave the defendants and Garelli, as members of the Penn Central Transportation Company's police force, "like police powers as those conferred upon the police of cities." Ill.Rev.Stat.1973, ch. 114, § 98.[1] In addition, Curotto was commissioned as a special police officer by the Chicago Police Department in 1966 and Hoffman in 1960. Those commissions were "renewed" or "updated" in 1973.

Defendants do not challenge the sufficiency of the evidence to show that they committed a number of assaults and batteries upon persons found on or near the property of Penn Central. Instead, they claim the evidence was insufficient to support a finding that they were

[1]In United States v. Belcher, 448 F.2d 494, we determined that railroad policemen have "authority as police officers under the Illinois Statutes."

acting under color of Illinois law with specific intent to deprive persons of rights secured by the Constitution of the United States. The evidence describes beating and other mistreatment of vagrants found on railroad property or adjacent thereto. As defendants' brief states, "All of these are undeniable examples of brutal assaults * * *."

The record shows that the defendants acted under color of state law. The acts charged occurred while they and Garelli were on duty and were armed with service revolvers while possessing the same powers as city police. One of their functions was to eject trespassers. They were required to submit daily time and activities sheets showing, *inter alia,* the number of trespassers ejected. They used the railroad police communication system to report their activities. Curotto attempted to justify his conduct to a fellow officer, stating that the trespassers were constant repeaters and that he had to use brutal tactics to keep them from returning. In sum, the acts alleged in the indictment occurred under the authority granted them as railroad policemen rather than as private persons. Under the applicable precedents, it is plain that the assaults occurred while they were cloaked with the authority of the state, thus constituting action under color of law within 18 U.S.C. §§ 241 and 242. Williams v. United States, 341 U.S. 97; Griffin v. Maryland, 378 U.S. 130.

Defendants rely on Ouzts v. Maryland National Insurance Co., 470 F.2d 790; Bichel Optical Laboratories v. Marquette National Bank, 487 F.2d 906; and Adams v. Southern California First Nat'l Bank, 492 F.2d 324. We need not decide whether we agree with those cases, for all are distinguishable. None of them involves a continuing delegation of the law enforcement power of the state. *Ouzts* involved a statute authorizing a bail bondsman to arrest a fugitive whose court appearance he had insured. *Bichel* and *Adams* involved secured creditor self-help repossession statutes. Common to each of these cases is a preexisting contractual relationship, and a narrow delegation to a private party of powers normally reserved to the state to enforce particular rights in each instance in which breach of contract is threatened. Defendants here, by contrast, are authorized on a continuing and full-time basis to search actively for criminals and trespassers and to use the powers of the state when their search is successful. Their territorial jurisdiction is limited, but unlike the defendants in *Ouzts, Bichel* and *Adams,* they are not limited to taking action only against certain previously identified persons for one narrowly defined offense.

We reject defendants' argument that they merely served the private interests of the railroad, and that what made their brutality possible was not their police power, but their private employment which gave them access to railroad property. Illinois has concluded that crimes against the railroad and its passengers and employees are a matter of public concern. Trespass on posted land is a misdemeanor. Ill.Rev.Stat. 1973, ch. 38, § 21-3. The statute delegating police power to defendants states that they are to "aid and supplement" municipal police forces. Ill.Rev.Stat. 1973, ch. 114, § 98. "If an individual is possessed of state authority and purports to act under that authority, his action is state action. It is irrelevant that he might have taken the same action had he acted in a purely private capacity * * *." Griffin v. Maryland, 378 U.S. at 135.

Defendants' argument that they could not have acted under color of law unless they initiated the formal processes of the criminal law is frivolous. The essence of their federal offense is precisely that they attempted to enforce the law by coercive means while bypassing the procedures designed to protect the rights of the trespassers.

Defendants assert that the evidence is insufficient for the jury to conclude that they intended to deprive their victims of rights secured by the federal Constitution. But defendants inflicted summary punishment under color of law, thus willfully intending to deprive their victims of due process of law. Crews v. United States, 160 F.2d 746; United States v. Delerme, 457 F.2d 156. As those cases hold, it is immaterial that defendants may have received personal gratification from the brutality.

Defendants also assail one of the intent instructions given by the district court. They acknowledge the correctness of the following instruction contained in the court's charge:

> "There must have been an intent on the part of the defendant willfully to subject the victim to a deprivation of a right, privilege or immunity secured or protected by the Constitution and the laws of the United States."

They complain that the force of this instruction "is immediately watered down" by the next instruction, which provided:

> "Now, 'specific intent' is required and the term means more than a general intent to commit the act. To establish specific intent the Government must prove that the defendant knowingly did an act which the law forbids, purposely intending to violate the law, but such intent may be determined from all of the facts and circumstances surrounding the case."

This latter instruction is said to permit the jury to convict without finding that the defendants' acts were specifically intended to deprive their victims of a constitutional right. However, when the two instructions are taken together, it is clear that the "act which the law forbids" in the second instruction refers to a deprivation of a constitutional right, as mentioned in the first instruction. This interpretation is reinforced by another instruction on intent reading as follows:

> " 'Intent' is merely the presence of a willingness to commit the act charged. It does not require knowledge that such an act is in violation of the law but it is necessary that the defendants had the actual knowledge—but it is necessary that the defendants have had the actual purpose of depriving the victims of their constitutional rights enumerated in the indictment."

Since the overall effect of the charge on intent stated the law with substantial accuracy, nothing more was required.

Finally, defendants request a new trial on the ground that the trial judge erroneously admitted evidence that Hoffman and Curotto had been appointed special policemen by the Superintendent of Police of Chicago in 1960 and 1966 respectively and that those appointments were renewed in 1973. As defendants observe, no evidence was adduced to show that the commissions in question were renewed annually under ch. 173-7[2] of the Municipal Code of Chicago through the period of time charged in the indictment. Another provision of the Municipal Code exempts special policemen of a common carrier from the licensing provisions.[3] It thus appears that defendants' commissions expired after one year, but that they were not required to renew their commissions annually because they were not required

[2]Ch. 173-7 provides:

> "The superintendent of police shall issue a special certificate of appointment to each person appointed as a special policeman, which certificate shall expire one year from the date of its issuance. The superintendent of police shall have power to renew any such appointment for a period of one year. He shall keep a correct list of all persons appointed as special policemen."

[3]Ch. 173-2 of the Municipal Code provides:

> "It shall be unlawful for any person to engage in the business of a special policeman without first being appointed and licensed therefor; provided, however, that no license shall be required of a special policeman engaged in the business of protecting persons, passengers, and property being transported in interstate or intrastate commerce within the city by a common carrier and the protection of the property of said common carrier within the city, but a special policeman engaged in such business shall comply with all the other provisions of this chapter applicable to him."

> Furthermore, ch. 173-12 permits the Superintendent of Police of Chicago to revoke a certificate of appointment for a special policeman of a common carrier only "for cause."

to be commissioned at all. It follows that these commissions were not admissible to show that defendants were granted law enforcement authority by the City of Chicago. But if there were any error here, it was harmless beyond a reasonable doubt, for defendants have not denied that they had law enforcement authority; their contention has been that they were not acting pursuant to that authority when they beat their victims. Furthermore, defense counsel objected to the admission of these documents only on the erroneous ground that the indictment did not "say anything about the City of Chicago."

Finally, the records were introduced expressly to prove that defendants were "commissioned special police officers for the Penn Central Transportation Company." The exhibits showed that Hoffman had been a Penn Central policeman for 12½ years prior to February 2, 1973, and that Curotto had been such for 7 years prior to July 12, 1973. The Government had to prove that defendants were railroad policemen to show that the Illinois statute granting the powers of city police was applicable. The exhibits were admissible for this purpose, and no limiting instruction was requested

Judgments affirmed.

CASE COMMENT

It is most important for the security manager to know each and every nuance of the state and local commissioning, licensing, and appointing laws and, as in this case, the non-license requirement that granted the authority. Only then can vulnerability to potential loss be realized. If a non-commissioned, non-licensed, non-appointed private citizen acts in concert with or participates with a government agent, that person may be considered a state actor.

Entrapment

Entrapment is the act of officers or agents of the government in inducing persons to commit crimes not contemplated by them for the purpose of instituting criminal prosecutions. This occurs when the criminal design originates with a government official and is implanted in the mind of an innocent person who does not otherwise have the predisposition to commit the offense charged. The idea of committing the crime originates with law enforcement officers or their agents who artificially propagate the inception of the crime. A law enforcement agent includes any person who acts in concert, in accordance, or in cooperation with the law enforcement official. A private citizen who does this becomes an extension of the law enforcement official's arm. Security managers should be aware of the cooperative activities of their staffs with law enforcement so as to prevent opening this affirmative defense to the potential defendant. Entrapment does not result from an act of inducement by a private citizen as is reported in the following case.

STATE v. ROCKHOLT
476 A. 2d 1236 (1984)

SCHREIBER, J.

Entrapment is appropriately characterized as the commission of a criminal act pursuant to improper police solicitation. Solicitation ordinarily is not a defense to a criminal prosecution. Rather, the principal remains guilty, regardless of the solicitor's influence, and the solicitor is subject to accomplice liability. Thus, when the solicitor is a private party, entrapment is unavailable as a defense to the solicited crime. It is only when the solicitor is a law enforcement official or someone acting as an agent of, or cooperating with, a law enforcement official that entrapment may provide a defense.

The inapplicability of the entrapment defense when the solicitor is someone other than a police officer demonstrates that inducement to crime does not negate the *mens rea* or mental culpability required for the substantive offense charged. The defendant still has acted with the requisite mental state to support a conviction. Who induced that mental state is a different question. As Justice Stewart noted in his dissent in *United States v. Russell*, 411 *U.S.* at 442:

That the defendant was induced, provoked, or tempted to do so by government agents does not make him any more innocent or any less predisposed than he would be if he had been induced, provoked, or tempted by a private person—which, of course, would not entitle him to cry "entrapment."

AFFORDING OPPORTUNITIES AND FACILITIES

In the following case private investigators were attempting to solve a suspected theft of shirts. In doing so they put the word out that they desired to "deal" in stolen shirts. What they were doing was affording opportunities and facilities for the commission of an ongoing criminal enterprise. The private investigators did not initiate the criminal design in the minds of the defendants, and in any event, entrapment does not apply to the actions of a private citizen who is not an agent of the government. Note in this case the inapplicability to private citizens of the *Miranda* decision. Also note the efforts made to accommodate the employees while they were being interviewed. They received their normal pay, including overtime. A TV room, sandwiches, and snacks were provided. Their freedom to leave was equivalent to that "while on the job."

UNITED STATES v. MADDOX
492 F. 2d 104 (1974)

RONEY, Circuit Judge:

Defendants James Maddox and Bradford Knowles were found guilty of conspiring to transport 10,000 stolen shirts in interstate commerce, knowing the shirts to be stolen.

Briefly, the facts are these. Suspecting theft as the reason for its inordinate inventory losses, shirt manufacturer Alatex, Inc., solicited the private investigative services of its parent corporation, Cluett-Peabody, Inc., to locate the culprits. Cluett-Peabody's private agents, making known their desire to "deal" in stolen shirts, were contacted by the defendants and arranged to "fence" the merchandise in Atlanta. The delivery of 300 stolen shirts to the security agents sufficiently fulfilled the conspiratorial overt act.

The defendants argue that the company's deep involvement in the conspiracy, to the extent of suggesting and arranging for the transportation, amounts to complicity and precludes their conviction because of entrapment as a matter of law. The argument overlooks the fact that private investigators, rather than governmental agents, participated in the arrangements. The entrapment defense does not extend to inducement by private citizens. Moreover, the defendants received the benefit of the defense when the District Court submitted the issue of entrapment to the jury for factual determination. The jury found against the defendants. In any event, the conduct of the private investigators merely afforded opportunities and facilities for the commission of the offense, a continuing illegal enterprise, without initiating the criminal design in the defendants' minds.

The voluntariness of Knowles' confession is challenged on appeal. The private investigators arranged for Alatex employee suspects to be questioned at a local motel concerning the missing merchandise. The employees, still on the company payroll and not under arrest, were maintained at company expense in a casual atmosphere. A T.V. room, sandwiches, and snacks were provided. The employees received their normal pay, including overtime during the questioning. Their freedom to leave was equivalent to that while "on the job." It was in this context that Knowles confessed his activities.

Defendants' objection is premised on the private investigator's failure to give *Miranda* warnings to Knowles. *Miranda* is inapplicable to non-custodial questioning by private citizens. The facts surrounding the confession were scrutinized by the trial judge at an out-of-the-presence-of-the-jury hearing on voluntariness requested by the United States Attorney. The jury was subsequently instructed as to voluntariness. The factual determination by the jury is not legally precluded.

CASE COMMENT

Knowledge by private investigators that entrapment does not apply to private persons and meticulous attention to the voluntariness rule in obtaining statements resulted in convictions that were upheld on appeal.

Legal and Other Resource Material

Dictionaries

1. *Black's Law Dictionary*, 5th Ed. St. Paul, MN: West Publishing Co.
2. *Words and Phrases*, St. Paul, MN: West Publishing Co.

Encyclopedias

3. *American Jurisprudence 2d.* Rochester, NY: The Lawyers Co-operative Publishing Co.
4. *Corpus Juris Secundum.* St. Paul, MN: West Publishing Co.

Reference Series

1. *American Law Reports.* Rochester, NY: The Lawyers Co-operative Publishing Co.
2. *American Jurisprudence Proof of Facts.* Rochester, NY: The Lawyers Co-operative Publishing Co.
3. *Restatement of the Law 2d: Agency.* Washington, DC: American Law Institute.
4. *Restatement of the Law 2d: Contracts.* Washington, DC: American Law Institute.
5. *Restatement of the Law 2d: Torts.* Washington, DC: American Law Institute.

Reporters: Federal

1. *United States Reports (U.S. Supreme Court).* Washington, DC: United States Government Printing Office.
2. *Supreme Court Reporter (U.S. Supreme Court).* St. Paul, MN: West Publishing Co.
3. *United States Supreme Court Reports, Lawyer's Edition (U.S. Supreme Court).* Rochester, NY: The Lawyers Co-operative Publishing Co.
4. *Federal Reporter (U.S. Appellate Courts).* St. Paul, MN: West Publishing Co.
5. *Federal Supplement (U.S. Trial Courts).* St. Paul, MN: West Publishing Co.

State Reports: Regional

1. West Publishing Co., St. Paul, MN
   Atlantic: Connecticut, Delaware, District of Columbia, Maine, Maryland, New

Hampshire, New Jersey, Pennsylvania, Rhode Island, Vermont.
Northeastern: Illinois, Indiana, Massachusetts, New York, Ohio.
Northwestern: Iowa, Michigan, Minnesota, Nebraska, North Dakota, South Dakota, Wisconsin.
Pacific: Alaska, Arizona, California, Colorado, Hawaii, Idaho, Kansas, Montana, Nevada, New Mexico, Oklahoma, Oregon, Utah, Washington, Wyoming.
Southeastern: Georgia, North Carolina, South Carolina, Virginia, West Virginia.
Southwestern: Arkansas, Kentucky, Missouri, Tennessee, Texas.
Southern: Alabama, Florida, Louisiana, Mississippi.

Index

1. *Index to Legal Periodicals.* New York, NY: H. W. Wilson Co.

Other Resource Material

1. *Private Security: Report of the Task Force on Private Security* (Washington, DC, National Advisory Committee on Criminal Justice Standards and Goals), Law Enforcement Assistance Administration, U.S. Department of Justice, 1976.
2. *Scope of Legal Authority of Private Security Personnel* (Washington, DC, Private Security Advisory Council), Law Enforcement Assistance Administration, U.S. Department of Justice, 1976.
3. William C. Cunningham and Todd H. Taylor, *The Hallcrest Report: Private Security and Police in America,* Portland, OR: Chancellor Press, 1985.
4. William C. Cunningham, John J. Strauchs, and Clifford W. Van Meter, *The Hallcrest Report II: Private Security Trends 1970-2000,* Boston, MA: Butterworth-Heinemann, 1990.

APPENDIX B

Settlements
(Security Related)

Association of Trial Lawyers of America. ATLA Law Reporter, 1050 31st St., N.W., Washington, DC 20007

1. Failure to have two full-time guards: $7.3 million, *32 ATLA L. Rep. 407, Nov. 1989.*
2. False arrest/imprisonment because security officers did not see receipt: $200,000, *31 ATLA L. Rep. 416, Nov. 1988.*
3. Inadequate training in proper security measures: $1,250,000, *32 ATLA L. Rep. 366, Oct. 1989.*
4. False arrest/imprisonment, couple arrested exchanging merchandise: $2,250,000, *32 ATLA L. Rep. 110, Apr. 1989.*
5. Assault and battery, negligent training and supervision: $100,000, *30 ATLA L. Rep. 272, Aug. 1987.*
6. Assault and battery, security beat visitor, alleged failure to conduct pre-employment investigation: $300,000, *30 ATLA L. Rep. 416, Nov. 1987.*
7. Assault by guard: $1.5 million, *31 ATLA L. Rep. 34, Feb. 1988.*
8. Killing of customer by security guard: $1.4 million, *31 ATLA L. Rep. 319, Sept. 1988.*
9. Misrepresentation of systems standards, negligent design and installation, negligent training of employees who improperly monitored, breach of the service contract: $12.3 million, *30 ATLA L. Rep. 262, Aug. 1987.*
10. Failure to have adequate security patrols, dimly lit side door, front door locked at 10:00 P.M., students not given front door keys: $577,000, *29 ATLA L. Rep. 374, Oct. 1986.*
11. Failure to teach use of alarm, failure to install centrally monitored alarm system, failure to provide trained and adequate security force, failure to provide adequately secure sliding glass doors: $4.2 million, *32 ATLA L. Rep. 20, Feb. 1989.*
12. False arrest and false imprisonment: $40,000, *29 ATLA L. Rep. 466, Dec. 1986.*
13. Wrongful death of suspected shoplifter shot by guard, negligent hiring, negligent training, negligent supervision: $500,000, *29 ATLA L. Rep. 39, Feb. 1986.*

Code Of Ethics*

PREAMBLE

Aware that the quality of professional security activity ultimately depends upon the willingness of practitioners to observe special standards of conduct and to manifest good faith in professional relationships, the American Society for Industrial Security adopts the following Code of Ethics and mandates its conscientious observance as a binding condition of membership in or affiliation with the Society:

ARTICLE I

A member shall perform professional duties in accordance with the law and the highest moral principles.

Ethical Considerations

I-1   A member shall abide by the law of the land in which the services are rendered and perform all duties in an honorable manner.

I-2   A member shall not knowingly become associated in responsibility for work with colleagues who do not conform to the law and these ethical standards.

I-3   A member shall be just and respect the rights of others in performing professional responsibilities.

ARTICLE II

A member shall observe the precepts of truthfulness, honesty and integrity.

*With permission from the American Society for Industrial Security, 1655 North Fort Myer Drive, Arlington, VA 22209.

Ethical Considerations

II-1 A member shall disclose all relevant information to those having a right to know.

II-2 A right to know is a legally enforceable claim or demand by a person for disclosure of information by a member. Such a right does not depend upon prior knowledge by the person of the existence of the information to be disclosed.

II-3 A member shall not knowingly release misleading information, nor encourage or otherwise participate in the release of such information.

ARTICLE III

A member shall be faithful and diligent in discharging professional responsibilities.

Ethical Considerations

III-1 A member is faithful when fair and steadfast in adherence to promises and commitments.

III-2 A member is diligent when employing best efforts in an assignment.

III-3 A member shall not act in matters involving conflicts of interest without appropriate disclosure and approval.

III-4 A member shall represent services or products fairly and truthfully.

ARTICLE IV

A member shall be competent in discharging professional responsibilities.

Ethical Considerations

IV-1 A member is competent who possesses and applies the skills and knowledge required for the task.

IV-2 A member shall not accept a task beyond the member's competence nor shall competence be claimed when not possessed.

ARTICLE V

A member shall safeguard confidential information and exercise due care to prevent its improper disclosure.

Ethical Considerations

V-1 Confidential information is nonpublic information the disclosure of which is restricted.

V-2   Due care requires that the professional must not knowingly reveal confidential information or use a confidence to the disadvantage of the principal or to the advantage of the member or a third person unless the principal consents after full disclosure of all the facts. This confidentiality continues after the business relationship between the member and his principal has terminated.

V-3   A member who receives information and has not agreed to be bound by confidentiality is not bound from disclosing it. A member is not bound by confidential disclosures made of acts or omissions which constitute a violation of the law.

V-4   Confidential disclosures made by a principal to a member are not recognized by law as privileged in a legal proceeding. The member may be required to testify in a legal proceeding to information received in confidence from his principal over the objection of his principal's counsel.

V-5   A member shall not disclose confidential information for personal gain without appropriate authorization.

ARTICLE VI

A member shall not maliciously injure the professional reputation or practice of colleagues, clients or employers.

Ethical Considerations

VI-1   A member shall not comment falsely and with malice concerning a colleague's competence, performance, or professional capabilities.

VI-2   A member who knows, or has reasonable grounds to believe, that another member has failed to conform to the Society's Code of Ethics shall present such information to the Ethical Standards Committee in accordance with Article XIV of the Society's Bylaws.

PRIVATE SECURITY CODE OF ETHICS**

Code of Ethics for Private Security Management

As managers of private security functions and employees, we pledge:

I   To recognize that our principal responsibilities are, in the service of our organizations and clients, to protect life and property as well as to prevent and reduce crime against our business, industry, or other organizations and institutions; and in the public interest, to uphold the law and to respect the constitutional rights of all persons.

II   To be guided by a sense of integrity, honor, justice and mortality in the conduct of business; in all personnel matters; in relationships with government agencies, clients, and employers; and in responsibilities to the general public.

III   To strive faithfully to render security services of the highest quality and to work continuously to improve our knowledge and skills and thereby improve the overall effectiveness of private security.

IV   To uphold the trust of our employers, our clients, and the public by performing our functions within the law, not ordering or condoning violations of law, and ensuring that our security personnel conduct their assigned duties lawfully and with proper regard for the rights of others.

V   To respect the reputation and practice of others in private security, but to expose to the proper authorities any conduct that is unethical or unlawful.

VI   To apply uniform and equitable standards of employment in recruiting and selecting personnel regardless of race, creed, color, sex, or age, and in providing salaries commensurate with job responsibilities and with training, education, and experience.

VII   To cooperate with recognized and responsible law enforcement and other criminal justice agencies; to comply with security licensing and registration laws and other statutory requirements that pertain to our business.

VIII   To respect and protect the confidential and privileged information of employers and clients beyond the term of our employment, except where their interests are contrary to law or to this Code of Ethics.

IX   To maintain a professional posture in all business relationships with employers and clients, with others in the private security field, and with members of other professions; and to insist that our personnel adhere to the highest standards of professional conduct.

X   To encourage the professional advancement of our personnel by assisting them to acquire appropriate security knowledge, education, and training.

Code of Ethics for Private Security Employees

In recognition of the significant contribution of private security to crime prevention and reduction, as a private security employee, I pledge:

**From *Private Security: Report of the Task Force on Private Security,* National Advisory Committee on Criminal Justice Standards and Goals, Washington, DC, 1976.

I   To accept the responsibilities and fulfill the obligations of my role: protecting life and property; preventing and reducing crimes against my employer's business, or other organizations and institutions to which I am assigned; upholding the law; and respecting the constitutional rights of all persons.

II   To conduct myself with honesty and integrity and to adhere to the highest moral principles in the performance of my security duties.

III To be faithful, diligent, and dependable in discharging my duties, and to uphold at all times the laws, policies, and procedures that protect the rights of others.

IV   To observe the precepts of truth, accuracy and prudence, without allowing personal feelings, prejudices, animosities or friendships to influence my judgements.

V   To report to my superiors, without hesitation, any violation of the law or of my employer's or client's regulations.

VI   To respect and protect the confidential and privileged information of my employer or client beyond the term of my employment, except where their interests are contrary to law or to this Code of Ethics.

VII To cooperate with all recognized and responsible law enforcement and government agencies in matters within their jurisdiction.

VIII To accept no compensation, commission, gratuity, or other advantage without the knowledge and consent of my employer.

IX   To conduct myself professionally at all times, and to perform my duties in a manner that reflects credit upon myself, my employer, and private security.

X   To strive continually to improve my performance by seeking training and educational opportunities that will better prepare me for my private security duties.

False Alarm Ordinance (Greenwich, CT)

CHAPTER 2A. ALARM DEVICES

Sec. 2A-1. Legislative determination.

It is determined that the number of false alarms being made to the Police and Fire Departments hinders the efficiency of those Departments, lowers the morale of Department personnel, constitutes a danger to the general public in the streets during responses to false alarms and jeopardizes the response of volunteers; and that the adoption of this chapter will reduce the number of false alarms and promote the responsible use of alarm devices in Greenwich.

Sec. 2A-2 Definitions.

For the purpose of this chapter, the following definitions shall apply:

(a) *Alarm device*—Any device which, when activated by a criminal act, fire or other emergency calling for Police or Fire Department response, transmits a signal to Police or Fire Department headquarters; transmits a signal to a person who relays information to Police or Fire Department headquarters; or produces an audible or visible signal to which the Police or Fire Departments are expected to respond. Excluded from this definition and the scope of this chapter are devices which are designed to alert or signal only persons within the premises in which the device is installed.

(b) *Alarm user*— The owner of any premises in which an alarm device is used, provided that an occupant who expressly accepts responsibility for an alarm device by registration pursuant to Section 2A-5 shall be deemed the "alarm user."

(c) *Automatic dial alarm*—A telephone device or attachment that mechanically or electronically selects a telephone line to Police or Fire Department headquarters and reproduces a prerecorded voice message to report a criminal act, fire or other emergency calling for Police or Fire Department response. Excluded from this definition are devices which relay a digital-coded signal to Police or Fire Department headquarters.

(d) *Central station*—An office to which remote alarm devices transmit signals where operators monitor those signals and relay information to the Police and Fire Departments.

(e) *Contractor*—Any person, firm or corporation in the business of supplying and installing alarm devices or servicing the same.

(f) *False alarm*—Any activation of an alarm device to which the Police or Fire Department responds and which is not caused by a criminal act, fire or other emergency, except an activation caused by malfunction of telephone equipment as verified by monitoring facilities at Police or Fire Department headquarters, a letter or other evidence from the telephone company or other proof; or power failure as verified by the administrator. A series of such activations attributable to the same cause and occurring under circumstances beyond the control of the responsible alarm user shall be deemed a single "false alarm."

Sec. 2A-3. Administrator.

(a) There shall be in the town an administrator for alarm devices which shall have the powers and duties granted to it under this chapter.

(b) The Finance Department shall be the administrator under the direction and control of the Board of Estimate and Taxation, which is authorized to adopt regulations for the administration of this chapter.

Sec. 2A-4. Alarm Appeal Board.

(a) There shall be in the town an Alarm Appeal Board, which shall have the powers and duties granted to it under this chapter.

(b) The Alarm Appeal Board shall consist of five (5) members who shall be appointed by the Representative Town Meeting on nomination by the Board of Selectmen. All members shall be electors of the town and shall serve without compensation. Three (3) members shall be appointed for terms expiring March 31, 1982, and two (2) members for terms expiring March 31, 1984. Further appointments, except to fill vacancies, shall be for terms of four (4) years, commencing on April 1. Appointed members shall serve until their successors shall have been appointed and qualified. Vacancies in the membership shall be filled for the unexpired portion of a term in the same manner as regular appointments.

(c) Three (3) members of such Board shall constitute a quorum. All decisions shall be by a majority of those present and voting.

Sec. 2A-5. Registration of alarm devices required.

Each alarm user shall register his alarm device or devices with the administrator prior to use.

Sec. 2A-6. Alarm device registration procedure.

(a) Alarm device registration shall be accomplished by filling out a form provided by the administrator to include such information concerning the identity of the prospective alarm user, the identity of the alarm user's contractor, if any, and the nature of the proposed alarm device as the administrator may require. The administrator shall issue the alarm user a written acknowledgment of proper registration.

(b) It shall be the responsibility of each alarm user to notify the administrator of changes in registration information.

Sec. 2A-7. Registration of central stations required.

Each central station which plans to transmit signals to the Police or Fire Department must register with the administrator before doing so.

Sec. 2A-8. Central station registration procedure.

(a) Central station registration shall be accomplished by filling out a form provided by the administrator to include such information as the administrator may require concerning the identity of the applicant, the type of its business organization (individual proprietorship, partnership, corporation), the principal place of business of the entity, the location of the office monitoring alarms, the staffing of that office and the alarm users in Greenwich served by the station. The administrator shall issue the central station a written acknowledgment of proper registration.

(b) It shall be the responsibility of each central station to notify the administrator of changes in the registration information, but such notification need not be given more frequently than once a month.

Sec. 2A-9. Registration of contractors required.

Each contractor which wishes to provide authorized inspection and repair services in accordance with Section 2A-17 shall register with the administrator. Certifications called for in Section 2A-17 shall be accepted from registered contractors only.

Sec. 2A-10. Contractor registration procedure.

(a) Contractor registration shall be accomplished by filling out a form provided by the administrator to include such information concerning the identity of the applicant, the type of its business organization (individual proprietorship, partnership, corporation), the principal place of business of the entity, the places of business from which Greenwich alarm users will be served, the types and makes of equipment sold and/or installed and the types and makes of equipment the contractor is qualified to service as the administrator may require. The administrator shall issue the contractor a written acknowledgment of proper registration.

(b) There shall be a fee of ten dollars ($10) for each registration accepted.

(c) It shall be the responsibility of each contractor to notify the administrator of changes in the registration information.

Sec. 2A-11. New automatic dial alarms prohibited.

No automatic dial alarm may be installed after October 10, 1980. No automatic alarm device in use on such date may remain in use after July 1, 1983.

Sec. 2A-12. Transmission of digital-coded signals prohibited.

(a) After the publication of this chapter, the administrator will not permit the registration of an alarm device which transmits a digital-coded signal to either the Police Department or the Fire Department unless the alarm user has received special authorization in accordance with Section 2A-12(b).

(b) A commercial establishment or a not-for-profit institution may have a direct line to the Police Department or Fire Department provided that:

(1) The connection is by a high grade, dedicated line meeting specifications that may be established by the departments concerned.

(2) The Police or Fire Department determines that the level of risk and exposure justifies a direct line.

(3) The Police or Fire Department has notified the administrator of its approval of such a direct line.

(c) After July 1, 1983, signals that result from the activation of an alarm device for which a direct connection has not been authorized in accordance with Section 2A-12(b) must be transmitted to a central station which, after such verification as is practicable, will transmit the alarm to the Police Department or Fire Department.

Sec. 2A-13. Exterior audible devices.

Unless required by law, no alarm device which produces an exterior audible signal shall be installed unless its operation is automatically restricted to a maximum of thirty (30) minutes.

Sec. 2A-14. Reporting of false alarms.

(a) The Police Department and Fire Department shall report false alarms to the administrator, based upon the report of the investigating officer.

(b) It shall be the responsibility of the central station to notify the alarm user or his designated keyholder whenever the central station reports an alarm activation to the Police Department or Fire Department.

Sec. 2A-15. Charges for false alarms.

When the administrator determines that the Police Department or Fire Department has responded to a false alarm, the administrator shall impose a charge on the responsible alarm user according to the following schedule:

(a) For the first three (3) false alarms within the town's fiscal year: no charge.

(b) For the fourth and subsequent such alarms: twenty dollars ($20).

Sec. 2A-16. Notification of charges.

(a) The administrator shall notify the responsible alarm user of any false alarm charge by mail. Within thirty (30) days after the mailing of such notice, the alarm user may file with the administrator information to show that the alarm was not a false alarm within the meaning of this chapter.

(b) The administrator shall consider such information, reaffirm or rescind the false alarm charge and notify the alarm user of its decision by mail. Within thirty (30) days after the mailing of such notice, the alarm user may file with the Alarm Appeal Board an appeal, in writing.

Sec. 2A-17. Required inspection; suspension of registration.

(a) If activations of any alarm device have resulted in five (5) false alarms within a single fiscal year of the town, the administrator shall, when notifying the alarm user of this fifth false alarm and the charge therefor, request that the alarm user arrange to have the alarm device inspected by a contractor registered in accordance with Section 2A-9, that the alarm device be adjusted or repaired if necessary and that the alarm user submit a certification in writing from the contractor that he has inspected the alarm device and that it is in proper working order. Such notification by the administrator shall be by certified or registered mail, return receipt requested.

(b) Such certification must be submitted within fifteen (15) days from the date of the return receipt for the administrator's letter. However, if the alarm user requests an extension of time to file the report because of absence from town or other satisfactory reason, the administrator shall extend, for a reasonable time, the date for filing.

(c) If the certification is not received within the fifteen-day period or permitted extension thereof, the administrator shall notify the alarm user that the registration of the alarm device is suspended and that thereafter the alarm device shall be deemed unregistered and, unless disconnected, subject to the penalties therefor. The suspension shall be lifted and the alarm user so notified when a satisfactory certification has been received by the administrator.

(d) If the alarm user believes that his registration has been suspended unjustifiably he may, within fifteen (15) days from date of mailing of notice of suspension, file with the Alarm Appeal Board an appeal in writing.

Sec. 2A-18. Appeals procedure.

(a) Upon receipt of a timely appeal from a false alarm charge or a registration suspension, the Alarm Appeal Board shall hold a hearing to consider it and shall mail notice of the time and place of said hearing to the alarm user taking the appeal at his last known address, at least fifteen (15) days before the hearing. On the basis of information provided by the alarm user and other information introduced at the hearing, the Board shall affirm the charge or suspension, if it finds that the charge or suspension was properly imposed, or rescind the charge or suspension, if it finds the charge or suspension was not properly imposed.

(b) There shall be a fee of ten dollars ($10) for each appeal to the Alarm Appeal Board.

(c) The amount of the fee for taking an appeal may be raised or lowered from time to time at the discretion of the Board of Estimate and Taxation without further approval of the Representative Town Meeting.

Sec. 2A-19. Notices to include instructions.

Each notice of a false alarm charge, the reaffirmation of such a charge by the administrator or the suspension of a registration shall refer to and provide instructions concerning the alarm user's right to further recourse by filing information with the administrator or an appeal with the Alarm Appeal Board, as the case may be.

Sec. 2A-20. Information to be confidential.

All information in the possession of the administrator, the Alarm Appeal Board, the Police Department or the Fire Department concerning particular alarm users and particular alarm devices shall not be divulged without the written consent of the alarm user or users concerned, except that information as to the frequency of false alarms experienced by an individual alarm user may be supplied to the contractor who installed or who currently has a contract to service that user's alarm device.

Sec. 2A-21. Information to be compiled.

The administrator, Police Department and Fire Department shall, with respect to each and every false alarm, compile information concerning alarm devices, contractors and sources of false alarms in a form such that the information may be evaluated in terms of relative reliability of different sorts of alarm devices and particular contractors and the frequency of false alarms attributable to different categories of sources.

Sec. 2A-22. Disclaimer of liability.

Notwithstanding the provisions of this chapter, the town, its departments, officers, agents and employees shall be under no obligation whatsoever concerning the adequacy, operation or maintenance of any alarm device or of the alarm-monitoring facilities at Police and Fire Department headquarters. No liability whatsoever is assumed for the failure of such alarm devices or monitoring facilities or for the failure to respond to alarms or for any other omission in connection with such alarm devices. Each alarm user shall be deemed to hold and save harmless the town, its departments, officers, agents and employees from liability in connection with the alarm user's alarm device.

Sec. 2A-23. Violations and penalties.

Any person who performs or causes to be performed any of the following acts shall be subject to a penalty not to exceed one hundred dollars ($100) for each such act:

(a) Failure to register an alarm device or give notice of changes in registration information as required by this chapter.

(b) Use of an automatic dial alarm or an exterior audible alarm device in violation of the provisions of this chapter.

Sec. 2A-24. Charges and fees to be paid into general fund.

Charges for contractor registration, charges for false alarms, appeal fees and penalties for violations shall be collected by the administrator and placed in the general fund.

Sec. 2A-25. Enforcement.

The town, upon authorization of the administrator, may institute civil proceedings to enforce the provisions of this chapter.

Sec. 2A-26. Applicability.

The provisions of this chapter shall not apply to alarm devices on premises owned or controlled by the town, including the Board of Education, the State of Connecticut or the government of the United States nor to alarm devices installed in a licensed motor vehicle, trailer or boat.

Selected Constitutional Amendments

The first 10 amendments, known as the *Bill of Rights,* were ratified on December 15, 1791. The fourteenth Amendment, dealing with the states, was ratified on July 9, 1868.

AMENDMENT 1

Congress shall make no law respecting an establishment of religion, or prohibiting the free exercise thereof; or abridging the freedom of speech, or of the press; or the right of the people peaceably to assemble, and to petition the Government for a redress of grievances.

AMENDMENT 2

A well regulated Militia, being necessary to the security of a free State, the right of the people to keep and bear arms, shall not be infringed.

AMENDMENT 3

No Soldier shall, in time of peace be quartered in any house, without the consent of the Owner, nor in time of war, but in a manner to be prescribed by law.

AMENDMENT 4

The right of the people to be secure in their persons, houses, papers, and effects, against unreasonable searches and seizures, shall not be violated, and no Warrants shall issue, but upon probable cause, supported by Oath or affirmation, and particularly describing the place to be searched, and the persons or things to be seized.

AMENDMENT 5

No person shall be held to answer for a capital, or otherwise infamous crime, unless on a presentment or indictment of a Grand Jury, except in cases arising in the land or naval forces, or in the Militia, when in actual service in time of War or public danger; nor shall any person be subject for the same offence to be twice put in jeopardy of life or limb; nor shall be compelled in any criminal case to be witness against himself, nor be deprived of life, liberty, or property, without due process of law; nor shall private property be taken for public use, without just compensation.

AMENDMENT 6

In all criminal prosecutions, the accused shall enjoy the right to a speedy and public trial, by an impartial jury of the State and district wherein the crime shall have been committed, which district shall have been previously ascertained by law, and to be informed of the nature and cause of the accusation; to be confronted with the witnesses against him; to have compulsory process for obtaining witnesses in his favor, and to have the Assistance of Counsel for his defense.

AMENDMENT 7

In suits of common law, where the value in controversy shall exceed twenty dollars, the right of trial by jury shall be preserved, and no fact tried by a jury, shall be otherwise re-examined in any Court of the United States, than according to the rules of the common law.

AMENDMENT 8

Excessive bail shall not be required, nor excessive fines imposed, nor cruel and unusual punishments inflicted.

AMENDMENT 9

The enumeration in the Constitution, of certain rights, shall not be construed to deny or disparage others retained by the people.

AMENDMENT 10

The powers not delegated to the United States by the Constitution, nor prohibited by it to the States, are reserved to the States respectively, or to the people.

AMENDMENT 14

Section 1. All persons born or naturalized in the United States, and subject to the jurisdiction thereof, are citizens of the United States and of the State wherein they reside. No State shall make or enforce any law which shall abridge the privileges or immunities of citizens of the United States; nor shall any State deprive any person of life, liberty, or property, without due process of law; nor deny to any person within its jurisdiction the equal protection of the laws.

Appendix F
Federal Deprivation of Rights Statutes

TITLE 42, UNITED STATES CODE, SECTION 1983 (CIVIL)

Every person who, under color of any statute, ordinance, regulation, custom, or usage, of any State or Territory or the District of Columbia, subjects, or causes to be subjected, any citizen of the United States or other person within the jurisdiction thereof to the deprivation of any rights, privileges, or immunities secured by the Constitution and laws, shall be liable to the party injured in an action at law, suit in equity, or other proper proceeding for redress. For the purposes of this section, any Act of Congress applicable exclusively to the District of Columbia shall be considered to be a statute of the District of Columbia.

TITLE 18, UNITED STATES CODE, SECTION 242 (CRIMINAL)

Whoever, under color of any law, statute, ordinance, regulation, or custom, willfully subjects any inhabitant of any State, Territory, or District to the deprivation of any rights, privileges, or immunities secured or protected by the Constitution or laws of the United States, or to different punishments, pains, or penalties, on account of such inhabitant being an alien, or by reason of his color, or race, than are prescribed for the punishment of citizens, shall be fined not more than $1,000 or imprisoned not more than one year, or both; and if bodily injury results shall be fined under this title or imprisoned not more than ten years, or both; and if death results shall be subject to imprisonment for any term of years or for life.

Statutory Arrest Authority of Private Citizens*

			Alabama	Alaska	Arizona	Arkansas	California	Colorado	Georgia	Hawaii	Idaho	Illinois	Iowa	Kentucky	Louisiana
Certainty of correct arrest		Probable cause													
		Reasonable grounds to believe person arrested committed	■					■	■		■			■	■
		Is in the act of committing													
		Summoned by peace officer to assist in arrest													
Major offense	**Type of Knowledge Required**	Is escaping or attempting							■						
		That felony has been committed in fact	■	■		■			■			■	■	■	■
		Reasonable grounds to believe being committed				■						■			
		View													
		Information a felony has been committed													
		Committed in presence							■	■					
	Type of Major Offense	Crime involving theft or destruction of property													
		Crime							■	■					
		Crime involving physical injury to another													
		Petit larceny													
		Larceny													
		Felony	■	■	■	■		■		■	■	■	■	■	■
Minor offense	**Type of Knowledge Required**	Upon reasonable grounds that is being committed									■				
		View													
		Immediate Knowledge													
		Presence	■	■			■	■			■	■			
	Type of Minor Offense	Indictable offense													
		Offense other than an ordinance										■			
		Offense							■						
		Public offense	■			■					■		■		
		Breach of the peace													
		Misdemeanor amounting to a breach of the peace			■										
		Crime		■					■	■					

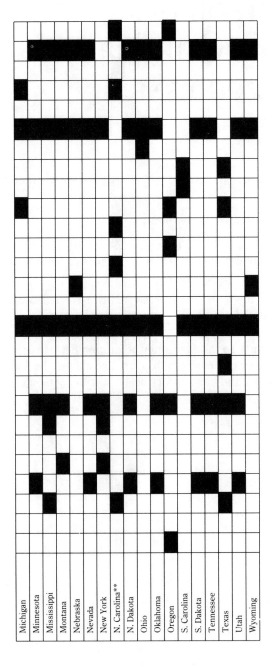

*For specific authority see referenced state code.

**Statute eliminates use of word arrest and replaces with detention.

*From Report of the Task Force on Private Security, National Advisory Committee on Criminal Justice Standards and Goals, Washington, D.C., 1976, p. 397.

Arrest by Private Persons California Criminal Procedure

§ 837. Private persons; authority to arrest.   ARREST BY PRIVATE PERSONS. A private person may arrest another:

1.   For a public offense committed or attempted in his presence.

2.   When the person arrested has committed a felony, although not in his presence.

3.   When a felony has been in fact committed, and he has reasonable cause for believing the person arrested to have committed it.

   § 847. Arrest by private person; duty to take prisoner before magistrate or deliver him to peace officer.   A private person who has arrested another for the commission of a public offense must, without unnecessary delay, take the person arrested before a magistrate, or deliver him to a peace officer.

Appendix I

Use of Physical Force Statute Connecticut Penal Code (Selected Portions)

Sec. 53a–19. Use of physical force in defense of person. (a) Except as provided in subsections (b) and (c) a person is justified in using reasonable physical force upon another person to defend himself or a third person from what he reasonably believes to be the use or imminent use of physical force, and he may use such degree of force which he reasonably believes to be necessary for such purpose; except that deadly physical force may not be used unless the actor reasonably believes that such other person is (1) using or about to use deadly physical force, or (2) inflicting or about to inflict great bodily harm.

(b) Notwithstanding the provisions of subsection (a), a person is not justified in using deadly physical force upon another person if he knows that he can avoid the necessity of using such force with complete safety (1) by retreating, except that the actor shall not be required to retreat if he is in his dwelling, as defined in section 53a-100, or place of work and was not the initial aggressor, or if he is a peace officer or a private person assisting such peace officer at his direction, and acting pursuant to section 53a—22, or (2) by surrendering possession of property to a person asserting a claim of right thereto, or (3) by complying with a demand that he abstain from performing an act which he is not obliged to perform.

(c) Notwithstanding the provisions of subsection (a), a person is not justified in using physical force when (1) with intent to cause physical injury or death to another person, he provokes the use of physical force by such other person, or (2) he is the initial aggressor, except that his use of physical force upon another person under such circumstances is justifiable if he withdraws from the encounter and effectively communicates to such other person his intent to do so, but such other person notwithstanding continues or threatens the use of physical force, or (3) the physical force involved was the product of a combat by agreement not specifically authorized by law.

Sec. 53a–20. Use of physical force in defense of premises. A person in possession or control of premises, or a person who is licensed or privileged to be in or upon such premises, is justified in using reasonable physical force upon another person when and to the extent that he reasonably believes it is necessary to prevent or terminate the commission or attempted commission of a criminal trespass by such other person in or upon such premises; but he may use deadly physical force under such circumstances only (1) in defense of a person as prescribed in section 53a–19, or (2) when he reasonably believes it is necessary to prevent an attempt by the trespasser to commit arson or any crime of violence, or (3) to the extent that he reasonably believes it is necessary to prevent or terminate an unlawful entry by force into his dwelling as defined in section 53a–100, or place of work, and for the sole purpose of such prevention or termination.

Sec. 53a–21. Use of physical force in defense of property.   A person is justified in using reasonable force upon another person when and to the extent that he reasonably believes it necessary to prevent an attempt by such other person to commit larceny or criminal mischief involving property, or when and to the extent he reasonably believes it necessary to regain property which he reasonably believes to have been acquired by larceny within a reasonable time prior to the use of such force; but he may use deadly physical force under such circumstances only in defense of person as prescribed in section 53a–19.

Sec. 53a–22. Use of physical force in making arrest or preventing escape.   (a) For purposes of this section, a reasonable belief that a person has committed an offense means a reasonable belief in facts or circumstances which if true would in law constitute an offense. If the believed facts or circumstances would not in law constitute an offense, an erroneous though not unreasonable belief that the law is otherwise does not render justifiable the use of physical force to make an arrest or to prevent an escape from custody.

(f) A private person acting on his own account is justified in using reasonable physical force upon another person when and to the extent that he reasonably believes it is necessary to effect an arrest or to prevent the escape from custody of an arrested person whom he reasonably believes to have committed an offense and who in fact has committed such offense; but he is not justified in using deadly physical force in such circumstances, except in defense of person as prescribed in section 53a–19.

Sec. 53a–100. Definitions.   (a) The following definitions are applicable to this part: (1) "Building" in addition to its ordinary meaning, includes any watercraft, aircraft, trailer, sleeping car, railroad car, other structure or vehicle or any building with a valid certificate of occupancy. Where a building consists of separate units, such as, but not limited to separate apartments, offices or rented rooms, any unit not occupied by the actor is, in addition to being a part of such building, a separate building; (2) "dwelling" means a building which is usually occupied by a person lodging therein at night, whether or not a person is actually present; (3) "night" means the period between thirty minutes after sunset and thirty minutes before sunrise.

Glossary

Agency   A voluntary, consensual legal relationship where one person is authorized to act for another and is subject to the other's control. Some of the relationships are principal and agent, master and servant (employer and employee), and proprietor and independent contractor.

Arrest   The deprivation of a person's liberty by legal authority. The seizing of an alleged offender or the taking into custody of a person to answer a criminal charge. The restriction of one's right to locomotion or restraint of full liberty. There must be an intent to arrest, under real or pretended authority, accompanied by a seizure (actual or constructive) of the person, and it must be understood to be an arrest by the person arrested.

Assault   An offer of the use of force; the threat to inflict injury on another, along with the apparent and imminent ability to do so.

Battery   The use of the force offered; unlawful application of force to another.

Breach of contract   A failure to perform on any promise; the non-performance of any contractual duty, or acting contrary to the provisions of the contract without a legal excuse or where a legal excuse in lacking.

Breach of peace   A violation of public tranquility or of laws enacted to preserve peace and good order. A disturbance of public order by an act of violence or by any act likely to produce violence or which, by causing consternation and alarm, disturbs the peace and quiet of the community.

Color of law   Pretense of law. Semblance, without substance, of legal right. Misuse of power made possible because the wrongdoer is clothed with the authority of state law. Color does not mean actual law. It means appearance as distinguished from reality.

Common law   Identifies with and consists of judicial opinions and decisions of courts. It consists not of absolute, fixed and inflexible rules but rather of broad and comprehensive principles based on justice, reason, and common sense. The principles are susceptible of adaption to new conditions, interests, relations, and usages as the progress of society may require. It is not static but rather dynamic and growing, and its rules conform to the changing conditions of society.

Compensatory damages   Actual damages given as the equivalent for the injury done; pecuniary compensation or recompense for the actual loss of injuries sustained.

Constructive force   Operates on the mind by putting a person in fear by use of threatening words, gestures, displays of force, menacing, or intimidation. Produces fear of personal violence sufficient to compel submission or to suspend the power of resistance or prevent the free exercise of will.

Contributory negligence   Conduct which involves an undue risk of harm to the person (complaining party) who sustains the harm; failure to use diligence and reasonable care to avoid the harm or injury; negligence on the part of the plaintiff which contributes to the injury sustained by him.

Contract   A voluntary, deliberate agreement between two or more competent parties to do or refrain from doing some act; a voluntary obligation the purpose of which is to define the promised performance.

Damages   Pecuniary compensation for a loss or injury sustained or suffered; relief which the law allows for the harm occasioned by the fault of another.

Defamation   The injuring of another's reputation; diminishment of that person's esteem and respect; the holding of a person to ridicule, scorn, or contempt; publication (oral or written) of a false statement, without privilege, which injures another.

Disclaimer   A device used to control, exclude, or limit a seller's liability by reducing the number of situations in which the seller is liable.

Duty   An obligation to conform to legal standards of conduct of reasonable persons under like circumstances; the exercise of reasonable care whenever it is foreseeable that one's conduct may cause harm to another. This duty adjusts to changing social situations and exigencies and man's relation to his fellow man.

Excessive force   Force used that is greater than necessary to accomplish the task. Force that is not justified in light of all the circumstances of the situation or that is beyond the need of the particular event.

Exculpatory   Tending to free from blame, guilt, or fault; tending to prove guiltless, clear, justify, or excuse.

Exemplary damages   Awarded over and above actual or compensatory damages. As an example, for deterrence or punishment. Arises from aggravating circumstances such as gross negligence, recklessness, willful, wanton, or malicious conduct. Synonymous with punitive or vindictive damages.

False arrest   Unlawful restraint of a person's freedom of movement or personal liberty. Because the freedom or liberty of the person is restrained, it is also false imprisonment.

False imprisonment   Unlawful detention of a person for any length of time; nonconsensual, unlawful confinement.

Felony   Distinguishes certain high crimes from minor offenses (see misdemeanors). More serious in nature than a misdemeanor. Generally any criminal offense for which the defendant may be executed or imprisoned for more than one year.

Foreseeability   To see or know beforehand; reasonable anticipation of danger; the ability to see or know in advance.

Imminent danger/peril   Danger about to be inflicted, more than a possibility and not remote or uncertain. A threatened and impending injury that would put a prudent and reasonable person on the defensive.

Implied   An indirect indication; where intent or intention is found from the surrounding circumstances and conduct of the parties, not by direct words.

Inculpatory   Tending to establish guilt, blame, or fault.

Independent contractor   One who contracts to work or render service to another, according to his own methods, and is subject to his employer's desires and controls only as to the results of his work.

Libel   Defamation expressed in writing.

Malicious prosecution   Prosecution instituted maliciously and without probable cause.

Misdemeanor   An offense lower than, or less serious in nature than, a felony. Punishment is generally imprisonment not to exceed one year and/or a fine.

Mitigation of damages   Where the injured party fails to exercise reasonable care to avoid the consequences of his injury.

Negligence   The absence of due diligence; the want of ordinary care; inadvertence, carelessness, heedlessness, inattention, thoughtlessness, oversight; the doing of a thing which a reasonably prudent person would not have done, or the failure to do a thing which a reasonably prudent person would have done in like or similar circumstances.

Outrageous conduct   Conduct exceeding all bounds usually tolerated by decent or civilized society; conduct done with a reckless indifference to the interests of others; atrocious conduct; conduct so extreme as to exceed all bounds of decency.

Presence   Within reach of the senses and not limited to sight alone. Perception by the use of all senses. Being near at hand. Not mere physical proximity but whether the offense is apparent to the citizens' senses.

Probable cause   Exists when facts and circumstances within one's knowledge and about which one has reasonably trustworthy information are sufficient in themselves to warrant a person of reasonable caution in the belief that a crime has been or is being committed. It is a practical and nontechnical concept based on conventional consideration of everyday life on which reasonable and prudent people, not legal technicians, act. It is good grounds for holding a person for trial and means having more evidence for than against. Probable cause, reasonable cause, and reasonable grounds may be used interchangeably in the context of legal justification, which is a defense to a false arrest action.

Reasonable force   The degree of force that is not excessive and that is appropriate in the particular circumstances of protecting oneself or one's property.

Remittitur   To decrease, slacken, or diminish damages awarded by a jury by remitting a portion of the award.

Respondeat superior   Let the master (employer) answer for the torts (wrongs) of his servant (employee) which are committed by the servant in the scope of his employment.

Scope of employment   Acts or conduct reasonably and fairly incident to or logically and naturally connected with the employment with some direct benefit to the employer; conduct furthering the master's business, where the master exercises control over the conduct.

Self-defense   A defensive, not offensive, act repelling an unprovoked attack or impending peril to one's person or property. The justified or excused use of a reasonable amount of force when non-aggressors reasonably believe they are in imminent danger of unlawful bodily harm and that force is necessary to avoid the danger.

Slander   Oral defamation.

Third-party beneficiary   One not privy to the contract who may benefit by it and who may bring a cause of action for its breach.

Tort   A civil wrong, other than breach of contract, resulting in damage; a breach or violation of a duty owing to the plaintiff. The elements are the existence of a legal duty, the breach of that duty, and damages as the proximate result of the breach.

Tortfeasor   A person who commits a tort.

Trespass   The unlawful intrusion of another's person, property, or rights.

Vicarious liability   Indirect legal responsibility; synonymous with *respondeat superior.*

Warranty   A promise that a proposition of fact is true. An affirmation of fact or promise made by the seller to the buyer that the goods shall conform to the affirmation or promise. A warranty is implied when the law derives it by implication or inference from the nature of the transaction or the acts or circumstances of the parties.

Table of Cases